THE
NEW BOOK
OF
KNOWLEDGE

THE NEW BOOK OF KNOWLEDGE

Scholastic Library Publishing, Inc.
Danbury, Connecticut

VOLUME 18

T

ISBN 0-7172-0540-1 (set)

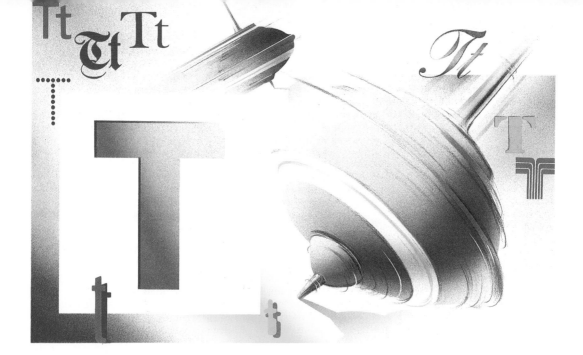

T, the 20th letter in the English alphabet, was the 22nd letter in the ancient Hebrew and Phoenician alphabets and the 19th letter in the classical Greek alphabet. The Hebrews and Phoenicians called it *taw.* The Greeks called it *tau.*

The Phoenicians used their letter names for words. In Phoenician speech the word *taw* meant "sign." Some language scholars say that the form of the letter represented a particular cross-shaped sign that the Phoenicians used to mark packages in commerce or to brand cattle. The letter *taw* looked like this: ✝

The Greeks based their alphabet on that of the Phoenicians. The Greek letter *tau* was written this way: T

The Romans learned the alphabet from the Etruscans, an ancient people who ruled in Rome in the 500's B.C. The Etruscan alphabet was based on a western Greek model. The Romans took over the letter T unchanged, giving it the same T sound that the Greeks had given the letter. It is the Greek-Roman T that is used in English today. In English, T is usually pronounced as in *toy.*

In certain English combinations the letter T has a SH sound. Examples are the words *inertia, partial, patient, lotion,* and *pretentious.* T also has a CH sound, as in *nature* and *question.* T is often combined with the letter H, as in *thank* and *then.*

The expression "to cross the T's" means to be very exact or to emphasize a point. The phrase "to a T" means just right, or properly.

The letter T is found in many abbreviations. In physics T stands for tritium and t stands for triton. In cooking, a large T often stands for tablespoon and a small t for teaspoon. In reference books, Old Testament is often written OT and New Testament is written NT. T can also be used to describe something shaped like the letter T, like a T-shirt or a T square, a tool used by carpenters.

Reviewed by MARIO PEI
Author, *The Story of Language*

See also ALPHABET.

TABLE SETTINGS. See ETIQUETTE.

SOME WAYS TO REPRESENT T:

The **manuscript** or printed forms of the letter (left) are highly readable. The **cursive** letters (right) are formed from slanted flowing strokes joining one letter to the next.

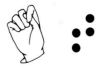

The **Manual Alphabet** (left) enables a deaf person to communicate by forming letters with the fingers of one hand. **Braille** (right) is a system by which a blind person can use fingertips to "read" raised dots that stand for letters.

The **International Code of Signals** is a special group of flags used to send and receive messages at sea. Each letter is represented by a different flag.

International Morse Code is used to send messages by radio signals. Each letter is expressed as a combination of dots (.) and dashes (– –).

TABLE TENNIS

Table tennis, also known as Ping-Pong, can be played anywhere. You need only a net, a celluloid ball, wooden paddles, and a table 9 feet by 5 feet (2.7 meters by 1.5 meters), with a playing surface that is 2½ feet (76 centimeters) above the floor. Two people may play singles, or four may play doubles.

Grips

There are two ways to hold, or grip, the paddle. One is the tennis grip, in which you grasp the paddle as though you were shaking hands. Your hand should fit the handle snugly with the index finger extended close to the edge of the blade. The thumb should rest diagonally on the opposite side of the paddle. The side where your thumb rests is the forehand side of the paddle, and the other is the backhand side.

The second grip is the penholder grip, in which the paddle is held as if it were a pen. Quickness and agility are needed for this grip. The player strikes the ball with the same side of the paddle for both forehand and backhand shots. Most Western players use the tennis grip, but the penholder grip is popular in Asia.

Strokes

The basic strokes are the forehand and backhand drives; the chop; the block shot, or half volley; and the smash.

The Forehand Drive. The drive is an attacking shot. Hold the paddle below the path of the ball, with the blade angled slightly forward. Hit upward and forward through the path of the ball. Time your swing so that the paddle makes contact with the ball at, or slightly before, the top of its bounce. Be sure to turn your wrist over as you strike the ball, and finish the stroke with the paddle well above your head. This gives the ball the topspin that makes it drop down on the other side of the net. At the finish of the swing, the back of the hand should be upward. Strive for lift, sharp wrist action, hitting from the elbow, and follow-through.

The Backhand Drive. The backhand shot is a necessity. The back of the hand leads and faces the net in making the swing, and the stroke starts on the left side of the body. The ball is hit like the forehand topspin drive, but it is hit with the other side of the paddle and, at the completion of the stroke, the palm of the hand is facing upward. For both strokes, your weight shifts from the rear foot to the front foot at the finish of the shot.

The Chop. This is a defensive stroke. The forehand chop is similar to chopping wood. Start with the paddle well above and behind the ball. Stroke down through the path of the ball and follow through after the paddle hits it. The backhand chop is the same but the paddle is held in the backhand position.

The Block Shot. When a ball is driven directly at you and there is no time to step to one side, you will probably have to block the ball back. The ball is usually blocked on the backhand. Keep the wrist locked, and push your forearm forward as you come into the ball.

The Smash. The smash is a kill shot used when the ball bounces unusually high. It is hit like the forehand topspin drive, except that the wrist is more rigid and there is little or no rotation of it as the ball is struck. Hit the ball with a flat paddle (the blade should be perpendicular to the desired flight of the ball), and take a long, sweeping stroke.

PAULINE BETZ ADDIE
Former World and U.S. Tennis Champion

TADPOLES. See FROGS AND TOADS.
TAFT, ROBERT A. See UNITED STATES, CONGRESS OF THE (Profiles: Senators).

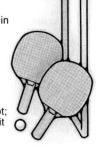

BASIC RULES

Scoring of Points • The first player to score 21 points wins the game. Players alternate serving every 5 points. If the score reaches 20–20, the winner will be the first player to score 2 points more than the opponent, and the service will change on each point, instead of after every 5.

Good Service • The server releases the ball by hand only. The ball must then be struck with the paddle so that it bounces first in the server's court, goes over or around the net, and then touches the other side of the table.

Good Return • A return is good if the ball is struck so that it passes directly over or around the net and directly touches the opponent's court.

Let • It is a let and the ball is served again if in passing over the net during a service, the ball touches the net before landing in the receiver's court, or if it is served before the receiver is ready and the receiver does not try to hit the ball.

Point • A player loses the point if the player fails to make a good service; fails to make a good return of the opponent's service or shot; or at any time **volleys** the ball (hits it before it touches the table).

WILLIAM HOWARD TAFT (1857–1930)

27th President of the United States

FACTS ABOUT TAFT

Birthplace: Cincinnati, Ohio
Religion: Unitarian
College Attended: Yale College, New Haven, Connecticut
Occupation: Lawyer
Married: Helen Herron
Children: Robert Alphonso, Helen, Charles Phelps
Political Party: Republican
Post Held Before Becoming President: Secretary of War
President Who Preceded Him: Theodore Roosevelt
Age on Becoming President: 51
Years in the Presidency: 1909–1913
Vice President: James S. Sherman
President Who Succeeded Him: Woodrow Wilson
Age at Death: 72
Burial Place: Arlington National Cemetery, Arlington, Virginia

DURING TAFT'S PRESIDENCY

Left: Robert E. Peary of the United States led the first successful expedition to the North Pole (1909). *Right:* The Boy Scouts of America was organized (1910). Roald Amundsen of Norway reached the South Pole (1911). *Below:* The British passenger liner *Titanic,* then the world's largest ship, sank after hitting an iceberg (1912), with the loss of more than 1,500 lives. New Mexico and Arizona became the 47th and 48th states (1912). The Sixteenth Amendment to the U.S. Constitution was ratified (1913), giving Congress the power to tax incomes.

TAFT, WILLIAM HOWARD. When William Howard Taft became president of the United States in 1909, great things were expected of him. The previous president, Theodore Roosevelt, one of the most popular in American history, had supported him enthusiastically, and Taft had promised to carry on Roosevelt's policies. Taft had already served the country for many years in a variety of important positions. In the 1908 election the people had chosen him over the Democratic candidate, William Jennings Bryan, by more than 1,000,000 popular votes. Yet Taft's administration was a disappointment to his supporters. He failed to win re-election in 1912 but later went on to a distinguished career as chief justice of the United States.

▶EARLY YEARS

Taft was born in Cincinnati, Ohio, on September 15, 1857. He came from an old and distinguished family, which traced its roots back to the 17th-century Puritan settlers of the Massachusetts Bay Colony. His father, Alphonso Taft, was a judge. Young William was intelligent and excelled at his studies. He graduated from Yale College in 1878, second in his class. He then returned to Cincinnati and became a lawyer. A big, heavy man, he eventually weighed more than 300 pounds (135 kilograms). He was friendly and warmhearted but rather lazy. His fine mind, however, soon made him a successful lawyer.

▶HIS PUBLIC-SERVICE CAREER

Taft became interested in Republican politics in Ohio, and in 1881 he was appointed assistant prosecutor in Hamilton County. In 1887 he was named a judge on the Ohio superior court. In 1890, President Benjamin Harrison offered him the post of solicitor general of the United States, the second-ranking office in the Department of Justice. Taft accepted, but in 1892 he resigned this important office to become a federal circuit court judge.

Taft would have happily spent his entire life in this post. In 1899 he even turned down an offer of the presidency of Yale College. How-

Helen Herron Taft was an attractive and ambitious woman. She urged her reluctant husband, William Howard Taft, to accept the nomination for the presidency.

ever, in 1900 he accepted President William McKinley's request that he become head of a special commission to oversee the government of the Philippine Islands. The Philippines had been acquired by the United States from Spain in 1898 after the Spanish-American War. In the Philippines, Taft demonstrated his ability as an administrator, and in 1901 he was appointed by McKinley as the first civilian governor of the islands.

Taft proved to be an excellent colonial governor. The Filipinos, objecting as much to American rule as to Spanish, were in rebellion against American troops when Taft arrived. Although he insisted that they lay down their arms, he developed a great affection for the people of the Philippines and carried out many important reforms. He saw to it that landless peasants were permitted to buy land at fair prices. He improved the school system, built many roads, and did everything possible to prepare the people for eventual independence. So interested was he in this work that he twice refused appointment to the United States Supreme Court—his highest ambition—because he felt that his work in the islands had not been completed.

However, in 1904 his friend Theodore Roosevelt, then president, appointed him secretary of war. This post enabled Taft to continue to supervise the Philippines. Heading the War Department also put him in charge of the building of the Panama Canal. He became one of Roosevelt's most trusted advisers, and soon he was being mentioned as a leading candidate for the office of president himself.

▶A RELUCTANT PRESIDENT

Taft did not want to be president. But his family, especially his wife, Helen Herron Taft, whom he had married in 1886, urged him to accept the nomination. When Roosevelt formally asked him to run, he reluctantly agreed.

This was a mistake. The hectic pressures of the White House made him an unhappy man. On the one hand, he spent too much time on the golf course. On the other, he complained that his work forced him to rush his meals and forego his afternoon nap. He hated to make speeches, and when he did, he was usually dull and long-winded. Too often he left important decisions to others. One critic called him "an amiable island completely surrounded by men who know exactly what they want." Taft had been an excellent administrator when working under someone else's direction. But he was not successful when faced with the final responsibility for establishing policy and directing the entire national government.

The Tariff

Taft's first move as president was to urge Congress to lower the tariff duties on foreign goods coming into the United States. Originally, high tariffs had seemed necessary to protect new American industries against European competition. But by 1900 American manufacturers were the most efficient in the world. High tariffs simply raised the cost of living for consumers and gave the manufacturers extra profits.

During the 1908 election campaign the Republican Party had promised to revise the tariff. This, everyone assumed, would mean lowering it. The new Payne-Aldrich tariff bill, however, made only very small changes in the law, and many reformers expected Taft to veto it. Taft was disappointed with the measure, but thought it at least better than the existing tariff. Therefore he signed it into law. Perhaps this was sensible. But Taft angered many citizens by actually praising the

Payne-Aldrich Act, even calling it "the best tariff bill the Republican Party ever passed."

The Pinchot Controversy

Next Taft angered the liberals by seeming to reverse Roosevelt's conservation policies. Roosevelt was a great nature lover. He had been disturbed by the rapid destruction of the nation's forest and mineral resources by lumber and mining companies and had established many large national parks and reserves in the West. His chief forester, Gifford Pinchot (1865–1945), was a leading conservation expert. Taft also believed in conservation, and he kept Pinchot on as chief forester. But his secretary of the interior, Richard A. Ballinger (1858–1922), who was Pinchot's superior, soon got into an argument with the chief forester over a large tract of public land in Alaska. When Pinchot accused Ballinger of allowing this land to be gobbled up by a big coal-mining company, Taft ordered an investigation. The inquiry convinced Taft that Ballinger had done no wrong, so he ordered Pinchot to stop his attacks. Pinchot refused, and Taft then removed him from office. While he was probably justified in doing so, his action cost him much support among liberal Republicans.

The opposition between Taft and Theodore Roosevelt for the Republican presidential nomination in 1912 is depicted in a political cartoon of the period.

Reforms

Taft did accomplish a number of major reforms. He was responsible for the creation of the Postal Savings System, which provided small depositors with a safe place for their savings. He strengthened the control of the Interstate Commerce Commission over the nation's railroads. He also continued and even expanded Roosevelt's "trust-busting" (antitrust) activities, which involved breaking up some of the large industrial monopolies that had grown up in recent years. But he came to rely increasingly on the conservative wing of the Republican Party and to criticize the reform, or progressive, wing. He believed the progressives were trying to ruin his administration and became so angry that he refused to invite them to White House dinners, receptions, and other social functions.

▶ THE FEUD WITH ROOSEVELT

The reformers turned to Roosevelt for help. After his term had ended, the former president had gone off to Africa to hunt big game and collect specimens for a museum. In 1910 he returned to find himself in the middle of a bitter political fight. Roosevelt genuinely liked Taft and tried to avoid opposing him. Yet all Roosevelt's progressive friends were insisting that Taft had sold out to the reactionaries. For a time Roosevelt tried to remain neutral. But this only angered Taft, who expected Roosevelt to back him up. Gradually they ceased to be friends. Mrs. Taft resented the fact that most people paid more attention to Roosevelt than to her husband. She made things worse by treating Roosevelt's wife and other members of his family coldly. Finally, in 1912, Roosevelt decided to oppose Taft for the Republican presidential nomination.

Taft would actually have been happy to retire from the race. But he felt that he could not honorably step down under the circumstances. He remarked angrily that even a rat will fight when cornered. In the campaign for the nomination Roosevelt won the votes of most of the delegates from states where presidential primaries were held. However, a majority of the convention delegates were not chosen by the voters but by local politicians. Taft won most of their votes because of his power as head of the party. At the convention Taft was nominated on the first ballot.

President Taft in 1909 with his two sons, Charles (*left*) and Robert.

Roosevelt felt that he had been cheated of the nomination. He therefore decided to form a new party and run for the presidency on his own. This Progressive, or Bull Moose, Party split the Republican vote, and the Democratic candidate, Woodrow Wilson, won the election. Taft ran a poor third, capturing only eight electoral votes.

▶ LAW PROFESSOR AND CHIEF JUSTICE

When his term ended in 1913, Taft became a professor of constitutional law at Yale. During World War I he served as joint chairman of the National War Labor Board. After the war he was a leading Republican supporter of Woodrow Wilson's League of Nations. The failure of the Senate to accept American membership in the league greatly distressed him.

Then, in 1921, President Warren Harding named Taft chief justice of the United States. This was the post he had always wanted, and the last 10 years of his life were probably the happiest. As a judge he was conservative. He opposed government control of business and objected particularly to laws giving special treatment to labor unions.

On the other hand, Taft succeeded in simplifying and making more efficient the procedures of the federal courts. Once again it was his skill as a manager, as distinct from ability to lead people, that came to the fore. He also persuaded Congress to construct the magnificent building that today houses the Supreme Court in Washington. Taft's administrative work while on the Supreme Court was probably his most important contribution in a lifetime devoted to public service.

Early in 1930 failing health forced Taft to retire. On March 8, 1930, he died in Washington, D.C., at the age of 72. He was buried in Arlington National Cemetery.

Taft was survived by his wife, two sons, and a daughter. His elder son, Robert Alphonso Taft (1889–1953), became a U.S. senator from Ohio and a leader of the Republican Party. His younger son, Charles Phelps Taft (1897–1983), was mayor of Cincinnati.

JOHN A. GARRATY
Columbia University

TAHITI. See PACIFIC OCEAN AND ISLANDS.

IMPORTANT DATES IN THE LIFE OF WILLIAM HOWARD TAFT

1857	Born in Cincinnati, Ohio, September 15.
1878	Graduated from Yale College.
1880	Admitted to the bar.
1881–1882	Assistant prosecutor, Hamilton County, Ohio.
1882–1883	Collector of internal revenue, 1st Ohio district.
1886	Married Helen Herron.
1887–1890	Judge of the Ohio superior court.
1890–1892	Solicitor general of the United States.
1892–1900	Federal circuit court judge.
1900	President of Philippines Commission.
1901–1904	Civil governor of the Philippine Islands.
1904–1908	Secretary of war.
1909–1913	27th president of the United States.
1913–1921	Professor of constitutional law, Yale University.
1921–1930	Chief justice of the United States.
1930	Died in Washington, D.C., March 8.

TAIPEI

Taipei is the capital and largest city of Taiwan, the main island of the Republic of China. It is a bustling city of 2.7 million people, situated on the Tanshui River, near the island's northern tip.

The City. Taipei municipality covers an area of 105 square miles (272 square kilometers). The city is continually being modernized, with skyscrapers replacing many old buildings. In 2003, Taipei 101, a 1,676-foot (511-meter) tower, became the world's tallest building to date.

Taipei is the home of National Taiwan University and many other educational and cultural institutions. The National Palace Museum houses a world-renowned collection of Chinese art. One of the city's most popular recreation areas, Yangmingshan Park, is flanked by two steep volcanic mountain peaks and is noted for its beautiful cherry and azalea trees. The National Chiang Kai-

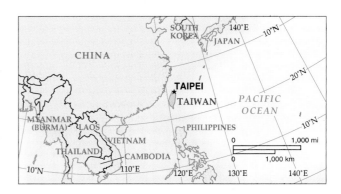

shek Cultural Center, which opened in 1987, provides space for various community activities and events. The Buddhist Lungshan Temple is famous for its stone columns, wood carvings, and statues. Other places of interest include the Taipei Fine Arts Museum; the National Museum of History; a school where children are trained in traditional forms of opera and acrobatics; a zoo; and a botanical garden.

Economic Activity. Taipei is the economic and financial heart of the Republic of China, as well as its political and cultural center. It is home to one of Asia's busiest stock exchanges. The island's thriving plastics, shipping, airline, and other industries maintain headquarters there and in the suburbs. Also nearby is Hsinchu Science Park, often called Taiwan's "Silicon Valley," and Keelung (Chilung). Keelung is Taipei's seaport and a center of overseas trade.

History. What is now known as Taipei was once inhabited by the Kaidagelan, a plains aboriginal people. Others who have occupied the region have included the Spanish, the Dutch, the Chinese, and the Japanese. Taipei became an important center of trade and commerce. It was officially named Taiwan's capital in 1891.

When the Chinese Communists took over the mainland in 1949 and founded the People's Republic of China, the Nationalists under President Chiang Kai-shek withdrew to Taiwan and established Taipei as the seat of government of the Republic of China. In the years since, the population, economy, and boundaries of the city have expanded enormously.

JUNE TEUFEL DREYER
Department of Political Science
University of Miami

Taipei, Taiwan's capital, is located on the island's northern tip. This busy city is also Taiwan's political, financial, cultural, and industrial center.

TAIWAN

Taiwan, sometimes called Formosa, is a large island in the South China Sea. Legend has it that the first Portuguese sailor to catch sight of the island proclaimed it *Ilha Formosa*, or "beautiful island."

Taiwan has served as the seat of the Republic of China (ROC) since 1949, when Communist forces took over the mainland and proclaimed the People's Republic of China.

▶ PEOPLE

The population of Taiwan is about 23 million. Nearly everyone is of Chinese descent, although there are also about 400,000 people of Polynesian heritage. Most of the Chinese immigrated to Taiwan mainly from the 1600's to the 1800's. Another 2 million arrived after the Communists took over the mainland in 1949.

The official language is Mandarin Chinese. Hokkienese is also widely spoken. Buddhism is the predominant religion, but there are also Taoists, Muslims, and Christians.

The government provides nine years of compulsory education. Taiwan has a number of colleges and universities. The state-run National Taiwan University is the largest and most prestigious.

▶ LAND

The ROC is made up of the principal island of Taiwan, plus the large islands of Matsu and Quemoy and the many small islands of the Pescadores. Taiwan island is about 240 miles (390 kilometers) long and about 90 miles (145 kilometers) wide. It has an area of about 13,885 square miles (35,961 square kilometers) and is approximately 100 miles east of the Chinese mainland, separated by the Taiwan (Formosa) Strait.

A mountain range extends the entire length of the island. The tallest peak, Yu Shan (Jade Mountain), is 13,113 feet (3,997 meters) high. Most of the eastern coast drops straight into the sea. The western coast is a plain extending fairly deeply inland in some places.

Taiwan's climate is subtropical. Temperatures vary little during the year, but sharp seasonal and regional variations in rainfall are caused by the monsoon winds. The average annual rainfall is about 100 inches (2,500 millimeters). The island is periodically battered by typhoons, especially in the summer. Taiwan also has many earthquakes.

▶ ECONOMY

Since World War II (1939–45), Taiwan has changed from a predominantly agricultural economy to one of the world's leading trading nations. The service sector, particularly the financial and stock markets, employs more than half the island's workforce. Taiwan is also a

Tea is harvested on a mountainside overlooking rice fields. Tea and rice are two of Taiwan's main crops.

world leader in computer manufacturing. Agriculture now accounts for less than 5 percent of Taiwan's total economy.

▶ MAJOR CITIES

Taipei is Taiwan's capital and largest city. A separate article on Taipei can be found in this volume. **Kao-hsiung** is Taiwan's second largest city and an important port.

▶ HISTORY AND GOVERNMENT

In addition to aboriginal (native) and Chinese influences, Taiwan was occupied by the Spanish, Portuguese, and Dutch, all of whom left their mark. In 1661 a Chinese army under Cheng Ch'eng-kung (Koxinga) drove out the Dutch. The Manchus overran Taiwan in 1683 and ruled it for more than 200 years.

Following China's defeat in the Sino-Japanese War (1894–95), Taiwan and other Chinese islands were ceded to Japan. After Japan was defeated in World War II (1939–45), Taiwan was returned to China and made a separate province. The Nationalists under Chiang Kai-shek established their government on Taiwan in 1949, after the mainland fell to the Communists.

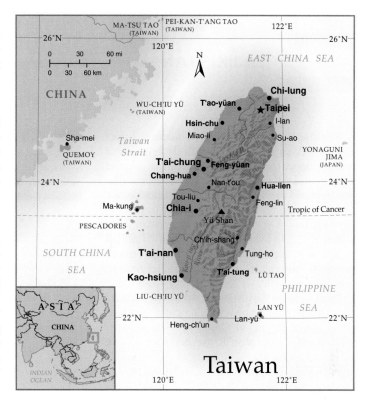

Taiwan

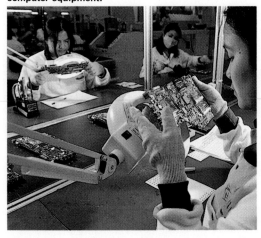

A worker inspects a circuit board in a computer factory. Taiwan is a world leader in the production of computer equipment.

Chiang served as president until his death in 1975. His son Chiang Ching-kuo was president from 1978 until his death in 1988. In 1971, Taiwan lost its seat in the United Nations to the People's Republic of China. The United States severed diplomatic relations with Taiwan in 1979.

In 1996, Chiang Ching-kuo's successor Lee Teng-hui won Taiwan's first direct presidential election. But in 2000, Chen Shui-bian of the Democratic Progressive Party was elected president, marking the first loss for the Nationalists in 50 years. Chen was re-elected in 2004, after the courts supervised a recount of the vote. Meanwhile, tensions with the mainland grew due to Chen's pro-independence views. Chen's government then changed the country's official name to the Republic of China (Taiwan), which implied a challenge to the mainland's "one-China" policy. In 2005, China passed a controversial law permitting the use of armed force against Taiwan should it continue to pursue independence.

JUNE TEUFEL DREYER
Department of Political Science
University of Miami

See also CHIANG KAI-SHEK; CHINA.

TAJIKISTAN

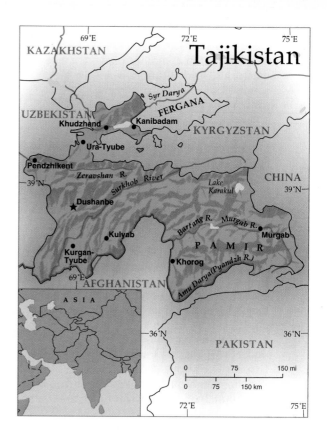

Tajikistan is one of the five former Soviet Central Asian republics, which declared their independence from a disintegrating Soviet Union in 1991. Tajikistan, however, is distinctive among the nations that once made up Soviet Central Asia, which also include Kazakhstan, Kyrgyzstan, Turkmenistan, and Uzbekistan. It shares a common political past with them, but in language and culture the Tajiks are related to Iranians rather than to the Turkic peoples of the region.

The People. Tajiks make up about 62 percent of the population. The largest minorities are Uzbeks (from neighboring Uzbekistan), with about 24 percent of the population, and Russians, with about 8 percent. The Tajiks and Uzbeks are Muslims; the Russians are Eastern Orthodox Christians. Considerable numbers of Tajiks also live in Afghanistan, to the south. Dushanbe is the capital and largest city, with about 600,000 inhabitants.

The Tajiks are among the most ancient peoples of Central Asia. Of Indo-European origin, they speak a language closely related to Persian. Although extended families still exist among them, the old structure of clans and tribes has been lost. Religious tradition is strong, but the idea of a separate Tajik nation

A narrow valley cuts through the high mountains that make up most of Tajikistan's landscape. Some of the mountains, part of the Pamir range, are eternally snow-covered.

The Tajiks are an Iranian people, who speak a form of Persian. They thus differ from most other peoples of Central Asia, who are Turkic-speaking.

did not exist until relatively recent times. Because of their rich Iranian heritage, many Tajiks, particularly in the cities, see themselves as culturally superior to their Turkic-speaking neighbors.

The Land. Tajikistan is a largely mountainous land of great scenic beauty. It stretches from the high Pamir range, where the country's highest peak reaches 24,590 feet (7,495 meters), to the fertile Fergana Valley. The major river is the Amu Darya. The climate varies according to the elevation—hot and dry in the lowlands and eternally snow-covered in the high mountains.

The Economy. Tajikistan's economy has traditionally been based on farming, in the irrigated lowland areas, cattle breeding, and silk cultivation. Cotton is the main crop, but rice and fruits are also grown. There are important mineral deposits, including gold, coal, and oil. Industry, developed during the Soviet period, revolves mostly around the processing of agricultural products, mining, and textile manufacturing. The country has large-scale hydroelectric power capability.

History and Government. Tajikistan's history dates back to the 100's B.C. Like other parts of Central Asia, it was often invaded. Arab conquerors brought Islam to the region in the

A.D. 600's, and Mongol invaders devastated the land in the 1200's. Early Tajik history was closely interwoven with that of the Uzbeks, since both were subjects of the same rulers and occupied the same cities.

Tajikistan fell under the domination of Russia in 1873, when the emir of Bukhara, one of the early states of the region, was forced to accept a Russian protectorate. With the overthrow of the Russian Empire in 1917, imperial rule was replaced by that of the Soviets. Tajikistan was made an autonomous republic within Uzbekistan in 1924. It became a separate constituent, or union, republic of the Soviet Union in 1929.

Tajikistan joined other Soviet republics in proclaiming its independence in 1991. In 1992 civil war broke out between the former Communists, Muslim fundamentalists, and Tajik nationalists. The former Communists, backed by Russia, assumed power in 1993. A 1994 constitution created a presidential system of government and established a two-house legislature, the Supreme Assembly.

Occasional fighting continued even after a cease-fire accord was signed late in 1996.

MICHAEL RYWKIN
City University of New York, City College
Author, *Moscow's Muslim Challenge: Soviet Central Asia*

FACTS and figures

REPUBLIC OF TAJIKISTAN is the official name of the country.

LOCATION: Central Asia.

AREA: 55,250 sq mi (143,100 km²).

POPULATION: 6,400,000 (estimate).

CAPITAL AND LARGEST CITY: Dushanbe.

MAJOR LANGUAGES: Tajik, Russian.

MAJOR RELIGIOUS GROUP: Muslim.

GOVERNMENT: Republic. **Head of state—**president. **Head of government—**prime minister. **Legislature—**Supreme Assembly.

CHIEF PRODUCTS: Agricultural—cotton, silk, rice, fruits, livestock. **Manufactured—**processed agricultural products, textiles. **Mineral—** gold, coal, oil.

The Taj Mahal, in Agra, India, is considered one of the finest examples of Islamic architecture. The white marble structure was built as a tomb in the 1600's.

TAJ MAHAL

The Taj Mahal has been called the most beautiful building in the world. Its gleaming white domes and slender minarets have thrilled visitors from many lands through the centuries. It has been described and praised in so many languages that the very words "Taj Mahal" have come to mean beauty.

"Taj Mahal" comes from Mum*taz Mahall* ("Ornament of the Palace"). This was the name given to Arjumand Banu, the favorite wife of Shah Jahan (1592–1666), a Mogul ruler of India. When she died, her grief-stricken husband decided to build the most beautiful tomb in the world to house her body. His monument to love was completed about 1648 by 20,000 laborers under the direction of skilled artisans from many lands.

The splendid white marble tomb is located in Agra, a city in north central India that was once the residential capital of the Mogul rulers. Like all fine Muslim architecture of the time, it has a great dome in the center. Four smaller domes surround the central one.

The Taj Mahal is noted for its harmonious proportions. It stands on a large white marble terrace and overlooks the peaceful Jumna River. Four slender minarets, each in a corner of the terrace, rise into the sky. The front of the Taj Mahal is reflected in the glistening waters of a long pool. Beautiful gardens studded with shrubs and dark green cypress trees form a lovely setting for the marble building.

Shah Jahan and his beloved wife lie buried beneath the floor of the building. Their tombs, side by side under the central dome, are enclosed by screens of pierced marble. The light filters softly through the holes, creating an atmosphere of peace and serenity. The walls are ornamented by delicate designs, many inlaid with semiprecious stones.

In recent times, air pollution from industries in Agra has marred the purity of the marble walls. Strict anti-pollution measures have been taken to try to protect the greatest masterpiece of Indian Mogul architecture.

ROBERT I. CRANE
Syracuse University

TALLAHASSEE. See FLORIDA (Cities).

TALLCHIEF, MARIA. See OKLAHOMA (Famous People).

TALMUD

Talmud is a Hebrew word that means "study" and "teaching." It refers to a large body of literature that is a record of the study and interpretation of Jewish oral traditions and all the books of the Hebrew scriptures.

The Talmud contains the fundamentals of Jewish law and ethics. It discusses daily life in the Jewish community and includes stories that elaborate on the biblical accounts of Abraham, Jacob, Moses, David, the prophets, and others. Many of these stories are derived from popular folktales.

There are also stories about the Talmudic teachers (rabbis) and the lessons they taught. One of the best known is about Rabbi Hillel (? B.C.–A.D. 9). He was once asked, "What is the principal message of Judaism?" He replied, "What is hateful to you, do not do to another. This is the law, all the rest is commentary. Now go and study." (Hillel's first sentence is a version of the Golden Rule.) Another story tells about Rabbi Akiba, who lived during the 100's. Until he was 40, he did not know how to read or write. Then he became the greatest Jewish scholar of his time.

The Talmud developed as Jews sought to understand and clarify the Bible, especially its laws. From about the 400's B.C. on, Jews regarded the Bible as God's primary revelation (statement) and laws for humanity, as revealed through the prophets. Because the Jews believed they had a special responsibility—to set an example for all people by obeying and serving God—they wanted to know what to do in every situation. For instance, what were one's obligations to God? How was one to celebrate sacred occasions? What things were permitted or forbidden?

At first these studies were conducted orally because the rabbis felt that interpretation of the Bible should remain separate from the Bible itself. Also, like many of the ancient Greeks, the rabbis felt that teaching by word of mouth was more effective. Gradually people began to make notes of the teachings they had inherited and memorized.

About the year A.D. 200, Rabbi Judah Ha-Nasi assembled all the records of Jewish traditions that were available in the academies and summarized them, then organized them into 60 treatises in six parts. This was called the Mishnah and was written in Hebrew. Since it was only a summary, and not a full discussion of the traditions, scholars from 200

The Talmud is a large body of literature that contains information about Jewish life, law, and ethics. It developed as Jews sought to understand and clarify the Bible. The Talmud has two parts, the Mishnah and the Gemara.

on had to interpret the Mishnah to make clear what its brief statements involved. Their discussions form the bulk of the Talmud. Gradually these discussions came to be called the Gemara, so that the Talmud was divided into two parts, the Mishnah and the Gemara.

By the year 400 a version of the Talmud existed in Palestine. Another version was developed in Babylonia 100 years later; it received wider circulation and acceptance. During the Middle Ages many copies were burned. Christian popes and kings ordered their destruction because the Talmud contained the main teachings of the Jewish religion. Eventually the Babylonian Talmud came to be regarded as the most authoritative version of the Talmud.

Reviewed by LAWRENCE GROSSMAN
The American Jewish Committee

TAMPA. See FLORIDA (Cities).

TANKS

A tank is a heavily armored combat vehicle that travels on tracks, or continuous metal belts, rather than wheels. With their powerful guns, tanks are important battlefield weapons for use against enemy troops and fortifications (buildings for defense).

The most common modern tanks are **main battle tanks** (MBT's). An MBT carries a crew of three or four—the tank commander, a driver, a gunner, and often a gun loader. There are smaller, lighter tanks for special uses.

▶ HOW TANKS MOVE

A tank's tracks consist of steel or rubber links that are moved by drive sprockets (engine-driven wheels with teeth that interlock with the links). The tracks run along a series of wheels called **bogie wheels,** which can move up and down to allow the tank to move smoothly over uneven ground.

The tracks give a tank great mobility over rough ground, but its movement may be restricted on some terrain. For example, a tank can bog down in muddy or swampy areas, where its tracks cannot always get a grip on the ground. Thick forests, dense jungles, and steep hills can also limit a tank's movements.

Tanks have diesel or gasoline engines, usually located in the rear of the vehicle. A tank's speed depends on its weight, the power of its engine, and the nature of the terrain. In the late 1980's, the fastest tank was the M1 Abrams, an MBT with a top speed of about 45 miles (72 kilometers) an hour.

▶ WEAPONS ON TANKS

Tanks may have various weapons, but most MBT's have main guns with calibers of 105 to 125 millimeters. (The caliber is the inside diameter of a gun's barrel, and it indicates what size shell the gun can fire.) Smaller tanks carry guns with calibers ranging in size from 75 to 85 millimeters. A few light tanks carry missiles, which are lightweight and very powerful. The missiles give the light tanks greater firepower than their regular guns. Missiles are not used on MBT's because the main guns of these tanks can give similar results for less cost. Besides the main gun, most tanks have one or more machine guns. The guns are usually mounted on a structure called a **turret** that can rotate in any direction.

Modern tanks are fitted with many devices to help them destroy enemy targets. For example, night sighting devices help locate enemy tanks by sensing the heat of their engines. These sights can also locate targets in dust, fog, smoke, and snow. When a target has been sighted, an automatic range finder measures how far it is from the tank, and a computer checks wind and weather conditions to increase the accuracy of the shot.

On some tanks a crew member loads the gun. On others, there is an automatic loader. The tank commander pushes a switch to select a shell, and it is automatically loaded into the gun. This allows a very rapid rate of firing.

▶ WEAPONS USED AGAINST TANKS

The main enemy of a tank is the gun of another tank. But other specialized weapons can also destroy or disable tanks. The most powerful of these weapons are missiles, some of which are guided by special controls and are very accurate. Artillery shells can also disable a tank. Certain shells can pierce a tank's armor or destroy the tank by exploding above it, where the armor is thinner.

Missiles may be fired from ground vehicles, airplanes, and helicopters or by foot soldiers. Foot soldiers may also carry small rocket launchers, popularly called bazookas, that fire armor-piercing shells. These weapons are deadly, but they must be fired at close range to be effective.

Mines—explosive devices buried in the ground—are not powerful enough to destroy a tank. But they can stop a tank by damaging its tracks, thus making it an easy target for other weapons.

As weapons used against tanks have become more effective, so has the armor used on tanks. The armor at the front of some tanks is 6 inches (15 centimeters) thick. But too much armor weighs a tank down. Among other solutions that have been tried are reactive armor, which explodes outward to destroy incoming shells, and armor made of dense uranium encased in steel.

▶ TYPES OF TANKS

Besides MBT's, there are battle tanks with special uses. For example, some tanks are fitted with anti-aircraft guns and radar for protection against attack from the air. These anti-aircraft tanks accompany the MBT's.

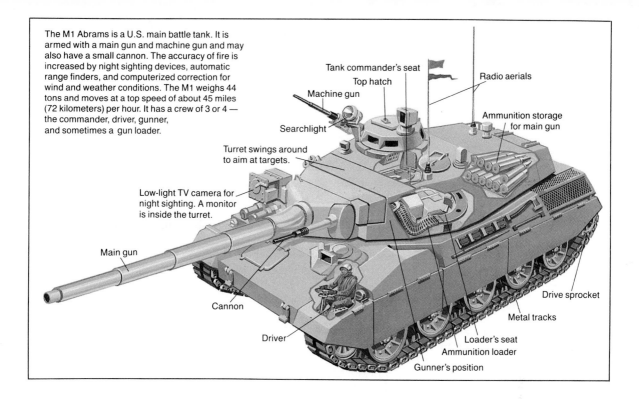

The M1 Abrams is a U.S. main battle tank. It is armed with a main gun and machine gun and may also have a small cannon. The accuracy of fire is increased by night sighting devices, automatic range finders, and computerized correction for wind and weather conditions. The M1 weighs 44 tons and moves at a top speed of about 45 miles (72 kilometers) per hour. It has a crew of 3 or 4 — the commander, driver, gunner, and sometimes a gun loader.

Tank commander's seat
Top hatch
Machine gun
Radio aerials
Ammunition storage for main gun
Searchlight
Turret swings around to aim at targets.
Low-light TV camera for night sighting. A monitor is inside the turret.
Main gun
Cannon
Driver
Gunner's position
Ammunition loader
Loader's seat
Metal tracks
Drive sprocket

Airborne tanks are lightweight vehicles that can be carried by aircraft. They may be unloaded when the plane lands or dropped by parachute if no landing field is available.

Some tanks are amphibious—they can travel through water as well as over land. Amphibious tanks are used to cross rivers or to land on beaches. They have snorkels—pipes that are raised above the surface of the water —to supply air for the engine and crew.

Other tanks are used for support rather than fighting. For example, tanks called bridge layers carry a folding bridge instead of a gun turret. The tank has armlike devices that lift the bridge and place it over a stream or gully that is to be crossed. After other tanks have crossed, the bridge layer picks up the bridge and follows the others to the next obstacle.

Some tanks are fitted with bulldozers and are used to dig fighting positions or to remove trees and other obstacles from the path of other tanks. The bulldozer may also be used to destroy enemy fortifications or to push earth over enemy pillboxes (low concrete platforms for machine guns and anti-tank weapons).

Because tanks are often damaged in battle, a tank recovery vehicle with a crane and power winch (a machine for hoisting) is kept a short distance behind the main tank group. When a tank is hit, the recovery vehicle moves forward to haul it to safety. The recovery vehicle carries spare parts, so that the damaged tank can be repaired and returned to battle.

▶ HISTORY

Tanks were developed by the British for use in World War I. To hide the true purpose of these early armored vehicles from German spies, the British called them water tanks— thus giving rise to the present name. Tanks were first used in 1916, at the Battle of the Somme in France. They terrified the German soldiers, but they were so clumsy and unreliable that they were successful in only a few battles after that.

Tanks played a major role in World War II (1939–45). The Germans used fast-moving tanks with other ground forces in their *Blitzkrieg* ("lightning war") tactics, rapidly gaining control of most of Europe in 1939–40. The Allies used similar tactics to eventually defeat the Germans. Tanks were later used in the Korean and Vietnam wars. They continue to be an important battlefield weapon, particularly in the desert regions of the Middle East.

JIM MESKO
Author, *Armor in Viet Nam*

TANNHÄUSER. See OPERA (Stories of Famous Operas).

TANTALUS. See GREEK MYTHOLOGY (Profiles).

TANZANIA

Tanzania is a nation in East Africa made up of the formerly separate countries of Tanganyika and Zanzibar. The former Tanganyika occupies a large area on the African mainland. Zanzibar consists of two islands in the Indian Ocean. Tanganyika won independence from Britain in 1961, and Zanzibar became independent in 1963. They formed a united country in 1964.

▶ PEOPLE

Most of Tanzania's 36.5 million people live on the mainland. Almost all are of African descent, but about 1 percent are of Arab, Indian, or European ethnic origin. Zanzibar's population includes Africans who trace part of their ancestry to Oman and Iran. Arabs from Oman colonized the islands in the 1800's. Both Arabs and Persians from Iran traded along the African coast in ancient times.

Language and Religion. The language most commonly spoken in Tanzania and the rest of East Africa is Swahili (or Kiswahili). Swahili belongs to the Bantu language family and contains many words from Arabic. Most Tanzanians also speak one or more other Bantu languages. Speakers of the Sukuma and Nyamwezi languages are among the most numerous. The Maasai (also spelled Masai) live on both sides of the border between Tanzania and Kenya. They speak a non-Bantu language. English is also widely spoken in Tanzania.

There are equal numbers of Christians and Muslims in Tanzania, and religious tolerance is well established. Muslims predominate along the coast and in Zanzibar. Estimates vary regarding how many Tanzanians are followers of traditional religions. Tanzanians of Indian ancestry include Hindus, Muslims, Sikhs, and Christians.

Education. Schooling is compulsory for Tanzanian children between the ages of 7 and 13. Enrollment has dramatically increased in recent years following the abolition of school fees. Tanzania has nine universities, the oldest of which is the University of Dar es Salaam. Almost 80 percent of Tanzanians age 15 and over can read and write.

Way of Life. Most Tanzanians live in rural areas. About one-quarter live in cities or towns. Most rural people are farmers who raise crops and livestock to feed themselves.

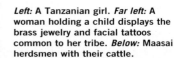

Left: A Tanzanian girl. *Far left:* A woman holding a child displays the brass jewelry and facial tattoos common to her tribe. *Below:* Maasai herdsmen with their cattle.

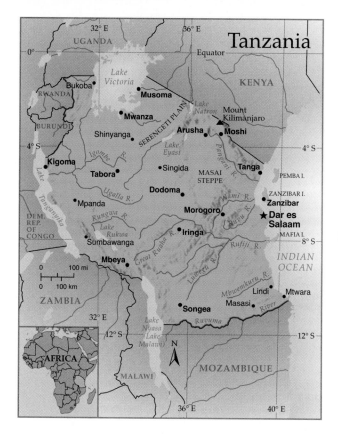

The country's staple food is *ugali*, which is made from ground corn and resembles the hominy grits eaten in the southern United States. The Maasai, who are semi-nomadic cattle herders, depend on their livestock for much of their diet of milk and meat.

Rural homes vary in size and shape but traditionally have earthen walls and roofs made of thatch, banana leaves, or tin. Houses on Zanzibar, reflecting Arab influence, are usually whitewashed structures, some with beautifully hand-carved doors.

Most Tanzanians wear modern-style clothing, but there are also many variations in dress. Women often prefer the cooler traditional costume made of brightly printed cloths called *kangas*. Men on the coast often wear sarongs, which are called *kikois*. Muslim men sometimes wear traditional white gowns. Some Muslim women wear *bui buis*, black gowns that cover their modern clothes when they go outdoors. Hindu women often wear saris, and Sikh men wear turbans.

Elephants walk across the vast Serengeti Plain. In the background is Mount Kilimanjaro, whose name means "shining mountain" in Swahili.

Health is an important social issue in Tanzania. Outside the highland regions, mosquitoes carrying malaria prey on the human population, and tsetse flies can cause sleeping sickness, a disease often fatal to humans and domestic animals. In addition to these longstanding health dangers, Tanzania has seen rising numbers of HIV/AIDS infections and deaths in recent decades. Today about 12 percent of the adult population is living with HIV/AIDS.

▶ **LAND**

Land Regions. The mainland of Tanzania consists of a long, narrow coastal plain, a low eastern plateau, and a higher central plateau, which is broken by the Great Rift Valley of East Africa. In the north, near the border with Kenya, Mount Kilimanjaro, Africa's highest peak, rises to 19,341 feet (5,895 meters). The most fertile soils on the mainland are found in the highland regions, where most of the inland population lives. Tanzania is also home to a vast region of grasslands and woodlands known as the Serengeti Plain, which is shared with Kenya.

The two islands of Zanzibar—Zanzibar and Pemba—are situated about 25 miles (40 kilometers) from the mainland. They are composed largely of coral.

Rivers and Lakes. Tanzania's rivers include the Mbwemkuru, Pangani, Rufiji, Ruvu, Ruvuma, and Wami. Three of Africa's largest lakes lie on Tanzania's borders—Lake Victoria in the northwest, Lake Tanganyika in the west, and Lake Malawi in the southwest.

Fishermen on the coast of Zanzibar attend to their *ngalawas*—canoes dug out of tree trunks and propelled by sails. Their catches include mackerel, parrotfish, and sharks.

Climate. Coastal Tanzania has a tropical climate, with high temperatures, humidity, and rainfall. The central plateau is hot and dry, with limited rainfall. The highland regions have a temperate climate.

Natural Resources. Tanzania has abundant mineral and water resources. Fish are plentiful in the Indian Ocean and Tanzania's lakes. The country also has some of the world's finest game parks, which are home to hundreds of species of wildlife.

▶ **THE ECONOMY**

In recent years, Tanzania has achieved strong economic growth and reduced poverty, but nearly one-third of Tanzanians remain too poor to buy basic necessities. The government plans to continue to pursue economic reforms designed to sustain growth and further decrease poverty.

Services. Services account for 40 percent of Tanzania's domestic output, but together with manufacturing they employ only 20 percent of its workers. Government workers and commerce account for most service jobs. Tourism is a growing source of employment. Many people earn a living by working as street vendors and craftspeople.

Manufacturing. Manufacturing is limited. The chief manufactures are textiles and processed agricultural products and other foods.

Agriculture. Despite the scarcity of cultivable land, agriculture accounts for more than 40 percent of Tanzania's domestic out-

put and employs 80 percent of its workers. Tanzania's principal food crops are corn and cassava (a starchy root). The country is one of the world's leading producers of sisal (a plant used in making rope and twine). Zanzibar is the world's largest producer of cloves.

Mining. Diamonds, gold, salt, and natural gas are all mined. There are undeveloped deposits of coal, iron ore, nickel, and uranium. Although development of natural gas has begun, no oil deposits have been found.

Energy. Tanzania relies on wood, oil and gas, and water power to produce energy.

Trade. Tanzania exports gold, coffee, tea, sisal, pyrethrum (used in making insecticides), cashew nuts, cotton, tobacco, sugarcane, and cloves. It imports machinery, raw materials, and crude oil.

Transportation. Tanzania has 54,800 miles (88,200 kilometers) of highways, only 5 percent of which are paved, and about 2,300 miles (3,700 kilometers) of railroads. Tanzania's lakes provide important ways to ship goods to neighboring countries.

Communication. Despite its large population, Tanzania has only about 1 million tele-

FACTS and figures

UNITED REPUBLIC OF TANZANIA is the official name of the country.

LOCATION: East Africa.

AREA: 364,900 sq mi (945,087 km²).

POPULATION: 36.5 million (estimate).

CAPITAL AND LARGEST CITY: Dar es Salaam (the capital is being transferred to Dodoma).

MAJOR LANGUAGES: Swahili (Kiswahili), English, various African languages.

MAJOR RELIGIOUS GROUPS: Christian, Muslim, local religions.

GOVERNMENT: Republic. **Head of state and government**—president. **Legislature**—National Assembly.

CHIEF PRODUCTS: Agricultural—coffee, tea, sisal, pyrethrum, cashew nuts, cloves. **Manufactured**—processed agricultural products, textiles, wood products. **Mineral**—diamonds.

MONETARY UNIT: Tanzanian shilling (1 T shilling = 100 cents).

phones, about 9 million radios, 100,000 television sets, and 250,000 Internet users.

▶ MAJOR CITIES

Dar es Salaam, with more than 1 million people, is Tanzania's capital, largest city, and main port. Its name means "Haven of Peace." **Dodoma**, in the central plateau, is being developed as Tanzania's future capital. Other important cities are **Tanga** on the coast, **Mwanza** on Lake Victoria, and **Arusha** in the northeast. The city of **Zanzibar** is the largest of Zanzibar's urban areas.

▶ GOVERNMENT

Tanzania's constitution provides for a president, elected for five years, and a separate president elected in Zanzibar who has authority over matters pertaining only to Zanzibar. Until 1992, Tanzania had only one legal political party, the Chama Cha Mapinduzi (CCM), or Revolutionary Party. In that year, the constitution was amended to provide for a multiparty political system.

▶ HISTORY

The East African coast and Zanzibar have had contact with people from many different lands since earliest times. By the A.D. 800's, perhaps earlier, the area began to be settled by people from the Arabian Peninsula. By the A.D. 900's most of the coastal Africans and Zanzibaris had been converted to the Muslim religion.

Portuguese interest in East Africa began in 1497. The struggle between Portugal and the Arabs for control of the Indian Ocean continued for more than 200 years. By the 1700's, the Arabs had forced the Portuguese almost entirely out of the region.

From 1804 until 1963, Zanzibar was ruled by a dynasty founded by Sultan Seyyid Said of Oman. A U.S. consulate was opened in Zanzibar in 1837 and a British one in 1841. Britain forced Zanzibar to abolish the slave trade. In 1890, Zanzibar became a British protectorate.

Germany gained influence in Tanganyika in 1884 and 1885, when the explorer Karl Peters signed treaties with twelve tribal chiefs. During World War I (1914–18), British and German troops fought each other in Tanganyika. After Germany's defeat, Tanganyika was made a mandate of the League of Na-

A view of the port of Dar es Salaam, the capital of Tanzania. The city's architecture reflects a mix of African, German, Asian, British, and other influences.

tions and was administered by Britain. In 1946, after World War II (1939–45), it became a trust territory of the United Nations under British administration.

In 1961, Tanganyika became the first British East African territory to win independence. Zanzibar became independent in 1963. The two joined to form the United Republic of Tanganyika and Zanzibar in 1964. The name was soon changed to Tanzania.

After independence, Tanzania was led by President Julius K. Nyerere. Under his leadership, the country carried out bold experiments aimed at preventing the growth of economic inequalities in Tanzanian society. These experiments to promote *ujamaa* (socialism) largely failed, but Nyerere became widely admired for his talents as a statesman. He retired as president in 1985 and was succeeded by Ali Hassan Mwinyi, who had previously served as president of Zanzibar.

Recent Events. The first multiparty elections, held in 1995, yielded an overwhelming victory for CCM presidential candidate, Benjamin Mkapa. In 2000, Mkapa was re-elected. The constitution prohibited him from pursuing a third term in 2005, but his party, the CCM, won both the presidential election and a parliamentary majority that year. Jakaya Kikwete became Tanzania's new president.

EDWARD J. MILES
University of Vermont
Reviewed by GAIL M. GERHART
Columbia University

TAPE RECORDERS. See SOUND RECORDING.

TAPESTRY

A tapestry is a handwoven textile. It is usually made with heavy threads of several colors. Most tapestries are hung on walls or suspended from ceilings.

The weaving of textile by hand requires much time and a great deal of skill. The weaver is limited by problems that other artists seldom face. He has no canvas to paint, no clay to model, no wood or stone to carve. Given only colored threads, he must manufacture and decorate his textile at the same time. Artists with patience, ability to plan, and skill to weave have always been rare, and tapestries traditionally are very expensive and precious.

In the days when the church and great royal houses ruled the world, tapestries were symbols of wealth. Whenever plays, official ceremonies, or public celebrations were held, tapestries lent beauty and richness to the events. Bishops and kings welcomed important visitors with red carpets flanked by tapestry displays. Religious processions followed routes marked with tapestries.

THE EARLIEST WEAVERS

In the ancient tombs of Egypt pictures have been found that show weavers making tapestries of linen. Only a few fragments of Egyptian tapestries survive, but the pictures indicate that the art of tapestry weaving is about 5,000 years old.

The Hebrews learned to make tapestries while they were living in either Babylon or Egypt. The Bible mentions this art several times, and other ancient writings refer to tapestry weaving among the people of Syria, Phoenicia, Persia, and India. Famous throughout the ancient Mediterranean world were the textiles that decorated the cities of Tyre and Sidon. These fabrics impressed the Greeks and Romans, who dominated the Mediterranean lands between 500 B.C. and A.D. 500.

During the medieval period Islamic warriors swept across the Middle East. These people developed a unique style of art. Because the Islamic religion was opposed to the reproduction of figures, tapestries were made with forms called arabesques, which are based on Arabic script, geometry, and abstract floral patterns.

Knights of the Crusades returning to Europe brought back an appreciation for many Eastern things. Among these newfound tastes was a delight in tapestries.

Although the returning Crusaders spread a desire for tapestries throughout Europe, an actual knowledge of the craft probably came from the Moors, Islamic people living in Spain. There are legends about tapestry workshops that were operating in southern France as early as the end of the 8th century, long before the Crusades. If these workshops did exist, they must have been operated by or influenced by the Moors.

The first tapestries that we are certain were made in Europe were woven in the workshops of monasteries. As the wealth of princes and merchants grew, so did the demand for more luxury goods. By the 14th century, Paris had become the main city of French tapestry production. From then until the present the history of tapestry has been centered mainly in France and Flanders (now Belgium and northern France).

THE GOTHIC ERA: GOLDEN AGE OF TAPESTRIES

Most early tapestry designs were simple patterns of geometric shapes and the symbols of heraldry. Around 1360, birds and small animals began to be represented more often. Then in less than 10 years most of the important factories began to produce tapestries woven in sets that illustrated religious texts, stories of knighthood, and scenes from contemporary life. Although these tapestries were more naturalistic than work from the previous era, they were still woven in the flat, decorative patterns typical of earlier work.

The Gothic period was a time of great cathedral building. To add color to the stone buildings, artists made beautiful stained-glass windows and hung tapestries. Pictures of Biblical scenes awed and educated churchgoers. Tapestries were also useful in sectioning off parts of large churches for special rites and ceremonies and in halting the drafts that flowed through the spacious churches.

THE RENAISSANCE

Good tapestries were woven in Italy but under the supervision of Flemish masters. So it was natural that Pope Leo X (1475–1521), deciding that he needed fine tapestries for the

Left: *Angeli Laudantes (Praising Angels)* (1881?), English tapestry designed by Burne-Jones. Victoria and Albert Museum, London. Right: *Hunt of the Unicorn: The Unicorn in Captivity* (detail) (French Gothic, c. 1500). The Cloisters, Metropolitan Museum, New York.

Sistine Chapel, should order them from Flanders. Along with the order he sent full-size designs (called **cartoons**) by the famous artist Raphael. The cartoons were actually paintings in the Renaissance style.

After this the Flemish weavers continued to work from cartoons painted by Italian artists. These artists used the same subjects and techniques as they did in their paintings, employing perspective as well as naturalistic rendering in their work.

Unfortunately, this marriage of Italian art and Flemish craft started a trend that almost ruined tapestry. The Gothic weaver had been free to choose his own colors and designs. Now *tapissiers* (tapestry weavers) had to make exact copies of Renaissance paintings, employing the technique of perspective. Robbed of its bold patterns and flat figures, tapestry lost much of its strength and uniqueness.

In addition to the decline in artistic quality, technical flaws began to creep in. Many col-

Gobelins tapestry *Story of the King: Louis XIV Entering Dunkirk* (France, 17th century).

21

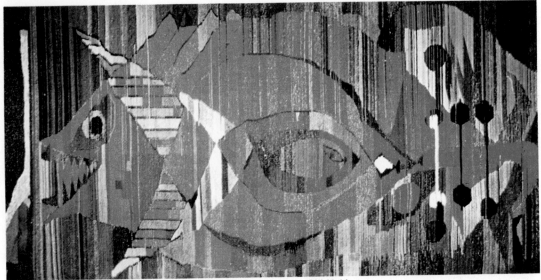
Purple Sea, a 20th-century Finnish tapestry designed and woven by Oili Maki.

ors came into use that were not chemically sound and quickly lost their brilliance. With the increase in orders for tapestries, speed— not artistry and skill—came to be expected from workers. Unsatisfactory sections were not rewoven, but instead were touched up with paints and dyes.

▶ 17TH, 18TH, AND 19TH CENTURIES

In 1662 Colbert, the first minister of Louis XIV of France, started a workshop on Avenue des Gobelins in Paris. It was owned by the government and produced furniture, tapestries, and other decorative products for royalty. The director of the Gobelins looms was the painter-designer Charles Le Brun (1619–90).

Political changes caused the Gobelins workshops to shut down between 1694 and 1697. When they reopened, few of the decorative arts except tapestry resumed production. Art in these years was rapidly moving away from the grand, dramatic style of the previous century. The playful and lightly elegant age of the rococo had arrived. The large wall hangings of Louis XIV's time gave way to much smaller panels, which were better suited to the more intimate rooms of the day.

The French Revolution brought work to a stop at the Gobelins and Beauvais workshops. Napoleon attempted to revive the factories under his personal supervision. He wished to glorify himself in great tapestries. None were completed before the emperor was exiled.

The best 19th-century tapestries were woven in England. The versatile artisan William Morris (1834–96) established a workshop at Merton Abbey in 1881. Morris loved all things medieval. His thorough study of Gothic methods resulted in lively tapestry designs based on Gothic style. After Morris died in 1896, Gothic principles were no longer followed closely.

▶ 20TH CENTURY: MODERN ART

The dramatic designs and bold, simple color schemes of abstract modern art helped bring back a strong decorative feeling in tapestry. In the 20th century there was a return to the principles—but not the style—of Gothic weaving.

The discovery of tapestries that were made by the Indians of Peru also influenced modern weaving. The Indians began making tapestry garments around A.D. 600 or 700. They used many deep colors and geometric abstractions or sets of animal patterns.

Since the late 1940's artists all over the world have been creating tapestries, using various materials and weaving techniques. The Scandinavians (people of Denmark, Sweden, and Norway), who are particularly active in the field, call upon their folk art for inspiration. After centuries of development, tapestry is once again at the forefront of the decorative arts.

RICHARD W. IRELAND
Maryland Institute College of Art

See also DECORATIVE ARTS; TEXTILES.

TAPEWORMS. See DISEASES (Descriptions of Some Diseases).

TARBELL, IDA (1857–1944)

Ida Minerva Tarbell, journalist, historian, biographer, and educator, was born on November 5, 1857, in Erie County, Pennsylvania. During the early 1900's, Tarbell was one of the primary leaders of the movement in American journalism known as **muckraking**, the public exposure of misconduct in politics and business.

After attending Allegheny College, Tarbell began her journalism career working as associate editor for *The Chautauquan*. In 1891 she decided to move to Paris to study the role of women in the French Revolution. While taking classes, Tarbell supported herself as a freelance writer.

In the spring of 1894, she took a position as associate editor for *McClure's Magazine*. Her early assignments included writing about Napoleon Bonaparte and Abraham Lincoln. The popularity of these articles led to their publication as books.

In 1904 Tarbell published *The History of the Standard Oil Company*, which also developed from articles written for *McClure's*

Magazine. As a result of her investigative journalism, Tarbell exposed dishonest and unlawful practices of the giant company owned by John D. Rockefeller. In 1911, the U.S. Supreme Court ordered that the Standard Oil Company, an oil **monopoly** with exclusive control over its industry, be broken up. In 1906, Tarbell and several muckraking journalists joined forces to purchase *American Magazine*, for which she contributed and edited articles until 1915 when the magazine was sold.

In later years, Tarbell became a lecturer and served as a member of several government conferences. In 1939 she published her autobiography, *All in the Day's Work*. She died of pneumonia on January 6, 1944.

Reviewed by JUDITH D. HINES
Education Manager, The Newseum

TARIFF

The term "tariff" generally refers to a tax on imports, or goods brought into a country. It may also be used, although more rarely, to tax exports, or goods sent out of a country. Tariffs may be applied in two main ways: as a percentage of the value of the imported product (called an ad valorem tariff) or as a specific amount of money for each unit of the imported article.

Tariffs traditionally have had two main functions: to produce government revenue (income) and to protect domestic producers from foreign competition. Revenue tariffs are no longer an important source of income for most countries. Today the main purpose of a tariff is protective. It adds to the cost of foreign products and thus discourages imports in favor of locally produced goods.

Those who support protective tariffs contend that they safeguard domestic jobs and protect wage earners against the competition of workers in countries with lower wages. In addition, they argue, certain industries may

become vital in case of war and should be protected in order to assure self-sufficiency.

Tariff opponents say that any advantages a country may receive from a protective tariff will only be temporary, and the results may actually be harmful rather than beneficial. For example, if country A reduces imports from country B by placing a tariff on them, country B will have less income with which to buy country A's products, and it might retaliate by raising tariffs on country A's exports.

This kind of economic warfare results in reducing the total amount of goods traded among nations. Most economists agree that tariffs usually lower the production rate of goods and the living standards of countries. Businesses suffer because they have fewer buyers, and consumers are hurt by having to pay higher prices for goods.

ALBERT ALEXANDER
New York City Council on Economic Education
See also INTERNATIONAL TRADE.

TASTE. See BODY, HUMAN (The Nervous System).

TAUSSIG, HELEN BROOKE (1898–1986)

Thousands of people are alive and healthy today because of the work of Dr. Helen Taussig. As the founder of pediatric cardiology, a branch of medicine that deals with heart problems in children, Dr. Taussig pioneered the heart surgery that gave children with no hope of survival the chance to live.

Born on May 24, 1898, in Cambridge, Massachusetts, Taussig's journey to becoming a doctor was littered with obstacles. As a child she was diagnosed with dyslexia, a learning disability that affected her throughout her life. She later faced sex discrimination as one of the few young women trying to enter a profession ruled by men. Many medical schools in the 1920's did not admit women. Women could take the medical courses offered at these universities, but the courses could not be used to obtain a medical degree. Taussig's search for a medical school that would admit her ended when she was accepted as a medical student at Johns Hopkins Medical School in Baltimore, Maryland. It was there that Taussig received her M.D. in 1927. Taussig spent her entire career at Johns Hopkins Hospital, serving as chief of the Pediatric Cardiac Clinic of the Harriet Lane Home, the children's division of Johns Hopkins, from 1930 until her retirement in 1963.

Practicing her profession proved to be a challenge for Taussig. She had a severe hearing impairment that resulted from childhood whooping cough. Just as she had managed to overcome other obstacles, Taussig overcame this one and, in fact, was able to develop expert diagnostic skills by "listening" to her young patients' hearts with her hands. Pressing against their tiny chests, she was able to detect heart murmurs and abnormal heartbeats by touch and visual examination.

Through her research, Taussig discovered that certain heart or blood vessel defects prevent the normal flow of blood through the heart and lungs, leading to a lack of oxygen in the blood, which in turn gives the skin a distinctive bluish color. Because of the characteristic skin color, children born with these defects were called blue babies. Taussig persuaded Dr. Alfred Blalock, a surgeon, to help find a way to correct the problem. They developed an operation, which was first performed in November 1944, known as the Blalock-Taussig shunt. The operation creates a bypass around the defective area, sending blood to the lungs so that the necessary oxygen can be picked up before the blood is carried throughout the body. Although it is not often used now, the operation has saved the lives of thousands of sick babies.

In the years that followed the development of the Blalock-Taussig shunt, Dr. Taussig turned her attention to teaching and writing. She developed close relationships with the young doctors she trained in the emerging field of pediatric cardiology and wrote what is considered the standard text for pediatric cardiology, *Congenital Malformations of the Heart* (1947). Throughout her career, Taussig's work had wide-ranging effects, even influencing U.S. policy on drugs. In the early 1960's, her investigation into, and later testimony about, an increase in the birth of infants in Germany with severely deformed limbs helped keep the drug Thalidomide from being sold in the United States.

In 1964, Taussig received the highest honor that can be bestowed on a civilian—the Medal of Freedom. Even though she retired in 1963, Taussig remained committed to her field, writing, researching, and lending her support to a variety of causes, especially those that affected children. Always politically active, Taussig was on her way to vote when she was killed in an automobile accident on May 21, 1986, in Kennett Square, Pennsylvania.

STEFFEN SMITH
Science Writer

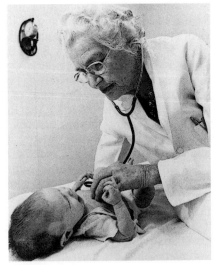

Using her watchful eyes and gentle hands, Dr. Taussig became an expert at diagnosis through touch and visual examination.

TAXATION

A tax is a charge or duty imposed by a government on income or property. Tax money is used to pay the expenses of government or for other public expenses. In countries that have a free-enterprise system of production, nearly all public services are paid for by revenue (income) from taxation.

Taxes differ in at least two ways from other funds collected by governments. When a tax is paid, the person paying the tax does not benefit directly. The taxpayer shares the benefits or services, such as public schools or sewer systems, with the community at large. When a non-tax payment is made to a government, the person paying it benefits directly. Good examples of non-tax payments are the fees that are paid for government documents, such as passports. Tax funds differ from non-tax funds in another way. A tax is compulsory —it must be paid. But an individual usually may decide whether or not to make a non-tax payment.

History of Taxes

Taxes are necessary to support public services. But taxes seldom have been popular with those who pay them. Throughout most of history the people had no voice in determining how, or how much, they would be taxed. In ancient times governments often took goods and services by force.

Objections by citizens to heavy or unreasonable taxation have been associated with many famous historical events. In the 1200's in England, the Magna Carta set forth the principle that members of a society, directly or through their representatives, should have a voice in deciding upon the taxes they pay. The English Bill of Rights strengthened that principle four centuries later. It was made illegal for the Crown to levy (impose and collect) taxes without the approval of Parliament. Issues concerning taxes also played a part in the Revolutionary War. The American colonists opposed the stamp tax in 1765 because this tax was imposed by the British Parliament, where the colonists were not represented. "Taxation without representation is tyranny," declared the American patriot James Otis. This statement became a rallying cry of the Revolution.

In modern times there is a close association between the right to vote and the duty to pay taxes. Traditionally, a government taxes only those persons who actually come under its legal authority.

Taxing Powers of Government

Independent governments have the right to collect taxes and to spend the funds in the public interest. But limitations may be placed on these rights. In the United States, Canada, and many other countries, the taxing powers are limited by the country's constitution. For example, the U.S. government could not levy a certain type of income tax without amending the Constitution. The taxing powers of each level of government—central, state or provincial, and local—also are limited.

Objects of Taxation

The forms of taxation most commonly used in the Western world are those on personal and business income; property; sales of goods and services; and transfers of estates, inheritances, and gifts. The large amounts collected from employers and employees for social security purposes may or may not be considered taxes. These payments are compulsory and must be made. On the other hand, the people who pay money into a social security system receive certain benefits when they retire or become disabled.

A tax paid directly by the person on whom it is imposed is referred to as a **direct tax**. Personal-income taxes generally are considered to be in this category. Some taxes may be passed along to persons other than those who pay the initial tax. These taxes are called **indirect taxes**. The manufacturer's excise tax is an example of an indirect tax. A familiar excise tax is the sales tax that is added to the price of many purchases. This tax is paid by the consumer.

The aim of most taxes is to produce revenue. But some taxes are imposed to control certain elements of use, production, or business conduct. Taxes of this type are said to be regulatory. In the early part of the 1900's, for instance, a tax was imposed in the United States to discourage the production of white phosphorus matches because their manufacture was harmful to the health of the people who made them.

Principles of Taxation

The burden of taxes should be distributed among various persons in a way that agrees with the goals of society. To guide governments in deciding the kind of taxes and the rate of taxes to be imposed, several principles of taxation have been established.

The best-known requirements of a good tax were set forth almost 200 years ago by the Scottish economist Adam Smith in his book *The Wealth of Nations* (1776). His principles —equality, certainty, convenience of payment, and economy—are still sound today.

Equality requires that people contribute to the support of their government in proportion to their ability to pay.

Certainty means that a tax should not be unreasonable or subject to sudden change. The time and manner of payment, and the amount, ought to be clear to everyone.

Convenience requires that a tax be levied at the time, and in the manner, most convenient for the taxpayer.

The government's costs in collecting a tax and the taxpayer's costs in paying it should be low compared with the amount the tax brings into the public treasury. The tax should not burden the people more than it benefits the government.

ELSIE M. WATTERS
Tax Foundation, Inc.

See also INCOME TAX; TARIFF.

TAXIDERMY

Have you ever seen a bear in the museum that looked so real it seemed ready to sit up and growl? If so, you have seen an example of taxidermy at its best.

Taxidermy is the art of preserving dead animals so that they seem almost alive. Contrary to common opinion, the animals that you see are not stuffed. Usually, what you are looking at is the skin of an animal fitted over a model made of clay, plastic, or wood.

These models are prepared in several ways. First, the bird, fish, or land animal is carefully measured because the model must be exactly the size of the animal if the skin is to fit. Then, a clay model is made that includes details of the animal's anatomy. After this, a plaster cast is made of the clay model. Then, the cast is split open and filled with several layers of burlap dipped in plaster or plastic. This form is light in weight and strong enough to support the animal's skin. Sometimes a wood model of the animal is made.

The skin, treated with preservatives or tanned and cured, is stretched over the model, and the eyes are reproduced in glass. The models are usually posed or carved in natural attitudes. When finished, the animals seem lifelike and on the verge of motion.

The ancient Egyptians embalmed dead animals, as well as people, and buried the animals along with their owners in fabulous tombs. But modern taxidermy did not appear until the late 1500's. About that time, animal skins were mounted on wires and stuffed with preservative spices. Even so, methods of taxidermy remained exceedingly crude until the 1800's, when the practice of carving models was developed.

Today large animals, such as elephants, tigers, and bears, are prepared almost exclusively by museums for natural history exhibits. Smaller animals, such as fish and game birds, are prepared by private taxidermists for use as home decorations. Some people who fish and hunt display fish, game birds, and mounted moose heads as trophies of their skill.

Reviewed by JOHN F. SCHNEIDER
John F. Schneider Taxidermy Studio

This leopard skin has been stretched over a model in a taxidermist's workshop in Kenya.

TAXONOMY

Taxonomy is the science of classifying living things. It is also the art of giving organisms names that indicate how they are classified.

Since ancient times, people have been describing living things and giving them names. One of the first to develop a usable system for classification was the Greek philosopher and naturalist Aristotle. Aristotle lived during the 300's B.C. At that time, the living world was divided into two groups, plants and animals. Aristotle further divided animals into those with red blood and those without red blood; plants were divided by size and appearance into groups of herbs, shrubs, and trees. For almost 2,000 years, this was the system used to classify organisms.

Modern classification began with the work of Carolus Linnaeus, a Swedish naturalist. In the early 1700's, he introduced a system of grouping organisms according to their structures and giving each kind of organism a unique two-part name. Since then the system has been somewhat modified, but it still follows his basic design.

▶ CLASSIFICATION OF THE LIVING WORLD

Using scientific classification, **biologists**, the scientists who study living things, are able to arrange the world's organisms in related groups. Early naturalists thought that all living things could be included in the two large groups, or kingdoms, of plants and animals. Over time, however, organisms were found that differed from plants and animals more than plants and animals differed from each other. New tools, such as microscopes, also extended the range of characteristics that could be used in identifying a living thing. Although Linnaeus based his classification on the visible structures of an organism, today's scientist examines the history of the organism's life, the patterns of development, and the internal structures, including those at the cellular level. By 1959, new knowledge and tools led to a system of five kingdoms: animals, plants, fungi, protists (such as many algae and protozoans), and monerans (such as bacteria). This system won broad support and remains popular, even though scientists continue to propose changes. For example, some scientists advocate a six-kingdom sys-

An extraordinary number of living things—about 2 million known species and perhaps as many as 100 million—inhabit this planet. One way to classify these many life-forms is with the well-known system of five kingdoms: (*from top*) protists, monerans, plants, fungi, and animals.

tem. (For more information, see the article KINGDOMS OF LIVING THINGS in Volume JK.)

Below kingdom, there are increasingly specific levels for classifying organisms. They include phylum or division, class, order, family, genus, and species. With each level, organisms become more closely related. With the final separation into species, the members share so many of the same basic characteristics that they look alike.

▶ CLASSIFYING AN ORGANISM

Scientific classification is used each time a taxonomist is called upon to classify (and therefore properly identify) a living thing. In

Classification of the Domestic Dog

Each type of living thing on Earth has its own unique classification. Knowing how an organism is classified provides a variety of information about an organism, such as its ancestry, structure, and development. Below is an example of how the domestic dog, which belongs in the kingdom of animals, is classified according to shared characteristics.

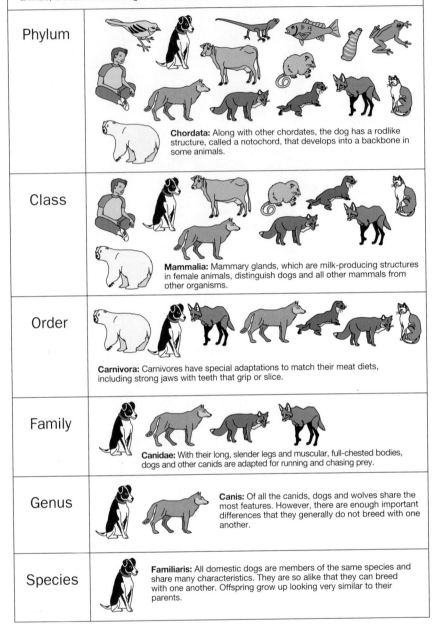

Phylum

Chordata: Along with other chordates, the dog has a rodlike structure, called a notochord, that develops into a backbone in some animals.

Class

Mammalia: Mammary glands, which are milk-producing structures in female animals, distinguish dogs and all other mammals from other organisms.

Order

Carnivora: Carnivores have special adaptations to match their meat diets, including strong jaws with teeth that grip or slice.

Family

Canidae: With their long, slender legs and muscular, full-chested bodies, dogs and other canids are adapted for running and chasing prey.

Genus

Canis: Of all the canids, dogs and wolves share the most features. However, there are enough important differences that they generally do not breed with one another.

Species

Familiaris: All domestic dogs are members of the same species and share many characteristics. They are so alike that they can breed with one another. Offspring grow up looking very similar to their parents.

animals than in any of the other kingdoms. So this living thing must be an animal and, therefore, belong to the animal kingdom. The examination shows that the animal has a notochord, which is a rodlike structure that in some animals develops into a backbone. Animals with a notochord belong to the phylum Chordata.

The taxonomist continues to examine the animal and observes that there are mammary glands, which are glands that in the female produce the milk used to nurse the animal's young. This tells the taxonomist that the animal belongs to the class Mammalia. It is also seen that the mammal's body is lean and strong and the head has powerful jaws and sturdy teeth designed for eating meat. Such an animal belongs to the order Carnivora.

As the observation continues, other features are revealed and examined until the taxonomist is able to place the mammal within its proper family (Canidae), followed by its genus (*Canis*) and species (*familiaris*). The scientist can now identify the animal as a domestic dog.

the illustration above, a domestic dog is used to show how one kind of organism is separated from other kinds of organisms as it is classified from kingdom to species.

The taxonomist first observes that the structure of the organism's body, pattern of growth and development, and behavior are more like those creatures in the kingdom of

Classifying an organism can be a difficult task. There may be several dozen different species that belong to a particular genus. A taxonomist has to then determine to which species a living thing belongs. This is accomplished by using a variety of sources that contain descriptions and names of the species belonging to that genus. A taxonomist may

Why are the scientific names of plants and animals in Latin?

The scientific names of plants and animals are Latinized because Latin was at one time the international language of scholars. In fact, the book Systema Naturae, in which Carolus Linnaeus described his system of classification and naming, was written in Latin. Translations of the Latin names of organisms are found in unabridged (complete) English dictionaries. Some of these scientific names are descriptive. A name may tell you something about the size, shape, or color of the creature or where it lives. Here are some examples of Latin names and their translations:

Lepidium campestre Lepidium means "little scale" (from the shape of the fruit of this plant); campestre means "of the field" (the plant is usually found growing in a field).

Canis familiaris Canis means "dog"; familiaris comes from the Latin word for "belonging to a family or a household." Canis familiaris, therefore, means "a household dog."

Sometimes a plant or an animal is named by a taxonomist in honor of a famous scientist. For example, the scientific name of the common butter-and-eggs plant is Linaria vulgaris. The name Linaria is in honor of Linnaeus. The species name, vulgaris, means "common."

Scientific names are not much more difficult to learn than English ones when you take the time to look up their meanings. Often you will find the scientific names delightfully poetic.

spend anywhere from an hour to several weeks studying these sources until a description is found that exactly fits.

▶ NAMING AN ORGANISM

Although common names may be used in everyday conversation, they do not positively identify an organism. Many living things have different common names in different places. Even when the same name is used, it may be applied to different things. The naming system developed by Linnaeus brings order to what is an incredibly diverse world. It gives scientists anywhere in the world, no matter what their native languages may be—French, Bulgarian, Russian, Chinese, Hindi, Swahili, Japanese, English—the ability to discuss any organism and know that they are talking about the same one.

By the beginning of the 1700's, when Linnaeus proposed binomial nomenclature, meaning "two-name naming," Latin was widely used in schools and universities, and it was already the custom to use Latin phrases to name plants and animals. Linnaeus continued the custom with his naming system. Each organism is identified, or named, by linking the name of its genus to the name of its species. The genus name always begins with a capital letter, and the species name always begins with a small letter. Both genus and species names are always underlined when written and are in italics when printed. For example, biologists would call your pet dog Canis familiaris. When the organism is being discussed in writing, the full name is given only once. In later references, the genus name may be abbreviated—C. familiaris.

▶ TAXONOMISTS AT WORK

As of the 1990's, descriptions of more than 1.5 million species of living things had been published. Among the species described are some that lived long ago but are now extinct. The descriptions and names can be found in books and journals that are in libraries. The number of plant and animal species alone is truly amazing. Did you know, for example, that there are descriptions and names of more than 2,000 kinds of mosquitoes? New species are being discovered and named all the time.

No one person can be an expert taxonomist for all the world's living things. Taxonomists must specialize. Among taxonomists, there are experts on bacteria, algae, flatworms, grasses, butterflies, fish, and many other groups. A good taxonomist usually knows more than the names and body structures of the organisms. He or she also knows where they may be found, what kind of environment they live in, how they reproduce, and how they are related to other organisms around them. Taxonomy is an important and active branch of biology.

ZACHARIAH SUBARSKY
University of Minnesota

See also KINGDOMS OF LIVING THINGS; LIFE; LINNAEUS, CAROLUS.

TAYLOR, MILDRED. See CHILDREN'S LITERATURE (Profiles).

ZACHARY TAYLOR (1784-1850)

12th President of the United States

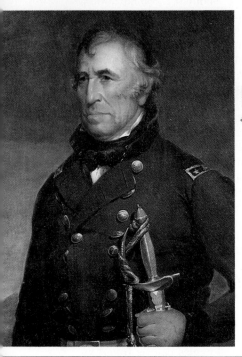

FACTS ABOUT TAYLOR

Birthplace: Near Barboursville, Orange County, Virginia (His boyhood home, *below,* was near Louisville, Kentucky.)

Religion: Episcopalian
Occupation: Soldier
Married: Margaret Mackall Smith
Children: Anne, Sarah, Octavia, Margaret, Mary, Richard
Political Party: Whig
Nickname: "Old Rough and Ready"
President Who Preceded Him: James K. Polk
Age on Becoming President: 64
Years in the Presidency: 1849–1850 (died in office, July 9, 1850)
Vice President: Millard Fillmore
President Who Succeeded Him: Millard Fillmore
Age at Death: 65
Burial Place: Springfield, Kentucky

Zachary Taylor

DURING TAYLOR'S PRESIDENCY

Thomas Ewing was appointed as the first secretary of the interior (1849). *Left:* The great California Gold Rush brought tens of thousands of gold prospectors, called forty-niners, into California (1849), seeking their fortunes; the gold had first been discovered in 1848 on the site of John Sutter's mill near Sacramento. *Below:* Congress heatedly debated measures intended to prevent a split in the Union between North and South over the issue of slavery in the western territories of the United States. The measures, known as the Compromise of 1850, were enacted shortly after Taylor's death in office.

TAYLOR, ZACHARY. Before he became president of the United States in 1849, Zachary Taylor served his country for nearly 40 years as an army officer. He fought with courage and honor in the War of 1812, The Black Hawk War, the Second Seminole War, and the Mexican War. At the close of the Mexican War he was the second highest officer in the United States Army. His term as president was cut short by death before much had been accomplished, but not before Taylor had made clear his devotion to the preservation of the Union, his absolute integrity, his unyielding firmness, and his modesty.

▶ EARLY YEARS

Taylor was born near Barboursville in Orange County, Virginia, on November 24, 1784. His father was Lieutenant Colonel Richard Taylor, a veteran of the Revolutionary War and a member of a long-established Virginia family. Through his father, Zachary Taylor was related to President James Madison and General Robert E. Lee.

In the spring of 1785, when Zachary was only a few months old, Richard Taylor took his family west to Kentucky (then a part of Virginia) to settle on lands he had received for his service in the Revolution. His new plantation was along the banks of the Muddy Fork of Beargrass Creek, a few miles east of the village of Louisville. Here Zachary Taylor spent his boyhood. At first the population of this wilderness region was small. But gradually the frontier was pushed back, and life for the Taylors became more comfortable. The family grew to include six sons and three daughters. Zachary probably had little, if any, formal education beyond that received at a small school in Louisville. Additional instruction was likely given him by his parents.

Zachary Taylor remained at home, assisting in the operation of the plantation, until 1808. In that year he was appointed first lieutenant in the 7th Infantry Regiment. The appointment marked the beginning of a military career that, except for one brief period, continued until Taylor's election as president 40 years later.

EARLY MILITARY CAREER

Between 1808 and 1837, Taylor was stationed at various army posts, mostly on the Northwest frontier but occasionally in the Southwest. During the War of 1812 (1812–14) he took part in a number of military campaigns against the British and their Indian allies. He slowly advanced in rank, receiving his commission as major in 1815. Later that year, when the Army was reduced to peacetime strength, he resigned rather than return to the rank of captain. But after less than a year in civilian life, which he spent growing corn and tobacco near Louisville, Taylor was appointed major in the 3rd Regiment. In 1819 he was promoted to lieutenant colonel.

By 1832, Taylor, now 47 years old, was a colonel, commanding the 1st Regiment. The Black Hawk War broke out the same year, and Taylor took part in the hard-fought campaign against Chief Black Hawk and the Sac Indians in Illinois.

HIS FAMILY AND HOME LIFE

This same period of nearly 30 years was important in Taylor's family and domestic life. In 1810 he married Margaret Mackall Smith, daughter of a Maryland planter. Five daughters and one son were born to them. Two of the daughters died in early childhood. A third, Sarah Knox, died only a few months after her marriage to Jefferson Davis, then a lieutenant in Taylor's regiment and later to

become the president of the Confederacy. The other two daughters also married army officers. Taylor's youngest child and only son, Richard, became a lieutenant general in the Confederate Army.

In addition to his military career, Taylor took an active interest in planting. In 1823 he purchased a 155-hectare (380-acre) cotton plantation in northern Louisiana. In later years he bought Cypress Grove, a much larger plantation in Mississippi.

THE SECOND SEMINOLE WAR

In the summer of 1837 Taylor was ordered to take his regiment to Florida. Since late 1835 the Army had been fighting the Seminole Indians, and reinforcements were needed. This was the start of events that were to make Taylor a national hero and carry him to the White House.

In December, 1837, with a force of nearly 1,100 men, including regular soldiers, volunteers, and some Shawnee and Delaware Indians, Taylor set out in search of the Seminole. On December 25, after hard marching through very rough and difficult country, he found the Seminole at Lake Okeechobee and defeated them in a desperate battle. This victory won for Taylor the thanks of President Van Buren and a brevet (honorary) commission as brigadier general. But the war continued, and in 1838 Taylor was placed in command. For 2 years he directed the fighting against the Seminole. His efforts were commended by the secretary of war, but he had no greater success in subduing the Seminole than had his predecessors. In 1840, at his own request, he was relieved of command and assigned to duty in the Southwest. Here his main concern once again was with the Indians.

THE MEXICAN WAR

In 1836, after winning its independence from Mexico, Texas had established itself as an independent republic. Early negotiations for Texas to join the United States had failed, but in 1844 these negotiations were renewed. Mexico, however, strongly opposed American annexation of Texas, and the Texans, fearing attack, requested protection from the United States.

Taylor was ordered to Fort Jesup, close to

IMPORTANT DATES IN THE LIFE OF ZACHARY TAYLOR

1784 Born near Barboursville, Orange County, Virginia, November 24.

1808 Appointed first lieutenant in the 7th Infantry Regiment.

1810 Married Margaret Mackall Smith.

1812– Served in War of 1812.
1814

1815 Resigned from the Army.

1816 Appointed major in the 3rd Infantry Regiment.

1832 Colonel commanding 1st Infantry Regiment; fought in the Black Hawk War.

1837 Defeated the Seminole Indians at Lake Okeechobee in Florida during the Second Seminole War; brevetted brigadier general.

1846 Won victories at Palo Alto and Resaca de la Palma during Mexican War; appointed major general.

1847 Defeated Santa Anna at the battle of Buena Vista.

1849 Inaugurated as 12th president of the United States, March 5.

1850 Died in office, July 9.

the Texas-Louisiana border. He remained there until July, 1845, when he was ordered to move his forces to the coast of Texas. Early in 1846 he was ordered to advance to the Rio Grande, the river that Texas claimed as its border with Mexico. On April 25, 1846, Mexican troops crossed the Rio Grande and attacked a U.S. detachment. In May a larger Mexican force crossed the river. Although badly outnumbered, Taylor gave battle, defeating the Mexicans at Palo Alto and Resaca de la Palma.

The American people hailed Taylor as a hero. Promoted to major general, he became the second ranking officer in the U.S. Army. He was outranked only by Major General Winfield Scott, the commanding general of the Army.

After Congress declared war on May 13, 1846, Taylor crossed the Rio Grande. On September 25, he captured the Mexican city of Monterrey. By November, 1846, he had advanced some 200 miles (320 kilometers) into Mexico.

Meanwhile, President James K. Polk had given General Winfield Scott command of a new Mexican expedition, and most of Taylor's best troops were transferred to Scott's forces. The angry Taylor claimed that Polk had acted so for political reasons. (Both Polk and Scott were Democrats.) Despite orders to remain on the defensive, Taylor advanced with his weakened forces. On February 22–23, 1847, at the battle of Buena Vista, he defeated a Mexican army under General Antonio

Mary Elizabeth Taylor Bliss was the Taylors' youngest daughter. Because Mrs. Taylor was a partial invalid, Mary Elizabeth served as the White House hostess.

López de Santa Anna that was four times larger than his own. This was Taylor's last battle of the war.

▶THE PRESIDENCY

Although Taylor had no political experience, leaders of the Whig Party urged his nomination for the presidency in 1848. Taylor at first refused but later accepted the nomination. In the election Taylor carried eight southern and seven northern states, exactly half of the total. But he won 163 electoral votes, 36 more than Lewis Cass, the Democratic candidate. Martin Van Buren, a former president, ran unsuccessfully as the Free Soil Party candidate.

The Slavery Crisis. When Taylor was inaugurated in 1849, the nation faced a crisis. Controversy between North and South over the question of slavery in the Western territories had grown increasingly bitter. Opponents of slavery insisted that Congress had the constitutional authority to keep slavery out of the territories. Southerners were equally certain that Congress had no such authority, and Southern extremists threatened secession (to leave the Union) if Congress took such action. Compromise proposals to settle this and other slavery problems were introduced into Congress by Henry Clay. Taylor opposed them. This was partly because he had already suggested a plan of his own, partly because of a growing feud with Clay, and partly because he believed that the Union could not be preserved by compromise reached in the face of threats of secession.

Though a Southerner and slaveholder, Tay-

A political cartoon of the time depicts the "race" for the presidency in the election of 1848: from left, Zachary Taylor, Lewis Cass, and Martin Van Buren.

lor had no sympathy with the southern position in this crisis. He was ready to take the field and lead the Army himself if rebellion occurred. The measures known as the Compromise of 1850 were not enacted until after Taylor's death, and his death was one of the factors that made their passage possible.

In the field of foreign affairs the chief accomplishment of the Taylor administration was the negotiation of the Clayton-Bulwer Treaty with Great Britain in 1850. The treaty provided that neither country would have exclusive control over any ship canal through Central America or could fortify such a canal. Trouble with Spain over Cuba threatened but was avoided, and honest friendship with all nations was maintained.

Taylor's Death

In his hard-fought campaigns against the Seminole, Taylor had won the nickname of "Old Rough and Ready." But by the time he entered the White House he was no longer in robust health. On July 4, 1850, he took part in the ceremonies at the laying of the Washington Monument cornerstone. After long exposure to the hot sun he returned to the White House. He developed a stomach ailment after dining and died on the evening of July 9, 1850. Vice President Millard Fillmore succeeded him as the 13th president.

Taylor was of medium height, short-legged, and heavy-set. He dressed plainly, at times carelessly, and made an undistinguished appearance. He was a man of absolute honesty, straightforward and simple in manner, strong-minded and firm almost to the point of obstinacy. He was not a military genius, but he was a hard-working, successful officer. He was not a great statesman, but he was a faithful servant of the people.

BRAINERD DYER
Author, *Zachary Taylor*

See also COMPROMISE OF 1850; MEXICAN WAR.

TAY-SACHS DISEASE. See DISEASES (Descriptions of Some Diseases).

TCHAIKOVSKY, PETER ILYICH (1840–1893)

Peter Ilyich Tchaikovsky, one of Russia's greatest composers, was born in Votkinsk on May 7, 1840. He studied the piano as a boy but showed no outstanding talent and did not think seriously of a musical career. At age 19 he took a post as a government clerk, studying music in his spare time.

By 1863, Tchaikovsky had decided to devote himself entirely to music, and he enrolled at the St. Petersburg Conservatory. After completing his studies three years later, he joined the newly opened Moscow Conservatory as a professor of harmony.

Slowly, Tchaikovsky's music began to win recognition. His first piano concerto (1875) was immediately successful. Among the admirers of his works was a wealthy widow named Nadezhda von Meck. For 14 years, Madame von Meck sent Tchaikovsky a generous allowance so that he could compose without financial worries. To show that her only interest was in his career, she insisted that they should not meet. Their long friendship was carried on entirely by letter.

In 1877, Tchaikovsky married Antonina Milyukova, a young conservatory student. It was a brief and unhappy marriage, lasting only about nine weeks. In that same year, Tchaikovsky's famous ballet music *Swan Lake* was first performed.

When his marriage ended, Tchaikovsky quit the conservatory and went on to write some of his most popular works. These include the Fourth Symphony, the opera *Eugene Onegin,* the Violin Concerto, the *1812 Overture,* and the overture-fantasy *Romeo and Juliet.* With these works, Tchaikovsky won world fame. Between 1888 and 1893, he toured Europe and the United States, conducting his own works. In 1891 he led four concerts in New York City to mark the opening of Carnegie Hall. His works of this period include the Fifth Symphony (1888) and the popular ballets *The Sleeping Beauty* (1889) and *The Nutcracker* (1892).

Returning to Russia, Tchaikovsky conducted the first performance of his famous Sixth Symphony ("Pathétique") in 1893. Less than two weeks later, on November 6, 1893, he died in St. Petersburg.

Reviewed by BARBARA-SUE WHITE
Founder, Princeton String Quartet

Tea pluckers must hand pick only the newest growth, or flush, of a tea plant. A machine would lack the careful eye needed to spot the plants with the freshest top leaves.

TEA

Tea is a beverage made from the dried leaves of the small evergreen tree *Camellia sinensis*. Tea leaves contain essential oils, which provide flavor; tannin, a chemical that provides color and a slightly bitter taste; and caffeine, a chemical that has a mildly stimulating effect. Next to plain water, tea is the world's most popular drink.

▶ THE TEA PLANT

The tea plant is native to Southeast Asia. It grows best in temperate and tropical zones where rain falls heavily throughout the year. Tea can be grown at various elevations, from sea level to about 7,000 feet (2,100 meters). However, the best quality tea is grown at the higher elevations.

How Tea is Grown. Tea plants are usually grown from seeds or cuttings taken from other tea plants. The tea seedlings, or young plants, are placed in well-drained, fertile soil and are shaded from the fierce heat of the sun. The plants can grow as tall as 30 feet (9 meters) high. However, on tea plantations (called tea gardens or estates) the plants are constantly cut back to produce low bushes, usually no more than 3 feet (1 meter) high, to make it easier for workers to pluck (pick) the leaves. The plants produce jagged, leathery dark green leaves; small, white, fragrant flowers; and seeds that resemble hazelnuts.

At least three years must pass before a tea plant is ready for plucking. During the growing season, the mature plants are plucked every ten days or so, depending on the climate and the height and age of each bush. Only the top two leaves are plucked each time. Some workers can pick up to 40 pounds (18 kilograms) a day. Forty pounds of freshly picked tea leaves yield about 10 pounds (4.5 kilograms) of dried tea.

▶ PROCESSING DIFFERENT TYPES OF TEA

There are three different types of tea—black, green, and oolong. The special appearance and flavor of each kind of tea come more from the method of processing than from the type of leaf used. However, certain varieties of tea leaves are better suited for making one or more of the three types of tea.

Black Tea. Black tea makes up about 95 percent of all the tea produced in the world. Four basic steps are used in making black tea from the raw leaf: withering, rolling, fermenting, and firing (drying).

First, the leaves are transported from the plantation to the factory as quickly as possible. They are spread on racks to wither, a process that removes about one third of the moisture and makes the leaves soft and flexible. Then

VARIETIES OF TEA

NAME OF TEA	KIND OF TEA	WHERE GROWN	FLAVOR
Assam	black	India	rich, pungent
Darjeeling	black	India	delicate, sweet
Earl Grey	black	India, Sri Lanka	richly fragrant
Gunpowder	green	Taiwan, China, Japan	delicate
Jasmine	oolong	Taiwan, China	delicate, scented
Keemun	black	Taiwan, China	delicately pungent
Lapsang souchong	black	Taiwan	rich, smoky
Oolong	oolong	Taiwan, China	pleasantly fragrant

the leaves are rolled by machine to break up the cells and release the juices. Afterward, they are spread out and kept under high humidity to promote fermentation, which develops the rich, hearty flavor of black tea. Finally, the leaves are fired (dried) to remove all of the remaining moisture.

Most black tea comes from India, Sri Lanka (formerly Ceylon), Indonesia, and from some countries in eastern Africa.

Green Tea. Green tea is made by steaming the leaves as quickly as possible after plucking to prevent fermentation. Then, like black tea, the leaves are rolled and fired until they are crisp. When brewed, green tea has a light green color and a delicate flavor.

Almost all of the tea produced in Japan is used to make green tea. The demand for it there is so great that little is left over to export.

Oolong Tea. Oolong tea is a cross between black tea and green tea. It is semi-fermented —that is, fermentation is stopped before the process is completed. This produces a brownish green leaf, whose flavor is richer than green tea but more delicate than black tea.

Most oolong tea is produced in Taiwan and in the People's Republic of China.

▶ PREPARING TEA FOR THE CUSTOMER

When tea is prepared for market, it is graded by size. Large and small, broken and unbroken leaves are mechanically sifted and separated to meet the preferences of buyers, who purchase the tea at auction for companies all over the world. Then the tea is packed in aluminum-lined, moisture-proof chests or bags made from layers of heavy paper, polyethylene, and aluminum foil. These packages are tightly sealed before being shipped to tea companies for blending.

Blending is an art that plays an important part in bringing enjoyment and satisfaction to tea drinkers. Most teas sold may be a blend of as many as 20 to 30 varieties of tea. Each variety is chosen for its color, flavor, aroma, or strength. Blending is based on selections made by expert tea tasters, who decide which kinds of tea leaves—and how many of each— make the best blend. Many different blends are created to please people's different tastes.

Blending is done in large mixing drums that can hold 3,000 pounds (1,350 kilograms) or more of tea at a time. After the tea is blended, machines measure the exact amount of tea to go into each package or tea bag.

Powdered instant tea, developed in the United States, is made from a strong brew of tea that is dried to remove all the water. Instant tea is usually packaged in glass jars. Iced-tea mixes, a combination of instant tea, flavorings, and sometimes sugar, are sold in jars, aluminum-lined envelopes and canisters, and in ready-to-drink cans. Decaffeinated teas appeared on the market in the mid-1980's.

▶ WORLD PRODUCTION AND USE

Today tea is grown and exported chiefly by Sri Lanka, the People's Republic of China, India, Kenya, Indonesia, Argentina, Bangladesh, Tanzania, Malawi, and Uganda. Other

Tea tasters need highly developed senses of taste and smell. They may sample great quantities—sometimes as many as 1,000 cups—of tea each day.

countries produce large quantities of tea but use most of what they produce, so they have little left to export. Among them are Turkey, Japan, Iran, Myanmar, Vietnam, and Taiwan.

Tea is used as a beverage in practically every country in the world. The United Kingdom is by far the largest importer, bringing in more than 400 million pounds (181 million kilograms) every year. The United States imports about half as much tea as the United Kingdom. All of the tea sold in the United States is imported and must pass inspection by the U.S. Food and Drug Administration, according to the Federal Tea Act of 1897.

▶ HISTORY

According to an ancient Chinese legend, tea was discovered by the Chinese emperor Shen-Nung in 2737 B.C. As the story goes, leaves from a wild tea bush fell into a pot of his drinking water as it was being boiled. This was, perhaps, the world's first cup of tea.

Many centuries later, tea was introduced into Japan by Chinese Buddhist monks. The Japanese developed a ritual tea ceremony, Cha No Yu, which remains a special part of their culture to this day.

In the 1500's, European sea merchants discovered tea in Asia and brought it back with them. It quickly became popular, and by the 1700's tea had become England's national beverage.

In 1650 the Dutch introduced tea into their colony New Amsterdam (now New York City). By 1670 the British had brought it to Massachusetts, where the colonists would boil and salt the leaves and eat them with butter on bread. In 1767, the British put a tax on the colonists' tea without their consent. This act provoked the 1773 Boston Tea Party, which eventually sparked the Revolutionary War.

In 1904 two important discoveries in the United States revolutionized the tea industry. On a blistery hot day at the Louisiana Purchase Exposition in St. Louis, Missouri, a young English tea merchant named Richard Blechynden discovered that he could attract thirsty customers by offering hot tea poured over ice. Thus, he invented iced tea. That same year, a New York City tea and coffee merchant, Thomas Sullivan, decided that it would be easier to send samples of tea to his customers in little hand-sewn silk bags, rather than in bulky canisters. When his customers

Afternoon tea featuring small sandwiches and sweets is a popular social custom, especially in Britain, where twice as much tea is consumed as in America.

WONDER QUESTION

How is tea made?

To make a good pot of tea, use fresh water and bring it to a full boil. Use a preheated pot for the tea. For each cup of water place one full teaspoon of loose tea into the pot or into a tea strainer in the pot. Pour the boiling water over the tea. Let the tea steep (soak) for 3 to 5 minutes. If the tea is steeped too long, it will have a bitter taste.

To make a cup of tea with a tea bag, use fresh water and bring it to a full boil. Preheat the cup before you put the tea bag in, and fill it with the boiling water. Steep for 3 to 5 minutes, then remove the tea bag.

Iced tea is made with 50 percent more tea leaves, to allow for the melting ice. The tea is poured into tall glasses that are two-thirds full of ice. Sliced lemons are served with it, and sugar may be added, according to individual taste. Flavorings of cloves, grated orange peel, or mint are sometimes added.

realized how easy it was to make a cup of tea by pouring boiling water over the sacks, tea bags instantly became popular. Today, more than half the tea sold in the United States is packaged in filter paper tea bags.

BERYL WALTER
Tea Council of the U.S.A.

Updated by DONALD A. WIEDERECHT
Tea Council of the U.S.A.

TEACHERS AND TEACHING

One day in 1925, a miner in the Kentucky hills was on his way to town with a wagonload of coal to sell. As he passed a one-room schoolhouse, he was stopped by the teacher, who was surrounded by his pupils.

"How much coal have you got in your wagon?" the teacher asked the miner. The miner said that he did not know how to figure that out, but that he guessed his wagon could hold about 25 bushels.

The teacher then told his students to use their newly learned arithmetic skills to figure out how much coal was in the wagon. They found that the wagon could hold 43 bushels. The miner had been cheated every time he had delivered a load—he had been paid for less coal than he actually had in his wagon.

This true story was told by Jesse Stuart, the teacher in the one-room school, in his autobiography, *The Thread That Runs So True*. It shows how important to daily life are the lessons learned in school. It also illustrates the most important job of the teacher: to help other people learn skills and knowledge that will help them lead rewarding lives.

▶ WHAT A TEACHER DOES

The profession of teaching is a varied one. The job of an elementary school teacher is very different from the job of a college professor—different material is taught, and different methods are used. But certain aspects of teaching are the same at all levels. Teachers must plan their lessons and present them in a way that interests students and helps them understand what is being taught. And they must measure, or evaluate, their students' progress.

Planning. A teacher's plan begins with a broad view of the material that students will be taught during the school year. The teacher then divides this material into units that will be covered in each grading period. These units in turn are divided into daily plans for the lessons to be covered that day and the methods and materials to be used. Each day's work should help achieve the goals that have been set for the grading period and the year. Lessons should also be planned to help students with different skill levels reach these goals.

Presentation. Because all children do not learn in the same way or at the same rate, lessons are presented in a variety of ways. The

Through effective teachers, the cultural heritage of a society is passed on to new generations.

teacher explains a subject to the class. Students read about the subject, discuss it, and write about it. They may work on problems, help each other in groups, or play a game in which they use what they have learned. They may see videotapes about the subject. Sometimes a class takes field trips to museums, zoos, or manufacturing plants. All these activities help make the subject more interesting and understandable to the students.

Evaluation. A teacher must measure each student's progress. This can be done by asking questions in class or on written tests. The teacher also observes how students participate in discussions, laboratory experiments, and other activities. The evaluation tells the teacher if the class is ready to move on to the next learning goal. It also helps the teacher decide if individual students need help.

▶ NEW ROLES FOR TEACHERS

Many communities have recognized the importance of making greater use of their teachers' knowledge and experience. Teachers now help plan their schools' goals. They help decide what books and materials will be used, how classes will be organized, and how to help less experienced teachers improve their skills.

Changes in society have presented teachers with new obligations. Because the numbers of working mothers and single-parent families have increased greatly, a teacher often spends more time each day with children than the parents can. Thus, a teacher must be alert for signs of physical and emotional problems that a parent might miss. Poor classroom performance may be a sign of illness, fatigue, or family problems. A child who squints when reading may need an eye examination.

Teachers are also important models for behavior. The way a teacher manages the problems of a normal school day can show the students the importance of being reasonable, consistent, pleasant, and firm.

Today teachers must be able to answer students' questions about important issues. Television, radio, and newspapers tell everyone about current events and problems. By being informed about these issues and discussing them, teachers can help calm students' fears and teach them valuable lessons. Students can learn the importance of getting facts and overcoming fear with knowledge.

▶ PREPARING TO BE A TEACHER

Teachers are required to have certain levels of skills and education. Private schools and colleges set their own requirements. For public schools in the United States, each state sets the requirements and **licenses,** or formally approves, teachers who meet them. Individual communities can add their own requirements.

All communities require teachers to have a college education, and many require advanced degrees. Different teaching methods are needed for different grades. For example, the skills needed to teach a first grader to write are different from those needed to teach composition to high school seniors. College programs for teachers usually include courses in education and in academic subjects appropriate to the age of the students they will teach.

In recent years, most states have increased their teacher licensing requirements. Many now give **competency tests** to new teachers, to be sure that they have certain basic skills.

▶ THE PAST AND FUTURE OF TEACHING

Throughout most of history, education was reserved for only a few. In ancient Greece, young men gathered around philosophers whose ideas inspired them. In Europe during the Middle Ages, education was centered in churches and monasteries. But some students formed associations and hired professors to broaden their learning. These associations later grew into universities.

In colonial North America, many children learned to read and write in **dame schools**— schools taught by women in their homes. Belief in the importance of education grew in the 1800's, and communities began to build schools and hire teachers. Most of these schools were one-room schoolhouses. The teacher often had just a high school diploma.

In those days, students were not expected to go much beyond the basics of reading and arithmetic. Even in 1940, only a fourth of adults in the United States were high school graduates. But by 1985, the figure was more than 75 percent. People had also come to expect more from schools—and from teachers.

In 1983 a special United States government panel on education released a study of the nation's schools. The study was called *A Nation at Risk* because it found that students were not learning what was required for their own needs or for the country's welfare. Advances in science and technology made it necessary to provide a higher level of education for more students.

In 1994 the U.S. Senate passed legislation setting national education goals for the end of the century. Among the "Goals 2000" were increased literacy and graduation rates and improved achievement in science and mathematics. Despite some progress, the nation's schools fell short of meeting these goals by 2000.

One problem in meeting these challenges was a critical shortage of new teachers, particularly in such subjects as science and mathematics. Many people who might have become teachers in the past began to choose better-paying jobs in other fields.

To attract qualified people to the teaching profession, many school districts have raised the salaries of teachers, given them a greater voice in deciding how schools are run, and provided on-the-job training.

In today's schools, as in Jesse Stuart's one-room schoolhouse, teachers have an important role to play. The teacher is the key to passing on to the next generation the best that people have thought and done.

ALBERT SHANKER
President, American Federation of Teachers

TEACHING MACHINES. See PROGRAMMED INSTRUCTION.

TECHNOLOGY

All people have the same basic needs: food, shelter, and safety. Beyond these basic needs, they have wants, such as knowledge, leisure, and good health. Technology is the term for all the methods people develop to satisfy their needs and wants. Technology is concerned with ways of making and doing things.

Technology has touched nearly every aspect of life, from the foods you have for dinner to the ways you spend your leisure time. Agriculture, industry, medicine, energy, transportation, and communication are some of the fields that have been most deeply affected by developments in technology.

Technology separates people from other animals. More than any other living things, human beings have the ability to create ways to live better in their environment. They can even change the environment to suit their needs and wants.

Technology may seem to be closely related to science, but it is actually quite different. People developed early technologies, such as basic methods of making metals, without knowing why they worked. The scientific principles behind new devices or techniques were not known. As science became more advanced, people developed organized ways of study to learn why things worked. Science also began to provide knowledge and information that could be developed into new technological advances. Technology, in turn, has provided better tools and methods to help scientists in their work.

▶ TECHNOLOGICAL CHANGE

The greatest reason for change in technology is people's desire to make their lives better and easier. Looking for better and easier ways of doing things seems to be a universal human trait. Over the centuries, people have greatly improved their lives through technology. Shelter improved—people moved from caves to structures they built. Food supplies improved when they developed ways to plant crops and raise animals.

Some changes in technology result from earlier developments. For example, early automobiles were a great improvement in transportation, but they were often uncomfortable and unsafe. New technologies were devel-

Technological advances over the past several decades produced a vast array of electronic devices, including circuit boards and robots.

This article defines technology, describes technological change, and highlights major technological achievements. It discusses the benefits as well as the harmful effects of technology.

Many articles in this encyclopedia give additional information about technology. Articles on specific products of technology include AIRPLANES; AUTOMOBILES; BATTERIES; COMPUTERS; SATELLITES, ARTIFICIAL; TELEPHONE; and TURBINES. More general coverage will be found in articles such as ELECTRONICS; MANUFACTURING; METALS AND METALLURGY; SPACE RESEARCH AND TECHNOLOGY; TELECOMMUNICATIONS; and TRANSPORTATION. Articles that give additional information about technological progress and change include AGRICULTURE; BIOTECHNOLOGY; ENGINEERING; INDUSTRIAL REVOLUTION; INVENTIONS; MEDICINE; and SCIENCE.

oped to solve these problems—ways of building better and smoother roads, better tires, shock absorbers, windshield wipers, safety glass, and so on.

Sometimes a change in one area of technology leads to change in others. Military needs brought about many changes in aircraft that were carried over into commercial aviation. Radar, developed to spot enemy aircraft, now helps control air traffic at busy airports. The need to shoot weapons accurately helped speed the development of computers. Foods, materials, and equipment developed for space travel have found many uses on earth.

The pace of technological change has increased in the 20th century. Before, many years might have passed between the development of a new device and its widespread use. The Chinese, for example, developed ways of making paper by about A.D. 100, but it took more than 1,000 years for this technology to reach western Europe.

Change now takes place rapidly, and the time between a discovery and its effect on people is very short. The airplane is an example. The Wright brothers made their first successful airplane flight in 1903, and airplanes were being widely used within a few years. Today air travel is commonplace. Technology itself is largely responsible for this faster pace of change, through improvements in communication, transportation, and methods of production.

▶ **MAJOR DEVELOPMENTS IN TECHNOLOGY**

Developments in technology are closely linked to changes in society. Early prehistoric people hunted animals and gathered wild plants for their food. Stone tools made by such people about 1,000,000 years ago are the oldest evidence of technology that we have. Prehistoric people also learned to use wood, bones, skins, and other natural materials to meet their needs. They learned to control fire, which provided the warmth that allowed them to live in cold climates.

What is high technology?

"High technology" is a term that loosely describes the application of the very latest scientific advances to make useful products and materials. The term is sometimes used in the shortened form, "high tech." Examples of high technology are computer hardware and software, genetic engineering, robotics, and electronics. Some home appliances and electronic devices, such as video-cassette recorders, may also be described as "high tech."

Sometimes the design of objects, such as furniture, or the design of entire rooms or buildings is called "high tech." This usually means that the object or structure has a very functional and streamlined or even futuristic appearance.

Some 8,000 to 10,000 years ago, people began to farm and raise domestic animals, such as sheep, goats, and pigs. This provided a more plentiful and reliable food supply. Instead of following roaming herds of wild animals, people began to settle permanently in villages. They gradually learned to build houses, to make pots and baskets for storing food, and to weave fabric.

Over the centuries, technology changed life in many other ways. The discovery of ways to make and use metals led to better tools and weapons. The development of the wheel made it easier to travel and carry heavy loads. The invention of writing brought changes in communication and knowledge. Ideas and information could be stored and read by many people.

The ancient Greeks and other people of the Mediterranean region developed many labor-saving devices, including the waterwheel and the pulley. Other advances in technology—including the invention of paper, cast iron, the wheelbarrow, gunpowder, and the compass—were made by the Chinese. The Chinese had a method of block printing before A.D. 900. The use of movable type and the printing press began in Europe in the 1400's, making books available to nearly everyone.

The Industrial Revolution, which began in Europe in the 1700's, was a time of rapid change. Textiles and other goods began to be produced by machine rather than by hand. The steam engine (and, later, electricity) made it possible to power many small machines for manufacturing. Large factories were built to house the machines, so that manufacturing no longer took place in homes and small shops. Many people moved from rural towns to cities in order to find work in the factories.

The development of factories led to assembly-line and mass-production techniques, and people began to produce goods faster and in greater quantities than ever before. Because mass-produced items were cheaper, more people could afford to buy them. And mass consumption (purchase and use) of the items was necessary; without it, the factories would go out of business.

Today many factories have been automated —that is, machines rather than people control the equipment. Automation began with the Jacquard loom, a cloth-making machine controlled by cards with holes punched in them.

Today computers control many kinds of complex machines, and robots have replaced many people on assembly lines.

The 20th century has brought an explosion of technology in many areas besides manufacturing. New machines and techniques for farming and medicine, automobiles and airplanes, telephones, and radio and television are just some of the developments. The computer has become a basic tool of research, education, communication, and business, as well as industry.

Technology has also allowed people to leave earth and make use of space for the first time. Rockets have launched people into space and carried them to the moon. Communications satellites can be placed in orbit to transmit information around the world. Satellites can also help people forecast the weather and locate mineral deposits. And by unlocking the secrets of the nucleus of the atom, people have developed new sources of energy—and powerful new weapons.

▶ **EFFECTS OF TECHNOLOGY**

Technological progress has not touched all people in the same way. Some societies have been able to make more use of technological developments than others. They have become richer, with a higher standard of living. Less-developed societies remain poor, with a lower standard of living. Moreover, technology can affect society in more than one way. It can produce benefits for many people, but it can have harmful affects.

Benefits. In industrial technology, mass production has made more products available to make life easier for more people. Machine production and automation have reduced the labor involved in manufacturing. Robots relieve people from boring or dangerous work, and they can do precision work faster and more accurately than people.

As a result, people now work fewer hours each week than they did 50 years ago, and they still produce more and better products. They have more leisure time—more time to rest, relax, and enjoy life. Even the ways in which people use their leisure time have been changed by new products made for recreation.

Technological advances have also resulted in better medical care. Modern surgical tools and machines make open-heart surgery commonplace, saving many lives. Diseases that once killed thousands of people are under control. People can live longer and healthier lives.

Changes in technology have made life better and easier in many other ways. Improvements in agriculture have increased the world's food supply. Improvements in transportation have allowed people to travel farther and faster than ever before. Improvements in communications have allowed people to speak directly with others thousands of miles away and to instantly spread information and ideas around the world.

Harmful Effects. Harmful effects often seem to accompany developments in technology. For example, the automobile has resulted in faster transportation, but it has also led to many highway deaths.

Mass production and automation have eliminated jobs for many people. New jobs in highly technological industries require complex new skills. People without these skills are put out of work. They must be retrained or be satisfied with menial jobs.

Other changes in technology have made some aspects of life less pleasant and have even harmed the environment. Automobiles and airplanes create noise and pollute the air. Industry pollutes the air and water. Mass production has used up natural resources to the point where many resources are in short supply. And mass consumption has caused large amounts of trash that must be disposed of.

The harmful effects of technology can be widespread. Pollution from factories can produce acid rain, which harms forests, lakes, and streams hundreds of miles away. An accident at a nuclear power plant can spread radiation over a wide area, affecting people, crops, and animals.

But technology also can provide ways to solve many of these problems. For example, materials can be recycled (used again). This preserves raw materials and often saves energy. New synthetic materials are being developed to replace natural materials that are in short supply. Technology can also provide better ways to limit pollution. The challenge is to make sure that the benefits of technological change outweigh the harmful effects.

ALLEN BAME
Virginia Polytechnic Institute
Author, *Exploring Technology*

TECHNOLOGY EDUCATION. See INDUSTRIAL ARTS.

TECUMSEH (1768?–1813)

In the late 1700's and early 1800's, American settlers pushed westward across the Appalachian Mountains. The Indians living in these regions were forced to give up large areas of their land. Tecumseh, son of a Shawnee chief, believed that a great union of Indian tribes could stop the settlers.

Tecumseh was born about 1768 near what is now Springfield, Ohio. As a young man he fought in border disputes against white settlers. He and his brother, known as the Prophet, grew up hating white people and fearing their influence on their ancient culture. Tecumseh and his brother urged their people to honor the ways of their ancestors and reject the advances of a different civilization.

During this period, William Henry Harrison, then governor of the Indiana Territory, arranged a series of treaties with some of the Indian chiefs. These treaties provided for United States control of large areas of land. Tecumseh believed that the land belonged to all the Indians and could be given up only if all the tribes agreed.

In a gigantic effort to slow the settlers' advances, Tecumseh tried to form a vast union of tribes from Florida to the Great Lakes. He traveled many miles winning supporters. While he was on one of his trips, news reached him that his brother, the Prophet, had been drawn into a conflict with Harrison in Indiana. The resulting battle of Tippecanoe brought defeat to the Indians and an end to Tecumseh's great plan.

Still hoping to limit the expansion of the United States into Indian lands, Tecumseh and his followers joined the British in Canada in the War of 1812 against the Americans. He was given the rank of brigadier general. In a general's uniform he led his troops against the Americans. Again and again the Indians and the British were forced to retreat. On October 5, 1813, at the battle of the Thames near Chatham, Ontario, Tecumseh made his last stand. Before leading his men into combat, he donned the battle dress of his tribe. The Americans, under Harrison, defeated the British, and Tecumseh was killed in the fighting.

Tecumseh was a brilliant and humane leader. At a time when white settlers feared the Indians, Tecumseh insisted on merciful treatment of captives. Americans respected his wisdom and honesty. Even his old enemy Harrison called him an "uncommon genius."

Reviewed by Daniel Jacobson
Montclair State College

TEETH

Clean, well-positioned teeth improve your physical appearance. They are the center of your smile. They also help you speak clearly. Most important of all, teeth enable you to chew your food properly, which in turn helps in swallowing and digesting.

Human beings grow two sets of teeth, a primary (first) set and a permanent (secondary) set. At birth no teeth are usually visible, but below the gums 20 primary teeth and 32 permanent teeth are beginning to form.

The primary teeth start to erupt, or grow out, between six months and a year after a baby is born. By the time children are 3 years old, they have a set of 20 teeth—10 in the upper jaw and 10 in the lower jaw.

At about 6 years of age, permanent teeth begin to erupt in the back of the mouth behind the last primary teeth. At about the same age the primary teeth in the front of the mouth begin to loosen. Eventually all the primary teeth become loose and fall out. Every time a primary tooth is lost, it is replaced with a permanent tooth. By the time most children are 11 years old, all their primary teeth have been replaced with permanent teeth.

The last permanent tooth to erupt in the mouth is the third molar. Third molars are often called wisdom teeth, because they erupt in the mouth when a person is in his or her late teens or early 20's—long after the primary teeth of childhood have been replaced.

▶TYPES OF TEETH

There are several varieties of primary and permanent teeth: incisors, cuspids, premolars, and molars. Each variety serves a different function.

Incisors are the squarish, sharp-edged teeth in the front of the mouth. There are eight incisors—four on the top and four on the bottom—in both primary and permanent sets of teeth. These teeth cut food, such as when you bite into an apple.

The **cuspids** are the pointed teeth that cut and tear food. In both primary and permanent teeth there are four cuspids, one on the side of each incisor, top and bottom.

In the back of the mouth are the **molars,** which have several points and grooves. These teeth are grinders. There are eight molars in the primary set (two on either side, top and bottom) and twelve in the permanent set (three on either side, top and bottom).

In the permanent set there are also eight **bicuspids,** or **premolars,** two on either side, top and bottom, between the molars and the cuspids. These teeth usually have two points and are used for tearing and grinding food.

▶ **PARTS OF THE TEETH**

All human teeth are made up of the same parts: a **crown** and one or more **roots.** The crown grows above the gums, and the root or roots grow in a socket in the jawbone.

The crown is covered by **enamel,** which is the hardest substance in the body. Enamel is made up of a combination of the minerals calcium and phosphorous. These minerals combine in a crystal structure called apatite. Enamel apatite is harder than bone. Because it has no nerves, this part of the tooth cannot cause pain.

The root has a protective outer layer called **cementum,** a hard, bonelike material. A third hard substance, called **dentin,** forms a continuous inner shell beneath the crown enamel and the root cementum. The dentin makes up most of the body of the tooth. It too is very similar to bone.

The inside of the tooth is filled with a soft tissue called dental **pulp.** Like other soft tissues in the body, dental pulp contains blood vessels and nerves. These connect with other blood vessels and nerves outside the tooth through a small opening at the bottom of the tooth's root. The blood vessels supply food and carry away waste products. When irritated, the nerves give the sensation of pain. Tooth decay, a sharp blow, or intense hot or cold may cause tooth pain. An interesting feature of a tooth nerve is that it cannot tell the difference between hot and cold. It registers both sensations only as pain.

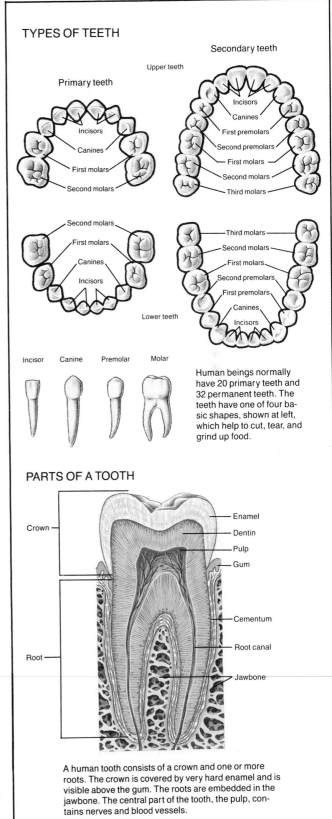

TYPES OF TEETH

Primary teeth

Upper teeth

Secondary teeth

Incisors
Canines
First molars
Second molars

Incisors
Canines
First premolars
Second premolars
First molars
Second molars
Third molars

Second molars
First molars
Canines
Incisors

Third molars
Second molars
First molars
Second premolars
First premolars
Canines
Incisors

Lower teeth

Incisor   Canine   Premolar   Molar

Human beings normally have 20 primary teeth and 32 permanent teeth. The teeth have one of four basic shapes, shown at left, which help to cut, tear, and grind up food.

PARTS OF A TOOTH

Crown

Enamel
Dentin
Pulp
Gum

Cementum

Root canal

Root

Jawbone

A human tooth consists of a crown and one or more roots. The crown is covered by very hard enamel and is visible above the gum. The roots are embedded in the jawbone. The central part of the tooth, the pulp, contains nerves and blood vessels.

As you look at the diagram of a tooth, you may wonder how the primary teeth can fall out. The roots of a tooth look very long and sturdy. After age 3, the roots of a child's primary teeth start to dissolve. As they dissolve, the permanent teeth grow into the space left by the roots of the primary teeth. When the entire root of a primary tooth has dissolved, nothing is left to hold it in the mouth. The crown of the tooth falls out.

▶ TOOTH DECAY

Healthy teeth are an important part of overall good health. When teeth are healthy, they do not ache or cause pain.

Pain in a tooth is a sign that you may have **tooth decay,** also known as **cavities.** A cavity is a hole in the enamel surface of the tooth. It is caused by bacteria that are always present in the mouth and on the teeth.

The bacteria that cause tooth decay thrive on some of the same foods you do. When they come in contact with cooked starch or sugar, the bacteria turn these foods into acid. The acid slowly causes the tooth's enamel to dissolve. One or more tiny holes, or cavities, are left behind. The term **caries** is used to describe this decay process, which is in fact a bacterial disease.

Caries usually start in the grooves of the molars or in places between the teeth or near the gums. This is because food particles are often caught in such places, giving the bacteria there plenty of food to turn into acid.

If the decay process is not stopped when the cavity is small, the decay may continue through the enamel to the dentin layer, causing a toothache. If the cavity reaches as far as the soft dental pulp, a serious infection may result and permanently damage the tooth. The infection also may spread to other parts of the body.

▶ CARING FOR TEETH

The best way to protect your teeth against cavities is to brush them carefully after each meal. When you brush you accomplish two things: (1) You remove excess bacteria from the tooth surfaces, and (2) you remove food particles that bacteria eat. Limiting the amount of sugary and starchy foods in your diet, such as cookies, pastries, candies, and soft drinks, will also help reduce the chance of getting cavities.

Another important way to care for your teeth is to have regular dental examinations. Your dentist will clean your teeth with special instruments. He or she will check the condition of your gums, which help hold your teeth firmly in place. If you have any cavities, the dentist will fill them so they do not become larger and the decay does not become more serious.

Fluoride

Fluoride is a mineral that occurs naturally in all water supplies. It makes your teeth stronger by causing some calcium and phosphorous that has dissolved from the tooth enamel to settle back onto the teeth. This process is known as **remineralization.**

The amount of fluoride in the water varies in different parts of the world. Scientists have found that if the water supply you drink contains 1 part of fluoride in 1,000,000 parts of water (abbreviated 1 ppm), you will very probably have fewer cavities than if your water contains only half that amount.

In many areas where the public water supply does not contain enough fluoride, the level is adjusted to about 1 ppm by adding fluoride to the water before it reaches your home. Because not everyone has a central water supply (some people get their water from a well), your dentist or physician can give you a prescription for a daily fluoride supplement. Your toothpaste should also contain fluoride.

Dental Sealants

Another helpful way to prevent cavities is to have dental sealants placed on your back teeth. If you look in a mirror at the biting surfaces of your molars, you will see a lot of tiny depressions and grooves. Dentists call these pits and fissures. Food and bacteria accumulate in the pits and fissures and cannot be removed easily with a toothbrush.

To prevent this accumulation, dentists can put a clear plastic material, called sealant, into these pits and fissures. The sealant stays permanently on the teeth, fills up the tiny spaces, and prevents cavity-causing bacteria from accumulating.

CHARLES I. STOLOFF, D.D.S.

Reviewed by STEPHEN J. MOSS, D.D.S.
Past President, American Academy of
Pediatric Dentistry

See also DENTISTRY; FLUORIDATION; ORTHODONTICS.

TEHRAN

Tehran (also spelled Teheran) is the capital and largest city of Iran and the political and economic center of the country. It is situated on the southern slopes of the Elburz Mountains, in the north, near the Caspian Sea. More than 6.5 million people live in the city proper. More than 12 million live in the greater metropolitan area. Tehran, whose name means "warm place," is hot in the summer and mild in winter. The area receives relatively little precipitation.

The City. Tehran is a lovely city, with tree-lined boulevards, ornamental gardens tucked away behind high walls, narrow canals filled with cool, rushing water, and exquisite mosques (Muslim houses of worship).

The city is divided into two sections. The old section, located in the southern part of the city, contains the great bazaar, or market-place. The old section also contains several museums that were once palaces of the former shahs (kings). The new city, located in the north, is very modern and has been built in the style of European cities. The two parts

of Tehran are joined at Maydan Sepah, a large, beautiful square. Tehran has several universities. The largest are Tehran University and the National University.

Economic Activity. More than half of Iran's manufactured goods are produced in Tehran. These include textiles, processed foods, chemicals, construction materials, transportation equipment, metal products, and military equipment. Oil refineries are also located in the area.

History. Tehran grew from a small village into an important city in the 1500's. It became the Iranian capital in 1788. The old city was originally surrounded by walls, which were torn down in 1926. Modern expansion began soon after.

In 1943, during World War II, the city was the site of the Tehran Conference. It was here that the allied leaders of the United States, Britain, and the Soviet Union discussed plans to invade western Europe.

In 1979, Tehran was the center of the revolution that overthrew the last shah, Mohammed Reza Pahlavi, and established an Islamic (Muslim) republic. Shortly thereafter, Iranians seized the U.S. Embassy in Tehran and held its American employees hostage for more than 14 months. Tehran also was caught up in Iran's long war with Iraq (1980–88). Parts of the city were destroyed and the economy was severely affected. By the end of the 1990's, much of the damage had been repaired, and a campaign to attract foreign investment was begun.

JAMES A. BILL
University of Texas at Austin

TEKAKWITHA, KATERI. See INDIANS, AMERICAN (Profiles).

TEKTITES. See COMETS, METEORITES, AND ASTEROIDS.

TEL AVIV. See ISRAEL (Major Cities).

Tehran's great marketplace is located in the old section of the city, where winding, narrow streets are lined with many small shops.

TELECOMMUNICATIONS

Without leaving their hospitals, doctors in distant countries share life-saving information over videoconferencing systems. At school, students use computers connected to the Internet to "visit" museums and other places around the world. At home, millions of television viewers watch as a robotic probe sends images of the planet Mars back to Earth.

The doctors, the students, and the robotic probe are all using technology that lets them communicate over sometimes great distances. This technology is called telecommunications. The term comes from the Greek word *tele*, meaning "far off," and the Latin word *communicare*, meaning "to share."

Familiar telecommunications devices today include the telephone, fax machine, radio, and television. The telegraph, too, was once an important means of communicating over long distances. In recent times, the computer has been increasingly used in telecommunications. Many telephones, computers, and other devices are now linked to one another in what are called **networks**, which allow people to share vast amounts of information.

▶ **COMMUNICATING BY ELECTRICITY**

All communication requires a sender, receiver, and **medium** over which messages can be transmitted. Early devices such as the telegraph used the flow of electricity, or electrical current, as a medium. These devices convert messages into electrical signals, transmit them over wires, and convert them back into their original form at the receiving end.

The Telegraph

Electrical communication began in 1837, when American inventor Samuel Morse developed the first practical telegraph. Operators tapped on keys to spell out messages in combinations of short and long electrical pulses, called dots and dashes. These corresponded to letters, numbers, and basic punctuation in a system called **Morse code**. The pulses traveled over wires to other telegraph instruments, where operators translated the code back into the original message.

Improvements in the telegraph came rapidly. A method called **multiplex telegraphy** made it possible to send many messages at once over the same wire. A device called the **teletypewriter**, or teleprinter, enabled an operator to type a message on a keyboard. The message was automatically coded and sent to other teleprinters, which printed it out.

The Telephone

By the 1870's, American inventor Alexander Graham Bell figured out how to transmit the human voice over telegraph wires. Long-distance telephone service soon followed.

This article provides an overview of telecommunications devices, such as the telephone and television. It also describes the transmission of telecommunications signals by means of electrical cables, optical fibers, and radio waves. And it discusses digital communications and computer networks.

Some telecommunications devices are covered in separate, more detailed articles. These are RADIO; SATELLITES, ARTIFICIAL; TELEGRAPH; TELEPHONE; and TELEVISION. Other applications of telecommunications are covered in the articles COMPUTERS and OFFICE MACHINES. The history of communication is found in the article COMMUNICATION.

Since then, many improvements have been made to the telephone. To keep up with the growing number of calls, engineers developed telephone carrier systems. These allowed many calls, or voice channels, to be carried on one pair of wires at the same time.

Later systems used coaxial cables, consisting of wires inside copper tubes filled with insulating material. One advantage of this design is that it helps prevent signals from radiating (spreading out) from the cable. As a result, signals can travel very far through coaxial cables without weakening much. The design also helps keep out signals from other sources (such as nearby cables), which can cause "cross talk," or interference, between signals. Today's telephone systems use a technology called fiber optics to carry even more calls over long distances. (See the section below on communicating by light waves.)

The Fax Machine

Another outgrowth of the telegraph was the facsimile, or fax, machine. Some early systems in the mid-1800's could reproduce messages that were written on metal plates and then transmitted over telegraph lines. Later facsimile devices used light-sensitive photoelectric cells to convert the light and dark areas on a page into telegraph or radio signals. Such systems enabled newspapers to exchange photographs of events around the world as they happened.

In the 1980's, many businesses, organizations, schools, and even home offices began using faster and cheaper fax machines that could send and receive documents over regular telephone lines. By the 1990's, faxes could also be sent and received using computers connected to phone lines.

▶ COMMUNICATING BY RADIO WAVES

In 1901, just as telegraph and telephone cables were spreading across the world, Italian inventor Guglielmo Marconi demonstrated his "wireless telegraph" by transmitting a dot-and-dash message across the Atlantic Ocean using radio waves. Radio broadcasts of voices and music soon followed, making radio a popular source of news and entertainment.

Radio Applications

Because radio needed no wires, it also became a vital communications link for vehicles such as ships, planes, and police cars. Today, amateur radio operators use radio to talk to others around the world and relay messages in times of disasters and emergencies. Over shorter distances, truck drivers and other travelers use citizens band (CB) radio.

Pocket-size radio devices called **pagers** allow people to be contacted even when they are on the move. If someone using a pager is wanted on the telephone, a radio signal is sent to the device, which buzzes, beeps, or displays the telephone number of the person calling. Newer two-way pagers also let people send brief text messages.

Cellular telephones are another application of radio. These portable devices connect to telephone networks through a series of

In early telephone systems, calls were connected manually by switchboard operators. Today's systems connect calls electronically, at much faster speeds.

radio transmitter-receivers that cover small areas, or cells. As a person moves from cell to cell, the call is automatically transferred from one transmitter-receiver to another. By the end of the 1990's, **satellite telephones** had become available. These phones send and receive signals through many satellites that, together, can cover almost the entire globe.

Television Broadcasting

In the early part of the 20th century, inventors began experimenting with ways of broadcasting moving pictures as well as voices over radio waves. By 1945, advances in technology and broadcasting standards made television widely available. Today, television reaches several billion people around the world and has become the leading source of news and entertainment.

At first, television sets needed to be close to a broadcasting station or use antennas to receive clear pictures and sound. In 1950, a method called **community antenna television**, or cable TV, brought television to isolated areas. Tall antennas would pick up distant television signals, amplify (strengthen) them, and feed them through coaxial cables to homes. Later, cable TV stations began picking up their signals from satellites.

Today, many people can receive television signals directly from satellites using dish-shaped antennas. These are particularly use-

Hair-thin glass strands called optical fibers transmit signals in the form of light pulses. These fibers can carry many more phone calls and other information than copper cables can.

ful in remote areas beyond the reach of ordinary television broadcast stations or cable TV. Satellite television service also provides many more channels.

Microwaves and Satellites

In order to transmit radio signals over long distances, two methods are used: microwave relay systems and orbiting communications satellites.

Microwaves are radio waves with very short wavelengths—less than 1 foot (0.3 meter) long. Waves that carry AM radio programs are about 1,000 times as long. Unlike ordinary radio signals that spread out in all directions from a transmitter, microwaves travel in narrow, straight lines just like light beams. Microwaves carrying the signals of telephones, radio and television stations, and computers are relayed between towers spaced many miles apart.

The other kind of relay system uses satellites in space instead of towers on the ground. Many satellites are positioned at a height of 22,300 miles (36,000 kilometers) above Earth. In this so-called geosynchronous orbit, satellites circle the planet at the same rate as Earth rotates, remaining over one fixed spot on the ground. As they receive microwave transmissions from ground stations, the transmissions are relayed to other stations.

▶ COMMUNICATING BY LIGHT WAVES

In the 1970's, a technology called **fiber optics** offered a new telecommunications medium: light. Fiber optics makes use of pulses of light generated by a tiny laser. These light pulses are transmitted over hair-thin strands of glass called optical fibers. At the receiving end, a device detects the light and converts the signals into electrical pulses.

Optical fibers can carry much more information than copper cables or even microwaves can. One optical fiber cable less than $\frac{1}{2}$ inch (1 centimeter) in diameter can carry more than a million conversations at a time. In 1989, the first undersea fiber-optic system connecting North America and Europe was completed, having several times the capacity of undersea coaxial cables.

▶ DIGITAL COMMUNICATIONS

In recent times, the greatest change in telecommunications has been the move from analog to digital signals. This move has greatly improved the quality and efficiency of telecommunications systems. It has also paved the way for telephones, computers, and other devices to work more closely together.

Analog signals are similar, or analogous, to the original sound or light waves of a voice or image. These signals can take the form of electrical currents or electromagnetic waves that change smoothly in their amplitude

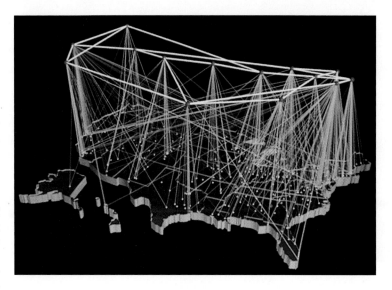

The colored lines in this image show some of the many connections between U.S. cities in the Internet computer network.

(height of the waves) or frequency (number of times the wave makes a complete cycle).

Digital signals, on the other hand, represent the original signals in strings of 1's and 0's. These bits (short for "binary digits") correspond to "on" and "off" electrical pulses. For example, a series of bits can represent the values of a sound wave's changing amplitude and frequency. Or they can represent the letters and numbers of computer data.

Speed and Accuracy

Because the telegraph worked with on-off pulses, the telegraph can be thought of as a forerunner to modern digital communications. In fact, transmission methods essential to digital communications came about as a result of telegraph improvements, based on a theory of information developed by American mathematician Claude Shannon in the 1940's.

Shannon's theory led to two important methods for sending messages faster and more accurately. One method was **data compression**, a technique that reduces the number of bits needed to send a message. For example, extra, or redundant, bits can be removed from a message so that it takes less time to transmit. The other method was **error correction**. This technique detects and fixes mistakes in transmissions, such as those caused by electrical interference.

By the end of the 1990's, digital information was routinely being transmitted at speeds of up to 100 million bits per second—almost a million times faster than was possible using the telegraph. Some advanced systems could transmit at a rate of more than a gigabit (1 billion bits) or even a terabit (1 trillion bits) per second. At this rate, the entire text of *The New Book of Knowledge* encyclopedia could be transmitted in less than a millisecond (thousandth of a second).

Switching Systems

Soon after the telegraph and telephone were invented, engineers realized that it would be too cumbersome for each device to be directly connected to every other one. By using central switching offices, connections could be more easily managed. The first switching systems were human operators. Their job was to connect one line to another as someone was placing a call.

Modern switching systems do the same job but at much faster speeds. While human operators took several seconds to connect calls, the first mechanical switching machines took a few milliseconds. The invention of the transistor in 1947 led to faster electronic switching machines. By the 1970's, these machines could make connections in microseconds (millionths of a second). Today's digital machines operate in nanoseconds (billionths of a second). A nanosecond is roughly the amount of time it takes light reflected off this page to reach your eyes.

Computer Networks

By the 1960's, advances in digital communications and switching gave rise to the first computer network, called ARPANET. Funded by the U.S. military, it was developed by researchers to share large amounts of scientific information across great distances. At first, the network connected only a few universities in the United States. However, it eventually grew to connect millions of computers around the world in what would become known as the **Internet**.

Using videoconferencing systems, doctors on opposite sides of the world can see each other and share information about patients.

viewed on a computer monitor. These pages are really computer files that can display text, pictures, and video on a monitor's screen. They can also contain sounds, such as music or speeches, that can be heard through a computer's speakers. Collections of such pages are called Web sites. These sites typically connect their pages to one another, or to those of other sites, using coded words or pictures called hyperlinks.

In the 1980's and 1990's, other computer networks called **online services** became available for personal computers in homes, schools, and businesses. Services such as America Online gave people access to its network, and later to the Internet, over regular telephone lines.

Computers can connect to these services through devices called **modems** (short for "modulate-demodulate"). When a modem sends information, it uses a process called modulation to convert digital data into analog signals that travel over telephone lines. When the modem receives information, it uses a process called demodulation to convert the analog signals back into a digital form that the computer can handle. More and more home computers are now connecting directly to the Internet and online services using digital cable and digital telephone connections, instead of analog-line modems.

Electronic mail, or e-mail, was one of the earliest uses of the Internet and other networks. It is a method of sending messages that can be typed on a computer keyboard, in much the same way that messages were once typed on teletypewriters. An e-mail message travels from a sender's computer over the network to a central computer. A recipient then uses his or her computer to retrieve the message from the central computer. Some e-mail systems also allow people to send voice messages, pictures, and videos in the form of attached computer files.

A more recent use of the Internet is the popular **World Wide Web**. It is a method of sharing information on "pages" that can be

▶ **TRENDS IN TELECOMMUNICATIONS**

Modern telecommunications systems combine many different technologies, from telephone wires between people's homes to communications satellites that orbit Earth. These systems can now handle a mixture of voices and other sounds, still and moving images, as well as computer text and other data—all in the same digital format.

As a result, many of these technologies are converging. Already, some television services provide access to computer networks. And some computers, equipped with microphones and cameras, allow people separated by great distances to see and hear each other at the same time. These videoconferencing systems are used by doctors to monitor the health of patients in remote locations, or by business people across the country to hold meetings without leaving their offices.

As the 21st century begins, radio- and satellite-based networks are ushering in a new era of wireless telecommunications. Some devices, such as cellular telephones and antenna-equipped portable computers, can now be used to access information virtually anywhere and anytime.

Telecommunications is even spreading out beyond Earth as space probes explore our solar system. Robotic spacecraft such as *Pathfinder*, which sent back television images of Mars in 1997, will extend our ability to communicate across even greater distances.

Reviewed by V. MICHAEL BOVE, JR.
Principal Research Scientist
MIT Media Laboratory
Massachusetts Institute of Technology

TELEGRAPH

The telegraph is a method of sending information in the form of electrical impulses. The word "telegraph" comes from Greek words meaning "writing" and "distance."

In the 1800's, telegraph systems were important to the growth of industry, the building of empires by European nations, and the settlement of the American West. Today, the telephone, the fax machine, and computer networks have replaced the traditional telegraph. But modern versions of telegraph services are still important for some uses.

▶ DEVELOPMENT OF THE TELEGRAPH

In the 1790's, the French engineer Claude Chappe invented the first visual telegraph, or semaphore, using tall poles spaced at intervals between cities. Blades on the poles could be moved into various positions standing for numbers and letters, so that a message could be relayed down the line of poles.

Discoveries about electricity and magnetism in the early 1800's led to a much faster way of communicating: the electric telegraph.

In this vintage photo, telegraph operators tap on keys to send messages and listen to the clicks of incoming messages made by devices called sounders.

In one early model, developed by British inventors William Cooke and Charles Wheatstone in 1837, five wires were connected to five compass needles mounted on a dial showing the letters of the alphabet. As current passed through wires, it turned the needles to point to various letters.

The Morse System. About the same time in the United States, inventors Samuel Morse, Joseph Henry, and Alfred Vail developed a more practical telegraph system in which messages could be sent over a single wire using a simple code. (A biography of Morse can be found in Volume M.)

In the Morse system, an operator would tap out a message on a telegraph key. Combinations of short and long intervals between taps represented letters and numbers. When the key was pressed down, it made a current flow over a wire to the receiver. There, the current passed through an electromagnet that moved a pencil, which marked a moving strip of paper with a dot or a dash. In later systems, the electromagnet moved a device called a sounder with a click. An operator at the receiving end would listen for the incoming clicks and translate them back into words.

Long-Distance Lines. Morse sent the first long-distance telegraph message in 1844, from Washington, D.C., to Baltimore, Maryland. By 1861, when the first transcontinental telegraph link was completed, much of the United States was linked by telegraph lines, most strung along railroad tracks. Gradually, many small companies that operated these lines consolidated into the Western Union Telegraph Company.

In 1866, a team led by American businessman Cyrus Field finally succeeded in laying the first successful transatlantic telegraph cable, from Newfoundland to Ireland. (A biography of Field appears in Volume F.) By the early 1900's, such cables made it possible to send a telegraph message around the world.

Multiple Messages. One of the important advances in early telegraphs was a system that could send more than one message over a single wire. The early duplex system could send two messages at a time. In 1874, Thomas Edison invented the quadriplex system, which allowed four signals to be sent simultaneously. A year later, French inventor Emile Baudot developed a multiplex system that could send five messages at once. Later systems could send thousands of messages at a time.

The Teletypewriter. Another important advance was the teletypewriter, a machine that could translate messages from plain language to code and back. By the early 20th century, teletypewriters came into widespread use,

Make Your Own Telegraph Set

You and a friend can make a simple telegraph set. You will need two electric buzzers, two 6-volt batteries, a roll of 18-gauge wire, two small blocks of wood, two thin strips of metal, and four round-head screws.

Make two sending keys. For each, use a block of wood as a base and a strip of metal as a sender. Ask an adult to cut the metal from the lid of a can. Bind the sharp edges of the metal with tape so you do not cut yourself. Sandpaper the lacquer off the underside of one end to allow the electric current to pass through. Screw one of the screws into one end of the block. Attach one end of the metal strip to the other end of the block with a second screw so that the unattached end of the strip is over the first screw. Bend the metal upward so that it will not make contact with the screw unless pressed down.

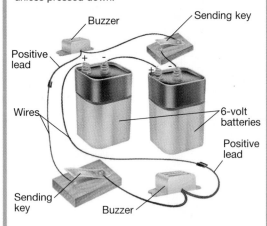

Attach the wires as shown in the diagram. Be sure to connect the positive (+) terminal of one battery with the negative (–) terminal of the other. Scrape off the insulation at the end of each wire so that its connection is made with bare wire. If your buzzers come with lead wires already attached, connect the positive (red) leads as shown. Twist the bare ends of the connecting wires together, and then cover the connection with tape. Now connect the wires to the sending keys by looping the bare wire under the head of each screw and tightening the screw against the wood.

When both keys are pressed to the contact screws, a complete electrical circuit is formed. Electric current flows through the circuit, and the buzzers sound. To send messages, use Morse code, keeping the key down longer for a dash than for a dot. (A table of the alphabet in Morse code can be found in the article RADIO, AMATEUR in Volume Q-R.) Messages can be sent by only one person at a time. When your partner is sending a message, you must hold your key down so that there will be a continuous electric circuit.

along with a number of wire services. They included stock tickers and news services that provided quick access to information for their subscribers. Services such as Telex were introduced in the 1930's to provide direct links between subscribers. These services have been largely replaced today by computer networks such as the Internet. These networks let people send electronic messages to others around the world almost instantly.

Wireless Telegraph. Perhaps the greatest advance came in the late 1890's, when Italian inventor Guglielmo Marconi developed a way to transmit telegraph signals using radio waves instead of wires. In 1901, Marconi received the first wireless telegraph signal sent across the Atlantic Ocean, from England to Newfoundland. His invention enabled ships and airplanes to communicate with one another and with stations on land. In the 1960's, satellites began relaying radio telegraph signals around the world. (A biography of Marconi appears in Volume M.)

The Fax Machine. As early as the mid-1800's, devices were invented to send written documents over telegraph lines. By the 1930's, improved facsimile systems—later called fax machines—could translate a picture into signals that were sent by radio. The receiving machine converted the signals and printed out a copy of the picture. Fax machines became popular in the 1980's, when faster equipment that worked over standard phone lines became widely available.

▶ **TELEGRAPH SERVICES**

Modern technologies have largely replaced the telegraph, but some telegraph services are still available. In the United States, for example, Western Union offices continue to offer telegrams for messages sent within the country or cablegrams for messages sent internationally. These are usually important messages sent to someone who may be otherwise unreachable. Instead of being tapped out on telegraph keys, they are now delivered via telephone by an operator or hand delivered by an agent. For special occasions, you can even send someone a "singing" telegram, which the agent sings to the person.

JAMES JESPERSEN
Coauthor, *Mercury's Web: The Story of Telecommunications*

See also TELECOMMUNICATIONS; TELEPHONE.

TELEPHONE

The word "telephone" comes from Greek words meaning "far" and "sound," and it describes what the telephone does: The telephone uses electricity to carry sound over great distances, so that people who are far away can talk to each other.

Alexander Graham Bell developed the first successful telephone in 1876. By the end of the 20th century, more than 800 million telephones were installed in homes, schools, and offices around the world. Today in the United States alone, the average telephone subscriber makes some 3,000 calls a year.

▶ **HOW THE TELEPHONE WORKS**

A telephone has three main parts: the **transmitter** (or microphone), the **receiver** (or speaker), and the connecting **wires**. The transmitter and receiver are both part of the **handset**, the part of the telephone that you hold. You speak into the transmitter, and you hold the receiver next to your ear. A dialing mechanism may be located in the handset or in a base unit.

When you speak into a telephone, the transmitter changes the sound waves of your voice into an electric current. The transmitter accomplishes this using a thin metal sheet, or **diaphragm**. In older telephones, the diaphragm covers a small cup containing carbon granules. Sound waves striking the diaphragm press the granules together, changing the amount of electric current flowing through them. In newer telephones, which have much smaller transmitters, the diaphragm is an electrically charged foil called an **electret**. The foil sits on top of a metal plate with holes. Sound waves make the foil vibrate in the holes and change the strength of an electric field between the foil and the plate. This changing electric field creates changes in the electric current flowing through the transmitter. In both types of transmitters, these changes in current form an electrical "pattern" of your voice.

From the transmitter, the fluctuating (changing) electric current travels over a pair of wires that connect your telephone to a telephone cable. The cable, which may be suspended from a series of telephone poles or buried underground, runs to a central telephone office, where calls are routed automat-

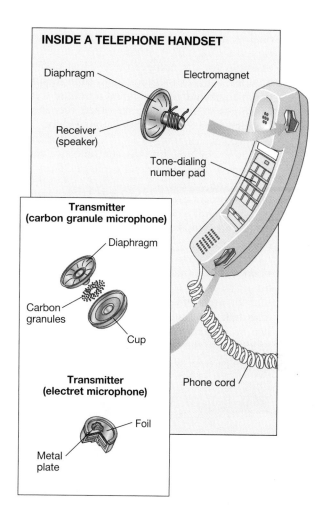

INSIDE A TELEPHONE HANDSET

Diaphragm
Electromagnet
Receiver (speaker)
Tone-dialing number pad

Transmitter (carbon granule microphone)
Diaphragm
Carbon granules
Cup

Transmitter (electret microphone)
Foil
Metal plate

Phone cord

ically through a network of telephone lines to other telephones.

When your call reaches another telephone, its receiver changes the fluctuating current carrying your voice back into sound waves. To do this, the receiver contains a permanent magnet, a diaphragm, and an **electromagnet**. An electromagnet is made of a coil of wire around a soft iron core. When current enters the receiver, it passes through the electromagnet, which creates a magnetic field that moves the diaphragm and makes the air vibrate. These vibrations reproduce the sounds of your voice.

A Telephone Call. When you lift the handset of a telephone to call a friend, you hear a **dial tone**, which tells you that the central telephone office is ready to handle your call. By dialing, you tell the office what phone you wish to reach. Some older phones use **pulse**

dialing, in which the electric current is interrupted for each digit—three interruptions, for example, for the number three. Most phones now use a faster method called **tone dialing**, in which each digit is assigned a unique tone. Machines at the telephone office recognize the digits and route the call automatically.

If you are making a local call, automatic switching equipment at the central office connects you to your friend's phone. Besides making the connection, the automatic switching equipment monitors the call. It provides a busy signal if your friend's phone is being used, and it makes records of long-distance calls for billing.

More advanced kinds of connections are needed when calling outside your local area. To make some long-distance calls, you must dial an **area code** before the local number. This tells the equipment at the telephone office what part of the country you wish to reach. From the central switching station near your home, a long-distance call is connected first to a long-distance carrier, which then routes the call to the appropriate town or city. International calls pass through special switching stations. Today, most parts of the world can be dialed directly.

Telephone Lines. A telephone call may travel in a variety of ways. Older long-distance telephone cables consist of thousands of copper wires or of special pipelines called coaxial cables. Each wire or pipeline can handle a number of calls at the same time. The calls do not interfere with each other because each one is transmitted at a slightly different frequency, or rate of vibration. Because the signals fade over distance, they are amplified, or made stronger, by devices called **repeaters** that are spaced along the line.

In many areas, copper and coaxial cables are rapidly being replaced with new **fiber-optic cables**. These are made up of optical fibers—fine, flexible glass strands that carry light in the same way a pipe carries water. A fiber-optic cable no thicker than your finger can carry some 50,000 phone calls at a time. It would take more than four copper cables, each as thick as your arm, to carry the same number of calls. In addition, fiber-optic cables require fewer repeaters.

In a fiber-optic system, the electrical signal produced by your voice is changed into a code made up of ones and zeros, like the code that operates computers. This **binary** (two-digit) code switches a tiny laser on and off thousands of times a second. Pulses of laser light travel down the optical fiber to their destination, where they are changed back into electrical signals.

Telephone cables may be strung from telephone poles, buried underground, or laid under the ocean. Sometimes, however, running cables is impractical. Long-distance telephone calls may also be transmitted by **microwave radio relay**. The signals are beamed through the air from one relay sta-

Alexander Graham Bell is shown making the first long-distance telephone call from New York to Chicago in 1892.

tion to another or to communications satellites, which act as relay stations.

HISTORY

The story of Alexander Graham Bell's invention of the telephone is told in the biography of Bell in Volume B. By 1878 there were 10,755 telephones in service in the United States. And in that year, the first commercial switchboard was built, in New Haven, Connecticut.

Since then, many improvements have been made. For example, in Bell's early telephones, the transmitter was also used as the receiver—the same instrument was held first to the mouth and then to the ear. Later designs had a more convenient separate earpiece, with the mouthpiece and the bulk of the set's equipment mounted on the wall. The handset, which combined the receiver and transmitter, was introduced for general use in 1928.

As telephones improved, so did telephone lines. In the early 1900's, the vacuum tube was invented, and an amplifier making use of it was developed. In 1915, this made it possible to talk across North America from coast to coast. In 1927, commercial radio telephone service spanned the Atlantic Ocean between New York City and London. Undersea telephone cables were first laid in the 1950's, and satellite transmission began in the 1960's.

Many changes have also been made in switching. In early switchboards, connections were made by hand. An operator sat in front of a board that had a **jack** (or socket) for each line served. When a subscriber wanted service, a light would flash at the appropriate jack, and the operator would ask the subscriber what number he or she wished to reach. Then the operator would connect the two lines by plugging the ends of a short wire into the two jacks. In

Radio waves provide a wireless connection to users of portable communications devices such as a doctor's pager, a businesswoman's cellular phone, or a girl's cordless phone at home. In each case, the device provides a link to telephone line networks.

the 1890's, much faster automatic switching devices came into use.

Today most telephone connections are made by electronic switches, which were introduced in the 1960's. These devices, which use transistors to perform switching operations in millionths of a second, can perform much more complicated operations than the older electromechanical switches. For example, by dialing a code, users can transfer calls from their homes to any other place where they may be. Conference calls can be set up between three or more telephones.

NEW TECHNOLOGY

Today telephones are available with many special features. Automatic dialers have tiny magnetic memory banks in which frequently called numbers can be stored. The user can then dial a number with a touch of one or two buttons. Some telephones have built-in answering machines, which record incoming calls and allow them to be played back later. In **voice-mail** systems, incoming calls are routed to a telephone company's central computer if there is no answer at the number being dialed or if the number is busy. The computer records the calls, which the user can later retrieve from any telephone.

Cordless home telephones are now quite common. A cordless telephone consists of a portable handset, complete with dialing and switch-hook mechanisms, linked to a base unit by a two-way radio connection rather than wires. Calls can be made and received within several hundred feet of the base unit.

Cellular telephones are portable units that can be used away from home. A cellular phone call travels by two-way radio to a tower at a transmitter-receiver base station. These stations are set up in a network, with each one covering a specific cell, or area. As the user moves from one cell to the next, the call is automatically connected to the nearest station, which relays the call to a central switching office. Older cellular networks use **analog** trans-mission, in which the radio signals travel in waves that are analogous, or similar, to the sound waves of the original call. Analog trans-missions are susceptible to a problem called interference, in which other signals combine with the transmissions and create static, like the noise heard between two stations on a radio.

By the mid-1990's, many cellular networks were using **digital** trans-mission, in which a person's voice is translated into a series of rapid radio pulses, similar to computer binary code. In digital trans-mission, computers check the signals for errors and automatically correct them. As a result, digital networks are able to provide cellular telephone users with much clearer calls, free of static. Digital networks also offer computer-based services, such as sending text messages that appear on a small screen on the telephone.

In the late 1990's, small mobile **satellite telephones** were introduced. Unlike cellular telephones, which have limited ranges, these new models can send and receive calls from virtually anywhere in the world. The calls are relayed by dozens of communications satellites orbiting Earth.

Other portable devices, called **pagers**, can alert users if someone is trying to reach them by telephone. In older pagers, the user is alerted by a beeping or buzzing sound. In newer models, a short text message from the person trying to reach the user may be displayed on a small screen, or a brief voice message may be heard.

Today, advances in computer technology are opening up a new world for telephone systems. People are now able to place voice and even video calls over computer networks such as the Internet. In these systems, special telephones or computers equipped with microphones, speakers, and video cameras let people both see and talk with each other.

JAMES JESPERSEN
Coauthor, *Mercury's Web: The Story of Telecommunications*

See also TELECOMMUNICATIONS.

Above: Satellites now let mobile phone users send and receive calls from virtually anywhere in the world. *Below:* Camera-equipped computers connected over networks let people place voice and video calls.

TELESCOPES

You can see planets, stars, and other objects in space just by looking up on a clear night. But to really see them—to observe the craters on the moon, the rings around Saturn, and the countless other wonders in our sky—you must use a telescope.

A telescope is an instrument used to produce magnified (enlarged) images of distant objects. It does this by gathering and focusing the light or other forms of electromagnetic radiation emitted or reflected by those objects. The word "telescope" comes from two Greek words meaning "far" and "see."

▶ KINDS OF TELESCOPES

There are many different types of telescopes, both optical and non-optical. Optical telescopes are designed to focus visible light. Non-optical telescopes are designed to detect kinds of electromagnetic radiation that are invisible to the human eye, such as radio waves, infrared radiation, X-rays, ultraviolet radiation, and gamma rays. The word "optical" means "making use of light."

Some telescopes are launched into space for clearer views and because some forms of

Telescopes produce enlarged images of distant celestial objects, allowing amateur astronomers in backyards (*above left*) and professional astronomers at observatories (*above*) to explore the depths of space.

electromagnetic radiation are absorbed by the Earth's atmosphere and do not reach the ground. For a detailed discussion of these telescopes, see the article SPACE TELESCOPES in Volume S.

Optical Telescopes

Different types of optical telescopes gather and focus light in different ways. Refracting telescopes, or refractors, use lenses. Reflecting telescopes, or reflectors, use mirrors. And catadioptric telescopes, or catadioptrics, use a combination of lenses and mirrors. The main lens or mirror in an optical telescope is called the **objective**.

Refracting Telescopes. A refracting telescope is typically a long, tube-shaped instru-

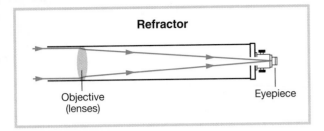

Refractor

Objective (lenses)

Eyepiece

ment. The objective is a system of lenses at the front end of the tube (the end facing the sky). When light strikes the lenses, it is bent and brought to a focus within the tube, forming an image of a distant object. This image can be magnified by the **eyepiece**, a group of small lenses at the back of the tube. A camera can replace or be added to the eyepiece so that photographs can be taken of celestial objects. For many years, these cameras used film. Today most are equipped with **charge-coupled devices** (CCD's), which use semiconductor chips to electronically capture images. CCD's are similar to the devices in home digital cameras and video camcorders, except that the CCD's used by astronomers are usually extremely sensitive to light.

Optical telescopes are frequently referred to by the diameter of their objective. A large objective gathers more light than a small one and allows astronomers to see more details or fainter objects. The objective lens of the refractor at the Yerkes Observatory in Wisconsin has a diameter of 40 inches (102 centimeters) and so is often called the Yerkes 40-inch refractor. The giant lens is mounted in a tube that is 63 feet (19 meters) long. This telescope is probably the largest refractor that will ever be built because it is extremely difficult and expensive to make bigger lenses. A bigger lens would sag out of shape from its own weight (which would prevent the light waves from being properly focused and produce a distorted image).

Reflecting Telescopes. In a reflecting telescope the objective is a large concave mirror at the back end of the tube. The mirror is shaped in such a way that when light strikes

its shiny surface and is reflected back up the tube, it focuses all the light rays to form a sharp image. A mirror with this shape is called a parabolic mirror.

But how can the image be viewed? A person who looks directly into the front end of the tube to see the image blocks the light going to the mirror. In 1668 the British scientist Isaac Newton solved this problem by placing a small flat secondary mirror at a 45-degree angle inside the tube at the point of focus. He made an opening in the side of the tube opposite the small mirror and set an eyepiece in the opening. The small mirror then reflected the image to the eyepiece. This style of telescope is now commonly known as a **Newtonian reflector**.

In 1672 the French scientist Sieur Cassegrain made a reflector with a small curved mirror (instead of a flat mirror) in the upper part of the telescope tube. The light reflected from the large mirror was then reflected off the small curved mirror back down the tube and through a small hole in the middle of the main mirror. The image formed by the light was viewed through an eyepiece behind the large mirror.

The world's largest optical telescopes are reflectors because it is easier and less expensive to create the mirror for a reflector than it is to create the lens for a refractor. A mirror will not bend under its own weight because its back can be supported, while a lens can be supported only around its edges. Because light passes through a lens, the glass must be perfect on both sides. But light strikes only one surface of the mirror, so the tedious process of grinding and polishing two sides of a lens is avoided.

The objective mirror of some large reflecting telescopes is actually formed by a group of smaller mirrors. The two main telescopes at the Keck Observatory on Mauna Kea in Hawaii have objectives made up of 36 six-sided mirrors, each 6 feet (2 meters) across, that together act as one large mirror more

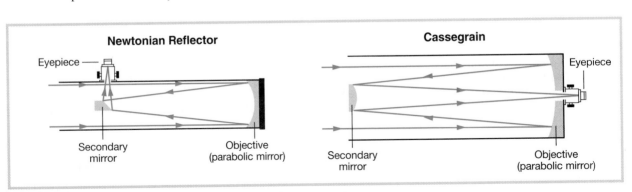

Newtonian Reflector

Eyepiece

Secondary mirror

Objective (parabolic mirror)

Cassegrain

Eyepiece

Secondary mirror

Objective (parabolic mirror)

The objectives of the Keck Observatory's two main telescopes are made up of 36 six-sided mirrors that together act as one large mirror.

than 32 feet (10 meters) across. Motorized controls keep the small mirrors properly positioned at all times so the light is focused correctly and forms a single image.

Catadioptric Telescopes. The objective of a catadioptric telescope is called a spherical mirror. Spherical mirrors are less expensive and easier to make than parabolic mirrors. However, the light rays reflected by a spherical mirror do not focus at one point, and this can produce blurry images. To fix this, a special lens called a corrector lens or corrector plate is placed at the other end of the tube.

In a **Schmidt-Cassegrain** telescope, the light enters through the corrector lens and hits the large objective mirror at the other end of the tube. The objective reflects the light back up the tube, where it hits a small secondary mirror on the back of the corrector lens. This mirror bounces the light back down the tube and through a small hole in the center of the objective mirror. A **Maksutov-Cassegrain** telescope functions in the same way, except it uses a thicker corrector lens with a reflective spot on its back that acts as the secondary mirror.

Non-Optical Telescopes

Non-optical telescopes are used to collect forms of electromagnetic radiation that are invisible to the human eye. Furthermore, while visible light is often blocked by dense clouds of dust and gas in space, other forms of radiation (especially radio and infrared radiation) can pass right through such obstacles and reveal a wealth of information about objects or regions of space otherwise hidden from sight.

A **radio telescope** works somewhat like a reflector. But instead of a mirror it has a metal structure, usually bowl-shaped, that is covered with wire netting or sheets of metal. This surface collects radio waves given off by objects in space and focuses them on a receiver that amplifies (strengthens) them. The amplified waves are changed to electric pulses, or signals, which are recorded by a computer. For more information, see the article RADIO ASTRONOMY in Volume QR.

Microwave telescopes are used to detect and map the very faint radiation given off at the time of the birth of the universe—the Big Bang. **Infrared telescopes** use a system of mirrors and electronic detectors to gather infrared radiation, or heat energy, emitted by

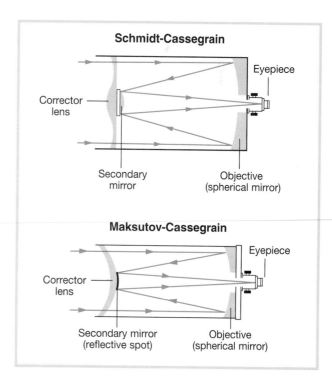

Schmidt-Cassegrain

Eyepiece

Corrector lens

Secondary mirror

Objective (spherical mirror)

Maksutov-Cassegrain

Eyepiece

Corrector lens

Secondary mirror (reflective spot)

Objective (spherical mirror)

celestial objects. Infrared radiation is even detectable from objects so cool that they emit little or no visible light. **Ultraviolet telescopes** use mirrors to collect ultraviolet light and change it to create an image. X-rays are highly energetic; if they struck a mirror head-on, they would not reflect off its surface like visible light but would instead pass through the mirror itself. **X-ray telescopes** have mirrors that are almost parallel to the path of in-coming X-rays; the X-rays glance off the mirrors' surfaces, like a rock skipping across water, and then form an image. Gamma rays are so energetic that they cannot be focused by lenses or mirrors, so **gamma-ray telescopes** track the electrons given off by gamma rays passing through special crystal or liquid detectors.

INTERFEROMETERS

An interferometer is an array, or group, of two or more telescopes whose observing capabilities are combined to create the equivalent of one large telescope. For example, the Very Large Array in New Mexico consists of 27 individual radio telescopes spread out over about 26 miles (42 kilometers). When the radio waves received by each telescope are combined, an image can be created that has greater detail than can be obtained by any of the individual telescopes alone.

Similarly, in optical interferometers, the light-collecting capability of all the telescopes in an array is combined. The European Southern Observatory's Very Large Telescope in Chile consists of four 26-foot (8-meter) telescopes that can operate individually or together as an interferometer.

TELESCOPES AND COMPUTERS

Computers play a vital role in telescopic observations today. They can be programmed with the precise positions of thousands of celestial objects and can aim the telescope at any of them in a matter of seconds. Computers can also control motors that move the telescope in tiny stages to track an object as it moves across the sky. Computers that perform these functions are standard accessories for many telescopes used by amateur, or backyard, astronomers.

Computers are also used to record, process, and analyze the images and other data obtained by telescopes. Data from telescope observations is often distributed over the Internet to personal computers around the world, which helps process the data at great speed. And in an activity called **remote observing**, astronomers can use computers to access and control telescopes miles—or even continents—away to make their own personal observations of the sky.

Galileo built his own telescopes and used them to make his historic celestial observations.

HISTORY OF THE TELESCOPE

No one is certain who invented the telescope. It is known, however, that in 1608 a Dutch eyeglass maker, Hans Lippershey, made a small optical telescope. There is a story that Lippershey's children accidentally discovered that when they held some lenses a certain distance apart, faraway things seemed much closer. This gave Lippershey the idea for making a telescope, which consisted of a long hollow tube with a lens set in each end.

The first person known to have used a telescope to look at the heavens was the Italian scientist Galileo. In 1609, Galileo heard reports about a telescope invented in the Netherlands. With his knowledge of light and lenses, Galileo was able to make his own telescopes without ever having seen one. Using various telescopes, Galileo discovered craters and plains on the moon, four moons in orbit around Jupiter, and the rings of Saturn. He also found that Venus goes through phases as it orbits the sun and that the Milky Way is composed of seemingly countless stars. Over the following centuries, telescopes grew ever larger and more refined. Today they allow us to explore our vast universe back to the edge of space and dawn of time.

COLIN A. RONAN
Fellow, Royal Astronomical Society
Reviewed and updated by WILLIAM A. GUTSCH
President, The Challenger Center for Space
Science Education

See also ASTRONOMY; LENSES.

TELEVISION

Can you imagine spending a day without encountering television? It is almost everywhere you turn.

Television is the most popular form of entertainment in the United States and most other countries. More than 98 percent of American homes have at least one television set. About three-quarters of those homes have at least two sets, some so portable they can be put in a pocket. The average family has television on about seven hours a day, about the same number of hours a student spends in school each day.

Television plays many important roles. It is the main source of news as well as entertainment for most Americans. Television is also used as a teaching tool in schools and businesses. At baseball, football, and basketball games, huge television screens help fans enjoy the action through close-ups and replays.

Television has important uses in industry and science, too. It allows workers to watch over radioactive materials or dangerous machinery from a safe distance. Surgeons use tiny television cameras to guide them during delicate operations. TV cameras have been placed aboard satellites to help meteorologists predict the weather, and they have traveled millions of miles into space to bring back scenes of Mars.

The word "television" comes from Greek and Latin words that mean "to see from far off." Television is a way of sending images (and sound) over distances. The images may be sent a short distance to just a few people, such as the workers who use television to watch over dangerous machinery. Or they may be sent over long distances to many people—the audience for an episode of a popular television show may number in the millions. Those images may also be saved and

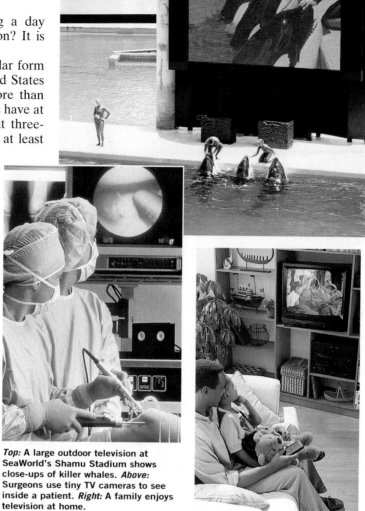

Top: A large outdoor television at SeaWorld's Shamu Stadium shows close-ups of killer whales. *Above:* Surgeons use tiny TV cameras to see inside a patient. *Right:* A family enjoys television at home.

watched later, using video recording systems. And now television is being used to transmit computer information as well as images.

▶ HOW TELEVISION WORKS

In television, images and sound travel electronically—that is, by means of electrical energy. A television camera changes the light that is reflected from a scene into electronic signals. Then a device called a transmitter sends out the signals (along with signals for the accompanying sound, which has been picked up by microphone). Finally, a television receiver (or set) in your home receives the signals and converts them back into images and sound.

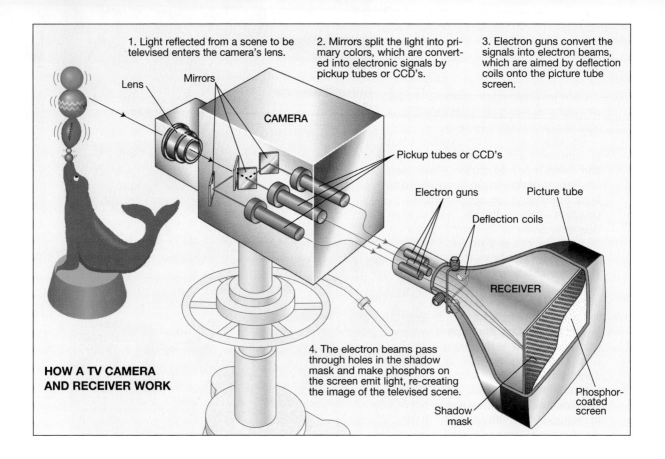

1. Light reflected from a scene to be televised enters the camera's lens.

2. Mirrors split the light into primary colors, which are converted into electronic signals by pickup tubes or CCD's.

3. Electron guns convert the signals into electron beams, which are aimed by deflection coils onto the picture tube screen.

Lens

Mirrors

CAMERA

Pickup tubes or CCD's

Electron guns

Picture tube

Deflection coils

RECEIVER

HOW A TV CAMERA AND RECEIVER WORK

4. The electron beams pass through holes in the shadow mask and make phosphors on the screen emit light, re-creating the image of the televised scene.

Shadow mask

Phosphor-coated screen

Creating Television Signals

A basic television camera consists of a lens, mirrors, image-sensing devices, various electronic circuits, and a viewfinder, through which the camera operator sees what the camera is looking at.

Light reflected from a scene passes through the lens, which focuses the image. In color television cameras, the light is then split into three beams by mirrors that separate the light into three basic, or primary, colors: red, green, and blue. Each colored beam strikes an image-sensing device. In older television cameras, these devices are glass vacuum tubes called **pickup tubes**. At one end, a pickup tube contains a light-sensitive material called a **target**. When incoming light hits the target, this material develops a pattern of positive electrical charges. At the back of the tube is a device called an **electron gun**, which shoots a beam of negatively charged particles called electrons across the target. The beam moves, or scans, much as your eyes do when you read. As it does so, it converts the pattern on the target into an electrical signal that is a "copy" of the original image.

Today, most television cameras detect images using electronic components called **charge-coupled devices** (CCD's), instead of pickup tubes. Developed in the 1970's, CCD's are small chips made of silicon that are divided into a grid of several million tiny squares called pixels, short for "picture elements." As light strikes the pixels, they build up a pattern of electrical charges that vary with the intensity of the light at any given spot. This pattern is then converted into an electrical signal.

Sending the Television Signal

In most cases, television signals are broadcast through the air. The video and audio (sound) signals travel from the camera to a transmitter, which turns the signals into electromagnetic waves. Electromagnetic waves radiate (travel in all directions) from their source, moving at the speed of light. This movement is expressed as **frequency**. Frequency is the number of cycles, or complete waves, transmitted in one second.

Television signals must be broadcast at a high frequency in order to carry the video information. The transmitter emits a **carrier wave**, a powerful high-frequency electromagnetic wave. Through a process called modulation, the video and audio signals are combined with the carrier wave.

The signal is sent out by a transmitting antenna, which is usually placed as high as possible because television signals move in a straight line. Hills, high-rise buildings, and even trees can interfere with the television signals. Generally, a clear picture can be received within a 50-mile (80-kilometer) radius of the transmitting antenna.

A group, or band, of frequencies that carries a television transmission is called a **channel**. Broadcast stations located in the same area are assigned separate channels so that their transmissions do not interfere with one another. In the United States, these assignments are made by the Federal Communications Commission (FCC), a government licensing body. For home television broadcasting, a station is assigned to one of twelve Very High Frequency (VHF) channels (channels 2–13) or to one of 56 Ultra High Frequency (UHF) channels (14–69).

Because the electromagnetic waves sent out by a transmitter cannot travel very far, television signals that must travel long distances are sent by other means. They may be carried by coaxial or fiber-optic cable. They may be sent by microwave relay (a system that relays signals through a series of tall towers spaced across the country). Or they may be transmitted to satellites that orbit Earth. The satellites receive the signals and bounce them down to receiving stations far away from the signal source.

The major U.S. and Canadian television networks use these methods to send signals to local stations, which then broadcast the signals to homes in their areas. Cable television companies also receive their programs via satellite. They then send them to their subscribers over cable.

Receiving the Television Signal

A transmitted television signal can be received through an antenna on the television set itself if the distance to the transmitter is

not too great. A roof-mounted antenna helps capture weak or distant signals. Today, television signals reach most North American homes via cable, and many homes now have satellite dishes that receive television signals directly from satellites.

The television receiver has a **tuner**, which picks up the frequency of the channel selected and blocks out other frequencies. As the video and audio signals are received, they are sent to a **demodulator**, a complex electronic circuit that allows the audio and video information to be processed.

The electronic video information is then sent to the receiver's screen, where the original image collected by the television camera is reconstructed. In most televisions, the screen is the front end of a large glass vacuum tube called the **picture tube**. The inside of the screen is coated with thousands of tiny **phosphors**, substances that emit light when struck by electrons. Each phosphor is responsible for reproducing either the color red, blue, or green. At the other end of a typical color picture tube are three electron guns, one for each of these three primary colors. Each gun shoots a beam of electrons at the screen, scanning it line by line.

As the beams race to the screen, they pass through a **shadow mask**, a thin screen pierced with hundreds of thousands of holes. The holes allow the beam from the red gun to hit only the red phosphors on the screen, the blue beam to hit only the blue phosphors,

Portable cameras allow television crews to cover news events wherever they happen. The images can then be transmitted "live" to a studio via satellite.

and the green beam to hit only the green phosphors. When each dot is hit, it glows with its respective color. Because the dots are so close together, the viewer's eyes see the mixture of primary colors as the whole range of colors that were in the original scene.

Because picture tubes are almost as deep as they are wide, they can be made only so large before they become too bulky to fit easily in most living rooms. However, some modern television sets, called projection TV's, overcome this problem by projecting images from small picture tubes onto a much larger screen. In this way, projection TV's can have screens as wide as 6 feet (nearly 2 meters) but still be only 2 feet (0.6 meter) deep.

In some new receivers, images are created without a picture tube, using a thin **flat-panel display** instead. Some displays are so thin, they can be hung on a wall like a painting. One type of display, also used in laptop computers, is the liquid crystal display, or LCD. It is made up of hundreds of thousands of cells in which crystal molecules "twist" light from a light source when an electrical charge is applied. The light passes through filters and appears as a red, green, or blue dot, depending on which direction the light was twisted.

A more advanced type of flat-panel display is the plasma monitor. It is like a honeycomb sandwiched between two sheets of glass. Each cell in the honeycomb represents a pixel and holds a gas mixture (such as neon and xenon) as well as a tiny phosphor in one of the three primary colors. When an electrical charge is applied, the gas mixture becomes a plasma—a hot gas in which the atoms are stripped of their electrons—and begins emitting ultraviolet light. That light, in turn, hits the phosphors, which then glow to create a picture.

▶ **DEVELOPMENT OF TELEVISION TECHNOLOGY**

In the early 1900's, inventors found that electrical signals could be transmitted through the air, as electromagnetic waves. At first, this discovery led to the wireless transmission of sound, as discussed in the article RADIO in Volume Q-R.

Soon, inventors began searching for ways of transmitting pictures as well. The problem was how to "scan" a scene line by line in order to turn it into electrical signals. The first television sets accomplished this mechanically, using large spinning disks with holes in them. An amateur Scottish inventor, John Logie

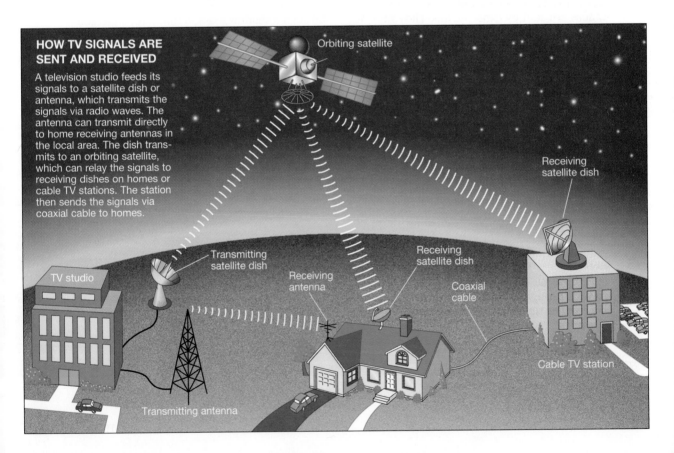

HOW TV SIGNALS ARE SENT AND RECEIVED

A television studio feeds its signals to a satellite dish or antenna, which transmits the signals via radio waves. The antenna can transmit directly to home receiving antennas in the local area. The dish transmits to an orbiting satellite, which can relay the signals to receiving dishes on homes or cable TV stations. The station then sends the signals via coaxial cable to homes.

Orbiting satellite

Receiving satellite dish

Receiving satellite dish

Transmitting satellite dish

Receiving antenna

Coaxial cable

TV studio

Cable TV station

Transmitting antenna

Baird, was the first to successfully use the disks, making them out of old hatboxes in his apartment. In 1925, at Selfridge's department store in London, England, Baird presented the world's first public demonstration of television. Viewers were able to see only crude outlines of shapes transmitted a few feet away.

Mechanical systems were too bulky to produce a good moving picture. However, electronic systems, which used vacuum tubes and electron beams, could scan many lines very quickly.

Two people were mainly responsible for developing electronic television. One was a self-educated Idaho farm boy named Philo T. Farnsworth, and the other was a successful engineer named Vladimir K. Zworykin, who had immigrated to America from Russia. In 1927, Farnsworth created the world's first all-electronic television system. He was able to transmit a single black line from one end of his lab to the other. Meanwhile, Zworykin was carrying out his own work at the electrical company Westinghouse and later at the Radio Corporation of America (RCA). He soon introduced his own television system.

During the 1930's, many manufacturers began producing television receivers, most based on either the Zworykin or Farnsworth system. However, these receivers could not process the same television signals. In 1941, the National Television Systems Committee (NTSC) established a national system that combined the best features of Farnsworth's and Zworykin's systems. In the NTSC system, television pictures are made up of 525 lines each, displayed at a speed of 30 pictures, or frames, per second. At that speed, the frames appear to blend smoothly.

Color television broadcasts began in the 1950's, and by 1965 the major U.S. networks were broadcasting nearly all their programs in color. By the late 1990's, 98 percent of American homes had color TV sets.

In 1956 another important breakthrough took place: the development of the videotape recorder (VTR). Before this time, all television programs had to be either broadcast "live" or recorded on motion picture film. Before film could be used for broadcast, it had to be developed. Then it was played back and converted into electronic images. The VTR records programs on videotape, which can be played back immediately.

Inventor Philo T. Farnsworth demonstrates an early television receiver. Images were displayed on a small round screen.

Meanwhile, closed-circuit television systems were becoming increasingly important in industry, medicine, and other fields. In these systems, television cameras are linked by cable to a limited number of receivers. Closed-circuit television is used in factories, to oversee assembly lines, and in hospitals, to monitor patients. It is an important part of many security systems.

There have been many other technological improvements since the early days of television. Lightweight, portable cameras, developed in the 1970's, allow television crews to travel almost anywhere to cover news or sports events. And many programs are now broadcast in stereo sound.

Alternate Delivery Systems

When television first became widely available in the 1940's and 1950's, it was distributed mostly over the airwaves. Today, new television technologies offer other ways for viewers to receive signals. These methods are referred to as alternate delivery systems.

Cable. One form of cable television, called community antenna television (CATV), was created in the 1940's to deliver broadcast signals to isolated places that could not receive them—in mountain valleys, for example. An antenna on a mountain picked up the broadcast signal and then sent it down a coaxial cable to the homes in the valley. Cable television did not experience rapid growth until some thirty years later. By the late 1990's, more than two-thirds of American households—some 63 million homes—relied on cable as their primary source of television.

Satellites. Television satellites are "parked" in geosynchronous orbit 22,300 miles (35,900 kilometers) above Earth. "Geosynchronous" means that as Earth rotates, the satellites follow and stay in exactly the same place over the ground.

Television stations send a powerful signal to a **transponder** on the satellite. The transponder receives the upcoming signal, amplifies (strengthens) it, and transmits it back down to Earth, where it can be received at the ground stations of cable systems that have dish antennas. Satellite signals can also be received directly by viewers, through home dish antenna systems. You can read more about cable and satellite transmissions in the article TELECOMMUNICATIONS in this volume.

Videocassette Recorders. Videocassette recorders (VCR's) for home use were introduced in the mid-1970's. By the late 1990's, more than 80 percent of American homes had at least one VCR. Viewers use VCR's to record programs for viewing at a later time and for viewing prerecorded tapes. Tapes of feature films—mostly in the video home system (VHS) format—are widely available for sale or rental. Many people also create their own tapes using home video cameras.

VCR's have also made television more useful in other settings. Teachers use VCR's in classrooms, and corporations use VCR's to train employees. You can find more information about VCR systems in the article VIDEO RECORDING in Volume U-V.

Laser Disk Players. Laser disks offer the highest-quality video and audio for home systems. They first became available in the United States in 1980 in the form of 12-inch plastic-and-metal disks called videodiscs. In the mid-1990's, smaller versions called digital video discs, or digital versatile discs (DVD's), were introduced. About the size of music compact discs (CD's), DVD's can store the

Flat-panel televisions, only a few inches deep, can be hung on a wall like a picture. The wide screen is specially designed for high-definition television.

video and audio of feature-length films as well as other information, such as background notes about a movie. Special players, connected to television sets or built in to some computers, are used to play DVD's.

High-Definition and Digital Television

In the 1990's, the television industry began preparing for high-definition television, or HDTV. This format uses more than twice the conventional number of scanning lines to produce better definition—that is, a sharper, clearer image and better color and brightness. HDTV also features a wider screen and theater-quality stereo sound.

HDTV was first developed in Japan in the 1980's. But the Japanese system was not compatible with U.S. broadcast standards.

By the late 1990's, HDTV became a reality in the United States, when the first stations began broadcasting digital television. Digital TV, or DTV, is a major change in the way television signals are sent and received. In conventional television, pictures and sound are converted into analog signals—electronic signals that are analogous, or similar, to sound and light waves. Digital TV converts pictures and sound into electronic pulses that stand for the digits 1 ("on") and 0 ("off"), like the binary code used by computers.

Televisions using liquid crystal displays can be made small enough to fit in the back of a headrest in a vehicle or even in the palm of your hand.

Digital TV signals can come in several formats. One is the HDTV format, which delivers high-quality video and audio, one program at a time. Other formats, however, allow networks to broadcast five or six programs at once with standard-definition video and audio, like those of conventional television. These formats use computers to compress TV signals: Each image is compared with the previous image, and only the visual information that has changed is transmitted. This savings in information means that more than one program can be transmitted at a time. It also means that, like DVD's, digital TV can display other information, such as captions in different languages.

In 1998, some stations started broadcasting digitally on a second channel while continuing to broadcast on their existing analog channels as well. Under a government plan, all stations were supposed to be broadcasting digitally as well as in analog by 2003, giving the public time to make the switch gradually. In 2006, analog transmissions would cease and all television would be digital—if, that is, at least 85 percent of American homes had digital TV's by then. In reality, the full transition to DTV could take much longer.

Television Controls and Features

One of the most important parts of a television system is the remote control, or, simply, the remote. Remote controls became practical in the mid-1950's, using high-frequency sound or electrical wires to transmit commands. In the 1970's, remote controls began using infrared light to send commands to television sets. And in the 1980's, remote controls could control not only televisions, but also VCR's and sound systems.

By the 1990's, remote controls were virtually in every home. Viewers use them to change channels, adjust the volume (or loudness), and mute the sound of commercials. Many viewers now switch programs at every commercial break. In this way, the remote control has changed the way people watch television, and also the way television programs are produced, as broadcasters struggle to keep viewers on their networks.

Other features developed in the 1980's and 1990's included picture-in-picture (a second program inset in the larger one), closed captioning for the hearing impaired (in which a program's dialogue is displayed on the screen as moving text), and the "V-chip." This term originally referred to a computer chip that would allow parents to block violent or other inappropriate programs, but it later came to mean any technology to achieve that aim. In the United States, the Telecommunications Act of 1995 mandated that such systems eventually be installed in all new TV sets.

▶ THE TELEVISION INDUSTRY

In many countries, television broadcasting is operated by the government. In the United States, the multi-billion-dollar television industry is privately owned. It includes broadcast networks, local television stations, production companies, and distributors such as cable and satellite services.

Commercial Television

For the most part, American broadcasting is a commercial system. That is, much of the cost of producing and distributing programs is paid for by advertising.

Most programs shown on commercial television come from large television networks. For forty years or so, there were three major networks: the Columbia Broadcasting System (CBS), Capital Cities/American Broadcasting Company (ABC), and the National Broadcasting Company (NBC). In the 1980's and 1990's, new networks were launched, such as Fox Broadcasting and the United Paramount Network (UPN). With the rise of cable television, large cable networks arose, such as Home Box Office (HBO), Turner Broadcasting, and the Discovery Channel. The networks distribute programming to affiliate stations all over the country, mostly via satellite. Independent stations are not affiliated with a network and obtain their programming from other sources.

Programming. Generally, the networks purchase the programs they broadcast from independent program producers. Many program producers are located in southern California—in or near Hollywood. News and public affairs programs, however, are usually produced by the networks themselves.

The networks and local stations hire audience research firms to help them determine how popular their programs are. (The process of rating television shows is described in the Wonder Question accompanying this article.) Ratings determine how much money advertisers pay to have their commercials broadcast.

Each broadcast day is divided into periods of time called dayparts. Programs shown during a certain daypart are planned to suit the interests of the audience watching at that time. The most important daypart is prime time, which runs from 8:00 P.M. to 11:00 P.M. That is when audiences are largest, and when advertisers must pay the most money.

Advertising. In the United States, television commercials are designed and produced by advertising agencies. The agencies also help choose the best programs on which to advertise their clients' products.

Educational and Public Broadcasting

Broadcast television in some countries has no advertising at all. Sometimes the government of a country pays for all costs of television. In other cases, noncommercial and commercial networks are in competition.

Public broadcasting in the United States began in the 1950's, when a few stations were created to provide educational programs for the public. These stations, some of which were associated with colleges or universities, broadcast instructional, arts, and public affairs shows. Since then, public broadcasting has played a small but important role.

In 1967, Congress passed a law forming the Corporation for Public Broadcasting (CPB), which in turn created the Public Broadcasting Service (PBS). PBS helps fund new programs and distributes them to more than 300 stations in the United States. Public stations are noncommercial; that is, they do not accept advertising. Money is raised through viewer contributions, grants, and funds from CPB.

Broadcast Regulation

Broadcasting is regulated by the government through an agency called the Federal Communications Commission (FCC), which administers broadcasting laws passed by Congress. Current federal regulation is based on the Communications Act of 1934, which established guidelines for broadcasters, and on later legislation. The Telecommunications Act of 1995 updated the laws to encompass new developments in television, such as digital television. The FCC issues licenses to qualified applicants to operate a television station. According to the law, broadcasters must operate in the public interest.

A television production technician watches several monitors while controlling a console. She is combining video camera images and sounds from a nearby studio.

What are television ratings?

Television audience ratings try to estimate how many people are watching various television programs. Companies that provide rating services survey a sampling of American families that own television sets. The best-known ratings service in the United States, the A. C. Nielsen Company, uses an electronic measuring device called the "people meter," which it installs in 1,200 American homes.

Ratings are complex, but the basic idea consists of two related concepts: the rating and the share. A **rating** is the percentage of all homes in a sampling that have television sets tuned to a particular program. A **share** compares homes with sets tuned to the program with only other homes whose sets are turned on during that time. For example, a program may have a rating of 19 and a share of 34 for a given week. This means that 19 percent of homes with televisions had the show tuned in that week. Of the homes with sets on while the show was airing, 34 percent were tuned to the program.

Why are ratings so important? They determine which programs get canceled and which remain on the air. Television programs with high ratings can charge advertisers more money to run commercials than can less popular shows. Because commercial television relies on advertising to pay for its costs, low-rated programs usually get canceled.

Television Production

Producing a television program combines creative, technical, and business skills. There are three basic types of television production: live, videotape, and film.

Some programs are broadcast live while an event is happening. Live broadcasts include news programs and events such as football games and parades. In the live-on-tape method, a program is videotaped, edited, and then broadcast later. For example, a week's worth of a daily game show might be videotaped on one day. Then the five shows are broadcast one at a time. A third method involves recording scenes on motion picture or video cameras. The recording is edited and then transferred to videotape for later broadcast.

People involved in a television production include the director, writer, producer, lighting director, camera operator, sound director, and editor. To get an idea of the people who work on television productions, read the credits at the end of a program.

Careers in Television

A wide variety of jobs are available in television. But because many people seek careers in the field, competition for jobs is high. Almost all these jobs require a high school education, and many require a college degree. Many schools and colleges offer programs in broadcasting and video production.

The main career areas in television are programming, sales, news, production, engineering, and management. Positions are also available in independent production companies, which hire people to write, produce, and direct television programs. Some companies hire people to produce video programs for businesses, governments, schools, and other groups.

▶ TELEVISION PROGRAMS

When television networks were formed in 1945–46, radio networks were already well established. Many radio programs and personalities simply moved to television.

The period up to 1956 was the era of live television. No videotape machines existed, so shows had to be performed in front of live cameras. During this period, called the Golden Age of television, many excellent live shows were turned out every week. One of the most notable was Milton Berle's comedy and variety show, *The Texaco Star Theater*. "Uncle Miltie" became so well liked by audiences that he earned the nickname Mr. Television.

The early years of television produced several types of programs that, with some variations, have remained popular ever since.

Beginning in the Golden Age, a number of memorable **situation comedies**, or **sitcoms**, were produced. *I Love Lucy*, starring Lucille Ball, may be the most famous, but there were many others—*The Honeymooners*, *Father Knows Best*, *Leave It to Beaver*. Sitcoms have been popular in every decade. Among the hits of the 1970's and 1980's were *All in the Family*, *Cheers*, and *The Cosby Show*. The

Above: Television's Golden Age produced some memorable situation comedies, or sitcoms, such as *I Love Lucy. Above right:* During the 1950's and 1960's, westerns such as *Gunsmoke* were very popular. *Right:* The series *Star Trek*, launched in the 1960's, became the most successful science fiction drama.

most successful sitcom of the 1990's was *Seinfeld*, starring comedian Jerry Seinfeld.

Toward the end of television's Golden Age, a craze developed for **quiz shows**, starting with *The $64,000 Question*, which awarded large sums of money and valuable prizes to winners. Many quiz and game shows, such as *Wheel of Fortune* and *Jeopardy*, continue to draw large audiences.

A great variety of **drama series** have also been produced. In the 1950's and 1960's, western dramas such as *Gunsmoke* were very popular. The 1960's and 1970's saw the rise of police dramas such as *Dragnet* and *Hawaii Five-O*, followed by shows such as *Miami Vice* and *Law & Order* in the 1980's and 1990's. Hospital dramas have also had a faithful following of viewers, from *Marcus Welby, M.D.* in the 1960's to *E.R.* in the 1990's. The most successful science fiction drama was the 1960's series *Star Trek*, which was revived with new characters in the 1980's and 1990's.

There have also been a number of daytime dramas, such as *The Young and the Restless*. They were originally called **soap operas** because many were sponsored by companies advertising soap and other household products. Dramas known as **miniseries** tell a story in several shows aired over a few days or weeks. One of the most widely watched shows ever was the 1977 miniseries *Roots*, which told the story of an African American family from the time of slavery to the present.

The longest-running television show of all time was a **news show**, *Meet the Press*. It started in 1947, featuring interviews with important leaders of American life. The investigative news program *60 Minutes* has had a loyal following since its debut in 1968. Many television stations now carry morning, evening, and late-night shows with local, national, and world news. In addition, there have been various **talk shows**, such as *The Tonight Show*, that include interviews with celebrities. Daytime talk shows, such as *The Oprah Winfrey Show*, also feature interviews with ordinary people who have moving stories to tell.

The 1950's saw the beginning of such **children's programs** as the beloved puppet shows *Kukla, Fran & Ollie* and *The Howdy Doody Show. Captain Kangaroo* and *The Mickey Mouse Club* also drew large audiences. Saturday morning cartoons first appeared in the 1950's and have remained popular. Cable television gave birth to children's networks such as Nickelodeon, the Disney Channel, and the Cartoon Network. One of the most

Above left: The children's show *Sesame Street* was created in the 1960's to both teach and entertain preschoolers. *Far left:* In the 1980's, cable television gave rise to a growing number of specialty channels, such as the Cable News Network. *Above:* In the 1990's, *Seinfeld* became the most widely watched sitcom. *Left:* Medical dramas continued to draw loyal viewers with shows such as *E.R.*

successful children's programs is PBS's *Sesame Street*, which helps preschoolers learn words and numbers.

Cable television led to the creation of single-purpose **specialty networks**. The Cable News Network (CNN), for example, is dedicated to 24-hour news. ESPN shows only sports-related programs. MTV and VH-1 feature music videos, concert broadcasts, and other shows for popular music fans. In addition, there are networks that are devoted to classic movies, history, cooking, weather, travel, home shopping, and other interests.

▶ **THE FUTURE OF TELEVISION**

With the advent of digital television, the home TV set will likely share more in common with the computer than with television's predecessor, the radio. In addition to offering entertainment programming, television services can now provide electronic mail (e-mail) and access to the Internet. Renting videocassettes and DVD's may become obsolete, as viewers "download" movies to their televisions without leaving the living room.

Some experts predict that "smart televisions" could one day scan through many hours of programming each day and pick out clips of particular interest to individual viewers.

Many people wonder about the influence of television. Do programs showing excessive violence make some viewers want to commit crimes? Do commercials make people want things they do not need or cannot afford? Do some programs show lifestyles that conflict with values taught at home and school?

Television is not by itself good or bad; it is merely a powerful communications tool. It is the people behind it, and the people watching it, who will determine whether its effects will be positive or negative.

JOHN P. FREEMAN
Texas Christian University
Reviewed by MARSHALL JON FISHER
Coauthor, *Tube: The Invention of Television*

TELSTAR. See COMMUNICATION; SATELLITES, ARTIFICIAL.

TEMPERATURE. See HEAT; THERMOMETERS.

TEMPLE, SHIRLEY. See MOTION PICTURES (Profiles: Movie Stars).

TEN COMMANDMENTS

The Ten Commandments are an ancient set of laws for living and worship that are found in the Bible. They are also called the Decalogue, from the Greek terms meaning "ten words." Both Christians and Jews believe the commandments were revealed by God to the prophet Moses. These laws became the terms of an agreement, or covenant, between God and the people of Israel.

According to the Bible, Moses received the commandments as he was leading the people of Israel out of slavery in Egypt. The Bible states that God called Moses to climb to the top of Mount Sinai, where he spent 40 days and nights. When he descended, he brought with him the Ten Commandments inscribed on two stone tablets. When he found his people worshiping an idol, Moses grew angry. He smashed the tablets, and new ones had to be created. These were placed in an ark, or chest, that was carried through the wilderness and later kept in the Temple (a place of worship in Jerusalem).

According to biblical tradition, this happened more than 3,000 years ago. Some people believe the commandments go back to that time. Others think the Decalogue shows the influence of later Hebrew prophets and was written about 600 B.C. or even later.

There may be some truth in both views. Some of the commandments are very short, and some are much longer. In Hebrew, the original language of the Bible, the short commandments contain as few as two words, and the longest more than 40. Once they may all have been short and easy to learn. In that simple form they may be very old. If so, the parts that seem to show later influences may be elaborations added in later biblical times.

The Ten Commandments of Chapter 20 of the book of Exodus are repeated in Chapter 5 of Deuteronomy. The two chapters are not exactly alike. The main differences are in the parts that may have been added to the earlier law. Whatever their age, they have exerted a great influence over the centuries.

▶ COUNTING THE COMMANDMENTS

In the feature on the opposite page are the Ten Commandments in a shortened form. The text is taken from the translation of the Hebrew original published by the Jewish Publication Society.

There is some uncertainty about how to count the ten. In Exodus 34:28 they are called the Ten Commandments, but they are not numbered in the Bible. As listed here, the first one seems more a statement than a commandment. The second and tenth each seem to be two commandments instead of one. The way they are listed here is the traditional Jewish way of counting the commandments. Christians usually say that "I the Lord am your God" is not a commandment but a kind of introduction. To make up the number, they divide either the second or the tenth into two commandments.

▶ WHAT THE COMMANDMENTS SAY

If anyone looks at the list of commandments and asks "Who says so?" the first commandment answers the question. "I the Lord," it says. It means "These are what God wants. These are what your religion requires of you." It shows that religion is not simply something that makes you comfortable. It is also something that makes demands on you. The commandments are a program for devout and moral living. The first four commandments speak of devotion to God; the rest, of people's behavior toward one another.

The first three form a group. The first says "Recognize God and listen to Him." The second says "Listen only to Him and to no substitute." The third says "Show your devotion to God by being honest and genuine and by always doing what you promise."

THE TEN COMMANDMENTS

1. I the Lord am your God. …
2. You shall have no other gods beside Me. You shall not make for yourself a sculptured image. …
3. You shall not swear falsely by the name of the Lord your God. …
4. Remember the sabbath day and keep it holy. …
5. Honor your father and your mother. …
6. You shall not murder.
7. You shall not commit adultery.
8. You shall not steal.
9. You shall not bear false witness against your neighbor.
10. You shall not covet your neighbor's house: you shall not covet your neighbor's wife … or anything that is your neighbor's.

The fourth connects the first group of three with the other six commandments. It speaks of a sabbath, a day of rest. The sabbath is a day that is holy—one day each week on which to think of God. It is also a day on which to think of other persons and take care that they, too, can rest—a day when all people are equal.

Next come the rules of behavior and ethics. They speak of the way people treat one another in a healthy and peaceful society.

The fifth and the seventh commandments concern family life. They mean more than they seem to say. The fifth commandment concerns the attitude of children to their parents, and the seventh concerns the love of parents for each other. Together the two commandments say that the love that unites a family should be whole and healthy.

The sixth commandment prohibits murder. It implies that every human life is precious. The ninth commandment is related to the sixth. It is not about murder, but it is about the damage that can be done to people and how they can be hurt by having things said about them that are not true. "Bearing false witness" means telling lies.

The two commandments that are left, the eighth and the tenth, are also related. Coveting means wanting something that belongs to someone else. Stealing means taking it. There are laws against stealing. People can be fined or jailed for taking other people's property. But no one can be punished by a court for coveting. Envy and covetousness are strong feelings, and they are hard to control. The tenth commandment encourages people to look deep inside themselves to see why they do wrong and how they can learn to do better.

The Ten Commandments are very meaningful for both Christians and Jews. According to the New Testament, Jesus said that keeping the commandments is part of what a person must do to "inherit eternal life." In synagogues a representation of the two tablets is often displayed as a symbol of their importance. Jewish chaplains wear this symbol the way Christian chaplains wear the cross. The tablets are frequently part of Christian church decoration as well.

Reviewed by KEVIN MADIGAN
Harvard Divinity School

See also MOSES.

TENNESSEE

Tennessee was named for the Cherokee village of Tanasi, which gave its name to the river and later to the whole state. The rich land and game-filled woods of what was called the Tennessee country drew natives and settlers alike. The nickname Volunteer State came from the large numbers of Tennesseans who enlisted in the War of 1812 and the Mexican War.

Tennessee is a land of great natural beauty where folk traditions, especially music, still thrive. Located in the south central United States, Tennessee forms a buffer between the Midwest and the Deep South. It is bordered by eight states—more neighbors than any other state except Missouri, which also has eight. Long and narrow in shape, stretching 432 miles (695 kilometers) from the Appalachian Mountains to the Mississippi River, Tennessee was a natural route for east-west migration. Even after its admission to the Union as the 16th state in 1796, Tennessee was considered part of the nation's western frontier.

Tennessee has in the last fifty years made the transition from an overwhelmingly rural state to an urban, high-growth part of the Sunbelt. Two-thirds of its people now live in cities. No longer dependent on farming, the state now possesses a diverse economy balanced among industry, finance, tourism, agriculture, and the music business.

Ironically, as the older rural culture has faded, its music has become popular around the world. The self-reliant pioneer tradition shaped the music of eastern Tennessee, just as the African American heritage of western Tennessee gave rise to the blues. The capital city of Nashville is widely known as the mecca of country music, while Memphis is the source of classic American jazz and blues music. W. C. Handy, Bessie Smith, Elvis Presley, and Dolly Parton are just a few of the famous music figures from Tennessee.

▶ LAND

Tennessee divides naturally into three areas: the upland, often mountainous east; the middle basin rimmed by hills; and the low plain of western Tennessee. Each of these geographical areas has a distinctive political and economic life. The Tennessee River, flow-

State flag

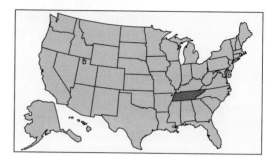

ing in a great arc across both the eastern and western sections, is one of the natural features that binds the state together.

Land Regions

The landscape of Tennessee varies from high peaks in the Blue Ridge to swamplands near the Mississippi River. The state's three "grand divisions" may be further broken down into six land regions: the Blue Ridge, the Ridge and Valley, the Appalachian Plateau, the Highland Rim, the Central Basin, and the Coastal Plain.

The Blue Ridge, which lies along the eastern border of the state, is rugged and heavily forested. It is made up of a series of short mountain ranges. The highest point in the state, Clingmans Dome, is in the Great Smoky Mountains; Roan Mountain is part of the lofty Unaka range. Within the mountains there are oval-shaped lowlands called coves.

The Ridge and Valley region lies to the west of the Blue Ridge. In this region, fertile valleys alternate with low, forested ridges. Some of the best farmland in the state is located in the valleys.

The Appalachian Plateau, also called the Cumberland Plateau, rises abruptly from the Ridge and Valley region. It is a flat to rolling

Opposite page, clockwise from top left: The 22,000-seat Pyramid sports complex is a Memphis attraction. Old-time country music is one of several strong musical traditions in Tennessee. The Great Smoky Mountains lie along the state's eastern border.

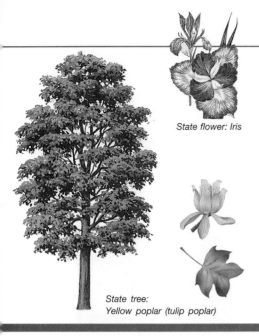

State flower: Iris

State tree:
Yellow poplar (tulip poplar)

FACTS AND FIGURES

Location: South central United States; bordered on the north by Kentucky and Virginia, on the east by North Carolina, on the south by Georgia, Alabama, and Mississippi, and on the west by Arkansas and Missouri.

Area: 42,146 sq mi (109,158 km²); rank, 36th.

Population: 5,689,283 (2000 census); rank, 16th.

Elevation: *Highest*—Clingmans Dome, 6,643 ft (2,025 m); *lowest*—182 ft (55 m) on the Mississippi River in the extreme southwestern corner of the state.

Capital: Nashville.

Statehood: June 1, 1796; 16th state.

State Motto: *Agriculture and commerce.*

State Song: "The Tennessee Waltz."

Nickname: Volunteer State.

Abbreviations: TN; Tenn.

State bird:
Mockingbird

A farm in Tennessee's fertile Central Basin. Despite a decline in the value of agriculture to the state economy, small farms still dominate the rural landscape.

tableland cut by deep valleys. Most of the coal mined in the state comes from this area.

The Highland Rim extends from the western edge of the Cumberland Plateau to the valley of the lower Tennessee River. Much of the area is forested and thinly populated, and some parts of the rim are extremely rugged.

The Central Basin lies about 300 feet (90 meters) below the level of the surrounding Highland Rim. The countryside is gently rolling, with some low hills. The Central Basin attracted many early settlers and is often called the Garden of Tennessee because of its productive farms.

The Coastal Plain is part of a large natural region that extends along the coast of the United States from Massachusetts to Texas. The southern part of this plain extends well inland and includes the part of Tennessee between the Mississippi and Tennessee rivers. The land surface of the coastal plain is flat to rolling. The Mississippi River flows through a low, flat area known as the Mississippi Alluvial Plain. This plain is quite narrow in Tennessee. On the east it is bordered by bluffs 150 to 200 feet (45 to 60 meters) high.

Rivers and Lakes

Tennessee's chief rivers are the Tennessee, the Cumberland, and the Mississippi. The Tennessee is formed by the joining of the Holston and French Broad rivers just east of Knoxville. Its major tributaries are the Clinch, Little Tennessee, Hiwassee, and Duck rivers. The Cumberland River flows in an arc through north central Tennessee. Both the Tennessee and the Cumberland enter the Ohio River in Kentucky. The Mississippi River forms the western boundary of the state. Its tributaries include the Obion and Hatchie rivers.

Tennessee has one large natural lake—Reelfoot Lake—in the northwestern part of the state. Earthquakes in the area in 1811–12 made a huge depression that forms the basin of the lake.

The Tennessee Valley Authority (TVA), a federal project established in the 1930's, and the U.S. Army Corps of Engineers have built many dams on the Tennessee and Cumberland rivers and their tributaries. These dams have created an impressive series of artificial lakes in Tennessee, sometimes called the Great Lakes of the South. Among the largest of these lakes are Kentucky, Cherokee, Chickamauga, Douglas, and Watts Bar.

Climate

Tennessee has a mild, humid climate. Summers are usually long and hot, and winters are short and fairly mild. The coolest part of the state is in the mountains, and the warmest part is in the extreme southwest. The average temperature is 37°F (3°C) in January and 79°F (26°C) in July. The growing season is long—190 to 200 days.

Most of the state's precipitation falls as rain during the winter and early spring. Summer also brings many heavy showers and numerous thunderstorms. Snowfall is light. Total precipitation averages about 50 inches (1,270 millimeters) statewide.

Plant and Animal Life

The great forests that originally covered Tennessee were some of the most diverse in North America. The yellow poplar, the state tree, grew to an enormous size and supplied the logs for many pioneer homes. Today forests cover half of Tennessee and support a thriving timber industry.

The chief areas of the original forest are in the eastern part of the state. Among the trees that grow there are hemlock, pine, and spruce and many hardwoods, such as elm, oak, beech, and cherry. Glades of red cedar trees are common in the central part of the state. The lowlands of western Tennessee contain stands of cypress, pecan, swamp locust, and other trees that thrive in moist areas.

A church nestles in the foothills of the Great Smoky Mountains. Much of the landscape of eastern Tennessee is rugged and heavily forested.

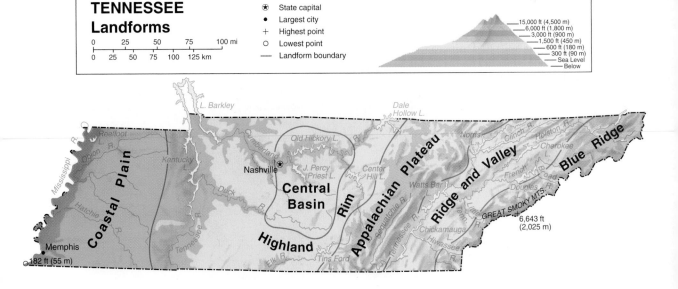

TENNESSEE Landforms

0 25 50 75 100 mi		
0 25 50 75 100 125 km		

⊛ State capital
• Largest city
+ Highest point
○ Lowest point
— Landform boundary

15,000 ft (4,500 m)
6,000 ft (1,800 m)
3,000 ft (900 m)
1,500 ft (450 m)
600 ft (180 m)
300 ft (90 m)
Sea Level
Below

A Tennessee Valley Authority (TVA) dam on the Ocoee River is part of a system of dams built to provide electric power and flood control in the Tennessee Valley region.

The state is famous for such native plants as ginseng, muscadine grape, and rhododendron. Spring and summer find the woods carpeted with trillium, violets, jack-in-the-pulpit, and the state wildflower, passion flower.

Tennessee's forests shelter a wide variety of wildlife. Black bears live in the high Smokies, and bay lynx, or bobcats, are fairly numerous in heavily wooded areas. There are large numbers of white-tailed deer, especially in the mountains. Smaller animals include raccoon, mink, skunk, opossum, and fox. Popular game birds are quail, ruffed grouse, wild turkey, bobwhite quail, and duck and goose. Some of the many fish taken by anglers are catfish, bass, crappie, and pike.

Natural Resources

In addition to a mild climate and an abundance of water, Tennessee's natural resources include fertile soils and minerals.

Limestone soils form the base for some of Tennessee's richest farmlands and pastures. These soils are found in the bluegrass region around Nashville and in the narrow valleys of the Ridge and Valley region. Rich alluvial soils are found on the

Mississippi River floodplain and on the major river bottoms.

Tennessee has reserves of zinc, copper, and manganese as well as stone, clays, sand and gravel, phosphate rock, and pyrite. Bituminous coal, petroleum, and natural gas are Tennessee's mineral fuels.

▶ PEOPLE

The Cherokee were the only native people to live in Tennessee during historic times. The early white settlers came across the Blue Ridge from the eastern states. They were descendants chiefly of English, Scotch-Irish, and German colonists. Most Tennesseans today come from these same ethnic groups.

African Americans, slave and free, were present from the earliest settlement, and by 1860, they made up 25 percent of the population. In later years, however, many blacks moved to cities in northern states; today about 16 percent of the state's people are African American.

Tennessee was once a completely rural state. But as industry developed, people began to move to the growing cities. At present nearly 70 percent of Tennessee's population is concentrated in metropolitan areas.

Education

The first regular school with graded classes was opened in 1780 by Samuel Doak, a Presbyterian minister. The state paid little attention to public education during the 1800's,

A nightclub on Memphis' historic Beale Street. The city is a center of many styles of American popular music, notably blues, soul, and rock and roll.

The Lady Vols of the University of Tennessee are one of the nation's top women's basketball teams. Their games draw large, enthusiastic audiences.

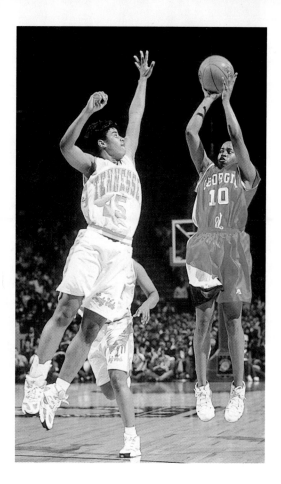

and private academies provided much of the schooling. To inadequate funding was added the further handicap of legally segregated schools, a system that was not fully eliminated until the 1970's. After a slow start, however, Tennessee has greatly increased its support for schools. Almost half of every state dollar now goes to public education.

The largest institution of higher education in the state is the University of Tennessee in Knoxville, founded in 1794. Its Center for the Health Sciences is in Memphis. Other University of Tennessee campuses are in Chattanooga and Martin. The Board of Regents system includes universities in Clarksville, Cookeville, Johnson City, Memphis, Murfreesboro, and Nashville and 14 community colleges distributed throughout the state.

Tennessee has many excellent private colleges and universities. Nashville is the home of Vanderbilt University, David Lipscomb University, Belmont University, Fisk University, and Meharry Medical College (the last two are historically black institutions founded after the Civil War). Others include the University of the South in Sewanee and LeMoyne-Owen College and Rhodes College, both in Memphis.

Libraries, Museums, and the Arts

Tennessee's first public library was established in Nashville in 1813. Today the state is served by some 250 public libraries, the largest of which are in Memphis, Nashville, Knoxville, and Chattanooga. The Tennessee State Library and Archives in Nashville has collections on the history of Tennessee and the South. Specialized libraries include the Oak Ridge Institute of Nuclear Studies Library in Oak Ridge and the Technical Library of the Tennessee Valley Authority in Knoxville.

The Parthenon, an art gallery in Nashville, is a full-size reproduction of the Parthenon in Athens, Greece. The Tennessee State Museum in Nashville and the Memphis Pink Palace Museum contain regional cultural and natural history exhibits. Other notable museums are the American Museum of Science and Energy in Oak Ridge and Nashville's Country Music Hall of Fame and Museum.

Tennessee long has been known as a center for many different kinds of music. The Fisk University Choir has done much to preserve spirituals. In Memphis, the Jazz and Blues Museum and the Sun Records Studio help

PEOPLE	Persons per sq mi		Persons per km²	
Population: 5,689,283 (2000 census).	over 250		over 100	
Density: 135 persons per sq mi (52 per km²).	50-250		20-100	
Distribution: 61% urban; 39% rural.				
Largest Cities (2000 census):	5-50		2-20	
Memphis 650,100 Clarksville 103,455				
Nashville 569,891 Murfreesboro 68,816	0-5		0-2	
Knoxville 173,890 Jackson 59,643				
Chattanooga 155,554 Johnson City 55,469				

Source: U.S. Bureau of the Census

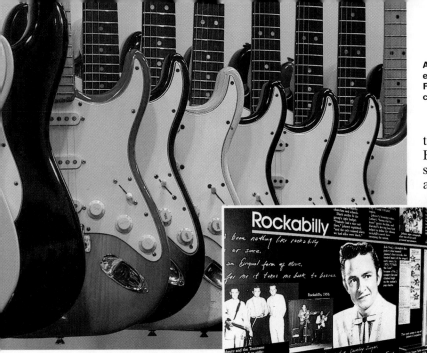

A display of electric guitars and an exhibit at the Country Music Hall of Fame are two sights of Nashville, the center of the country music industry.

keep alive the legacy of early rhythm and blues. Nashville is the international capital of the country music industry. For many years, the goal of almost every country singer has been to perform at Nashville's Grand Ole Opry, now part of a musical theme park called Opryland U.S.A. Tennessee also boasts five full-time symphony orchestras.

▶ ECONOMY

Before the Civil War, Tennessee was a leading farming state. By the 1960's, the state had the nation's 16th largest industrial economy. This transformation is the story of Tennessee's economy in the 20th century.

Services

The service sector employs well over half of all Tennesseans who work and is expected to grow well into the future. Business, social, and personal services, especially health care, are leading service activities. Wholesale and retail trade have also expanded rapidly, as have finance, insurance, and real estate. The state's fastest-growing category of service workers has been government employees.

Manufacturing

The leading industry in the state is the production of chemicals and such chemical products as plastics, industrial chemicals, and synthetic fibers. Food processing is next in importance. Plants throughout the state turn out meat and dairy products, soybean and cottonseed oil, and canned and frozen vegetables and fruit. Automotive manufacturing is one of the state's fastest-growing industries; Smyrna and Spring Hill are the sites of major car and truck assembly plants. Other important manufactured goods include fabricated metal products, machinery, and clothing and textiles. Kingsport has one of the country's largest book-printing establishments.

Agriculture

The small owner-operated farm, more than in most states, still dominates the rural landscape in Tennessee. About half of total farm

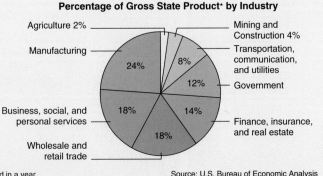

PRODUCTS AND INDUSTRIES

Manufacturing: Chemicals and chemical products, food products, fabricated metal products, motor vehicles and equipment, industrial machinery and equipment, clothing and other textile products, paper and paper products.

Agriculture: Cattle and hogs, dairy products, cotton, tobacco, soybeans, poultry and eggs, corn, snap beans, tomatoes, greenhouse nursery products.

Minerals: Coal, stone, zinc, cement, clays, phosphate rock, sand and gravel, petroleum, natural gas.

Services: Wholesale and retail trade; finance, insurance, and real estate; business, social, and personal services; transportation, communication, and utilities; government.

Percentage of Gross State Product* by Industry

Agriculture 2%
Manufacturing — 24%
Mining and Construction 4%
Transportation, communication, and utilities 8%
Government 12%
Finance, insurance, and real estate 14%
Business, social, and personal services — 18%
Wholesale and retail trade — 18%

*Gross state product is the total value of goods and services produced in a year.

Source: U.S. Bureau of Economic Analysis

income is derived from the sale of livestock and livestock products. The bluegrass areas of the Central Basin and the valleys in the Ridge and Valley region provide excellent pastures for cattle and dairy cows. Large numbers of hogs are raised in the corn-growing northwest, while poultry and eggs are produced in all areas.

Cotton and soybeans, the leading crops, are grown in the fertile lowlands of western Tennessee. Tobacco is grown mainly in north central and eastern Tennessee. Other important crops are corn, greenhouse and nursery products, and vegetables.

Mining and Construction

The coalfields of the Cumberland Plateau yield large amounts of bituminous coal, the most valuable mineral. Stone ranks next in value. The Knoxville area is a center of marble quarrying. Tennessee is the leading U.S. producer of zinc, mined in the central and eastern parts of the state.

Together with mining, construction employs almost 100,000 people in the state. Suburban counties, such as Williamson, have been the most active residential construction markets. Building along urban beltways also has created many construction jobs.

Transportation and Communication

Tennessee's early roads followed bison and Indian trails. By 1800, rough roads extended as far west as Nashville. One of the most famous early roads was the Natchez Trace, which ran from Natchez, Mississippi, to Nashville. It is preserved today as a part of the National Park System.

Tennessee's major rivers—the Mississippi, the Tennessee, and the Cumberland—are important transportation corridors. Memphis is a major port on the Mississippi. Barge traffic on the Tennessee-Tombigbee inland waterway can go directly from the Tennessee River to the Gulf of Mexico.

Late in building railroads, Tennessee by 1865 was connected by railway with the East Coast and with cities to the north. By 1920 more than 4,000 miles (6,400 kilometers) of track crisscrossed the state. But the amount of track has decreased since that time because trucks and buses have taken a great deal of the railroads' business. Tennessee's modern highway system and its central location with regard to eastern markets are among the state's chief advantages in recruiting business.

Scheduled airline service in the state began in 1925. Major airports include Memphis International Airport, Nashville International Airport, and Lovell Field in Chattanooga.

The first newspaper in Tennessee was the Knoxville *Gazette*, founded in 1791. Today the leading newspapers in Tennessee include the Memphis *Commercial Appeal*, *The Tennessean* and *The Banner*, both published in Nashville, *The Knoxville News-Sentinel*, *The Chattanooga News-Free Press*, and *The Chattanooga Times*.

Tennessee's first radio station began broadcasting from Knoxville in 1922. At present the state has about 150 AM stations and 130 FM stations. There are approximately 60 television stations.

▶ CITIES

Tennessee has four major cities—Memphis, Nashville, Knoxville, and Chattanooga. Many

An assembly line and workers in a Nissan automotive plant in Smyrna. Car manufacturing is one of the state's fastest-growing industries.

Places of Interest

Great Smoky Mountains National Park

Incline Railway, Lookout Mountain

Graceland, Memphis

Shiloh National Military Park

American Museum of Science and Energy, in Oak Ridge, is filled with models, films, demonstrations, devices, gadgets, and machines, all designed to tell the story of energy and its uses.

Big South Fork National River and Recreation Area (shared with Kentucky) preserves a wild, free-flowing stream that has created unusual scenic features in the northern Columbia Plateau.

Casey Jones Home and Railroad Museum, in Jackson, is the restored home of railroad engineer John Luther "Casey" Jones, whose death in a train wreck inspired a popular ballad. The home, now a railroad museum, has a replica of Casey's steam engine.

Cherokee National Forest covers more than 600,000 acres (240,000 hectares) in the eastern part of the state along Tennessee's border with North Carolina. It contains a wide variety of recreation areas.

Chickamauga and Chattanooga National Military Park is the oldest and largest military park in the nation. It was established in 1890 to preserve important battlefields of the Civil War. Most of the park is in northwestern Georgia, and the remainder is in southeastern Tennessee. Many markers and monuments tell the story of important events and battles.

Graceland, in Memphis, was the home of singer Elvis Presley. Guided tours include the first floor and basement of the mansion as well as Meditation Garden, where Elvis and members of his family are buried. Elvis' personal touring bus; his private jet, the *Lisa Marie*; and his car collection are also on view.

Great Smoky Mountains National Park covers a vast stretch of forestland in the Great Smoky Mountains. Somewhat less than half this area lies in Tennessee; the rest is in North Carolina. The park is noted for its excellent trails and roads and its remarkable variety of plants and animals.

The Hermitage, near Nashville, was the estate of Andrew Jackson. The stately mansion, with its original furnishings, and grounds are maintained as Jackson left them. The tombs of President and Mrs. Jackson are in the garden of the estate.

Lookout Mountain, near Chattanooga, was the site of a Civil War battle known as the Battle above the Clouds. An incline railway carries visitors to the top of the mountain. Point Park, a federal reservation on the mountaintop, includes a museum and an observatory with spectacular views.

Natchez Trace Parkway, which runs from Nashville to Natchez, Mississippi, follows the route of the historic Indian and pioneer trail. Along the way are picnic sites, nature trails, museums, and historic sites pertaining to the history of the Natchez Trace. One site, the Meriwether Lewis Monument near Hohenwald, marks the grave of the co-leader of the Lewis and Clark expedition.

Opryland USA, in Nashville, is the nation's only musical show theme park. It offers fully staged musicals and shows as well as gardens, restaurants, shops, and rides. The Opryland complex includes the Opryland Hotel, the Grand Ole Opry House, and the Nashville Network television studios.

Shiloh National Military Park, near Savannah, was the site of a major Civil War battle—the Battle of Shiloh, or Pittsburg Landing—on April 6–7, 1862. The park includes Shiloh National Cemetery.

State Areas. Tennessee has more than 20 state parks and forests. For more information, contact the Tennessee Department of Tourism, P.O. Box 23170, Nashville, Tennessee 37202.

of the state's large industries are located in these cities. But smaller cities such as Clarksville, Jackson, Johnson City, Murfreesboro, and Kingsport also have become manufacturing and trade centers.

Nashville, the capital, is located on the banks of the Cumberland River near the center of the state. Long known as the Athens of the South, Nashville today is the capital of country music and home to some of the South's outstanding medical facilities. An article on Nashville appears in Volume N.

Memphis, Tennessee's largest city, is located on the bluffs of the Mississippi River at the mouth of the Wolf River. The modern city is known as a leading cotton market and is also an important livestock center. Memphis has many colleges and universities and is noted as a medical center. An article on Memphis appears in Volume M.

Knoxville is located on the upper Tennessee River in the eastern part of the state. It was established as a frontier outpost about 1786. In 1790, streets were laid out, and the new town was named Knoxville in honor of Henry Knox, the first U.S. secretary of war.

Today Knoxville is the hub of the valley region of eastern Tennessee. It is an important livestock center and tobacco market. Large marble quarries are located nearby. Factories in the city produce textiles, clothing, and furniture and other hardwood products. Knoxville is the headquarters of the Tennessee Valley Authority. In 1982 the city was the site of a world's fair, for which it underwent extensive rebuilding. The fair was the first to be held in a southern U.S. city.

Chattanooga is situated on the Moccasin Bend of the Tennessee River, close to the Georgia border. In the early 1800's, a Cherokee trading post known as Ross's Landing was established on the site. The town was laid out in 1838 and given the name Chattanooga. The name is said to have come from a Native American word that described Lookout Mountain, southeast of the city.

Chattanooga has excellent transportation facilities and abundant electric power. These two assets have helped to make the city one of the South's most important manufacturing centers. Several important battlefields of the Civil War are in the area.

▶ **GOVERNMENT**

Tennessee has had three state constitutions since its admission to the Union in 1796. The present constitution was adopted in 1870.

The executive branch of the state government is headed by the governor, who is elected by the people. The speaker of the state senate serves as lieutenant governor. Three executive officers—the secretary of state, the treasurer, and the comptroller—are chosen by the legislature. The attorney general is selected by the state supreme court.

The state legislature is called the General Assembly. This branch of government is made up of a 33-member senate and a 99-member house of representatives.

Tennessee's highest courts are the state supreme court and court of appeals. Others are chancery courts, circuit courts, criminal courts, and various general sessions courts.

▶ **HISTORY**

Following the last Ice Age, Tennessee's game-filled woodlands provided a rich environment for Native Americans. Abundant spear and arrow points, pottery, and burial sites attest to 12,000 years of native life before the appearance of Europeans. In historic times, Tennessee became a great hunting ground for powerful southern tribes such as the Cherokee, Chickasaw, and Creek.

The state capitol building at Legislative Plaza, Nashville. The city, the second largest in Tennessee, is the center of state government.

GOVERNMENT

State Government
Governor: 4-year term
State senators: 33; 4-year terms
State representatives: 99;
  2-year terms
Number of counties: 95.

Federal Government
U.S. senators: 2
U.S. representatives: 9
Number of electoral votes: 11

For the name of the current governor, see STATE GOVERNMENTS in Volume S. For the names of current U.S. senators and representatives, see UNITED STATES, CONGRESS OF THE in Volume U-V.

INDEX TO TENNESSEE MAP

● County Seat   Counties in parentheses   ★ State Capital

Discovery and Exploration

British and French fur traders were the first Europeans to take an interest in the area. In 1673 two Virginia traders, James Needham and Gabriel Arthur, visited southeastern Tennessee. In the same year the French explorers Father Jacques Marquette and Louis Jolliet canoed down the Mississippi River and touched the western edge of what is now Tennessee. In 1682 Robert Cavelier, Sieur de La Salle, built Fort Prud'homme at the mouth of the Hatchie River.

The Indians supplied British and French traders with furs, becoming dependent on the guns and tools they received in return. European rivalries led to the French and Indian War (1754–63) between the French and British and their Indian allies. Involvement in the war, which was eventually won by the British, reduced the power and independence of the Cherokee, whose land lay squarely in the path of westward migration.

Colonial Times

The first permanent settlers came into Tennessee about 1769. William Bean, James Robertson, and other pioneers started settlements in northeastern Tennessee along the Watauga, Nolichucky, and Holston rivers. In 1772 the newly arrived settlers formed their own government, known as the Watauga Association. Two famous frontiersmen, John Sevier and James Robertson, headed the association. Soon after the start of the Revolutionary War, the group organized the district of Washington, which became part of North Carolina. In 1779 Robertson led the first band of settlers to Middle Tennessee, where they drew up the articles of self-government that are known as the Cumberland Compact.

During the Revolutionary War, the frontiersmen from the Tennessee border took part in several important campaigns, including the Battle of Kings Mountain (1780) in South Carolina. This battle was a turning point of the Revolution.

North Carolina took little interest in its far western counties during the 1780's, when the young Tennessee settlements nearly were destroyed by Indian warfare. Left without protection, the frontiersmen organized an independent state known as Franklin in 1784.

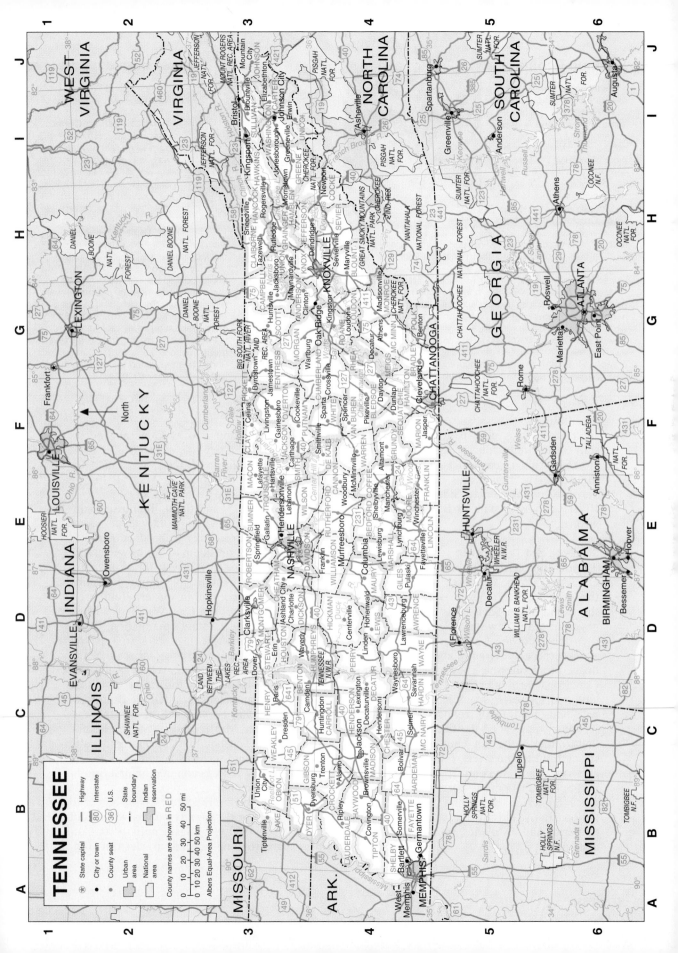

Famous People

Tennessee claims three presidents of the United States—Andrew Jackson, James K. Polk, and Andrew Johnson. They were born in neighboring states but spent most of their lives in Tennessee. Biographies of the presidents appear elsewhere in this encyclopedia.

Biographies of pioneer Davy Crockett, naval hero David G. Farragut, U.S. secretary of state Cordell Hull, U.S. vice president Albert Gore, Jr., and the Indian leader Sequoya, all Tennesseans, are included in other volumes.

James Agee (1909–55), born in Knoxville, was an author and critic. He is perhaps best known for his nonfiction work on the Great Depression, *Let Us Now Praise Famous Men* (1941). He was awarded the Pulitzer Prize for the autobiographical novel *A Death in the Family* (1957). Agee was also a film critic for the

Bessie Smith

Dolly Parton

magazines *Time* and *The Nation* and the author of several screenplays, including *The African Queen* (1951).

Nathan Bedford Forrest (1821–77), born in Bedford County, was a Confederate general known for his brilliant cavalry raids during the U.S. Civil War. He fought at Fort Donelson (1862), Shiloh (1862), and Brice's Cross Roads (1864). When asked to explain his success in battle, Forrest famously replied, "Get there first with the most men." Forrest later became

the first Grand Wizard of the Ku Klux Klan, a society of white supremacists.

W. C. (William Christopher) Handy (1873–1958), born in Florence, Alabama, was a composer who is known as the Father of the Blues. Working in Memphis, he popularized the blues style with such songs as "Memphis Blues" (1912) and "St. Louis Blues" (1914). He was one of the first publishers of music by black composers.

Dolly Parton (1946–), born into a poor mountain family in Locust Ridge, became a world-famous country music recording star. She sang and played guitar from early childhood. Immediately after graduating from high school she went to Nashville, where she achieved great success as a singer-songwriter. Parton has also acted in motion pictures, notably *Nine to Five* (1980).

John Sevier was chosen governor. But the state lasted only four years, at which time North Carolina reasserted control. In 1790 the Tennessee region was organized as the Territory of the United States South of the River Ohio, with William Blount as the first governor.

Statehood and Development

Soon the territory applied for statehood. On June 1, 1796, Tennessee was admitted to the Union as the 16th state, with Knoxville as the capital. John Sevier was elected the first governor of the new state.

In the following years, settlers from other states, especially Virginia and the Carolinas, flocked to Tennessee. They came overland in Conestoga wagons or poled up the Cumberland and Tennessee rivers in boats piled high with household goods. Tennessee, along with Kentucky, was called the Old Southwest, the first frontier of the new United States. On the strength of its fine rivers, Tennessee soon became an important commercial center for the mid-South. Prosperous corn and hog farms made Tennessee the leading farm state in the nation. Early industries, such as gristmills, tanneries, and distilleries, were also based on agriculture.

Tennessee troops led by General Andrew Jackson played a key role in the War of 1812. When the governor of Tennessee called for troops during the Mexican War (1846–48), thousands of Tennesseans responded.

Between 1815 and 1860, Tennessee supplied many political and military leaders for a young nation expanding its borders. Three of the first 17 U.S. presidents—Andrew Jackson, James K. Polk, and Andrew Johnson—were Tennesseans. Cotton plantation farming proved very successful in western Tennessee, and on the eve of the Civil War, slaves made up 25 percent of the state's population.

Tennessee was the last state to separate from the Union before the outbreak of the Civil War. During the war, well over 400 battles and skirmishes were fought on Tennessee soil. Major campaigns included the capture of Fort Henry and Fort Donelson and the battles of Shiloh, Murfreesboro (Stones River), Chickamauga, Chattanooga, Franklin, and Nashville. Tennessee was readmitted to the Union in July 1866, becoming the first Southern state to rejoin.

The war had devastated Tennessee, and farm output and property values would not reach their 1860 level again until 1900. Cotton sharecropping spread in western Ten-

James Robertson (1742–1814), born in Brunswick County, Virginia, was a frontiersman and the cofounder of Nashville, along with John Donelson. He is known as the Father of Tennessee. His leadership was crucial in holding the early Tennessee settlements together.

John Ross (1790–1866), born near Lookout Mountain, was a Cherokee chief who united the eastern and western branches of his tribe. He commanded a Cherokee regiment under General Andrew Jackson in the War of 1812. Ross resisted the U.S. government's removal of the Cherokee from their Tennessee and Georgia homeland but led his people to Oklahoma when his legal appeals failed.

Wilma Rudolph (1940–94), born in Clarksville, was a star Olympic athlete. She contracted polio as a child and had to wear a leg brace. She later became a champion sprinter, winning three gold medals in the 1960 Olympic Games and setting the world record for the 100-meter dash in 1961.

John Sevier (1745–1815) was born in Virginia but moved to the Tennessee frontier in 1773. He served as an officer in the Revolutionary War and later led expeditions against the Indians. Sevier was governor (1784–88) of the short-lived state of Franklin, which became part of Tennessee. In 1796 he was elected the first governor of the state of Tennessee. Sevier also was a member of the U.S. House of Representatives (1789–91 and 1811–15).

Bessie Smith (1894–1937), born in Chattanooga, was the leading female blues singer of the 1920's. Known as the Empress of the Blues, she sang on Beale Street in Memphis and made her first recording, "Down Hearted Blues," in 1923. In more than 150 other recordings, she performed with top jazz musicians of her day.

Sergeant York

Nancy Ward (1738–1824), born in the Cherokee village of Chota, was known as Beloved Woman. During the Revolutionary War, she saved the white Watauga settlement by warning them of a planned attack by the pro-British Cherokees.

Alvin Cullum York (1887–1964), born in Pall Mall, is famous as Sergeant York, the best-known hero of World War I. On October 8, 1918, in the Battle of the Argonne in France, he led a small detachment of troops against a German machine-gun battalion. York alone shot some 25 enemy soldiers and captured 132 prisoners. He was made a sergeant and received more than 50 military decorations.

---

nessee, and the lives of farmers worsened. Along with these problems, Memphis suffered a series of yellow fever epidemics in the 1870's that killed thousands of people. Many others fled the city and never returned.

Modern Times

Cultural issues dominated the early decades of the 1900's. In 1920, Tennessee was the deciding state to pass the 19th Amendment, giving women the right to vote. Five years later, the trial of Dayton high school teacher John T. Scopes received national attention. Scopes was charged with teaching the theory of evolution, banned by state law because it contradicted the teachings of the Bible. He was defended by Clarence Darrow, a famous attorney. The so-called monkey trial was one reflection of the clash between the traditional beliefs of rural Tennesseans and those of an emerging urban culture. Agriculture based on sharecropping had begun to break down after World War I (1914–18), and large numbers of rural people started migrating to cities.

Another significant event was the creation by Congress of the Tennessee Valley Authority (TVA) in 1933. The goal was to develop the Tennessee River system, mainly for electric power and flood control, and to stimulate economic growth in the region. World War II (1939–45) also spurred industrial development and the migration from the country to the city. After 1942, the city of Oak Ridge played a leading role in building the atomic bomb and developing the nation's nuclear energy program.

Perhaps the greatest social event of the postwar era was the civil rights movement. Desegregation of Tennessee public schools began in Clinton in 1957, ending 75 years of legal segregation in the state. Other notable victories were gained by sit-down strikes in Nashville (1960) and voter registration drives in Fayette County (1963). The murder of civil rights leader Martin Luther King, Jr., in Memphis in 1968 was a tragic reminder of the seriousness of the nation's racial problems.

Tennessee enjoyed one of its strongest periods of business prosperity in the 1980's, when the state became a prime market for Japanese investment and a center of automotive manufacturing. As it embarks on the new century, Tennessee's rich history and strong traditions of community are among its greatest assets.

WAYNE C. MOORE
Tennessee State Library and Archives

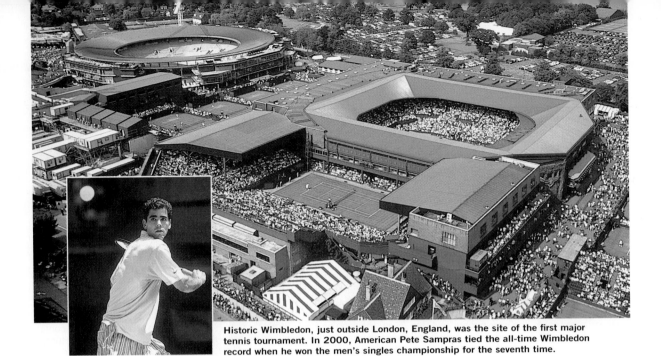

Historic Wimbledon, just outside London, England, was the site of the first major tennis tournament. In 2000, American Pete Sampras tied the all-time Wimbledon record when he won the men's singles championship for the seventh time.

TENNIS

Tennis is the most popular of the racket sports. It is played by people of all ages and levels of skill. Millions of people enjoy watching outstanding players in national and world competitions including the Olympic Games.

▶ HOW THE GAME IS PLAYED

Tennis is played on a rectangular court by two people (singles) or two teams of two players each (doubles). The players use rackets to hit a ball back and forth across a net. The object is to hit the ball into the opposing court in such a way that the opposing side cannot return it. The side that does this wins a point. A **game** is completed when one side wins four points with a two-point lead. The first to win six games with a two-game lead wins a **set**. In most women's competitions, the first to win two sets wins a **match**. In most men's competitions, the first to win three sets wins a match.

Service. Play begins with the service (delivery) of the ball. Each game is served by only one player. The service alternates between sides and, in doubles play, between the partners. A coin toss or similar method determines the first server. The server begins by serving from the right side of the court. The serve then alternates between the left and right sides after each point.

The server stands behind the **baseline**, between imaginary extensions of the center mark and sideline. In singles play the inner sidelines mark the boundaries of the court. In doubles the boundaries are the outer sidelines. If the server's foot touches any of these lines or the court inside the lines during the serve, or if the server walks or runs before the racket strikes the ball, a **foot fault** is declared.

The server tosses the ball into the air and strikes it with the racket. The ball must cross the net without touching it and bounce in the **service court** diagonally opposite the server. A ball landing on a boundary line of the service court is considered good. If the ball does not land in the service court, a **fault** is declared and the player gets a second serve. If the player then commits a fault or a foot fault, a **double fault** is declared, and the receiver is awarded the point. A **let** is declared if the ball strikes the net and falls into the service court or if the receiver was not ready. In the case of a let, the service is repeated.

The Return. The receiver must allow the ball to bounce once in the service court before striking it back. In any play after the service, the ball may land anywhere within the outside boundaries of the opponent's court. It may be struck in the air (called a **volley**) or after one bounce (called a **ground stroke**). Any ball struck before bouncing is considered within the boundaries. If the ball hits the net but rolls over into the correct court, it is legal and should be returned (struck back). The players continue to **rally** (hit the ball back and forth) until the ball is not returned or goes out of bounds. A point goes to the last player to make a legal return. The server continues to serve from alternate sides of his or her court until one player or team has won the game.

Scoring. If there is no umpire, the server calls the score before each serve, calling the server's score first, then the receiver's. A score of 0 is called **Love**, one point is called **15**, two points are called **30**, and three points are called **40**. If the game is tied at 40–40, the score is called **deuce**. The next point is called **ad** (or **advantage**). If the score ties again, the score is again deuce. To win the game, a player or team must get two ad points in a row following deuce.

Examples of the score call are: Love–15 (Server has 0, receiver has one point); 15–15 (each side has one point); 30–15 (server has two points, receiver has one point); 40–15 (server has 3 points, receiver has 1 point). **Game** is called when either side has gained the fourth point and is two points ahead.

When there is no umpire, scoring is done on an honor system. Players determine whether a ball is inside or outside the boundaries on their own side of the net.

Boris Becker, known for his powerful serves, waits for the ball in the ready position. He holds his racket out in front of him and cradles its throat in his free hand. His knees are slightly flexed and his legs are wide apart so he can move quickly in any direction.

▶**PREPARATION**

Returning the ball requires preparation, concentration, and good form for each stroke. As you await your opponent's shot, you should assume the **ready position**, demonstrated by Boris Becker in the photograph above. From the ready position you can quickly adjust to make the correct stroke for your return shot.

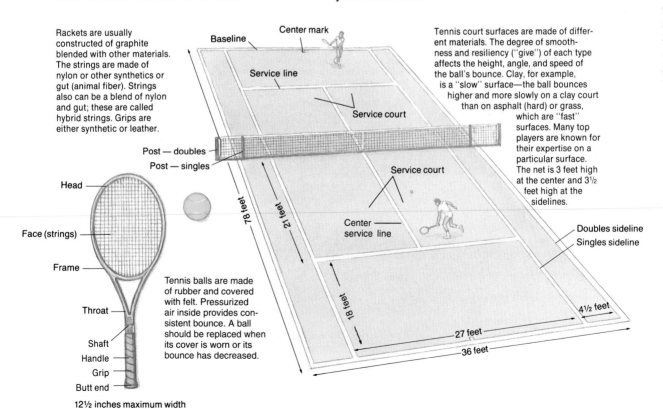

Rackets are usually constructed of graphite blended with other materials. The strings are made of nylon or other synthetics or gut (animal fiber). Strings also can be a blend of nylon and gut; these are called hybrid strings. Grips are either synthetic or leather.

Tennis court surfaces are made of different materials. The degree of smoothness and resiliency ("give") of each type affects the height, angle, and speed of the ball's bounce. Clay, for example, is a "slow" surface—the ball bounces higher and more slowly on a clay court than on asphalt (hard) or grass, which are "fast" surfaces. Many top players are known for their expertise on a particular surface. The net is 3 feet high at the center and 3½ feet high at the sidelines.

Tennis balls are made of rubber and covered with felt. Pressurized air inside provides consistent bounce. A ball should be replaced when its cover is worn or its bounce has decreased.

Center mark
Baseline
Service line
Service court
Service court
Post — doubles
Post — singles
Head
Center service line
Face (strings)
Frame
Throat
Shaft
Handle
Grip
Butt end

Doubles sideline
Singles sideline

78 feet
21 feet
18 feet
27 feet
36 feet
4½ feet

12½ inches maximum width
32 inches maximum length

The most important lesson to learn is to keep your eye on the ball from the time it leaves your opponent's racket through its contact with your own racket. In addition to helping you strike the ball in the center of your racket, concentration on the ball helps you know where to go on the court and which stroke to use.

▶THE BASIC STROKES

There are six basic tennis strokes—the **serve**, **forehand** and **backhand ground strokes**, **forehand** and **backhand volleys**, and **overhead smash**. Each requires preparation, a correct **grip** (position of the hand on the racket), and the correct movements of the whole body in order to obtain the best results. Figures 1 through 5 that follow illustrate the strokes for right-handed players. Left-handers reverse the directions.

The Serve

The serve (or **service**), shown in Figure 1, begins the play for every point. Two serves are allowed to get the ball into the opponent's service court. The server tries to put the receiver on the defensive by the speed and placement of the shot. A fair serve that the receiver is unable to touch is called an **ace**. A player's fastest and best-placed serve is usually the most difficult to make, so you can try for the ace on your first serve. However, it is generally better to have a high number of successful first serves rather than to always try for the more difficult ace. If the first serve fails, then be more cautious on the second. If that misses the service court, you will have double-faulted and your opponent gains a point.

If your first serve is not good, reduce your hitting power a little and concentrate on ball control. Use a **topspin** or **slice** on your second

Chris Evert

Figure 1

The Serve

A. Position: Both feet are on an imaginary line leading to your opponent's service court. Hold your racket over that same line.
B. Toss: Extend your arm fully and toss the ball. It should rise in a straight line above and to the right of your left foot to a point about 6 inches past your racket's reach. As your tossing arm goes up, start your backswing. Watch the ball.
C,D. Backswing: Sweep your racket back and up behind you until the head nearly touches your back. Bend your knees.
E. Stroke: Bring your racket up, straighten your knees, and reach high.
F. Contact: Hit the ball at the top of your reach. See the contact.
G. Follow-through: Continue the swing. Shift your weight to your left foot and turn your shoulders to face the net.
H. Finish with your racket to your left. Step into the court on your right foot.

Continental Grip

Turn the racket on its edge and grasp the handle as if you were shaking hands. Rotate your hand counterclockwise until the "V" of the thumb and forefinger is on the left side of the top plane of the racket grip. Beginners may find that the Eastern forehand grip gives them more control.

Figure 2
Forehand Ground Stroke

A. Preparation: Start from the ready position. Keep your eye on the ball from the moment your opponent strikes it.

B. Backswing: Turn to the right, pivoting on your right foot as you bring your racket back. Keep your elbow relaxed.

C. Stroke: Step forward on your left foot as you bring your racket forward to meet the ball. Tighten your grip; keep your wrist firm and your elbow bent slightly through the contact.

D. Contact: Hit the ball forward of your left foot. Try to see the ball hit the center of your racket.

E. Follow-through: Bring the racket through in the direction of the target. Finish with the racket face at or above head height. Your elbow will be straight and your shoulders turned to the net. Your right foot will move forward as you return to the ready position.

Bjorn Borg

Eastern Forehand Grip

Stand the racket on its edge and grasp the handle as if you were shaking hands. The "V" formed by the forefinger and thumb rests on the right edge of the top plane of the racket handle. Your palm should rest on the diagonal and side planes of the racket handle. This grip produces a powerful stroke for both high and low balls.

A B C D E

serve and place the ball where it will be hard for your opponent to return. For example, if the receiver has a weak backhand, you should try to serve to that side.

Ground Strokes

Ground strokes are made after the ball has bounced once. They are usually made near the back of the court. Forehand strokes (Figure 2) are made with the palm of the hand toward the incoming ball. Backhand strokes (Figure 3) are made with the back of the hand toward the incoming ball. As you move from the ready position to prepare to hit a ground stroke, your eye will be on the ball. If it is high as it crosses the net toward you, it will probably bounce high. If it is low, it will probably bounce low.

Begin your backswing as soon as you know whether you will hit a forehand or backhand shot. Use your knees as elevators to raise or lower yourself to the ball.

It is important to maintain your balance. Your body should be inclined only slightly forward. If you must bend over or lunge at the ball, your free arm and leg will act as counterweights. However, it will be more difficult to control your shot.

In a correctly executed ground stroke, your arm is never straight when the racket strikes the ball. A slight bend of the elbow permits easier and more powerful hitting. The grip and the wrist must be firm to control the racket head.

Because most players are stronger on the forehand than the backhand, an opponent will usually attack your backhand. Therefore you would be wise to develop a strong backhand ground stroke.

Volleys

Volleys, illustrated in Figure 4, are return shots made anywhere between your feet and head and before the ball bounces in your court. Volleys are usually made near the net, where you have the best chance to hit the ball at an angle that puts it out of your opponent's reach.

Because you are near the net, you have less time to prepare, so the backswing on a volley must be short. Instead of swinging at the ball, you punch it. Keep your racket head up, even with or above the level of your wrist. If the ball is low, bend your knees to get down to it instead of dropping the head of your racket.

The volley is an opportunity to put the ball where your opponent cannot reach it. If that is not possible, try to force him or her in a direction that opens up (leaves unprotected) enough court area for your next volley to be a winner. Otherwise, your opponent may do the same to you.

The Overhead Smash

The overhead smash (Figure 5) is the answer to a **lob**—a ball that arcs high over your head. The stroke resembles that of a serve, but you usually make it when moving rather than from a stationary position as in the serve. A powerful smash is not always the best response to the lob. If it bounces high, your opponent may have time to reach it and lob in return. A well-placed smash may win a point more quickly than one hit with all your force.

Steffi Graf

Figure 3
Backhand Ground Stroke

A. Ready Position: Switch to the backhand grip. Keep your left hand on the throat of the racket. Watch the ball.
B. Preparation: Shifting your weight to your left foot, turn to your left. Your right shoulder points toward the ball.
C, D. Backswing: Bring the racket back to the height of your left shoulder, keeping your left hand on the racket throat. Your right shoulder follows through so that your back is to the ball. Your weight is on your left foot.
E. Stroke: Your left hand releases the racket. Swing the racket forward, tighten your grip, keep your elbow relaxed, and shift your weight to your right foot.
F. Contact: The ball meets the center of the racket, in front of your right hip. Try to see the contact.
G. Follow-through: Your racket head should follow through in the direction of the ball's flight. Finish with your arm extended and the racket above head height. Your left foot moves forward naturally, and you return to the ready position.

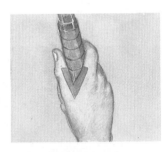

Eastern Backhand Grip

Hold your racket with the Eastern forehand grip described in Figure 2. Then rotate your hand counterclockwise until the "V" of the thumb and forefinger is on the diagonal plane of the racket handle.

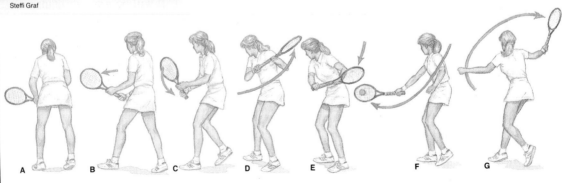

A   B   C   D   E   F   G

Figure 4
Volleys

Use the continental grip (Figure 1). Assume the ready position, but bend your knees more and hold your racket higher and more forward. Keep the backswing short and the racket head above wrist level. For low balls, bend your knees rather than the racket head. Hit the ball with a punching motion. Return quickly to the ready position for a return volley.

Forehand Volley

A. Backswing: With your weight on your right foot, bring your racket back.
B. Stroke and Contact: Step across with your left foot and punch the ball.
C. Follow-through: Make a short follow-through in the direction of the ball's flight.

Backhand Volley

A. Backswing: With your left hand on the throat, draw the racket back to your left.
B. Stroke and Contact: Step across with your right foot and punch the ball.
C. Follow-through: Make a short follow-through in the direction of the ball's flight.

Figure 5
Overhead Smash

A. Preparation: Move into position behind and below where the ball will drop. Turn right, lining up your shoulders with the ball's path.
B,C. Backswing: Point at the ball with your left hand as you sweep the racket up behind your back. Adjust your position with short steps.
D. Stroke: Bring the racket up, dropping your left arm. Keep your eye on the ball and hit it at your full reach.
E. Follow-through: Bring the racket down in an arc to your left side. Step through on your right foot.

Arthur Ashe

Figure 6

Racket Control

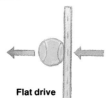

Flat drive

The flight path of your ball is greatly affected by the angle and motion of the racket face at contact. The flat drive is hit with the racket face perpendicular to the ground. The ball travels straight until gravity pulls it down.

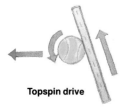

Topspin drive

If the racket face is closed (tilted down), the ball will be driven down unless topspin is applied. This is done by brushing upward on the back of the ball at contact. Topspin causes the ball to drop sooner and bounce higher than a flat hit.

Slice shot

If the racket face is open (tilted up), it will drive the ball up unless underspin is applied. This is done by brushing downward on the back of the ball at contact. Underspin causes the ball to bounce lower.

▶ STROKE PRODUCTION

The flatter the ball is hit, the greater are its **speed** and **pace**. Speed is the swiftness of the ball through the air, and pace is the swiftness of its bounce off the court. The speed and pace produced by a **flat shot** enable you to keep your opponent from attacking and perhaps force him or her to make errors or to become tired. It is important to learn the flat shot first.

Although the ball is round, you must think of it as having a front, back, top, and bottom. Figure 6 shows how the racket hits the back of the ball in a flat shot. It also shows how the racket meets the ball in a **topspin** and **slice shot**.

Topspin makes the ball rotate forward. It will drop sharply into the court after crossing the net. The ball with topspin will bounce high and forward sharply after it bounces.

A slice shot has a backward and sometimes a sideways spin. When it hits, it bounces low and slow.

HELEN HULL JACOBS
Former United States and Wimbledon Champion

Reviewed and updated by RHONDA K. MILLER
Staff Reporter, *Tennis* magazine

▶ HISTORY

Games similar to tennis were played in ancient Egypt, Greece, and Persia. In the 1100's, French and English nobility played an indoor game called court tennis or royal tennis. The name tennis is said to have come from the French expression *"Tenez!"* ("take"). The player preparing to hit the first ball called this to the receiver.

In 1874, a British army officer, Major Walter Clopton Wingfield, patented in London a game he called lawn tennis. It was played on an hourglass-shaped court divided by a high-hung net. The game required ease of movement, speed, and accuracy in hitting the ball.

There are several theories on how tennis was introduced in America. Some historians think it was first played by Dr. James Dwight in 1874 in Massachusetts. Others think the first player was Mary Outerbridge, who saw the game in Bermuda in 1874 and brought it to New York. Documents also show that tennis was played in 1874 in the Arizona Territory by Ella Wilkins Bailey, the wife of an army officer. Whatever its origin, the game spread quickly in the eastern United States and was being played in California by 1879.

Early National Championships

In 1877 the first lawn tennis championship match was held in Wimbledon, a suburb of London, England. It was played on a rectangular court with a net that was lower than those used earlier. The tournament, after a men's singles match, became an annual event. Men's doubles were added in 1879, women's singles in 1884, and women's doubles and mixed doubles in 1913. The All England tournament soon came to be known simply as Wimbledon, and it is still considered the most important tennis championship in the world.

The United States National Lawn Tennis Association (now the United States Tennis Association, or USTA) was formed in 1881 and held its first championships that year in Newport, Rhode Island. Richard D. Sears won and continued as champion for seven years. Ellen F. Hansell won the first U.S. women's championships in 1887 at the Philadelphia Cricket Club in Chestnut Hill, Pennsylvania.

In the meantime, tennis was being played around the world, and several other countries had established national championships. The New Zealand championships began in 1886,

The U.S. Open is held every fall at the National Tennis Center (*above*) in Flushing Meadow, New York. Among the top-ranked players who triumphed there were Steffi Graf (*top*), who won the women's singles title five times (1988–89, 1993, 1995–96), and Monica Seles (*right*), who won it twice (1991–92).

the French and South African championships in 1891, the German championships in 1892, and the Australian in 1905.

The Changing World of Tennis

For its first 50 years, tennis was largely a pastime for wealthy people. But as it spread across the United States, it also became more popular with many others. Programs for junior players were started, and the number of courts in public parks increased steadily.

By the early 1920's a few players had risen to world fame, creating wider public interest in the game. Among them were William ("Big Bill") Tilden of the United States and Suzanne Lenglen of France.

The first big professional promotion was launched in 1926, with prominent players touring. Other well-known players turned professional. However the professional matches lacked the prestige of the main amateur events, and only a few players shared the big cash prizes each year.

Then Britain demanded the right to stage Wimbledon as an open event, meaning that both amateurs and professionals could compete. In 1968 the International Tennis Federation, which governs tennis worldwide, agreed. The winners of the singles titles in the first open Wimbledon were Billie Jean King of the United States and Rod Laver of Australia. In the first U.S. Open, also in 1968,

GREAT PLAYERS IN THE HISTORY OF TENNIS

The International Tennis Hall of Fame was established in 1954. It is located at the Newport Casino in Newport, Rhode Island, which was the site of the first recognized U.S. men's tournament, known as the National Championships. Since that tournament in 1881, the grass courts of the casino have been used by amateur and professional players. Many of the best players in tennis history are honored in the Hall of Fame. A biography of Althea Gibson, an important member, is in Volume G. Some of the players profiled here are also members.

JIMMY CONNORS

MARGARET SMITH COURT

STEFAN EDBERG

CHRIS EVERT

BILLIE JEAN KING

ARTHUR ASHE (1943–93), the first African American male to win a major singles tennis title, won his first U.S. Open and the U.S. Amateur title in 1968 and shared the world's No. 1 ranking with Rod Laver. Ashe was ranked No. 1 again in 1975. During his career he won 33 titles, including the Australian Open in 1970 and Wimbledon in 1975. In doubles, he captured the 1971 French and 1977 Australian crowns. Ashe was a member of 11 U.S. Davis Cup teams, including 5 championship teams, 2 while he was captain (1981–82). He was elected to the Hall of Fame in 1985.

BJORN BORG (1956–) has the most consecutive title wins, 5, in men's singles at Wimbledon (1976–80). His fifth came after a historic 34-point tiebreaker in the fourth set against John McEnroe, after which he won the fifth set. During the late 1970's and early 1980's, the native of Sweden also won a record 6 French Opens. He retired in 1983 with 62 tournament titles and was elected to the Hall of Fame in 1987.

MAUREEN CONNOLLY (1934–69), nicknamed Little Mo, was the first woman to claim a Grand Slam by winning the 1953 Australian and French Opens, Wimbledon, and the U.S. Open. The strong American baseline player held the U.S. No. 1 ranking from 1951 to 1953, won the Australian doubles crown in 1953, and the singles, doubles, and mixed doubles titles at the French Open in 1954, retiring after an accident that year. She was elected to the Hall of Fame in 1968.

JIMMY CONNORS (1952–) had 109 career wins and 8 Grand Slam titles, including the Australian Open in 1974, Wimbledon in 1974 and 1982, and the U.S. Open in 1974, 1976, 1978, 1982, and 1983. Partnered with Ilie Nastase, Conners also

ARTHUR ASHE

BJORN BORG

MAUREEN CONNOLLY

won doubles titles in 1973 at Wimbledon and in 1975 at the U.S. Open. During his career, Connors was ranked among the top 10 players in the world 16 times, holding the No. 1 slot a total of 268 weeks. He was elected to the Hall of Fame in 1998.

MARGARET SMITH COURT (1942–), known as the Arm for her incredible reach, is the only player to win a Grand Slam in singles (1970) and mixed doubles (1963). She holds the record in men's and women's tennis for most wins in Grand Slam events, with a total of 62 in singles, doubles, and mixed doubles. This outstanding Australian won 24 Grand Slam singles titles during the 1960's and the early 1970's. From 1962 to 1973, she was ranked No. 1 in the world 7 times. She was elected to the Hall of Fame in 1979.

STEFAN EDBERG (1966–), a native of Sweden, was the first player to win a Junior Grand Slam as the world's No. 1 junior before turning pro in 1983. He then won the Australian Open singles crown in 1985 and 1987, Wimbledon in 1988 and 1990, and the U.S. Open in 1991 and 1992. He also won the 1987 Australian Open and U.S. Open doubles titles and the bronze medal at the 1988 Olympics. After retiring in 1996, Edberg set up a foundation to help educate and nurture young Swedish tennis players.

CHRIS EVERT (1954–), in 1970 at age 15, defeated Margaret Court, then the world's No. 1 player. She went on to win 157 pro singles titles, with a 309–145 win-loss record, one of the highest winning percentages in tennis history. Ranked No. 1 in the world during the late 1970's and early 1980's, the American holds 21 Grand Slam titles and was the first player to win more than 1,000 singles matches and 150 tournaments. She holds the record on clay with a 125-match winning streak, set from 1973 to 1979. Evert retired in 1989 and was elected to the Hall of Fame in 1995.

BILLIE JEAN KING (1943–), the American trailblazer in women's tennis who helped found the WTA, won a record 20 titles in singles, doubles, and mixed doubles at Wimbledon. She won her first Grand Slam tournament in 1966 by taking the singles title at Wimbledon, where she won again in 1967, 1968, 1972, 1973, and

1975. She also won several French, Australian, and U.S. Open titles in the 1960's and 1970's and was undefeated in 27 Fed Cup matches. King was elected to the Hall of Fame in 1987.

JACK KRAMER (1921–) began his career as a teenager when he was asked to play doubles for the U.S. Davis Cup team. The American became known as a power player, rushing the net behind his serve and attacking the return. His singles titles include Wimbledon in 1947 and the U.S. Open in 1946 and 1947, the same two years he was ranked No. 1 in the world. His doubles crowns include 2 at Wimbledon and 5 at the U.S. Open. One of the founders of the ATP Tour, he was elected to the Hall of Fame in 1968.

ROD LAVER (1938–) won the Grand Slam in 1962 as an amateur and won it again in 1969 as a pro, becoming the only double Grand Slam winner. During his career, the Australian won 18 singles, doubles, and mixed doubles titles at Grand Slam events between 1959 and 1969, placing him among the all-time male winners. He also won 10 out of the 12 Davis Cup challenge matches he played. Laver was ranked No. 1 in the world in 1961, 1962, 1968, and 1969. He was elected to the Hall of Fame in 1981.

IVAN LENDL (1960–) won 94 titles in his career and held the world No. 1 ranking for a total of 270 weeks. The Czech-born Lendl (later a U.S. citizen) played in 8 consecutive U.S. Open finals, equaling a record set by Bill Tilden in the early 1900's. He won the Australian Open in 1989 and 1990, the French Open in 1984, 1986, and 1987, and the U.S. Open in 1985, 1986, and 1987. Citing chronic back problems, Lendl retired in 1994.

JOHN McENROE (1959–) was as famous for his fiery temperament as he was for his exceptional play. At the U.S. Open, the American won four times each the singles title (1979–81, 1984) and the doubles title (1979, 1981, 1983, 1989). At Wimbledon, he won the singles title three times (1981, 1983–84) and the doubles five times (1979, 1981, 1983–84, 1992). He was also a member of the Davis Cup team 12 times (1978–84, 1987–89, 1991–92). He was elected to the Hall of Fame in 1999.

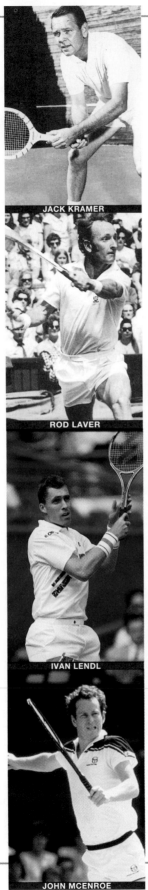

JACK KRAMER

ROD LAVER

IVAN LENDL

JOHN MCENROE

HELEN WILLS MOODY

MARTINA NAVRATILOVA

STAN SMITH

BILL TILDEN

HELEN WILLS MOODY (1905–98) did not lose a set in singles from 1927 to 1932, making her one of the best female tennis players in her day. By 1938, she had won 52 of 92 tournaments and had a 398-35 win-loss match record. During the 1920's and 1930's, Moody won 8 singles titles at Wimbledon, 7 at the U.S. Open, and 4 at the French Open, also winning doubles titles at Wimbledon and the U.S. Open. The American was elected to the Hall of Fame in 1959.

MARTINA NAVRATILOVA (1956–) was one of the best players in the history of tennis. She was as skilled in singles play, in which she won 167 titles, as she was in doubles, in which she won 165 titles. She holds the record for most match victories in both categories (1,438 singles, 1,111 doubles) and was ranked the No.1 singles player for 331 weeks. The Czech native (later a U.S. citizen) also won 56 Grand Slam titles in singles, doubles, and mixed doubles, and in 1987 she won the triple crown (all three events) at the U.S. Open. Navratilova was named Female Athlete of the Decade for the 1980's by the National Sports Review, the Associated Press, and United Press International. In 2000, she was elected to the Hall of Fame.

STAN SMITH (1946–) was one of the best U.S. Davis Cup players in history, with 35 singles and doubles victories in 13 years on the team. He also won singles titles at the 1971 U.S. Open and at Wimbledon in 1972. In doubles, he won titles at both the Australian Open and the U.S. Open. Between 1968 and 1980 this top American tennis player won 100 pro singles and doubles titles. He was elected to the Hall of Fame in 1987.

BILL TILDEN (1893–1953), nicknamed Big Bill for his fierce serve and tall, lanky build, dominated men's tennis from 1920 to 1926, with wins at the U.S. Open, Wimbledon, and in Davis Cup matches. Tilden won 138 out of 192 tournaments from 1912 to 1930. He was ranked among the world's top 10 players from 1919 to 1930, holding the No. 1 slot 6 times from 1920 to 1925. He was in the U.S. top 10 for 12 consecutive years, ranking No. 1 a total of 10 times, and was elected to the Hall of Fame in 1959.

ATP   Association of Tennis Professionals
WTA   Women's Tennis Association

THE WILLIAMS SISTERS

Venus and Serena Williams are two of the world's most talented tennis stars, and since 1999 they have taken the women's tennis circuit by storm.

Both sisters had outstanding junior careers. Venus (1980–) turned pro in 1994 and Serena (1981–) in 1997. They soon began winning major championships, in both singles and doubles play.

At the 1999 U.S. Open, in her first Grand Slam final, Serena beat the then number-one player Martina Hingis and became the first African American woman to win a Grand Slam event since Althea Gibson, in 1958. She then teamed with Venus to win the tournament's doubles championship. It was the first time in 101 years that sisters had taken the title.

The year 2000 brought more firsts. Venus won her first Grand Slam at Wimbledon, and the sisters again went on to win the doubles—the first time in history that sisters had won a doubles championship there. At the 2000 U.S. Open, Venus won the singles crown, and weeks later won the singles title at the Summer Olympics in Australia. When she and Serena took the doubles title there as well, they became the first sisters ever to

win an Olympic doubles championship. And Venus became the first woman since Helen Wills (Moody) in 1924 to win both the singles and doubles championships at the same Olympic Games.

Venus won the Wimbledon singles title again in 2001. Later that year at the U.S. Open, Venus and Serena became the first sisters in 117 years to play against each other in a Grand Slam singles final. Venus won the title for the second year in a row.

Virginia Wade of Britain and Arthur Ashe of the United States were the winners.

The British went a step further in 1968. They ended all distinctions between amateurs and professionals. All were simply players. In a short time amateur tennis declined as a major attraction. Scores of players began to win prize money they had never dreamed of. Tennis became a full-fledged professional sport.

Women generally receive less prize money than men. But women have organized themselves and pressed their demand for equal prize money. This was first achieved in 1974, when Billie Jean King and Jimmy Connors of the United States were awarded identical cash prizes as the singles champions at the U.S. Open. The U.S. Open and the Australian Open are the only Grand Slam tournaments to currently award the same amount of prize money to both men and women.

▶ TENNIS COMPETITION TODAY

An important reason for the popularity of tennis since the 1960's has been the increase in professional competition. Professionals play for pay. Amateurs may only have their expenses paid by sponsors and do not receive cash prizes. Today amateurs are mostly college and junior players.

As soon as major competitions became **open events**—entered by both amateurs and professionals—big corporations began to sponsor tournaments and offer large cash prizes. Promoters created new events, and these, with traditional events, created worldwide professional tournament circuits (tours). More than 1,000, including all the famous players, now compete throughout the year. Television coverage has also increased. New champions emerged from countries that had never before produced exceptionally strong players.

Tournaments and Champions

When open tennis began in 1968, most of the great champions were from the United States and Australia. The Australian Open and the U.S. Open, along with the French Open and Wimbledon, make up what is called the **Grand Slam** of tennis. To win a Grand Slam, a player has to win all four of the titles in a single calendar year. This has been accomplished by only five players: Don Budge (1938) and Maureen Connolly (1953) of the United States, Rod Laver (1962 and 1969) and Margaret Court (1970) of Australia, and Steffi Graf (1988) of Germany.

In the 1970's, champions began emerging from other countries. The most successful was Bjorn Borg of Sweden, who won Wimbledon five years in a row (1976–80) and the French Open a record six times. John Newcombe of Australia and Guillermo Vilas of Argentina were followed in the 1980's and early 1990's by Ivan Lendl and Martina Navratilova of Czechoslovakia (now both U.S. citizens), Boris Becker and Steffi Graf of Germany, Stefan Edberg of Sweden, Arantxa Sanchez Vicario of Spain, and Monica Seles of Yugoslavia (now a U.S. citizen). By the end of the 1990's, Switzerland's Martina Hingis and Russia's Yevgeny Kafelnikov were among the top players in the world.

Meanwhile, Jimmy Connors, Chris Evert, and John McEnroe succeeded Arthur Ashe, Stan Smith, and Billie Jean King as top U.S. stars. They were followed in the 1990's by Jim Courier, Michael Chang, Andre Agassi, and Pete Sampras. At the close of the decade, Lindsay Davenport and newcomers Venus and Serena Williams joined Sampras and Agassi as the top American players.

The Davis Cup, the most famous trophy in men's tennis, was donated in 1899 by an American, Dwight W. Davis. Sixteen nations, called the World Group, play in the tournament each year. Other nations compete in qualifying matches to win a spot in the World Group. Until the 1970's only four countries had won the Davis Cup—Australasia (Australia and New Zealand), France, Britain, and the United States. Since then, it has been won by South Africa, Italy, Czechoslovakia, Sweden, and Germany. The United States has won the trophy a record 31 times.

The Federation Cup (Fed Cup), a women's tournament comparable to the Davis Cup,

When he won the French Open in 1999, Andre Agassi became one of only five male tennis players to win all four Grand Slam tournaments during his career. That same year, Agassi went on to win the U.S. Open for the second time.

was begun in 1963 by the International Tennis Federation. The United States has won the Fed Cup a record 16 times.

In 1988, tennis became a full Olympic sport for the first time since 1924. Tennis professionals competed in the 1988, 1992, and 1996 Summer Games.

▶ TENNIS FOR EVERYONE

According to a nationwide survey, there were about 5.6 million tennis players in the United States in 1965. By 1995 there were almost 23 million. They were attending tennis schools and camps and playing at commercial clubs and public tennis courts. A nationwide program directed at the public schools had introduced many children to the game. Newspapers, magazines, and television provided publicity for the game.

Tennis appeals to many people because it can be played and enjoyed at all levels of skill. It can be played year-round indoors or outdoors. It is a game that contributes to one's physical fitness and pleasure for a lifetime.

ALLISON DANZIG
Member, National Tennis Hall of Fame
Reviewed and updated by RHONDA K. MILLER
Staff Reporter, *Tennis* magazine

Alfred Tennyson was one of the most influential poets of his day. He was appointed England's poet laureate and was made a baron by Queen Victoria. His poems, including *In Memoriam* and *Idylls of the King*, continue to be admired today.

TENNYSON ALFRED, LORD (1809–1892)

Alfred Tennyson, one of England's greatest poets, was born in Somersby, a village in northern Lincolnshire, on August 6, 1809. He was the fourth of twelve children of the rector of Somersby.

When Alfred was 7, he went to live with his grandmother at Louth and attended the grammar school there. The masters and the older boys bullied him cruelly. He was miserably unhappy and often just sat in a corner, reading a book. When he was 11, he returned home and was taught mostly by his father. He read widely from his father's library and began to write verses, plays, and ballads.

In 1827, Alfred published a volume of poems with his brothers Frederick and Charles. The next year Alfred entered Trinity College, Cambridge University. There he met Arthur Henry Hallam, the son of a well-known historian, who became his closest friend. Hallam encouraged Tennyson to write and to enter into university society. Both joined ''The Apostles,'' a literary club, and Tennyson's poetry was highly praised by other club members.

Tennyson won a prize, the Chancellor's Medal, for his poem *Timbuctoo* in 1829. He published *Poems, Chiefly Lyrical* the following year. In 1831 his father died, and Tennyson left Cambridge before obtaining a degree and returned home to Somersby. The next few years were difficult for Tennyson. He was distressed by harsh reviews of his next book, *Poems*, published in 1833. But the sudden death of his friend Hallam later the same year was an even greater blow. Although Tennyson continued to write, he published nothing for almost ten years.

Poems, Two Volumes (1842) proved a great success and established Tennyson as the foremost poet of the Victorian age. His status was confirmed in 1850 with the publication of *In Memorium*, his great elegy to Arthur Hallam, which he had begun in 1833, and with his appointment as England's poet laureate. The year 1850 was important for Tennyson for another reason: his marriage to Emily Sellwood, whom he had loved for many years.

Tennyson's later years were happy and productive. He and his wife had two sons. The family lived on the Isle of Wight and in a second home built in 1868 in Aldworth, Surrey. Tennyson wrote, received many distinguished visitors, and traveled. As poet laureate, he wrote many patriotic poems, the most famous of which is *The Charge of the Light Brigade* (1854). But his greatest work of this period is *Idylls of the King* (1859–85), a series of poems about King Arthur and the Round Table. Among Tennyson's admirers was Queen Victoria, who made him a baron in 1884. He died on October 6, 1892, and was buried in Poets' Corner in Westminster Abbey.

Reviewed by JEROME H. BUCKLEY
Author, *Tennyson: The Growth of a Poet*

Examples of Tennyson's poetry follow.

Crossing the Bar

Sunset and evening star,
　And one clear call for me!
And may there be no moaning of the bar,
　When I put out to sea,

But such a tide as moving seems asleep,
　Too full for sound and foam,
When that which drew from out the boundless deep
　Turns again home.

Twilight and evening bell,
　And after that the dark!
And may there be no sadness of farewell,
　When I embark;

For though from out our bourne of Time and Place
　The flood may bear me far,
I hope to see my Pilot face to face
　When I have crost the bar.

From *The Lady of Shalott*

On either side the river lie
Long fields of barley and of rye,
That clothe the wold and meet the sky;
And through the field the road runs by
    To many-towered Camelot;
And up and down the people go,
Gazing where the lilies blow
Round an island there below,
    The island of Shalott.

Willows whiten, aspens quiver,
Little breezes dusk and shiver
Through the wave that runs for ever
By the island in the river
    Flowing down to Camelot.
Four gray walls, and four gray towers,
Overlook a space of flowers,
And the silent isle imbowers
    The Lady of Shalott.
     •   •   •

There she weaves by night and day
A magic web with colours gay.
She has heard a whisper say,
A curse is on her if she stay
    To look down to Camelot.
She knows not what the curse may be,
And so she weaveth steadily,
And little other care hath she,
    The Lady of Shalott.
     •   •   •

A bow-shot from her bower-eaves,
He rode between the barley-sheaves,
The sun came dazzling through the leaves,
And flamed upon the brazen greaves
    Of bold Sir Lancelot.
A red-cross knight for ever kneeled
To a lady in his shield,
That sparkled on the yellow field,
    Beside remote Shalott.
     •   •   •

She left the web, she left the loom,
She made three paces through the room,
She saw the water-lily bloom,
She saw the helmet and the plume,
    She looked down to Camelot.
Out flew the web and floated wide;
The mirror cracked from side to side;
'The curse is come upon me,' cried
    The Lady of Shalott.

In the stormy east-wind straining,
The pale yellow woods were waning,
The broad stream in his banks complaining,
Heavily the low sky raining
    Over towered Camelot;
Down she came and found a boat
Beneath a willow left afloat,
And round about the prow she wrote
    The Lady of Shalott.

And down the river's dim expanse
Like some bold seër in a trance,
Seeing all his own mischance—
With a glassy countenance
    Did she look to Camelot.
And at the closing of the day
She loosed the chain, and down she lay;
The broad stream bore her far away,
    The Lady of Shalott.

Lying, robed in snowy white
That loosely flew to left and right—
The leaves upon her falling light—
Through the noises of the night
    She floated down to Camelot:
And as the boat-head wound along
The willowy hills and fields among,
They heard her singing her last song,
    The Lady of Shalott.
     •   •   •

TERMITES. See HOUSEHOLD PESTS.

TERRARIUMS

A terrarium is a container made of clear glass or plastic that houses a group of small plants (and occasionally small animals such as snails) belonging to the same natural environment. When properly set up, a terrarium requires very little care and will provide years of enjoyment.

▶ MAKING A TERRARIUM

Just about any kind of natural environment can be re-created in a terrarium. Before setting up your terrarium, you must decide which kind you want, because the plants or animals that live in each kind of environment have their own special requirements. This article will discuss creating a terrarium for common houseplants.

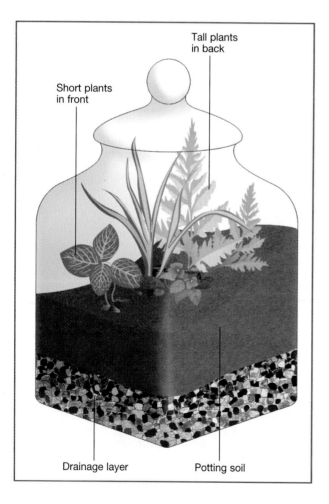

Tall plants in back

Short plants in front

Drainage layer

Potting soil

The container you use will determine the number and sizes of the plants you have. It could be a small jar or a large fish tank. It can have straight or rounded sides.

After thoroughly cleaning the container, cover the bottom with a layer of drainage material. A drainage layer provides a place for excess water to accumulate. It is made of gravel or sand mixed with small pieces of broken flower pot and pieces of charcoal to help eliminate odors. Make the drainage layer about 1 inch (2.5 centimeters) thick. Cover this with a layer of potting soil that is at least 2 inches (5 centimeters) thick.

The best place to get the plants for your terrarium is at a florist or nursery. The people who work there will be happy to help you pick out plants that belong in the same kind of environment and will not outgrow your terrarium. Among the small houseplants that work well in terrariums are begonias, ferns, African violets, and ivy.

Plant your terrarium soon after you get your plants. Form the potting soil into hills and valleys, and arrange small rocks or pieces of bark on the surface. Set your plants lightly where you think they should go. Larger plants should be put in the back of the terrarium so they do not block your view of the smaller plants. The more natural the arrangement of plants, the more attractive your terrarium will be.

Once you are satisfied with the arrangement, make holes for the plants, insert them carefully, and press the soil firmly around them. Spray your new garden well with water, but do not make it soggy. Cover the terrarium with a piece of glass. When the temperature in the terrarium rises, the water will evaporate, and when the temperature goes down, the water will condense on the glass and run down into the soil. If the glass becomes too cloudy, remove the cover for a while to let some of the water evaporate. If very little or no water collects on the glass and the plants look dry, spray them lightly with water. You will probably not need to do this more than once a month, because the plants in the terrarium make their own climate and set up an effective water cycle. Place the terrarium in a cool place with good light, but not in direct sunshine.

ESTHER MARCUS
Board of Education, City of New York

In the 1840's a westward movement began, inspiring thousands of pioneers to migrate toward the Pacific. The term "Manifest Destiny" was invented, which implied it was God's will to settle the entire continent. Later the term was used to justify expansion overseas.

TERRITORIAL EXPANSION OF THE UNITED STATES

The United States has changed greatly since it declared itself an independent nation in 1776. In little more than 200 years it has grown more rapidly than any other nation in history. What started out as 13 British colonies scattered along the Atlantic coast has developed into a country that stretches across the North American continent, from the Atlantic to the Pacific Ocean and beyond. Americans have come to believe that it was their "manifest destiny" (their right and duty) to expand westward and settle new frontiers.

▶ WESTWARD EXPANSION TO THE PACIFIC

Before the Revolutionary War began in 1775, some of the 13 colonies, such as Rhode Island, New Jersey, and Maryland, had very definite borders. The borders were established in charters granted by the king or queen of England. But some of the other colonies had vague boundaries. Some charters granted land that spread "from sea to sea." These had been written long before anyone knew how much land there was between North America's coastal seas. Nobody had yet explored the interior of the continent.

Some charters even seemed to give the same land to more than one colony. Virginia, Massachusetts, and Connecticut all claimed land that is now part of Ohio and other midwestern states. New York, on the basis of its treaties with Indian tribes, also claimed land in Ohio. Georgia and the Carolinas claimed land that stretched far to the west of their original settlements and their modern borders.

As a result, several colonies argued with each other over their conflicting claims. Many colonies were also ready to argue with King George III when, in 1763, he closed off much of this western land to settlement. By order of the King, settlers were forbidden to move across the Appalachian Mountains. This made the colonists resentful of British rule. Thus the argument about colonial land grants helped to bring on the Revolutionary War.

The Revolutionary Settlement

After the Revolutionary War the United States appeared for the first time on the map of the world. It was a large country from the start. Although there were only 13 colonies involved in the Revolution, these colonies took up a land area now occupied by 25 states.

Drawing the new country's boundaries was one of the main tasks of the peace conference that ended the war. This conference was held in Paris in 1783. The American and British statesmen who met at the conference drew the boundaries very well, considering the fact that they based their treaty on bad maps and poor information. They set the western boundary of the United States at the Mississippi River. The northern boundary ran through the Great Lakes, along the St. Lawrence River, and across the top of New York, Vermont, and New Hampshire. This boundary is almost unchanged today. On the south, the United States was bounded by the northern border of Spain's Florida colony.

These boundaries seemed reasonable to the statesmen. However, one secret agreement and two problem areas led very quickly to a great deal of trouble. The secret agreement concerned the border between the United States and Spanish Florida; the two problem areas were the northern and eastern borders separating the United States and Canada.

Establishing a Border with Spanish Florida

At the time of the peace treaty between Britain and the United States, Spain and Britain were at war. The secret part of the peace treaty was an agreement that if Florida was still in Spanish hands when that war ended, Britain would recognize the line of 31° north latitude as the Florida–United States border. But if Britain won control of the Florida colony, the United States would agree to a border farther north.

The war between Britain and Spain ended with Florida in Spanish hands. Then the secret agreement between the United States and Britain caused trouble between the United States and Spain. Naturally, Spain did not like a settlement that cut down the size of its Florida colony. However, there were few Spaniards in the area, and many Carolinians and Georgians. Thus the Spanish were not able to hold onto their claim very long. In 1795 a treaty between the United States and Spain recognized the American claim to the disputed part of Florida, which included southern portions of modern-day Alabama and Mississippi.

The Northwest Angle

One of the two problem areas that emerged following the 1783 peace conference was where the northwestern border between British Canada and the United States had been established. The statesmen who wrote the peace treaty used a map drawn in 1755. The map showed the Mississippi River starting well north of the Canadian border. Therefore the statesmen agreed that the border would extend from the Lake of the Woods to the Mississippi River by a line drawn due west of the lake. They believed the river ran that far north. In fact, they were so sure of this that they gave the British and Americans equal rights to use the Mississippi River. When it was later discovered that the Mississippi rises in what is now northern Minnesota, not in Canada, the border question had to be resettled.

The Canadians and British were dismayed when they found that the Mississippi River could not be reached from Canada. The countries could not agree on a solution until 1818. Then they drew the boundary as it now appears, near the Lake of the Woods: a line due south from a northwestern corner of the lake to the line of 49° north latitude.

At that time the 49° line was decided on as the border. As a result, a small part of modern Minnesota (about 130 square miles, or 335 square kilometers) is cut off from the rest of the United States by a bay of the Lake of the Woods. This section is called the Northwest Angle. As in the Florida dispute, serious trouble was avoided by a treaty, but only after a long argument.

The Maine Boundary

The other area that posed a problem following the 1783 peace conference was in Maine at the eastern end of the boundary with Canada. The peacemakers in Paris had agreed that the border should run up the St. Croix River to its source. From the source the boundary would go along the divide to the northwestern headwaters of the Connecticut River. (This divide separates the streams that flow into the St. Lawrence River from those that flow into the Atlantic Ocean directly.) The problem arose from the fact that the St. Croix River has branches that were not shown on the map used in Paris. As a result, there soon were arguments about where this border between the United States and Canada should be established. The statesmen went back to their maps. In 1798 they finally agreed on where the St. Croix River really ran.

When Maine became a state in 1820, the border was still in question. Peace was threatened, as Maine sent its police and settlers into the disputed area. The dispute grew so serious that American and Canadian soldiers marched to the border in 1839, ready to fight. However, war was prevented, and an agreement was reached in 1842 as part of the Webster-Ashburton Treaty. This treaty finally solved the problem written into the first peace treaty, signed 59 years earlier.

The Louisiana Purchase

When the Revolutionary War ended, many Americans moved across the Appalachians into previously unsettled lands. As they moved farther west, trading goods with people in the east became difficult. There were no railroads. It was almost impossible to carry goods over the few trails and paths that crossed the mountains.

However, the rivers were fine highways. Barges or boats could be built from trees growing along the riverbanks. Most midwestern rivers flowed into the Mississippi River, which led to the Gulf of Mexico and the markets of the world. The Mississippi River, therefore, was an important trade route. However, the mouth of the river was controlled by Spain.

The same treaty that settled the Florida border gave Americans the right to deposit goods at Spanish-held New Orleans without paying special taxes, if the goods were not sold in Spanish territories. This right of deposit was very valuable. It meant that Americans could move westward and use the great river system as a cheap and dependable route to market.

In 1800, however, Spain made an agreement giving to France the mouth of the great river, including New Orleans and all of the Louisiana Territory. The Americans feared that Napoleon, the French ruler, might cut off their right of deposit at New Orleans. President Thomas Jefferson decided to try to buy a port on the Gulf of Mexico from France. Such a port would be a permanent deposit point for Americans.

The American diplomat James Monroe was sent to Paris to help Robert Livingston, the United States minister to France, solve the New Orleans problem. They were surprised to find that Napoleon was anxious to sell all of the Louisiana Territory, not just part of it. Napoleon was planning a war with Britain. He thought it would be wiser to sell Louisiana

In 1803, American troops raised the flag over New Orleans after the United States purchased the Louisiana Territory from France for $15,000,000. The Louisiana Purchase doubled the size of the United States.

than to risk losing it and his fleet in battle with the British in American waters.

The American agents had no official orders to buy the Louisiana Territory. But they signed the agreement anyway, purchasing all French claims to the territory for $15,000,000. Today that seems a small price for land that included large parts of 13 modern states. Fifteen million dollars was more money than the United States Government had ever raised in taxes in any one year. After some worry about the purchase, President Jefferson agreed to the treaty. In one stroke the territory owned by the United States doubled in size; its boundary problems, however, doubled as well.

Boundary Problems

Nobody knew how far north the Louisiana Territory extended. In the past, French explorers had gone very far north indeed. Canada, owned by Britain, also laid claim to the territory explored by the French.

After the War of 1812, British and American diplomats agreed on the northern boundary during the Convention of 1818. This

TERRITORIAL GROWTH OF THE UNITED

CANADA

TREATY LINE OF 1846 49°N

49°N TREATY LINE OF 1818

Northwest Angle

Lake of the Woods

L. Superior

CEDED BY GREAT BRITAIN 1818

OREGON TERRITORY

AMERICAN TITLE ESTABLISHED 1846

ROCKY

CONTINENTAL DIVIDE

ADAMS-ONÍS TREATY LINE OF 1819

42°N

LOUISIANA PURCHASE FROM FRANCE 1803

L. Michigan

MEXICAN CESSION ACQUIRED FROM MEXICO BY TREATY 1848

MTS.

ADAMS-ONÍS TREATY

LINE OF 1819

BOUNDARY OF 1803

RED RIVER

MISSISSIPPI RIVER

GILA RIVER

GADSDEN PURCHASE FROM MEXICO 1853

RIO GRANDE

TEXAS

ANNEXED 1845

CEDED B

TH

NUECES RIVER

31°N

New Orle

PACIFIC OCEAN

MEXICO

GULF O

MEXIC

| | 0 | | 250 |
| 0 | 250 | | 500 K |

ALASKA	HAWAII	PUERTO RICO	VIRGIN ISLANDS
BOUGHT FROM RUSSIA 1867	ANNEXED 1898	CEDED BY SPAIN 1898	BOUGHT FROM DENMARK 1917

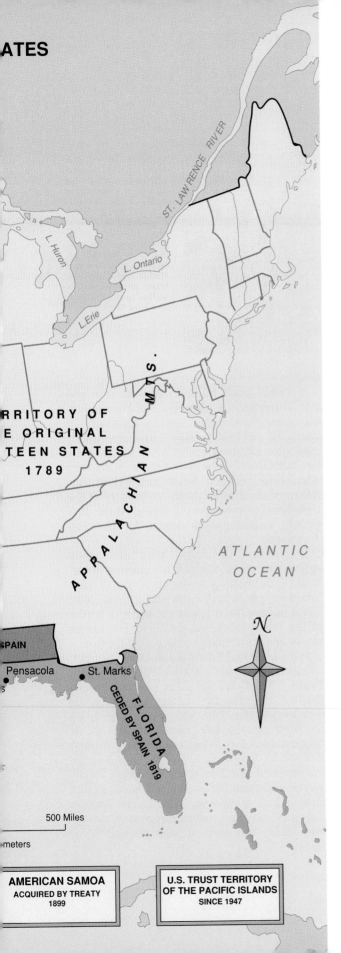

ST. LAWRENCE RIVER

L. Huron

L. Ontario

L. Erie

RRITORY OF
E ORIGINAL
TEEN STATES
1789

APPALACHIAN MTS.

ATLANTIC
OCEAN

SPAIN

Pensacola   St. Marks

FLORIDA
CEDED BY SPAIN 1819

N

500 Miles

meters

AMERICAN SAMOA
ACQUIRED BY TREATY
1899

U.S. TRUST TERRITORY
OF THE PACIFIC ISLANDS
SINCE 1947

convention also created the Northwest Angle. It set 49° north latitude as the border between the Louisiana Territory and Canada, west to the Rocky Mountains. Beyond the Rockies the land then called Oregon would be open to both Americans and British. This meant that neither nation owned Oregon completely. People from both Canada and the United States could settle in the vast reaches of that unknown land.

When the United States bought the Louisiana Territory, it inherited a source of trouble with the Spaniards, who controlled Texas and Mexico. The Spaniards also held West Florida, the territory along the Gulf of Mexico near the Mississippi River. Americans felt this was really part of Louisiana. Few Spaniards lived there. So Americans simply moved south along the streams from the Louisiana Territory and took over West Florida between 1803 and 1818. This area includes the southernmost parts of modern Alabama and Mississippi that border on the Gulf of Mexico.

Florida and Texas

The boundary between the United States and Spanish territory was an old problem. Any Americans found in Florida's border area were open to arrest and were often attacked by Indians friendly to Spain. After the War of 1812, Florida Indian tribes raided American settlements in Georgia, Alabama, and Mississippi.

In 1818, General Andrew Jackson chased a war party of Seminole Indians back into the Spanish colony. He also captured the Spanish towns of St. Mark's and Pensacola. This invasion in time of peace could have led to open war. Instead it led to a solution of the border problem, by encouraging the two governments to make a treaty. The treaty is called the Adams-Onís Treaty, after its authors, John Quincy Adams and the Spanish minister Luis de Onís. It helped to settle the map of the United States across the whole continent. Under its terms the United States gained all of Florida. Although Florida was well known, it was not thought to be valuable. Except for a few forts and trading posts the peninsula was mostly Indian country. It was held by fierce tribes and did not look like a good place for settlement.

When Spain gave up Florida, the United States in return accepted Spain's claim on the Texas-Louisiana border. An irregular line was

In 1847 during the Mexican War, General Winfield Scott's troops landed at Veracruz on their way to occupation of Mexico City. The treaty of Guadelupe Hidalgo (1848), which ended the war, ceded to the United States the territory that is now California, Utah, and Nevada, as well as most of Arizona and New Mexico.

drawn through the open ranges of Texas, Oklahoma, and Colorado and through part of Kansas, separating the United States from Mexico. Westward to the Pacific Ocean, the northern limit of Spanish Mexico was set at 42° north latitude. This meant that the United States took over all of Spain's claim to the Oregon Territory. Spain was credited with $5,000,000 to seal the bargain. The United States agreed to use the money to pay Americans for debts owed them by the Spanish Government.

Texas Joins the Union

Soon after the Adams-Onís Treaty, Spain's empire in America began to fall apart. Mexico became an independent republic, and Texas was part of it. In the 1820's, 300 American families settled in Texas as part of an agreement between Stephen Austin and the Mexican Government. By 1835 the Texas population had grown to about 50,000. Many of the Texas settlers became dissatisfied with Mexican rule and rebelled. In 1836, after a short, bitter war, Texans under General Sam Houston won their freedom and declared Texas an independent nation called the Lone Star Republic. Later that year, Texans voted to be annexed to the United States, but the U.S. Congress delayed its approval due to controversy over slavery in Texas and other western territories. Texas was finally admitted to the Union as the 28th state in 1845.

Oregon

By 1845 small numbers of American and British trappers and farmers had been jointly occupying the Oregon Territory for nearly 30 years. In the 1840's more and more Americans traveled the Oregon Trail to Oregon's fine farmlands. At the end of the trail, disputes often arose between Americans and British. Britain wanted to establish a boundary at the Columbia River but finally settled on the 49th parallel because the fur yield to the south had diminished.

By 1844, Americans were sufficiently aroused to make Oregon an election issue. James Polk, running under the slogan "Fifty-four forty or fight," was elected president. North latitude 54° 40′ was the northern border of the jointly occupied territory. The slogan meant that Americans wanted all of Oregon.

But the United States did not have to fight, though war threatened after Polk's election. Nor did Americans get all of Oregon. Instead the two countries, by an 1846 agreement, divided the region. The United States accepted the 49th parallel (49° north latitude) as its northern boundary. This was the same parallel that the 1818 agreement had set as the northern limit of the Louisiana Territory. At its westernmost end the line jogged south, so that Britain kept Vancouver Island. The Oregon Territory took in modern Oregon, Washington, Idaho, and parts of Montana and Wyoming.

Mexican Cession

While the Oregon question was settled peacefully, another border dispute, this time with Mexico, erupted into war in 1846. When Texas joined the Union, the United States took over Texan claims to western and southern borderlands where the boundary line with Mexico was still unsettled. Soon fighting broke out in the disputed area between the Rio Grande and the Nueces River.

During the Mexican War (1846–48) drastic changes were made in the map of North America. American settlers led a revolt in the Mexican province of California—the Bear Flag Revolt. It resulted in the capture of California for the United States. By 1848, Mexico was defeated and American troops occupied huge stretches of Mexican territory.

The war officially ended with the Treaty of Guadalupe Hidalgo (1848). By this treaty, Mexico ceded to the United States all of modern California, Utah, and Nevada and most of present-day Arizona and New Mexico. In return the United States paid Mexico $15,000,000.

In 1844, at the beginning of President Polk's administration, the United States covered 1,788,000 square miles (4,631,000 square kilometers). By 1848, with the acquisition (gain) of Texas, Oregon, and the Mexican Cession, the United States covered nearly 3,000,000 square miles (7,770,000 square kilometers), increasing the size of the country by about 67 percent.

Gadsden Purchase

The war with Mexico had just ended when gold was discovered in California. The Gold Rush of 1849 brought thousands of Americans to the region. One of the overland routes ran through Mexican territory. To avoid further warfare and to prepare for the building of a railroad in the future, President Franklin Pierce sent his minister to Mexico, James Gadsden, to buy the land along the route to California. According to the treaty Gadsden arranged in 1853, the United States bought 45,535 square miles (120,000 square kilometers) of unsettled land along the southern border of New Mexico and Arizona. The price was $10,000,000—a large sum, considering that the United States paid $15,000,000 for the vast Louisiana Territory and $15,000,000 for the Mexican Cession.

ALASKA

BOUGHT FROM RUSSIA 1867

0   500 Miles

0   500 Kilometers

Alaska

By 1848 the United States, stretching "from sea to shining sea," spread to nearly its present shape on the map. But all of the added territory bordered on land that was already largely in American hands. The United States had no territories separated from the nation by other countries or by oceans. It already had more living space than its people needed at the time.

The first change in this pattern came in 1867, when the United States bought Alaska from Russia for $7,200,000. A little larger than all of the territory ceded from Mexico, Alaska was mostly unexplored and unsettled. Americans thought of it as a huge frozen wasteland. Many criticized Secretary of State William Seward, who arranged the purchase. They called Alaska "Seward's Folly" and "Seward's Icebox."

For years Alaska drew little attention. It was administered in turn by the Departments of War, Treasury, and Navy. In 1884 it became a separate civil district with its own officials.

Then, in 1896, gold was discovered in the Klondike Valley of Alaska. Other gold strikes later were made at Nome (1899) and Fairbanks (1903). The Alaskan gold rush drew many adventurers. Americans grew excited about Alaska, and businessmen and farmers

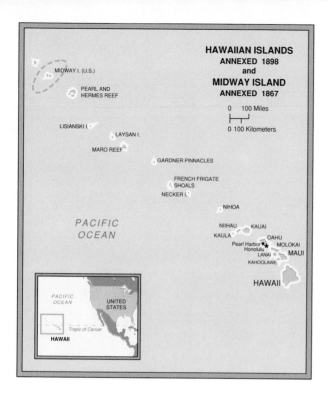

HAWAIIAN ISLANDS
ANNEXED 1898
and
MIDWAY ISLAND
ANNEXED 1867

0   100 Miles

0 100 Kilometers

PACIFIC OCEAN

followed the gold seekers. People saw that Alaska was a 20th-century frontier, rich in natural resources and opportunities.

In 1912, Alaska became an official territory instead of a civil district. As its population grew, Alaskans began demanding statehood. In 1959, Alaska became the 49th state. One fifth the size of the rest of the nation, it is the largest state of the Union, twice as big as Texas. ''Seward's Icebox'' was a better bargain than anyone had guessed in 1867.

▶EXPANSION OVERSEAS

Although Seward's opponents had not been able to stop him from buying Alaska, they did block his efforts to acquire Hawaii and other islands. Throughout the 19th century whaling ships and merchantmen sailed the Pacific, stopping for trade and supplies at islands. Americans settled on some islands, such as Hawaii. They sometimes moved to little islands that did not seem to belong to anyone. For example, they occupied Midway Island in 1867. But they generally regarded islands as good places for ships to take on water and fuel, rather than as possessions.

In the late 19th century many European nations were claiming colonies and building empires. Industrial nations desired colonies as markets for manufactured goods and sources of raw materials. The United States was slow to join the race for colonies. It did not claim lands beyond North America until the 1890's. Then, nearly 30 years after Seward bought Alaska, other Americans began to revive his dream of expansion in the Pacific and the Caribbean.

Hawaii

Overseas expansion began with a revolt in Hawaii in 1893. As early as the 1840's, American merchants, sugar planters, and missionaries had settled in the Hawaiian Islands, which were under native rule. In 1893 a few American settlers who had become rich and powerful supported a successful revolt against Hawaii's Queen Liliuokalani. The queen lost her throne, and the Republic of Hawaii was established in 1894. An American, Sanford Dole, became its first president.

When William McKinley was elected president of the United States in 1896, public sentiment in favor of annexing Hawaii (making it part of United States territory) was growing. But many other Americans claimed the United States had no right to take over foreign lands. On July 7, 1898, however, after a heated debate, Congress voted to annex Hawaii.

On June 14, 1900, Hawaii became a United States territory, and Hawaiians became American citizens. Sanford Dole served as its first governor. Hawaii prospered and in 1959 became the 50th state of the Union.

War with Spain Brings New Additions

The Spanish-American War of 1898 rose out of conflicts in the Caribbean and left the United States with an overseas empire. Cuba, a Caribbean island that was owned by Spain, had been torn by uprisings for years. Individual Americans had been involved on both sides of Cuba's revolts. The United States carried on a sizable trade with Cuba, and Americans had sugar plantations on the island. Therefore certain American businessmen wanted a stable government, such as Spain's, to protect their investments. Other Americans, however, favored a *Cuba libre* (''free Cuba'') —free from Spanish rule.

On February 15, 1898, the United States battleship *Maine* was blown up in Havana Harbor. Although no one knew what caused the explosion, Spain was blamed. With the war cry ''Remember the Maine!'' the United

The sinking of the *Maine* in 1898 sparked the Spanish-American War. At the end of the war Spain ceded the Philippines, Guam, and Puerto Rico to the United States.

States went to war against Spain. American forces took Cuba and occupied Puerto Rico, another Spanish island in the Caribbean. Meanwhile in the Pacific Ocean, in the Spanish-owned Philippines, Admiral George Dewey captured Manila, the capital city. When the war ended that summer, the American flag flew in several remote parts of the world. By the terms of the peace treaty the United States paid the government of Spain $20,000,000. In return Spain gave up control of Cuba and ceded the Philippines, Guam, and Puerto Rico to the United States. After four years of American military rule, Cuba became a republic. But the United States kept the right to intervene in Cuba to protect U.S. citizens and their property until 1934. The United States also obtained exclusive use of a naval base at Guantánamo Bay for 99 years.

The Philippines

In 1898 the United States claimed the right to rule the Philippines as the successor to Spain. But the Philippines had declared its independence. Winning the islands from the Filipinos proved much harder than winning them from Spain. About 60,000 American troops fought the Filipino forces for more than three years. The islands finally came under American control in 1902.

Many Americans were shocked by their country's role in the Philippines. The United States Government took the view that the

Filipinos should be independent eventually but were not yet ready to govern themselves. The United States sent teachers, lawyers, doctors, and judges to train the Filipinos in democratic self-government. In 1916 the Philippines was promised independence. Congress passed a law in 1934 providing for complete independence in twelve years.

In 1941, Japan invaded the Philippines. Filipinos and Americans fought side by side during World War II to free the islands from the Japanese. The Philippines became fully independent on July 4, 1946.

Puerto Rico

The development of Puerto Rico, also taken from Spain in 1898, was quite different. In 1900, Puerto Rico became an unorganized territory. The United States appointed a governor and council (upper house of lawmakers), while Puerto Ricans elected their lower house. Puerto Rico became an organized territory in 1917, with Puerto Ricans gaining full American citizenship. They also began electing both houses of their legislature.

Some Puerto Ricans have wanted statehood. Other groups have called for complete independence. Today the island is a self-governing commonwealth of the United States. Because their island is small and overcrowded, Puerto Ricans have had a hard time

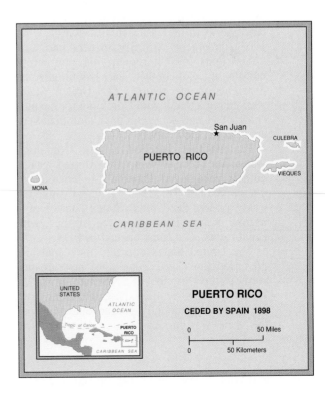

ATLANTIC OCEAN

San Juan

CULEBRA

PUERTO RICO

VIEQUES

MONA

CARIBBEAN SEA

UNITED STATES

ATLANTIC OCEAN

Tropic of Cancer

PUERTO RICO

CARIBBEAN SEA

PUERTO RICO

CEDED BY SPAIN 1898

0   50 Miles

0   50 Kilometers

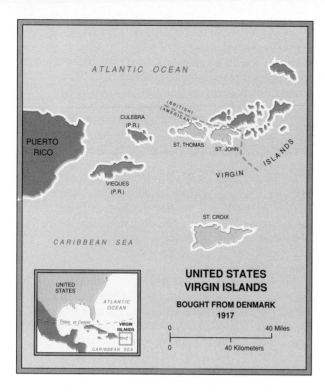

ATLANTIC OCEAN

CULEBRA
(P.R.)

(BRITISH)
(AMERICAN)

PUERTO
RICO

ST. THOMAS

ST. JOHN

VIRGIN

ISLANDS

VIEQUES
(P.R.)

ST. CROIX

CARIBBEAN SEA

**UNITED STATES
VIRGIN ISLANDS**

**BOUGHT FROM DENMARK
1917**

UNITED
STATES

ATLANTIC
OCEAN

Tropic of Cancer

VIRGIN
ISLANDS

CARIBBEAN SEA

0   40 Miles

0   40 Kilometers

improving its economy, even with American help. Because they are American citizens, they can emigrate freely to the United States.

The Panama Canal

Since the 1850's the United States had wanted to build a canal across the Isthmus of Panama, which was then part of Colombia. Such a canal would greatly cut the sailing distance between the east and west coasts. Until 1901, agreements with Britain, who had territorial rights in that region, did not permit building a canal. In that year, Britain gave up its rights in the region. The United States worked out a treaty with Colombia for the purchase of a canal zone. But the Colombian Senate rejected the treaty in 1903.

Panama then rebelled against Colombia. When the rebels won, the United States quickly recognized Panama's independence. On November 18, 1903, Panama signed a treaty giving the United States control of a narrow strip of land across the isthmus, with canal rights. The canal opened in 1914.

The United States operated the canal and governed the Canal Zone until new treaties were ratified by the U.S. Senate in 1978. Under the new treaties, the Canal Zone government was gradually phased out. Much of the zone was turned over to Panama. The

canal is now operated jointly by the United States and Panama. But the canal and any remaining parts of the zone will come under Panamanian control by the year 2000.

U.S. Island Possessions and Territories

Except for the U.S. Virgin Islands, island possessions and territories of the United States are controlled by various agencies of the federal government. These possessions and territories do not hold equal status with the states, nor are they represented in Congress.

The U.S. Virgin Islands. In 1917 the United States bought from Denmark a group of about 65 small islands in the Caribbean. The U.S. Virgin Islands, tiny as they are, cost the United States $25,000,000. This amount was $10,000,000 more than the cost of the Louisiana Territory. Virgin Islanders are American citizens. They elect their own governor and members of a territorial legislature.

American Samoa. In the late 1800's, steamships on long voyages across the Pacific Ocean often needed to stop for refueling. Because the steamships burned coal, the island ports where they stopped were called coaling stations.

In 1878 a treaty with chiefs of the Samoan islands gave the United States a naval station at the port of Pago Pago. During the 1880's, Germany and Britain also had coaling stations in Samoa. All three countries controlled the islands until 1899, when they signed a treaty that divided the islands between Germany and the United States. Britain gave up its claims in return for rights in the Pacific and West Africa. The United States kept the eastern islands, which are now known as American Samoa.

American Samoa is an unincorporated territory of the United States and is administered by the Department of the Interior. American Samoans are nationals, but not citizens, of the United States. Since 1977 they have elected their own governors.

Islands Claimed by the Guano Act. In 1856 the United States Congress passed the Guano Act. This act provided a way for the United States to claim sovereignty (possession) over unoccupied and unclaimed islands containing large deposits of guano (natural fertilizer). The island of Navassa in the Caribbean, which is administered by the U.S. Coast Guard, and Baker, Howland, and Jarvis islands in the Pa-

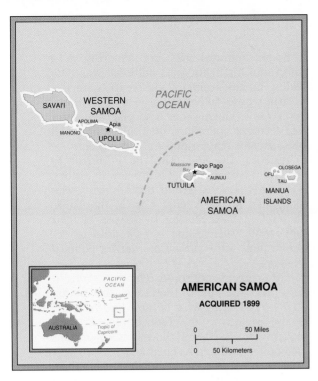

WESTERN SAMOA

SAVAI'I
APOLIMA
MANONO
UPOLU
APIA
Apia

PACIFIC OCEAN

Massacre Bay
TUTUILA
Pago Pago
AUNUU

OFU
TAU
OLOSEGA
MANUA ISLANDS

AMERICAN SAMOA

PACIFIC OCEAN
Equator
AUSTRALIA
Tropic of Capricorn

AMERICAN SAMOA

ACQUIRED 1899

0   50 Miles
0   50 Kilometers

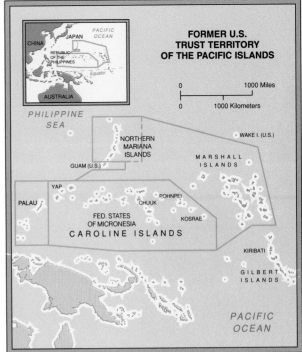

CHINA
JAPAN
REPUBLIC OF THE PHILIPPINES
AUSTRALIA
PACIFIC OCEAN
Equator

FORMER U.S. TRUST TERRITORY OF THE PACIFIC ISLANDS

0   1000 Miles
0   1000 Kilometers

PHILIPPINE SEA

NORTHERN MARIANA ISLANDS

GUAM (U.S.)

WAKE I. (U.S.)

MARSHALL ISLANDS

PALAU

YAP

POHNPEI
CHUUK
KOSRAE

FED. STATES OF MICRONESIA

CAROLINE ISLANDS

KIRIBATI

GILBERT ISLANDS

PACIFIC OCEAN

cific, which are administered by the Department of the Interior, are among the U.S. island territories claimed under the Guano Act.

Wake and Midway Islands. Wake Island in the Pacific was seized from Spain by the United States in 1898. In 1941 an air base was built there. The island has been administered by the U.S. Air Force since 1972. Midway Island, also in the Pacific, was annexed by the United States in 1867. As a naval base during World War II, it was vital to U.S. defense in the Pacific. Today Midway is administered by the U.S. Navy.

Guam. The island of Guam serves as an important American air and naval base in the Pacific. It was ceded to the United States from Spain in 1898 following the Spanish-American War. Guam was declared a territory in 1950, and its people became American citizens. The people elect their own governor and one-house legislature. The island is administered by the U.S. Department of the Interior.

Trust Territory of the Pacific Islands

The Trust Territory of the Pacific Islands was a United Nations Trusteeship administered by the United States. It included the Caroline Islands, the Mariana Islands (excluding Guam), and the Marshall Islands. These island groups were once claimed by Spain. However, all of the islands became German possessions in the late 1800's. After World War I (1918), Japan administered the islands (excluding Guam) under a League of Nations mandate.

The United Nations took title to the islands after World War II (1945). The United States administered them as a trust territory under U.N. supervision. The Trust Territory was later divided into four internally self-governing parts. Two—the Federated States of Micronesia in the Carolines and the Republic of the Marshall Islands—entered into a Compact of Free Association with the United States in 1982 (effective 1986). Under this agreement, they are self-governing, but rely on the United States for defense and financial assistance. The Northern Marianas (except for Guam, which remains a U.S. territory) became a commonwealth of the United States that same year. It has self-government, but the United States is responsible for its defense and foreign affairs. The last U.S. Pacific trust territory, the Republic of Palau, also gained its independence in free association with the United States, in 1994.

See the articles on the Marshall Islands and the Federated States of Micronesia in Volume M and the one on Palau in Volume P.

JOSEPH F. X. McCARTHY
Coauthor, *Man the Citizen*

TERRORISM

Although it has no single, generally accepted definition, terrorism can be described as the unlawful use of fear or force to achieve certain political, economic, religious, or social goals. The methods used by individual terrorists or terrorist groups include threats, bombings and other destruction of property, kidnappings, taking hostages, spreading harmful chemicals or diseases, executions, and assassinations. Terrorists, unlike other criminals, claim to be dedicated to some higher cause rather than to personal gain. But their actions typically harm innocent people.

Some countries may use terrorism as a substitute for fighting a traditional war, providing money, training, and weapons to terrorists whose activities serve their national aims. Governments may also plan and carry out terrorist operations themselves, although they usually deny responsibility for them.

Historical Overview. The use of terror to achieve a particular goal is not new in history. One early terrorist group, the Assassins, who flourished in the Middle East in the 1100's and 1200's, used murder to dispose of their opponents. Their name is now used to describe those who commit murder for political reasons.

Government-sponsored terrorism dates at least from the time of the French Revolution (1789–99). During what became known as the Reign of Terror, the French revolutionary government executed thousands of citizens whom it considered its enemies.

Acts of terrorism have also been committed by individuals or groups seeking national independence. One such act altered the course of history. The assassination in 1914 of the Archduke Francis Ferdinand, heir to the throne of Austria-Hungary, was the primary event that led to the outbreak of World War I. The assassin, Gavrilo Princip, had sought to win the independence of Bosnia (now part of Bosnia and Herzegovina) from Austrian rule.

Modern Terrorism. Terrorism became global in its extent in the late 1960's. It grew rapidly between 1970 and the late 1980's, when terrorist incidents swelled from a few hundred to several thousand a year. It has since continued to grow steadily.

Modern terrorism has retained elements of historical terrorism, although today it is more likely to affect innocent people. For example, the practice of hijacking commercial airliners and holding their passengers and crews hostage has become increasingly common. Typically, if the terrorists' demands are not met, the hostages face the threat of death.

In recent decades, some terrorists have carried out attacks seemingly for the sake of destruction alone. No demands were made prior to or following the events. Crowded commercial airliners have especially been targeted, such as Pan Am flight 103, which exploded over Lockerbie, Scotland, in 1988. Suicide bombings (also known as homicide bombings) are another growing trend. In

Opposite page: This photograph, taken in New York City on September 11, 2001, shows the World Trade Center at the moment terrorists crashed a hijacked jetliner into the South Tower (background). The North Tower (foreground) had been similarly attacked a short time earlier. Both towers soon collapsed, killing thousands trapped inside.
Right: In 2001, Israeli volunteers searched through debris following a terrorist bombing in Jerusalem.
Below: A terrorist held a gun to the head of an airline pilot after hijacking TWA flight 847 in 1985.

such cases, the terrorist dies along with his victims. Many suicide bombers think of themselves as martyrs fighting for a religious cause.

Attacks by foreign terrorists against the United States have included the bombings of the World Trade Center in New York City in 1993 and the U.S. embassies in Kenya and Tanzania in 1998. The worst calamity occurred on September 11, 2001, with the complete destruction of the World Trade Center and part of the Pentagon building outside Washington, D.C. These horrific acts were linked to Osama bin Laden, head of a radical anti-American terrorist organization known as Al Qaeda. Al Qaeda may also have been responsible for the bombings in 2002 of a nightclub in Bali, Indonesia, that killed some 200 people.

Not all terrorist attacks are made by foreigners. President Anwar el-Sadat of Egypt was killed in 1981 and Israeli prime minister Yitzhak Rabin in 1995—both by political extremists from their own countries. Also, in 1995, Timothy McVeigh, a U.S. veteran with extreme anti-government views, exploded a car bomb, destroying the Alfred P. Murrah Federal Building in Oklahoma City.

Bioterrorism. Governments have long studied the possibilities and consequences of biological, or germ, warfare. Anthrax, smallpox, and bubonic plague are among the most feared biological agents. These diseases can spread quickly, and all can be deadly if not treated promptly.

Public concerns over bioterrorism—the purposeful spreading of disease by terrorists—are on the rise. Following the attacks of September 11, unknown terrorists mailed anthrax in powdered form to selected U.S. government and media offices, causing several deaths. The mysterious and random nature of these attacks heightened the public's anxiety about bioterrorism. Many people feared the possibility of more widespread disasters, such as biological contamination of food and water supplies, though none were reported.

The Future of Terrorism. It is unlikely that terrorism will end in the near future. Many of the causes that motivate terrorists remain unresolved, such as the territorial conflict between Israelis and Palestinians in the Middle East. Furthermore, terrorist attacks have proved successful in attracting publicity and disrupting governments. And international networks have facilitated the financing and undertaking of terrorist activities.

There are no simple solutions to this age-old problem. But what is required first of all is the insistence by the international community on upholding the rule of law at all times. After the September 11 attacks in the United States, President George W. Bush formally declared war on terrorism. His first objective was to capture Osama bin Laden, the world's "most wanted" man. He also vowed to conduct war against any nation that harbored or supported known terrorists. For more information, see the article TERRORISM, WAR ON following this article.

YONAH ALEXANDER
State University of New York (Oneonta)
Author, *International Terrorism*

See also HIJACKING.

TERRORISM, WAR ON

On September 20, 2001, before a joint session of the United States Congress, President George W. Bush announced that the United States was at war against terrorism. The president's declaration came in response to the September 11 terrorist attacks on the World Trade Center in New York City and the Pentagon outside Washington, D.C., in which more than 2,700 innocent people were killed. It was soon confirmed that the Al Qaeda network, organized by the known Saudi terrorist Osama bin Laden, was responsible. The declaration of war, however, targeted every terrorist group throughout the world.

After the attacks occurred, it was discovered that Al Qaeda had members in more than 60 countries. Most of these countries were unaware of Al Qaeda's activities. But some others, such as Afghanistan, openly aided the terrorists. The Taliban, the group then ruling Afghanistan, allowed Al Qaeda members to live and work in their country and even to operate terrorist training camps. The United States declared that the war on terrorism would begin in Afghanistan and continue, if needed, against any other nation that continued to support or protect Al Qaeda and any other terrorist group.

The United States Builds an International Coalition. The first step in the war was to build a worldwide coalition of nations against terrorism. Under the leadership of U.S. secretary of state Colin Powell, nearly every nation in the world offered some form of assistance. This even included Pakistan, a nation with close ties to the Taliban. A number of nations, including Great Britain, France, Germany, Italy, Canada, Australia, and Japan, committed military forces. Many others provided financial and legal support and agreed to share information gathered by intelligence and law enforcement agencies.

Military Campaigns. The global war on terrorism began in Afghanistan on October 7, 2001, when the United States and its coalition allies launched Operation Enduring Freedom. The coalition included the Northern Alliance, an Afghan fighting force that had long opposed the

Osama bin Laden, leader of the Al Qaeda terrorist network, became the world's most wanted man after he sponsored the September 11, 2001, attacks on the United States.

Taliban. The operation's goal was to liberate Afghanistan from the rule of the Taliban and destroy the Al Qaeda terrorist network there. Fighting was heaviest in the eastern region, particularly in and around the cities of Kandahar, Mazar-e Sharif, and Kabul, the capital.

Within six weeks, the coalition forces, commanded by U.S. general Tommy Franks, defeated the Taliban, eliminated Afghanistan's terrorist training camps and facilities, and allowed for the creation of a transitional Afghan government. Further attacks, such as Operation Anaconda, helped prevent the return of the Taliban, destroy remaining Al Qaeda forces, and protect the newly installed government.

The military campaign against terrorism, however, extended far beyond Afghanistan. Within months, U.S. military personnel were sent to the Philippines, Yemen, and the Republic of Georgia to support local efforts against terrorist groups. The United States also warned that it might attack countries such as Iraq that it believed were both supporting terrorism and trying to build weapons of mass destruction.

Nonmilitary Strategies. The coalition took steps to improve the ability of law enforcement organizations to identify terrorist "cells," uncover their plots, and arrest suspects. In the United States new laws, notably the Patriot Act, were passed that allowed police and the Federal Bureau of Investigation (FBI) to pursue suspected terrorists more aggressively. Within weeks of September 11, U.S. officials had detained 500 people for questioning. Hundreds more were arrested throughout the world, and numerous terrorist plots were uncovered.

The United States government installed additional protection measures. It created a new cabinet-level department, the Department of Homeland Security. It strengthened the Coast Guard, Border Patrol, Customs Services, and other federal agencies responsible for securing America's borders. The National Guard secured airports, landmarks, and important buildings. Air Force fighters patrolled the skies over major cities. Naval forces patrolled the world's oceans. And tribunals (military courts) were authorized to prosecute foreign terrorists arrested outside the United States.

One of the most effective nonmilitary strategies was targeting the terrorists' financial resources. This involved locating and

In 2001, the Northern Alliance, an Afghan group allied with U.S. forces, used Soviet howitzers from a previous war to help fight the Taliban.

freezing the terrorists' assets (such as bank accounts) and preventing terrorists from transferring funds or raising money.

Progress. In 2003, a report on global terrorism that showed that the war, although far from being won, was achieving significant goals. In that year alone, more than 300 Al Qaeda suspects were arrested in more than 100 countries. Among them was Khalid Shaikh Mohammed, the suspected mastermind of the September 11 attacks. By 2004, some reports claimed that more than 70 percent of Al Qaeda's leaders had been captured or killed.

DANIEL GOURÉ
Vice President, The Lexington Institute

See also IRAQ WAR; TERRORISM.

TESTS AND TEST TAKING

This is an age of test taking. Students are tested throughout their school careers to measure what they have learned. Tests help determine which students will be admitted to college and which applicants will be hired for certain jobs. Lawyers, doctors, pilots, electricians, and many others must pass tests before they are allowed to work in their fields.

Tests can also help you know yourself. They can help you discover your talents, what jobs you might like to do, and how you feel about things. A combination of tests can help you choose a career.

A test score does not always reflect a person's true talents. But if you know how to use them, tests can help you demonstrate your abilities. You must understand how to prepare for tests and how to take them. You should know the various kinds of tests, what information about you each kind can give, and the best ways of taking each kind of test.

▶ KINDS OF TESTS

Achievement tests measure what you have learned about specific subjects, such as English, history, or mathematics. Tests to measure achievement in schoolwork include those created by teachers for use in their classes. Other achievement tests are developed and produced by test publishers and are intended for wide use in schools. Tests for several subjects may be given together in groups called **test batteries.** One such achievement battery is the California Test of Basic Skills (CTBS). These tests help schools plan programs and place students in them. The American College Testing Program Tests (ACT) are used by some colleges to select students for admission.

Performance tests are used to select persons for jobs that require some skill or group of skills. Typing tests and driving tests are of this kind. To pass, a person must demonstrate the skills associated with the job or task.

Mental ability tests were once called intelligence tests. Today, many factors are thought to contribute to a person's intelligence, factors that cannot be completely or accurately measured by these tests. When combined with other information, mental ability tests can be used to predict how a person is likely to perform on a school-type task. But these kinds of tests can also be misused to label students as

Tests are a necessary part of our lives, both in and out of school. Learning how to prepare for tests and how to take them can boost confidence and improve scores.

over- or underachievers. Traditionally, the results on a mental ability test have been expressed as an intelligence quotient (IQ). The IQ score is no longer recommended as a way of scoring mental ability tests. Instead, a special score called the Deviation IQ (DIQ) is often used by test publishers today.

Aptitude tests try to predict a person's ability to succeed in future study or work. They focus on a specific ability or group of abilities in such areas as art, music, mathematics, languages, law, and medicine. The Scholastic Aptitude Test (SAT), along with other information, is used by some colleges to select students for admission. The General Aptitude Test Battery (GATB) is used to help those seeking jobs to find suitable careers.

Not all tests are concerned with some form of achievement. **Interest inventories** such as the Strong Vocational Interest Blank are meant to determine a person's likes and dislikes for various activities. The profile of interests obtained from an interest inventory can be used to help a person choose a career.

Personality tests are designed to help you understand yourself: how you feel about yourself, what makes you happy or sad, and what makes you feel afraid or confident. Some tests, such as the Minnesota Multiphasic Personality Inventory (MMPI), measure a number of these aspects, while others may focus on a single attitude. Scores on **attitude scales** show how persons feel or say they feel about persons, places, or things. One can like or dislike a city or a painting or a subject in school.

On some tests, the pattern of answers is more useful than the score. **Diagnostic tests** that pinpoint specific weaknesses in mathematics or reading are of this type. The Rorschach Test, a personality test, consists of ten pictures of ink blots. Test takers are shown the pictures and asked to tell what each shape looks like to them. A trained psychologist can use the responses to help clients better understand their feelings.

▶ SCORING TESTS

To be useful, scores on tests must be reliable. This means that whenever the test is given, essentially the same results should be obtained. One way to increase the reliability of scores on a test is to "standardize" it, that is, to make sure that the testing materials, the way the test is given, and the way it is scored are the same for all who take the test.

When scoring a test, the first step is to count up the number of correct answers to obtain the **raw score.** The raw score alone may not be meaningful, however. A student having a raw score of 150 on a test did well if the best possible score is 150. But if the best possible score is 1500, the student did not do so well. The raw score must be transformed, or changed, to make it more useful in interpreting test results.

Test results may be interpreted in various ways. For example, a teacher creates a test for a particular class that is designed to measure whether students have learned the material taught in that class. A percentage score is often used as the transformed score for interpreting this kind of test. If a test has 10 questions, and a student answers 7 questions correctly, the student has a raw score of 7 and a transformed score of 70 percent.

In other kinds of tests, the transformed score shows how your performance on a test compares with that of a group of test takers. This group, called the **norm group,** is chosen as a representative sample. In these kinds of tests, known as norm-referenced tests, a com-

monly used transformed score is the **percentile rank score.** If you are ranked at the 80th percentile, this means that 79 percent of those taking the test scored lower than you did and 19 percent scored higher. A 50th percentile rank is at the middle; that is, just as many test takers scored above you as scored below you. Norm-referenced tests are designed so that few test takers can answer all the questions correctly. One way of doing this is to make the test long enough so that most cannot finish it.

Most kinds of published tests (sometimes called "standardized" tests) are norm-referenced. But a growing number of published tests are used to measure a test taker's mastery of a subject, rather than how his or her performance compares with that of a norm group. For example, several U.S. states require students to pass a competency test to demonstrate that they have reached a minimum level of achievement set by the state before they can graduate from high school.

▶ WHAT A TEST SCORE MEANS

A test score does not tell everything about a person. Your performance throughout your school career, as well as your personality, interests, and activities, combine to give information about you and your abilities.

Test scores are affected by many factors. Being mentally prepared to take a test can improve your score. Feeling ill or upset when taking a test can prevent you from doing your best work. Cultural, regional, or economic differences among test takers may also affect scores. A test taker's score could be misinterpreted if his or her environmental background is very different from that of the norm group with which the score is compared.

A person may do poorly on a test not because of the difficulty of the test material, but because of a physical problem such as difficulty in seeing or hearing. A careful teacher or psychologist will consider such possibilities when interpreting test scores.

JOHN R. MCGOWAN, ED.D.
Chairman, Department of Elementary Education
Southern Connecticut State University

▶ SAMPLE TEST QUESTIONS

The two types of tests students most often encounter are achievement tests and scholastic aptitude tests. Achievement tests usually contain questions on factual information learned in school. Therefore, it is possible to study for an achievement test by reviewing facts in the subject area covered on the test (although your entire experience in the area tested is more important). For example, an achievement test question might ask:

Which is *not* a power granted to the federal government under the U.S. Constitution?
(A) The power to regulate interstate commerce
(B) The power to tax imports and exports
(C) The power to negotiate foreign commercial treaties
(D) The power to establish uniform weights and measures

To choose the correct answer (choice B), you must be familiar with the specific facts.

Other kinds of achievement test questions are designed to see if you can punctuate, capitalize, and express a sentence correctly:

In the following sentence there may be an error in wording. If there is an error, choose the underlined part that should be changed to make the sentence correct. If there is no error in the sentence, choose D.
Everyone <u>in the</u> classroom <u>were</u> surprised to see
        A   B
a monkey <u>walk into</u> the room. <u>No error.</u>
          C   D

You can choose the correct answer (choice B) only if you know that "everyone" must take a singular verb.

Aptitude tests, on the other hand, usually do not contain questions on specific facts such as history facts or English grammar. Memorizing information or studying will not help you prepare for an aptitude test. But in order to be judged fairly and accurately by the test, you should be familiar with the rules and methods for taking these tests. Learning these test-taking skills will make you more confident when taking the test and will help you increase your score.

Scholastic aptitude tests typically test verbal skills with four types of questions: analogies (word relationships), vocabulary, reading comprehension, and sentence completion. They measure mathematical ability with questions that require mathematical skills and strategies. They may also ask questions that require logical reasoning or common sense. This section gives examples of each kind of question.

Analogies

To answer an analogy, you must understand the relationship between a pair of words and find a similar relationship between two other words. Here is an example from a third-grade aptitude test:

Find a relation in the choices that matches the relation you find in the CAPITALIZED WORDS.
PENCIL: PAPER :: (A) pen : ink
                  (B) crayon : art
                  (C) writing : print
                  (D) chalk : blackboard

If you are not using the correct thinking skill, you can easily get lured into choosing a wrong answer. You may think, "PENCIL is like a pen, and ink is used to write on PAPER." This reasoning would lead you to pick choice A, which is incorrect. But there is a simple technique that will help you answer analogies correctly. Always put the analogy in the form of a sentence; PENCIL is used to write on PAPER. Then try to put the words in each choice into the same sentence form:

(A) A *pen* is used to write on *ink*. This does not make sense, so go on to B.

(B) A *crayon* is used to write *art*. No. Try C.

(C) *Writing* is used to write on *print*. Wrong.

(D) *Chalk* is used to write on a *blackboard*. This is the only choice that fits the same sentence form. Here are examples of analogies for higher grades. See if you can answer them using this strategy.

Grades 6–9	Grades 9–12
CHILD : ADULT ::	ROBBERY : THIEF ::
(A) man : boy	(A) burglar : diamonds
(B) servant : master	(B) hostage : kidnapper
(C) kitten: cat	(C) crime : prison
(D) actor : director	(D) capture : criminal
	(E) forgery : counterfeiter

For the first example, use the sentence, "A CHILD grows up to become an ADULT." For the second example, use the sentence, "A ROBBERY is committed by a THIEF." (Answers: C; E)

Vocabulary

Vocabulary questions test whether you know the meanings of certain words. Aptitude tests often contain many different types of vocabulary questions. It is essential to build your vocabulary, both to do well on these tests and to communicate well in other areas. One important way to build vocabulary is to read widely and always look up the meanings of unfamiliar words in a dictionary. To prepare for aptitude tests, some students try to memorize long lists of words. But research suggests that, over time, students tend to forget the words they learned using this method.

A much more effective technique is to learn the prefixes (beginning syllables) and roots of words. Knowing certain key prefixes and roots can help you figure out the meanings of many different words. For example, on an aptitude test you may be asked the meaning of PRE-CURSORY. By knowing that the prefix PRE-means "before" and that the root CURS means "to run," you can determine that PRE-CURSORY means "running (or going) before." Other key prefixes to know are: ab-(away from), anti- (against), con- (with), circum- (around), dis- (apart; not), ex- (out of), in- (into), mal- (bad), pro- (forward), re-(back), sub- (under), trans- (across), and un-(not). Key roots are cred (believe), dict (speak), duc (lead), fac (make or do), par (equal), spec (see), and ten (hold).

Reading Comprehension

Reading-comprehension questions test your ability to understand what a written passage is about. Usually, you will be asked to read a passage of about 50 to 300 lines and answer questions about what you have read. Most often, the questions will test the following four abilities:

(1) Your ability to identify the **main idea** of a passage. Typical questions would begin, "The main idea of the passage is . . ." or "The writer's main point is that . . ."

(2) Your ability to **spot details** and identify specific information in the passage. A typical question might begin, "The word *warlike* in line 10 refers to . . ."

(3) Your ability to **draw inferences**—understand things about the passage that are not directly stated. You might be asked what the writer assumes or believes, or what the passage implies.

(4) Your ability to identify the **mood** or **tone** of the passage. You might be asked to identify the writer's attitude or whether the passage is serious, sad, or funny.

As you read a passage, be aware of these four elements so that you will be prepared to answer questions about them. Another useful technique is to underline key words or phrases in the passage so that you will be able to spot things quickly when answering questions. For example, when you see the word "however," you may want to underline it, because it signals a place where a contrast may occur.

Sentence Completions

In a sentence completion, you are asked to find the missing word or words that make sense when inserted in the sentence. Here is an example for the fifth-grade level:

Although she is really _____, she does not do well on exams.
(A) likable   (B) smart   (C) rich   (D) tough

The technique for answering this kind of question is to watch for key words that tell what is happening in the sentence. In this example, the word "although" signals a contrast between the first part of the sentence (before the comma) and the second part. The only word among the choices that will give such a contrast is "smart" (choice B).

Other key words and phrases that signal a contrast or an opposing thought are "however," "in spite of," "rather than," "nevertheless," and "but." Other key words signal a phrase that supports the rest of the sentence. These words include "moreover," "besides," "additionally," "and," and "furthermore." Words that signal a result are "therefore," "so," "when," "because," and "since."

Mathematics

Mathematics questions test how well you can compute or calculate something and how well you can reason using mathematical rules. They may also measure how quickly and logically you can solve a problem, using the least amount of calculating.

To do well on mathematics questions, you must be familiar with important mathematical concepts and rules. You must also develop the critical-thinking skills that will help you use these concepts and rules correctly.

Here is an example:
    Which is greater, A or B?
(A) $6 \times 7 \times 8$ (B) $7 \times 9 \times 6$

One way of solving this problem is to multiply the numbers in each choice and compare the products to see which is greater. But this method is time-consuming and unnecessary. You are asked only to find which choice is greater, not to calculate. And comparing is much simpler and faster than calculating. How do you compare two quantities easily? Look for similarities. You can see that there is a 7 and a 6 in both choice A and choice B. Cross off the 7 and the 6 in both groups. You are left with an 8 in choice A and a 9 in choice B. Now it is easy to see that choice B is the correct answer—9 is greater than 8.

Questions that require the strategy of canceling (crossing off) common terms appear on many standardized tests, in many different grade levels. Here is an example of a question on an eighth-grade aptitude test:

Which is greater: 66×79 or 79×65? Remember, to find the answer, just cancel the common term: 79.

This example is for the eleventh- and twelfth-grade level:

Is A greater, equal to, or less than B?

(A) $77 \times 89 \times 66$ (B) $89 \times 77 \times 65$

Just cross off common terms: 89×77.

Here is another way of simplifying two quantities so that you can compare them:

Which is greater, (A) or (B)?

$$(A) \ \frac{7}{12} - \frac{5}{11} \quad (B) \ \frac{2}{11}$$

You could find a common denominator for $\frac{7}{12}$ and $\frac{5}{11}$, subtract, and then compare the result with $\frac{2}{11}$ to see which is greater. But in this case it is easier to add than subtract. Add $\frac{5}{11}$ to both quantities to cancel out the $-\frac{5}{11}$ in choice A. You now get:

$$(A) \ \frac{7}{12} \quad (B) \ \frac{2}{11} + \frac{5}{11} = \frac{7}{11}$$

B is greater than A because it contains a smaller denominator with the same numerator.

Here is an example that requires multiplying each quantity by the same number:

Which is greater, (A) or (B)?

$$(A) \ \frac{4}{7} \quad (B) \ \frac{5}{9}$$

To solve this problem quickly, eliminate the denominators. First, multiply both quantities by 7 to cancel the denominator in choice A:

$$\frac{4}{7} \times 7 = 4 \quad \frac{5}{9} \times 7$$

Then multiply both by 9 to get rid of the denominator in choice (B):

$$4 \times 9 = 36 \quad \frac{5}{9} \times 7 \times 9 = 35$$

36 is greater than 35, so choice A is correct.

Here is an example of a mathematics problem that is stated mostly in words. This type of mathematics question causes more difficulty than most others among students of all ages.

What is 20 percent of 200?

To solve word problems, substitute mathematical symbols for words. Translate "what" to "?" or "x." Translate "is" to "equals" ($=$), "percent" to "over 100" (/100), and "of" to "times" ($\times$).

Thus,   What is 20 percent of 200 becomes

$$? \ = 20 \ \frac{}{100} \times 200$$

$$? \ = \frac{20}{100} \times 200$$

$$? \ = \frac{20}{100} \times 200$$

$$? \ = 20 \times 2 = 40$$

Many other words and phrases can be translated into mathematical symbols. "Added to," "gained," and "increased by" become "plus" ($+$); "decreased by" and "less than" become "minus" ($-$); "x years ago" becomes "minus x" ($-x$); and "x years from now" becomes "plus x" ($+x$).

Logical Reasoning

Logical reasoning questions test your ability to think logically or use common sense.

Here is an example:

What is the next number in the following sequence: 1, 2, 3, 5, 8, 13, 21, 34, ?
(A) 48   (B) 51   (C) 55   (D) 56   (E) 60

The key to answering this type of question correctly is to observe: Look for a relationship among the numbers that will connect one number with another. You will see that adding the first number to the second gives you the third. Adding the second number to the third gives you the fourth, and so on. Thus, you can conclude that the last number of the sequence is obtained by adding the two preceding numbers. Therefore your answer is $21 + 34$, or 55 (choice C).

Do not rush into an answer without thinking carefully. Ask yourself, "Have I really examined all the possibilities?'' Here is an example from a test for grades 3–5:

What is the smallest amount of an American coin that is greater in value than an American nickel?
(A) 6 cents   (B) 7 cents   (C) 8 cents   (D) 9 cents   (E) 10 cents

Did you choose (A) 6 cents? Before you rush into a seemingly good answer, be sure that you have read the problem carefully. In the preceding problem, note that you are asked to choose the amount of an American *coin*. The only American coin listed that is greater in value than five cents is a dime, or ten cents. Choice E is the correct answer.

Here is an SAT example, for grades 9–12:

Think of a digital clock. And think of the times when the hour digit is the same as the minutes digit, such as 7:07 or 8:08. What is the smallest time between any two ''double times'' like 7:07 and 8:08?
(A) 61 minutes   (B) 191 minutes   (C) 57 minutes   (D) 60 minutes   (E) 49 minutes

The answer is E. Did you consider 12:12 and 1:01?

▶ GENERAL STRATEGIES

The following are some general test-taking strategies:
(1) Always read directions carefully and make sure that you understand them. If possible, try to become familiar with the directions to each type of question before you actually take the test. Try to obtain a description of the questions from the test makers or find a workbook that offers practice questions similar to those on the test.
(2) Before you start the test, find out if there is a penalty for guessing. If there is no penalty, it is advisable to guess even if you have no clue as to how to answer a question. If there is a penalty for guessing, it is advisable to guess if you can eliminate one or more of the choices.
(3) Always write as much as you want in your test booklet. Extend lines in diagrams and label sides of geometry figures. Circle key words and underline prefixes and roots of words. Underline specific statements or phrases in reading-comprehension passages. If you are not allowed to write in your test booklet, use scratch paper.

(4) As you work through the test, put check marks next to questions you think you answered correctly, question marks next to those you are not sure of, and double question marks next to questions that have you completely stumped. This will give you a quick indication of which questions to go back to when you review your answers. Skip difficult questions and answer the easy ones first. You can always go back to the harder ones later.
(5) Do not spend too much time on each question. Look at the total number of questions on the test and estimate how long you can take for each question. For example, if there are 30 questions and you have 60 minutes to answer them, you have about two minutes to spend on each question. Of course, some items will take longer than others, but your estimate is a useful guide.

Many books, computer programs, and coaching courses exist to help students prepare for tests. Be careful in choosing these study aids—many do not provide questions that accurately represent those you will find on the test. Others contain gimmicks or rely on a strict drill and practice approach. The best material should help you develop thinking skills and test-taking strategies that can be used for many different questions. These abilities will help you throughout your test-taking career.

GARY R. GRUBER
Author, *Gruber's Complete Preparation for the SAT; Dr. Gruber's Essential Guide to Test Taking for Kids* (Grades 3–5; 6–9); *Gruber's Super Diagnostic Test for the SAT*

TETANUS.   See DISEASES (Descriptions of Some Diseases).

TEXAS

In its history, Texas has been claimed by six different nations—Spain, France, Mexico, the Republic of Texas, the Confederate States of America, and the United States. The Spanish, who claimed Texas in 1519 and ruled there until 1821, adopted the name "Texas" from the Caddo Indians. It was a word that meant "friend" or "ally."

In 1836, while rising up against Mexican rule, Texas rebels used a flag that carried a single five-pointed star. This symbol, a "star of destiny," was officially adopted by the Texas Republic in 1839, and it became a part of a blue, white, and red flag. Later, in 1845, when Texas became a part of the United States, the same flag was used. Texas then became known as the Lone Star State.

State flag

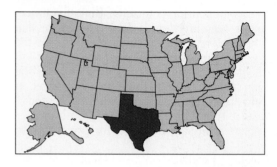

Texas is where the South meets the West. It is bordered by Arkansas and Louisiana on the east, Mexico on the south, New Mexico on the west, and Oklahoma on the north. Texas is the second largest state in the nation, after Alaska, and the second most populous state, after California. Most Texans live in the eastern part of the state, along the coast, and in the cities—Dallas, Houston, Fort Worth, San Antonio, and Austin, the state capital.

In Texas, the landscape and climate change dramatically from east to west. The eastern part, which has higher rainfall, attracted early cotton planters, who brought slaves to work the fields. The drier western portion became the land of ranches, cowboys, and cattle. After the Civil War (1861–65), Texas developed a legendary cattle trade that involved driving herds of Texas-bred longhorns northward to shipping yards in Kansas.

In the early 1900's, oil was discovered with a spectacular gusher at Spindletop, near Beaumont. Soon Texas became the largest oil producer in the world. This was particularly important during World War II (1939–45), when Texas became a major supplier of materials for rubber and fuel made from petrochemicals. The U.S. government established navy, army, and air force bases in Texas as well as shipbuilding facilities for the war effort. The economy and population boomed as a result, and the state continued to grow with additional manufacturing and businesses for the remainder of the century.

▶ LAND

Texas is one of the states known as the West South Central States. It lies along the southern border of the nation, to the west of the Mississippi River. In shape, Texas roughly resembles a giant arrowhead, with a broad handle, known as the Panhandle of Texas. From sea level in the southeast, the surface of Texas rises northwestward to an elevation of more than 8,700 feet (2,600 meters).

Land Regions

Texas is divided into four major physical regions—the West Gulf Coastal Plain, the Great Plains, the Interior Plains, and the Basin and Range region.

The West Gulf Coastal Plain is marshland, separated from the Gulf of Mexico by lagoons, bays, and long, low ridges of sand and shells called barrier beaches. One of the well-known barrier beaches is Padre Island, which is separated from the mainland by Laguna Madre. Some of the bays are San Antonio, Matagorda, and Galveston. In the marshlands there are hills known as salt domes that are sometimes capped by thick layers of nearly pure sulfur. The low plains along the eastern coast are usually wet from the plentiful rainfall in that area. To the south the plains grow

Opposite page, clockwise from top left: Dallas, the second largest city in Texas, is headquarters to many industries. Oil and the products made from it profit the state's economy. An ocotillo plant grows in the dry, rocky soil of Big Bend National Park.

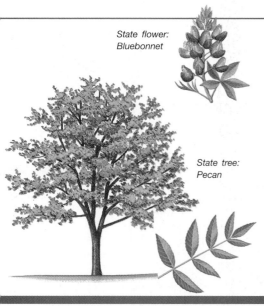

State flower:
Bluebonnet

State tree:
Pecan

FACTS AND FIGURES

Location: West South Central United States; bordered on the north by Oklahoma, on the east by Arkansas and Louisiana, on the south by Mexico and the Gulf of Mexico, and on the west by Mexico and New Mexico.

Area: 267,277 sq mi (692,248 km^2); rank, 2nd.

Population: 20,851,820 (2000 census); rank, 2nd.

Elevation: *Highest*—8,751 ft (2,667 m) at Guadalupe Peak; *lowest*—sea level, along the Gulf of Mexico.

Capital: Austin.

Statehood: December 29, 1845; 28th state.

State Motto: *Friendship.*

State Song: "Texas, Our Texas."

Nickname: Lone Star State.

Abbreviations: TX; Tex.

State bird:
Mockingbird

Above: The Rio Grande, one of the principal rivers of Texas, forms the state's border with Mexico. *Below right:* Wild Texas bluebonnets bloom in the Hill Country. *Bottom:* Claret cup cacti grow in the Chihuahuan Desert in the southwestern part of the state.

south of the Canadian River is known as the Llano Estacado, or Staked Plain.

The Interior Plains, which lie to the east of the High Plains, feature a low, rolling landscape, most of which is flat enough for agriculture. It is part of a large region of the interior United States known as the Central Lowland.

The Basin and Range, at the western edge of Texas, is quite different from the plains areas. It is part of a large region of the western United States. There the land is dry and rocky, with ranges of mountains rising above broad basins. The Guadalupe Mountains in the north contain Guadalupe Peak, the highest point in the state. To the south are the Davis Mountains, with other high peaks, and the Chisos Mountains in the Big Bend of the Rio Grande. Some geographers consider these mountains the southern portion of the Rocky Mountain system.

drier, and near the Rio Grande, they become semi-arid. Inland from the Gulf of Mexico, the land rises gently. To the north and west it becomes rolling and then hilly.

The Great Plains extend into central Texas, especially in the area known as the Hill Country, where there are sharp valleys and steep, rocky cliffs and peaks. Some parts of the land are even mountainous in appearance. An interesting feature of the Panhandle is the Balcones Escarpment, which overlooks the Coastal Plain. This escarpment (a long series of cliffs and hills rising from the flat plains) extends from the Rio Grande near Del Rio northeastward to the vicinity of Austin. It received the Spanish name *Balcones* because it was thought to resemble balconies.

The High Plains occupy most of the Texas Panhandle and the area to the south. This part of Texas is higher in elevation than the other plains sections. It is separated from them by another escarpment known as the Cap Rock. Most of the Panhandle is flatlands. Cotton fields and grainfields stretch level as far as the eye can see. But some parts are sharply cut by canyons, such as the colorful Palo Duro Canyon, near Amarillo. The section of the High Plains

Rivers, Lakes, and Coastal Waters

Texas has few large rivers for a state of its size. The Rio Grande forms all the boundary between Texas and Mexico. This river rises in the mountains of Colorado and empties into the Gulf of Mexico. Its main tributary in Texas is the Pecos River, which flows through the western part of the state. Most of the rivers broaden in the east, where the rainfall is greater. The Brazos and Colorado rivers stretch almost across Texas.

The Trinity and Sabine are the chief rivers of eastern Texas, with the Sabine River forming part of the eastern boundary with Louisiana. The Red River, named for its rust-colored waters, flows eastward between Texas and Oklahoma.

Texas also has few large natural lakes. The largest is Sabine Lake on the Texas-Louisiana border. However, there are more than 200 reservoirs (lakes formed by dams on rivers and streams). The largest include Toledo Bend Reservoir, on the Texas-Louisiana border, and Lake Texoma, which Texas shares with Oklahoma.

Texas' total shoreline, including the shoreline of bays and islands, is 3,359 miles (5,405 kilometers). Along the coast, the water is generally too shallow for large ships to approach the land. Channels have been dredged, or dug, in rivers and bays for ships to come into the cities, such as Houston and Corpus Christi. The Intracoastal Waterway follows bays and canals just inside the barrier beaches. It is part of a system of waterways that extends around the coast of the United States from Massachusetts to Brownsville, Texas.

Climate

Texans living in the mountainous desert region of the west rarely see rain. Some places usually receive less than 10 inches (254 millimeters) of precipitation during an entire year. However, the woodlands of eastern Texas receive about five times as much. Between those two extremes, most of the state has moderate precipitation.

Along the coast, freezing weather is rare and there is hardly any snow. In the extreme south, the average January temperature is 61°F (16°C). During the same month, the Panhandle and other northern regions may be swept by blizzards. Cold waves in Texas

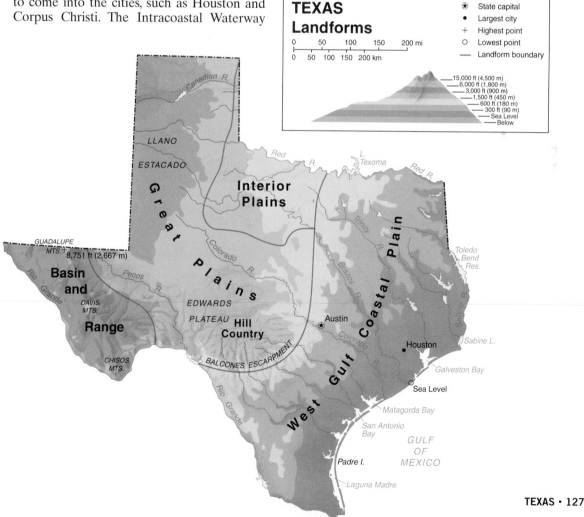

TEXAS Landforms

State capital
Largest city
Highest point
Lowest point
Landform boundary

15,000 ft (4,500 m)
6,000 ft (1,800 m)
3,000 ft (900 m)
1,500 ft (450 m)
600 ft (180 m)
300 ft (90 m)
Sea Level
Below

are called northers because they usually come in on strong winds from the north.

Summer days are hot almost everywhere in the state. From June until November, the coastal areas are in danger of hurricanes, while West Texas suffers from tornadoes in late spring and early summer.

The nine-banded armadillo, a Spanish word meaning "small armored one," is a familiar sight in Texas.

Plant and Animal Life

Oaks, pecans, hickories, and elms are just a few of the many trees that grow in Texas. In the west, where the climate is drier, mesquite and sagebrush dominate along with various native grasses such as sideoats and buffalo grass. On the High Plains, the tall spikes of the yucca plant give the land the name the Staked Plains.

Wildlife thrives in many parts of Texas. Armadillos and various kinds of snakes and lizards are widespread. Deer are especially numerous in the Hill Country. Opossums, rabbits, raccoons, muskrats, and javelinas (a kind of wild pig, also called jabalina and peccary) are also common.

Many kinds of wildfowl make their winter home in the salt marshes along the coast. They are protected in state and national refuges. The Aransas National Wildlife Refuge is famous as the winter home of the nearly extinct whooping crane.

Freshwater fish are abundant, especially in the reservoirs. The waters along the coast are full of shellfish—shrimp, oysters, and crabs—and many varieties of saltwater fish, such as red snapper, flounder, Spanish mackerel, and tarpon.

Natural Resources

Much of the history of Texas is linked to its natural resources of water, land, and minerals. Freshwater was needed by the first settlers, and they established their towns near streams and springs. As towns and cities grew, the citizens pumped water from underground water sources, called aquifers. In the 1900's they built dams and reservoirs along the rivers.

In the early 1900's, overcutting for construction depleted the East Texas pine forests. As a result, the landowners and lumber companies learned to replant the land. The forests returned, and at present, the amount of timber cut comes close to the amount regrown each year. Today trees cover about 13 percent of the land.

Although Texas produces a variety of mineral resources, the most important is petroleum. The state provides almost one-fourth of the oil and natural gas produced in the nation. The average depth of an oil well is 5,000 feet (1,524 meters), but some go as deep as 30,000 feet (9,144 meters). Most wells yield natural gas, and some produce only gas. Gas became valuable for heating purposes in the early 1940's, during World War II, and pipelines were constructed to carry the gas to the eastern United States.

Next in importance to petroleum are minerals available for construction—sand, gravel,

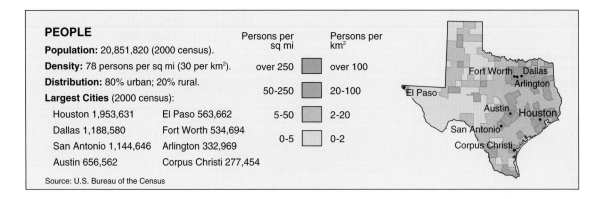

PEOPLE

Population: 20,851,820 (2000 census).

Density: 78 persons per sq mi (30 per km²).

Distribution: 80% urban; 20% rural.

Largest Cities (2000 census):

Houston 1,953,631	El Paso 563,662
Dallas 1,188,580	Fort Worth 534,694
San Antonio 1,144,646	Arlington 332,969
Austin 656,562	Corpus Christi 277,454

Source: U.S. Bureau of the Census

Persons per sq mi		Persons per km²
over 250		over 100
50-250		20-100
5-50		2-20
0-5		0-2

A Mexican-style mariachi band plays at the River Festival in San Antonio.

clay, gypsum, and other materials used in making cement and bricks. Two other important minerals are salt and sulfur, which are mined along the Gulf Coast. These are basic components of the petro-chemical industry, which produces plastics and fuels. Somewhat more unusual is the helium taken from wells in the Panhandle. Among its uses is to maintain the pressure in the fuel tanks of rockets. Magnesium, extracted from seawater by chemical plants on the coast, is used in building aircraft, automobiles, tools, and other equipment.

The Western style of clothing, characterized by cowboy hats and boots, is traditional dress among Texans.

▶ PEOPLE

The ancestors of most present-day Texans came from other parts of the United States or from neighboring Mexico. But some areas of central Texas were settled largely by Germans and Czechs, who came directly from Europe. Most of the first English-speaking settlers who came to Texas before the Civil War were natives of the southeastern states. They brought with them the way of life they had known in their former homes. They grew corn and cotton and used slaves. It was in this way that blacks were introduced to Texas. Because of this historical background, Texas joined the South during the Civil War. Today, African Americans make up 12 percent of Texas' population.

For many years, Texas has drawn increasing numbers of new residents from all parts of the United States as well as from Mexico. Today more than one-quarter of all Texans are of Hispanic origin. Most of them have Mexican ancestors or were born in Mexico themselves. Many speak both Spanish and English, and a number of Spanish-language newspapers and magazines are published.

Texas was the home of Native American peoples long before Europeans came. Only 66,000 descendants of these earliest people live in the state today.

Education

With more than 1,000 school districts, Texas maintains one of the largest public school systems in the nation. Like other large states, especially in the West, Texas once found it difficult to provide enough schools in thinly settled areas. After the Civil War, the laws of the state required segregation in public education. This requirement was declared illegal by a 1954 decision of the U.S. Supreme Court.

The oldest state-supported institutions of higher education in the state are Texas A&M University and the University of Texas. Today the University of Texas system, with its central office in Austin, includes university campuses in Arlington, Austin, Brownsville, Dallas, El Paso, Odessa, San Antonio, and Tyler, as well as health science centers at Dallas, Houston, and San Antonio and a medical branch at Galveston. The Texas A&M Uni-

Every year on New Year's Day, the Cotton Bowl college football game is played in Dallas' State Fair Park. Texans also support two professional football teams, the Houston Oilers and the Dallas Cowboys.

Methodist University in Dallas, Texas Christian University in Fort Worth, and St. Mary's University of San Antonio and Trinity University, both in San Antonio.

Libraries, Museums, and the Arts

Texas has about 500 public libraries and an even larger number of primary- and secondary-school libraries. The Texas State Library in Austin is the oldest of the public libraries. It is noted for valuable manuscripts on Texas history. The University of Texas at Austin has the largest library collections in the state. One of these is the Lyndon B. Johnson Library, which contains a collection of the former president's official papers. The Armstrong Browning Library at Baylor University in Waco contains original works of the English poets Robert and Elizabeth Barrett Browning.

The Amon Carter Museum of Western Art and the Kimbell Art Museum in Fort Worth and the Menil Collection in Houston are among the nation's leading art museums. Notable collections of European and American art may also be seen in museums in Dallas and San Antonio. Throughout the state there are museums specializing in regional or state history and natural history.

Sports

Widespread sports activity can be found throughout the educational system. The most popular sport for fans is football, with so-called college "shootouts" drawing large crowds. Professional sports teams include the

versity system has its main campus at College Station and other campuses at Prairie View, Corpus Christi, Canyon, Kingsville, Stephenville, and Galveston. There are more than 20 other state universities, including the University of North Texas and Texas Woman's University, both in Denton, and the University of Houston system, with four campuses in the Houston area. Public two-year colleges number about 50.

Some of the oldest private colleges and universities are Austin College in Sherman, Baylor University in Waco, and Southwestern University in Georgetown, all founded in the 1840's. Other well-known private institutions include Abilene Christian College in Abilene, Rice University in Houston, Southern

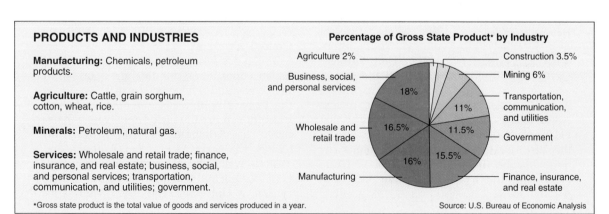

PRODUCTS AND INDUSTRIES

Manufacturing: Chemicals, petroleum products.

Agriculture: Cattle, grain sorghum, cotton, wheat, rice.

Minerals: Petroleum, natural gas.

Services: Wholesale and retail trade; finance, insurance, and real estate; business, social, and personal services; transportation, communication, and utilities; government.

*Gross state product is the total value of goods and services produced in a year.

Percentage of Gross State Product* by Industry

- Agriculture 2%
- Construction 3.5%
- Mining 6%
- Business, social, and personal services 18%
- Transportation, communication, and utilities 11%
- Wholesale and retail trade 16.5%
- Government 11.5%
- Manufacturing 16%
- Finance, insurance, and real estate 15.5%

Source: U.S. Bureau of Economic Analysis

Houston Astros and Texas Rangers major league baseball teams; the Dallas Mavericks, Houston Rockets, San Antonio Spurs, and Houston Comets basketball teams; the Dallas Cowboys of the National Football League; and the Dallas Stars of the National Hockey League.

▶ ECONOMY

Most Texans are employed in services, wholesale and retail trade, government, and manufacturing. Agriculture and the production of minerals, especially petroleum, are im-

important service is government, which alone employs about 1.4 million Texans. Most of these jobs are at the county and city level. The federal government also maintains more than a dozen military bases in Texas, including the three largest—Fort Bliss in El Paso, Fort Sam Houston in San Antonio, and Fort Hood in Killeen.

Manufacturing

Most significant in terms of product value has been the output of Texas' petrochemical industry. Chemicals made from oil and gas

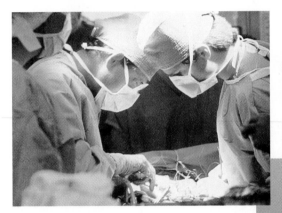

Far left: The Texas Medical Center is Houston's largest employer. *Left:* Texas grows more cotton than any other state. *Below:* Petrochemicals, made from oil and gas, are the most profitable products manufactured in Texas.

portant in the amount of revenues they bring to the state, but because of efficient technology, these areas employ fewer people.

Services

A majority of Texans are employed in a wide variety of service industries—from banking, real estate, transportation, and trade to hotels, restaurants, grocery stores, clothing stores, and auto repair shops. The most important service category, however, is health care. The Texas Medical Center in Houston, for example, administers more than 50 hospitals and facilities and is the leading employer in the city. It is also the most significant medical complex in Texas, with a worldwide reputation for work in cancer and heart disease. Tourism, the state's second most important economic activity, supports hotel employment, amusements, transportation, and dining. Another

are called petrochemicals because they are based on petroleum. More petrochemicals are made in Texas than in any other state. These chemicals are the base materials for plastics, nylon and other synthetic fibers, paints, antifreeze fluids, plant fertilizers, medicines, insecticides, and many other useful products.

Food processing, which includes grain milling and the canning and freezing of fruits and vegetables, is also important to the econ-

Places of Interest

Padre Island National Seashore

Lyndon B. Johnson Space Center, near Houston

The Alamo, San Antonio

The vast size, varied landscape, and colorful history of Texas provide many places of unusual interest. Texas has four national forests, all in eastern Texas. They are the Angelina, Davy Crockett, Sam Houston, and Sabine.

The Alamo, in San Antonio, preserves the site where more than 180 rebels, including William B. Travis, Davy Crockett, and James Bowie, died fighting in the Texas Revolution. The Alamo (the Spanish word for "cottonwood") is Texas' most popular tourist attraction.

Big Bend National Park, in southwestern Texas, lies within the Big Bend of the Rio Grande. The park is famous for rock-walled canyons, rugged mountains, and desert scenery.

Big Thicket National Preserve protects part of an area in southeastern Texas. It includes forests, swamps, creeks, and bayous.

Chamizal National Memorial, at El Paso, commemorates a treaty signed there by the United States and Mexico in 1963, settling a century-old boundary dispute.

Dallam-Hartley XIT Museum, in Dalhart, provides a display of equipment and activity from the famous XIT ranch in West Texas. Emphasis is on cowboy life around 1900.

Fort Davis National Historic Site, near Fort Davis in West Texas, preserves a fort that guarded the San Antonio-El Paso road from 1854 to 1891.

Guadalupe Mountains National Park includes Guadalupe Peak, the state's highest mountain, and significant fossil remains of dinosaurs.

Lyndon B. Johnson National Historical Park is made up of two units, about 15 miles (24 kilometers) apart—the boyhood home of President Johnson in Johnson City and the LBJ Ranch, the site of his birthplace and grave.

Lyndon B. Johnson Space Center, south of Houston, is the location of the control center for NASA space explorations. A visitor center exhibits moon rocks and historic space equipment.

Padre Island National Seashore, in the Gulf of Mexico, is noted for its beaches and bird and marine life.

Palo Duro Canyon State Park, cut by the Red River, represents four geologic ages in its layers of rock.

San Antonio Missions National Historical Park, at San Antonio, preserves four Spanish missions from the 1700's. A historic dam and aqueduct system are part of the park.

San Jacinto State Park, near Houston, preserves the battlefield where Texas won independence from Mexico in 1836. The San Jacinto Monument, which commemorates the battle, is an impressive tower, with a historical museum in the base. The USS *Texas*, moored nearby, is a battleship that played a part in World Wars I and II.

The Sixth Floor, a museum in downtown Dallas, commemorates the life and death of President John F. Kennedy. It is located in the former Texas School Book Depository, the building from which the gunshots that killed Kennedy were fired.

Texas Ranger Hall of Fame and Museum, in Waco, presents 150 years of Texas Ranger history with displays of guns and photographs of these frontier law enforcers.

State Recreation Areas. Texas has an extensive system of state parks and other recreation areas. For more information, contact Texas Parks and Wildlife Department, 4200 Smith School Road, Austin, Texas 78744.

omy. Texas' cattle industry provides beef for meatpacking plants throughout the state.

Aircraft building is an important occupation for people living in the Dallas–Fort Worth area. Nonelectrical machinery, especially construction and oil-field equipment, and electric and electronic equipment are other major products.

Agriculture

Texas' most valuable crops are cotton, corn, and grain sorghum. Texas usually leads the nation in cotton production and grows about 25 percent of the national total. It is cultivated mainly on the high plains and harvested with machines. Much of the crop is exported to Japan, South Korea, and Mexico. The corn and sorghum are used as feed for livestock. Rice grown along the Gulf Coast was an important crop until the 1980's, when farmers began to produce more wheat, peanuts, and hay.

Farms in various parts of Texas grow large quantities of vegetables and fruit. Truck farms produce tomatoes, watermelons, onions, carrots, and spinach to be sent to market. Pecans are grown in central and south Texas. The Rio Grande Valley produces citrus fruit. Another important product is rosebushes. Each year, the rose farms near Tyler ship millions of bushes to nurseries and gardeners all over the nation.

Mining and Construction

Much of the mining activity in Texas involves the drilling of oil, although this industry began to decline in the 1980's. The mining of sand and gravel for use in concrete, clays for making bricks and tile, sand for making glass, and gypsum for use in plaster for the construction industry continues to play an important part. Construction activity,

Ice-skaters enjoy a turn on the indoor rink at the Galleria in Houston, a 45-acre (18-hectare) shopping center and business complex. Retail sales account for nearly 10 percent of the state's economy.

particularly for homes, employs more than twice the number involved in the oil business. Home construction is a reflection of the growth in Texas' population.

Transportation

As might be expected of such a large state, Texas leads the nation with 13,000 miles (20,922 kilometers) of railroads and 220,000 miles (354,056 kilometers) of roads. Texans own about 15 million motor vehicles, second only to Californians.

The Dallas/Fort Worth International Airport, Texas' busiest airport, handles 55 percent of the air traffic of Texas and is one of the busiest airports in the nation. Houston International Airport, Texas' second busiest airport, handles 25 percent of the traffic.

The 13 deepwater seaports along the coast provide harbors for hundreds of oceangoing freighters and even more barges. Strings of barges, usually laden with heavy mineral products, are towed along the coast by way of the Intracoastal Waterway. The Port of Houston, with its ship channel through Galveston Bay, is ranked the second busiest port in the nation, mainly due to oil shipments.

Communication

The *Gaceta de Texas* (Texas Gazette), published in Nacogdoches in 1813, was Texas' first newspaper. The first English-language paper was the *Texas Republican*, also pub-

Fort Worth, in north central Texas, is an industrial city known especially for the manufacture of aircraft. It is also a major distribution center for grain and oil.

lished in Nacogdoches, in 1819. Today, more than 100 newspapers are printed daily. Among those with the widest circulation are the *Dallas Morning News*, *Fort Worth Star-Telegram*, and *Houston Chronicle*.

Texas' first radio station was WRR in Dallas, which began broadcasting in 1920. Television first appeared in Fort Worth in 1948. The state now has more than 500 radio stations and about 70 television stations.

▶ CITIES

Texas has three cities with more than 1 million people and 21 additional cities with populations exceeding 100,000. Most Texans live in the cities or close to them.

Austin, the capital city, is located on the Colorado River in south central Texas. The original settlement was founded in 1839. In 1840, Mirabeau B. Lamar, president of the Republic of Texas, recommended the site as the capital and renamed it in honor of Stephen F. Austin, a leader in Texas' struggle for independence. The present capitol build-

ing, constructed of red granite in 1888, was designed to resemble the U.S. Capitol in Washington, D.C. Today, Austin is a center of high-technology industry and research. The main campus of the University of Texas is located there.

Houston, the largest city in Texas, is also the fourth largest city in the United States. A 50-mile (80-kilometer) ship channel that links the city to Galveston Bay and the Gulf of Mexico has made Houston one of the busiest deepwater port cities in the nation and a center of the petro-chemical industry. An article on Houston appears in Volume H.

Dallas is Texas' second largest city. Located in the north central part of the state, it is a major manufacturing, distribution, banking, and insurance center of Texas and the Southwest. An article on Dallas appears in Volume D.

San Antonio, in southern Texas, was established in 1718 with the founding of the mission of San Antonio de Valero, later called the Alamo, and a military post. Today, San Antonio is a center for trade, culture, and tourism. Many military bases are located in its general vicinity. An article on San Antonio appears in Volume S.

El Paso, Spanish for "the Pass," is located on the Rio Grande at the lowest natural pass through the mountains at the western tip of Texas. It is an important gateway between the United States and Mexico. An article on El Paso appears in Volume E.

Fort Worth, known as the town "Where the West Begins," is located on forks of the Trinity River, about 30 miles (50 kilometers) west of Dallas. Founded as an army post in 1849, the present city was incorporated in 1873. After the Civil War, it became an important cattle town. During World War II, many military bases were established there, and it became a center for aircraft manufacture, grain milling, and the oil industry of West Texas.

▶ GOVERNMENT

The state government of Texas is guided by an unusually detailed constitution that includes more than 350 amendments.

TEXAS

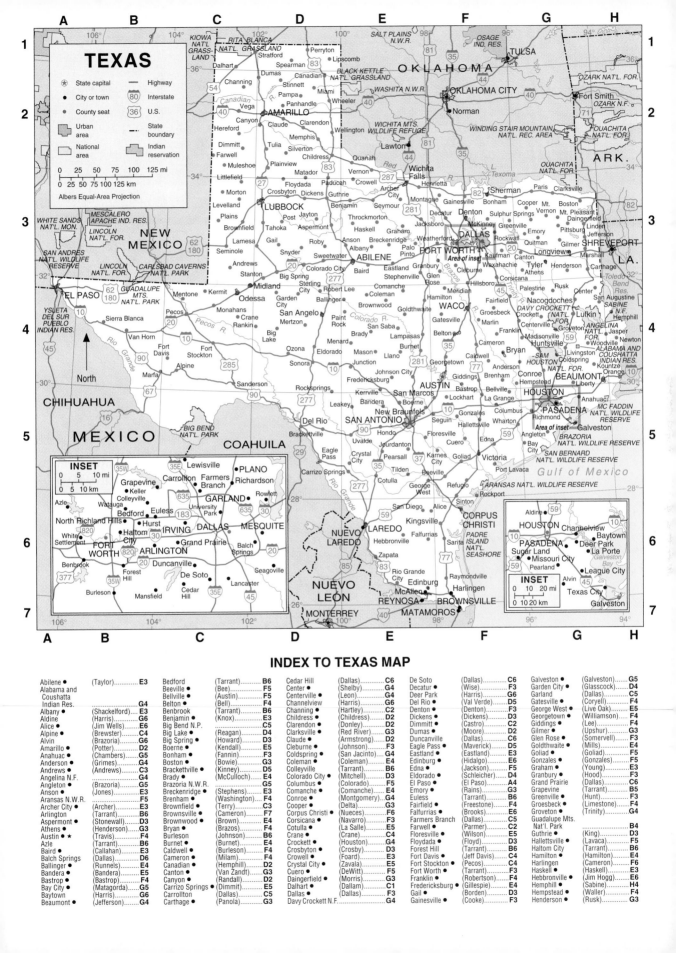

INDEX TO TEXAS MAP

Henrietta • (Clay) **E3**
Hereford • (Deaf Smith) **C2**
Hillsboro • (Hill) **F3**
Hondo • (Medina) **E5**
Houston • (Harris) **G5**
Huntsville • (Walker) **G4**
Hurst • (Tarrant) **B6**
Irving • (Dallas) **C6**
Jacksboro • (Jack) **E3**
Jasper • (Jasper) **G4**
Jayton • (Kent) **D3**
Jefferson • (Marion) **G3**
Johnson City • (Blanco) **E4**
Jourdanton • (Atascosa) **E5**
Junction • (Kimble) **E4**
Karnes City • (Karnes) **F5**
Kaufman • (Kaufman) **F3**
Keller • (Tarrant) **B5**
Kermit • (Winkler) **C4**
Kerrville • (Kerr) **E4**
Kingsville • (Kleberg) **F6**
Kountze • (Hardin) **G4**
La Grange • (Fayette) **F5**
La Porte • (Harris) **G6**
Lamesa • (Dawson) **D3**
Lampasas • (Lampasas) **E4**
Lancaster • (Dallas) **C6**
Laredo • (Webb) **E6**
League City • (Galveston) **G6**
Leakey • (Real) **E5**
Levelland • (Hockley) **C3**
Lewisville • (Denton) **C5**
Liberty • (Liberty) **G4**

Linden • (Cass) **G3**
Lipscomb • (Lipscomb) **D1**
Littlefield • (Lamb) **C3**
Livingston • (Polk) **G4**
Llano • (Llano) **E4**
Lockhart • (Caldwell) **F5**
Longview • (Gregg) **G3**
Lubbock • (Lubbock) **D3**
Lufkin • (Angelina) **G4**
Madisonville • (Madison) **G4**
Mansfield • (Tarrant) **C6**
Marfa • (Presidio) **B4**
Marlin • (Falls) **F4**
Marshall • (Harrison) **G3**
Mason • (Mason) **E4**
Matador • (Motley) **D2**
McAllen • (Hidalgo) **E6**
McFaddin N.W.R. **G5**
McKinney • (Collin) **F3**
Memphis • (Hall) **D2**
Menard • (Menard) **E4**
Mentone • (Loving) **B4**
Meridian • (Bosque) **F4**
Mertzon • (Irion) **D4**
Mesquite • (Dallas) **D6**
Miami • (Roberts) **D2**
Midland • (Midland) **C4**
Missouri City • (Fort Bend) **G6**
Monahans • (Ward) **C4**
Montague • (Montague) **F3**
Morton • (Cochran) **C3**
Mt. Pleasant • (Titus) **G3**
Mt. Vernon • (Franklin) **G3**

Muleshoe • (Bailey) **C2**
Nacogdoches • (Nacogdoches) .. **G4**
New Braunfels • (Comal) **E5**
Newton • (Newton) **H4**
N. Richland Hills • (Tarrant) **B6**
Odessa • (Ector) **C4**
Orange • (Orange) **H4**
Ozona • (Crockett) **D4**
Padre Island Nat'l. Seashore **F6**
Paducah • (Cottle) **D2**
Paint Rock • (Concho) **E4**
Palestine • (Anderson) **G4**
Palo Pinto • (Palo Pinto) **E3**
Pampa • (Gray) **D2**
Panhandle • (Carson) **D2**
Paris • (Lamar) **G3**
Pasadena • (Harris) **G5**
Pearland • (Brazoria) **G5**
Pearsall • (Frio) **E5**
Pecos • (Reeves) **C4**
Perryton • (Ochiltree) **D1**
Pittsburg • (Camp) **G3**
Plains • (Yoakum) **C3**
Plainview • (Hale) **D2**
Plano • (Collin) **C5**
Port Lavaca • (Calhoun) **F5**
Post • (Garza) **D3**
Quanah • (Hardeman) **D2**
Quitman • (Wood) **G3**
Rankin • (Upton) **D4**
Raymondville • (Willacy) **F6**
Refugio • (Refugio) **F5**

Richardson • (Dallas) **C5**
Richmond • (Fort Bend) **G5**
Rio Grande City • (Starr) **E6**
Rita Blanca N.G. **C1**
Robert Lee • (Coke) **D4**
Roby • (Fisher) **D3**
Rockport • (Aransas) **F5**
Rocksprings • (Edwards) **D4**
Rockwall • (Rockwall) **F3**
Rowlett • (Dallas) **D6**
Rusk • (Cherokee) **G4**
Sabine Nat'l. For. **H4**
Sam Houston N.F.
San Angelo • (Tom Green) **D4**
San Antonio • (Bexar) **E5**
San Augustine • (San Augustine) **G4**
San Bernard N.W.R. **G5**
San Diego • (Duval) **E6**
San Marcos • (Hays) **F5**
San Saba • (San Saba) **E4**
Sanderson • (Terrell) **C4**
Sarita • (Kenedy) **F6**
Seagoville • (Dallas) **D6**
Seguin • (Guadalupe) **F5**
Seminole • (Gaines) **C3**
Seymour • (Baylor) **E3**
Sherman • (Grayson) **F3**
Sierra Blanca • (Hudspeth) **B4**
Silverton • (Briscoe) **D2**
Sinton • (San Patricio) **F5**
Snyder • (Scurry) **D3**
Sonora • (Sutton) **D4**

Spearman • (Hansford) **D1**
Stanton • (Martin) **D3**
Stephenville • (Erath) **E3**
Sterling City • (Sterling) **D4**
Stinnett • (Hutchinson) **D2**
Stratford • (Sherman) **C1**
Sugar Land • (Fort Bend) **F6**
Sulphur Springs • (Hopkins) **G3**
Sweetwater • (Nolan) **D3**
Tahoka • (Lynn) **D3**
Throckmorton • (Throckmorton) .. **E3**
Tilden • (McMullen) **E5**
Tulia • (Swisher) **D2**
Tyler • (Smith) **G3**
University Park • (Dallas) **C6**
Uvalde • (Uvalde) **E5**
Van Horn • (Culberson) **B4**
Vega • (Oldham) **C2**
Vernon • (Wilbarger) **E2**
Victoria • (Victoria) **F5**
Waco • (McLennan) **F4**
Watauga • (Tarrant) **B6**
Waxahachie • (Ellis) **F3**
Weatherford • (Parker) **F3**
Wellington • (Collingsworth) **D2**
Wharton • (Wharton) **F5**
Wheeler • (Wheeler) **D2**
White Settlement • (Tarrant) **B6**
Wichita Falls • (Wichita) **E3**
Woodville • (Tyler) **G4**
Ysleta Del Sur Pueblo Ind. Res. **A4**
Zapata • (Zapata) **E6**

● County Seat   Counties in parentheses   ★ State Capital

TEXAS COUNTIES

The state capitol building, completed in 1888, is located in the heart of Austin, which also served as the seat of government for the Republic of Texas from 1840 to 1845.

GOVERNMENT

State Government
Governor: 4-year term
State senators: 31; 4-year terms
State representatives: 150;
 2-year terms
Number of counties: 254

Federal Government
U.S. senators: 2
U.S. representatives: 32
Number of electoral votes: 34

For the name of the current governor, see STATE GOVERNMENTS in Volume S. For the names of current U.S. senators and representatives, see UNITED STATES, CONGRESS OF THE in Volume U-V.

The chief executive officer of the state is the governor. Other executive officers elected by the people include the lieutenant governor, attorney general, and treasurer.

The legislative branch, or the state legislature, is made up of a senate and house of representatives. Legislators meet in January of odd-numbered years for no longer than 140 days, although special sessions may be called.

The judicial branch of the state government is headed by a supreme court, which has a chief justice and eight associate justices. The highest criminal court is the court of criminal appeals. There are also many districts, each with its own court of appeals. Other courts include county, municipal, justice of the peace, and criminal district courts.

▶ **HISTORY**

No one knows exactly how or when the earliest people came to what is now Texas. Cultural remains indicate that people lived there at least 11,000 years ago. A variety of Native American groups were living in Texas when the first European explorers arrived in the early 1500's. Among them were the Apache and the Comanche, the famous hunting peoples of the Great Plains in western Texas, and the Caddo, who lived in earthen houses in eastern Texas.

Spanish and French Exploration

The coast of the Gulf of Mexico was one of the first parts of North America to be explored by the Spanish. In 1519, Alonso de Piñeda sailed along the coast to the mouth of the Rio Grande. Nine years later another Spanish expedition along the coast was shipwrecked. Some of the survivors were washed ashore, probably on Galveston Island. One of these was the famous Álvar Núñez Cabeza de Vaca, who later led a small expedition across Texas to Mexico.

During the next 150 years, Spanish missionaries and settlers came to various parts of present-day Texas. They claimed the area for Spain, but they did not believe that the land was of much value. The first permanent settlement was made about 1682 near present-day El Paso by Spanish people who were driven out of New Mexico by a revolt of the Pueblo Indians.

The period of Spain's undisputed claim to Texas ended in 1685, when an expedition led by the French explorer Robert Cavelier, Sieur de La Salle, landed by accident at Matagorda Bay while seeking the mouth of the Mississippi River. La Salle founded a little settlement near Matagorda Bay, but it failed due to illness, poor management, and the hostility of the native population.

Spanish Settlement

Meanwhile the Spanish in Mexico were disturbed to learn that the French were invading what they felt was Spanish land. To block settlement by other nations, the Spanish began building missions and villages in

Famous People

Consult the Index for more information in *The New Book of Knowledge* about the following people who were either born in Texas or are associated with the state: frontiersman Davy Crockett (1786–1836); soldier and statesman Samuel Houston (1793–1863); short-story writer O. Henry (1862–1910); Vice President John Nance Garner (1868–1967); Speaker of the House Sam Rayburn (1882–1961); Presidents Dwight D. Eisenhower (1890–1969), Lyndon B. Johnson (1908–72), George Bush (1924–), and George W. Bush (1946–); First Lady Claudia ("Lady Bird") Johnson (1912–); baseball great Rogers Hornsby (1896–1963); industrialist Howard Hughes (1905–76); public official Oveta Culp Hobby (1905–95); civil rights leader James Farmer (1920–99); athlete Mildred ("Babe") Didrikson Zaharias (1914–56); and rock and blues singer Janis Joplin (1943–70).

Stephen Fuller Austin (1793–1836) was born in Virginia. He grew up in Missouri, where his father, Moses Austin, was a merchant and mine owner. Moses Austin went to Texas in 1820 to obtain

Lyndon B. Johnson

permission from the Spanish governor to settle American families there, but he died the next year. Stephen F. Austin took up his father's plans and led many colonists to Texas. Later he became a leader in Texas' struggle for independence from Mexico. Among the places named for him are the capital city, Austin College in Sherman, and Stephen F. Austin State Park.

Judge Roy Bean (1825?–1903) was born in Mason County, Kentucky, but made a name for himself as justice of the peace at the small railroad town in West Texas called Vinegaroon. He was also the town's saloonkeeper and coroner. An eccentric who called himself the only "Law West of the Pecos," Bean administered justice in a loose manner. According to legend, he fined a corpse $40 for "concealing a weapon." He also renamed his town Langtry after Lillie Langtry, an actress with whom he had fallen in love.

Michael Ellis DeBakey (1908–) was born in Lake Charles, Louisiana, but became famous as a heart surgeon at the Baylor Medical School in Houston.

Texas. In 1690 the mission San Francisco de los Tejas was founded near present Nacogdoches, but it was abandoned a few years later. Beginning in 1718, several missions were established in or near what is now San Antonio. Spanish missionary priests moved into Texas to try to bring Christianity to the native peoples.

Mexican Rule

As time passed, the power of Spain declined both in Europe and in America. By the year 1800, the settlement at present-day San Antonio was one of the few Spanish colonies in Texas. At this time, the United States was expanding rapidly to the west, and English-speaking Americans began to come into the Spanish land.

In 1821, Mexico overthrew the Spanish government and became an independent nation that included Texas. In that same year, Stephen F. Austin brought settlers to Texas from the United States under arrangements with the new Mexican government. In the years that followed, so many families from other states moved into Texas that the Mexican authorities became disturbed. In an at-

The struggle for the Alamo was the most dramatic battle of the Texas Revolution. More than 180 men, including James Bowie and Davy Crockett, were killed.

Between 1948 and 1981, he performed close to 40,000 heart surgeries. He pioneered the coronary bypass operation and helped develop the artificial heart.

José Ángel Gutiérrez (1944–), a Chicano civil rights leader, was born in Crystal City. In 1970 he founded the political party *La Raza Unida* ("people together"), which supported Mexican-American candidates in the Southwest. That same year, Gutiérrez was elected president of the school board in Crystal City and later ordered that classes there be given in both Spanish and English.

Barbara Charline Jordan (1936–96), a politician and educator, was born in Houston. A Democrat, she was the first African American woman from the South to win election to the U.S. House of Representatives. During her three terms (1973–79), Jordan promoted civil rights legislation and defended the needs of the

Barbara Jordan

Sam Houston

poor. Known for her dignity and eloquence, she delivered the keynote addresses at the 1976 and 1992 Democratic national conventions.

Mirabeau Buonaparte Lamar (1798–1859), born in Georgia, visited Texas in 1835 and returned there the next year to join Sam Houston's army. Lamar commanded the cavalry at the Battle of San Jacinto. He served as vice president (1836) of the new Republic of Texas and then as president (1838–41). Lamar was also a poet, diplomat, and

educator. He is remembered especially for his work in founding the public education system of Texas.

Audie Leon Murphy (1924–71), born in Farmersville, won more recognition for heroism than any other soldier during World War II. Single-handedly, he turned back a German infantry attack by firing machine guns from the top of a burning tank destroyer, killing fifty of the enemy. In all, he was awarded three French, one Belgian, and twenty-four U.S. medals, including the Medal of Honor. After the war he became an author and a movie actor.

(Henry) Ross Perot (1930–), born in Texarkana, was a popular but unsuccessful independent candidate for president of the United States in 1992 and 1996. A self-made billionaire, he founded Electronic Data Systems (EDS) in 1982, which was acquired by General Motors in 1984 for more than $2.5 billion.

tempt to control Texas, they passed strict laws, causing the Texans to rise in rebellion.

The Fall of the Alamo

The Texas Revolution began when skirmishes broke out in many of the settlements. Many Texans banded together and in 1836 declared their independence. Samuel Houston was named commander in chief of the Texas forces. The Texas rebels laid siege to the Mexican stronghold of San Antonio and captured it. This event alarmed the Mexican president, Antonio López de Santa Anna. He took charge of the Mexican Army and marched northward to win San Antonio back and to defeat the Texans.

Inside the walls of the old Spanish mission San Antonio de Valero, known as the Alamo, a small band of Texas soldiers was besieged by an army of several thousand Mexicans. The Mexican commander, Santa Anna, demanded a surrender. William B. Travis, leader of the Texans, vowed he would never surrender or retreat.

On the morning of March 6, 1836—the 13th day of the siege—Santa Anna's troops stormed the walls. The battle raged from building to building in the old mission compound. The chapel was the last to fall. By the end of that day, the Texans had not surrendered. As a result of this battle, more than 180, including Travis, James Bowie, and Davy Crockett, were killed.

The Republic of Texas

Six weeks later—rallying other Texas forces with the cry "Remember the Alamo!"—Sam Houston gathered about 900 men and encamped near the coast where the San Jacinto River flows into Buffalo Bayou. Nearby was Santa Anna with a force of 1,400 men. In the famous Battle of San Jacinto (April 21, 1836), the rebels defeated the Mexicans and won their independence. The independent Republic of Texas soon was recognized by the United States and other countries. Once Texas became independent, people from the United States arrived in larger numbers than before.

Statehood and Later Times

Almost as soon as Texas had won its independence, it sought to join the United States. But several of the northern states did not

In the early days of settlement, Texas Rangers defended settlers from hostile Mexicans and Native Americans and helped keep law and order on the frontier. Today the Rangers are part of the Texas state police force.

(10 kilometers) out into the Gulf.

Modern Times

In the 1940's, Texas became a focal point in national politics when one of its U.S. representatives, Sam Rayburn, became Speaker of the House. He went on to serve in that position longer than any other speaker in history. In the 1950's, another Texan, Lyndon B. Johnson, became the majority leader in the Senate. He later was elected vice president and became president after the assassination of President John F. Kennedy in Dallas in 1963.

In the early 1960's, the nation became focused on the expansion of a national space program. In order to direct space exploration, the National Aeronautics and Space Administration (NASA) constructed the Manned Spacecraft Center (later renamed the Lyndon B. Johnson Space Center) near Houston in 1961–62.

A worldwide oil depression in the 1980's, along with declining oil reserves, forced Texas to diversify its economy. The result was a rapid development of electronic and computer industries, health and education services, and tourism, among other activities. Texas also experienced a sharp increase in population, as many people moved to the state to find greater economic opportunity and to take advantage of the mild climate. For many years, Texas was the third most populous state in the nation. But by 1995, its population had surpassed that of New York, making Texas second only to California in number of residents.

LORRIN G. KENNAMER, JR.
ROBERT H. RYAN
University of Texas at Austin
Reviewed by DAVID G. MCCOMB
Author, *Texas: A Modern History*

See also DALLAS; EL PASO; HOUSTON; SAN ANTONIO.

want to admit Texas because some Texans owned slaves. Finally, on December 29, 1845, Texas joined the Union, but this event aroused the government of Mexico, which still claimed Texas for itself. The United States then found itself at war with Mexico. The story of the Mexican War, which ended in 1848, is told in Volume M.

Peace existed for a while, but it was not to last. In 1861, Texas seceded from the Union to join the Confederacy in the Civil War (1861–65). After the war, Texas was readmitted to the Union in 1870.

During the years 1866–85, the colorful Texas cattle industry was most active. It was during this time that cowboys drove vast herds of longhorns northward from southern Texas to the Kansas cow towns of Abilene, Wichita, and Dodge City. Also during this era, the Texas Rangers became famous as a special state law-enforcement agency.

The Discovery of Oil

By 1900, Texas was a well-developed agricultural state. Then, in 1901, the large-scale discovery of oil began with a gusher at Spindletop, near Beaumont. The oil business changed the face of Texas in many ways. Oil refineries and other industrial plants were built, Texas seaports became increasingly important, and cities grew.

During and after World War II, the petrochemical and natural-gas industries stimulated further economic growth. In 1953, Texas finally won a long legal battle for possession of the oil-rich tidelands in the Gulf of Mexico. This encouraged underwater oil drilling on the continental shelf that extended 6 miles

TEXTILES

Almost every culture makes or uses textiles in some form. They can be made by hand or by machine, from several sets of yarns and a loom, or from one yarn and a hooked stick. The word "textile" comes from the Latin word *texere*, meaning "to weave." Textile, fabric, and cloth—words that are generally interchangeable—are used to refer to anything made from fibers or fibrous materials. Denim jeans, knitted shawls, wool rugs, and lace wedding veils are just a few examples of textiles.

A tunic made by the Chimu in pre-Columbian Peru combines two types of fibers and two types of weaving. The tassels were applied after the weaving.

▶ HOW TEXTILES ARE MADE

Textiles may be made from either natural or synthetic fibers. Until the late 1800's, all textiles were made from natural fibers, even though as early as 1664, English naturalist Robert Hooke had tried to produce a fiber to imitate silk. Finally, in 1889, French chemist Count Hilaire de Chardonnet perfected the first "artificial silk," which became known as rayon.

Materials

Many natural materials are used to make textiles. Some, such as linen, cotton, ramie, and raffia, come from the stems, seeds, bark, or leaves of plants. Silk comes from silkworm cocoons. Wool, mohair, and cashmere are among the fibers that come from the fleece of sheep, goats, and other animals. After the synthetic fibers in rayon were introduced, scientists found other ways to produce fibers from combinations of chemical compounds. Acetate, nylon, acrylic, and polyester are a few of these synthetic fibers.

In the 1980's, microfibers, which are extremely small in diameter, were produced. During the same decade, American scientist Sally Fox began to develop machine-spinnable cotton that is colored naturally in shades of green and brown.

Most textiles are created from fibers that have been spun into yarns. Yarns composed of plant fibers and animal hair are made by aligning these relatively short fibers into a bundle by carding or combing them. A few fibers are drawn from the bundle to begin the process of spinning, in which the fibers are twisted together to form long lengths of yarn. Single yarns may be used alone or retwisted with another yarn or yarns in a process called plying.

A ceremonial dancing blanket (*left*), made by the Chilkat from the northwest coast of North America, is an example of twining. Beaten barkcloth is made in Polynesia, Indonesia, and parts of Africa. This Polynesian example is decorated with designs (*below*).

Construction Techniques

One way to classify textiles is to analyze how they are made. The two broad categories of construction are nonwoven and woven.

Nonwoven Techniques. Nonwoven textiles may be made from fibers, single yarns, or a single set of yarns. Common nonwoven construction methods are felting, looping, knotting, and oblique interlacing. In **felting**, loose fibers or fibrous strips are arranged to form a mat, which is treated with friction, moisture, and heat to compress and lock the fibers together. Felt made of wool or fur is often used for hats. The nomadic peoples of central Asia make their yurts, or tents, from felted wool. Beaten barkcloth, called tapa in Polynesia, is a felted material made from fibrous strips of the inner bark of plants such as the paper mulberry or the wild fig. The strips are placed side by side, with the edges overlapping, on a hard surface. Then they are beaten with a mallet to felt the overlapped fibers.

Using the **looping** method, a textile can be made from a single yarn or from two single yarns. Rows of loops may be built up on one another by using one yarn threaded through a needle or shuttle. This technique is used in many kinds of nets. In a second method, one yarn may be looped around a second, or foundation, yarn. This method is used to make needle-lace and coiled baskets. In a third method, the yarn is wound into a skein, and the free end is used to make a loop. A second loop is made lower on the yarn and is pulled through the first. Knitting and crocheting are examples of this type of construction.

Tie-dyeing is a resist-dyeing technique used in many cultures to make patterns on traditional clothing. These women's trousers were tie-dyed in Uzbekistan.

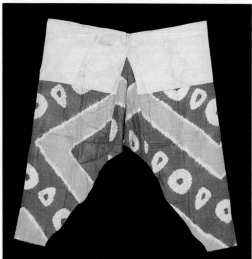

Textiles made by **knotting and interknotting** may be as simple as a fishing net or as complex as a macramé wall hanging. A knotted net is usually made from a single yarn, which is twisted or looped around itself and is knotted at each contact point. Tatting, a type of lace, is also made by knotting a single yarn. In interknotting, often called macramé, individual yarns within a set are arranged side by side. Each yarn then is knotted around an adjacent yarn. Different knots can be used to produce a variety of surface textures and patterns.

In **oblique interlacing**, a single set of yarns arranged side by side are interlaced with one another on the diagonal. The techniques known as braiding, finger-weaving, and bobbin lace produce this type of structure. These techniques are useful in the production of narrow fabrics.

Woven Techniques. Woven textiles may be interlaced, twined, or wrapped, but they always require the use of at least two sets of yarns. The two types of sets are the warp and weft. In **weaving**, the warp and weft are interworked at right angles. The warp yarns are held in place on a loom, and the weaver inserts the weft yarns. Simple weaves are plain weave, twill weave, and satin weave. Compound weaves are formed by adding extra sets of warp and weft yarns to the fabric during the weaving process. These extra yarns can create flat patterns on the surface of the cloth, or they can be pulled up to form loops of yarn, called pile, which can be left as loops or cut open. Velvet, corduroy, and some rugs and carpets are examples of pile fabrics.

Twining and **wrapping** also use a set of warp yarns and a set of weft yarns. In weft-twining, two or three weft yarns spiral around each other, enclosing the warp yarn within the twist. In wrapping, the weft yarn moves forward over and backward under the warps, instead of interlacing with them.

Dyeing and Printing

Adding color to fibers, yarns, and finished textiles can be done by dyeing or printing. Prior to the 1800's, all dyes came from natural sources such as plants, insects, and minerals. The first synthetic dye, a purple color called "mauveine," was invented in England in 1856 by W. H. Perkins. Today most people, even in nonindustrial countries, use synthetic dyes that produce an enormous range of bright, long-lasting colors. When dye is used to paint or print cloth, it is mixed with a thickening agent to prevent the color from spreading out. Pigments may also be used to paint or print on cloth. However, pigments do not bond chemically with the cloth, as dyes do, and they may flake or rub off.

This relief sculpture from Susa, which was a city in ancient Iran, dates from the 700's or the 600's B.C. It shows a woman using a spindle to spin yarn, just as many people do today.

Dyeing Methods. Dyes add color to yarns or to finished fabrics. Solid colors are produced by immersing an entire skein of yarn or length of cloth into a vat of dye. Patterns are made by treating yarns or fabrics with a substance that will resist penetration by the dye, in order to leave some areas uncolored. Many types of resists, including tightly tied cords, hot wax, or a paste of starch, are used. Resists and dye may be reapplied to yarn or cloth several times to create multicolored patterns. Ikat is the Indonesian word for resist-dyeing yarns bound with cords. This technique is also used in India, Central America, Central Asia, and Japan. In tie-dyeing, a technique common in many cultures, cords are wrapped around sections of a finished cloth before dipping it in dye. Wax resist, better known by its Indonesian name, batik, and paste resist also are used in many parts of the world. In these two methods, the wax or paste is used to draw or stamp patterns on the fabric before it is dyed.

Printing Methods. Printing textiles with dyes or pigments probably originated in China or India before the 1st century A.D. Europeans first used carved wooden blocks to print linens with a one-color pattern during the 1300's. However, it was not until trade routes opened with India in the 1600's that Europeans discovered the multicolored painted and printed cotton wall hangings and clothing fabrics of India, which became fashionable in Europe in the 1600's and 1700's. Because of the popularity of these fabrics, Eu-

Dry climates have helped preserve textiles from ancient times. These textiles were found in present-day Nevada with a mummified body more than 9,400 years old.

ropean artisans struggled to compete with the Indian fabrics.

In 1752, Francis Nixon, an Englishman working in Ireland, invented the technique of copperplate printing, using large engraved plates that printed finely drawn, single-color patterns. Both copperplate and woodblock printing were important industries in England and France during the late 1700's, but they were replaced in the early 1800's by mechanized printing machines that used metal or wooden rollers instead of flat plates. Roller printing, in turn, has largely been replaced by silk-screen printing since the 1930's.

▶ THE HISTORY OF TEXTILES

The making of textiles can be traced to prehistoric times. Evidence found by archaeologists in Europe shows that people used plant fibers to make cords and fishing nets around 8000 B.C. The use of linen in Ancient Egypt is known from mummy wrappings and garments that have survived from that time, from wall paintings and tomb models illustrating how cloth was made, and from spindle whorls (disks that act as pulleys) and loom weights found in excavated villages and temples. Chinese tradition dates the beginning of sericulture, the raising of silkworms for their cocoons, to between 3000 and 2000 B.C. Extraordinary examples of embroidered, tapestry-woven, and tie-dyed textiles of cotton and camelid (llama and alpaca) fibers have been found in excavations of sites in Peru dating from between 1500 B.C. and A.D. 1530. Sandals, socks, and pouches made of yucca and cotton fibers have been found at sites of early North American Indian groups, including the Anasazi, Mound Builders, and Basketmakers.

Textiles Before the Industrial Revolution

By the A.D. 100's, the Byzantine and Persian empires ex-

Adire cloth is made by the Yoruba people of Nigeria. They use a resist paste to mark designs on the cotton cloth before dyeing it in indigo.

ploited their positions at the crossroads of Europe and Asia by acting as mediators in the trade of silks coming from China. By the 300's, however, the Byzantine cities of Constantinople (now Istanbul, Turkey), Antioch (now Antakya, Turkey), and Damascus (in Syria) were established silk-weaving centers.

Their competitors were the Persians, who may have started their textile industry with Byzantine weavers captured from Syria. The tradition of fine weaving survived wars and conquests in both regions. From the 1500's to the 1800's, Safavid Iran and the Ottoman Empire had strong textile industries based on centuries of skill and artistry.

The Arab conquest of Syria, Iraq, Iran, and Egypt in the 600's led to the spread of silk weaving from those areas to Spain and Sicily after they also were conquered by the Arabs, in the 700's. Most of Europe, however, produced only linen and woolen cloth, and imported silk goods. Tapestry weaving flourished in Flanders (now parts of Belgium, France, and Holland), France, and Germany. Holland, Flanders, and Ireland had important linen industries, producing both yarn and cloth. England initially sold raw wool to weavers in Italy and Holland. However, in the 1500's, after skilled Protestant weavers emigrated from Catholic France, England began to export fine finished cloth.

Silk weaving in Sicily and southern Italy was well established by the 1200's, and after

GLOSSARY OF TEXTILE TERMS

BLOCK PRINTING: the process of printing with carved wooden blocks; sometimes pins or strips of metal are added to produce fine lines or dots.

CARDING: the process of brushing fibers to remove materials such as bits of seeds or twigs and to untangle and straighten the fibers and produce a "sliver" about an inch in diameter.

COMBING: a process done to carded slivers to remove the shorter, undesirable fibers and produce a smoother, stronger yarn.

FIBER: a flexible, threadlike strand of material much longer than it is wide, but of limited length.

FILAMENT: a single fiber of indefinite length.

LOOM: a frame that holds the warp threads taut to allow the weaver to insert the weft threads.

PIGMENT: an insoluble coloring material that does not combine chemically with the object it is used to color, but instead sits on the surface.

PILE: the soft, brush surface on fabric, formed by yarns that have been cut straight across, as in velvet, or left standing in loops, as in terrycloth.

PLYING: the process of twisting together two or more individual yarns to produce a thicker or stronger yarn.

ROLLER PRINTING: the process of printing fabric with engraved metal rollers that are attached around a core cylinder; a separate roller is used for each color.

SHUTTLE: a device used in weaving to hold the weft yarn and pass it from one side of the warp to the other.

SILK-SCREEN PRINTING: a stencil-like process using fine mesh cloth stretched in a frame; the negative areas of a design (areas that are not to be printed) on the mesh are coated with a substance that prevents ink from passing through those areas, and color is pushed through the uncoated areas of the screen.

Detail, Java batik

SKEIN: yarn or thread wound into a loose coil or figure eight.

SPINDLE: a rod, usually of wood, used to twist yarn as it is spun and also the rod on which the yarn is wound.

WARP: the set of yarns placed lengthwise in a loom, crossed by and interworked with the weft, and forming the lengthwise thread of a woven textile.

WEFT: the set of yarns carried by the shuttle and interworked at right angles with the warp.

1314, it spread northward. Italy was the most important European silk-weaving center for more than 400 years, producing damasks, brocades, and velvets. France became the leader in both style and technology in the mid-1600's, as designs and innovations by people such as Jean Berain and Jean Revel became known. In the 1700's, England maintained a small but thriving silk center, established in part by a second wave of refugees from religious persecution in France. Handmade lace, another important luxury item, was made in Italy, France, Flanders, and England from the late 1500's into the 1800's.

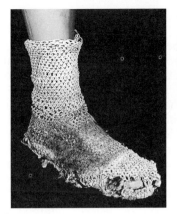

Looping was a technique known to early Native American cultures. This shoe-sock was made by the Anasazi about A.D. 1100–1300 (*left*). Ribbons and velvets designed by Gertrude Rapp won many medals in the 1800's at industrial exhibitions (*above*).

The Industrial Revolution and Modern Times

Inventions of the 1700's such as the flying shuttle, spinning jenny, and power loom were vital to the rapid mechanization in the 1800's of the textile industry. Great Britain and other colonial powers profited from the industrialization of textile making. The colonies provided raw material for European mills as well as markets for finished goods. Cotton and wool were the mainstays of British industry until the late 1800's, when American cotton manufacturing came of age. Silk and other luxury fabrics, which were helped along by Parisian high fashion, continued as important textile products in the 1800's and 1900's. Germany and Italy also maintained leadership roles in textile production in the 1900's.

▶ THE TEXTILE INDUSTRY IN NORTH AMERICA

Early North American colonists imported most of their cloth from their European homelands. As settlements became more stable, small workshop production of linen and woolen cloth began, but luxury fabrics continued to be imported. Raw materials, particularly furs and raw cotton, were exported. British laws did not allow colonists to import most machinery used to make textiles or to establish industries that would be in competition with British companies. In 1774, in defiance of these laws, John Hewson, an Englishman who had immigrated to Philadelphia, opened a textile printing workshop that existed into the 1800's.

After the American Revolution, textile manufacturing slowly changed from local hand-weaving to industrial production in large mills. The first water-powered cotton-spinning mill was opened in Rhode Island by Samuel Slater in 1790. The invention of the cotton gin by Eli Whitney in 1793 led to the expansion of cotton plantations in the southern states. As supplies of raw materials grew, so did the production of yarns and fabrics. At first the products tended to be of a lower quality than the European imports, but after the Civil War, high-quality cottons and woolens were produced in the northern states. Attracted by lower wages and fewer regulations, mills that manufactured simple fabrics and relied on unskilled labor began to move south in the late 1800's.

This cotton coverlet was block printed with fashionable flower and bird designs by Englishman John Hewson in Philadelphia in the late 1700's.

Gertrude Rapp, a member of the Harmonist society in Old Economy, Pennsylvania, and one of the first silk producers in America, manufactured silk ribbons and velvets during the 1830's. Silk, however, did not become a major industry until the 1880's, when tariffs, or taxes, were imposed on imported silks, and skilled weavers were encouraged to emigrate from Europe. Paterson, New Jersey, known as the Silk City, was the leading producer of silk in America between the 1880's and the 1920's. After the 1920's, however, the Great Depression of the 1930's and the competition from new artificial fibers caused the silk industry to decline.

The textile industry has expanded everywhere. New fibers, computer-driven looms, and computer-aided design point the way to the future. But not all textiles—even in industrialized nations—are produced by machine. Hand-weaving, knitting, embroidery, quilting, and other techniques and construction methods continue to be used by fiber artists and craftspeople around the world.

Many societies have maintained or revived their traditional crafts, making and using textiles the way they have for centuries. But choices of designs and materials are often influenced by outside sources. Modern themes and images may be depicted using ancient techniques, just as centuries-old designs may be constructed using new materials. Although times change and textiles change, people still make and appreciate textiles for their utility and their beauty.

MADELYN SHAW
Collections Manager and Collections Gallery Coordinator, The Textile Museum

See also CLOTHING; COTTON; CROCHETING; DYES AND DYEING; FIBERS; INDUSTRIAL REVOLUTION; KNITTING; LACE; NYLON AND OTHER SYNTHETIC FIBERS; RUGS AND CARPETS; SILK; TAPESTRY; WEAVING; WOOL.

THACKERAY, WILLIAM MAKEPEACE (1811–1863)

William Makepeace Thackeray, one of the greatest English novelists of the Victorian period, was born in Calcutta, India, on July 18, 1811. His father, who was in the British civil service in India, died when William was 4. The next year, William was sent to England to live with relatives. His mother remained in India and remarried. William did not like school and was not an outstanding student. In 1829 he entered Trinity College, Cambridge, but left after one year.

Thackeray traveled, studied law for a while, ran a newspaper, and studied art in Paris. He soon spent the fortune he had inherited, and to earn a living, he began writing for newspapers. In 1836 he married Isabella Shawe. They had three daughters (one died in infancy) before Mrs. Thackeray became mentally ill and had to be hospitalized.

Thackeray's first book, *The Paris Sketch Book*, was published in 1840. He then became a regular contributor of stories and drawings to *Punch*, a humor magazine started in 1841. He wrote a number of Christmas stories, including *The Rose and the Ring*. *The Luck of Barry Lyndon*, a novel about the adventures of a handsome rogue, was published in 1844.

Thackeray's masterpiece, the novel *Vanity Fair*, was published in monthly parts during 1847 and 1848. Through the character of the ambitious and amoral Becky Sharp, the novel satirizes English society of the 1800's. His later novels include *Pendennis* (1848–50), *Henry Esmond* (1852), and *The Newcomes* (1853–55).

In 1852, Thackeray went to the United States on a lecture tour. It was such a success that he made a second tour in 1855. He was made editor of a new magazine, the *Cornhill*, in 1860. Poor health forced him to retire in 1862, but he continued to write for the *Cornhill* until his death in London on December 24, 1863.

Reviewed by JULIET MCMASTER
University of Alberta (Canada)

▶ VANITY FAIR

Becky Sharp, the main character in Thackeray's social satire, is a penniless young woman who schemes to win the affections of wealthy men. Her first victim is Joseph Sedley. In the excerpt on the following page, which includes an illustration by the author, Joseph has just come home from India, and Becky is visiting his sister Amelia.

The first move showed considerable skill. When she called Sedley a very handsome man, she knew that Amelia would tell her mother, who would probably tell Joseph, or who, at any rate, would be pleased by the compliment paid to her son. All mothers are. If you had told Sycorax that her son Caliban was as handsome as Apollo, she would have been pleased, witch as she was. Perhaps, too, Joseph Sedley would overhear the compliment—Rebecca spoke loud enough—and he *did* hear, and (thinking in his heart that he was a very fine man) the praise thrilled through every fibre of his big body, and made it tingle with pleasure. Then, however, came a recoil. "Is the girl making fun of me?" he thought, and straightway he bounced towards the bell, and was for retreating, as we have seen, when his father's jokes and his mother's entreaties caused him to pause and stay where he was. He conducted the young lady down to dinner in a dubious and agitated frame of mind. "Does she really think I am handsome?" thought he, "or is she only making game of me?" We have talked of Joseph Sedley being as vain as a girl. Heaven help us! the girls have only to turn the tables, and say of one of their own sex, "She is as vain as a man," and they will have perfect reason. The bearded creatures are quite as eager for praise, quite as finikin over their toilets, quite as proud of their personal advantages, quite as conscious of their powers of fascination, as any coquette in the world.

Downstairs, then, they went, Joseph very red and blushing, Rebecca very modest, and holding her green eyes downwards. She was dressed in white, with bare shoulders as white as snow—the picture of youth, unprotected innocence, and

humble virgin simplicity. "I must be very quiet," thought Rebecca, "and very much interested about India."

Now we have heard how Mrs Sedley had prepared a fine curry for her son, just as he liked it, and in the course of dinner a portion of this dish was offered to Rebecca. "What is it?" said she, turning an appealing look to Mr Joseph.

"Capital," said he. His mouth was full of it: his face quite red with the delightful exercise of gobbling. "Mother, it's as good as my own curries in India."

"Oh, I must try some, if it is an Indian dish," said Miss Rebecca. "I am sure everything must be good that comes from there."

"Give Miss Sharp some curry, my dear," said Mr Sedley, laughing.

Rebecca had never tasted the dish before.

"Do you find it as good as everything else from India?" said Mr Sedley.

"Oh, excellent!" said Rebecca, who was suffering tortures with the cayenne pepper.

"Try a chili with it, Miss Sharp," said Joseph, really interested.

"A chili," said Rebecca, gasping. "Oh, yes!" She thought a chili was something cool, as its name imported, and was served with some. "How fresh and green they look," she said, and put one into her mouth. It was hotter than the curry; flesh and blood could bear it no longer. She laid down her fork. "Water, for Heaven's sake, water!" she cried. Mr Sedley burst out laughing (he was a coarse man, from the Stock Exchange, where they love all sorts of practical jokes). "They are real Indian, I assure you," said he. "Sambo, give Miss Sharp some water."

The paternal laugh was echoed by Joseph, who thought the joke capital. The ladies only smiled a little. They thought poor Rebecca suffered too much. She would have liked to choke old Sedley, but she swallowed her mortification as well as she had the abominable curry before it, and as soon as she could speak, said, with a comical, good-humoured air:

"I ought to have remembered the pepper which the Princess of Persia puts in the cream-tarts in the *Arabian Nights*. Do you put cayenne into your cream-tarts in India, sir?"

Old Sedley began to laugh, and thought Rebecca was a good-humoured girl. Joseph simply said, "Cream-tarts, miss? Our cream is very bad in Bengal. We generally use goats' milk; and, 'gad, do you know, I've got to prefer it!"

"You won't like *everything* from India now, Miss Sharp," said the old gentleman; but when the ladies had retired after dinner, the wily old fellow said to his son, "Have a care, Joe; that girl is setting her cap at you."

THAILAND

Thailand is an ancient kingdom in Southeast Asia. It is approximately the size of France and has a population of about 62 million. Known for hundreds of years as Siam, the country changed its name in 1939 to Thailand, meaning "Land of the Free." The name is appropriate, for Thailand is the only Southeast Asian nation never to have been a European colony.

▶ PEOPLE

Most of Thailand's people belong to the Thai/Lao ethnic group. There are also people of Chinese, Malay, Khmer (Cambodian), and Vietnamese

ancestry. Smaller numbers of other ethnic groups are also present.

About half of Thailand's population lives in or near urban areas in modern buildings. Others live in rural villages. Traditional village homes are built of wood or bamboo, with roofs made of thatch or corrugated iron.

Although Western-style dress is now common, some Thai in rural areas wear traditional clothing. Both men and women wear long, flowing garments called sarongs, and men sometimes wear loin-

Clockwise from right: An elderly villager from a rural area of Thailand. A vendor in Chiang Mai displays fans for sale. Bangkok, Thailand's capital and chief port, is one of the largest cities in Southeast Asia.

148

cloths. In private homes, family members and guests do not wear footwear.

Language. The country's official language is Thai. Most people speak the Bangkok dialect. English is widely taught in schools and many Thai speak it fluently.

Religion. Most Thai are Buddhist. The entire country is dotted with thousands of Buddhist temples called **wats**. Every Thai male is expected to serve in a wat for at least three months. About 4 percent of Thailand's population is Muslim.

Education. Thailand's school system has three major levels of education—primary, secondary (including high school), and higher education. In the past, only primary education was required. Since 1997, however, education up to high school (twelve years) has been compulsory. It is also free.

Thailand has many universities. The oldest and most prestigious are Chulalongkorn and Thammasat, both in Bangkok. The Thai respect for education is reflected by the country's high literacy rate (the number of people who can read and write), which is above 90 percent.

Food. Rice is the staple food. Thai cuisine is very spicy and usually includes lots of vegetables with fish, pork, or chicken. Fish sauce, hot peppers, and chili pastes are principal ingredients in Thai cooking. Tropical fruits are also part of the Thai diet.

Sports and Recreation. Favorite sports in Thailand include traditional Thai boxing and *takraw*, a cross between soccer and volleyball. Western sports such as basketball and tennis have also become popular.

▶ **LAND**

Thailand is situated in the center of Southeast Asia, bordering Myanmar, Laos, Cambodia, and Malaysia.

Land Regions. The country consists of four distinct land areas. The central plains region is the country's most populous and fertile area. The northwestern region is mountainous and includes most of the country's tropical forest. Thailand's highest point, Doi Inthanon, which rises to 8,512 feet (2,594 meters), is located there. The northeastern region, or Khorat Plateau, has poor soil that cannot be used to grow crops. The southern region is a narrow strip of land on the Malay Peninsula, which Thailand shares with

Thailand

Malaysia. It consists of heavily forested mountains.

Rivers and Coastal Waters. Thailand has two major river systems—the Chao Phraya (or Me Nam) and the Mun. Together with its four largest branches, the Chao Phraya

FACTS and figures

KINGDOM OF THAILAND is the official name of the country.

LOCATION: Southeast Asia.

AREA: 198,455 sq mi (514,000 km²).

POPULATION: 62,400,000 (estimate).

CAPITAL AND LARGEST CITY: Bangkok (Krung Thep).

MAJOR LANGUAGE: Thai.

MAJOR RELIGIOUS GROUP: Buddhist.

GOVERNMENT: Constitutional monarchy. **Head of state**—king. **Head of government**—prime minister. **Legislature**—National Assembly (composed of the Senate and House of Representatives).

CHIEF PRODUCTS: Agricultural—rice, cassava, rubber, corn, sugarcane, coconuts, and soybeans. **Manufactured**—textiles, beverages, tobacco products, cement, jewelry, electric appliances and components, computers and computer parts, integrated circuits, furniture, and plastic. **Mineral**—tin, tungsten, natural gas.

MONETARY UNIT: Baht (1 baht = 100 satang).

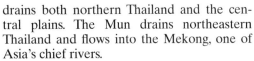
Above: Workers harvest rice, Thailand's chief agricultural export. Most rice is grown in the central plains region.
Right: Thailand's lush rain forests are becoming an increasingly important resource for medicines, obtained from plants that grow there.

drains both northern Thailand and the central plains. The Mun drains northeastern Thailand and flows into the Mekong, one of Asia's chief rivers.

Thailand also has about 2,000 miles (3,200 kilometers) of coastline along the Gulf of Thailand and the Andaman Sea. Phuket, the country's largest island, is off the southwestern coast in the Andaman Sea.

Climate. Thailand has a tropical climate with three seasons: hot, rainy, and cool. Average temperatures for most of the country range from about 65 to 95°F (18 to 35°C), depending on season and elevation. Yearly rainfall varies widely, from about 40 inches (1,000 millimeters) in the central plains to about 220 inches (5,600 millimeters) in the southern peninsula.

Natural Resources. Fertile soil is Thailand's chief natural resource. The central plains region is one of the world's most productive areas for growing rice. Thailand's coastal waters are rich in marine life, although it has been depleted in recent years. Tin is the country's most important mineral and a major export. Thailand is the world's second largest producer of tungsten and third largest producer of tin. Other mineral deposits include natural gas, lignite (brown coal), and gypsum. Forests were once a source of teak and other valuable woods. But logging and farming have drastically reduced the country's forested areas. Logging was banned in 1989, and Thailand's remaining rain forests are becoming an increasingly important resource for medicines.

▶ **ECONOMY**

Since the 1960's government policies have converted Thailand from an agricultural to an industrial nation. Between 1985 and 1995, it had one of the world's highest rates of economic growth. This was largely fueled by the manufacture of goods for export, including clothing, toys, integrated circuits, and consumer electronics parts.

Since 1997, however, the economy has declined. The value of Thailand's currency dropped, due in part to excessive growth and unprofitable corporate investment in the previous decade. Many businesses have gone bankrupt and unemployment is widespread. Although economic recovery is under way, progress has been limited by several factors, including corruption, an inefficient banking system, the decline of the tourist industry (due in part to terrorist activity and war), and the worldwide economic slowdown.

Services. Services account for about 50 percent of Thailand's economy. They include personal and business services, wholesale and retail trade, finance, insurance, real estate, transportation, utilities, and communications. Businesses related to tourism are also included in the service sector.

Manufacturing. Manufacturing accounts for 40 percent of Thailand's economy. Manufactured items include textiles and garments, beverages, tobacco products, cement, jewelry, electric appliances and components, computers and computer parts, integrated circuits, furniture, and plastic.

Agriculture. Although Thailand's economy is no longer based on agriculture, more than half the population is still involved in some agricultural activity. Thailand remains one of the world's major exporters of farm products such as rice, cassava (a starchy root), rubber, sugarcane, soybeans, and fruits.

▶ **MAJOR CITIES**

Bangkok is Thailand's capital, largest city, chief port, and economic and cultural center. It is also one of Southeast Asia's major cities. The Bangkok metropolitan area, which includes parts of several adjacent cities—**Nonthaburi**, **Pathum Thani**, **Samut Prakan**, and **Nakhon Pathom**—has a population of 10 to 12 million. The Thai name for Bangkok is Krung Thep, or "City of Angels." People from all over the country come to work, study, and visit, or worship at its many beautiful Buddhist temples. For more information, see the article BANGKOK in Volume B.

Other important cities include **Chiang Mai**, a cultural and religious center in the north. Its hundreds of Buddhist temples make the city one of the region's most important tourist destinations; **Songkhla**, on the peninsula, a trade center and port; **Nakhon Si Thammarat**, also on the peninsula, one of Thailand's oldest Buddhist centers; and **Nakhon Ratchasima** in the east, a trade and industrial center.

▶ **CULTURAL HERITAGE**

Music. Although Thai folk music is popular with most Thai, especially in the northeast, many Thai listen to pop and rock music. Classical Thai music, once limited to the royal court, is also popular. Musicians often perform in ensembles called *piphats*, which include cymbals, gongs, drums, and a wind instrument similar to an oboe.

Art. Traditional Thai art is religious and includes sculpture, painting, and temple architecture. Thai craftspeople are known for their beautiful textiles, particularly silks, as well as bamboo and rattan furniture.

Literature. Thailand's earliest written literature dates back to the 1200's and often features themes related to religion or the monarch. Notable modern writers include Dok Mai Sot, Si Burapha, Kukrit Pramoj, and Jit Phoumisak.

Theater and Dance. The best-known form of traditional Thai theater is *khon*, a precisely choreographed drama based on Hindu themes, performed by dancers in elaborate costumes and masks. Other forms of theater include *lakhon* and *likay*, which are more informal. These also dramatize a wider range of subjects.

▶ **GOVERNMENT**

Until 1932, Thailand was ruled as an absolute monarchy. In 1932, following a bloodless revolution, the government became a constitutional monarchy. The king now serves as head of state but possesses little political power. Thailand's present monarch is Bhumibol Adulyadej (Rama IX), who came to the throne in 1946. He is the world's longest-serving living monarch.

The legislative body is the National Assembly, which is composed of two chambers, the Senate and House of Representatives. Senators, formerly appointed by the king, have been elected since 2000 to 6-year terms. Members of the House of Representatives are elected by the people to 4-year terms. The prime minister, who is the head of government, must be a member of the House of Representatives and is chosen by that body.

Thai dancers in traditional costume. Dance is an important art form in Thailand.

▶ HISTORY

Archaeological finds indicate that bronze metalworking was flourishing in the area of present-day Thailand by about 2000 B.C. About 1,000 years later, the inhabitants of what is now northeastern Thailand cultivated rice. These two factors fueled the development of social and political systems.

A Powerful Kingdom. By the 1200's the Thai had established several small kingdoms, such as Chiang Mai and Sukhothai in the upper and lower Chao Phraya regions. The kingdom of Ayutthaya was founded in 1350 and remained one of the most dominant powers in the region for some 400 years. Bangkok was founded as the capital by the Chakri dynasty in 1782. In the 1800's the British and French began to build colonial empires in the region. Although the Thai kingdom (then known as Siam) kept its independence, the Thai state—particularly its economy—was strongly influenced by European colonialism.

Modernization began under King Mongkut (Rama IV), who ruled from 1851 to 1868. Mongkut (the model for the king in the musical *The King and I*) promoted new ideas and scientific knowledge and paved the way for reform. His son, Chulalongkorn (Rama V), who ruled from 1868 to 1910, promoted sweeping changes in government administration, education, transportation, and the armed forces. He abolished slavery, emphasized Western education, and laid the foundation for a modern economy.

Revolution and Reform. By 1932, during the reign of King Prajadhipok (Rama VII), dissatisfaction with the absolute monarchy and exposure to Western ideas led to the revolution that created the current constitutional government. This revolution also launched the continuing struggle between military and civilian groups for government control. Since then, there have been several violent clashes between both groups, more than 20 military coups, and 17 constitutions.

Modern Thailand. Although modernization has improved living conditions for many Thais (including better education and health

King Chulalongkorn (Rama V), who ruled Thailand from 1868 to 1910, promoted sweeping social and economic reforms.

care), it has also created greater gaps between rich and poor and urban and rural societies, as well as damage to the environment. An increasingly global economy threatens to destroy local cultures.

Thailand also faces unrest among Muslims in the southern provinces (the ethnic Malay), who have been discouraged from expressing their cultural identity and have little voice in the government. Ethnic minorities in the northwest have also been denied basic rights.

Drug abuse is a serious problem in Thailand, and this has contributed to a high incidence of AIDS. The country, nevertheless, is known for its efficient health care system.

Recent Events. Thailand's constitution was adopted in 1997 during a period of strong public protest against the government's response to the nation's economic crisis. The first to be written with public input, it stresses greater civil liberties and provides for direct elections to the Senate (members were previously appointed by the king). The 2001 elections were the first in which a single political party (the Thai Rak Thai) won more than half the seats in the legislature. Party leader Thaksin Sinawatra became prime minister.

In early 2004, Thailand reported its first human case of influenza A (H5N1), a deadly virus more commonly known as bird flu. By 2005, the government had implemented an emergency program to help stop the spread of the disease.

On December 26, 2004, a violent earthquake in the Indian Ocean caused tidal waves that in Thailand alone killed more than 5,300 people. The island of Phuket was especially devastated.

In 2005, the Thai Rak Thai party won re-election, giving Thaksin an unprecedented second term as prime minister. This historic election ended half a century of constant political upheaval.

Reviewed by THONGCHAI WINICHAKUL
Center for Southeast Asian Studies
University of Wisconsin, Madison

The holiday of Thanksgiving dates back to 1621 when the Pilgrim settlers celebrated their first harvest by enjoying a bountiful feast with their native American friends.

THANKSGIVING DAY

On Thanksgiving Day, American people gather together with their family and friends to share food and to give thanks for the blessings of the past year. In kitchens across the country, people work to prepare such traditional foods of the season as turkey, cranberry sauce and pumpkin pie. This American holiday has been celebrated since the early days of the Pilgrims, who set aside a time of festive thanksgiving in response to a plentiful harvest.

The Pilgrims held the first Thanksgiving festival at Plymouth, Massachusetts, in October of 1621. They had arrived there from England the year before on the ship *Mayflower*. The harsh winter, sickness, and hunger caused the death of over half of the original 100 settlers in their first year there.

By the fall of 1621 their lives had improved greatly. The seeds planted earlier in the year had produced a harvest that allowed the settlers to increase their meager food rations, thereby improving their health. Houses were constructed, promising adequate shelter for the upcoming winter. A long-lasting peace treaty was arranged between Massasoit, head

chief of the Wampanoag Indians, and the new settlers, allowing the settlers to hunt for food in the surrounding woods in safety.

Because of their good fortune, the Pilgrims decreed a holiday on which all might, "after a more special manner, rejoice together."

William Bradford, the governor of the colony, sent men out to hunt for waterfowl and wild turkeys. The women went about the work of preparing foods for the upcoming feast. Chief Massasoit was invited to the feast, and he brought with him 90 brightly painted male warriors, about four times the number of Pilgrim men living in the settlement at that time. The Indians contributed to the feast by going into the surrounding forest to hunt deer, so the feast would include venison.

This bright festival took place in an open field along the north bank of Town Brook. There was target shooting with guns and bows and arrows as well as games of skill and chance. The Indians entertained with some of their dances. Captain Miles Standish staged a military review of his tiny force of men.

For three days the festivities went on, with

the Pilgrims and their guests gorging themselves on venison cooked on a spit over a blazing open fire, roast ducks and geese, clams and other shellfish, smoked eel, groundnuts (a kind of potatolike root), baked in hot ashes, peas, salad greens, herbs, corn pones, and "Injun" (corn-rye) bread. The Pilgrims served wine made from wild grapes.

There were cranberries by the bushel in neighboring bogs. But it is doubtful that the Pilgrims had yet found a tasty way of using them. It is also doubtful that the feast included another delicious invention—pumpkin pie. If such pie was served, it is certain that it was not topped with rich whipped cream, for the Pilgrims had no cows as yet and would not have any for another three years.

After that first New England Thanksgiving, the custom spread throughout the colonies, but each region chose its own date. In 1789, George Washington, the first president of the United States, proclaimed November 26 a day of Thanksgiving. His proclamation still expresses the spirit of the feast:

Whereas it is the duty of all nations to acknowledge the providence of Almighty God, to obey his will, to be grateful for his benefits, and humbly to implore his protection and favor . . . now therefore I do recommend and assign Thursday, the 26th day of November next to be devoted by the people of these States to the service of that great and glorious Being, who is the beneficent Author of all the good that was, that is, or that will be; that we may then all unite in rendering unto him our sincere and humble thanks for his kind care and protection of the people of this country. . . .

Thanksgiving Day continued to be celebrated in the United States on different days in different states until Mrs. Sarah Josepha Hale, editor of *Godey's Lady's Book,* decided to do something about it. For more than 30 years, she wrote letters to the governors and the presidents asking them to make Thanksgiving Day a national holiday.

Finally, in 1863, President Lincoln issued a White House proclamation calling on the "whole American people" wherever they lived—north, south, east, or west—to unite "with one heart and one voice" in observing a special day of thanksgiving.

Setting apart the last Thursday of November for the purpose, the President urged prayers in

Americans have set aside the fourth Thursday in November as an official day of thanks for their blessings. Many families celebrate Thanksgiving Day with a delicious turkey dinner.

the churches and in the homes to "implore the interposition of the almighty hand to heal the wounds of the nation and to restore it . . . to the full enjoyment of peace, harmony, tranquility and union." He also asked that people express heartfelt thanks for the "blessings of fruitful fields and healthful skies."

In 1939, President Franklin D. Roosevelt advanced Thanksgiving Day one week. However, since some states used the new date and others the old, it was changed again two years later. Thanksgiving Day is now celebrated on the fourth Thursday in November.

The theme of Thanksiving has always been peace and plenty, health and happiness. To be truly observed, it involves not merely "thanks" but "giving," too. It is a time for special generosity in remembering and helping the less fortunate.

GEORGE F. WILLISON
Author, *Saints and Strangers: Lives of Pilgrim Fathers and Their Families*

THANT, U (1909–1974)

U Thant was a Burmese diplomat and secretary-general of the United Nations. He took over the United Nations post at a difficult time, following the death of Secretary-General Dag Hammarskjöld in a plane crash.

Thant was born on January 22, 1909, in Pantanaw, Burma (now Myanmar). In Burmese, "U" means "Mr." or "uncle." Thant attended University College in Rangoon (now Yangon). He then became a teacher, and later, headmaster at his former high school. After Burma became independent in 1948, Thant held several posts in the government. He became Burma's permanent representative to the United Nations in 1957. Following Hammarskjöld's death in 1961, Thant became acting secretary-general after weeks of disagreement between the United States and the Soviet Union over the post. Thant was elected secretary-general in 1962 and re-elected in 1966.

As secretary-general, Thant was faced with a number of international crises. He played a key role in helping to avert war between the United States and the Soviet Union during the 1962 Cuban missile crisis. But he was frustrated by the inability of the United Nations to help end the war in Vietnam. One of Thant's most controversial decisions as secretary-general concerned the U.N. peacekeeping force stationed in the Gaza Strip and Sinai peninsula. Egypt and Israel had fought over the territory, and the U.N. force had been sent to prevent further fighting. At the insistence of the Egyptian government, Thant had the peacekeeping force withdrawn. Soon after, the 1967 Arab-Israeli War broke out.

Thant's term of office as secretary-general ended on December 31, 1971. He died in New York City on November 25, 1974.

MICHAEL J. BERLIN
United Nations Correspondent
The Washington Post

THATCHER, MARGARET (1925–)

Margaret Thatcher was the first woman prime minister in British history (1979–90) and the first British prime minister in more than 150 years to win three consecutive elections. She was born Margaret Hilda Roberts on October 13, 1925, above a shop in Grantham, England. Her father was a grocer. Margaret won a scholarship to Oxford University and later worked as a research chemist.

An active member of the Conservative Party, Thatcher tried but failed to win election to Parliament in 1950 and 1951. She then studied law and married Denis Thatcher, a businessman. In 1953 she gave birth to twins, Mark and Carol. By the time she won a seat in Parliament in 1959, she was a practicing barrister (trial lawyer) and an expert in tax law.

In the House of Commons, Thatcher soon made her mark as a forceful speaker and tireless worker. When the Conservatives returned to power in 1970 under Prime Minister Edward Heath, she served as secretary of state for education and science.

In 1975, Thatcher became the first woman to head a major British political party. At that time, the British people watched with alarm as prices rose steeply. They felt that Thatcher, with her conservative ideas and determination, was the best person to deal with the problem of inflation. After the election of May 1979, Thatcher became prime minister. She cut taxes and some social services and reduced government spending and inflation. But she was criticized for failing to deal with widespread unemployment.

In 1982, Britain won a short but difficult war against Argentina in the Falkland Islands. The British approved of Thatcher's firm handling of the crisis, and her party won easy political victories in the elections of 1983 and 1987.

Thatcher, however, later lost support due to an unpopular citizens' poll tax, continuing unemployment, and her opposition to participate fully in a new European monetary system. In November 1990, she was forced to resign as party leader. Thatcher was succeeded as prime minister by her protegé John Major. After her retirement, she was given the title Baroness Thatcher of Kestevan. She has published two memoirs, *The Downing Street Years* (1993) and *The Path to Power* (1995).

GEORGE MALCOLM THOMSON
Author, *The Prime Ministers*

A theater with an arena stage (*top right*) makes the audience feel a part of the action. The classic proscenium stage (*below right*) "frames" the play like a picture frame. The thrust stage (*below*) is most like the stage of Shakespeare's day.

THEATER

A theater is a place in which actors perform for an audience. A theater can be located anywhere—indoors or outdoors, in a specially constructed space or a place chosen on the spur of the moment. An audience might consist of one person or thousands. Although the word "theater" refers specifically to the place in which actors perform, it is also used to describe the entire process of dramatic production and performance.

▶ THE BUILDING

A typical theater building has a stage, an auditorium, and a backstage area.

The Stage. The space in which actors perform is called a stage. Although variations exist, three basic types of stage are used today: the **arena** stage, sometimes called theater-in-the-round; the **thrust** stage; and the **proscenium**, or "picture frame," stage.

In a theater with an arena stage, the audience sits around the performers. This form was first used 2,000 years ago by the ancient Greeks. Because the audience surrounds the stage, there is little room for scenery. Arena productions therefore depend more on costumes and lighting to suggest the setting and mood of the play.

In a theater with a thrust stage, the audience sits on three sides of the stage. The fourth side is placed against a wall or an opening through which the audience can see the scenery.

The proscenium stage is usually in a fan-shaped auditorium, with the stage at the narrow end of the fan. The audience is separated from the stage by a wall with an opening in it, called the proscenium arch, which frames the stage and supports the curtain.

The Auditorium. The part of the theater where the audience sits is called the auditorium. The first floor of a proscenium theater is called the orchestra. Musicians sit in the orchestra pit, which is usually located slightly below the front of the stage. Sound-control equipment is often located at the rear of the orchestra. Above the orchestra floor and extending over part of it is the balcony. This level is often called the mezzanine. Lighting-control equipment is sometimes placed here. Some theaters have another level, called the second balcony or, if the second level is referred to as the mezzanine, the balcony.

Backstage. "Backstage" is the term used for the space behind the stage. Here are the dressing rooms, the sound and lighting boards (if they are not located in the main auditorium), and the scenery and properties.

In the dressing rooms, actors apply makeup and change into the clothes they wear on stage. Properties, or **props**, may be kept in a special room called the prop room. Big props —such as tables, chairs, and pictures—are part of the stage set. Smaller props—such as books, letters, and swords—which actors can carry on the stage, are called hand props.

Above the stage are the **flies**, the space from which scenery is lowered, or "flown" down, and where it is often stored when not in use.

▶ **PEOPLE**

Playwright. The playwright, also called the dramatist, writes the play. It is called a straight play if it is performed without music and a book if it is a musical. Through the characters, the playwright portrays the life and people of the time in which the play is set.

Producer. In the United States, the producer is responsible for the entire process of presenting the play. In commercial theater, the producer raises the money needed to put on the show. The producer either selects a play or musical (usually called a property) that has already been written or develops one for production. The producer selects the director, rents the theater, and pays salaries and bills. In England, the producer is called the manager. In amateur and not-for-profit theaters, the producer often directs as well and may be called the artistic director.

Director. The director brings the playwright's words to life. The director works with the actors, staging the play and interpreting the playwright's intentions. The director selects the actors and coordinates the tasks of everybody involved in the production, including the scenic, costume, lighting, and sound designers. Before the mid-1900's, many actors formed their own theater companies and were called actor-managers. They directed the plays in which they performed.

In England the director is usually called the producer, in Europe the *régisseur*.

Actors. Actors are either amateur or professional. An amateur actor receives no pay for performing and often holds another job. A professional actor, on the other hand, is paid and works as an actor full-time. Acting is an ancient tradition. Thousands of years ago,

The audience never sees many of the people who work to put on a theatrical production. They include (*left*) the director and (*right*) the costume designer.

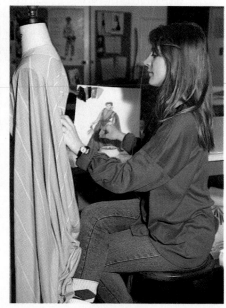

the first actors danced, chanted, and sang in religious ceremonies. Over time, acting became a recognized craft requiring discipline and a great deal of hard work. Actors study voice and speech so that their enunciation (pronunciation of words) is clear and their voices can project to the last row of a theater. They study characterization in order to understand the parts they play. And they study body movement or dance so that they know how to move on the stage.

Set Designer. The set designer, sometimes called the scenic designer, plans and designs the scenery. The designer makes a drawing of the proposed setting and builds a miniature set with every piece of furniture or scenery in place. The setting may be realistic, such as a living room that looks just like one in a real home, or it may be nonrealistic, merely suggesting a living room.

Lighting and Sound Designers. In addition to making sure that the audience can see the action on stage, the lighting designer helps create the mood of the play. Different lighting would be used for a grim murder scene, for instance, than for a happy party scene.

Sound designers create a balance between the actors' voices and musical instruments, emphasize certain sound elements, and create special sound effects. When necessary, sound may be amplified (made louder) with microphones, either installed on the stage or worn by performers.

In addition to establishing characterization, stage makeup defines actors' features so that the audience can see their facial expressions from a distance.

Costume Designer and Makeup Artist. The costume designer designs the clothes worn by the actors on stage. The costumes are either purchased, rented, or constructed in special costume shops. In addition to ensuring that costumes are historically correct, the designer must make sure that the actors can make quick changes when necessary and move easily when in costume.

Makeup is an important part of any stage performance. **Straight makeup** brings out the actor's own features and helps the audience see his or her facial expressions more clearly. **Character makeup** is used to transform an actor's appearance and may include wigs, false noses, and the like. Actors often design and apply their own makeup, but a makeup artist may be hired for certain productions.

Stage Manager. The stage manager assists the director at rehearsals and is in charge backstage after the play opens. The stage manager gives cues (signals) for changes in lighting, for opening and closing the curtain, and for sound effects. The stage manager or an assistant follows the script during the performance and prompts any actor who forgets a line.

Backstage Crew. "Backstage crew" is the general name for the people who work at the back of the stage. They include the stagehands, who carry scenery and furniture on and off the stage and who operate the curtain; the electricians, who control the lighting on the stage and in the auditorium; and the person in charge of props.

A set designer works with a scale model and blueprints. The set, or scenic, designer is responsible for creating the setting in which the play is staged.

▶ **THEATER AROUND THE WORLD**

Every country in the world has some form of theater. Like music and painting, it is an art and part of a nation's culture.

Most countries have theaters subsidized, or financed, by their governments. Some theaters are supported by a combination of government funds and private donations. These theaters do not exist to make money and are therefore called not-for-profit. Often a resident group of actors, directors, and designers works on all the productions presented by the theater. Some not-for-profit theaters are **repertory** companies, which present a series of different plays. The actors play a variety of parts during a season. Both new works and classic plays may be presented.

An individual, a group of people, or a business organization raises the money to produce a play in a commercial theater. The production continues only as long as it makes a profit. After salaries, rent, and other bills are paid, the profits are distributed among the people who invested in the show.

Almost every country has theater festivals, usually held in the summer so that tourists and vacationers can attend. Some are world famous, notably Scotland's Edinburgh Festival; the festival of Greek classics at Epidaurus, Greece; and the Théâtre des Nations (Theater of the Nations) held annually in Paris. In the United States, the Williamstown Theater Festival, in Massachusetts, is well known. In Canada, an important event is the Shakespeare Festival in Stratford, Ontario.

United States. The United States had a government-subsidized theater from 1935 to 1939, when the Federal Theater Project was created by an act of Congress to give work to the theater people during the Depression. During its existence, it brought living theater to almost every part of the nation and employed more than 10,000 actors, playwrights, directors, and designers.

In 1964, Congress created the National Endowment for the Arts (NEA), a federal agency that promotes and supports the arts. Funds from the NEA helped build and support the John F. Kennedy Center for the Performing Arts in Washington, D.C. The NEA and state arts councils award monetary grants to not-for-profit theaters. This has spurred the development of more than 100 regional professional theaters throughout the nation. These theaters present new works, revivals, and the classics. They are financed by a combination of government funds, foundation grants, and private contributions. Some of the better-known regional theaters include the Long Wharf and Yale Repertory theaters in New Haven, Connecticut; the Guthrie Theater in Minneapolis; the American Conservatory Theater in San Francisco; the Mark Taper Forum in Los Angeles; and the Alley Theater in Houston, Texas.

New York City's theater district is concentrated in a Manhattan area called Broadway. Scattered throughout the city are off-Broadway and off-off-Broadway theaters. On an average evening in New York City, it is possible to choose from more than 80 productions, ranging from hit musicals to lower-priced experimental works.

Many towns have amateur community theaters. Before the start of the resident theater movement, community theaters in the United States provided a place for playwrights to stage new plays. Many well-known modern playwrights, including Tennessee Williams and William Inge, staged their first works in these small theaters. Eugene O'Neill, one of America's greatest dramatists, had his first plays performed by an amateur group in Massachusetts. This group later became the famous Provincetown Players.

The United States has more university theaters than any other country because of its many college and university drama departments. University theaters are nonprofessional because their casts and crews are students.

There is a long tradition of touring theater in the United States. National companies of hit Broadway shows play major cities throughout the nation, and "bus and truck" productions travel to smaller towns and college campuses. These tours are called bus and truck because the cast travels by bus, and the sets and props are transported by truck. One form of touring theater that has almost vanished is the showboat. During the late 1800's and early 1900's, showboats played up and down the large rivers, bringing theater to frontier settlements along the riverbanks.

Another form of theater, seen mostly in the summer, is stock. Stock companies flourished between 1890 and 1925 and provided training for aspiring actors. Today, some sum-

Sarah Bernhardt as Tosca

Helen Hayes

Sarah Bernhardt (1844–1923), a world-renowned French actress, was born Henriette Rosine Bernard in Paris. Called the Divine Sarah, she was known for her *voix d'or* ("golden voice"). She acted with the Comédie Française (1874–80), touring Europe and the United States with great success. She was noted for her performances in plays by Hugo, Sardou, Rostand, and Racine. Despite a leg amputation in 1915, she continued her acting career. She wrote memoirs and several plays and managed her own theater in Paris.

Edwin Thomas Booth (1833–93), born in Bel Air, Maryland, was the greatest American actor of his day and the first to win international recognition. Known especially for Shakespearean roles, he set a record in 1864 when he played Hamlet in 100 consecutive performances. He built the Booth Theater in New York City (1869) and founded the Players Club there (1888). Booth was the son of noted actor Junius Brutus Booth and the brother of John Wilkes Booth, the assassin of Abraham Lincoln.

Eleonora Duse (1858–1924), born in Vigevano, Italy, was considered the greatest actress of her era. She specialized in tragedies and was known for her restrained and subtle performances. Two of her best-known roles were the leads in *La Gioconda* and *Francesca da Rimini*, plays written especially for her by Gabriele D'Annunzio, with whom she had a long love affair. Duse retired in 1909 but returned to the stage in 1921 and died while on tour in the United States.

Helen Hayes (1900–93), born in Washington, D.C., was known as the First Lady of the American theater. She began acting professionally at age 5 and made her New York stage debut in 1909. Her notable performances included roles in *What Every Woman Knows* (1926), *Mary of Scotland* (1933), *Victoria Regina* (1935), and *A Touch of the Poet* (1957). A Broadway theater was named in her honor. Hayes also appeared in films, winning an Academy Award as best actress in 1932 and as best supporting actress in 1970. She wrote two novels and three autobiographies.

Edmund Kean (1787–1833), born in London, England, was the outstanding tragedian of his day, noted for his passionate portrayals of Shakespearean characters. He achieved his first success in 1814 playing Shylock in a production of *The Merchant of Venice* at London's Drury Lane Theatre. He went on to play many other classic roles, notably Iago, Macbeth, and Richard III.

Fanny Kemble (1809–93), born in London, England, came from a famous theatrical family. Known for her beauty as well as for her talent, Kemble's popularity saved her father's theater from bankruptcy. In 1832 she toured the United States, where she was an immediate success. Her marriage to a Southern

mer theaters present revivals of well-known musicals and light comedies—their stock. Others present touring attractions.

England. In 1963, national theater in England became a reality. The National Theatre, under the direction of Sir Laurence Olivier, replaced the famous Old Vic Company in London, which since 1914 had staged outstanding productions of the classics. Another subsidized British theater is the Royal Shakespeare Company. In 1961 it took over the operation of the Shakespeare Memorial Theatre, which since 1879 had presented Shakespeare's plays at Stratford-on-Avon.

London's commercial theaters are in a part of the city known as the West End. Elsewhere in London there are important smaller theaters, such as the Royal Court Theatre.

Repertory theater got its start in England in the early 1900's. The National Theatre and the Royal Shakespeare Company are repertory. Birmingham, Nottingham, and other cities have their own repertory companies.

France. France's most famous theater, the Comédie-Française, began in 1680 under the patronage of King Louis XIV and has continued ever since. A repertory theater, it is noted for its productions of the great French dramatists Corneille, Racine, and Molière.

Paris has approximately 80 commercial theaters. In addition to the Comédie-Française, there are two other important government-sponsored theaters: the Théâtre National Populaire, founded in 1920, and the Odéon-Théâtre de France, formed in 1959.

After World War II the government established theater centers in five places in France so that theater would be available to more people. Since 1959, France has had a minister of state for cultural affairs, who supervises all government-supported theaters and keeps the standards of production high.

planter in 1834 exposed her to the evils of slavery, which she later chronicled (1863). She also published *Journal of a Residence in America* (1835), which was critical of the young United States. Kemble's aunt, **Sarah Kemble Siddons** (1755–1831), born in Brecon, Wales, was a leading English actress noted especially for her portrayal of Lady Macbeth.

Alfred Lunt (1893–1977), born in Milwaukee, Wisconsin, and **Lynn Fontanne** (1887?–1983), born in Woodford, England, were a celebrated acting duo. Married in 1922, they first acted together a year later, in a New York production of *Sweet Nell of Old Drury*. Their later successes include *Arms and the Man* (1925), *Design for Living* (1933), and *The Visit*, which opened New York's Lunt-Fontanne Theatre in 1958.

Laurence Olivier (1907–89), born in Dorking, Surrey, England, was one of the finest English actors of the 1900's. He achieved early success on the London stage, joining the Old Vic theater company in 1937. He won critical acclaim for his work in both Shakespearean and modern drama. He was director of the National Theatre Company (1962–73). Olivier also acted in films, including *Wuthering Heights* (1939) and *Pride and Prejudice* (1940). He was knighted in 1947 and made a peer in 1970.

Laurence Olivier as Hamlet

The Redgraves

Michael Redgrave (1908–85), born in Bristol, England, was a schoolmaster before joining an acting company in 1934. Best known for Shakespearean and other classical stage roles, he was knighted in 1959 for his contributions to the British stage. He also appeared in films. **Vanessa Redgrave** (1937–   ), born in London, England, is a daughter of Michael Redgrave and the actress Rachel Kempson. A highly accomplished stage and screen actress, she also gained notoriety for her leftist political views. Her stage work includes leading roles in plays by Shakespeare and Chekhov. She won an Academy Award for best supporting actress in *Julia* (1977) and an Emmy Award for the television movie *Playing for Time* (1980). Another

daughter, **Lynn Redgrave** (1943–   ), born in London, specialized in comedies, on stage as well as in films and television. Vanessa's daughter **Natasha Richardson** (1963–   ) is a member of the family's third generation of performers. Her stage roles include the title role in *Anna Christie* (1993). Richardson also acts in films.

Konstantin Stanislavski (1863–1938), a famous actor and director who developed an influential acting technique, was born in Moscow, Russia. His original family name was Alekseyev. A cofounder (1898) of the Moscow Art Theater, he directed and acted in many plays. He trained the actors in his company to explore the inner thoughts and feelings of a character to achieve a more naturalistic performance. Stanislavski wrote about his acting system in *An Actor Prepares* (1926) and other books. The technique became popular in the United States, where it was known as method acting or the Method.

Germany. Although Germany has close to 300 theaters, it has no main theater center. One reason is that Germany was not a unified nation until after the Franco-Prussian War in 1870. Before that time, each kingdom or principality supported its own theaters. Many theaters in western Germany were built after World War II, during the period when Germany was divided into two nations.

One of the most famous theaters in Germany is the Berliner Ensemble in Berlin. Founded in 1947 by Bertolt Brecht, one of the great modern playwrights, the Berliner Ensemble has been very influential, both in its productions of Brecht's works and in those of contemporary German playwrights.

Italy. Italy prefers opera to theater. Almost every large town has an opera house. But Italy was the birthplace of the *commedia dell'arte* (first performed in the 1500's), a comedy of improvisation made up by the ac-

tors as they played before audiences. Improvisational theater still exists today.

Italy has two important theater centers, Rome and Milan. One of the most famous theaters in Milan is the Piccolo Teatro (Little Theater), a repertory company supported by government and city funds.

Ireland. Ireland's famous Abbey Theatre, which was organized in the early 1900's, stages plays by Irish writers. Like many famous repertory companies, it started with amateurs, who became professional simply by continuing to act with the company. Among the Irish playwrights who had their works staged there were William Butler Yeats, John Millington Synge, and Sean O'Casey. A second well-known theater, the Dublin Gate, opened in 1928.

Russia. Konstantin Stanislavski is the name associated with the most famous Russian theater, the Moscow Art Theater. He founded it in 1898 with Nemirovich-Danchenko and shaped it into one of the finest acting companies in the world. The Moscow Art Theater has been called the theater of Chekhov because it staged the first successful productions of Anton Chekhov, Russia's greatest playwright, and has continued to present them to the public.

Russia has many theaters, all of which under the Soviet Union were financed and controlled by the government. The main theater centers are Moscow and St. Petersburg.

China. Theater in China is often called opera because for hundreds of years actors did not speak on stage. They sang their parts. Traditional or classical theater in China is a blending of song, gesture, and music performed in stylized forms. The Peking Opera is the best-known example of classical Chinese theater.

The Chinese stage is bare—a platform with a table, one or two chairs, and a curtain at the back. Musicians sit at one side of the stage. Changes in scenery are made in front of the audience by men who move furniture and give hand properties, such as swords or fans, to the actors.

The Chinese actor uses traditional gestures that have been handed down for centuries. For example, in classical Chinese theater, a real or painted horse is not brought on stage when a horse is needed. Instead, a switch—a kind of riding crop—is used. The way the actor moves with it tells the audience when the actor is getting off the horse and when he is riding away.

One of the most famous Chinese theater forms is the shadow puppet play. Behind a lighted screen, cloth or paper figures move as the puppeteer sings and talks. This kind of play is especially popular with children.

India. Dance is the most important part of theater in India and other Southeast Asian countries. There are three elements in a classical theater performance in India: poetry, music, and dance. A storyteller is often a part of the traditional Indian theater performance. He recites certain poetry passages and serves as a narrator.

Two great epic poems, the *Ramayana* and the *Mahabharata*, have been the basis of classical Indian dance-drama for more than 2,000 years. Filled with adventure, the poems are still performed today.

Japan. The two most famous forms of Japanese drama are the No and the Kabuki. The No plays, written and acted in the Middle Ages, use ancient Japanese language and are performed very slowly in nonrealistic style. For example, a kimono on a stage means a sick person. The lifting of a hand indicates crying. The No plays are performed on a roofed platform stage. The audience sits around the stage on two sides.

Through its tours, Kabuki theater is better known to Western audiences than the No plays. Kabuki plays were written in the 1500's and 1600's—about the time that Shakespeare wrote in England. Kabuki plays have more action than No plays, and their language is more modern.

Bugaku, a theater form older than Kabuki or No, is still performed today. Dating from the 400's, it is a form of dance to music called Gagaku. The dances and music have remained unchanged since their beginnings.

Japan's puppet theater is called Bunraku. It uses puppets of almost life size. Three operators are needed to work each of the main puppets. These puppeteers begin training for their profession in childhood.

Japan's modern theater uses the Western style of staging and produces many plays translated from the West, as well as works by contemporary Japanese playwrights.

Other Theaters. Austria, Belgium, Denmark, the Netherlands, Norway, and Sweden all have fine national repertory theaters financed by the government. In Canada, the Canada Council funds professional theater companies throughout the country.

Theater in Latin America has existed ever since the Spanish and Portuguese colonized the countries. In origin the plays are Native American, Spanish or Portuguese, or by modern Latin American playwrights.

The Australian Elizabethan Theatre Trust is Australia's national theater. It is government-subsidized and was founded in 1955.

In Africa, theater is emerging as an important art form, particularly in Nigeria and Ghana. South African theater also flourishes.

LEOTA DIESEL
Managing Editor, *Theatre Arts*
Updated by JAN GREENBERG
Author, *Theater Business: From Auditions Through Opening Night*

See also DRAMA; PLAYS; PUPPETS AND MARIONETTES.

THERMOMETERS

A thermometer is an instrument used to measure temperature, that is, to determine how hot or how cold something is. It indicates temperature based on a scale, such as degrees Fahrenheit (°F) or degrees Celsius (°C), two commonly used temperature scales. A temperature scale usually has an indication for two fixed points, such as freezing and boiling points, and the space between them divided into a number of degrees.

▶ MEASURING TEMPERATURE

Temperature is invisible and it is unrelated to the size of an object, so it is difficult to define and measure directly. For example, we cannot weigh something to determine its temperature the way we are able to determine its mass (mass is the quantity of matter in an object), so we must use an indirect method. The way to determine the temperature of an object or a substance is to measure a property of that object or substance that depends on temperature. For example, we can measure at what temperatures some substances become solids, liquids, or gases.

Water is one of many substances that can transform from a solid to a liquid to a gas, depending on its temperature. It can freeze (change from a liquid to a solid), melt (change from a solid to a liquid), boil (change from a liquid to a gas), or condense (change from a gas to a liquid). The freezing and melting points of water are the same, 32°F (0°C). The boiling and condensation points of water are also the same, 212°F (100°C). The Celsius scale used to be called the centigrade scale because there is a 100-degree difference between its freezing and boiling points.

The coldest possible temperature is generally considered to be –459.67°F or –273.15°C, at which there is an absence of all heat. It is known as absolute zero. Two other temperature scales, the Kelvin scale and the Rankine scale, are based on absolute zero. Kelvin scale temperatures are indicated by a K without the degree symbol, so absolute zero is noted as 0K. The freezing point of water is 273.15K, and the boiling point of water is 373.15K. The Kelvin scale is used for many basic scientific calculations. On the Rankine scale, 0° equals –459.67°F, and its degree intervals are equal to those of the Fahrenheit scale.

▶ TYPES OF THERMOMETERS

Different types of thermometers have been developed to be used for various purposes.

Liquid-in-Glass Thermometers

The liquid-in-glass thermometer, the most common type, has a glass bulb at one end containing a liquid, usually mercury or alcohol, whose volume expands when heated and contracts when cooled. The liquid in the bulb flows into a small glass tube—the capillary tube—that is inside the stem. A change in the volume of the liquid causes the column of liquid to rise or fall within the capillary tube. The level of the column is measured on the thermometer's stem, which is marked in degrees. There are many types of liquid-in-glass thermometers, including indoor and outdoor thermometers used to measure the temperature of the air and fever thermometers used to measure a person's temperature.

Dial Thermometers

Dial thermometers, often used in ovens, measure temperature by responding to the changing length of strips of two different metals as they react to temperature changes. The metals, fastened together to form a single bimetallic (two-metal) strip, expand and contract at different rates when the temperature changes. This causes the bimetallic strip to bend. If the strip is wound into a

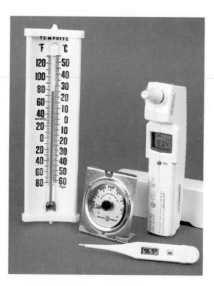

Thermometers you may have at home are the liquid-in-glass (far left) to measure outdoor air temperatures; the dial (center), whose bimetallic strip measures oven temperatures; and two fever thermometers to measure your body's temperature—one that detects infrared radiation from your ear (left) and one with a thermistor sensor in its tip that you put in your mouth (resting on table).

spiral, the bending causes the spiral to rotate. A needle connected to the end of the spiral indicates temperature in degrees on the dial.

Electrical Thermometers

Three types of thermometers indicate temperature by measuring electrical properties that change with temperature. Metal resistance thermometers indicate temperature by measuring electrical resistance, which is the resistance the metal offers to a flow of electricity. These thermometers are based on the principle that the electrical resistance of metals increases with increased temperature. The platinum resistance thermometer, the most reliable of these devices, is often used by laboratories as a standard for calibrating other thermometers. To **calibrate** means to determine and mark temperature levels by careful comparison with a known standard. Metal resistance thermometers are often used in automobiles, airplanes, and spacecraft.

Thermistors, which also measure electrical resistance, are tiny ceramic semiconductor devices made out of metal oxides. They can determine temperature by measuring the amount of electrical resistance in the ceramic material. The ceramic material's resistance to the flow of an electric current decreases with increased temperature, just the opposite of what happens in metals. Thermistors are very sensitive to changes in temperature, so they are often used in fever thermometers.

Diode and transistor thermometers are based on the principle that the maximum amount of current that can flow through a diode or transistor depends upon temperature. Thus by measuring the current flowing through a diode or transistor, you can determine temperature. For this reason, these tiny thermometers often are used in other electronic devices to detect temperature changes.

Gas Thermometers

Gases expand when heated and contract when cooled. This is the basic principle of gas thermometers, which measure the volume of a gas in relation to changes in temperature. Gas thermometers are rarely used for practical applications since the volume of gas in them must be fairly large. However, they often are used in laboratories for the precision calibration of other devices.

Thermocouple Thermometers

A thermocouple is a device consisting of two wires of different alloys, or combinations of metals, joined at both ends to form two junctions. A difference in temperature between these junctions will produce a small electrical voltage. The amount of the voltage depends on the difference in temperature. Using one junction as a reference point, a thermocouple can determine temperature by measuring the voltage at the other junction. Thermocouples are widely used in furnaces and water heaters, where they convert heat energy to electricity. The electrical voltages they produce can be used to indicate or control temperature.

Radiation Thermometers

Radiation thermometers indicate temperature by measuring electromagnetic radiation. They are based on the principle that the intensity and wavelength of radiation shift with temperature changes. As temperature increases, radiation becomes more intense and wavelengths become shorter. Devices that measure radiation can receive all wavelengths, a single wavelength, or a band of wavelengths. A common type, the infrared radiation thermometer, detects long, invisible wavelengths of light known as infrared radiation. Among the many types of infrared radiation thermometers is a fever thermometer that detects infrared radiation from the ear.

THOMAS D. MCGEE
Author, *Principles and Methods of Temperature Measurement*

See also ELECTRICITY; HEAT; LIGHT; TRANSISTORS, DIODES, AND INTEGRATED CIRCUITS.

THERMOSTATS. See HEATING AND VENTILATING SYSTEMS.

THESEUS. See GREEK MYTHOLOGY.

THIAMINE (Vitamin B_1). See VITAMINS AND MINERALS.

TEMPERATURE SCALE CONVERSIONS

- To convert a temperature reading from °Celsius to °Fahrenheit, multiply it by 9, divide the new number by 5, then add 32.
- To convert a temperature reading from °Fahrenheit to °Celsius, subtract 32 from it, multiply the new number by 5, then divide by 9.
- To convert a temperature reading from °Celsius to Kelvin, add 273.15 to it.
- To convert a temperature reading from °Fahrenheit to °Rankine, subtract –459.67 from the Fahrenheit temperature.

THIRTEEN AMERICAN COLONIES

The winter of 1587 was past, and spring had come to England. The countryside was fresh and green with new leaves on the trees and flowers in bloom. Farmers were planting their fields. Newborn lambs frolicked in the pastures.

This year, however, one group of English subjects had no time to enjoy the beauty of the spring. This group of men, women, and children were about to sail for America. Sir Walter Raleigh was sending them to build what he hoped would be the first successful English colony in the New World.

Sir Walter Raleigh

Sir Walter Raleigh was a born leader. Handsome, intelligent, and wealthy, he was afraid of nothing. Raleigh hoped that some day England would become a mighty empire with many colonies across the seas.

In 1583 an expedition commanded by Raleigh's half brother, Sir Humphrey Gilbert, sailed to Newfoundland. Sir Humphrey had

Sir Walter Raleigh was a soldier, poet, and colonizer, who sponsored the first English settlements in North America. Although Raleigh himself never saw the New World, the expeditions he sent explored much of the Atlantic coast.

been looking for a place to start a colony. On the return voyage, however, Gilbert's ship and all on board were lost at sea.

Raleigh received permission from Queen Elizabeth I to carry on Sir Humphrey's work. In April, 1584, he sent an expedition to America to find the best location for a colony. Avoiding the cold, bleak shores of Newfoundland, Raleigh's expedition explored the coasts of what are now North Carolina and Virginia.

The Virginia Colony

The expedition returned to England with glowing reports of the New World. They said that America was a rich land. The soil was the best in the world. The trees were larger than any they had ever seen, and herds of deer roamed the forests. The Indians were "gentle, loving, and faithful."

Raleigh was delighted with the good news. The country was named Virginia to honor Queen Elizabeth, who was sometimes called the Virgin Queen.

Raleigh was now ready to start his colony. He chose Sir Richard Grenville and Ralph Lane to lead the expedition. With 108 men aboard their ships, Grenville and Lane sailed from England in April, 1585. They reached Roanoke Island, off what is now the North Carolina coast, in July. Grenville then returned to England with the ships, leaving Lane in charge of the settlement.

The "Lost Colony." Raleigh's success quickly turned into a series of misfortunes. The first came in the spring of 1586, when the settlers abandoned the colony and sailed back to England. In spite of this blow, Raleigh sold more of his property and borrowed from his friends to raise money for another expedition. In May, 1587, a group of 117 colonists sailed from England, led by their newly appointed governor, John White.

Shortly after the colonists arrived at Roanoke Island in August, John White's daughter

The original 13 American Colonies as they appear today as states of the United States.

Canada

New Hampshire

Massachusetts

New York

Rhode Island

Connecticut

Pennsylvania

New Jersey

Maryland

Delaware

Virginia

North Carolina

South Carolina

Georgia

Eleanor, wife of Ananias Dare, gave birth to a little girl. She was named Virginia for her birthplace and her queen. Virginia Dare was the first English child born in what is now the United States.

From the day they landed, the colonists had trouble. Many Indians had learned to fear and hate the English. The colonists had to be on guard day and night and had no time to build houses or plant crops. Driven to desperation, they asked John White to return to England to bring back more people and supplies.

White soon discovered that England was at war with Spain, and he could not arrange for a rescue ship until three years had passed. Finally, late one night in the summer of 1590, he reached Roanoke Island. Through the darkness, the crew could see the light of a campfire burning on shore. When they rowed ashore, they discovered the island was deserted. The houses and fort were in ruins. The only clue they found was the word CROATOAN carved on a tree, which was the name of a nearby island. Although White wanted to search for the settlers, his ship had to return to England before the winter storms began. No one ever learned what had become of the lost colonists.

▶ **THE SETTLERS AND WHY THEY CAME**

In 1606 the east coast of North America was an almost unbroken wilderness. A handful of Spaniards lived in the small fort of St. Augustine, Florida. Some French people lived in Port Royal, Nova Scotia. But from Florida to Canada, there was only an immense forest. In all this vast wilderness, no European footprint marked the earth. No European voice echoed down the forest trails. North America still belonged to the first Americans, the American Indians.

In 1607, however, great changes began to take place. Between 1607 and 1733, the English established 13 prosperous colonies. By 1750 nearly 2,000,000 men, women, and children were living there. Raleigh's dream had come true. Between New France in the north and Spanish Florida in the south, North America was indeed ''an English nation.''

During the first 150 years of colonial history, most of those who settled in America came from the British Isles. They came from England, Scotland, Ireland, and Wales. Many came from other countries in Europe, too. Still others came from Africa. Most of the Africans were transported to the New World as slaves.

John White, the leader of the ''lost colony'' of Roanoke Island, returned to Virginia in 1590 and found the settlement deserted. The fate of the colonists remains a mystery.

Many settlers came to the New World because they were denied religious freedom at home. In their colony of Plymouth, Massachusetts, the Pilgrims could worship in their own way.

America: Land of Opportunity

Why did the settlers come? Why did they leave their homes and their friends in the Old World to come to a strange and distant land?

Opportunity was the magic that drew people to America. It drew English nobles who dreamed of carving great new estates out of the wilderness. It drew carpenters, masons, bakers, tailors, and other skilled workers who could not find work in England. Most of all, it drew the poor and the homeless from the farmlands and villages of Europe. It offered them a chance for a better life than they could hope for in the Old World.

At the time Sir Walter Raleigh was trying to build his colony in Virginia, most people in England were farmers. A few wealthy nobles owned most of the land. The owners of these large estates rented small areas of land to tenant farmers.

But England was changing. Many of the rich landowners could make more money by raising sheep than they could by renting their land to tenant farmers. The landowners turned the plowed fields of the small farms into pastures. As a result, the tenant farmers and their families lost their houses and their way of making a living.

Some former tenant farmers found work in the towns and cities. But there were not enough jobs for all of the homeless people who wandered the roads of England looking for work. For these people America was indeed a land of hope in which there would be work for everyone.

America: Promise of Religious Freedom

Many settlers came to the English colonies in search of religious freedom. They wanted the right to worship God in their own way in their own churches.

In Europe at this time each nation had an official state church. In most European countries the Roman Catholic Church was the official, or established, church. In England it was the Church of England, or Anglican Church. The government collected taxes to support the state church. Every citizen had to pay these taxes, even if he did not want to worship in that way. The government also expected every citizen to attend the state church. Those who refused were sometimes sent to prison.

Many people were unhappy with this situation. English Roman Catholics, Methodists, Baptists, Presbyterians, Quakers, and other religious groups wanted to attend their own churches. Many discontented religious groups started their own colonies in America. These colonies attracted people from all over Europe as well as from England.

Each man and woman who crossed the sea had his or her own reason for beginning life again in the New World. Some came to improve their fortunes. Others came in search of land and jobs. Still others came in search of freedom. But for all of them America was the land of opportunity.

▶ VIRGINIA: THE FIRST SUCCESSFUL COLONY

The English built their first successful colony in Virginia, in the same general area where Sir Walter Raleigh had earlier tried and failed.

In 1606, King James gave two business companies the right to settle and trade along the Atlantic coast. To the London Company he gave the right to settle all the land from what is now Cape Fear, North Carolina, northward to Long Island. To the Plymouth Company he gave the right to settle all the land from what is now Maine southward to Chesapeake Bay.

These two grants overlapped. Both companies had the right to build and trade in the area between what are now the states of Virginia and New York. In order to prevent

The introduction of Negro slavery into the American colonies occurred in 1619 when a Dutch ship put 20 Africans ashore at Jamestown, Virginia.

trouble, the King ruled that neither company could build a settlement within 100 miles (160 kilometers) of the other's.

The directors of the London Company decided to build their first settlement in the south, where the climate was warm. They planned to sell shares of stock to anyone who was willing to buy them. As for the settlers, in 1606 many people were more than willing to risk their lives in the hope of improving their fortunes.

By December, 1606, three ships—the *Goodspeed* (or *Godspeed*), the *Susan Constant* (also known as the *Sarah Constant*), and the *Discovery*—swung at anchor in the Thames River, ready for a long voyage. The ropes and rigging had been tarred to protect them from the weather. Water and food had been packed in the holds. The colonists, 120 men in all, were waiting to sail.

Finally the moment arrived. Captain Christopher Newport gave the order to raise the anchors. One by one the vessels swung into the ebbing tide and began to float down the Thames toward the sea.

For four months the three ships moved slowly across the Atlantic Ocean. Day after day and week after week the passengers and crews saw only the immense dome of sky above them and the immense expanse of sea on every side. Sixteen men died during the long voyage. At last, late in the month of April, the vessels sailed between two capes of land into the mouth of Chesapeake Bay.

Captain Newport named the capes Cape Henry and Cape Charles, in honor of King James's two sons. Then, after crossing the bay, he sailed up a river that he named the James, in honor of the King himself.

The directors of the London Company had given the colonists strict orders to build their settlement well inland. There they would be safe from Spanish warships that might try to destroy the colony. Captain Newport sailed about 30 miles (50 kilometers) up the river to a marshy island, where he and the other leaders decided to build their settlement. They named the future colony Jamestown.

Jamestown Struggles to Survive

It was springtime, and the weather was mild. The colony might have prospered, but in their ignorance the colonists made many mistakes. These mistakes cost them dearly.

By the end of the year only one third of those who had sailed from London were still alive. Some had been killed by Indians. Most had died from hunger and disease.

The first serious mistake was the poor location of the colony. To be sure, the island could be defended easily against attack by Indians. But the settlers could not defend themselves against the clouds of mosquitoes that carried deadly malaria out of the surrounding marshes.

The settlers made other, equally bad mistakes. Instead of digging a well to get pure water, they drank from the river and swamps. Instead of planting gardens and raising food, they explored the surrounding country in search of gold and jewels. As a result, when winter came, those who were still alive were poorly sheltered and had little food to eat.

The settlers were not entirely to blame for their troubles. The directors of the company in London should have sent skilled workers to build the colony. Instead they sent people who had never held a saw or an ax or a hoe in their hands before. And many did not even try.

The directors made another mistake when they ordered that all supplies must go into a common storehouse. Everyone received an equal share, whether they worked or not. This discouraged those who were willing to work hard. Why should they work, they asked, when the others were roaming the forest in search of gold or resting in the shade of a tree?

If it had not been for John Smith, every one of the first settlers might have died. When the situation became desperate, Smith made himself the leader of the colony. He was a hard ruler. He took charge of the lazy ones and made them work whether they wanted to or not. Every morning he lined them up in front of the little fort. Then, in military fashion, to the beat of a drum, he marched them to their jobs. He made them dig a well, build shelters, and plant gardens. The men grumbled, but John Smith's rule was no work, no food, and so they worked. In the meantime Smith himself traveled to nearby Indian villages, where he traded glass beads and iron knives and kettles for corn, meat, and fish.

Under John Smith's leadership, conditions improved. But after he was injured in an explosion and returned to England, in the autumn of 1609, the situation became more desperate than ever. The winter of 1609–10 was the darkest period in Jamestown's history. So many died during that terrible winter that the survivors called it the starving time, and in the spring they decided to abandon the colony. Just then, however, ships from England brought new settlers and fresh supplies of food, clothing, and tools.

Up to this point the colony of Jamestown had been a bitter disappointment to the directors and stockholders of the London Com-

The English soldier and explorer Captain John Smith was a founder of Virginia. He became the colony's leader when he saved it from starvation by making the settlers work for their food. But Smith is best known from the tale of his rescue from the Indians by the chief's daughter, Pocahontas.

pany. Instead of making a profit on their investment, they had lost a great deal of money. Fortunately, during these years the directors learned several important lessons.

For one thing, they realized that people worked harder when they had land of their own to farm. As a result, the London Company made each settler responsible for a particular area of land.

The directors also realized that married men made the best settlers. In 1621, therefore, the company sent the first shipload of women to America. The women soon married and began to raise families. They made homes out of the bare cabins and helped their husbands in the fields.

In 1619 the directors of the London Company made another very important decision. They gave the settlers a share in their own government. By then more than 1,000 settlers were living in Virginia. Their settlements stretched along the James River for about 20 miles (30 kilometers). In each settlement the men were allowed to elect two of their number to represent them in the government. These 22 representatives, who called themselves burgesses, traveled to Jamestown to meet with the colonial governor and help to make the laws. In this way representative government had its beginning in America in the colony of Virginia.

Virginia Begins to Prosper

Both the London Company and the settlers in Virginia were learning the lesson John Smith had once tried to teach them. From the beginning Smith believed that the true wealth of Virginia lay in its forests and fertile soil. While he was still in Jamestown, he warned the directors, "There is nothing to be gained here except by hard work." John Smith was right.

Tobacco was the settlers' first "money crop"; it transformed the struggling settlements into a prosperous colony. American Indians had been smoking long before the first Europeans arrived in the New World. When tobacco was introduced to the Old World, many Europeans at first objected. King James of England warned that smoking was "hateful, harmful to the brain, and dangerous to the lungs." But each year Englishmen bought more tobacco. As the demand for tobacco increased, the price climbed higher and higher.

One of the early Jamestown settlers, John Rolfe, decided to try growing tobacco. He planted the first seeds in 1612 and discovered that this valuable plant grew well in the soil and the mild, moist climate of Virginia. Other settlers quickly followed his example. Within a few years Englishmen began to call Virginia their tobacco colony.

▶ NEW ENGLAND

In 1607, only a few weeks after the first settlers landed at Jamestown, another band of English settlers arrived off the coast of what is now Maine. They had been sent by the Plymouth Company to start a colony. They built a fort and a few huts near the mouth of the Sagadahoc River, later called the Kennebec. But they were no better prepared to build a settlement in the wilderness than the Jamestown colonists had been. To make matters worse, the winter was bitterly cold. Many of the hungry, half-frozen settlers died. The survivors returned to England.

The Pilgrims

Meanwhile, a small group of English Separatists who lived in the farming village of Scrooby were having their own troubles. They were called Separatists because they wanted to separate from the Church of England. Today we know them as the Pilgrims because they traveled from place to place seeking somewhere to settle where they would be free to worship God in their own way.

Their troubles began with the adoption of a law compelling all English subjects to attend the Church of England. The Pilgrims refused to obey this law. They gathered secretly in one another's homes to worship in their own way. Those who were caught were fined and thrown into jail. In 1608 they fled from England to Holland.

The Pilgrims lived for a year in Amsterdam and then moved to the smaller city of Leyden. In Holland they were allowed to worship as they chose. The Dutch, a tolerant people, gave shelter to religious and political refugees from many nations.

But the Pilgrims were not completely happy in the Netherlands. Most of them had been farmers in England, and they found it hard to earn a living at other trades. It disturbed them to see their children growing up Dutch instead of English. So the Pilgrims decided to move again, this time to America.

The Pilgrims could not afford to hire ships and to buy supplies for their colony. Fortunately, a company of English businessmen, looking for colonists, was willing to finance the venture. In return the Pilgrims agreed to work for the company for seven years. During this period all the profits from trade with the Indians and from fishing, lumbering, and farming were to belong to the company. It was a hard bargain, but the best the Pilgrims could make.

The Pilgrims left Holland and sailed first to the English seaport of Southampton. There they joined another group of Pilgrims. On August 15, 1620, they sailed for America on two vessels, the *Speedwell* and the *Mayflower*. But the smaller of the two ships, the *Speedwell,* sprang a leak, and both ships turned into the port of Dartmouth. As soon as repairs had been made the Pilgrims sailed again. The *Speedwell* still leaked, however, and the vessels turned back a second time, this time to the port of Plymouth. There the Pilgrims decided to abandon the *Speedwell*. Leaving 20 of the passengers behind, the remaining travelers—101 in all—crowded on board the *Mayflower*.

On September 16 the *Mayflower* left Plymouth and headed west into the open sea. In one terrible storm a main beam of the ship split wide open. The vessel seemed doomed.

After two stormy months at sea aboard the *Mayflower* (*above*), the Pilgrims (*left*), led by William Bradford, signed the Compact establishing the Plymouth Colony.

But the Pilgrims and the crew managed to repair the damage, and the *Mayflower* continued on its way.

At last, on November 19, after more than two months at sea, the Pilgrims caught their first glimpse of land. In the distance they saw the long, sandy peninsula of Cape Cod. They had intended to settle much farther south, but winter was close at hand. They decided to land and begin their colony as soon as possible.

The next day the *Mayflower* rounded the tip of the cape and anchored in what is now the harbor of Provincetown. There, before they landed, the Pilgrims made a solemn promise to one another. One by one the men stepped forward in the ship's tiny cabin to sign an agreement known as the Mayflower Compact. They pledged to obey all the laws that they themselves would adopt. With this agreement the Pilgrims took a long step along the road toward a system of self-government and democracy.

Plymouth Colony

The next day was Sunday, and the Pilgrims spent the time aboard ship in prayer and thanksgiving. But early Monday they went ashore. While the men stood guard with loaded muskets, the women washed clothes and the children played on the beach.

The *Mayflower* remained in Provincetown harbor for several weeks. During this period Captain Miles Standish and a number of the men explored the coast. Finally they chose Plymouth as the place to build their colony. Captain John Smith had visited the site of Plymouth in 1614 and had given it the name it bears to this day. It was an ideal location, with a good harbor, brooks of clear water, and fields cleared by the Indians.

Late in December the *Mayflower* crossed Massachusetts Bay and anchored in Plymouth Harbor. On December 25 work began on the first building, a "common house." During the following weeks the first rough cabins began to take shape. But the Pilgrims suffered from the bitter cold and sickness. Before spring arrived only half of those who sailed in the *Mayflower* were still alive. But not one of the survivors returned to England when the *Mayflower* sailed in April.

All through that cruel winter the Pilgrims had lived in constant fear of the Indians. Guards stood on watch day and night. The little graveyard on the hill grew larger and larger. But only the Pilgrims knew it was there, for they had carefully covered the scarred earth with leaves and grass. They did not want the Indians to learn how many of their number had died and how few were left.

Toward the end of winter, however, the settlers learned that the Indians living around Plymouth were friendly. They taught the Pilgrims how to hunt game and trap fish. They told them what berries and nuts were good to eat. They gave them seeds of pumpkins,

After their first harsh winter in New England, the Pilgrims began to build a permanent colony. They traded with the Indians, who taught them to hunt and plant crops.

squash, beans, and corn and taught them how to plant and cultivate the crops.

With the Indians helping them, the Pilgrims began to prosper. They caught and dried fish. They cut down trees and sawed the logs into planks. They traded with the Indians and collected bundles of furs. All these were carefully stored until they could be sent to the company in England. When autumn came, seven houses and a church faced the street that led to the water. Three other buildings, all storehouses, were filled with the harvest from the fields and with fish, furs, and lumber.

By November, 1621, the Pilgrims had been in the New World an entire year. A ship from England had just landed 30 new settlers and fresh supplies. The storehouses were filled to overflowing. William Bradford, the governor, decided to set aside several days for recreation and giving thanks to God. And so, with nearly 100 Indians for company, the Pilgrims held the first Thanksgiving celebration in America.

After 1621 other ships brought more men, women, and children to the colony. Plymouth itself grew larger. New villages sprang up nearby. There on the shores of Massachusetts Bay the Pilgrims found the religious freedom and the new way of life they had been seeking.

Massachusetts Bay Colony

The Pilgrims led the way. The Puritans soon followed. The Puritans, like the Pilgrims, were dissatisfied with the Church of England. Unlike the Pilgrims, however, they were willing to remain members of the church. But they wished to simplify and purify the church service. This is why they were called Puritans. Finally they decided to move to the New World. They did not wish to go to Virginia, because there the Church of England had already been established as the official church. They decided, therefore, to follow the Pilgrims to New England.

In 1629 the Puritan leaders secured a charter from the King of England. This charter gave them a grant of land in New England and the right to build a colony. The leaders of the Massachusetts Bay Company, as it was called, then began to make plans to settle in America.

With the help of the Indians, the Pilgrims were soon able to send furs and other goods to England.

In 1628, even before the King gave a charter to the company, a number of Puritans had moved to New England. About 40 settlers, led by John Endecott, had started the village of Naumkeag, later called Salem, on the northeast coast of Massachusetts.

The first large group of Puritans sailed for the New World in the spring of 1630. They were led by John Winthrop, their first governor. There were nearly 1,000 men, women, and children aboard the fleet of ships that carried them on their great venture.

Many of the Puritans were well educated. Many were wealthy. They brought with them everything they needed to start a successful colony. They brought large supplies of food,

John Winthrop brought 1,000 Puritans to New England aboard the Arbella in 1630. He was governor of the Massachusetts Bay Colony for more than 20 years. Winthrop also helped to settle Boston and to establish the Congregational Church in New England.

plows and other tools, seeds, cattle, horses, and oxen. They brought furnishings for the homes they planned to build.

During the next few years thousands of other Puritans arrived in America. By 1640 more than 20,000 settlers were living in the growing towns of Boston, Charlestown, Newtown (Newton), and other settlements.

During the first few years, John Winthrop and other Puritan leaders tried to keep the control of the colony in their own hands. They refused to allow people of other religions to settle in the colony. They punished Puritans who did not agree with them, sometimes whipping them in public, sometimes driving them out of the colony. They permitted only a small, selected group of settlers to vote and to hold public office.

Many settlers objected to this strict rule. They demanded the right to share in the government. Finally, as the protests increased, the leaders agreed to meet these demands. They allowed all Puritan men to vote. They gave each town the right to send representa-

tives to the legislature of the colony. And they gave each town the right to govern itself through town meetings. At these town meetings the citizens reached decisions by a majority vote. So in Massachusetts Bay Colony, as earlier in Virginia, the settlers began to develop a democratic form of government.

Rhode Island

Massachusetts Bay Colony was only a year old when, in 1631, a young clergyman named Roger Williams arrived in New England. He began to trade with the Indians around Narragansett Bay and soon learned their language. Because he was always fair in his dealings with them, the Narragansetts became his firm friends.

On Sundays Roger Williams preached in a church in Salem. From the beginning he was in trouble with the Puritan leaders. He taught that the settlers had no right to the land unless they bought it from the Indians. He made the Puritan leaders even angrier when he insisted that they had no right to compel the colonists to attend the Puritan church. He argued that every individual had the right to worship in his own way and to say what he

Roger Williams founded Rhode Island after he quarreled with the Puritan leaders of the Massachusetts Bay Colony. Williams believed that the Indians should be treated fairly and that the colonists should not be forced to attend the Puritan Church.

believed to be true. The Puritan leaders repeatedly warned Roger Williams that he must stop teaching these beliefs. When he refused to be silent, the Puritans decided to banish him from their colony.

On a wintry night in 1635, a friend knocked on the door of Roger Williams' home. He warned Williams that officers were on the way to arrest him. Williams hastily gathered a few belongings and fled into the forest. He made his way through the snow-covered wilderness to his friends, the Narragansett Indians, and lived with them for the rest of the winter.

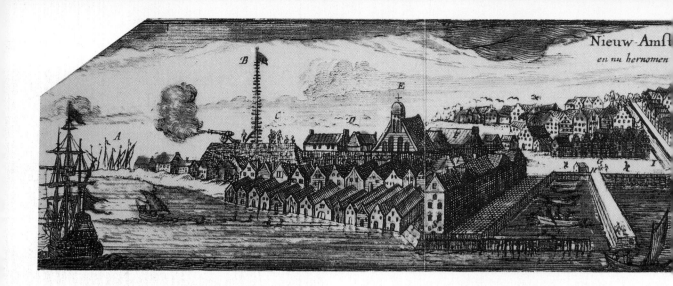

Nieuw-Amf[...]
en nu hernomen

In the spring Roger Williams bought land from the Indians. With a group of friends from Massachusetts he started the settlement of Providence on the shores of Narragansett Bay. Other exiles from Massachusetts built other villages around the bay. In 1644 the King of England gave Roger Williams a charter for the colony of Rhode Island.

Rhode Island became a model of freedom. Every man had the right to vote and to hold public office. Individuals could worship as they pleased, and they were free to say what they believed without fear of arrest.

Connecticut

In 1636, the same year that Roger Williams started Rhode Island, another group of people from the Massachusetts Bay Colony settled on the banks of the Connecticut River. This group of about 100 men, women, and children had heard of the rich soil in the Connecticut Valley. Led by Thomas Hooker, the pastor of their church, they traveled westward along Indian trails through the forest. On the banks of the Connecticut River they built a village called Hartford.

Other pioneers soon started settlements nearby. In 1662, after 15 towns had been settled, the English King gave the new colony a charter. This charter gave the Connecticut colonists the right to govern themselves.

Maine and New Hampshire

In 1622 the King gave Sir Ferdinando Gorges and John Mason the right to settle the vast wilderness that in time became the states of Maine and New Hampshire. Seven years later the two men divided the land. Gorges took the northern, or Maine, section. Mason took the New Hampshire area.

During the 1630's pioneers from Massachusetts Bay Colony moved northward and started the towns of Portsmouth, Exeter, and Hampton, in New Hampshire. Other pioneers built farms and villages. Like the settlers of Rhode Island, many of these people were escaping from religious persecution. It was not until 1679, however, that New Hampshire became a separate colony.

During these same years fishermen, traders, and pioneers from Massachusetts started a number of villages and towns in Maine, mostly along the coast. But Massachusetts claimed the entire area, and Maine never became a separate colony.

▶ **THE MIDDLE COLONIES**

Settlers from the Netherlands and Sweden, rather than from England, built the first settlements in the area that later became the middle colonies—New York, New Jersey, Pennsylvania, and Delaware.

New Netherland

In 1609, when Jamestown was only two years old, a Dutch ship called the *Half Moon* sailed from the Netherlands. Henry Hudson, the captain of the ship, was an Englishman. He had been hired by the Dutch East India Company to explore the Atlantic coast of the New World. The owners of the company hoped that Hudson would find a passage through America that would give them a shorter trade route to the East Indies.

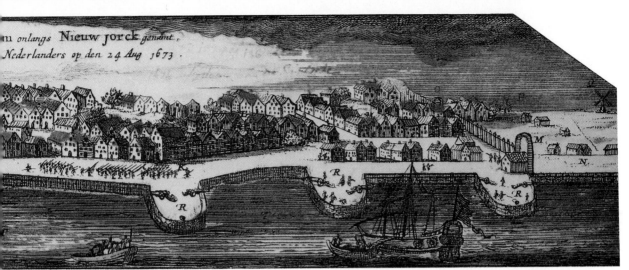

m onlangs Nieuw jorck genant,
Nederlanders op den 24 Aug 1673.

The Dutch settled New Amsterdam, in their colony of New Netherland, in 1625. The British took over the prosperous town in 1664 and renamed it New York.

Henry Hudson failed to find the passage. But he did explore two rivers, the Delaware and the river that bears his name, the Hudson. He also discovered that the land around these rivers was more fertile than any he had seen in Europe. Even more important, the Indians were friendly and eager to trade their furs for European goods.

The Dutch claimed all the territory Hudson had explored and called it New Netherland. Dutch businessmen immediately organized a new trading company, the Dutch West India Company. Since the King of England had granted the same land to a company of London businessmen, there was certain to be trouble in the future. But at the time the land belonged to the Indians, and no European settlements had been started.

During the next few years, traders sent out by the Dutch West India Company built forts and trading posts along the Delaware, Hudson, and Connecticut rivers. They built their largest fort on an island near the mouth of the Hudson. The Indians called the island *Manahatta,* which meant "the heavenly land." The Dutch called the fort and the land around it New Amsterdam. In 1626, Peter Minuit, the governor of the colony, bought all of this area from the Indians with knives, beads, colored cloth, and food, worth about $24.

The Dutch West India Company was eager to strengthen the colony of New Netherland. It offered huge areas of land along the Hudson River to any member of the company who would settle at least 50 tenants on the land. The patroons, as these landowners were called, soon built a number of large estates along the banks of the Hudson. But most of the Dutch were unwilling to give up the freedom they had in the Netherlands to work as tenants for wealthy landowners in America. As a result, New Netherland grew only slowly.

New Sweden

The Swedes as well as the Dutch were interested in building trading posts in the New World. In 1638 two Swedish ships sailed up the Delaware River. On the site of present-day Wilmington, the passengers started a settlement called Fort Christina, in honor of the Queen of Sweden. They gave the name New Sweden to the area they settled along the Delaware River.

New Sweden lasted only a few years. Dutch traders resented the competition from the Swedes. In 1655, Dutch troops seized the Swedish settlements.

England Conquers New Netherland

In the meantime, English settlers in the New World were becoming more and more concerned about the growth of New Netherland. The English insisted that the Dutch had no right to be there and that the land belonged to England.

In 1664 a powerful fleet of English warships sailed into the harbor of New Amsterdam. The commander of the fleet ordered the Dutch to surrender. The Dutch looked at the warships and at their own weak defenses. They realized that it would be hopeless to fight. So the Dutch governor, Peter Stuyvesant, hauled down the Dutch flag, which for 50 years had flown over New Netherland. Without a shot being fired, the colony passed into the hands of the English.

New York and New Jersey

The King of England gave all of what had once been New Netherland to his brother James, the Duke of York. The new colony was named New York in the duke's honor. The old Dutch city of New Amsterdam was renamed New York City. The Duke of York then made a gift of some of the land to two of his friends, Lord John Berkeley and Sir George Carteret. Carteret had once been governor of the island of Jersey in the English Channel. In honor of this English island, he named the colony New Jersey.

New York City had a splendid harbor and a central location. It grew rapidly and soon became one of the largest English seaports in America. New Jersey grew as settlers moved in from New England.

William Penn Founds Pennsylvania

William Penn was the son of a wealthy admiral in the English Navy. He devoted his life to helping others less fortunate than himself and to defending the cause of religious freedom.

William Penn was a Quaker who worked for religious tolerance and political freedom in England. In 1681, he was granted a charter to establish a new colony, which was named Pennsylvania in his honor. Penn drew up the constitution for his colony.

Penn was still a young man when he left the Church of England. His father was shocked at his son's behavior. He was even more shocked when, a few years later, the young man joined the Society of Friends, or Quakers. The Quakers believed that in the eyes of God all people were equal. Quakers wore plain dress and refused to take off their hats even in the presence of the King.

Because he was a Quaker, Penn was jailed several times. On one occasion he was told that he would be kept in prison for the rest of his life unless he abandoned his Quaker beliefs. Penn refused. "My prison shall be my grave before I will budge one jot," he said.

When his father died, William Penn became a rich man. He decided to build a colony where Quakers could worship as they pleased. He asked King Charles II for a grant of land in America. The King had owed Penn's father a large sum of money, and Penn offered to take the land instead. This was an easy way for King Charles to pay off his debt. It was also an easy way for him to get the troublesome Quakers out of England.

In 1681 the King gave Penn a large grant of land west of the Delaware River. The King himself named the land Penn's Woods, or Pennsylvania, in honor of William Penn's father. Penn was disappointed that his colony did not have a coastline. In 1682 the King's brother, the Duke of York, solved this problem by giving Penn another grant of land, on Delaware Bay, south of Pennsylvania. This land, at first called the lower counties, in time came to be known as Delaware.

From the beginning Penn invited people from many different countries to settle in his colony. He wanted honest and hardworking people. He gave them land, as much as 500 acres (200 hectares) a family. He promised them that in Pennsylvania they could worship in their own way and share in the government.

The first group of settlers started Philadelphia, The City of Brotherly Love, on the banks of the Delaware River. Others followed by the hundreds and then by the thousands. Many who came were Quakers, but there were also large numbers of other Protestant groups as well as Catholics and Jews. They came from all over Europe.

One of the largest groups was made up of German and Swiss farmers from the Rhine Valley. After they arrived in Pennsylvania, the colonists from the Rhineland continued to speak German, or *Deutsch,* as they called it. According to one story, their English-speaking neighbors misunderstood them and thought they said "Dutch." So it was that the German-speaking settlers in Pennsylvania came to be known as the Pennsylvania Dutch.

William Penn kept his promises, not only to the colonists but to the Indians as well. He

An Exact Prospect of CHARLES TOWN, the Metropolis of the Province of SOUTH CAROLINA.

Charles Towne was the early capital of South Carolina, founded by the English in 1670. The waterfront of Charleston today is still lined with warehouses and docks.

had promised the Indians that he would buy land from them and not take it by force. As a result, for many years the colonists lived at peace with their Indian neighbors and the colony prospered.

▶ THE SOUTHERN COLONIES

While New England and the Middle Colonies were growing, other Englishmen started other colonies in the warmer, milder regions to the south. One of these was George Calvert, whose title was Lord Baltimore.

George Calvert, Lord Baltimore, was a member of the British Parliament who took a great interest in colonial affairs. He wanted to establish a haven for Roman Catholics, and in 1632 he was granted territory that was later overseen by his son and named Maryland.

Lord Baltimore Founds Maryland

George Calvert was a good friend of the English king, Charles I. Calvert was a Roman Catholic. He wanted to build a colony in which all Christians, including Catholics, could worship in their own way. In 1632 King Charles I gave him a large land grant just north of Virginia.

George Calvert framed a charter for his province, but he died before he could send out his first group of settlers. But his son, Cecil, the second Lord Baltimore, carried on the work his father had started. He named the colony Maryland in honor of Henrietta Maria, the wife of Charles I.

The first group of about 200 settlers, including Catholics and Protestants, landed near the mouth of the Potomac River on March 25, 1634. They called their settlement St. Mary's.

The Calverts had learned from the earlier experience of the settlers in Jamestown. As a result, Maryland, with Cecil Calvert's younger brother Leonard as its first governor, prospered from the beginning. The settlers bought land from the Indians. They cleared the land and built large farms, called plantations, along the banks of the Potomac and other rivers. As in Virginia, tobacco became the most important cash crop.

In 1649, Lord Baltimore urged the Maryland legislature to adopt a law that came to be known as the Toleration Act. This act guaranteed religious freedom to all Christians who settled in Maryland.

North and South Carolina

In the meantime, restless pioneers from Virginia had been moving into the wild, unsettled country to the south of their colony. They built log cabins and cleared a little land. They lived by hunting, fishing, and raising crops in the forest clearings.

The early settlers had moved into country where there was no government. Some of them led lawless lives. The rivers and creeks became favorite hiding places for pirates.

But most of the settlers were hardworking men and women. Some of them planted small patches of tobacco, which they sold as a cash crop. Others earned a living by selling forest products to shipbuilders in England. They sold lumber and tall, straight pine trees for shipmasts. They sold resin and turpentine, which they got from the sap of the pines.

In 1663 the King of England renamed this region Carolina. He gave it to eight of his friends, all wealthy noblemen. The new owners advertised for settlers, offering land on easy terms to all who came to the colony.

The southern area of Carolina at first attracted most of the new settlers. They built a seaport, which they named Charles Towne (later shortened to Charleston), that soon became the most prosperous southern seaport. Settlers from many different countries and of many different religious beliefs moved to the city and into the surrounding countryside.

Many of the wealthy settlers started large rice plantations on the rich swampland along the coast. Before long they began to bring in slaves to work on the plantation. By this time the tobacco planters in Maryland, Virginia, and the northern part of Carolina were also using slave labor. So in the early years of colonization slavery became firmly established in the southern colonies.

Although Carolina became a thriving colony, the proprietors had difficulty governing it from overseas. Finally they returned it to the King, who divided it into two royal colonies. In 1721 he created South Carolina, and in 1729 he created North Carolina.

Georgia, Last of the 13 Colonies

Three years after North Carolina became a separate royal colony, James Oglethorpe started the last of the 13 colonies along the Atlantic coast. Oglethorpe was a wealthy Englishman. He and a number of his friends were deeply troubled over conditions that existed in English prisons. In those days debtors (people who owed money they could not repay) were sent to jail until they repaid their debts. But since they could not earn money in prison, those who had no friends to help them remained behind bars for years.

James Oglethorpe founded Georgia, the last of the 13 American colonies, in 1733. He accompanied the first settlers there and settled Savannah. Oglethorpe wanted Georgia to provide a home for debtors, where they could start life over instead of suffering in English prisons.

Oglethorpe had visited such prisons. He knew that many of the prisoners were poor but honest and could become good citizens if given a chance. He decided to start a colony where debtors could begin life again.

In 1732, King George II of England gave Oglethorpe and several of his friends a large grant of land. This land, known as Georgia for the King, lay between South Carolina and the Spanish colony of Florida. The King realized that English settlements in Georgia would help to protect the other English colonies from Spanish attack.

James Oglethorpe himself led the first group of debtors to the new colony. They arrived in 1733 and settled at a site they called Savannah. Each person received 50 acres (20 hectares) of land. Oglethorpe and the other owners (trustees) were determined to make Georgia a model colony. They refused to allow slavery or the sale of rum and brandy.

Settlers from New England and from Europe, as well as debtors from English prisons, moved to Oglethorpe's colony. Savannah became a thriving seaport. Farms and farming villages of free people spread inland. In 1752, Georgia became a royal colony.

In 1606 the coast of North America was a wilderness, except for the settlements in Florida and Canada. Less than 150 years later, the English flag was flying over 13 colonies along the coast. These 13 colonies were the new homeland of nearly 2,000,000 men, women, and children. The colonists were building a new way of life in the New World. Although they did not know it, they also were building a new nation, one that would become the United States of America.

LEWIS PAUL TODD
Author, *New Ways in the New World*

See also COLONIAL LIFE IN AMERICA; JAMESTOWN; MAYFLOWER; PLYMOUTH COLONY.

Magdeburg, pictured here during a siege in 1631, was one of the many German cities and towns destroyed in the Thirty Years' War (1618–48). The war began as a religious conflict but eventually expanded to involve all of Europe.

THIRTY YEARS' WAR

The Thirty Years' War (1618–48) began as a religious conflict but grew into a widespread war that eventually engulfed all of Europe. Its causes were confused and its results were generally disastrous, especially for Germany, where the war centered.

Historical Background. Germany at the time was not a nation in the modern sense, but a very loose confederation of states, ruled by princes. The head of the confederation, in theory, was the Holy Roman emperor. But the emperor's power came mainly from two other sources. His own possessions in Austria, Hungary, and Bohemia (now part of the Czech Republic) were one source of power. The other was the fact that he was a member of the powerful Habsburg family, which also ruled in Spain, Italy, and parts of what are now Belgium, the Netherlands, and France. This meant that quarrels among the German states merged into the long-standing conflict between Spain and France and thus gradually came to involve the rest of Europe.

Origins of the Conflict. In the beginning the main cause of the war was the bitter religious differences between Catholics and Protestants, which were really an extension of the religious wars of the previous century. The Habsburgs were Catholic, but many of the German princes were Protestant. In 1618 the Protestant nobles of Bohemia asked the Elector Palatine, Frederick V, a German Protestant prince, to be their king, in preference to their Habsburg ruler, the soon-to-be Emperor Ferdinand II. The crowning of Frederick led to the first outbreak of war. The first battle, the Battle of the White Mountain, was a defeat for Frederick and the Bohemians. But it was only the beginning of a long conflict, as Catholic and Protestant states lined up on one side or the other. France, guided by its chief minister, Cardinal Richelieu, although Catholic, sided with the Protestants against its enemy Spain.

The War Expands. Gradually a series of wars developed, which were often less religious in origin than the result of the rivalry between particular states, princes, or generals. In 1630 the Protestant king of Sweden, Gustavus Adolphus, invaded Germany. He won famous victories over the Catholic armies at Breitenfeld and Lützen but was killed at Lützen. As the war continued, the armies on both sides increasingly became the followers of independent generals fighting for their own advantage. One of the most extraordinary was the Catholic general Albrecht von Wallenstein. A brilliant soldier, he was eventually murdered by three of his own officers.

Peace of Westphalia. The combatants, exhausted by the years of war, finally signed a peace at Westphalia in 1648.

The war solved no problems. The extreme Protestants and Catholics were both left unsatisfied. The Holy Roman Empire had disintegrated, and the Habsburgs were reduced in power. The war had been a catastrophe for Germany, which was still splintered into many small, despotic states. Hordes of undisciplined soldiers had plundered the land for a generation. The numbers of people killed, villages burned, and towns destroyed can never be known. In time the physical damage was repaired, but the horror of the war long remained a part of German consciousness.

C. V. WEDGWOOD
Author, *The Thirty Years War*

THOMAS, CLARENCE. See SUPREME COURT OF THE UNITED STATES (Profiles).

THOMAS, DYLAN (1914–1953)

The poet Dylan Thomas was born on October 27, 1914, in Swansea, Wales. Dylan was educated at Swansea Grammar School, where he edited and wrote many poems for the school magazine.

After leaving school, Thomas worked as a reporter for a newspaper in Swansea. During this time, when he was between the ages of 16 and 20, he wrote a great deal of poetry. After he became famous, he revised and published some of these early poems.

His first poem, "And Death Shall Have No Dominion," appeared in a London magazine in 1933, when he was 19. He contributed poems to several magazines, and one of them awarded him a prize by publishing his first book, *18 Poems*, in 1934. His highly original poems were widely praised, and Thomas soon became well known. He published a second book, *Twenty-Five Poems*, two years later.

After marrying Caitlin Macnamara in 1937, Thomas moved to the small Welsh town of Laugharne. During World War II he lived in London, wrote film scripts, and worked in radio broadcasting while continuing to write poetry. Thomas also wrote fairy tales, short stories, essays, and a short novel.

Some of Thomas' best work deals with his early life in Wales. The poems "Fern Hill" and "Over Sir John's Hill" describe the Welsh landscape. The book of stories called *Portrait of the Artist as a Young Dog* (1940) is based on events of his youth.

In 1949, Thomas moved back to Laugharne. Some of his best-known works were written during this time. One is *Under Milk Wood*, a radio play (first broadcast in 1954) about the people in a small Welsh town like Laugharne. Another is the sketch called "A Child's Christmas in Wales" (1955).

Thomas was famous as a fine public reader of poetry. He made three tours of the United States, giving readings to enthusiastic audiences. He died of pneumonia on the last of these tours, in New York City on November 9, 1953.

JACOB KORG
Author, *Dylan Thomas*

THOMAS, HELEN. See JOURNALISM (Profiles).

THOMPSON, BENJAMIN (1753–1814)

Benjamin Thompson was an American-born British diplomat and scientist known for his research on heat. He was born in North Woburn, Massachusetts, on March 26, 1753. As a young man, Thompson was a schoolteacher in Rumford, New Hampshire.

In 1775 the American Revolutionary War broke out, but Thompson did not support the American patriots. He fled to England where he entered government service. In 1784, Thompson was knighted by King George III in England and given permission to serve the government in the German state of Bavaria. In Bavaria, Thompson received the title of Count Rumford.

Thompson introduced important reforms in the Bavarian army and later served as minister of war. Always interested in science, he conducted experiments at a weapons factory, studying the heat that was produced when cannons were being bored (drilled out). The results of these studies led Thompson to the theory about heat for which he is famous. He said that the hotness of an object is due to the vibrating motion of the particles in the object. This theory is now called the kinetic theory of heat.

Thompson was a founder of the Royal Institution of Great Britain. He also financed the Rumford medals that are awarded for outstanding achievements in physics.

In 1805, Thompson married the widow of the French chemist Antoine Lavoisier. He died near Paris on August 25, 1814.

DUANE H. D. ROLLER
The University of Oklahoma

See also HEAT.

THOMPSON, DAVID. See FUR TRADE IN NORTH AMERICA (Profiles).

THOMPSON, ERA BELL. See NORTH DAKOTA (Famous People).

THOMPSON, JENNY. See OLYMPIC GAMES (Profiles).

THOMPSON, SIR JOHN. See CANADA, GOVERNMENT OF (Profiles).

THOMSON, SIR JOSEPH JOHN. See PHYSICS, HISTORY OF (Profiles).

THOR. See NORSE MYTHOLOGY (Profiles).

THOREAU, HENRY DAVID (1817–1862)

The American writer and naturalist Henry David Thoreau is best known for his book *Walden*, an account of his two-year experiment in simple living on Walden Pond, in Massachusetts.

Thoreau was born in Concord, Massachusetts, on July 12, 1817. He was one of four children. The Thoreau family was not wealthy. Thoreau's father kept a store and manufactured pencils in a shed attached to the house. The family took in boarders to earn extra money.

Henry was the best student in his school, so it was decided that he should go to college. He was given aid from college funds and entered Harvard at age 16. During vacations he taught school to help pay for his education.

Soon after he graduated from Harvard, Thoreau and his older brother, John, started a school in their home. They taught the usual courses—Latin, Greek, mathematics—but they also held classes in natural history and took their pupils on field trips. This was a new idea at the time. Soon the school was so successful that they rented the Old Academy building in Concord and filled it with scholars. But when John became ill in 1841, the school was given up.

Thoreau became a friend of the writer Ralph Waldo Emerson, who also lived in Concord. Through Emerson, he became involved in transcendentalism, a movement of New England writers and philosophers. (For more information on this movement, see the feature on transcendentalism in the article AMERICAN LITERATURE in Volume A.) Emerson encouraged Thoreau to become a writer.

In 1845, Thoreau built a tiny cabin on land owned by Emerson on Walden Pond, just outside Concord village. He wanted to live simply, without spending much money, and devote his time to observing nature and writing. Thoreau lived at Walden for a little more than two years. He studied the plant and animal life around him and kept a written record of all he saw and thought. He also wrote his first book, *A Week on the Concord and Merrimack Rivers* (1849), about a trip he had taken with his brother in 1839. Later, Thoreau put his experiences at Walden into his masterpiece, *Walden; or, Life in the Woods* (1854). The two books are much admired today. But

The American writer Henry David Thoreau was a naturalist as well as a political thinker. He is best known for his book *Walden*, in which he advocates living simply and in harmony with nature. His essay on civil disobedience is also an important contribution to American literature.

when Thoreau wrote them, few people appreciated what he had to say.

Thoreau's ideas were very advanced for his time, and most people thought them strange. He stressed the importance of living in harmony with nature at a time when America was becoming more and more industrialized. He observed the ways of deer, beaver, woodchucks, and other wild creatures when most people thought of animals mainly as things to hunt and kill. He studied the history of North American Indians at a time when no one seemed to care how the Indians had lived before the first European settlers arrived.

Thoreau publicly opposed slavery before the idea of abolishing it was generally accepted. He once went to jail for refusing to pay his taxes, saying the government would use the money to support slavery. In the essay *Civil Disobedience* (1849), he explained his view that a person has a right to protest unjust laws by disobeying them. Many years later, this technique of passive resistance was adopted by such reformers as Martin Luther King, Jr., and Mohandas Gandhi.

Thoreau died of tuberculosis on May 6, 1862. When all his writings were published, they filled 20 volumes. His writings, in addition to their literary value, have been influential in the areas of individual liberties and land conservation. There is now a public park at Walden Pond.

LOUISE HALL THARP
Author, *Tory Hole, The Peabody Sisters of Salem*

The following pages contain excerpts from *Walden*.

Thoreau lived in this tiny cabin beside Walden Pond, near Concord, Massachusetts, for a little more than two years. The drawing is by his sister Sophia.

I went to the woods because I wished to live deliberately, to front only the essential facts of life, and see if I could not learn what it had to teach, and not, when I came to die, discover that I had not lived. I did not wish to live what was not life, living is so dear; nor did I wish to practise resignation, unless it was quite necessary. I wanted to live deep and suck out all the marrow of life, to live so sturdily and Spartan-like as to put to rout all that was not life, to cut a broad swath and shave close, to drive life into a corner, and reduce it to its lowest terms, and, if it proved to be mean, why then to get the whole and genuine meanness of it, and publish its meanness to the world; or if it were sublime, to know it by experience, and be able to give a true account of it in my next excursion.

.   .   .

I had three chairs in my house; one for solitude, two for friendship, three for society. When visitors came in larger and unexpected numbers there was but the third chair for them all, but they generally economized the room by standing up. It is surprising how many great men and women a small house will contain. I have had twenty-five or thirty souls, with their bodies, at once under my roof, and yet we often parted without being aware that we had come very near to one another. Many of our houses, both public and private, with their almost innumerable apartments, their huge halls and their cellars for the storage of wines and other munitions of peace, appear to me extravagantly large for their inhabitants. They are so vast and magnificent that the latter seem to be only vermin which infest them. I am surprised when the herald blows his summons before some Tremont or Astor or Middlesex House, to see come creeping out over the piazza for all inhabitants a ridiculous mouse, which soon again slinks into some hole in the pavement.

One inconvenience I sometimes experienced in so small a house, the difficulty of getting to a sufficient distance from my guest when we began to utter the big thoughts in big words. You want room for your thoughts to get into sailing trim and run a course or two before they make their port. The bullet of your thought must have overcome its lateral and ricochet motion and fallen into its last and steady course before it reaches the ear of the hearer, else it may plow out again through the side of his head. Also, our sentences wanted room to unfold and form their columns in the interval. Individuals, like nations, must have suitable broad and natural boundaries, even a considerable neutral ground, between them. I have found it a singular luxury to talk across the pond to a companion on the opposite side. In my house we were so near that we could not begin to hear,—we could not speak low enough to be heard; as when you throw two stones into calm water so near that they break each other's undulations. If we are merely loquacious and loud talkers, then we can afford to stand very near together, cheek by jowl, and feel each other's breath; but if we speak reservedly and thoughtfully, we want to be farther apart, that all animal heat and moisture may have a chance to evaporate. If we would enjoy the most intimate society with that in each of us which is without, or above, being spoken to, we must not only be silent, but commonly so far apart bodily that we cannot possibly hear each other's voice in any case. Referred to this standard, speech is for the convenience of those who are hard of hearing; but there are many fine things which we cannot say if we have to shout. As the conversation began to assume a loftier and grander tone, we gradually shoved our chairs farther apart till they touched the wall in opposite corners, and then commonly there was not room enough.

.   .   .

The phenomena of the year take place every day in a pond on a small scale. Every morning, generally speaking, the shallow water is being warmed more rapidly than the deep, though it may not be made so warm after all, and every evening it is being cooled more rapidly until the morning. The day is an epitome of the year. The night is the winter, the morning and evening are the spring and fall, and the noon is the summer.

The cracking and booming of the ice indicate a change of temperature. One pleasant morning after a cold night, February 24th, 1850, having gone to Flint's Pond to spend the day, I noticed with surprise, that when I struck the ice with the head of my axe, it resounded like a gong for many rods around, or as if I had struck on a tight drumhead. The pond began to boom about an hour after sunrise, when it felt the influence of the sun's rays slanted upon it from over the hills; it stretched itself and yawned like a waking man with a gradually increasing tumult, which was kept up three or four hours. It took a short siesta at noon, and boomed once more toward night, as the sun was withdrawing his influence. In the right stage of the weather a pond fires its evening gun with great regularity. But in the middle of the day, being full of cracks, and the air also being less elastic, it had completely lost its resonance, and probably fishes and muskrats could not then have been stunned by a blow on it. The fishermen say that the "thundering of the pond" scares the fishes and prevents their biting. The pond does not thunder every evening, and I cannot tell surely when to expect its thundering; but though I may perceive no difference in the weather, it does. Who would have suspected so large and cold and thick-skinned a thing to be so sensitive? Yet it has its law to which it thunders obedience when it should as surely as the buds expand in the spring. The earth is all alive and covered with papillae. The largest pond is as sensitive to atmospheric changes as the globule of mercury in its tube.

THORPE, JAMES FRANCIS (JIM) (1888–1953)

Jim Thorpe was perhaps the greatest American athlete of all time. It is difficult to believe that one person could be so outstanding in running, jumping, shot-putting, pole vaulting, swimming, and skating and also excel in archery, boxing, football, handball, hockey, lacrosse, and rifle shooting. But there was no sport that Jim Thorpe could not do well. When he first tried golf, he shot in the low 80's, and he bowled in the 200 class.

James Francis Thorpe was born on an Indian reservation near Shawnee, Oklahoma, on May 28, 1888. His mother was a granddaughter of the Sauk chief Black Hawk. His father was half Indian and half Irish. Young Jim's tribal name was Bright Path. Jim began to ride when he was 3 and to swim soon after.

After attending school on the reservation and at the Haskell Institute in Lawrence, Kansas, Jim went to the Carlisle Indian School in Pennsylvania. There, in 1907, his amazing football career began when he was sent into a game as a substitute and won an upset victory for his team. Walter Camp chose Jim for the All-American teams of 1911 and 1912. It has been said that trying to catch Thorpe when he ran was like trying to clutch a shadow.

Jim Thorpe was the marvel of the Olympic Games held in Stockholm, Sweden, in 1912. He won the decathlon and the pentathlon—the only time both contests ever were won by the same man. In the pentathlon (five events), he won four out of the five events. In the decathlon (ten events), he scored a remarkable 8,412 points. But in 1913, it was charged that Jim Thorpe had been a professional athlete before he competed in the Olympics—he had played semiprofessional baseball in 1909. He had to return his medals, and his Olympic deeds were erased from the records. But in 1982 the International Olympic Committee restored the medals to Jim Thorpe's family.

Jim Thorpe played professional baseball (1913–19) and football (1915–29).

In 1950 the Associated Press named Jim Thorpe the greatest football player and all-around male athlete of the first half of the 20th century. He died on March 28, 1953, in Lomita, California.

Reviewed by BOB MATHIAS
Olympic Decathlon Champion (1948, 1952)

Jim Thorpe won both the decathlon and the pentathlon at the 1912 Olympic Games. A great all-around athlete, he also played professional football and baseball.

Lightning is a huge electric spark—a single flash between cloud and ground may be 9 miles (14 kilometers) long and discharge about 100,000,000 volts of electricity.

THUNDER AND LIGHTNING

A brilliant flash of lightning followed by a deafening roll of thunder is one of nature's most dramatic displays. It is no wonder that in ancient times people thought thunder and lightning had supernatural causes. The early Greeks believed that the god Hephaestus made lightning bolts in his workshop and that Zeus, the father of the gods, hurled these lightning bolts at his enemies.

Today we know there is nothing supernatural about thunder and lightning. Lightning is simply a series of huge electric sparks. The sparks are similar to the tiny spark that passes between your finger and a metal doorknob after you have scuffed your feet on a carpet. (This kind of electricity is called **static electricity.**) The crackle you hear as the spark jumps from your finger corresponds to thunder.

When a large amount of static electricity builds up in a storm cloud, a giant spark—the lightning flash—appears. The lightning may jump from one part of the cloud to another part, or it may jump from cloud to cloud. The lightning we usually see jumps between the storm cloud and the ground.

Benjamin Franklin, the famous American statesman and inventor, was the first person to prove that lightning is electricity. In his famous experiment in 1752, Franklin sent a kite high into the air during a thunderstorm. Electricity from the storm clouds traveled down the wet kite string and through a key that Franklin had tied near the end of the string. It was a dangerous experiment. Franklin could have been electrocuted.

▶ WHAT IS THUNDER?

A lightning flash heats the air along its path by many thousands of degrees. The heat causes the air along the lightning flash to expand very quickly. The rapid expansion causes nearby air particles to crowd together, forming a sound wave. As the sound wave moves outward from the flash region and reaches your ears, you hear thunder. If the storm is right overhead, you hear a loud crack. If the storm is far away, the sound wave is weak by the time it reaches your ears. You hear a booming noise.

Because the usual flash of lightning follows an irregular, jagged path, there may be sudden changes in the nature of the sound waves. This brings about some of the rolling and rumbling effects of thunder that last for several seconds. Echoes from hills, mountains, or buildings may cause these sound effects to continue even longer. Sometimes a rapid series of lightning flashes takes place, also causing long thunder.

When lightning flashes inside a cloud, you may not see it. But you do hear the thunder.

▶ CHARGES AND SPARKS

How does a little spark from your finger or the big spark of lightning jump from one place to another? The answer has to do with atoms.

All things are made of atoms. And all atoms are made of even smaller things. When scientists talk about electricity, they are chiefly concerned with two parts of an atom—electrons and protons, each of which carries an electrical charge. Electrons carry a negative ($-$) charge, and protons carry a positive ($+$) charge. Usually an atom has the same number of electrons and protons. The negative charges balance the positive charges, and the atom is neutral—that is, it does not have a net, or overall, charge.

Electrons, however, can be added to atoms or taken away. When an atom gains or loses electrons, we say it becomes **charged.** If it gains electrons, it becomes negatively charged. If it loses electrons, it becomes positively charged.

Atoms with unlike charges attract each other. It is also true that electrons can flow from a region of many electrons to a region of few electrons. Thus, electrons flow from a negatively charged object to one with a positive charge. That is what causes the spark between your fingers and the metal doorknob.

When you scuff your feet across a carpet, you scrape electrons off the carpet and onto your shoes. These extra electrons flow all over you. Like an atom that has been given extra electrons, you become negatively charged. If you stand still or just walk around, the electrons gradually leave your body, and we say you have become **discharged.** The electrons simply attach themselves to atoms in the air around you or to atoms in the carpet. In this way you become discharged slowly.

But if you touch a doorknob right after scuffing your shoes on the carpet, you become discharged quickly. The extra electrons on your body jump in the form of a spark from your fingers to the doorknob.

If the charges are strong enough, the charged objects do not have to touch for a spark to occur. The electrons jump across the space between them, making a spark. That is what happens with lightning.

How Does a Cloud Become Charged?

A storm cloud, often called a thundercloud, can build up great charges of electricity. The electricity is discharged as lightning, but the cloud can recharge itself time and time again. How does the charging and recharging take place?

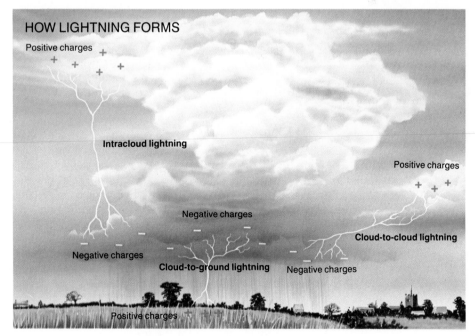

HOW LIGHTNING FORMS

Lightning occurs when electrons flow rapidly between regions of positive and negative electrical charge. This can occur within a single cloud (*left*), between a storm cloud and the ground (*middle*), or between two clouds (*right*). Cumulonimbus clouds are the most common producers of lightning.

Positive charges

Intracloud lightning

Positive charges

Negative charges

Negative charges

Cloud-to-cloud lightning

Cloud-to-ground lightning

Negative charges

Positive charges

Above: Tall objects, such as trees, make excellent targets for lightning. Keep this in mind—never seek shelter under a tree during a thunderstorm!

Left: Trees can sometimes survive being struck by lightning. This large oak tree bears the scar of a lightning strike along its trunk.

Many scientists believe that a thundercloud becomes charged because of ice particles and water droplets in the cloud. A single thundercloud may hold hundreds of tons of water in the form of water droplets, hail, and ice crystals. All of this material is in constant, rapid motion.

How can you tell how close a thunderstorm is to you?

During a storm you can try to figure out how far away the thunderclouds are. It is easy to do if you remember these facts. Light travels so quickly that you see a flash of lightning almost at the moment it occurs. Sound travels much more slowly. It takes about 5 seconds to travel 1 mile (1.6 kilometers), while light travels 186,000 miles (about 300,000 kilometers) in 1 second. To find out how far away a storm is, all you have to do is time the number of seconds between the flash and the thunderclap. Divide the number of seconds by 5. The result will be the distance in miles. (Multiply this number by 1.6 to get the distance in kilometers.)

Laboratory experiments have shown that in a mixture of water and ice, the water has a positive charge and the ice has a negative charge. The interaction of water and ice particles causes positive and negative charges to separate. This suggests what happens inside a thundercloud. When hailstones and other heavy ice particles in the cloud come in contact and collide with tiny water droplets, the ice particles become negatively charged. Because of their weight they fall to the bottom of the cloud. The lighter particles rise, giving the top of the cloud a strong positive charge.

Not all scientists agree with this explanation. Some believe that the violent air movements in the thundercloud cause positively and negatively charged particles to separate.

Building up an electrical charge in a thundercloud may last for more than an hour. When the top of the cloud is positively charged and the bottom of the cloud is negatively charged, there may be a voltage difference of 100,000,000 volts.

▶THE LIGHTNING STROKE

A thundercloud's electrical strength is in the top and middle sections of the cloud. This is the region where most lightning occurs. When the charges are strong enough, electrons flow from the negatively charged section to a positively charged one. That is, a rapid discharge takes place, which is the lightning flash.

Cloud-to-ground lightning has been extensively studied by scientists using special photographic equipment. Their studies have revealed in detail what happens during a stroke of lightning. Lightning usually appears as a jagged streak that moves in quick steps, spurting and halting along a zigzag path. The first stroke, or **step leader,** which is invisible, finds the path of least resistance (the shortest, easiest path) through the air. It clears the way for other strokes that follow.

When the step leader nears the ground, a strong charge from the ground surges up the jagged path to the cloud. It is this return stroke that you see as the lightning flash. Secondary leaders usually move down the same path as the step leader, and more return strokes result. These occur within fractions of a second. The return strokes follow each other so quickly that there may be from 3 to 30 or more return strokes in what we see as a single flash of lightning. And depending on conditions, one flash of lightning may be as much as 100 miles (150 kilometers) long.

Kinds of Lightning

There are several kinds of lightning. A jagged flash of lightning is called **streak lightning**. Sometimes as lightning seeks the path of least resistance, it forks out. This is **forked lightning. Chain,** or **bead, lightning** is closely related. It begins as a streak and ends up looking like a string of beads.

St. Elmo's fire is a form of lightning that does not flash. It is seen as a glow on pointed objects such as church steeples, poles, and the masts of ships. St. Elmo's fire forms when the negative electrical charges at the base of a cloud attract positive charges from the ground below. The positive charges accumulate on pointed objects and slowly leak away (discharge) into the air. When this discharge is visible, it is called St. Elmo's fire.

Ball lightning is another unusual type of lightning that does not flash. It appears as a round glowing ball that floats along the ground or through the air. Ball lightning usually lasts less than 5 seconds and disappears silently or with a small explosion.

▶SAFEGUARDS AGAINST LIGHTNING

At any one time, as many as 2,000 thunderstorms are occurring in various parts of the world. About 100 flashes of cloud-to-ground lightning are occurring every second. These enormous sparks of electricity can be very destructive. In the United States alone, between 100 and 200 people are killed each year by lightning. Property damage caused by lightning reaches several hundred million dollars each year.

Safety Precautions During a Thunderstorm

To protect yourself from possible injury during a thunderstorm, you should observe some important rules.

First, do not believe the old saying, "Lightning never strikes twice in the same place." It can and does.

If you are out in the open, do not try to keep dry by standing under a lone tree. This can be a dangerous place, because tall objects make good targets for lightning. It is better to lie low and get wet.

Low places, such as a valley between hills, are safer than high places. Woods are safer than open places.

Do not go near beaches, swimming pools, or lakes. Keep away from wire fences. Avoid small sheds that are out in the open.

Do not take a bath or shower during a thunderstorm because water is an excellent conductor of electricity. Keep away from the fireplace and from electrical outlets. Do not use the telephone unless necessary.

The safest place to be during a thunderstorm is in the house or in a large building.

Thousands of forest fires also are caused by lightning, although such fires can sometimes produce beneficial effects. For example, the heat from lightning-caused forest fires can help distribute certain kinds of plant seeds by causing the plant's seedpods to burst. In addition, the electrical discharge from lightning causes chemical reactions that speed the recycling of important plant nutrients.

The principal protection for property against lightning damage is the lightning rod, which was invented by Benjamin Franklin. It consists of a metal rod extending up from the roof or other high point on a building. A heavy wire connects to the rod. The other end of the wire is buried in the ground. (The rod on the roof is then said to be **grounded.**) The lightning rod provides an easy route (to the ground) for the lightning, so it will not take a destructive path if it strikes the building.

A steel-frame building is safe in an electrical storm. This is because a lightning stroke will pass safely through the steel framework and into the ground.

Roy A. Gallant
The Natural History Press
Reviewed by Jerome Spar
New York University

See also Electricity.

THURBER, JAMES (1894–1961)

James Grover Thurber, the celebrated American humorist, was born on December 8, 1894, in Columbus, Ohio. For most of his life he lived in or near New York City. He wrote many of his stories and sketches for *The New Yorker*, a weekly magazine edited by his friend Harold Ross.

Thurber was a newspaper reporter from 1920 to 1927, when he joined the staff of *The New Yorker*. He wrote his first children's story, *Many Moons* (1943), for his daughter Rosemary. Four other stories followed—*The Great Quillow* (1944), *The White Deer* (1945), *The 13 Clocks* (1950), and *The Wonderful O* (1957). He also wrote two books of fables. One of his fables, "The Moth and the Star," follows the article FABLES in Volume F.

Thurber's 14 books for adults recall his boyhood in Ohio, his experiences as a student at Ohio State University, and his life as a civilian code clerk in Paris after World War I. He wrote about ordinary people in everyday situations. Automobiles, shower faucets, politicians, and other complications of the modern world almost defeat Thurber's characters. But no matter how bad their dilemmas, Thurber makes us laugh. He even laughed about his own loss of sight and eventual blindness, caused by a childhood accident. Thurber also drew cartoons of men, women, and sad-faced dogs. The dog below is typical.

Thurber's most famous story is "The Secret Life of Walter Mitty." While Mitty drives his wife on a shopping trip, he imagines himself flying a navy airplane and performing other brave deeds. His wife thinks about overshoes, puppy biscuits, and taking Mitty's temperature.

With Elliott Nugent, Thurber wrote a play, *The Male Animal* (1940). He acted in *A Thurber Carnival,* a Broadway revue based on his own stories, in 1960. He told about his early life in *My Life and Hard Times* (1933) and about his *New Yorker* experiences in *The Years with Ross* (1959). Despite his blindness, he worked continuously until his death in New York City on November 2, 1961.

RICHARD C. TOBIAS
Author, *The Art of James Thurber*

▶THE GREAT QUILLOW

One of James Thurber's books for children is *The Great Quillow*. The story begins:

> Once upon a time, in a far country, there lived a giant named Hunder. He was so enormous in height and girth and weight that little waves were set in motion in distant lakes when he walked. His great fingers could wrench a clock from its steeple as easily as a child might remove a peanut from its shell. Every morning he devoured three sheep, a pie made of a thousand apples, and a chocolate as high and as wide as a spinning wheel. It would have taken six ordinary men to lift the great brass key to his front door, and four to carry one of the candles with which he lighted his house.
>
> It was Hunder's way to strip a town of its sheep and apples and chocolate, its leather and cloth, its lumber and tallow and brass, and then move on to a new far village and begin his depredations again. There had been no men strong enough to thwart his evil ways in any of the towns he had set upon and impoverished. He had broken their most formidable weapons between his thumb and forefinger, laughing like the hurricane. And there had been no men cunning enough in any of the towns to bring about his destruction. He had crushed their most ingenious traps with the toe of his mammoth boot, guffawing like a volcano.
>
> One day Hunder strode hundreds and hundreds of leagues and came to a little town in a green valley. It was a staunch little town and a firm little valley, but they quaked with the sound of his coming. The houses were narrow and two stories high; the streets were narrow and cobbled. There were not many people in the town: a hundred men, a hundred women, a hundred children.

One of the 100 men in the little town was Quillow, the toymaker. The other men used to make fun of him, calling him the Great Quillow. But it was Quillow who rid the town of Hunder, the giant. How he did it, only Thurber can tell.

THURMOND, STROM. See SOUTH CAROLINA (Famous People).

TIBET

Tibet is a rugged, mountainous land in Central Asia. Consisting of a vast plateau surrounded by the world's highest mountains, it has often been called the Roof of the World. Tibet was long an independent country with its own distinctive culture and way of life, developed during centuries of isolation from the rest of the world. It has been occupied by China since 1950.

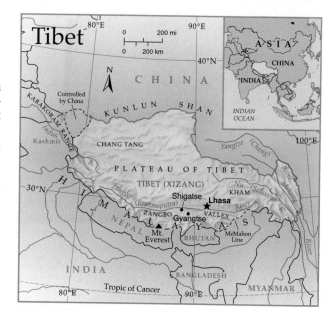

▶ PEOPLE

The population of the Tibetan Autonomous Region (one of five such regions in China) is estimated at about 3 million. Another 2 million Tibetans live in adjacent provinces. Approximately 130,000 Tibetans live in exile around the world.

Most Tibetans are farmers or nomadic herders of yaks (a variety of long-haired oxen), sheep, and other livestock. They belong to the large Mongoloid group of peoples who inhabit Central and East Asia as well as parts of Southeast Asia.

Language. Tibetan is one of the Sino-Tibetan family of languages, which also includes Chinese, Thai, and Burmese. The Tibetan alphabet, however, is based on the ancient Sanskrit alphabet of India.

Religion. Religion has always been important in Tibet. At one time there were many monasteries throughout the country. Tibetans practice Lamaism, a form of Buddhism. The word "lama" refers to priests and monks of high rank. The Tibetan religious leaders are the Dalai Lama and the Panch'en Lama. The Dalai Lama was also the political ruler of Tibet. The present Dalai Lama (the 14th, installed in 1940) established a government-in-exile in India in 1959, following an unsuccessful revolt against Chinese rule.

Tibetans have a distinctive culture and way of life. They belong to the Mongoloid group of peoples who live in Central and East Asia and parts of Southeast Asia.

Way of Life. Chinese Communist rule radically changed Tibetan society. Most of the monasteries were closed, although some have reopened. The nobility and the lamas, many of whom were large landowners, were removed from power. Their estates were broken up, to be redistributed among the landless farmers.

▶ **LAND**

The Tibetan plateau averages about 15,000 feet (4,500 meters) in elevation, making it one of the highest regions on Earth. It covers an area of close to 500,000 square miles (1.3 million square kilometers). It is bounded by

Tibet consists of a large plateau surrounded by mountains. Many Tibetans are farmers, although farming is limited because of the severe climate.

the Kunlun mountains in the north and the Himalayas in the south. To the west is the Karakoram mountain system. Tibet is the source of many of Asia's great rivers, including the Yangtze (Chang), Mekong, Brahmaputra (called Zangbo in Tibet), Salween, and Indus.

Tibet is composed of three main regions: the Zangbo Valley, Chang Tang, and Kham. The Zangbo Valley is the economic, cultural, political, and religious center of Tibet. The major cities, including Lhasa, the capital, are located in this region. Chang Tang, or the Northern Plain, is a barren, cold, and windswept area, with many salt lakes. Kham, the eastern part of Tibet, has dense forests,

abundant grazing land, and some of Tibet's most important mineral deposits.

Climate. Much of Tibet is cold and dry through most of the year. With the exception of the Kham region and parts of the Zangbo Valley, rainfall is slight. Temperatures can vary widely. Areas such as Lhasa have moderate temperatures, but winter lows of –40°F (–40°C) and summer highs of 90°F (32°C) have been recorded in other parts of Tibet.

▶ **ECONOMY**

Tibet has an agricultural economy. Barley, wheat, and millet are the chief crops and dietary staples. However, farming is limited because of the severe climate. Tibet has rich mineral resources, including coal, oil, iron ore, manganese, gold, borax, and salt. Also, tourism has recently become an important economic activity. But Tibet's economy still remains largely undeveloped.

Transportation has long been Tibet's most difficult problem. Under the Chinese two major roads have been constructed, and air service now links Tibet with Beijing, Shanghai, and Hong Kong in China, and with Kathmandu (or Katmandu) in Nepal. A railroad is now being built that will link Lhasa with other Chinese cities.

▶ **MAJOR CITIES**

Lhasa, Tibet's capital and largest city, lies in the sheltered valley of the Zangbo River in southern Tibet. Overlooking the city is the Potala, a gold-roofed, many-windowed palace that is the traditional residence of the Dalai Lama.

Shigatse is the second largest city. The famous monastery Tashi Lumpo, headed by the Panch'en Lama, is located nearby.

Gyangtse, the third largest city, is also in the Zangbo Valley. It is known for its hand-loomed woolen cloth and carpets.

▶ **GOVERNMENT**

As part of the People's Republic of China, Tibet is technically part of a Communist republic and socialist nation. It currently has twenty delegates to the National People's

Lhasa, Tibet's capital, was established in the 600's. Overlooking the city is the Potala palace, the traditional residence of the Dalai Lama.

Congress (NPC), China's legislature. Under a new constitution adopted in 1982, a president serves as head of state, and a prime minister is appointed as head of government.

▶ HISTORY

Early History. One of the first great rulers of Tibet, Songtsan Gampo, established a kingdom in the Zangbo Valley in the A.D. 600's. He made Lhasa the capital and expanded his empire. Buddhism, introduced from India and China, became the religion of the royal court. Tibet was a great power in the region, until wars with China and internal conflicts led to its decline. In the 1200's Tibet was conquered by the Mongols.

In 1270, Kublai Khan, the Mongol ruler who became emperor of China, adopted Lamaism as the state religion of his empire. For the next several centuries Tibet was ruled by its lamas under China's protection. It remained largely isolated from the world by its high mountains and the choice of its lamas.

By the end of the 1800's, China, weakened by the Opium Wars and other conflicts, was losing control of Tibet. However, as the British attempted to establish themselves in the region during the early 1900's, China reasserted its sovereignty. In 1914 a dispute arose between China and India when a boundary between Tibet and India was defined. China refused to recognize this boundary, called the McMahon Line, which has remained a source of conflict. In 1962 this led to a border war between China and India.

Chinese Occupation. In 1911, Tibet declared its independence from China, which it maintained until Chinese forces invaded in 1950. In 1951 it signed a treaty making it a self-governing region of China. In reality, however, it was not; the Dalai Lama had no political power. In 1959, Tibetans revolted against Chinese rule. The uprising was quickly crushed and the Dalai Lama fled to India. In 1965, Tibet was officially made an autonomous region of China. New revolts against the Chinese have broken out several times since. In 1989 the Dalai Lama was awarded the Nobel Peace Prize for his efforts in trying to find a solution to the problem.

In 1994 the Chinese government placed stricter limits on the number of monks and nuns allowed to study in Tibet's monasteries. In 1995 it selected its own candidate for Panch'en Lama.

In 2001 the Dalai Lama met with U.S. president George W. Bush, who supported the Tibetan exile community. This further angered China at a time of increasing U.S.-Chinese tensions. Meanwhile, the Chinese government continues to promote an economic policy in Tibet that includes natural resource development and industrialization.

Reviewed by DAVID ZURICK
Eastern Kentucky University

See also CHINA.

TICKS

Ticks are small animals that feed on the blood of mammals, birds, reptiles, and amphibians. Although they resemble small insects, ticks belong to a group called **arachnids**, which includes spiders, scorpions, and mites.

Most kinds of ticks live in forests and grassy fields where they attach themselves to another animal, called a **host**, in order to feed on its blood. (The tick is called a **parasite** because it feeds on other organisms.) The tick's mouth is a short tube covered with sharp spines for cutting through the animal's skin. Some ticks transmit diseases to the animals they bite.

Ticks are divided into two types. Hard ticks are those that feed on the blood of dogs and other mammals as well as birds, reptiles, and amphibians. Soft ticks feed mostly on poultry and a few other kinds of birds. More than 1,000 species of ticks are known. Most live in tropical and subtropical regions.

Life Cycle

Tick reproduction begins on the host animal when the female tick is engorged (swollen) with blood. After mating, the female drops off the host, crawls to a secluded place, and lays up to 6,000 tiny eggs, each about the size of the period at the end of this sentence.

Newly hatched ticks, sometimes called seed ticks, are about $1/16$ inch (2 millimeters) long. These are the larvae, one of two immature forms. To find a host, the three-legged larvae climb up a blade of grass or other vegetation. When a suitable animal passes by, they attach themselves to its skin and begin to feed.

The larvae grow into nymphs, a second immature form, by shedding their covering in a process called **molting**. After several molts, the tick is a full adult. An engorged adult tick may be $3/4$ inch (20 millimeters) long.

Most ticks live less than a single year. The male dies after mating. After the eggs are laid, the female tick dies. Sometimes ticks have difficulty finding hosts and may remain active, living as long as three years without food before finding a host, maturing, and laying eggs. They hibernate in the winter and resume activity in the spring. Some kinds of soft ticks may live as long as 11 years.

Ticks have few natural enemies. The only known predators are certain tickbirds, a type

Ticks are not insects. They are part of an animal group called arachnids, which includes spiders, scorpions, and mites. All ticks, such as this American dog tick, feed on the blood of other animals.

How to Safely Remove a Tick

If you find a tick on yourself or your pet, you should remove it as soon as possible. Ticks are easy to spot on people but not very easy to see under the fur of dogs or cats. Check your pet's skin periodically, especially during early spring when ticks are abundant. (If you live in a tick-infested area, your veterinarian can recommend preventive treatments to help keep ticks off your pet.)

Do not pull an engorged (swollen) tick off your body or your pet's body. The tick's head may remain in the skin, a potential source of infection. Instead, cover the tick with mineral oil, rubbing alcohol, or even nail polish remover. These substances will cause the tick to disengage its mouthparts. The tick can then be removed and killed.

---

of starling, found in tropical regions. Tick eggs are sometimes eaten by insects.

Diseases

Lyme disease, Rocky Mountain spotted fever, and tularemia are three diseases carried by ticks, which transmit the diseases from infected animals to healthy ones.

Particularly widespread across the United States is Lyme disease, which is caused by a microscopic bacterium. Tiny deer ticks can carry this organism and infect rodents, dogs, deer, and humans as well. Symptons can include a rash at the site of the tick bite, headaches, fatigue, fever, and chills.

Antibiotics can usually treat the disease if it is detected early. But left untreated, it can cause serious long-term health problems. In the late 1990's, scientists developed a vaccine that can prevent Lyme disease. However, the best protection is to wear long pants and long sleeves when playing or hiking in areas where ticks thrive, and to check your body afterward.

Ross H. Arnett, Jr.
Author, *American Insects*

TIDAL WAVES. See Ocean (Tsunamis).

TIDES

Nearly three fourths of the earth's surface is covered by oceans and seas. The level of these waters is called **sea level.**

Sea level is always changing. Each day a rhythmic rise and fall of sea level takes place in all the ocean waters of the world. This rhythmic rise and fall of the ocean waters is known as the **ocean tides.**

▶WHAT ARE OCEAN TIDES?

To understand what the tides are, let us take an imaginary trip to an ocean beach somewhere on the Atlantic Ocean coast of North America.

Suppose you arrive at 10:00 A.M. According to a sign, this is just the time of **high tide,** or **high water.** You choose an uncrowded spot not far from the water's edge, and there you leave your belongings while you go for a swim. When you come out, you notice that your belongings are farther from the water's edge than they were when you entered the water. You sit down on the beach and watch the ocean. The sea level is steadily going down. More and more of the beach is being exposed, and the water's edge is receding (drawing back) farther and farther. The tide is going out. It continues to do so for about 6 hours 13 minutes. Then it comes to a level at which further movement ceases. The ocean here is now at **low tide,** or **low water.**

Now the tide goes no lower. Instead, it begins to rise. It continues to do so until once again it reaches a high-water, or high-tide, mark. The time taken to go from low water to high water is nearly 6 hours 13 minutes—just about the same as the time taken to go from high water to low water.

By now you have undoubtedly left the beach, for nearly 12½ hours have passed since you arrived and night has long since fallen. But if you were still present, you would be able to observe the high-water level. While it is not exactly the same height as the first high water you observed, it is close to that level.

Again the tide goes out and comes in. Each time it takes about 6 hours 13 minutes for its rise or fall. Thus, two consecutive (one following the other) high waters are about 12 hours 25 minutes apart. And it is twice that time—roughly 24 hours 50 minutes—from one day's high water to the next day's.

Water levels during high tide and low tide vary greatly in some locations. In Friendship, Maine, the levels change by about 10 feet (3 meters) every 6 hours.

Suppose that you return to the beach at 10:00 A.M. the next day. The tide will be rising at this time, but it will not reach high water until about 10:50 A.M. In other words, high tide (and low tide, too) comes about 50 minutes later from one day to the next.

▶TIDES AND THE MOON

What causes the tides? Although the question is a very old one, no satisfactory answer was given until 1687, when Sir Isaac Newton published his law of gravitation. Long before Newton, however, astronomers had noted many facts that suggested a relation between the tides and the moon. They noticed that the lunar day—the time from moonrise to moonrise on two consecutive nights—averaged 24 hours 50 minutes. This was the same amount

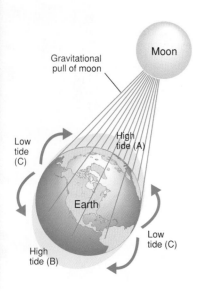

Gravitational
pull of moon

Moon

Low
tide
(C)

High
tide (A)

Earth

Low
tide (C)

High
tide (B)

HOW TIDES FORM

A. Waters on the side of
the earth nearest the moon
are attracted more strongly
than the solid earth. A bulge
of water – high tide – forms.

B. The solid earth is
attracted toward the moon
more strongly than waters
on the farthest side.
Another high tide forms.

C. Two low tides are formed
by waters flowing toward
the two high tide locations.
As the moon revolves around
the earth, the locations of
high and low tides change.

of time as that between high water one day
and high water the next. Both moonrise and
high water came about 50 minutes later each
day.

Astronomers also observed that the tidal
range and the phase of the moon seemed to be
related. (The **tidal range** is the difference in
height between high water and low water at a
given place.) They noticed that the tidal range
varied with the phases of the moon. The tidal
range was greatest at the times of full moon
and new moon. It was least at the times of first
quarter and last quarter.

These observations strongly suggested that
the moon caused the tides. But it remained for
Newton to provide an explanation.

How the Moon Causes the Tides

Newton's law of gravitation states that
every object in the universe attracts every
other object with a gravitational force. The
larger the mass of an object is, the greater the
force with which it attracts any other object.
(Mass is the total amount of material in an
object.) The greater the distance is between
two objects, the less the force between them.

The earth and moon, which both have a
great amount of mass, attract each other according to Newton's law, even though they
are, on average, 237,100 miles (381,493 kilometers) apart. This attraction causes tides on
earth. (If there were bodies of water on the
moon, tides would exist there, too.)

As suggested by Newton, the ocean tides
result from differences in the gravitational attraction exerted by the moon on three different
parts: the solid earth, the waters on the near
side of the earth, and the waters on the far
side. These differences are due to the different
distances between the moon and these three
parts of the earth. The ocean waters on the
side of the earth facing the moon are nearest
to the moon. They are therefore attracted most
strongly by the moon. The ocean waters on
the far side of the earth are attracted least, for
they are about 8,000 miles (12,800 kilometers) farther away from the moon. The solid
earth is attracted at its center of gravity, which
is midway between. This means that every
part of the solid earth is attracted as if it were
located at the center of the earth, about 4,000
miles (6,400 kilometers) from either side.

Because of these differences the moon attracts the ocean waters on the near side of the
earth more than it attracts the solid earth. As a
result, the waters on the near side rise, forming the bulge in the ocean surface that we call
a high tide. On the far side of the earth the
moon attracts the ocean waters less than it attracts the earth. This again results in a movement of ocean waters toward the part of the
earth that is in line with the moon. Here, too,
a high tide forms directly opposite the first.
Halfway between the two high-tide locations,
two areas of low tide are formed. They are the
result of the outward flow of ocean waters
from these places to the high-tide locations.

Why the Tides Rise and Fall

Suppose that the moon stood still while the
earth rotated on its axis. The earth's rotation
takes about 24 hours. In 6 hours a place that
had started by being in line with the moon
would move from a high-water point to a low-
water point. During this time its sea level
would gradually lower as an outgoing tide. In
the next 6 hours it would move from a low-
water point to a high-water point and it would
have an incoming tide. Then it would again go
from high to low and from low to high.
Twenty-four hours later it would have returned
to its starting point, having completed a cycle
of high-low-high-low-high.

But the moon is not standing still. It is revolving around the earth. While the earth rotates once on its axis, the moon revolves about
13 degrees in the same direction. So the earth

must rotate an additional 13 degrees before our first high-water point comes back in line with the moon. The additional rotation adds about 50 minutes to the completion of the cycle. The total time is about 24 hours 50 minutes—a lunar day. ("Lunar" comes from *luna,* the Latin word for "moon.") Divide this time by 4, and you get about 6 hours 13 minutes. This is the time required to go from high water to low water or from low water to high water.

▶ HOW THE SUN AFFECTS TIDES

The sun's gravitational attraction also affects the tides, but not to the same degree as the moon. The sun's great distance from the earth reduces its tide-producing force to less than half that of the moon.

The sun's tide-making force can add to or oppose that of the moon. When the sun is in line, or nearly in line, with the moon and the earth, its tide-making forces strengthen those of the moon. When the sun is far out of line with the moon, the sun's tide-making forces oppose and weaken those of the moon.

The moon and the sun most strengthen each other when the moon is new and again when the moon is full. When the moon and sun work together, we have our highest high tides and our lowest low tides. These unusually large tides are called **spring tides.** They come approximately every 2 weeks and have nothing to do with the spring season of the year.

The moon and sun oppose each other most when the moon is in its first quarter and again when it is in its third quarter. During those phases, imaginary lines joining moon, earth, and sun form a right angle. The sun's force then raises somewhat the low-tide levels made by the moon. It lowers somewhat the high-tide levels made by the moon. As a result, the high tides are usually the lowest of the month and the low tides are the highest of the month. In other words, the high tide is not very high, and the low tide is not very low. These tides are called **neap tides.** Scientists also refer to spring tides and neap tides as **long period tides.**

▶ HEIGHT OF SUCCESSIVE HIGH AND LOW WATERS

The tide-making forces that produce the high-tide bulges on opposite sides of the earth are approximately equal. Therefore the two high-tide bulges should be—and are—about the same height.

Yet two successive high waters may not be equal for a given place. The reason has to do with the location of the tidal bulges, and the location has to do with the moon's orbit.

The moon's orbit is inclined (at an angle) to the earth's orbit. As a result, the moon moves north and south of the earth's equator during the course of each month. When the moon is in line with the earth's equator, the tidal bulges are evenly placed on opposite sides of the earth. A given place on the earth's surface moves in 12 hours 25 minutes from one high-tide bulge to another of equal height.

But when the moon is north or south of the equator, the tidal bulges are not evenly placed. One is in the Northern Hemisphere and the other is in the Southern Hemisphere. At such a time there is likely to be a marked difference in level between two successive high waters or between two successive low waters.

The highest high tides are called spring tides. They are caused by the combined gravitational pull of the sun and moon. They occur when the moon is positioned between the earth and the sun (new moon) or when the moon is on the opposite side of the earth farthest from the sun (full moon). The lowest tides are called neap tides. They occur when the pull of the moon and the pull of the sun partially neutralize each other's effects. Neap tides occur when the pull of the moon and the sun are at right angles to each other (first and last quarter moons).

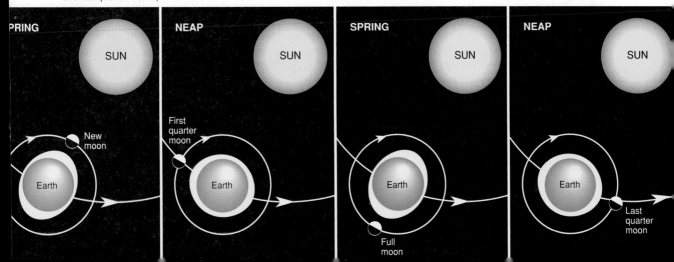

The movement of tidal waters can provide power to produce electricity. This hydroelectric tidal power plant, the first one in North America, is in Nova Scotia.

The same thing happens with solar tides for the same reason. The orbit of the earth around the sun is inclined by about 23°. This influences the tidal bulges but to a lesser degree than does the inclined orbit of the moon.

▶ **IRREGULAR TIDES**

It seems as if each seacoast in the world should have two high tides and two low tides every 24 hours 50 minutes. There are, however, many exceptions to this. Most of them occur where the effect of the moon's position north or south of the equator is very strong.

Along the Atlantic coasts of both eastern North America and western Europe, two daily high tides and two daily low tides are usual. Most of the Pacific coast of North America also has two daily highs and two daily lows. But here two consecutive highs or lows are much more likely to be unequal in height. Even more irregularity occurs on many Pacific Ocean islands that have only one high tide and one low tide daily.

▶ **TIDAL RANGE**

Lakes also have tides for the same reasons that oceans have tides. In small lakes, however, the tides are so small as to be unnoticeable. Even large lakes, such as Lake Superior, have tidal ranges of only a few inches.

In the open ocean the tidal range averages between 2 and 3 feet (0.6 and 0.9 meter). But in bays and gulfs and on the shores of continents and islands there are vast differences in tidal range. In places such as the Gulf of Mex-

ico, the tidal range may be as little as 1 foot (0.3 meter). At the other extreme, in the Bay of Fundy, between New Brunswick and Nova Scotia, the difference between high tide and low tide may reach 50 feet (15 meters) or more.

▶ **Tidal Resonance**

Scientists have determined that these great differences in tidal range are caused mainly by differences in the shape and size of bays, gulfs, or other parts of the ocean basins. The Gulf of Mexico, they point out, has a comparatively narrow mouth and wide shoreline. The tidal waters that enter the mouth are spread thin along the shoreline. Gulfs and bays with similar shapes should have similarly small tidal ranges.

The Bay of Fundy is V-shaped. Water entering its wide mouth from the open ocean is squeezed into less and less space as it moves into the head of the bay. Therefore a large tidal range might be expected along the shoreline. But shape appears to be only part of the explanation of the enormous tidal range, for many other V-shaped bays do not have large tidal ranges. The rest of the explanation is related to something called tidal resonance.

Perhaps the best way to understand resonance is to think of making waves in the bathtub. Suppose you start a wave at one end. It travels to the other end of the tub, is reflected, and comes back. Now suppose with careful timing you make the second wave. You make it at the very instant the first wave starts to move away from you again. The second wave moves in time with the first—this is resonance. The first and second waves reinforce each other. If you keep on making new waves that move in time with the others, the movement of water gets bigger and bigger.

Very much the same thing happens in the Bay of Fundy. The bay has a natural period of oscillation of about 12 hours. This means that it takes 12 hours for a wave to travel the full length of the bay and back again. But the tide-making forces also have a period of about 12 hours. Resonance occurs, and great quantities of water move into and out of the bay.

▶ **TIDAL BORES**

In some parts of the world tides from the oceans are funneled into the mouth of a river. Under certain conditions this action creates a huge wall of water that moves quickly up the river. The wall of water is called a tidal bore. Four very famous tidal bores are those on the Severn River in England, the Amazon in South America, the Tsientang Kiang in China, and the Petitcodiac, which empties into the Bay of Fundy.

A tidal bore may occur where there is a large tidal range in the open ocean. Or it may occur where the shores of the bay funnel large amounts of tidewater toward the mouth of the river. When the high tide nears the river, it runs into shallows. It also meets water being carried down by the river. Often the result is that the tide is held back. The water builds up and reaches a considerable height. Then it forces its way up the river at great speed. The tidal bore on the Amazon is sometimes 16 feet (4.9 meters) high and 1 mile (1.6 kilometers) wide. At the time of a spring tide the Tsientang bore can be 25 feet (7.6 meters) high.

▶ EARTH TIDES

The solid part of the earth is not a rigid, motionless mass. It too is influenced by the gravitational attraction of the moon and the sun. The entire earth from its center to its outer crust deforms (changes shape) periodically under the influence of the moon and sun. This phenomenon is called earth tides.

Earth tides are not noticeable to us, even though the ground beneath our feet is moving very slowly up and down twice a day. The movement is greatest near the equator and much less in the polar regions. In the United States, for example, earth tides cause an up and down movement of about 16 inches (40 centimeters). It happens so slowly that we cannot feel it, although sensitive scientific instruments can detect it.

Earth tides and ocean tides as well influence all precise measurements that scientists make as they stand on the surface of the earth. Research efforts are now focused on understanding the effects of tides on these measurements and how to accurately correct for them.

SAMUEL N. NAMOWITZ
Author, *Earth Science*
Reviewed by PAUL MELCHIOR
Director, International Center for Earth Tides
Author, *The Tides of the Planet Earth*

TIENTSIN

Tientsin (Tianjin) is one of China's largest cities. It is a major industrial center and an important railroad junction and port as well. The municipality of Tientsin, which includes the surrounding area, has a population of about 8,000,000. The city proper has more than 5,000,000 inhabitants.

Located in northern China, on the Hai River, Tientsin lies about 70 miles (115 kilometers) southeast of Peking (Beijing), the capital. Railroads link Tientsin with Peking, the industrial centers of the northeast, and large cities in the south. Its chief products are iron and steel, machinery, farm equipment, textiles, chemicals, and processed foods.

History. Tientsin was a relatively small town until the middle of the 19th century. In 1860, treaties with Western nations opened Tientsin and other Chinese ports to international trade. Foreign merchants settled in Tientsin, and it became a thriving city. Part of Tientsin was destroyed during the Boxer Rebellion of 1900, an uprising by Chinese against foreigners. But it was rebuilt over a

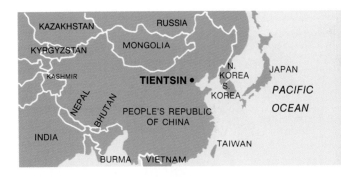

period of years into a modern city with wide boulevards and Western-style buildings.

After the establishment of the People's Republic of China in 1949, hundreds of new factories were built in the area. Tientsin was merged with surrounding towns to become one of China's three municipalities, which are administered directly by the central government in Peking. (The other two are Peking itself and Shanghai.) Tientsin was badly damaged again in 1976, when an earthquake struck the region, but it has since been rebuilt.

HYMAN KUBLIN
City University of New York, Brooklyn College
Author, *The Rim of Asia*

TIGERS

Tigers vary in size and appearance. The Siberian tiger weighs up to 650 pounds (295 kilograms) and may be 13 feet (4 meters) from its nose to the tip of its tail. It is the largest of all cats. Indian, or Bengal, tigers may weigh from about 300 to 550 pounds (about 135 to 250 kilograms) and are about the size of a lion. Tigers in Malaysia and Indonesia are smaller.

The background of the tiger's coat is usually a bright reddish orange or a pale yellow-brown. The stripes that mark the body and limbs are usually black.

The appearance of the tiger depends to a great extent on where the animal lives. Tigers that live in cold regions are pale in color and large in size. Their fur is long and thick. In warmer climates tigers are smaller and more colorful. They have shorter, thinner fur.

Like all cats, tigers have sharp claws and teeth, and they can move quickly and quietly. Springing with ease, tigers may cover 15 feet (4.5 meters) in one leap. They rarely climb trees but are very good swimmers.

The regal-looking tiger is an adaptable animal that can live in a variety of habitats as long as it has food, water, and shelter from the searing heat of the sun.

Tigers usually stalk their prey alone and at night. To make a kill, the tiger leaps on the animal, biting its neck. It then takes the slain prey to some hidden spot. If it is a large animal, the tiger may feed on it for several days. Tigers eat deer, pigs, cattle, goats, and some smaller animals.

Young tigers, or cubs, are born from 100 to 112 days after the parents have mated. One to six young may be in a litter, but the usual number is two or three. Cubs weigh a couple of pounds when they are born. The tiny cubs open their eyes about 10 to 16 days after birth. At the age of 6 or 8 weeks, the young begin to go on hunting trips with their mother. After about a year, they can hunt for themselves. At 3 or 4 years of age, young tigers are ready to raise their own families.

In zoos tigers may live to be 20 years old. They seldom live to be this old in the wild.

Tigers live in jungles or forests. Their striped bodies blend well with the underbrush. They prefer places near water.

Tigers are found only in Asia, where their numbers have fallen drastically since the late 1800's. Hunting and habitat destruction have already driven some tigers, such as the Caspian tiger, to extinction. Wildlife preserves and international laws now protect many tigers, but illegal poaching continues to endanger them.

Reviewed by ROBERT M. McCLUNG
Author, science books for children

See also CATS, WILD.

Sumatran tiger

Manchurian tiger

Indian tiger

Caspian tiger

Keeping track of time is important to most people. Clocks and watches help us do that. But have you ever stopped to think what time really is? If you have, you know that defining time is not as easy as it may seem.

TIME

What is time? Does it exist? We say that it does. But can we see it, touch it, feel it, smell it, hear it, or taste it? If not, then how do we know that it is there?

We say, "We exist in time." But are we actually in time as we are in air or as a fish is in water? We have physical evidence of the existence of air and water, but time is different. It does not seem to be a thing or a substance. It is not composed of matter—atoms and molecules.

We also say, "Time passes. It flows or goes on." But can we see it pass as an automobile passes? Do our eyes go from one direction to another as it passes? Yet if time does not move, how can it stand still, begin, or end?

We say that we "save time," "spend time," "kill time," "lose time," and "have a good time." Could we save enough time so that we would never grow old? If we lost time, could we find it again? What we say about time does not seem to be much help in proving its existence.

▶ A DEFINITION OF TIME

It is circular to define time in terms of other time words, such as "Time is hours, minutes, and seconds," "Time is duration," or "Time is past, present, and future." It does no good to say, "Time is duration," because duration is a time word also. Circular statements may seem to give us new knowledge, but instead they give a synonym, that is, they just repeat the word to be defined.

We must do two things in order to understand time: answer the above questions, and define time without using time words. We can do this by describing what we actually *do* when we "tell time." The procedure must be described without using any time words. If we can do this, then we can see what time actually means.

A useful way to understand time is to think of a clock with a round face, two moving hands (or pointers), and the numbers 1 through 12 positioned on the face. If both hands point to 12, we say, "It is 12 o'clock," which means "12 of the clock." A clock of this type is simply a set of pointers that move to line up with numbers.

Time, then, is the change that is indicated by the movement of the pointers (or by the electronic change of numbers if we use a digital clock). All we actually do when we "tell time" is tell about clock changes. In this sense, contrary to common belief, clocks do not actually "tell time," nor do they actually measure time. Clocks are standards of change.

Time Defined as Relations of Change

The clock represents not just any change, but one that people select in order to measure other changes.

If we time a runner, we relate the change of the runner to the change of the clock. It is a correlation, or ratio. We summarize the number of changes by saying, "He ran one mile in 5 minutes." We do not relate the change of the runner to time, but to the clock. Thus, time may be defined as: **a chosen change of any**

object as a standard of change, by means of which we can measure other changes.

Instead of saying, "The clock shows the time," it would be more correct to say, "The clock is the standard of change." In using the word "time," we must understand it to mean change, rather than a mysterious thing or object.

A Test of the Definition

Suppose one clock is chosen as the standard of time (change). Call it Big Ben. If this clock is then broken, or stops, would time stop? Most people would say that time keeps going on. They feel that even when Big Ben is in pieces, time still passes, as if time were some invisible fluid.

The surprising answer is that if the clock stops, time stops. This is because we have chosen the clock as the standard. If the clock had not been chosen, there would have been no standard, and thus, no time. In this sense, we would live in a timeless world. If the clock stops, there are other standards of change we could select—but unless we choose one, there is no time.

▶ HOW MECHANICAL TIME IS DETERMINED

There are basically two types of changes that can be selected as the standard of time. One is physical change or motion; the other is psychological, such as experienced change or emotion. Physical standards are based on either (a) existing movements of natural objects, such as the movement of the sun, or (b) mechanical instruments we construct, such as clocks.

Early Natural Clocks

The first people on earth had no difficulty living without a time standard. They merely observed the relations of things to each other. They learned how to find food, protect themselves from the weather, and keep themselves warm. The first clocks were just relations of changes, and no special standard was chosen.

Eventually people observed the changes of light and darkness, and they produced a standard we call day and night. Moon changes, or lunar time, were also noted. One could count moons instead of days. In some cultures, one said, "We will meet in three moons."

The moon changes its appearance in an orderly way each month from partial moon to full moon. Thus, the word "month" derives from "moon." A month is the change between successive full moons. When counting began, it was thought that about thirty moons constitute a month and that twelve months make up a year. A year was also connected with changes of the season: spring, summer, winter, fall. These were nature's clocks that were chosen as standards of changes.

Early Artificial Clocks

Artificial clocks were also created. People observed that trees and other objects cast shadows, which moved with the sun. In 1500 B.C., the Egyptians constructed shadow clocks. A vertical polelike object, or obelisk, cast shadows on marked areas of the ground as the sun moved. Later there were sundials, which consisted of a pointer that cast shadows on a marked dial. Some sundials were as large as a building and others as small as a ring.

Sundials were used by the ancient Egyptians to tell time. As the sun moved across the sky during the course of a day, the shadow cast by a pointer moved around a marked dial. Unfortunately, these time-keepers were useless on cloudy days and at night.

The sundial works only on sunny days and when it is light. The ancient Egyptians solved the problem of telling time at night or on a cloudy day with the use of a water clock. The water clock operates by measuring water that trickles regularly from one container to another. In A.D. 725 the Chinese had an elaborate waterwheel clock, and later they built a 40-foot (12-meter)-high, pagoda-like observatory water clock. The Saxons in Europe also used water clocks. Like the sundial, the water clock had its disadvantages. It would freeze in colder climates and could not easily be used on moving objects, such as ships.

Construction of mechanical clocks, such as our modern ones, began in the 14th century, although there were some primitive versions as early as 200 B.C. The first mechanical clocks were sound clocks. They had no faces or hands to look at but a bell that rang a number of times each day. More advanced versions of bell clocks were driven by a weight attached to a cord that was wrapped around a cylinder. The weight pulled down the cord to ring the bell. Such clocks were not very regular or efficient.

Modern clocks with hands and a dial were developed and powered in different ways. In 1656, Christiaan Huygens, a Dutch scientist, built the first pendulum clock. In 1675 he built a clock powered by a spring that regularly coiled and uncoiled.

Watches were first made by Peter Henlein around A.D. 1500 in Germany. They were elaborate, expensive toys of the rich that kept time quite poorly. You can read more about these timekeeping devices in the articles CLOCKS and WATCHES.

The Development of Units of Time

Along with different clocks, different units of time were developed. Almost everywhere today a year is divided into 12 months, or 52 weeks, or 365 days. There are 7 days in a week, 24 hours in a day, 60 minutes in an hour, and 60 seconds in a minute.

But this division is not necessary. A year could be constructed with 365 days and no months or weeks. And our present year could be year 4,500,000,000—the approximate age of the earth.

In 1792 the French established a week of ten days, with 10 hours per day, 10 minutes per hour, and 10 seconds per minute. It was a metric day based on the decimal system. The twelve months were given names that related to the weather or agriculture, such as vintage month, fog, frost, snow, rain, seed, blossom, pasture, harvest, heat, and fruit. This system lasted only 13 years.

The calendar is like a map of the year. It assigns names and numbers and an order to the days, weeks, and months of each year. Other facts may be added to the calendar to show what happens on a certain day, such as holidays, the time the sun rises and sets, high and low tides, phases of the moon, when crops should be planted, or the beginning of each season.

Modern Artificial Clocks: Atomic Time

The early clocks were not very regular or accurate. They were affected by gravity, location, movement, wear, and temperature, and they needed constant correction. A pendulum clock would be of little use in a tossing ship at sea. The movements of such things as a shadow, sand, water, fire, sun, moon, and stars are not sufficient to measure the changes of atomic particles or the movement of bodies in outer space.

For these purposes, scientists needed a steady and detailed standard that also was affected as little as possible by external influences. They eventually found the answer in atoms themselves. Scientists determined that the regular, predictable vibrations (also called waves, cycles, oscillations, and resonations) of certain elements could function as a time standard.

The number of oscillations of the element Cesium in one second is 9,192,631,770. In 1967 this number of oscillations was adopted in the International System of Units (SI) as the definition of one second. Years are now officially measured in seconds. The earlier definition of a second, which at one time was based on astronomical observation, was given up, although it is still used for certain purposes.

The atomic clock is only inaccurate by one second in many thousands of years. This is quite good, but we have not seen the end of clocks. New ones are already being developed. Clocks will change with new discoveries and needs. No one clock can meet all of the needs of everyone. There is no perfect clock or absolute time.

Modern Natural Clocks: Astronomy

Atomic clocks have great accuracy for certain purposes, but we also wish to relate their movements to the movements of our solar system. The earth traveling (revolving) once around the sun is called a solar year. In a year the earth rotates on its axis slightly more than 365 times. Thus, there are 365 days, 5 hours, 48 minutes, and 46 seconds in a year. This is called the tropical year and is used for our calendar.

However, not all years are exactly equal in length. This is caused by a number of factors: (1) the earth "wobbles" irregularly on its axis; (2) the earth is tilted on its axis; (3) the earth's orbit around the sun is elliptical (oval shaped), so the earth travels faster when it is near the sun; (4) there is tidal friction, causing the rotation of the earth to slow down slightly; and (5) there is irregular movement due to motions of the earth's liquid core.

As a result, corrections must constantly be made to account for these deviations from regularity. This correction process results in **universal time**. To bring universal atomic time in line with solar time, fractions of seconds have to be added to, or subtracted from, solar time each year. This correction produces **coordinated universal time**. This corrects atomic time consistently with the natural movements of the solar system.

▶ TIME ZONES AND STANDARD TIME

The earth is divided into approximately equal sections by imaginary circular lines running through the north and south poles. These lines are called **meridians**. (See the world time zone map on the opposite page.) They look like vertical lines on a flat map. The distance to the right or left between these meridians is called degrees of longitude.

There are 360 degrees around the earth. The earth rotates from west to east once every 24 hours to turn a full 360 degrees. The earth is divided into 24 sections, each 15 degrees wide. It takes one hour for the earth to rotate 15 degrees of longitude.

Each 15 degrees, then, is specified as a different time zone. The time zone extends 7½ degrees on either side of the meridian. Anywhere in that zone and in that zone only, is the time **standard**, or the same. The time

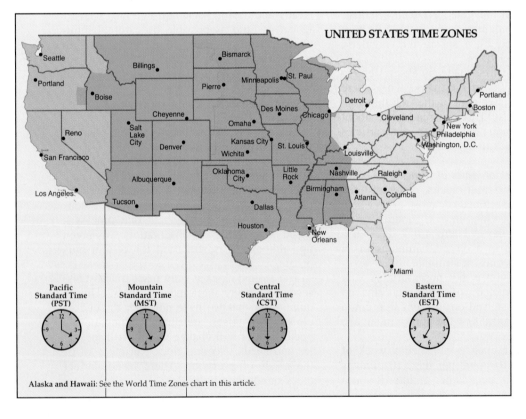

UNITED STATES TIME ZONES

Imaginary lines separate regions into time zones. There are four different standard time zones in the continental United States: (from east to west) Eastern, Central, Mountain, and Pacific.

Pacific Standard Time (PST) — Mountain Standard Time (MST) — Central Standard Time (CST) — Eastern Standard Time (EST)

Alaska and Hawaii: See the World Time Zones chart in this article.

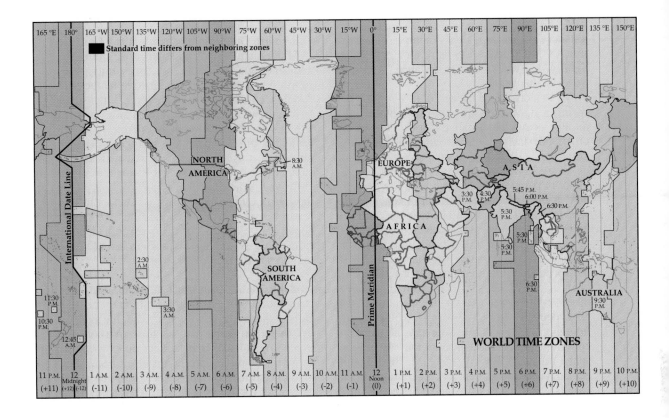

WORLD TIME ZONES

| 11 P.M. (+11) | 12 Midnight (+12)(-12) | 1 A.M. (-11) | 2 A.M. (-10) | 3 A.M. (-9) | 4 A.M. (-8) | 5 A.M. (-7) | 6 A.M. (-6) | 7 A.M. (-5) | 8 A.M. (-4) | 9 A.M. (-3) | 10 A.M. (-2) | 11 A.M. (-1) | 12 Noon (0) | 1 P.M. (+1) | 2 P.M. (+2) | 3 P.M. (+3) | 4 P.M. (+4) | 5 P.M. (+5) | 6 P.M. (+6) | 7 P.M. (+7) | 8 P.M. (+8) | 9 P.M. (+9) | 10 P.M. (+10) |

zones are zigzagged for convenience so that large cities will not have two different times. Some countries use ½-hour time zones of 7½ degrees. India and the countries in the Far East do this. However, standard time officially applies for them as well.

If it is 7 A.M. in Washington, D.C., it will be noon in London, England. As we travel east, time is later in the day. As we travel west, it is earlier. This is for convenience, since it would not be practical to have noon everywhere on earth at the same time, especially if it is night-time on half of the earth.

The meridians begin at Greenwich, England. All other meridians are either east or west of this. Thus, standard time is sometimes called Greenwich Time.

International Date Line

If you travel halfway around the earth, 180 degrees from Greenwich, you will travel through twelve time zones and arrive at the side of the earth opposite Greenwich. This particular meridian is called the International Date Line. This means you have traveled one full day of time zones. If it is 5 P.M. Friday on the western side of the date line, it is 5 P.M.

Thursday on the eastern side. When the date line is crossed going westward, the date must be advanced one day. This means the loss of a calendar day. If it is crossed moving eastward, a full day is gained.

Daylight Saving Time

In summer when days lengthen, many countries set their clocks ahead one hour. This provides one more hour of daylight in the evening rather than in the morning. The sun will then set one hour later. It may also serve to save fuel and electricity.

▶ RELATIVE TIME

Physicists, following the great scientist Isaac Newton, once thought that time is absolute, that everywhere it is the same. Relativity physicists, following the scientist Albert Einstein, now say that there is no absolute time. Rather, time is relative to each situation.

This theory applies especially to travel in space and takes the movement of light as the universal standard of time. Light (in a vacuum) is regarded as having the greatest known speed in the universe. It travels at 186,282 miles per second (approximately 300,000 kilometers per second) in a vacuum. As a measure of large distances, astronomers use the **light year,** which is the distance light can travel in one year.

As objects come close to moving at the speed of light, they are said to become "infinitely" heavy and smaller. Clocks as well as other physical processes are said to slow down.

An example that demonstrates this idea is the twin paradox. According to the twin paradox, if one twin were to travel in space at the speed of light and the other twin were to remain on earth, the space traveler would age more slowly than the earthbound twin. In other words, if the space traveler left earth at the speed of light and returned ten earth years later, it would seem to the astronaut to have taken only a few days. At the speed of light, all processes slowed down. However, earth time did not slow down, so everyone on earth continued to age at the normal rate. When the space traveler returned, the earth twin would be ten years older than the other twin. Each twin had a different clock and a different time.

The purpose of relativity theory is to tell us that (1) the speed of light can be used as a constant time standard, (2) clocks approaching this speed alter their movements, and (3) time is not absolute but requires a frame of reference. It should not, however, be assumed that humans could survive light-speed travel. It also should not be assumed that there is time itself independent of change (which can slow down) or that objects actually contract "infinitely" and become "infinitely" heavy. These ideas about relative time are either theoretical assumptions or they are untrue.

Time Reversal and Time Travel

As a result of relativity theories, physicists are debating and speculating on the astounding possibility that if something can travel faster than the speed of light, it will go back in time. This is referred to as time reversal.

Generally, time is thought of as an arrow that goes in one direction, that is, linear time. However, no time machines are possible because time is just change. And changes take place according to the laws of nature. Birds cannot be made to fly backwards. An egg cracked into a pan will not come back together again. Trees will not ungrow to become acorns again.

The Fourth Dimension: Mathematical Time

Mathematics and geometry use numbers and diagrams to represent time units. The fourth dimension is an imaginative mathematical concept. We think of the three dimensions —length, width, and depth of a solid object. Time is the fourth dimension. Time is represented as the movement or change of a solid object. If this movement is selected as the standard, it is time. If not, it is just a change. However, scientists do not agree about what the fourth dimension means or whether or not it can be sensed. Similar questions are raised about a fifth, sixth, or even seventh dimension. This is largely a question about what numbers and mathematics mean.

▶PSYCHOLOGICAL TIME AND REMEMBERING

In addition to mechanical and natural clocks, there is psychological time, the subjective (personal) experience of time. We confuse psychological with mechanical time when we eat not because we are hungry, but because it is dinnertime. Similarly, we may be in a hurry, but for no reason. Instead of enjoying a discussion, we may be distracted by constantly looking at the clock.

Psychological time is change that is felt and experienced. It often takes the form of an emotion. We say, "The train was five minutes late, but it seemed like an hour." What we are saying is that by the mechanical clock it is five minutes late and that we wish that it had been on time. Our wish, or being disappointed because the train was late, is an experienced emotion about clock time. Similarly, we find that "time goes fast" when we are enjoying ourselves. In a fearful situation, time may "seem to stop."

Remembering is the psychological equivalent of the past. But when we do this, the remembering is all going on in the present. The difference between the past and the present is the difference between having a mental image of someone and actually seeing them in front of you. Thus, past, present, and future may be seen as three different kinds of immediate experience or change.

WARREN SHIBLES
University of Wisconsin—Whitewater
Author, *Time: A Critical Analysis
for Young People*

See also CALENDAR; CLOCKS; INTERNATIONAL DATE LINE; SEASONS; WATCHES.

TIME MANAGEMENT

How many times have you heard someone complain, "I just don't have enough time"? The truth is that everyone has exactly the same amount of time. Everyone has 60 minutes in each hour and 24 hours in each day. Yet we all know people who seem to make the most of their time. Often, it is the busiest people who can take on new jobs and get them done. These people seem to have time to do all the things they must do and still have time to do the things they want to do.

The reason is that these people, although they have only the same amount of time as everyone else, have learned to manage their time. Time management is a skill that anyone can master. By learning to manage your time, you can catch up on chores and schoolwork—and still have plenty of time left for sports, hobbies, or simply relaxing.

▶ FINDING TIME

The first step in time management is proving to yourself that you can find time in your life, no matter how busy you are. Try keeping a "time log" for a few days to discover exactly how your time is spent each day. Divide your log into the following categories, leaving some space between each item: Before Breakfast, Breakfast Time, Breakfast to Lunch, Lunchtime, Lunch to Dinner, Dinnertime, Dinner to Bedtime, Bedtime. Make a copy for each day you plan to continue the experiment. A week should be long enough.

Begin the log on Day 1 by writing down all the things you do that day. Put each in the proper time slot, and note how much time each took. Repeat the process on Day 2, Day 3, and so forth, using a separate sheet of paper for each day. Be sure to list activities as you do them so you do not forget what you did. If you stop to talk to friends, list it. If you feed the dog, list it. If you deliver papers, work at the grocery store, or help your mother or father, list it.

At the end of the week, go over your log carefully. Find ways to pick up time by eliminating unnecessary activities and by using your time more efficiently. For example, in reading over his log one boy noticed that he was going out to feed the dog, then coming back later to take out the trash. The trash area was not far from the dog house. The boy com-bined the two jobs and saved almost the entire time for one of them.

But, as you go over your activities, be sure to give yourself enough time to do each job well. Nothing is as great a time waster as doing a job carelessly and having to do it over.

▶ GETTING THINGS DONE

Ask a busy person who gets things done how he or she can possibly take on other jobs with such a full schedule. Chances are the answer will be, "By making lists of what needs to be done and crossing jobs off as I do them."

Making a list of jobs to be done is one of the best ways to organize your time. List items in order of priority—that is, decide how important a job is and when it must be completed. For example, if your science project is due this Friday and your reading assignment is due next week, list the science project first. List both these jobs ahead of something less important, like re-arranging your room.

Make a new list at the beginning of each week, or each day if you have a very busy schedule. Try to work steadily at each job until it is completed, and move promptly to the next one on your list. Putting things off or wasting time only prolongs an unpleasant job, leaving you with less free time. After you have crossed off the last job on your list, reward yourself by doing something you really enjoy.

▶ MAKING A DECISION

A person who is able to make decisions is a person who is using time to its best advantage. The longer you must struggle with a decision, the more time you are wasting. Consider making a decision using this method:

Use a sheet of paper for each possible choice. If you must decide, for example, between joining the drama club or the cheerleading squad, label one paper "drama" and one paper "cheerleading." Make two columns on each sheet, one labeled "pro" and the other "con." Now write down all the good things that will happen, including things that will happen inside yourself, under the pro column. List all the bad things under the con column. Do this on both sheets of paper. Take your time and fill out the sheets carefully. You will be saving time in the long run, because with just a little bit of study it will become obvious to you which choice is best.

Monday		
	ACTIVITY	TIME
Before Breakfast	shower and brush teeth	10 min.
	get dressed	10 min.
Breakfast time	feed cat; eat breakfast	15 min.
	review homework; pack bookbag	25 min.
Breakfast to Lunch	ride school bus	30 min.
	Geography	45 min.
	Math	45 min.
	Reading	45 min.
	English	45 min.
Lunchtime	Eat lunch; talk with friends	15 min.
	play ball	30 min.
Lunch to Dinner	Science	45 min.
	Social Studies	45 min.
	Computers	45 min.
	ride school bus	30 min.
	play with friends	1 hr.
	Karate lesson	1 hr.
Dinnertime	eat dinner	30 min.
	help clean up; take out garbage	30 min.
Dinner to Bedtime	do homework	2 hrs.
	watch TV	1 hr.
Bedtime	sleep	10 hrs.

Keeping a daily log is a good way to find out how you are spending your time. The example above shows how a student kept track of her activities during one day.

▶MANAGING TIME AT SCHOOL

Use school for schoolwork. Students who use time wisely do not doze, chat, or read novels or comic books during class. Paying attention in class saves time in the long run, because you are learning while you are listening. It will save study time later on.

Good time managers use free periods and study hall to do homework assignments. Students who do this often manage to complete much of their homework at school and have more free time in the evening.

Do not take on more activities than you can handle. If you are already a member of the soccer team and the debating club, you may not have time to be in the school play, too. Learn to reserve some free time for yourself.

Make the most of time spent going to and from school. If you ride the bus, use the time to study or review an assignment. If you walk,

think about the day's lessons. At lunchtime, if you finish eating early, use the extra time to talk to a friend, to read, to study, or to play a game. Make the time pay off.

▶MANAGING TIME AT HOME

Time managers agree on one point: You need a desk, or even a drawer, that is all yours. In this place keep everything you need to organize your time—pencils and pens, a memo pad or notebook, a calendar to mark important dates. An accordion-pleated file with sections labeled for each month is very handy for filing important papers, clippings, and projects.

Does your room look messy or disorganized, cluttered with papers, magazines and books, clothes, posters, knickknacks, and sporting and hobby equipment? Putting your possessions in their proper place and throwing out unneeded items are two good ways to get organized. It is easier to think and work in a clean, tidy area. If you have doubts about throwing certain things away, store them in a box. If you have not used them after a month or two, throw them away.

If you can, do tomorrow's work today. For example, decide tonight what clothes you will wear tomorrow and lay them out before you go to bed. Pack your book bag, making sure it contains everything you need for the next day. And do not wait until morning to ask your parents to sign permission slips or give you lunch money.

Set limits for your telephone conversations and television viewing and stick to them. Try not to let friends get in the habit of calling you every night for a lengthy chat. Choose one or two favorite television programs to watch per day. When they are over, get up and walk away from the television set or turn it off if possible.

Learn to trade tasks with other family members. If you hate to vacuum and your brother hates to mow the lawn, try switching jobs. Each of you may work more efficiently if you enjoy what you are doing.

And remember, you do not have to be doing something every minute to be spending time wisely. Take a break, relax, and enjoy yourself. This, also, is a wise use of time.

ROSS R. OLNEY
PATRICIA J. OLNEY
Authors, *Time: How to Have More of It*

TIMOR, EAST (TIMOR-LESTE)

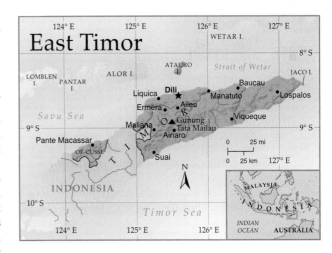

East Timor (Timor-Leste in Portuguese) is the world's newest nation. It occupies the eastern half of Timor, an island of Southeast Asia between Indonesia and Australia.

East Timor's road to independence was one of the most tragic in recent history. In 1975, just as Portugal was about to free East Timor after 400 years of colonial rule, it was invaded and forcibly annexed by Indonesia. As a result, one-third of the East Timorese lost their lives. After voting for independence in 1999, East Timor was nearly destroyed in a rampage carried out by pro-Indonesian militias and regular troops. But today, with economic aid from the international community, the East Timorese are beginning to rebuild under a liberal democratic government.

▶ **PEOPLE**

The people of East Timor are mostly of Malay and Papuan origin. They speak at least 15 different languages, including Tetum and Portuguese, the official languages. English and Indonesian are also widely spoken.

About 75 percent of East Timorese practice Lulik, the native animist religion. (Animists believe that spirits reside within all objects.) A small number of people practice Islam. Most others combine Roman Catholic and Lulik beliefs.

▶ **LAND**

East Timor, which is about the size of the U.S. state of New Jersey, occupies the eastern half of Timor, the largest and easternmost of the Lesser Sunda Islands. The country also includes Oé-Cusse (a separate enclave surrounded by Indonesian West Timor) and two offshore islands, Atauro and Jaco.

East Timor is rugged and mountainous. The country's highest peak, Gunung Tata Mailau, rises 9,719 feet (2,962 meters). From October or November to May, northwest monsoon winds bring moisture to the island.

▶ **ECONOMY**

Most East Timorese live in scattered farming villages. They grow corn, rice, cassava (a starchy root), sweet potatoes, and yams to eat, and garden vegetables to sell in local markets. They raise pigs, goats, and chickens for ceremonial occasions. They also raise Timorese mountain ponies to ride and to transport goods, and water buffalo to work their fields. Coffee, tea, rubber, sandalwood, and marble are exported.

During the 1999 attack by pro-Indonesian militias, East Timor's economy was virtually destroyed. Homes, businesses, schools, government buildings, and hospitals were burned and looted. Unemployment soared to 80 percent, leaving East Timor dependent on international

East Timor is a nation of Southeast Asia. It occupies the eastern half of Timor, the largest of the Lesser Sunda Islands in the Indian Ocean.

assistance. One hope for East Timor's economic future lies with the valuable petroleum and natural gas deposits contained in the Timor Sea.

▶ **MAJOR CITIES**

Dili, the capital and largest city of East Timor, has a population of about 45,000. Located on the island's northern coast, Dili is a major seaport and has an international airport, making it a center of commerce. It is home to the University of East Timor.

▶ **HISTORY AND GOVERNMENT**

Timor was first populated at least 13,000 years ago. About 4,000 years ago, seafarers sailing in dugout canoes from the islands of Indonesia and Melanesia began to settle Timor. The Portuguese arrived in the 1500's. They were followed in the 1600's by the Dutch, who occupied the western part of the island. During World War II (1939–45), the Japanese briefly occupied Timor and other islands of Southeast Asia.

In 1949, Indonesia gained its independence, and in 1950 it took control of West Timor, while East Timor remained under the control of Portugal. In 1975, however, Portugal withdrew from East Timor, and the Revolutionary Front of Independent East Timor (Fretilin) declared the nation's independence.

On May 20, 2002, the East Timorese celebrated their independence from Indonesia, which had ruled the former Portuguese colony since 1976.

Indonesia then invaded East Timor and in 1976 made it a province of Indonesia.

The United Nations and most foreign governments did not recognize Indonesia's claim to East Timor. The East Timorese fought back under a rebel army led by José "Xanana" Gusmão. In 1996 Timorese bishop Carlos Ximenes Belo and independence leader José Ramos-Horta shared the Nobel Peace Prize for their efforts to bring peace to the region.

Finally, in 1999, Indonesia allowed the East Timorese to decide their own future. The United Nations then held a ballot in which 78.5 percent of the voters chose independence. Following the vote, pro-Indonesian militias supported by the Indonesian military retaliated. Some supporters of independence were murdered. More than 200,000 people either fled or were forced across the border into West Timor. Most towns were leveled. Under international pressure, Indonesian forces withdrew, and the United Nations took over day-to-day administration. Indonesia formally gave up control of East Timor in 1999.

In 2001, East Timor held its first free parliamentary elections, and a new constitution was written in which executive power was to be shared by a prime minister and a president. In 2002, Xanana Gusmão was elected East Timor's first president, and on May 20 the nation celebrated its hard-won independence. East Timor was admitted to the United Nations the same year.

EUGENE AMMARELL
Ohio University

FACTS
and figures

DEMOCRATIC REPUBLIC OF EAST TIMOR (REPÚBLICA DEMOCRÁTICA DE TIMOR-LESTE) is the official name of the country.

LOCATION: Southeast Asia.

AREA: 7,300 sq mi (18,907 km²).

POPULATION: 800,000 (estimate).

CAPITAL AND LARGEST CITY: Dili.

MAJOR LANGUAGES: Tetum, Portuguese (both official).

MAJOR RELIGIOUS GROUPS: Lulik, Roman Catholic.

GOVERNMENT: Parliamentary democracy. **Head of state**—president. **Head of government**—prime minister. **Legislature**—Legislative Assembly.

CHIEF PRODUCTS: Agricultural—corn, rice, cassava, sweet potatoes, yams, garden vegetables, coffee, tea, rubber, sandalwood.

MONETARY UNIT: U.S. dollar (1 dollar = 100 cents).

TIN

Pure tin is a shiny, silvery white metal. It is very soft and malleable (easy to shape). It can be rolled into sheets of foil as thin as 1/5,000 of an inch (0.005 millimeter). Adding small amounts of other materials to tin affects the metal in different ways. Lead, for example, makes tin softer; arsenic and zinc harden it. Mixing copper with tin makes tin stronger and forms bronze or any one of a number of other alloys, depending on the proportions of copper and tin.

Because tin resists corrosion, it is used as a coating to protect other metals from corrosion. Metal machine parts that are subject to wear, such as the pistons in airplane engines, are often plated with tin because tin helps give a lubricating effect.

Most metals can be coated with tin, but its major use is in making **tinplate**. This is steel sheeting with a thin coating of pure tin. Most tinplate is used to make tin cans for foods and beverages. Because tin is not poisonous, it is safe to use for packaging foods.

Many other everyday items are made of steel or brass coated with tin. These include paper clips, staples, and safety pins.

The second most important use of tin is in **solders**. These are alloys of tin and lead that have a low melting point. Solders are used to join pieces of metal together.

Pewter is a tin alloy with antimony and copper. It can be worked into almost any shape. Polishing gives it a shiny surface that remains bright indefinitely. Pewter is used for candlesticks, mugs, and many other articles.

Another important use of tin is in stannous fluoride. This chemical compound of tin and

BASIC FACTS ABOUT TIN

CHEMICAL SYMBOL: Sn (from the Latin *stannum*).
ATOMIC WEIGHT: 118.69
SPECIFIC GRAVITY: 7.29 (about 7¼ times as heavy as water).
COLOR: Silvery white with a bluish tinge.
PROPERTIES: Soft and malleable; melts at a little over twice the boiling point of water; at very low temperatures, crumbles into a gray powder.
OCCURRENCE: Not found in nature in metallic form; occurs in various minerals.
CHIEF ORE: Cassiterite.
CHIEF SOURCES: Malaysia, Brazil, Bolivia, China, Indonesia, Thailand, Russia.

fluorine is added to toothpastes to aid in the prevention of tooth decay.

The leading tin-producing country is Malaysia. Other major producers are Brazil, Bolivia, China, Indonesia, Thailand, and Russia. Tin is found in several mineral ores, but the only one that is commercially important is **cassiterite**, a dark-colored compound of tin and oxygen. Almost all cassiterite is found in streambeds or on plains where it was deposited by running water. Some deposits of cassiterite lie beneath the sea, carried there by rivers.

The earliest known use of tin was about 3500 B.C., when people made bronze. The Romans mined large quantities of tin in Spain. Besides bronze, they made solder and tinned-copper containers.

Reviewed by JON C. VAN LOON
University of Toronto

See also ALLOYS; BRONZE AND BRASS.

Tin is widely distributed in small amounts throughout the world, but only a few deposits are large enough to be commercially important. One of these deposits is found in Catavi, Bolivia, site of one of the world's largest tin mines.

TIN PAN ALLEY. See United States, Music of the.

TINTORETTO (1518–1594)

When the Venetian painter Tintoretto was born in 1518, the Italian Renaissance was coming to a close. During that age, artists had developed many new painting techniques. Skillfully using these techniques, Tintoretto added to them and helped to produce the style of the 1500's known as mannerism.

Tintoretto's real name was Jacopo Robusti. Because his father was a dyer of silks, Jacopo was nicknamed Tintoretto, which means "little dyer." At 14 young Tintoretto studied briefly with the master painter Titian.

Mannerist painters, among whom Tintoretto was a leader, stressed technique. Tintoretto worked very quickly and often painted the same subject time and time again. With each picture the sense of depth was increased with daring use of perspective. Figures were shown in twisted, sometimes violent motion. Important action was illuminated by glaring rays of light, which were like spotlights on a stage. Tintoretto's color effects were veiled, mysterious, and unearthly, with brilliant streaks of heavenly light.

Tintoretto also painted many pictures on ceilings, often using illusionism. This form of painting creates the illusion (leads the viewer to believe) that what is painted is actually real. By 1548, Tintoretto's work was in great de-

Christ in the House of Martha and Mary by Tintoretto. Light relfecting from the figures makes them seem alive and almost in motion. Alte Pinakothek, Munich.

mand, so he opened a workshop in Venice and took student assistants. At least two of his own eight children worked in the studio. Tintoretto, who had produced some of the great glories of Venetian painting, died on May 31, 1594.

Reviewed by Howard Hibbard
Columbia University

TIRES

Rubber tires are found on almost every kind of vehicle wheel. They are found on lawn mowers and wheelchairs as well as tractor trailers and airplanes. Tires are part of bicycles, motorcycles, automobiles, buses, farm tractors, and hundreds of other kinds of wheeled vehicles.

Most tires used today are **pneumatic tires.** A pneumatic tire is a round, airtight, air-filled rubber tire on which vehicles roll smoothly and safely. "Pneumatic" comes from the Greek word meaning "wind" or "air." The inventor of the pneumatic tire, Robert William Thomson, was so far ahead of his time that his

patent, taken out in 1845 for a rubber tire described as a "hollow belt," went almost unnoticed.

More than 40 years later, in 1888, John Boyd Dunlop of Belfast, Ireland, made an experimental hollow rubber tire for his son's tricycle. He made his tire by placing an inner tube in a casing of Irish linen fabric, which he laced to the wheel. The air-filled rubber tube cushioned the bumpy ride over Belfast's rough cobblestone streets and made pedaling easier. Dunlop went into business manufacturing pneumatic tires for bicycles, and this time the idea caught on.

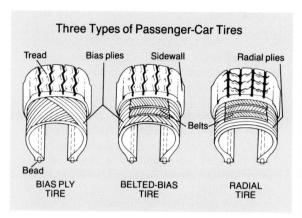

Three Types of Passenger-Car Tires

Tread   Bias plies   Sidewall   Radial plies

Belts

Bead

BIAS PLY TIRE   BELTED-BIAS TIRE   RADIAL TIRE

The age of the automobile was beginning at about this time, too. The first cars slowly rolled along on solid rubber tires, but the automobile manufacturers soon adopted the pneumatic tire because it had more resiliency, or "bounce." For many years, automobile tires were made in two parts. They had a heavy outer casing of rubber as well as a light inner tube. In 1955 the tubeless tire became standard equipment on new passenger cars. Tubeless tires are safer than inner-tube tires because they are more resistant to leaks and punctures.

▶PARTS OF A TIRE

Three types of pneumatic tires are now in use for passenger cars. They are the bias-ply tire, the belted-bias tire, and the radial tire. Each of these tires is made up of the same four main parts: the **body plies** (and often **belts** as well), which give the tire strength; the **beads**, which are wire rings that hold the tire to the wheel's metal rim; the airtight **inner liner;** and the **tread** and **sidewall** unit, which is the only part that is visible when the tire is mounted on the car.

The body plies and belts form the main body of the tire. The plies are rubber-covered cord fabrics that are cut into strips. The arrangement of the plies and of reinforcing belts (made of glass fiber, steel, or other materials) determines the tire's type. The bias-ply tire has plies running across the tire at an angle, or bias. The belted-bias tire has plies in this same arrangement but includes reinforcing belts located between the plies and the tread. The belts give added strength and stability to the tire. A radial tire also has belts under the tread,

There are more than 3,500 kinds and sizes of pneumatic tires. They range from 1½-pound airplane tail wheels to the giant 3-ton tires used on earth-moving equipment.

but its plies run straight across the tire, perpendicular to the tread. This arrangement makes a radial's sidewalls a bit more flexible than other tire types and gives the radial a slightly under-inflated look. The advantage of radial tires is that they usually provide greater traction and longer wear.

The tire's tread is designed to grip the road surface and minimize sliding on a wet road. The grooves that make up the tread provide channels that direct water outward from the tire. Without a tread, tires would ride on a thin layer of water instead of on the road surface. This would create a slippery and extremely hazardous driving condition. Snow tires have especially deep treads and sometimes even metal cleats or studs to help the tires grip the road.

The tire's sidewalls flex up and down to cushion the vehicle from bumps in the road. But the sidewalls must also be relatively rigid to withstand the activities of driving, such as turning, braking, and accelerating. At their innermost edges, the sidewalls meet the tire's beads.

ASSEMBLING A TIRE

The process of assembling the parts of a tire is called building a tire. It begins with the placement of two beads on a collapsible metal drum. The drum is then expanded, and the airtight inner liner is placed around the drum. The first ply is placed over the liner. A second ply is laid over the first, with the cord running in a different direction to make the tire stronger. In a radial tire the cords of the body plies are placed at right angles to the side of the tire, instead of at a diagonal angle, as in conventional or belted-bias tires. The number of plies depends on the type of tire. Tires for earth-moving equipment can have as many as 48 plies.

Mechanical devices fold the two outside edges of the plies over the beads on the drum and stitch them into place. For belted-bias and radial tires, the belts are then added in the area that will be covered by the tread. The belts and plies are then covered with the strips of special rubber tread and sidewall compounds. The tire, whose parts are now assembled, is known as a **green tire,** meaning that it is not yet **vulcanized** (cured).

The green tire is removed from the drum and placed in a giant vulcanizing press. Inside the press, a bladder inflates. This pushes the tire into the mold, where the desired tread design is pressed into the surface of the tire.

Intense heat and steam fuse the fabric, rubber, chemicals, and wire into a solid mass. When the tire is removed from the press, it is inspected for a variety of potential defects before it is sent to the warehouse for shipment to customers.

SAFETY AND MAINTENANCE

The quality and safety of tires have improved greatly since the early 20th century. In 1910 the best pneumatic tires could be expected to last about 3,000 miles (4,800 kilometers). Today, passenger-car tires are good for 40,000 miles (64,000 kilometers) or more if given proper care.

Tires developed for highway use must meet safety standards to ensure their reliability for extended use. The greatest enemy of tire safety is heat buildup inside the tire. This causes the tire to wear out prematurely. Heat buildup is usually caused by driving at high speeds for a long time or by using too much or too little air in the tires. Car owners should check the air pressure regularly and before long trips. This should be done when the tires are cool because when tires become hot from driving, the pressure increases.

Motorists should inspect the tread on their tires, checking for uneven wear. Periodic rotation of the tires (moving tires from one position on the vehicle to another, usually in a certain pattern) helps ensure even tread wear and long tire life. When the tread is worn out so that the grooves are less than $1/16$ inch (1.6 millimeters) deep, the tires should be replaced promptly.

RICHARD A. RILEY
Firestone Tire & Rubber Company
See also RUBBER.

TIRPITZ, ALFRED VON. See WORLD WAR I (Profiles: Central Powers).

TITIAN (1488?–1576)

Tiziano Vecelli, known as Titian, was the most important Venetian painter of the Italian Renaissance. Titian was born near Venice about 1488. As a boy he studied with the foremost Venetian painter of the time, Giovanni Bellini.

In 1508, Titian began working with another great Venetian artist, Giorgione—but as an associate, not as a pupil. Giorgione died two

years later, and Titian completed several of his colleague's unfinished paintings. In 1511, Titian was invited to Padua to paint frescoes of the miracles of Saint Anthony. His fame spread. When Bellini, official painter of the Republic of Venice, died in 1516, Titian was appointed his successor.

In 1525, Titian married a barber's daughter named Cecelia. They had three children.

One, their daughter Lavinia, was a frequent subject of Titian's paintings.

Titian has been described as a feverish worker. Painting with oils, he sometimes worked on several pictures at once, starting with a rough underpainting and then refining it with layer after layer of color. He was very critical of himself and sometimes would turn a canvas to the wall for months before going back to it and revising it. Titian blended colors skillfully to achieve the rich and strong effect he wanted. The warm red that seems to glow in his pictures, for example, was made with many layers of transparent colors.

Titian's fame spread through Europe. At various times he was court painter to the pope and to the rulers of Austria, the Netherlands, and Spain. Despite his great success, he was constantly and restlessly creative. Even when he grew old and partially crippled, he continued to explore new techniques.

Titian died in Venice on August 27, 1576.

Reviewed by S. J. FREEDBERG
National Gallery of Art (Washington, D.C.)

Detail from Titian's *Madonna with a Rabbit* (about 1530). The color of the madonna's gown, a blend of yellow, red, and brown, is often called titian, after its creator.

TITO (1892–1980)

Marshal (or Commander) Tito brought the Communist Party to power in the former nation of Yugoslavia, where he ruled for nearly 35 years. His strong leadership helped unify Yugoslavia and restore it to prosperity after World War II (1939–45).

Tito was born Josip Broz on May 25, 1892, in Kumrovec, Croatia, which was then part of Austria-Hungary. At 15, he became a metalworker, studying politics and languages at night. In 1913 he was drafted into the Austro-Hungarian Army.

During World War I (1914–18), Broz was taken prisoner by the Russians. When the Russian Revolution broke out in 1917, he joined the Red Army. After returning home in 1920, he worked for the outlawed Communist Party. He was often arrested, and he changed his name many times before adopting the name "Tito." In 1937 he became secretary-general of Yugoslavia's Communist Party.

During World War II, Italy and Germany invaded Yugoslavia. Tito organized a strong resistance movement, and many Yugoslavs came to regard him as a savior. But Draža Mihajlović, a resistance leader loyal to the exiled king, opposed Tito's rise to power. After a bitter civil war, the Communists gained control of the government. Tito became both prime minister and defense minister in 1945, and the following year, Mihajlović was shot for treason. In 1953, Tito was named president for life.

Tito asked the Soviet Union to help rebuild the war-torn country. But in 1948, when he refused to take orders from Soviet leaders, Yugoslavia was expelled from the international Communist organization. He then asked non-Communist countries for aid and received it. He also helped organize a group of nonaligned nations (nations opposed to dividing the world into Communist and non-Communist blocs). Tito developed his own form of Communism, in which workers helped manage the economy. He remained president until his death on May 4, 1980.

Reviewed by JULES ARCHER
Author, *Red Rebel: Tito of Yugoslavia*

See also YUGOSLAVIA.

TOADS. See AMPHIBIANS; FROGS AND TOADS.

The machine at left is "topping" tobacco plants—that is, removing their flowers in order to promote the growth of larger leaves. It is the leaf of the tobacco plant that is used commercially, mainly for smoking materials. The harvested leaves are hung to cure for a period of time after which they are auctioned to manufacturers of cigars and cigarettes.

Leaves hung for curing

Cured leaf

TOBACCO

When Christopher Columbus landed in the West Indies in 1492, he found that the people there smoked the dried leaves of the tobacco plant, rolled up into a small tube. The tobacco plant was unknown in Europe at that time, although tobacco had been smoked, probably chewed, and used as snuff in the Americas for about 2,000 years. The explorers took the seeds of the plant back to Spain with them. Over the next century, the use of tobacco in Europe grew with each voyage of Europeans to the New World.

The first varieties of the tobacco plant found by Spanish and Portuguese traders were harsh and strong. In 1612 a new, milder variety was planted in the Jamestown colony in present-day Virginia by John Rolfe. Rolfe probably got his seeds from the Caribbean island of Trinidad, but it is believed that the plant originally came from Brazil. The new kind of tobacco became one of Jamestown's most valuable crops in its trade with England. Later tobacco came to be grown in other areas in the eastern part of North America and in other parts of the world. Smoking tobacco became a widespread pastime.

▶THE PLANT

More than 60 species of tobacco grow today in places as far apart as Canada and India. The most common commercial tobacco species, called *Nicotiana tabacum,* is related to tomatoes, potatoes, and eggplants.

Tobacco plants may grow to about 6 feet (1.8 meters) high. The leaves may be more than 3 feet (1 meter) long and half as wide. The leaves are covered with tiny hairs that give off a gummy wax. The light pink flower produces a seed pod with thousands of seeds.

How Tobacco is Grown

Tobacco seeds are too small to be sown in a field. Therefore, they are first mixed with water or fertilizers. Then they are seeded in a bed covered with a light mulch, cotton cloth, or plastic sheet. In six to ten weeks, the seedlings reach a height of 6 to 8 inches (15 to 20 centimeters). Then they are transplanted to fields, either by hand or with the aid of transplanting machines. Tobacco can be grown in any one of a variety of soils during the frost-free period of the year.

As the plants begin to flower, they are usually **topped**—that is, the budding seed heads are removed. This promotes the growth of the leaves, but it also stimulates the growth of suckers—new stems and leaves, which interfere with the development of the plant. Suckers must be removed by hand or controlled with chemicals. Tobacco grown for cigar wrappers and the aromatic (fragrant) tobaccos of the Middle East are not topped.

Tobacco that is produced for cigar wrappers is grown in the shade. It is transplanted under cheesecloth strung over wire frames held upright by high poles. The cloth filters the sunlight and protects against the loss of moisture, which is needed for the flexible, light-colored, fine-textured leaves used for cigar wrappers.

Three to four months after the tobacco seedlings have been transplanted, they are ready for harvesting, either by **priming** or by cutting down the whole plant. Priming means harvesting two to four leaves each week. It may take five to eight weeks to harvest all the mature leaves on a plant by priming. Tobaccos for the interior parts of cigars are harvested by cutting off the mature plant at the soil line.

The tobacco plant is attacked by many insect, weed, and disease pests. The farmer controls these by planting disease-resistant varieties of tobacco, by cultural practices, and by the use of pesticides. Common insect pests include flea beatles, hornworms, and aphids.

▶ CURING TOBACCO

Curing is the process by which harvested tobacco is prepared for market. When the leaf is properly cured, it takes on the desired color, aroma, elasticity, and finish to make good-quality smoking products.

The three most common methods of curing tobacco are by air, flue, or fire. In the air-curing method, the leaf is dried by leaving it out in the sun for several days until it wilts. Then it is hung in a well-ventilated barn for several months.

In flue-curing, green leaves are hung in small, insulated barns heated by oil- or gas-burning heating systems. This method gets its name from the long iron flues (pipes) that were once used to carry heat from furnaces. Flue-cured tobacco is blended with other types of tobacco in the manufacture of cigarettes.

Fire-curing is similar to flue-curing, except that the leaves are exposed to smoke from fires lighted on the soil floors of the barn. Fire-cured tobacco is used to make snuff, chewing tobacco, and strong cigars.

▶ MARKETING TOBACCO

Most of the tobacco grown in the United States, Canada, Africa, and Australia is sold by farmers at auction warehouses. On auction day, farmers deliver their cured tobacco leaves, which are separated into bundles, or "sheets." The sheets are then graded by government inspectors according to quality standards for the intended use of the tobacco.

The auctioneer calls out bids in a rapid, sing-song voice. After the tobacco is sold to buyers from tobacco product manufacturers, it is shipped to plants where it is cleaned, sorted, and redried. Then it is packed for storage and aged for as long as several years before being made into cigarettes or other products.

Today more than 7 million tons of tobacco are produced each year in some 130 countries. Most of it is used in smoking products. Some is processed to extract the protein in the green leaves to be used as a supplement in both human and animal food. Among the world leaders in tobacco production are China, the United States, India, Brazil, and Turkey. Other tobacco-growing countries include Zimbabwe, Indonesia, Greece, and Italy.

Tobacco Use

Tobacco smoking is a widespread habit, which many people find physically stimulating. This effect is caused by nicotine, an addictive substance in the plant's leaves. (An article on smoking appears in Volume S.) In recent years, however, tobacco use has declined as a result of increased concern about the health hazards of smoking, particularly lung cancer. Such concern has led to restrictions on cigar and cigarette advertising and smoking in public places. Many countries also have high taxes on tobacco products to discourage smoking as well as to raise revenue. In addition, individuals and governments have taken legal action against tobacco companies to recover health-care costs related to smoking.

Future uses of tobacco may include nicotine drugs, which have shown promise in treating certain mental illnesses, such as Alzheimer's disease. Also, researchers are using a technique called genetic engineering to develop varieties of tobacco plants from which certain medicines could be extracted.

W. K. COLLINS
Coauthor, *Principles of Flue-Cured Tobacco*

TOBAGO. See TRINIDAD AND TOBAGO.

TOGO

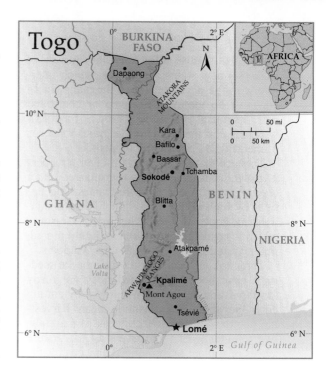

Togo is a small nation in West Africa, situated on the Gulf of Guinea, an inlet of the Atlantic Ocean. It is the second smallest country in the region, after The Gambia.

▶ PEOPLE

Togo's people belong to a number of different ethnic groups. The largest and most important of these is the Ewe, who live mainly in the densely populated southern part of the country. They are related to Ewe people living in the neighboring nation of Ghana. Other important ethnic groups are the Mina, who live mostly in the south, and the Kabre, who live mostly in the north.

French is the country's official language, but other languages are also spoken. The most important of these are the African languages Ewe and Mina in the south and Kabye and Dagomba in the north. About half the people practice traditional African religions. About 30 percent are believed to be Christian and 20 percent Muslim (followers of Islam).

▶ LAND

Togo occupies a long, narrow strip of land, about 70 miles (113 kilometers) across at its widest. It has 35 miles (56 kilometers) of

A woman spreads out corn to dry in the sun. About two-thirds of Togo's workforce is engaged in agriculture, which includes farming and raising livestock.

coastline along its southern border, the Gulf of Guinea. It is bounded by Ghana on the west, Burkina Faso on the north, and Benin on the east.

The Gulf of Guinea coast is flat and sandy, with stands of coconut palms and numerous lakes and lagoons. North of the coastal region are plateaus, which rise to a chain of high hills. The hills, known as the Atakora Mountains in the north and the Togo Mountains in the south, run diagonally across the country. They include Togo's highest point, Mount Agou, which has an elevation of 3,937 feet (1,200 meters). They are also the source of several rivers. The most important are the Mono in the south and the Oti in the north.

Southern Togo has a hot, humid climate, with average temperatures of 70° to 87°F (21° to 31°C). The climate is generally cooler in the north. Rainfall is heaviest in the hilly regions.

▶ ECONOMY

About two-thirds of Togo's workforce is engaged in agriculture. The most important cash crops are coffee, cocoa, and cotton. Major food crops include yams, cassava (a starchy root), corn, beans, rice, and millet. Livestock raising and fishing are important activities.

FACTS and figures

TOGOLESE REPUBLIC is the official name of the country.

LOCATION: West Africa.

AREA: 21,925 sq mi (56,785 km^2).

POPULATION: 5,700,000 (estimate).

CAPITAL AND LARGEST CITY: Lomé.

MAJOR LANGUAGES: French (official), Ewe, Mina, Kabye, Dagomba.

MAJOR RELIGIOUS GROUPS: Traditional African religions, Christian (mainly Roman Catholic), Muslim.

GOVERNMENT: Republic. **Head of state**—president. **Head of government**—prime minister. **Legislature**—National Assembly.

CHIEF PRODUCTS: Agricultural—coffee, cocoa, cotton, yams, cassava, corn, beans, rice, millet, sorghum, livestock, fish. **Manufactured**—processed foods, cement, handicrafts, textiles, beverages. **Mineral**—phosphates, limestone, marble.

MONETARY UNIT: African Financial Community (CFA) franc (1 CFA franc = 100 centimes).

Services account for nearly 40 percent of Togo's economy. They include personal and business services, trade, finance, insurance, real estate, transportation, utilities, and communications. Businesses related to tourism are also significant.

Togo has limited industry. The chief manufactured goods are processed foods, cement, handicrafts, textiles, and beverages. The country also has petroleum refining facilities.

Phosphates, used in making fertilizers, are Togo's most important mineral resource and a chief export. Marble and limestone are also mined. There are untapped deposits of iron ore and bauxite (aluminum ore).

▶ **MAJOR CITIES**

Lomé, Togo's capital and only major city, has a population of about 375,000. Situated on the Gulf of Guinea, it is one of the leading port cities of West Africa. **Sokodé**, Togo's second largest city, has about 46,000 residents.

▶ **HISTORY AND GOVERNMENT**

The Ewe and related peoples began migrating to the region in the 1100's. Togo's colonial history began in 1884, when a treaty with Ewe kings gave Germany a protectorate over a small region on the coast. The Germans gradually acquired additional territory, which became German Togoland. The colony was bordered by the British Gold Coast colony (now Ghana) and the French colony of Dahomey (now Benin).

In 1914, at the beginning of World War I, Britain and France, who were at war with Germany, took over German Togoland. In 1922 the League of Nations gave Britain the authority to govern its western portion and France the authority to govern its eastern portion. This partition split the Ewe's traditional homeland. In 1946, the two areas became trust territories of the United Nations.

Independence. When Ghana won its independence in 1957, British Togoland became part of the new nation. French Togoland gained independence in 1960 as Togo.

The years following independence were stormy. Togo's first president, Sylvanus Olympio, was assassinated in 1963. His successor, Nicolas Grunitzky, was overthrown in a military coup in 1967. General Gnassingbe Eyadema assumed the presidency and was elected, without opposition, in 1979 and 1986.

Recent Events. Widespread protests against Eyadema's repressive one-party rule resulted in the adoption of a new constitution in 1992. It called for a president to serve no more than two 5-year terms and to share power with a prime minister in a multiparty political system. In the first elections held under the new constitution, in 1993, opposition parties refused to take part and Eyadema remained president. He was narrowly re-elected in 1998. In late 2002, Parliament voted to allow Eyadema to run for a third term. He then won the 2003 presidential election, which his opponents contested.

When Eyadema died in 2005, the legislature passed a constitutional amendment to allow his son, Faure Gnassingbe, to serve out his father's term. This act led to riots in the capital and was condemned by other West African leaders. The amendment was quickly overturned, and Abass Bonfoh stepped in as interim leader. An election returned Gnassingbe to office, although his victory was accompanied by protests and violence.

PAUL J. KAISER
African Studies Center
University of Pennsylvania

TOJO, HIDEKI. See WORLD WAR II (Profiles: Axis Powers).

The dazzling neon-lit Ginza is Tokyo's main shopping and entertainment district. It offers a wide array of department stores, boutiques, theaters, restaurants, and nightclubs.

TOKYO

Tokyo, the capital of Japan, is one of the world's largest and most exciting cities. It is the political, cultural, and industrial heart of the nation. Approximately 8 million people live within the city limits, and more than 28 million live within its greater metropolitan region.

The city covers an area of 223 square miles (578 square kilometers). Some of the land was created by filling in parts of Tokyo Bay. Hills and mountains enclose the city on three sides. On a clear day, the majestic snow-capped peak of Mount Fuji, Japan's highest mountain, can be seen to the southwest.

Tokyo was nearly destroyed at the end of World War II (1939–45), but it has since been rebuilt and has become a thriving and modern urban center. Its government has found it difficult to keep up with the city's rapid growth and the constant demand for new housing, schools, playgrounds, parks, and improved mass transit systems. But although Tokyo has many problems to resolve, it remains one of the great cities of the world.

The City. Tokyo is made up of a tremendous cluster of towns, suburbs, and other communities. Many people spend their entire lives in the city without getting to know all its sections. It consists of 23 *ku* (wards), 26 cities, five towns, eight villages, and the Izu and Ogasawara Islands. The *ku* make up the center of the *to* (metropolis) and what many people regard as the actual city of Tokyo.

The main subdivision of the *ku* is the district, called a *cho* or *machi*. A person's address includes the names of both the ward and the district. The final part of an address is the house number. Few streets have names. To add to this confusion, buildings and houses on a street are numbered not consecutively but according to the order in which they were built.

The city has many famous buildings and landmarks. The most popular shopping and recreation area is the Ginza, the busiest and most famous street in Japan. The Imperial Palace, home of the emperor of Japan, is situated in the heart of downtown Tokyo. It is one of the few historic buildings still standing. To the south are several foreign embassies and the imposing National Diet Building, which houses Japan's parliament. Farther south is the Tokyo Tower, a 1,092-foot (333-meter) structure with observation platforms that provide spectacular views of the city and Tokyo Bay.

The Marunouchi district, in the east part of town, is headquarters of the Nikkei Stock Exchange and other important financial institutions. To the north are dozens of Japan's best schools of higher learning, including Tokyo University. Notable museums include the Tokyo National Museum, the National Science Museum, and the National Museum of Western Art. The library at the National Diet (Parliament) is the largest in the country.

Tokyo has many parks. The most famous, Ueno Park, boasts lovely gardens, ponds, and a zoo. Hibiya Park is often used for public meetings. Yoyogi Park, on the west side of the city, contains the Meiji Shrine, dedicated to the emperor Meiji (1852–1912). The Japanese people donated more than 100,000 trees to the park when the shrine was built in 1920.

The Outer Garden of the Meiji Shrine, now known as Meiji Olympic Park, has many sports facilities. The complex was built for the 1964 Olympic Games. Tokyo Dome also hosts sports events. Just west of the city, in Urayasu, is Tokyo Disneyland. It has been one of Tokyo's most popular parks since it opened in 1983.

The city has excellent transportation systems. There is a fine subway in the midtown area. Bus and streetcar lines crisscross the city and extend into the suburbs. But traffic jams are frequent because of the great number of vehicles on the narrow streets. Some relief has been provided by a system of elevated highways.

Electric trains are speedy and inexpensive. More than 1 million passengers use the Tokyo Railroad Station every day. Haneda Airport and the New Tokyo International Airport at Narita offer national and international service.

The Economy. Tokyo is one of the major industrial centers of Japan. Plants, mills, and

Traditional neighborhoods in Tokyo have shopping arcades lined with small businesses, such as this convenience store. But in recent years, small, family-owned stores have faced stiff competition from modern chain stores and giant supermarkets.

workshops located throughout the city produce iron and steel goods, machines, tools, electrical equipment, chemicals, textiles, optical goods, and foodstuffs. These products are sold all over Japan and are transported in the many ships that leave Tokyo Bay daily. The industrial sections of Tokyo, like those in many other cities of the world, are unattractive. The buildings are often drab and grimy, and clouds of smoke hover above them.

Japan's publishing industry, centered in Tokyo, produces books and magazines that are distributed throughout the nation and the world. Many different daily newspapers are published and sold in Tokyo. Several radio and television stations broadcast from there. Tokyo Tower serves as an antenna for a number of the main radio and television stations. Tokyo is also the center of Japan's flourishing film industry.

History. During the greater part of Japan's history, Kyoto was Japan's capital. In 1603, Tokyo, then known as Edo, became the political and military headquarters of the Tokugawa shoguns (military rulers) of Japan. During the next 265 years, Edo grew into one of the great cities of the world. In 1868, Edo became the imperial capital of Japan. It was renamed Tokyo, meaning "eastern capital," to distinguish it from Kyoto, the western capital.

Tokyo underwent many changes after it was made the imperial capital. The new central government was determined to modernize Japan. Tokyo became a model for the entire country. Many of the homes of the former feudal lords were converted into government offices and schools. Numerous Western-style buildings gradually altered the appearance of the city. Some of these buildings are still standing. Others were destroyed by the many earthquakes and resulting fires that strike the city every year. The most terrible of these disasters took place on September 1, 1923, when more than 100,000 people were killed or injured. Large parts of the city were reduced to ashes.

During the last months of World War II, the city was repeatedly bombed. Much of Tokyo became a vast wasteland. After the war, the city was rebuilt and expanded with remarkable speed. Today Tokyo is larger and more modern than ever before.

HYMAN KUBLIN
City University of New York, Brooklyn College

TOLEDO. See OHIO (Cities).

TOLKIEN, J. R. R. (1892–1973)

Although J. R. R. Tolkien was a professor at England's Oxford University and a respected scholar of medieval literature, he is best known as the author of the fantasy novels *The Hobbit* and *The Lord of the Rings*.

John Ronald Reuel Tolkien was born on January 3, 1892, in Bloemfontein, South Africa. At the age of 3 he moved with his mother to Sarehole, a village outside Birmingham, England. It was there that Ronald developed the deep love for English country life that is reflected in his stories.

Tolkien had a skill for languages; he even made up his own private words and alphabet in a language he called Naffarin. While a student at King Edward's School in Birmingham, he excelled in Latin, Greek, German, and Middle English. His skill with words earned him a scholarship to Oxford, where he majored in philology, the study of language. He studied the great medieval literatures that would provide the background for his own writings, in which he created a world with its own languages.

Tolkien graduated in June 1915 and, as World War I had begun, enlisted in the army. Before going to France as a signal officer, he married his childhood sweetheart, Edith Bratt. During the war, Tolkien contracted trench fever, remaining ill for nearly a year. During that time he began *The Book of Lost Tales* (later renamed *The Silmarillion*). After the war, Tolkien returned to Oxford, becoming professor of Anglo-Saxon in 1925.

Outwardly a popular lecturer and scholar, Tolkien also had an inner life filled with fanciful stories. Borrowing material from the unfinished manuscript of *The Silmarillion*, he began telling his children tales about a funny little creature named Bilbo Baggins, who found a magic ring that made its wearer invisible. These stories became *The Hobbit* (1937). Later he invented the evil Sauron, whose efforts to obtain the ring are dramatically told in three novels, together called *The Lord of the Rings* (1954–55). The three are *The Fellowship of the Ring, The Two Towers,* and *The Return of the King.*

Tolkien retired from Oxford in 1959, devoting his last years to work on *The Silmarillion* —a task he was unable to finish before his death on September 2, 1973. The novel was edited by his son Christopher and published in 1977 as the final offering of one of the most beloved and widely read authors in the world.

RANDEL HELMS
Author, *Tolkien's World*

In this excerpt from *The Hobbit,* Bilbo Baggins is lost in the Goblin caves under the Misty Mountains. Trying to find a way out, he stumbles onto Gollum's lair.

Deep down here by the dark water lived old Gollum, a small slimy creature. I don't know where he came from, nor who or what he was. He was Gollum—as dark as darkness, except for two big round pale eyes in his thin face. He had a little boat, and he rowed about quite quietly on the lake; for lake it was, wide and deep and deadly cold. He paddled it with large feet dangling over the side, but never a ripple did he make. Not he. He was looking out of his pale lamp-like eyes for blind fish, which he grabbed with his long fingers as quick as thinking. He liked meat too. Goblin he thought good, when he could get it; but he took care they never found him out. He just throttled them from behind, if they ever came down alone anywhere near the edge of the water, while he was prowling about. They very seldom did, for they had a feeling that something unpleasant was lurking down there, down at the very roots of the mountain. They had come on the lake, when they were tunnelling down long ago, and they found they could go no further; so there their road ended in that direction, and there was no reason to go that way—unless the Great Goblin sent them. Sometimes he took a fancy for fish from the lake, and sometimes neither goblin nor fish came back.

Actually Gollum lived on a slimy island of rock in the middle of the lake. He was watching Bilbo now from the distance with his pale eyes like telescopes. Bilbo could not see him, but he was wondering a lot about Bilbo, for he could see that he was no goblin at all.

Gollum got into his boat and shot off from the island, while Bilbo was sitting on the brink altogether flummoxed and at the end of his way and his wits. Suddenly up came Gollum and whispered and hissed:

The evil Gollum is a "small slimy creature . . . as dark as darkness, except for two big round pale eyes . . ."

"Bless us and splash us, my precioussss! I guess it's a choice feast; at least a tasty morsel it'd make us, gollum!" And when he said *gollum* he made a horrible swallowing noise in his throat. That is how he got his name, though he always called himself 'my precious'.

The hobbit jumped nearly out of his skin when the hiss came in his ears, and he suddenly saw the pale eyes sticking out at him.

"Who are you?" he said, thrusting his dagger in front of him.

"What iss he, my preciouss?" whispered Gollum (who always spoke to himself through never having anyone else to speak to). This is what he had come to find out, for he was not really very hungry at the moment, only curious; otherwise he would have grabbed first and whispered afterwards.

"I am Mr. Bilbo Baggins. I have lost the dwarves and I have lost the wizard, and I don't know where I am; and I don't want to know, if only I can get away."

"What's he got in his handses?" said Gollum, looking at the sword, which he did not quite like.

"A sword, a blade which came out of Gondolin!"

"Sssss" said Gollum, and became quite polite. "Praps ye sits here and chats with it a bitsy, my preciousss. It like riddles, praps it does, does, it?" He was anxious to appear friendly, at any rate for the moment, and until he found out more about the sword and the hobbit, whether he was quite alone really, whether he was good to eat, and whether Gollum was really hungry. Riddles were all he could think of. Asking them and sometimes guessing them, had been the only game he had ever played with other funny creatures sitting in their holes in the long, long ago, before he lost all his friends and was driven away, alone, and crept down, down, into the dark under the mountains.

"Very well," said Bilbo, who was anxious to agree, until he found out more about the creature, whether he was quite alone, whether he was fierce or hungry, and whether he was a friend of the goblins.

"You ask first," he said, because he had not had time to think of a riddle.

So Gollum hissed:

> *What has roots as nobody sees,*
> *Is taller than trees*
> > *Up, up it goes,*
> > *And yet never grows?*

"Easy!" said Bilbo. "Mountain, I suppose."

"Does it guess easy? It must have a competition with us, my preciouss! If precious asks, and it doesn't answer, we eats it, my preciousss. If it asks us, and we doesn't answer, then we does what it wants, eh? We shows it the way out, yes!"

TOLSTOI, LEO (1828–1910)

Russia's best-loved novelist, Leo Tolstoi, was also an important philosopher and social reformer. He was born on his family's estate, Yasnaya Polyana, south of Moscow, on August 28, 1828. Both his parents died before he was 9 years old. He was brought up by his relatives and was educated by French and German tutors. At 16 he enrolled at Kazan University, but he did not finish his studies.

Tolstoi wrote his first novel, *Childhood* (1852), while serving in a military regiment in the Caucasus. It was praised for being very lifelike. *Boyhood* and *Youth* followed.

In 1859, Tolstoi started a school at Yasnaya Polyana. There were no free schools then for peasant children in Russia, so he went abroad to study educational methods in other countries. Back home, he built a schoolhouse and prepared a curriculum and textbooks that were used widely. His school became a model for other village schools. In 1862, Tolstoi married Sofya Bers. They had 13 children.

Tolstoi's first long novel, *War and Peace* (1869), created a sensation. When it was followed by *Anna Karenina* (1877), Tolstoi was acknowledged as Russia's greatest novelist. *War and Peace* is a sweeping historical epic of Russian life in the time of Napoleon I. *Anna Karenina* tells of a society woman's unhappy marriage and love affair. In these novels, Tolstoi created a new, realistic literary style. All the characters—more than 500 of them in *War and Peace*—become wonderfully alive and familiar people to the reader.

In spite of his success, Tolstoi gave up fiction for several years. Instead he wrote moral essays that reflected his search for a religious faith and a purpose in life. He dropped his inherited title of count, dressed simply, and worked with the peasants in the fields to show that he was no better than they. He began publishing inexpensive illustrated booklets so that the poor could have good literature and art. The church and the government did not like Tolstoi's ideas and persecuted his followers. His works were censored.

Tolstoi quarreled with his wife over his habits. Finally he left home secretly one night, only to fall ill of pneumonia at a nearby railway station. He died in the stationmaster's house on November 7, 1910.

THAÏS S. LINDSTROM
Author, *A Concise History of Russian Literature*

TOMATOES

Probably no other vegetable has as many uses as the tomato. It can be served raw, stewed, baked, fried, or in meat dishes. Tomatoes are made into soups, juice, catsup, relish, pickles, sauces, and paste.

The tomato is a member of a group of plants known as the nightshade family. Other members of this family are the pepper, potato, eggplant, and tobacco plants. The tomato fruit is a pulpy berry that varies from about ¾ inch to 6 inches (2 to 15 centimeters) in diameter. The tomato is usually round, but some are shaped like pears or plums. Most people think of ripe tomatoes as being bright red. But there are also tomatoes that turn pink, yellow, or white when ripe. Tomatoes grow on a vine that looks like a spreading bush.

▶ **HISTORY OF THE TOMATO**

The tomato is native to South America. Both the Incas and the Aztecs grew and ate tomatoes. Spanish explorers carried tomato seeds back to Spain. English colonists later took tomato seeds from Europe to plant in the gardens of their settlements in North America. But in both Europe and North America the tomato was grown only as a curiosity. Few people tried tasting the fruit because it was thought to be poisonous.

Superstition was not the only reason that people were slow to try tomatoes. The early tomatoes were very watery and had an acid taste. In the 1800's, growers began to try to produce bigger and tastier tomatoes. They hunted through each crop for plants that bore large, round, juicy, and good-tasting tomatoes. Seeds from these plants were used in the next planting. Gradually tomatoes became rounder, juicier, and tastier. Different varieties of tomato have been crossed to improve the yield, flavor, shape, and resistance to diseases. Varieties that can withstand cold have also been developed, since tomatoes are easily killed by frost. Using a technique called genetic engineering, scientists have even produced tomatoes that ripen without softening. This new variety is easier to store and ship, since it does not need refrigeration.

▶ **HOW TOMATOES ARE GROWN**

Tomatoes grow best in a warm climate with plenty of sunlight, and they thrive in almost any kind of soil. Tomato seeds may be sowed, or planted, directly in the field or garden. But most tomato seeds are planted in fine, loamy soil in special seedbeds that can be covered in case of frost. The young seedlings must be kept in full sunlight during the day for good, sturdy growth. Plants are ready to be transplanted when they are 6 to 7 inches (15 to 18 centimeters) high, about six weeks after seeding. The seedlings are watered with a fertilizer solution as soon as they have been transplanted.

Tomato plants produce a heavier yield if they are allowed to sprawl. But some growers save space by training tomato vines on stakes or tying them to trellises with wire and string. Some tomatoes in northern areas are grown entirely in greenhouses.

The first tomatoes ripen about three months after the seeds are planted. The plant bears tomatoes continuously for two to three months and then dies. Tomatoes to be sold fresh are picked when fully grown but still green or just beginning to color. They are usually carefully picked by hand because they are easily squashed or bruised. Tomatoes that will be canned or processed in some other way are picked when they are fully ripe. They are often picked by a mechanical harvester.

Italy was the first country to regard the tomato as a useful food. It is the leading producer in Europe. China, the United States, and Turkey are the world's largest producers of tomatoes.

The tomato is an excellent source of vitamins A and C and the antioxidant lycopene.

RAYMON E. WEBB
United States Department of Agriculture

TOMPKINS, DANIEL D. See VICE PRESIDENCY OF THE UNITED STATES.

TONGA

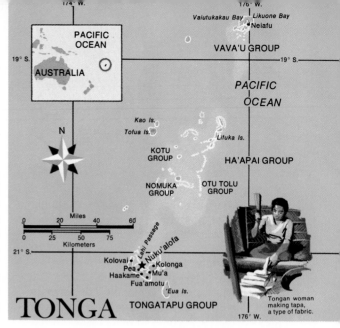

Tongan woman making tapa, a type of fabric.

Tonga is an island kingdom in the southern Pacific Ocean. It is composed of about 150 small islands, of which less than one-third are inhabited. Tonga was once known as the Friendly Islands, a name given it in the 1700's by the British explorer Captain James Cook, who found its people especially hospitable.

People. The Tongans are Polynesians. Their language is Tongan, but English is also widely used. Most of the people are Protestants; a minority are Roman Catholics.

Land and Climate. There are three main groups of islands: Vava'u in the north, Ha'apai in the center, and Tongatapu in the south. Nearly two-thirds of the people live on Tongatapu, the largest island and the site of the capital, Nuku'alofa. Most of the islands are low-lying coral atolls. A few of the islands are mountainous, some with active volcanoes.

Tonga's climate is tropical, with temperatures averaging about 73°F (23°C). Rainfall is moderate.

Economy. Tonga's economy is based on agriculture. The chief exports are coconuts and coconut products, including copra (dried coconut meat) and coconut oil; bananas; and vanilla beans. The main food crops are sweet potatoes, taro and cassava (starchy roots), and yams. Tourism is becoming an important source of income.

History and Government. The early Tongans were warriors and seafarers, whose ancestors may originally have come from Asia. The first Europeans to see the islands were Dutch navigators in the 1600's. British explorers arrived in the late 1700's, followed by Christian missionaries.

The islands were united by conquest under King George Tupou I, who came to the throne in 1845 and was the founder of the present Tongan royal house. A constitution was adopted in 1875. Tonga was a British-protected state from 1900 to 1970, when it regained complete independence. Tonga joined the United Nations in 1999.

The government of Tonga is a mixture of Polynesian tradition and Western-style democracy. The king is the head of state and governs with the aid of the Privy Council, which serves as a cabinet and is led by an appointed prime minister. The lawmaking body is the Legislative Assembly. It includes the members of the Privy Council; nine nobles elected by all the hereditary nobles of Tonga; and nine additional representatives elected directly by the Tongan people.

JOHN MILES
Senior Political Affairs Officer, United Nations

FACTS and figures

KINGDOM OF TONGA (Pule'anga Tonga) is the official name of the country.

LOCATION: Southern Pacific Ocean.

AREA: 270 sq mi (699 km²).

POPULATION: 102,000 (estimate).

CAPITAL AND LARGEST CITY: Nuku'alofa.

MAJOR LANGUAGES: Tongan, English.

MAJOR RELIGIOUS GROUP: Christian (mainly Protestant).

GOVERNMENT: Constitutional monarchy. **Head of state**—monarch (king). **Head of government**—monarch and Privy Council (including prime minister). **Legislature**—Legislative Assembly.

CHIEF PRODUCTS: Coconuts and coconut products, including copra (dried coconut meat) and coconut oil; bananas; vanilla beans.

MONETARY UNIT: Pa'anga (Tongan dollar) (1 T dollar = 100 seniti).

TONGUE TWISTERS

A tongue twister or tongue tangler is a group of words that is difficult to repeat rapidly several times. The harder a person tries to pronounce a twister correctly, the sillier he or she sounds. This is one reason why tongue twisters are such a popular form of word play.

"Black bug's blood" is one of the more difficult tongue twisters. "Miss Smith dismissith us" is another.

There are tongue twisters in almost every language and in almost every country. *Mi mama me mima mucho* is a Spanish twister that means "My mother spoils me a lot." *Le ver vert va vers le verre vert* is a popular French twister that means "The green worm goes to the green grass."

A tongue twister may be a single word, like "gigwhip," or a phrase or one or more sentences. It also may rhyme. Some twisters are simple statements. Others are stories that often may involve strange situations and weird characters. One such twister story begins this way:

Mr. See owned a saw
And Mr. Soar owned a seesaw,
Now See's saw sawed Soar's seesaw
Before Soar saw See . . .

One of the longest twisters has 418 words, each beginning with the letter "s." It is the story of a shy seller of saddles named Samuel Short who wished to marry a woman named Sophia Sophronia Spriggs.

Some tongue twisters are very old. One of the most famous twisters in the English language, the Peter Piper twister, first appeared in 1674 in an English grammar book. That version went this way:

Peter Piper picked a peck of pickled pepper,
A peck of pickled pepper Peter Piper picked,
If Peter Piper picked a peck of pickled pepper,
Where is the pickled pepper Peter Piper picked?

This tongue twister was one of several "charms" recommended as a cure for hiccups. Another twister in this ancient group is still known today:

Hickup, snickup,
Rise up, right up,
Three drops in the cup
Are good for the hiccup.

About 150 years after its first appearance, Peter Piper turned up in an English booklet of 23 twisters, each starting with a different letter of the alphabet. It was called "Peter Piper's Practical Principles of Plain and Perfect Pronunciation." Together the 23 made up one of the earliest alphabet rhymes. Each told about one character—Andrew Airpump, Oliver Oglethorpe, Questing Quidnunc, Walter Waddle, and others. But of all these characters, only Peter is still with us.

No one knows how many tongue twisters there are, but it is accurate to say that there are thousands. Nor does anyone know just who made most of them up. But usually it was an ordinary person who loved word play. If he or she created a good twister, it passed from person to person by word of mouth.

In the late 19th century some people wrote down the twisters they liked and wanted to remember in a "scribble-in" book and, in turn, passed them on. When people moved from one region or one country to another, they took their tongue twisters with them. The famous Peter Piper twister was brought to America from England in this manner.

As tongue twisters move about, people tend to change them in small and large ways. For example, in some places Peter Piper's pickled pepper may be purple pepper or peppercorns or prickly prangly pears or served off a pewter plate. And the tongue twister that starts "Betty Botter bought some butter" also may have a heroine named Betsy Butter or Betty Botta, depending on where it is told. Her problems with butter also may be different.

In such ways tongue twisters have become part of our folklore and have been passed from generation to generation as a traditional means of having fun.

Tongue twisters also have been used for serious purposes. One is to improve a person's pronunciation. Opera singers, actors, and announcers on radio and television may use them in their training. Some specialists have used them in trying to help people with speech problems. At least one dentist had his patients try tongue twisters to test the false teeth he had made for them. And some people still believe that using a short tongue twister, like "a knapsack strap," will cure the hiccups if it is repeated rapidly while holding a breath.

When Poland was conquered by Nazi Germany during World War II, the Poles who

FIVE TOUGH TONGUE TWISTERS

Rubber baby-buggy bumpers.
Rubber baby-buggy bumpers.
Rubber baby-buggy bumpers.

Six crisp snacks.
Six crisp snacks.
Six crisp snacks.

A tutor who tooted the flute
Tried to tutor two tutors to toot.
Said the two to the tutor,
"Is it harder to toot or
To tutor two tutors to toot?"

Fried fresh fish,
Fish fried fresh,
Fish fresh fried,
Fresh fried fish.

Mr. See owned a saw, and Mr. Soar owned a see-saw. Now See's saw sawed Soar's seesaw before Soar saw See, which made Soar sore. Had Soar seen See's saw before See saw Soar's seesaw, then See's saw would not have sawed Soar's seesaw. But See saw Soar's seesaw before Soar saw See's saw, so See's saw sawed Soar's seesaw. It was a shame to let See see Soar so sore because See's saw sawed Soar's seesaw.

continued to resist the invaders used a Polish tongue twister as a secret password. It was *Chrazaszcz brmzi w trzcinie,* which means "The beetle buzzes in the thicket." When German spies tried to pass as resisters, most could not pronounce the password properly and were found out.

Thousands of years earlier ancient Hebrews had used a similar tongue-trapping password to identify their enemies the Ephraimites. They asked suspects to pronounce the Hebrew word for a flooding stream, which was *shibboleth.* But the Ephraimites pronounced the word as *siboleth,* and this pronunciation gave them away.

▶ **CREATING YOUR OWN TONGUE TWISTERS**

It is not difficult to make up your own tongue twisters, just as people have always done. If the subject of a twister is a silly one, it will add to the fun. But what is most important is that the sounds are arranged so that they will tangle a tongue. By studying how twisters work, you will find many methods you can use.

One of the easiest is to write a brief sentence in which each word begins with the same letter or sound, like the twister "Men munch much mush" or "Old Oily Ollie oils old oily autos."

Another approach is to use the same word again and again in the same sentence. For example, "This can opener can open any can that any can opener can open."

By varying the sounds in a sentence slightly, you can write a really difficult tongue twister. "*Shy sly She*ila" is an example. It starts with a "sh" sound, shifts to a "sl" sound, and returns to "sh." The famous tongue twister "*She sells seashells* by the *seashore*" follows a similar pattern, as does "*Bl*ack *bug's bl*ood."

A twister should be repeated at least three times. The faster you recite it, the more likely it is that you will use the wrong sound in the wrong place and twist your tongue. This will cause everyone to laugh at how silly you sound, which is the main purpose of tongue twisters.

ALVIN SCHWARTZ
Author, *A Twister of Twists,*
A Tangler of Tongues

TONSILLITIS. See DISEASES (Descriptions of Some Diseases).

TOOLS

A tool is a device used to carry out a task. Devices such as pens, pencils, pots, pans, electric irons, and even computers might be considered tools. Usually, however, the term "tool" refers to implements such as hammers, screwdrivers, saws, and drills that are used to make, repair, and maintain many different types of objects. People have been using tools to accomplish such tasks for more than 12,000 years.

The ability to make and use tools is one of the significant differences between human beings and animals. Some animals use sticks and stones to accomplish simple tasks, but this is the extent of their tool use. From the earliest tools people devised to make fire, build shelters, and make clothing, to the most modern tools they manufacture and use today to produce computers, skyscrapers, and spaceships, human beings have been able to invent and use tools to shape and change their environment and to make their lives easier and more interesting.

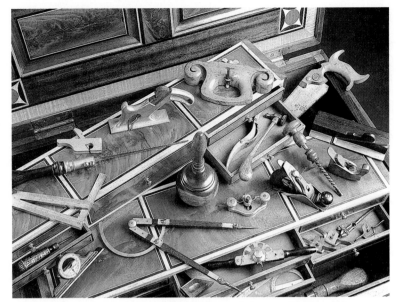

There are many types of tools of various shapes and sizes used to saw, drill, measure, hold, turn, and shape wood or metal. Tools help people shape their environment and make their lives easier.

▶ HAND TOOLS

There are many types of hand tools. Tools held in a worker's hand are used to accomplish various tasks, including pounding, cutting, shaping, drilling, holding, turning, and measuring.

Hammers and mallets are made of various materials, including wood, brass, lead, and rawhide. They also come in many shapes and sizes.

Hammers and Mallets

Hammers and mallets are pounding tools. They are among the oldest tools and have changed very little over the years. Hammers come in many shapes and sizes. The claw hammer, the most common type, has a flat end for pounding or driving nails and a forked claw on the other end for pulling nails. The ball-peen hammer, which has a rounded knob at one end instead of a claw, is used primarily for shaping metal.

Mallets are large hammers with two flat striking surfaces. The surfaces usually are made of wood, but they can also be plastic, rubber, or even iron. A carver's mallet has a ball-type head, which makes it easier to hit a chisel squarely from any angle. Rubber mallets often are used to bang out dents in metal.

Axes, Hatchets, and Adzes

Axes, hatchets, and adzes are called edge tools because they have sharpened edges for cutting and shaping wood. A tapered blade of varying width is attached to the long handle of an ax. This tool is used primarily for felling trees and shaping logs. A hatchet is a smaller type of ax, with a shorter handle. Held with only one hand, hatchets have a number of uses, including cutting firewood and making the initial rough cuts in large wood carvings. An adze is similar to an ax and a hatchet except that the blades are perpendicular, in-

An ax (*above*) is similar in design to a hammer, but it is sharpened on the striking edge. A hatchet (*right*) is a smaller type of ax that is held with only one hand.

stead of parallel, to the handle. Not widely used today, the adze was used in the past to square the sides of beams and to smooth floors and the decks of ships. Small adzes, called hand adzes, were designed to hollow out bowls and other utensils.

Chisels and Gouges

Chisels and gouges are also edge tools. A chisel has a long, flat blade with a sharp beveled, or slanted, end. There are many different shapes and sizes of chisels. They are used to cut grooves in wood and to do fine shaping work. A gouge is a special type of chisel with a hollow blade that is shaped somewhat like a long spoon. Found in many shapes and sizes, gouges also are used to carve and shape wood.

Saws

Saws are used to cut wood or metal to a certain length or width. A handsaw has a long, thin, flexible blade attached to a handle. The cutting edge of the blade consists of sharp teeth, arranged so that the teeth stick out slightly on either side of the blade. This helps prevent the blade from becoming stuck in the cut.

The two basic types of saws designed for cutting wood are the ripsaw, which cuts with the grain of the wood, and the crosscut saw, which cuts across the grain.

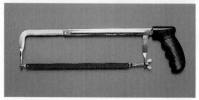

A handsaw (*top*), which has a long, flexible blade attached to a handle, is used for cutting wood; a hacksaw (*bottom*) is used mostly for cutting metal.

The difference between these saws is the shape of their teeth. The teeth of a ripsaw are shaped like tiny chisels, while the teeth of a crosscut saw are shaped like tiny knives.

Other types of saws are used for more accurate cutting. A backsaw has a reinforcing strip on the top of the blade that steadies the blade for greater accuracy when cutting wood. A miter saw is a larger, heavier backsaw used with a miter box, a device that guides the blade to ensure a precise cut. A coping saw has a very thin blade that is held in a C-shaped frame. It is used for very fine work and for cutting small curves in thin pieces of wood. A keyhole saw has a narrow tapered blade that can fit into a hole and then cut outward to create a desired shape. A hacksaw has very fine teeth and is used almost exclusively for cutting metal.

A block plane, which is held with only one hand, is used to smooth and shape the surfaces of wood.

Planes

Planes are one of the most important tools in woodworking. They are used to smooth and shape the surfaces of wood and to straighten the edges of boards so that they can be joined and fitted together precisely.

A plane is basically an adjustable chisel blade held in place by a frame, or body, which always keeps the blade at the angle and cutting depth at which it is set. A bench plane, the oldest and most common type, is so named because it is generally used on the workbench. It has a flat bottom, a chisel-edged blade that is wedged or held in the body of the plane, and an opening at the top of the plane to allow wood shavings to escape. Most bench planes have a rear handle. A block plane, another common type, is similar to a bench plane except that it is smaller, is used with only one hand, and rarely has a handle.

Some types of planes can be fitted with different blades to cut curves and grooves into wood. There are many different types of planes that can be used for almost every woodworking activity.

Files and Rasps

Files and rasps are used for smoothing and shaping metal and wood, for removing marks left by other tools, and for sharpening other tools. A file has a series of sharp-edged ridges, or teeth, along the faces and sides of its blade. These teeth cut away tiny chips of the material being filed. There are many sizes and shapes of file blades, including flat, three-cornered, half-round, and round. A rasp—a type of file with large teeth—is used for the coarse shaping of wood.

Drills and Braces

Drills and braces are used to make holes. The key part of a drill or brace is a **drill bit**, a sharp-tipped rod of steel that usually has a spiraling groove. Drill bits are interchangeable and come in many sizes. As the drill bit is rotated, it bores into the wood, forming a hole. The spiraling groove on the drill bit helps remove the wood chips from the hole as the bit descends into the wood. The drill bit is held in place by a mechanism called a **chuck**. Turning the chuck or the chuck screw tightens or loosens the bit, allowing it to be changed quickly.

The most common hand drill, which looks somewhat like an eggbeater, has a geared mechanism with a handle attached to it. Turning the handle of an eggbeater-gear drill moves the gears and causes the drill bit to

When the handle of an eggbeater-gear drill is turned, the gears move and make the drill bit rotate. As shown in the left corner, the bits come in various sizes.

rotate. A brace is a type of drill with a U-shaped frame and no gears. When the frame is turned by the handle in the center, the drill bit rotates. Modern braces usually have a screw-tipped bit that pulls itself into the wood as it turns and cuts the hole. Braces are used for making large holes, while hand drills are used for making smaller holes.

Wrenches come in many shapes and sizes. These very versatile tools are used to turn or hold bolts and nuts.

Screwdrivers and Wrenches

Screwdrivers, which are used to turn screws, come in many sizes and shapes. Standard screwdrivers have a flat blade that fits into a single slot in the head of a screw.

Phillips-head screwdrivers, which first appeared in the 1930's, have an X-shaped blade tip that fits into crossed slots in the head of screws. Spiral screwdrivers, which were invented in the mid-1800's, have a device that causes the blade to turn automatically when the handle is pushed down.

Wrenches are used to turn or hold bolts and nuts and sometimes pipes. Some wrenches have open ends, usually U-shaped, that slip onto the head of a nut or bolt. There are hundreds of styles and sizes of adjustable and nonadjustable wrenches. These include adjustable pipe wrenches, adjustable monkey wrenches, and adjustable and nonadjustable crescent wrenches. Box wrenches, another group, have a closed multisided opening that fits around nuts and bolts. Box wrenches come in various sizes. Socket wrenches have a ratchet handle that moves back and forth, which makes them useful for working in hard-to-reach places, and a set of interchangeable sockets of different sizes.

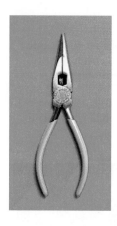
Pliers are used to hold or to bend objects. The long, thin jaws of needle-nose pliers make this tool useful for reaching into tiny spaces.

Pliers

Pliers are used for holding and, sometimes, for bending objects. The most common are standard adjustable pliers, which come in various sizes and designs. Needle-nose pliers have long, thin jaws that can reach into tiny holes. Some types of pliers have a fixed joint that allows them to open in only one position. Combination pliers have a special joint that allows the jaws to open in two or more wider positions. Locking pliers, or vise grips, have a mechanism that allows the jaw opening to be locked in position.

Measuring Tools

There are many different types of measuring tools. **Rules** are flat, straight pieces of metal or wood with number markings along the edge. Produced in many sizes and designs, some rules can be folded into sections, and others, called tape rules, can be rolled in and out of a case.

Levels are used to determine whether horizontal surfaces are level and whether vertical surfaces are plumb, or square to the Earth's surface. Generally made of wood or metal, levels contain a vial of liquid with a bubble of air trapped inside. The position of the bubble inside the vial indicates whether or not a surface is level.

Squares are used to check the straightness of an edge or to mark and check a right angle. Found in sizes ranging from 3 inches (8 centimeters) to 24 inches (61 centimeters), they have a metal blade and a wooden or metal handle perpendicular to the blade. A combination square has an adjustable sliding blade and a level that fit into the handle.

Bevel gauges are used to scribe, or mark, angles on a board. They have a steel blade that can be swiveled to any angle and then locked in place with a wingscrew—a screw with a wing-shaped head. The use of a bevel

gauge allows many boards to be cut at the same exact angle.

Dividers have a pair of straight, sharp-pointed metal legs that are hinged together at one end. These legs can be set various distances apart. Dividers are used to determine exact measurements that can then be accurately transferred somewhere else.

Calipers have two hinged, curved legs and a screw device to lock the legs in position. They are used mostly to measure round objects. The legs of the calipers are closed around an object and then removed. The distance between the tips of the legs is then measured.

A **marking gauge** has a steel point at the end of a wooden stem. The gauge can be adjusted to scribe lines on wood without the need for a ruler or pencil.

The position of the bubble inside the vial of a level indicates whether or not a horizontal surface is level or a vertical surface is plumb.

Hand Power Tools

The greatest change in hand tools in the 1900's was the development of powered hand tools. These tools, which are driven by small electric motors, are light, fast, and powerful. One of the most versatile hand power tools is the electric drill. It can be fitted not only with drill bits but also with screwdriver bits, wire brushes, grinding wheels, sanding disks, rotary rasps, and other devices. There are also power saws that can cut wood to exact dimensions and routers with bits of various shapes that are used to cut shapes or molding on wood surfaces.

▶ MACHINE TOOLS

Machine tools are large stationary devices that are designed to do much of the same type of work as hand tools. Because of their size and power, they can do a job much faster than a worker with hand tools, and the results are more consistent and precise. Machine tools can also handle much larger pieces of work, and since they can produce hundreds of identical parts, they are used for mass-production purposes.

While some machine tools are extremely large and dwarf their operators, there are a number of small machine tools that can be used in home workshops.

Two common types of hand power tools are the circular saw (*left*), which is used for cutting wood, and the electric drill (*below*), which has many uses, including sanding, drilling, and grinding.

Machine Tools for Wood

The oldest type of machine tool is the lathe, which is used for turning wood and metal to produce a round shape. The material to be turned is held on the lathe by a spindle at each end. As the lathe revolves, a cutting tool is pressed against the material to shave thin layers from it. Among the objects made on a lathe are furniture legs, baseball bats, and axles. A lathe can also be used to make open-faced objects, such as wooden bowls and dishes.

The ancient Egyptians were among the earliest people to use a crude type of lathe. This lathe was turned by hand by a worker pulling on a cord wound around the material to be cut. Another worker handled the cutting tool. Over time, lathes were improved and redesigned so that they could be operated by one person. They also became powered by water and then by electricity.

Water-powered mechanical saws for cutting logs into planks were developed in the 1400's, but they did not come into full use until the 1800's. One of the first types of mechanical saw was the circular saw, which has a thin round blade with sharp teeth. A circular saw mounted in a stationary position on a metal table is known as a table saw. The wood to be cut is pushed across the table into the saw. A radial-arm saw is similar to the table saw, except that the blade is movable rather than stationary.

Another type of mechanical saw is the band saw, so named because the blade is a long band of steel with teeth along one edge. This blade, which is connected in a closed loop, is stretched between two wheels that support and drive it as they turn. The powered jigsaw has a short thin blade that moves up and down rapidly in a vertical position.

The drill press is a power drill mounted above a metal tablelike pedestal that adjusts in height. The drill is moved up and down by

CATEGORIES OF MODERN TOOLS

Cutting Tools

Adze
Ax
Backsaw
Band saw
Chisel
Circular saw
Coping saw
Drawknife
Gouge
Hacksaw
Handsaw
Hatchet
Jigsaw
Keyhole saw
Miter saw
Radial-arm saw
Table saw

Drilling Tools

Brace
Drill press
Eggbeater-gear drill
Electric drill
Reamer
T-auger

Holding Tools

Box wrench
Combination pliers
Crescent wrench
Flat-blade screwdriver
Monkey wrench
Needle-nose pliers
Phillips-head screwdriver
Pipe wrench
Socket wrench
Spiral screwdriver
Vise grip

Measuring Tools

Bevel gauge
Caliper
Divider
Flat rule
Level
Marking gauge
Plumb bob
Square
Tape rule

Pounding Tools

Ball-peen hammer
Carver's mallet
Claw hammer
Rubber mallet
Wood mallet

Shaping and Smoothing Tools

Belt sander
Bench plane
Block plane
File
Grinder
Grooving plane
Jointer
Lathe
Miller
Planer
Rasp
Router
Shaper
Shaping plane

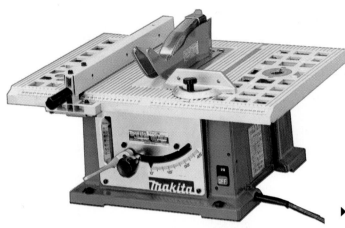

The table saw, a popular machine tool, is a circular saw that has been mounted on a metal table. The wood to be cut is pushed across the table into the saw.

a geared handle that can be adjusted so that the drill will cut into the object to the desired depth.

There are several types of power grinding and sanding machines used to smooth or polish the surfaces of wood or metal. The work is done by rapidly revolving grinding wheels or belts made of an abrasive material that has tiny, sharp grains. These act like a cutting tool to chip away the surface. Grinding machines can be fitted not only with grinding wheels but also with other types of wheels, including cloth wheels that can be used to buff, or polish, a surface.

Planers and jointers are used for smoothing flat surfaces. The wood to be worked is moved against a rotating shaving tool. Shapers and routers cut intricate shapes into wood for moldings and trims. Small routers are held in the hand and worked around the wood. Larger routers and shapers are stationary, and the work is fed into them.

Machine Tools for Metal

Machine tools for working with metal are similar to the tools used with wood, except that they are often stronger and designed so that the work will be more exact. The cutting tools of metal lathes, for example, are mounted solidly on posts rather than being held in the worker's hands. This allows the worker to make precise cuts.

Milling machines, or millers as they are called, are designed to make fine, complicated cuts in metal. For example, they are used for cutting teeth into gears, for making

spiral edges on drill bits, and for making machine parts. The cutting tool in milling machines is a rotating wheel or cylinder with many sharp teeth. The cutters come in different shapes and sizes. The vertical miller looks somewhat like a complicated drill press. Its cutting tool moves up and down, and the table that the work is mounted on can move forward and backward as well as left and right. More sophisticated millers allow the work to tilt at an angle.

▶ HISTORY OF TOOLS

Historians think people began to use sticks and stones as tools as early as 1 million years ago. These tools were used to kill animals and to dig up food. Over time, people learned that certain jobs could be done faster and better by using tools with special shapes. They learned how to chip and split stones into thin blades to use as knives and scrapers, and into sharp points to make holes in skins and wood. They used thick, sturdy stones as hammers and axes. This idea of specialization—using the right tool for a specific job—has been the basis of tool design from early to modern times.

Although people have used simple tools for hundreds of thousands of years, it was not until about 10,000 B.C. that they began to make tools similar to those we know today. Since that time, there have been several periods in which toolmaking and the use of tools have undergone important changes. The tool periods used here are broad categories. Because the development of tools usually occurred at different times at different locations around the world, the time periods noted for each category often overlap one another.

Stone Age Tool Period

Many tools were developed and used between approximately 10,000 and 4000 B.C., a time known as the Stone Age Tool Period because most of the tools were made of stone. However, stone was not the only material used for tools. Wood, bone, ivory, and shell were also used, but most tools made of these materials have decayed and disappeared with the passage of time.

Among the Stone Age tools were hammers, scrapers, drills, chisels, knives, awls, adzes, axes, and saws. The first hammers, which were simply stones that fit easily into a

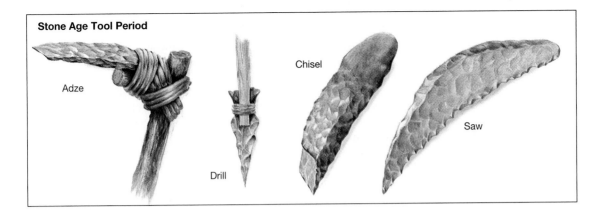

Stone Age Tool Period

Adze

Drill

Chisel

Saw

person's hands, were used mostly to break up firewood and to shape other tools. Toward the end of the Stone Age period, wooden handles were added to hammers, as well as to other tools, to make them more comfortable to work with and to allow the user to apply greater force.

Stone Age scrapers were stones chipped on one side to create a sharp edge. They were used to remove flesh from animal hides, which were then used to make clothing. Needlelike pieces of bone or antler served as awls to make holes in the hide, allowing narrow strips of hide or vines to be threaded through them to fasten the hides together.

The first drills were long pieces of stone shaped into sharp points, which were simply twisted back and forth in the hand. Later, sharp stone points were lashed to slender sticks with rawhide, and the sticks were spun between the palms of the hands.

To cut and shape wood, Stone Age people sharpened stones to create edges of various sizes and shapes. These stones were used as chisels, knives, axes, and adzes. The saw, an ingenious tool of the period, was a long, flat stone in which teeth had been chipped out. In rare cases, the saw blades were made from very sharp volcanic glass.

Copper and Bronze Age Tool Period

In the Copper and Bronze Age Tool Period, about 4000 to 1000 B.C., tools were made from copper and bronze. At the beginning of this period, people discovered how to use fire to separate copper ore from rock, leaving just the copper. By melting copper and pouring the molten metal into clay molds, people were able to create metal devices of various shapes. This discovery led to the first metal tools. About a thousand years later, it was dis-

covered that by adding tin to molten copper, a stronger, harder metal—bronze—could be formed.

The use of metals brought great changes in the design of tools and the kinds of work they could be used for. While stone tools were thick and heavy, metal tools were thinner, lighter, and easier to handle. They could also do finer, more precise work.

With the introduction of metal, many new specialized tools, including flat-bladed handsaws for cutting wood and files for shaping and smoothing wood, were produced. A type of drill known as the bow drill was also introduced during this period. It had a metal drill bit and a bow with a rawhide cord that was wrapped around the shaft that held the drill bit. When a person pushed the bow back and forth, the drill bit rotated with it.

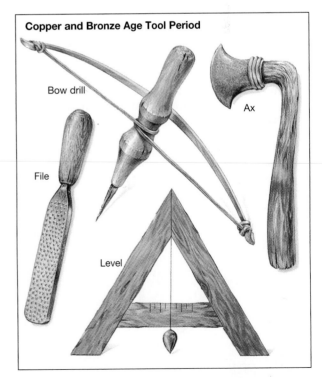

Copper and Bronze Age Tool Period

Bow drill

Ax

File

Level

One of the earliest measuring tools developed in this period was the measuring rod, a wooden rod marked off at regular intervals. Wooden and bronze rulers were used by the early Egyptians, who were also the first people to use a square to measure right angles.

To determine whether the vertical surfaces of buildings were straight and the horizontal surfaces were level, early builders used a tool called a plumb bob. This was simply a string with a weight on the end. Similar plumb bobs are still used today. The Egyptians developed an A-shaped wooden level with a plumb bob hung from the center point at the top. When the string of the plumb bob crossed the horizontal line of the A exactly at a middle mark, the surface was level.

Iron Age Tool Period

During the Iron Age Tool Period, about 1000 B.C. to the A.D. 400's, iron replaced copper and bronze as the metal for tools. Iron is very strong, and tools made from it had sharper edges and points that lasted longer, which made it easier to do precision work. Many of the tools from this period are of Roman origin, and they closely resemble a number of tools we use today. The Romans were also the first people to use iron nails.

One of the important achievements of the Iron Age was the development of the plane. Its adjustable blade could be used to make shallow or deep cuts, and its body kept the blade at the same angle and depth while cutting. The use of the plane made it possible to create tight joints between pieces of wood.

A number of other specialty tools were developed during this period. Most notable was the drawknife, a flat-bladed tool with two handles used to cut away large quantities of wood with just a few controlled strokes. The handles were at a 90-degree angle to the flat

of the blade, an awkward position that was later changed. Other innovations were the frame saw—a saw blade attached to a wooden frame that gave the user greater control of the blade—and the claw hammer, with its forked claw for pulling nails out of wood.

Medieval Tool Period

For much of the Medieval Tool Period, which lasted from about the 400's to the 1500's, tools remained very similar to those designed and used by the Romans. Only toward the end of the period, in the 1400's and 1500's, were certain adjustments introduced. At that time, for example, planes became very popular and were modified for special uses. Ax heads also were modified, becoming more flared.

A number of new boring tools—tools for making holes—were developed in the period. These included T-augers and reamers. T-augers are simply drills attached in a T shape to a handle. Reamers are similar to augers except that they have hollow, tapered blades, which are shaped like a long pointed spoon. They are used to enlarge or taper holes.

Transitional Tool Period

The Transitional Tool Period, the 1600's and 1700's, was a time when toolmaking became a separate trade and people trained for years to learn the craft of making tools. Tools were also improved and refined in order to be capable of creating the detailed architecture and ornate furniture of the time.

Among the advancements in tools during this period were modified planes that could cut grooves and joints for fitting together pieces of wood. They could also cut complex shapes used to create moldings and pieces of trim. Saw blades became thinner, allowing woodworkers to cut very thin slices of fine

Iron Age Tool Period

Drawknife

Hammer

Frame saw

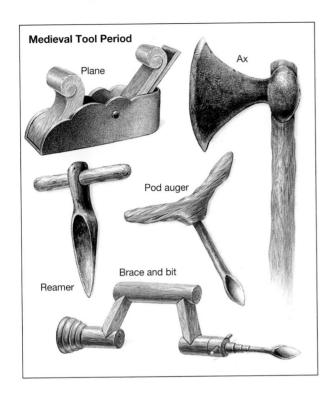

Medieval Tool Period

Plane

Ax

Pod auger

Reamer

Brace and bit

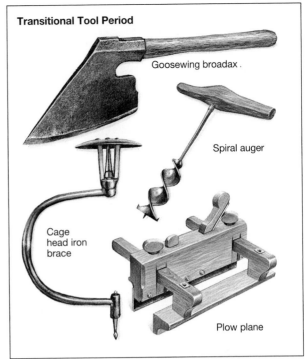

Transitional Tool Period

Goosewing broadax

Spiral auger

Cage head iron brace

Plow plane

wood, called veneer, for use on furniture. A common building tool of the period was the broadax, which has a broad blade used for shaping beams for houses and barns. Braces, as well as augers and reamers, became larger and stronger during this period.

Lathes for turning metal appeared in the 1600's and were used first by clockmakers. Metal lathes, however, were not widely used until the late 1700's. Another innovation of the period was the use of steel for making tools. Steel was used on the edges of most cutting tools, greatly improving their effectiveness because steel holds a sharp edge much longer than iron does.

Industrial Tool Period

The Industrial Tool Period, during the 1800's, marked the transition between hand-made tools produced by a single craftsworker and tools made by many workers in large shops and factories. As a result, more tools were made than ever before.

A major advancement of the period was the ability to cast, or mold, iron instead of shaping it by hand with hammers. This enabled many tools to be made completely of iron. Standardization was another important innovation. As parts such as drill bits, nuts, and bolts became standardized in size, manufac-

turers were able to interchange them, thereby reducing the number of different sizes of a tool. Specialization and assembly-line techniques made more tools more widely available.

Modern Tool Period

Many of the tools used today are not that different from those produced in the 1800's. The most significant difference has been in the development of electric power tools. However, the modern period has also seen the development of automated machines and robots, some operated by computers. In many factories, the entire production process is automated, and computer programs tell the machines exactly what to do.

Tools continue to play an important role in our lives because we depend on them to help us accomplish many important tasks. The versatility of today's tools has also enabled millions of people to do work that only skilled craftspeople could do in the past.

HERBERT P. KEAN
Author, *Collecting Antique Tools*

See also AUTOMATION; GRINDING AND POLISHING; METALS AND METALLURGY; ROBOTS; WOODWORKING.

TOOMER, JEAN. See WASHINGTON, D.C. (Famous People).

TOPEKA. See KANSAS (Cities).

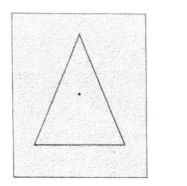
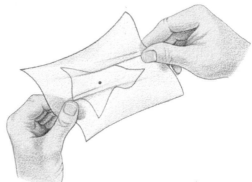

If a dot is drawn inside a triangle, the dot remains inside the triangle even if the triangle itself is forced out of shape. The location of the dot is invariant.

TOPOLOGY

Topology is a field of mathematics. It is a branch of geometry.

Topology deals with properties (characteristics) of figures, properties that do not change even though the figures themselves change. These unchanging properties are said to be **invariant**. The word "invariant" means "not changing."

It is easy to understand invariance from the illustration above. Think of a simple closed shape, such as a triangle, drawn on a thin sheet of rubber. There is a dot inside the triangle. No matter how you twist and stretch the rubber sheet, the dot always remains inside the triangle. The location of the dot, therefore, is called invariant.

Another example of invariance can be seen in the illustration below. Since the "dough-nut" is made of soft clay, you can shape it into any other figure you wish. But if you want to preserve the hole in the doughnut, then the new figure must have a hole similar to the doughnut's. For example, you can shape the doughnut so that it looks like a cup with a handle. The hole is preserved. It is invariant. The cup is said to be **topologically equivalent** to the doughnut. ("Equivalent" means "the same.")

The molding of the doughnut into a cup is called a **topological deformation**. (A deformation is a change of shape.) In a topological deformation, you can bend, squeeze, or stretch figures. But you cannot tear, cut, or join figures. For if you tear, cut, or join figures, you are making new figures. You are not deforming them.

You can shape a clay doughnut so that it looks like a cup with a handle. By preserving the hole as an invariant, the cup and doughnut are considered to be topologically equivalent.

▶THE SEVEN BRIDGES OF KÖNIGSBERG

A famous example in topology concerns seven bridges in Königsberg, Germany (now the Russian city of Kaliningrad).

Many years ago the people of Königsberg enjoyed taking Sunday strolls. They liked to walk over the seven bridges that connected the main parts of town and two islands in the Pregel River. During their strolls, some of the people used to try to cross all the bridges without crossing any one bridge twice. No one succeeded in doing it, but the townspeople were unable to prove whether the walk was possible. A map of the seven bridges appears below.

Finally, someone sent the puzzle to the famous Swiss mathematician Leonhard Euler (1707–83), who was then working in the Russian Academy in St. Petersburg. Euler proved mathematically that what the townspeople of Königsberg were trying to do was impossible. He went on to prove that the bridges cannot be crossed in a single trip if more than two of the land areas they connect—either islands or riverbanks—have an odd number of bridges leading to them.

▶EULER'S THEOREM

The map of the bridges of Königsberg has been redrawn as a **network**. In topology a network is a figure that has a definite number of lines and vertices. (The singular of "vertices" is "vertex." The points at which lines and curves meet are called vertices.)

Each line and curve in the network drawing below represents a bridge. The number of lines and curves is represented by E. The number of vertices is represented by V. The number of numbered areas is represented by F. Euler found an important relation between V, E, and F. The relation, which is called Euler's theorem, is this:

$$V + F - E = 2$$

The network has four vertices and seven lines. There are five areas, counting the area outside the figures. So we have $4 + 5 - 7 = 2$.

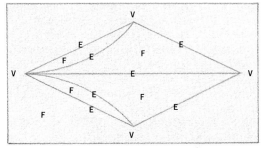

The map of the bridges of Königsberg redrawn as a network.

In Euler's theorem the "2" is an invariant for networks. The bridges form a two-dimensional network. ("Two-dimensional" means that the network lies on a two-dimensional plane. The plane has two dimensions, such as length and width.) The "2" is also invariant for certain kinds of three-dimensional networks.

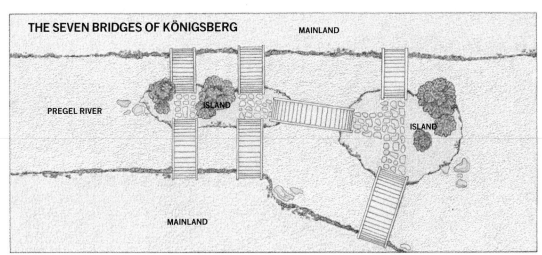

THE SEVEN BRIDGES OF KÖNIGSBERG

MAINLAND

PREGEL RIVER

ISLAND

ISLAND

MAINLAND

Leonhard Euler proved mathematically that it was impossible for the people of Königsberg to cross all of the bridges shown on this map without crossing any of them twice.

THE MÖBIUS STRIP

Another famous example in topology is the Möbius strip, named after the German mathematician August F. Möbius (1790–1868). To make a Möbius strip, take a strip of paper, give one end half a turn, and glue the ends together.

The Möbius strip has a very strange property. It seems to have two sides but actually has only one. You can see that the Möbius strip has only one side by drawing a pencil line along the side of the strip. Draw the line, without taking your pencil from the paper, until your pencil comes back to the starting point. There is a pencil line along what appears to be the second side of the strip. Yet you made this line without lifting the pencil from the paper or crossing the edge of the strip.

A Möbius strip also has only one edge. You can see this by running your finger along the edge. Do not lift your finger. When you return to the starting point, you will have touched all points along the edge.

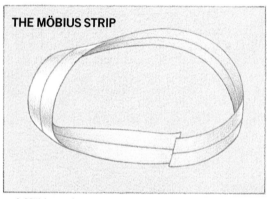

THE MÖBIUS STRIP

A Möbius strip seems to have two sides but actually has only one. You can see this by following a pencil line along the strip. It also has only one edge.

THE FOUR-COLOR MAP PROBLEM

A third example of topological study is the four-color map problem. Different colors are often used on a map so that the boundaries between states or countries will be easy to recognize. On maps where there are many countries crowded together, as in the one above, it is necessary to use several colors if there is to be a different color on each side of the boundary lines.

Mapmakers have long known that four colors are enough for even the most complicated

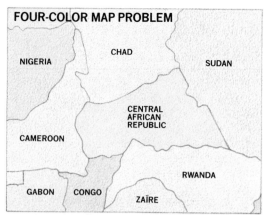

FOUR-COLOR MAP PROBLEM

NIGERIA CHAD SUDAN
CENTRAL AFRICAN REPUBLIC
CAMEROON
RWANDA
GABON CONGO ZAÏRE

In 1976, mathematicians proved that a mapmaker needs only four colors to draw a flat map on which no neighboring regions have the same color.

maps. Mathematicians tried for more than a century to prove this fact. Finally the proof was worked out in 1976, using computers to do the enormous number of calculations.

THE JORDAN THEOREM

Another important theorem is the Jordan theorem. French mathematician Camille Jordan said, in 1892, that a simple closed curve, such as a circle, on a plane (flat) surface always divides the plane into two regions as in the example drawn below. One region contains all the points inside the curve. The other region contains all the points outside the curve.

In topology the phrase "simple curve" means a curve that does not cross itself. Thus a circle is a simple curve, but a figure such as an 8 is not. A simple closed curve, however, may not always look simple to you. A topologist can include an extremely complicated,

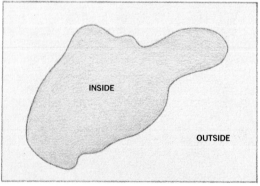

INSIDE

OUTSIDE

A simple closed curve divides a flat surface into two regions: One contains all points outside the curve, and the other contains all points inside the curve.

twisted maze in defining a simple closed curve such as the one at the left below. You can check to see if this maze is a simple closed curve by placing the tip of a pencil at any point in the curve. Mark this point and follow the curve around. If you can get back to the starting point without lifting your pencil and without crossing any parts of the curve, the curve is a simple closed one. If you cannot get back to the starting point this way, the curve is not a simple closed one.

Jordan's theorem helps make it possible to find out quickly if a particular point in the maze is inside or outside the closed curve. Simply draw a straight line from the point to any side of the maze and count the number of lines (parts of the curve) it crosses. If the number is even, the point is outside the closed curve. If the number is odd, the point is inside the curve.

How does Jordan's theorem give this result? The easiest way to understand this is to work backward from outside the maze. With a pencil make a mark at point A in the figure at the right below. The mark is outside the closed curve. Now move the pencil point toward point B until you cross a part of the curve. Since Jordan's theorem says the line separates the outside region from the inside region, the pencil must now be inside the curve. Move the pencil again until you cross another part of the curve. Now the pencil is

outside the curve again. Crossing a third part of the curve puts the pencil back inside. Therefore, if you cross an odd number of lines (parts of the curve) to get from point A to point B, point B must be inside the curve.

Jordan's theorem is true for a flat surface. The theorem, however, does not always hold for three-dimensional objects.

▶PUTTING TOPOLOGY TO WORK

Topology shows that many figures, though they seem quite different, have features in common. These features are the invariants. By using invariants, topologists can solve many problems in which they seem to have little information to go on.

Invariants are important in sciences such as astronomy and in engineering. Electrical engineers, for example, use topology in designing electrical circuits. The circuits can be thought of as networks. The wires and junctions are, topologically speaking, simply lines and vertices. Calculators, digital watches, radios, computers, and other electronic devices make use of tiny circuits.

Topology is still being applied to new areas of science and engineering. Scientists hope it will give them a new way of looking at many things in the universe.

Reviewed by MURRAY R. SPIEGEL
Rensselaer Polytechnic Institute

See also GEOMETRY; MATHEMATICS.

This figure is a simple closed curve because you can follow the curve back to a starting point without lifting your pencil or crossing a line.

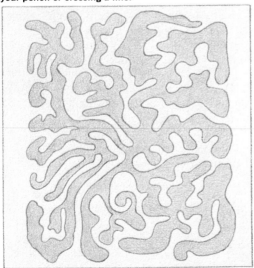

You cross an odd number (3) of lines to get from A to B and an even number (6) to get from C to D. So B is inside the curve and D is outside.

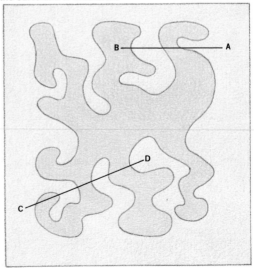

TOPS

Tops have amused both young and old for hundreds of years. For ages the spinning top has been found throughout the world, used for gaming and sport by adults and enjoyed as a toy by children.

There are many different kinds of tops. Some are plain and some are decorated with bright colors. But all of them are based on the same principle of design—a round, oval, or cone shape with a point or peg on which to spin. Most tops today are made of plastic,

There are many different kinds of tops. *Left:* This painted wooden top dates from about 1840. Above it is the separate hand grip that sets it spinning. *Below:* When this modern top spins, the little figures inside go round and round. *Bottom:* The large top on the left is a spindle top. Beneath it are two finger tops. Next are a large finger top, a string-wound top, a metal finger top, and a gyroscope top.

wood, or metal. Tops have also been made of a variety of other materials, including shells, gourds, nuts, bamboo, and stone.

Many games, requiring varying degrees of skill, use tops that are set spinning in a variety of ways. String-wound tops are twirled by a sudden pull on the string wrapped around the top. Other tops are spun by a twist of the hand or the action of an inside spring. The whipping top is turned around and around by being whipped with a lash. Holes cut into tops give them "voices" to hum or roar while they are spinning. A whistle inside a top adds music to the spinning.

No one is sure exactly when or where the top was first invented. Some historians believe the string-propelled top originated in Japan and was taken to Europe by Dutch sailors who traveled to Asia. It is known that children in England played with tops from the 1100's on. In the 1500's in England, large whipping tops were kept for adults to use in cold weather. The exertion provided a fine warming-up exercise. Humming tops were extremely popular toys in Victorian nurseries. Tops were among the earliest toys to be patented in the United States.

In Japan, *koma asobi*, top spinning, was popular among adults as well as children. About a century ago there were professional top spinners in Japan, who earned their living by performing tricks with tops. The Maori of New Zealand enjoyed a kind of spinning top called a *potaka*. Some of their tops were pointed at both ends and were made to reverse by a whip.

The gyroscope, used to help stabilize boats and ships, is based on the principle of the spinning top.

JOHN DARCY NOBLE
Curator of Toys
Museum of the City of New York

See also GYROSCOPE.

TORNADOES

A tornado is a type of violent windstorm in which a rapidly rotating column of air extends from the base of a thunderstorm to the ground. Like a hurricane, a tornado is a type of cyclone—a low-pressure area (a region in which warm, light air is rising into the atmosphere) with winds spiraling around the center.

Tornadoes can be various sizes, shapes, and colors, and they can occur in most parts of the world, except in the polar regions. Most tornadoes, however, occur in the United States, where they are sometimes called twisters. Every year, there are about 1,000 tornadoes in the United States, especially in the Midwest. Most of them occur between March and June, but they can form at any time of the year.

How Tornadoes Form

Tornadoes typically develop within a large-scale low-pressure system. Winds circling this "low" bring warm humid air from one direction and colder dry air from another direction. In the Northern Hemisphere, winds circling counterclockwise bring warm humid air from the south to the eastern side of the low and colder dry air from the north to the western side of the low. Sometimes hot and dry air enters the low-pressure system from the southwest.

As these streams of air meet, they can form thunderstorms. If the temperature conditions are just right and strong jet stream winds are blowing, massive thunderstorms that extend 50,000 feet (15,240 meters) or more into the atmosphere can develop. Under certain conditions, these massive thunderstorms develop a rotation, and smaller rotations, or tornadoes, may form within the larger rotation.

These types of conditions occur most frequently in "tornado alley," an area that runs northeastward from northern Texas into Illinois. About half of all tornadoes in the United States are reported in these eight states: Texas, Oklahoma, Arkansas, Kansas, Missouri, Nebraska, Iowa, and Illinois.

Experts think that a tornado breaks up when it becomes filled with dust and debris, as shown here. Then it begins to lose its momentum.

Characteristics of Tornadoes

Most tornadoes begin as a funnel-shaped cloud extending from the base of a thundercloud. At times, this funnel reaches the ground. At other times, it simply dangles from the base of the thundercloud. In general, if the funnel extends more than halfway down from the thundercloud, the circulating air of the tornado has already reached the ground. The only clue to its presence may be dust swirling on the ground. Tornadoes occur individually or in small groups. Sometimes outbreaks, or swarms, of many tornadoes may occur within a short period of time. For example, on April 3–4, 1974, almost 150 tornadoes were reported east of the Mississippi River, and on April 26–27, 1991, an outbreak of 54 tornadoes occurred within tornado alley.

THE FUJITA SCALE

- **F0 Light:** 40–72 mph (64–116 kph). Chimneys and windows damaged; shallow-rooted trees pushed over.
- **F1 Moderate:** 73–112 mph (117–180 kph). Surfaces peeled off roofs; mobile homes pushed off their foundations or overturned; trees snapped or broken.
- **F2 Considerable:** 113–157 mph (181–253 kph). Roofs torn off some houses; mobile homes demolished; light objects fly through the air and become dangerous missiles.
- **F3 Severe:** 158–206 mph (254–332 kph). Roofs and some walls torn off well-constructed houses; trains overturned; most trees uprooted.
- **F4 Devastating:** 207–260 mph (333–419 kph). Well-constructed houses leveled; cars thrown and demolished; trees carried away.
- **F5 Incredible:** 261–318 mph (420–512 kph). Strong frame houses carried away and demolished; automobile-sized missiles airborne for more than 300 feet; bark torn off trees; odd phenomena, such as straws pushed into trees like metal spikes.

TORNADO SAFETY RULES

- **Near a Tornado Cellar:** When time permits, go to a tornado cellar or other shelter.
- **In Open Country:** Do not try to outrun a tornado! Lie flat in the nearest depression, such as a ditch or ravine.
- **In a City or Town:** Seek shelter, preferably in a strongly reinforced building. Go to a small interior room on the lowest floor of the building. Stay away from windows!
- **In Homes:** The corner of the basement toward the tornado can offer some safety. The safest places in homes without basements are closets and bathrooms without windows. Cover yourself with a sturdy piece of furniture, a mattress, or other cushioning object. Stay low!
- **In Schools:** If a school building is strongly reinforced, stay inside and away from the windows. Go to interior rooms on the lowest floor. Avoid auditoriums, gyms, and cafeterias.
- **In Vehicles and Mobile Homes:** Get out of a vehicle or mobile home immediately and lie flat in a nearby ditch or depression. A mobile home offers little protection even if it is tied down.
- **Keep Looking and Listening:** Tornadoes sometimes develop rapidly. Remain alert for signs of an approaching tornado, such as dust swirls or a loud roaring sound. Keep tuned to a radio or television station for the latest information.
- **Keep Calm.**

These rules are based on publications from the United States Department of Commerce, the NOAA, and the Red Cross.

The rotating winds of tornadoes may range from about 40 miles (64 kilometers) per hour to more than 300 miles (480 kilometers) per hour. The extremely high winds of some tornadoes can cause enormous destruction, flattening everything in their path and tearing apart buildings with explosive force.

Most tornadoes travel along the ground in a northeasterly direction at speeds averaging about 30 miles (48 kilometers) per hour. Some may remain almost stationary for periods of time, while others race along at more than 50 miles (80 kilometers) per hour.

Tornadoes can be various colors. If they are illuminated by the sun, they appear to be white like other clouds. When filled with soil and debris, they appear to be shades of black, dark brown, gray, or even red. A fully developed tornado, with its twisting funnel and its hissing and roaring sound, is very frightening.

A tornado that forms over water is called a **waterspout**. Most waterspouts are weaker than land tornadoes, and they often form in fair weather. **Dust devils** are similar to fair-weather waterspouts except that they form over very dry ground, usually in desert areas.

Classification of Tornadoes

Tornadoes are classified according to the Fujita Scale. This scale, developed in the late 1960's by Theodore Fujita, a University of Chicago scientist, classifies tornadoes according to their wind speeds and damage. The classification also indicates the typical sizes and lifetimes for tornadoes of different strengths. For example, F0 and F1 tornadoes are the smallest. These tornadoes can vary in width from 10 feet (3 meters) to several hundred feet; they last only a few minutes and have paths only a few miles long. The largest tornadoes, classified F4 and F5, can be more than a mile wide, last up to an hour or more, and travel over paths averaging 30 to 35 miles (48 to 56 kilometers) long. The more violent and long-lived the tornado, the greater the potential for damage and loss of life.

Tornado Warnings and Protection

Meteorologists and emergency management officials have created an effective system to alert citizens to tornadoes or to the possibility that they might occur. Tornado watches indicate areas where tornadoes may form within a certain period. The watches are issued by the Storm Prediction Center in Norman, Oklahoma, which is run by the National Oceanic and Atmospheric Administration (NOAA). Using this data and other information from storm spotters and Doppler radar, local offices of the National Weather Service (NWS) issue tornado warnings for specific parts of counties or states. Warnings indicate that a tornado has formed and is moving on the ground. People in areas that receive tornado warnings should seek shelter at once and follow tornado safety rules.

H. MICHAEL MOGIL
Meteorologist, How the Weatherworks

See also HURRICANES; JET STREAMS; WEATHER; WINDS.

TORONTO

Toronto is the capital of the province of Ontario. Situated on the northwest shore of Lake Ontario, it is one of the leading ports on the St. Lawrence Seaway. The city is Canada's largest metropolis and its most important economic center. The name "Toronto," of Huron Indian origin, is usually translated "place of meeting."

▶ HISTORY

The French explorer Étienne Brûlé is thought to be the first European to visit the area, in 1615. In 1793, Upper Canada's first governor, John Graves Simcoe, founded the town of York. In 1834, York was incorporated as the city of Toronto, and William Lyon Mackenzie became the first mayor. (For more information, see the article on William Lyon Mackenzie in Volume M.)

Toronto was settled by people from Great Britain and Ireland. Since World War II (1939–45), the city has changed its staid image to that of a truly cosmopolitan and multicultural metropolis. This is due mainly to waves of immigration from various parts of the world.

More than 50 percent of Toronto's people trace their roots to countries other than Britain. Ethnic groups include Italians, Chinese, Jews, Portuguese, French, Germans, and Native Americans. A growing number of people come from the West Indies.

▶ METROPOLITAN TORONTO

In 1953 a distinctive system of municipal government was established for Toronto and the surrounding municipalities. A regional government, the Municipality of Metropolitan Toronto (commonly known as Metropolitan Toronto) includes the cities of Toronto, Scarborough, York, North York, Etobicoke, and the borough of East York. Today the city of Toronto has a population of 2.5 million, and the population of the Toronto metropolitan area is almost 5 million.

As the capital of Ontario, Toronto is the seat of provincial law and government. Its television and radio stations, newspapers, and magazines put it at the center of Canada's English-language communications.

Toronto is Canada's main financial center. Banks, insurance companies, and Canada's largest stock exchange are headquartered there. The city is also Canada's chief manufacturing center. Among the leading indus-

Toronto is the capital of the province of Ontario. The city is also home to the CN Tower, which is the tallest freestanding structure in the world.

A woman dressed in a colorful costume participates in the Caribana parade, one of Toronto's most popular summer attractions.

tries are automobile assembly and parts, food processing, chemical and oil refining, publishing and printing, and the manufacture of machinery, aircraft, and electrical and electronic equipment.

Among Toronto's educational institutions are the University of Toronto, established in 1827; York University; Ryerson University; and several community colleges.

Getting around Toronto is made easy by the Toronto Transit Commission, whose system and operation serve as a model for large cities around the world. Subway, bus, and streetcar routes provide safe, efficient, and clean transportation to all points of the city's 248 square miles (642 square kilometers).

▶ PLACES OF INTEREST

There are many places of interest in Toronto. The most visible is the CN (Canadian National) Tower, one of the tallest freestanding structures in the world. Next to it is Rogers Centre, a sports stadium with the world's first retractable roof. Exhibition Place is the site of the annual Canadian National Exhibition. Toronto's City Hall is an imposing modern structure with two semicircular towers.

Toronto offers a rich variety of museums and art galleries. The Royal Ontario Museum, one of Canada's largest, is renowned for its Chinese collection as well as for the research work sponsored by the museum at archaeological digs throughout the world. The Art Gallery of Ontario boasts the world's largest collection of works by the sculptor Henry Moore, numerous old master paintings, and a wing devoted to Canadian art.

Among other Toronto museums are the George R. Gardiner Museum of Ceramic Art, the Marine Museum of Upper Canada, the Bata Shoe Museum, and Casa Loma ("house on the hill"), a large, ornate castle that was once a residence.

Toronto's history is on display at Montgomery's Inn, Scarborough Historical Museum, Old Fort York, and other sites. At Black Creek Pioneer Village, restored buildings form a living museum of rural life in Canada before Confederation (1867).

Toronto is the home of the Canadian Opera Company and the National Ballet of Canada. The Roy Thomson Hall is a glamorous showcase for the Toronto Symphony Orchestra and for visiting international performers. Prominent theaters are the Princess of Wales Theatre, the Royal Alexandria Theatre, and the Canon Theatre.

Sports and Recreation

Professional sports are popular in Toronto. Fans support the Maple Leafs (hockey), the Argonauts (football), the Blue Jays (baseball), and the Raptors (basketball).

The city's waterfront provides many recreational opportunities, such as Harbourfront's sailing schools, theaters, and arts and crafts galleries. Ontario Place, located on a series of artificial islands in Lake Ontario, includes marinas, Adventure Island, an open-air theater, and a Cinesphere housing a six-story–high motion picture screen.

Each year in June, Toronto celebrates its diversity of nationalities during the Caravan, a two-week festival featuring arts, ethnic foods, traditional costumes, and entertainment. Another summer celebration is the Caribana, a West Indies festival with a colorful parade as its highlight.

KENNETH H. PEARSON
Editor in Chief, *Encyclopedia Canadiana*
Reviewed by JAMES T. LEMON
Professor of Geography, University of Toronto
See also ONTARIO.

TORTOISES. See TURTLES.

TOSCANINI, ARTURO (1867–1957)

Arturo Toscanini, the Italian conductor who won recognition as a great interpreter of opera and orchestral music, was born in Parma, Italy, on March 25, 1867. He studied at the Parma Conservatory and graduated with a first prize in cello in 1885.

In 1886, when Toscanini was a cellist in the orchestra of an Italian opera company performing in Rio de Janeiro, Brazil, he was called on to take over a performance of Verdi's *Aïda* from a conductor whom the audience noisily rejected. He not only conducted this performance from memory but continued as conductor of the following performances. The singers' reports of his achievements when they returned to Italy brought Toscanini occasional engagements to conduct in minor opera companies. These led to his appointment as musical director at the Teatro Regio in Turin in 1895 and at La Scala in Milan in 1898. In these theaters he conducted operas and orchestral music from many nations.

From 1908 to 1915, Toscanini conducted historic performances of opera at the Metropolitan Opera in New York City. In 1913 his performance of Beethoven's Ninth Symphony with the Metropolitan's orchestra, chorus, and solo singers was praised as having "revealed in the fullest measure the qualities of a great symphonic conductor."

After World War I, Toscanini returned to La Scala as its artistic director. In 1926 he also began to conduct the New York Philharmonic Orchestra for part of each year. Under his baton the Philharmonic's playing in Europe was considered the greatest that musicians there had ever heard.

Toscanini resigned from La Scala in 1929 but conducted opera at the Wagner Festivals in Bayreuth in 1930 and 1931 and at the Salzburg Festivals of the Vienna Philharmonic and State Opera from 1934 to 1937. In 1936 he resigned from the New York Philharmonic. From 1937 to 1954 he conducted the NBC Symphony in radio broadcasts. For years after, NBC Symphony musicians spoke of having been moved and inspired by his conducting. Toscanini died in New York City on January 16, 1957.

B. H. HAGGIN
Author, *The Toscanini Musicians Knew*

TOUCH. See BODY, HUMAN (The Nervous System).

TOULOUSE-LAUTREC, HENRI DE (1864–1901)

The French artist Henri de Toulouse-Lautrec was born in the town of Albi on November 24, 1864. He came from a noble family and grew up on one of his family's estates. His father was a great sportsman who liked riding horses and hunting falcons. But Henri was small and sickly, and took little part in the many social and sporting activities of his wealthy family. When he was 14 years old, Henri slipped and broke one of his thigh bones, and the following year, he broke the other one. Because of a bone disease, his legs never mended properly. They remained short and stumpy, while the rest of his body grew to full size. His deformed appearance affected him his whole life.

Henri had always liked to draw. After his accident he began to paint a great deal, and art became the center of his life. In 1882 he went to Paris to study. He rented a studio in Montmartre, a colorful section of the city filled with

Jane Avril is one of the many posters created by Henri de Toulouse-Lautrec to advertise the music halls and cabarets of Paris in the 1890's.

artists, musicians, dance halls, and cabarets. Among his friends were the poor entertainers who lived in the neighborhood and the very rich who went there to be entertained.

Toulouse-Lautrec was not interested in painting grandiose subjects, nor did he like to use posed models. He wanted to depict the life and the people around him. The cafés, dance halls, and theaters of Montmartre provided him with subjects for his paintings. He drew pictures of bartenders and customers, singers, dancers, clowns, and musicians. He used bright, flat colors and forceful, energetic lines to show the rhythm and excitement of Paris nightlife.

When Toulouse-Lautrec made a picture, he was not interested in putting down the small details of his subject, but rather the most important aspects. He simplified forms, intensified colors, and emphasized lines. For him, line was never simply an outline but was important in its own right. It was decorative and expressive and suggested the movement of his figures.

The bold style of Toulouse-Lautrec was especially suitable for the design and printing of posters. One of the artist's favorite cafés was the Moulin Rouge (''Red Mill''). In 1891 the owner persuaded him to design posters advertising the place. These posters were a great success, and Toulouse-Lautrec went on to create posters for other music halls and cafés.

Beginning in 1898 Toulouse-Lautrec's health began to suffer because he drank too much liquor. While being cared for in a clinic, he made a series of circus drawings from memory. After his recovery, however, he began drinking again. When he died on September 9, 1901, he was only 37 years old. He left behind a vivid picture of life in Paris in the 1890's and raised poster making to the level of art.

LYNNE PUDLES
University of California—Berkeley

TOUSSAINT L'OUVERTURE (1743–1803)

Toussaint L'Ouverture helped to bring about the liberation of Haiti, the only country in modern history born out of a slave revolt. According to legend, Toussaint was descended from an African king. But he was born a slave.

Pierre Dominique Toussaint grew up on a plantation in Saint-Domingue, the French part of the West Indian island of Hispaniola. (The rest of the island was controlled by the Spanish.) Toussaint taught himself to read and write. He also learned so much about horses that he was made the plantation's coachman, a rare position for a black slave. In 1791 he was a leader of a slave revolt against the French. Later he became known as Toussaint L'Ouverture (*l'ouverture* means ''opening''), possibly for his skill in parting and dispersing the ranks of the enemy.

The Spaniards, fighting the French for control of Hispaniola, recognized Toussaint's growing power among his people and made him a lieutenant general in their army. But they would not agree to Toussaint's lifetime dream of freedom for the slaves. When France agreed to free the slaves, Toussaint joined the French Army as a brigadier general. His military skills and cleverness helped bring about the defeat of Spanish and British forces fighting the French. And he outwitted the slave leaders, French officials, and former slaveholders who opposed him. By 1801, Toussaint had gained control of the entire island and declared himself governor general for life.

Toussaint was an excellent leader. He brought prosperity and peace to his war-torn land. Although he was a kind person, he made his people work hard so that they might remain free. But Toussaint stood in the way of Napoleon Bonaparte's colonial ambitions in the Americas. In 1802, Napoleon sent French troops to invade Saint-Domingue. After heroic resistance, Toussaint was arrested. Later he was imprisoned in France, where he died on April 7, 1803.

Toussaint L'Ouverture's cause did not die with him. Shortly after his death, his native army defeated the French. In 1804, Saint-Domingue, restored to its Indian name, Haiti, became the first independent state in Latin America.

ÉMILE SAINT-LOT
Former Haitian Ambassador to Ethiopia

See also HAITI.

Toy boats have been favorites in many times and places. These, sporting colorful sails, dot an artificial pond in Paris. Like other good toys, the boats give children simple pleasure and also help them learn about the world around them.

TOYS

A walk through any toy store shows the huge variety of toys that are available today. There are puzzles, pegboards, and colored blocks. Old-fashioned dolls in lace dresses sit next to dolls wearing the latest styles. In the next aisle are plastic figures of aliens from outer space. Shelves are stacked high with electronic games and toys that mirror all the inventions of the modern world, from submarines to spacecraft. But old favorites such as kites, wagons, and roller skates are still here, too.

A toy is an object that is intended for play. Its main purpose is to provide fun and amusement. But toys also play an important part in education. Through play, children at every stage learn about themselves and others and about how things work. They need a variety of toys that challenge them to use their minds, bodies, and feelings.

▶CHOOSING TOYS

With so many toys available, selecting the right ones can be difficult. Toy manufacturers advertise heavily, on television and elsewhere. But a toy that looks wonderful on television may not be as good as it appears. In the same way, the most expensive toys are not necessarily the best ones. Good toys allow children to use their imaginations. Even simple household objects—pots and pans and cardboard boxes —can be good toys. A plain cardboard carton can become a dollhouse, a wagon, a pirate ship, or a space station in the hands of an imaginative child.

A good toy should meet certain standards. First, it should be sturdily built of materials that will stand up under several years of hard wear. A broken toy is a disappointment. It may also be dangerous.

All toys should meet certain safety standards. In the United States, the Consumer Product Safety Commission sets standards for toys. But it tests only toys with suspected safety hazards, after they are in toy stores. Thus toys should be examined closely for features that might lead to accidents. These include sharp edges, wires, pins, and protruding nails that might cut a child, and strings, cords, or elastic that might become tangled in hair or clothing.

Take special care in choosing toys for infants and toddlers, who are apt to put their playthings in their mouth. Toys should not be so small that they could be swallowed and should be painted only with nontoxic paints. Avoid toys with small parts that could come off. Such toys are usually labeled "not for children under 2," but many children of 3 or 4 still put toys in their mouth. Balloons can present a choking hazard if they burst.

Some toys for older children may be dangerous as well. These include toys that shoot rockets or darts with force, those that use light bulbs as heating elements, and chemistry sets that require adult supervision.

▶TOYS FOR ALL AGES

Children of different ages enjoy playing with, and can learn from, different types of toys. Thus toys should be chosen with a knowledge of how children grow and develop. Toys that are too babyish or too complicated may sit on the shelf or produce more frustration than enjoyment.

Infants and Toddlers. Young babies begin to learn about the world around them through their senses. They focus on color, sound, and motion. Toys that provide these elements—crib mobiles, squeak toys, and rattles—are the ones they enjoy the most. As they become older, infants enjoy objects that they can grasp and handle: fabric and plastic blocks, boxes and containers, balls, and activity boards with doors, buttons, wheels, and knobs. Simple water toys, such as a set of plastic cups, help make bath time fun.

Once a child begins to walk, new possibilities open up. Push toys are popular with young toddlers, as are bags, boxes, and wagons that can be filled with blocks and other objects and carried about. Toddlers also enjoy soft dolls and stuffed animals, ''shape sorters'' that allow them to manipulate various shapes, and blocks for stacking and building.

Older toddlers begin to enjoy games of pretending. Toy versions of common items such as dishes and telephones help in these games. Children at this age also like to experiment with basic art materials, such as crayons. Fat crayons are easiest to hold at first, and those with flat sides are less likely to roll away.

Children enjoy different toys at different ages. Simple blocks and containers (*left*) are popular with infants. Preschoolers (*below*) enjoy working with paints. For slightly older children (*bottom left*), construction sets make good toys. They can be used to build towers, bridges, and other structures.

Dolls are classic toys that are popular with children at many ages. Younger children enjoy playing make-believe games with dolls. Many older children build collections of their favorite dolls.

Preschool Years. In the preschool years—ages 3 to 5—variety is important. The best toys are those that can be used in a number of different ways and that invite children to use their imaginations.

Preschoolers are an active group. They enjoy running, jumping, and climbing indoors and out. Climbing equipment, swings, and riding toys such as tricycles and toy trucks help them work off what may seem to be endless supplies of energy. Children at this age also love to dance, sing, and play along with music. Simple tape and record players, drums, chimes, and horns provide the means for this type of play.

Make-believe play is important for preschoolers. Toy brooms, ironing boards, and playhouses are popular. Toy trucks and cars and miniature scenes—a farm with toy animals or an airport with toy airplanes—provide other opportunities for pretending.

Boys as well as girls enjoy playing with dolls at this age. Accessories such as doll clothes, strollers, and cradles add to the fun. Plush stuffed animals are also appreciated by preschoolers. Often, a child will adopt one stuffed animal as a favorite.

As children become more skilled in manipulating objects, they enjoy solving simple jigsaw puzzles. Interlocking blocks and simple construction sets also make good toys at this point. With them, a child can build an endless variety of castles, towers, and bridges.

Preschoolers also become more interested in artwork. They enjoy working with crayons, pencils, and poster paints. As a rule, they prefer drawing freehand to coloring in the figures in coloring books. They also enjoy finger paints, modeling clay, and using blunt scissors to cut out shapes from colored paper.

Early School Years. Many toys for this age group—6 to 7 years old—are designed to help children master basic skills in reading and mathematics. Electronic toys that beep and buzz and light up when answers are given are especially appealing. However, many toys that provide drill in spelling and arithmetic are not as popular with children as they are with parents. Children in the early school years still need a variety of playthings for fun and amusement.

Bicycles, skates, scooters, and similar toys provide physical activity, as do balls, simple sports and fitness equipment (such as a jump rope or an exercise mat for tumbling), and ringtoss and similar games. The early school years are also a time when children become more curious about the world around them. Simple tools such as a magnifying glass or a pair of binoculars can help them begin to study nature. Magnets, compasses, prisms, and periscopes are fascinating. Many children this age enjoy growing plants from seed or collecting rocks or shells.

Make-believe and fantasy play are still important. In addition to dolls, props for dressing up and pretending, and miniature settings, many children enjoy figures modeled on characters from their favorite stories. Besides drawing and painting, they like to try their hand at simple woodworking projects and crafts, such as weaving and sewing. At this age, however, such projects should not be too complicated.

Middle Years. From age 8 to age 11, children gradually move from toys to real equipment. For example, they may prefer a basketball from a sporting goods store or paints from an art supply shop to toy versions of these items. However, many kinds of toys are still popular with this age group. And children in the middle years are more apt to choose their own toys than let their parents or others choose for them.

Many children become collectors—of traditional items such as coins, stamps, dolls, and animal figures or of the latest "action" figures of robots and aliens from outer space. Children at this age also enjoy staging their own theatrical productions. Magic tricks, juggling sets, costumes and makeup, and other show-business equipment are welcome. Electric trains, race cars that run on tracks, and remote-control vehicles have great appeal.

Some of the best toys in the middle years are those that allow children to create things with their hands. Jewelry-making, needlework, leather-tooling, and woodworking kits are popular. Children in this age group are also ready for more advanced art materials, such as charcoal, pastels, and calligraphy sets. They may want to take on more complicated sewing and weaving projects or put together model ships, airplanes, and spacecraft. Telescopes, microscopes, and other science equipment; more complicated puzzles; and board and word games all have growing appeal.

▶ THE HISTORY OF TOYS

Great discoveries in science and important events in history are mirrored in the world of toys. Thus toys tell the story of the growth of civilization.

Primitive people, engaged in the difficult struggle to keep alive, had little time for the art of toy making. It is likely that Stone Age children are amused by the sound of seeds rattling in a gourd. Perhaps they used small stones as toy tools in make-believe games, imitating their parents.

There is evidence that some simple toys were made thousands of years ago. Crude, flute-shaped musical instruments and balls stuffed with dried husks have been found. The children of ancient Egypt, Greece, and Rome played with more complicated toys. Archaeologists have found carvings that show children playing with clay or wooden balls and pulling simple wheeled carts. In Egypt, miniature cooking utensils and other items resem-

Many of today's toys depend on electronics. *Above:* In an updated version of an old favorite, an electric train carries a tiny camera that gives the operator a view of the track ahead. *Left:* Video games, introduced in the 1970's, now rank among the most popular toys.

Toys have changed a great deal since early times, but they have always mirrored everyday life. Mechanical toys, such as this bank (*left*), were popular in the 1800's. A toy horse from ancient Cyprus (*right*) is made of terra-cotta and is at least 3,000 years old.

bling household equipment have been unearthed. Many museums display ancient wooden dolls with movable arms and legs, animals with jaws that open and close, puppets, and tiny chariots. The Etruscans of ancient Italy made small metal soldiers more than 2,000 years ago.

Some of the miniatures of these early civilizations probably were not toys. Many were used in religious ceremonies. Others were copies of people's possessions, buried with the owners when they died. But many objects were created specifically for the enjoyment of children. Children of the ancient world tossed small bones or chips of stone in an early version of jacks or dice, games that are known in one form or another all over the world today.

In Asia the history of toys goes back at least as far as it does in the West. Some of the earliest toys known have been found in India. In China and Japan, children were flying kites thousands of years ago. And paintings show that folk toys of many kinds were common more than 700 years ago.

In medieval Europe, the toys that children played with varied according to the child's place in society. For children of poor families, peddlers sold simple folk toys. For children of noble families, skilled workers made elaborate toys—dolls with silken robes, toy soldiers with suits of armor and miniature horses, miniature weapons and furniture. Few toys from this time survive. But hobbyhorses, tops, balls, rattles, bowling pins, bubble pipes, stilts, and skates are shown in paintings or mentioned in written records.

From the late Middle Ages on, the production of toys of all kinds increased rapidly. A large toy-making center developed in southern Germany. There, all the people of the village might be engaged in making toys that would be shipped to children all over the world. The city of Nuremberg became famous for distributing the toys made in this region.

Advertisements in early New England newspapers show that toys from Europe found their way to the New World. Dolls, Noah's arks, musical instruments, forts, stables, puppets, and dollhouse furnishings were popular.

In the 1700's and 1800's, the principles of clockwork were adapted to make mechanical toys. Animated dolls and animals were produced. The new inventions of the Industrial Revolution were copied in toys that included miniature trains.

The invention of new machines made it possible to produce toys in greater variety than ever before. Toy stores opened in cities and towns everywhere. For many years the words "Made in Germany" stood for excellence in the manufacture of toys. In the early 1900's, Britain, Japan, and the United States also began to manufacture toys on a large scale. The development of new materials such as plastic further increased the variety of toys.

More recently, people have become concerned about choosing toys that have educational value. Some parents and teachers have questioned whether toy guns and other "war" toys might promote violence. However, these toys remain popular. And developments in technology, especially in electronics, have changed the world of toys. Computer games and "interactive" toys (toys that respond when the child presses a button or, in some cases, speaks) are among the latest arrivals.

Reviewed by JOANNE F. OPPENHEIM
Author, *Buy Me! Buy Me! The Bank Street Guide to Choosing Toys for Children*

See also BALL; DOLLS; TOPS.

Contests for men or women based on running, jumping for height and distance, and throwing for distance make up the sport of track and field. Competitions in track and field are called meets. The track events (those involving running) take place on an oval course, while the field events (those involving jumping and throwing) usually take place at the same time in the center of the track or nearby. Clockwise from left, the photos show the pole vault, running, the shot put, and the discus throw.

TRACK AND FIELD

Nothing is known of the first sports contest, but it might well have been a footrace. Today one person racing another is still the simplest of all sports and the most universal. Foot racing makes up more than half the events in the sport of track and field. Besides racing on a track, this sport includes hurdling and jumping, vaulting, and weight throwing on a field that the track usually surrounds.

In the beginning, primitive people had no time for sports. But they did run to catch the animals they ate or to flee their enemies. It is easy to imagine what happened when people found time for fun. One hunter, envious of the reputation of a neighbor, tried to prove he could run faster. "I'll bet that I can run to the river before you can" might have been the challenge that led to the first sports contest of any kind.

Other track-and-field events grew out of the natural activities of human beings. Throwing a spear was once the way to kill game or make war. Today it is known as the javelin throw, and its only purpose is to see who can throw the steel-tipped spear the farthest. Once people jumped over ditches or fallen trees because they had to. Now they want to see how far or how high they can jump in three of the main field events.

The shot put had its beginning in the hurling of stones as deadly weapons. Hurdling and steeplechasing, modern track events in which athletes race over a series of obstacles, are natural sports for the descendants of people who had to jump creeks, rocks, or other barriers when running away from or after their enemies.

Running, jumping, and throwing have been organized contests for nearly 3,000 years. They played a prominent part in the original Olympic Games, which were held in Greece from 776 B.C. to A.D. 394. Then, as now, the Olympic Games brought together in competition the speediest, strongest, and most skillful of all young athletes.

For a long period after the ancient Olympic Games ended, there is little record of organized track competition. But young men continued this natural activity, and by 1825 it once more was formally organized. From then on, it increased rapidly in importance.

TRACK AND FIELD TODAY

Today track and field holds a high position in the world of sports. It takes place in every part of the world and is the leading sport in the Summer Olympic Games. Men and women, boys and girls, take part, and the majority of women's track-and-field events are the same as those in the men's competition.

The main purpose of track and field rules is to make sure that all contests are fair. In its simplest form, track requires no uniform, no special playing area, and very little equipment. In highly organized competition, it requires special conditions, but neither the sport nor its surroundings are ever complex.

CLOTHING

A pair of shorts and a sleeveless shirt are the usual clothing worn while competing. Shoes are special equipment. They are as light as possible and often fitted with tiny metal or plastic spikes to provide better footing for all events except the shot put and the hammer and discus throw. These are usually thrown from a hard surface, and athletes wear shoes without spikes. Spiked shoes are not necessary for younger athletes, especially on today's tracks. A variety of running shoes that provide good traction and support are available.

THE TRACK

Running tracks are oval, consisting of two straight stretches, called straightaways, connected by two curved sections. Outdoor tracks are usually 400 meters around. Track composition varies widely. Many, especially in Australia and Britain, are grass playing fields on which the running track is outlined. The better tracks are all-weather tracks made of asphalt and rubber. They need little maintenance. Starting and finishing lines and other markers on them are painted on permanently. Older tracks still in use are made of dirt, clay, cinders, crushed brick, or other materials.

Most tracks in the United States surround football fields. The inner area is used for the field events. All-weather runways for the jumps and concrete circles for the throws are desirable, but dirt and grass are widely used.

The long jump is one of eight field events. At the 1991 World Championships, Mike Powell broke Bob Beamon's 23-year-old record for the longest jump.

In *The New Book of Knowledge*, customary, or English, measurements are generally given first, followed by their metric equivalents in parentheses. However, because the distances of track-and-field races are measured in metrics, they are given in metrics in this article. For quick reference, the following chart lists some common track-and-field distances; their customary equivalents appear in this chart rather than in the text.

60 meters = 65 yards	5,000 meters = 3.1 miles
80 meters = 90 yards	6,000 meters = 3.7 miles
100 meters = 110 yards	10,000 meters = 6.2 miles
110 meters = 120 yards	20,000 meters = 12.4 miles
150 meters = 165 yards	25,000 meters = 15.5 miles
200 meters = 220 yards	30,000 meters = 18.6 miles
300 meters = 330 yards	50,000 meters = 31 miles
400 meters = 440 yards	
800 meters = 875 yards	5 kilometers = 3.1 miles
1,000 meters = 1,095 yards	8 kilometers = 5 miles
1,500 meters = 1,640 yards	15 kilometers = 9.3 miles
1,600 meters = 1 mile	16 kilometers = 10 miles
3,000 meters = 1.9 miles	42 kilometers 195 meters =
3,200 meters = 2 miles	26 miles 385 yards

TRACK EVENTS

Learning how to perform track-and-field events varies in difficulty. In the simplest track events, the athlete has to learn to become a skilled runner. Field events are more difficult and involve a variety of skills.

Racing distances range from 100 meters to 42 kilometers 195 meters—the distance of the classic marathon race. But the marathon is run on roads, not on the track, and is not part of the usual track meet. In all important track meets, the lengths of the races are measured in meters. The lone exception is the mile run (1,609 meters).

Sprints

Any race up to 400 meters is called a sprint or a dash. In these races, runners begin from a crouched position, pushing off from two triangular starting blocks to get the fastest possible start. Sprinters go at full speed nearly all the way. They run with long strides, raise their knees high, pump their arms vigorously, and lean forward.

A good start and smoothness of style are helpful to the sprinter. But sprinting is mainly a contest of sheer speed. The best possible technique and the hardest training in the world will not enable the naturally slow runner to achieve victory over the naturally fast athlete in a sprint.

Distance Runs

Distance runs are usually regarded as races that are 3,000 meters long or longer. Here athletes depend on endurance rather than speed. They build stamina by training nearly every day of the year and running several kilometers every day. It is not unusual for a champion distance runner to run 15 kilometers or more daily.

Distance runners must learn to keep a proper pace, expending energy at a steady rate. They also need to have enough strength left at the end of the race to finish quickly in order to achieve their best time.

Middle-Distance Runs

Between the sprints and distance runs are the middle distances—800 and 1,500 meters. In many track meets, the 1-mile run, which is an especially popular event, is substituted for the 1,500-meter run.

In high school track meets, middle-distance runners often compete in the 1,600-meter run, which is slightly less than a mile. At the level of international competition—but not in the Olympics—the 1,000-meter and the 2,000-meter runs are occasionally contested.

Middle-distance races call for some of the speed of the sprints and some of the endurance of the distances. Hard training is required, and racing strategy plays a major role. In these events more than in any others in the sport, victory can be achieved by an inferior athlete who uses superior strategy.

▲ The strength and endurance needed for the 10,000-meter run shows on the face of Kenya's Moses Tanui, competing here at the 1993 world championships in Stuttgart, Germany.

▶ Correct technique is essential in the standard start for all sprint and hurdle races—On your mark (far right), set (center), go!

SPRINT

Above: Kevin Young of the United States, a world champion in the 400-meter hurdles, shows the running and jumping skills needed for this event. *Right:* Hurdle races call for exact technique as well as speed. A good hurdler jumps over the hurdle straight on, maintaining speed and balance by thrusting one arm forward toward the lead leg.

HURDLE

Hurdle Races

The hurdle races, events in which runners must jump over obstacles called hurdles, call for a combination of speed and skill. Women run the 100-meter and the 400-meter hurdles. Men run the 110-meter and the 400-meter hurdles. Each race has a series of ten hurdles that are evenly spaced along its course. The hurdler must learn to clear each obstacle with the same number of steps or strides in between jumps. In the women's 100-meter hurdle race, the barriers are 84 centimeters (2 feet 9 inches) high, and in the women's 400-meter event, they are 76 centimeters (2 feet 6 inches) high. In the men's 110-meter race, the hurdles are 1.07 meters (3 feet 6 inches) high, and in the men's 400-meter event, they are 91 centimeters (3 feet) high.

Steeplechases

Historically, steeplechasing has been limited to men, but women are now trying it. The athlete runs 3,000 meters and jumps 35 hurdles. There are seven water jumps, in which a firmly anchored barrier is followed by a pool of water 3.6 meters (12 feet) long.

Relay Races

Relay races are among the most exciting events at track meets. They are the only team sport in track. Four people form a team, each running in turn and passing a stick called a baton from one to the next. Relays are run at various distances, but the most common are the 400-meter relay, in which each athlete runs 100 meters, and the 1,600-meter relay, in which each athlete runs 400 meters.

Cross-country and Road Racing

Cross-country running and road racing are two other areas of the sport. These two areas, however, do not actually take place on an oval track.

Most cross-country races cover from 5 to 16 kilometers. Road racers cover from 5 kilometers to the full marathon distance and even farther.

▶ WALKING EVENTS

In the walking races, the athlete must have at least one foot on the ground at all times. While the foot is on the ground, the leg must be straight. If both feet are in the air at the same time, the athlete is really running, and he or she will be disqualified from the race.

Walking races usually leave the track and follow streets and roads near the stadium. Judges are positioned along the route to make sure the racers do not break form. Men's races cover distances from 10,000 to 50,000 meters. Women's races range from 5,000 to 10,000 meters.

▶ JUMPING EVENTS

There are eight field events. Not all of them are always on the schedules of track meets, especially in competition among schools. Four

High jumper Javier Sotomayer of Cuba, an Olympic gold medalist and world record holder, demonstrates the grace and control needed to clear the crossbar.

are jumping events, and four are throwing. All eight require a combination of strength and skill, and each has its own requirements.

High Jumping

The object in high jumping is to see how high an athlete can jump over a thin metal stick called a crossbar. This crossbar is set atop two standards (supports), and the jumper attempts to jump over the bar without knocking it down. After each successful jump, the height of the bar is increased by 2.5 or 5

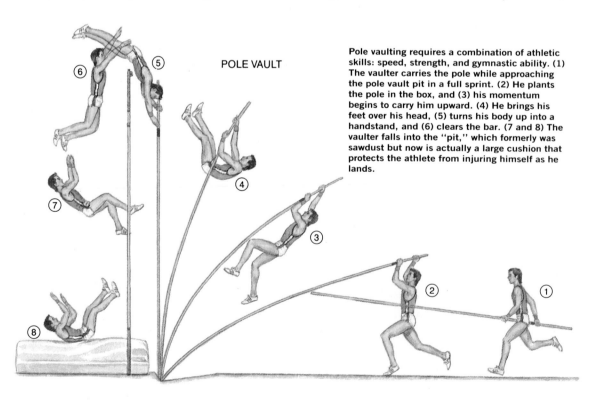

POLE VAULT

Pole vaulting requires a combination of athletic skills: speed, strength, and gymnastic ability. (1) The vaulter carries the pole while approaching the pole vault pit in a full sprint. (2) He plants the pole in the box, and (3) his momentum begins to carry him upward. (4) He brings his feet over his head, (5) turns his body up into a handstand, and (6) clears the bar. (7 and 8) The vaulter falls into the "pit," which formerly was sawdust but now is actually a large cushion that protects the athlete from injuring himself as he lands.

centimeters (1 or 2 inches). A jumper is eliminated after three straight misses. Whoever has cleared the greatest height wins.

Pole Vault

The pole-vaulter's aim, also, is to go as high as possible over a crossbar. But the vaulter is aided by a long, thin pole. Generally made of fiberglass, the vaulting pole may be up to 5.5 meters (18 feet) long, but usually it is shorter, depending on the strength and size of the athlete. Vaulters have soared to over 6.15 meters (20 feet 2 inches). The vaulter grips the pole near one end, sprints about 35 meters (40 yards), and jams the pole into a small box set into the ground. The end of the pole swings the athlete high into the air. The vaulter performs a series of difficult gymnastic movements to achieve the proper position at the greatest possible height. At the peak of the vault the athlete, arched over the bar, releases the pole and prepares to drop into a cushioned landing area.

Long Jump

Long jumping is one of the simplest of the field events. The jumper sprints along a smooth runway and jumps as far as possible into a sandpit. The jumper must take off from behind the front edge of a board 20 centimeters (8 inches) wide, and the jump is measured from the board to the landing place.

Triple Jump

The triple jump uses the same pit and runway as the long jump, but the takeoff board is farther away from the pit. The athlete jumps from one foot and lands on the same foot, then continues forward, landing on the other foot. Finally, in the third part of the movement, the jumper leaps forward and lands on both feet. The distance is measured from the takeoff board to the jumper's landing point.

▶ THROWING EVENTS

There are four throwing events, in which the athlete throws an implement as far as possible. The javelin is thrown from behind a line after a short run. The shot and the hammer are thrown from within a circle having a diameter of 2.14 meters (7 feet). The discus is thrown from within a circle having a diameter of 2.5 meters (8 feet 2½ inches).

Javelin Throw

The javelin is a slim wooden or metal spear. The men's javelin must be at least 2.6 meters (8 feet 6⅜ inches) long and must weigh at least 800 grams (28¼ ounces). The women's javelin must be at least 2.2 meters (7 feet 2⅝ inches) long and must weigh at least 600 grams (1 pound 5¼ ounces). A new rule requires the men's javelin to stick in the ground, resulting in shorter throws than under the old rules.

The javelin throw requires speed, strength, and coordination. The athlete runs through a short sprint, reaches top speed, and throws the javelin before crossing a "foul line." All throws are measured from the line.

The discus throw (*right*) and the shot put (*far right*) require explosive speed and strength. A discus thrower spins to gather momentum and then throws the discus with a sidearm motion. A shot putter holds the shot against the neck, moves quickly across a small circle, and then pushes, or "puts," the shot as far as possible.

Shot Put

The shot is a metal ball that weighs between 3.63 and 7.26 kilograms (8 and 16 pounds). The size used depends on the age and sex of the user. Women use a shot weighing 4 kilograms (8 pounds 13 ounces). Men use a 7.26-kilogram shot. It is not thrown but is pushed straight out from a position between chin and shoulder.

Discus Throw

Discus throwing is the oldest of the throwing events and was a classic contest in the first Olympic Games in ancient Greece. The discus is shaped like a pie that is thickened in the middle and sloped toward the narrow rim. The men's discus weighs about 2 kilograms (4 pounds 6 ounces) and is about 22 centimeters (8⅝ inches) in diameter. The women's discus weighs about 1 kilogram (2 pounds 3 ounces) and is about 18 centimeters (7 inches) in diameter. The thrower spins around one and a half times to gain momentum and releases the discus at arm's length with a sweeping, sidearm motion.

Hammer Throw

The hammer throw is perhaps the most spectacular throwing event. The hammer consists of a metal ball attached to one end of a chain that is about 1.2 meters (3 feet 11 inches) long. The men's hammer weighs 7.26

kilograms (16 pounds), and the women's weighs 4 kilograms (8 pounds 13 ounces). The thrower grips a handle at the other end of the chain, twirls the ball and chain around the head, spins rapidly in the circle, and throws.

▶ DECATHLON AND HEPTATHLON

The most unusual of all events is the decathlon, which is actually ten events combined in one. Competitors take part in five events on each of two successive days. On the first day, they do the 110-meter dash, the long jump, the shot put, the high jump, and the 400-meter dash, in that order. On the second day, they do the 110-meter hurdles, the discus throw, the pole vault, the javelin throw, and the 1,500-meter run, in that order. Points are awarded to each athlete according to how well the athlete performs in each event. The contestant with the highest total for the ten events is the winner.

Women take part in a heptathlon, a series of seven events—100-meter hurdles, shot put, high jump, and 200-meter dash on the first day; long jump, javelin throw, and 800-meter run on the second day.

▶ INDOOR TRACK AND FIELD

During the winter, athletes prepare for the outdoor track-and-field season by competing in indoor meets. For some, these meets are just as important as the outdoor ones.

GREAT ATHLETES IN THE HISTORY OF TRACK AND FIELD

The National Track and Field Hall of Fame honors great American athletes in all track and field events. Originally located in Charleston, West Virginia, it is now located in New York City. A few of the best American and international athletes in track-and-field history are profiled here. Biographies of Hall of Famers Jesse Owens and Jim Thorpe are in volumes O and T.

BOB BEAMON (1946–) shattered the long-jump record at the 1968 Olympics when he jumped 29 feet 2½ inches (8.9 meters), setting a record that lasted until 1991. Prior to that Olympics, the American had won 22 out of 23 meets, despite going months without coaching. He was elected to the Hall of Fame in 1977.

SERGEI BUBKA (1963–) set his first world pole-vaulting record in 1983, then established himself as one of the best vaulters by breaking his own records 8 times over the next 5 years and winning the gold medal at the 1988 Olympics. The Ukrainian broke world indoor and outdoor pole-vaulting records 35 times, being the first to clear the barrier at 19 feet 8 inches (6.0 meters) and then at 20 feet (6.1 meters).

SEBASTIAN COE (1956–) set a record in 1979 when he won the 800-meter event in 1 minute 42.33 seconds. Two weeks later, he broke the record for the mile and helped forge the British domination of middle-distance running in the early 1980's. At both the 1980 and 1984 Olympics, he won gold medals in the 1,500 meters (the first athlete to win that event twice) and silvers in the 1,800 meters.

JACKIE JOYNER-KERSEE (1962–) set an American pentathlon record of 6,520 points in the 1984 Olympic trials and won a silver medal at that Olympics. In 1986, she became the first American to hold the pentathlon world record by scoring 7,148 points at the Goodwill Games in Moscow, and at the 1988 Olympics she won gold medals in the long jump and the

BOB BEAMON

SERGEI BUBKA

SEBASTIAN COE

JACKIE JOYNER-KERSEE

MARITA KOCH

CARL LEWIS

NOUREDDINE MORCELI

heptathlon. At the 1992 Olympics, she again won the heptathlon and took the bronze in the long jump, then won a bronze in this event at the 1996 Olympics as well. She was the first woman to win multi-event titles at two Olympics and the first athlete, male or female, to win multi-event medals in three Olympics. In 1986, she received the Sullivan award.

MARITA KOCH (1957–) won the gold medal in the 400-meter event at the 1980 Olympics, also winning the silver medal in the 1,600-meter relay. At the World Cup in 1985, the German ran the 400 meters in 47.60 seconds, a record that still stands. During her career, Koch broke 11 world records in the 200-meter and 400-meter events and achieved 5 relay records.

CARL LEWIS (1961–) duplicated Jesse Owens' 1936 Olympics feat by winning 4 gold medals in the same 4 events, the 100 and 200 meters, the long jump, and the 4 x 100-meter relay, at the 1984 Olympic Games. In 1986, the American won national titles in the 100 meters and the long jump, also winning the long jump at the 1987 World Cup. At the 1988 Olympics, Lewis won 2 gold medals, in the 100 meters and the long jump, and a silver medal in the 200 meters. He won 2 more golds for the long jump and the 4 x 100-meter relay at the 1992 Olympics. At his last Olympics, in 1996, Lewis won a 9th gold medal by winning the long jump again. He won the Sullivan award in 1981 and was elected into the Hall of Fame in 2001.

NOUREDDINE MORCELI (1970–) set many world records in middle-distance running in the 1990's, including, in 1993, running the mile in 3 minutes 44.39 seconds. The Algerian runner won most of the events he entered, including the 1,500-meter run at the 1996 Olympics. He was also world champion in the 1,500-meter event three times (1991, 1993, 1995).

EDWIN MOSES (1955–) won a gold medal for the 400-meter hurdles in a record 47.64

JAMES E. SULLIVAN MEMORIAL TROPHY, awarded annually by the Amateur Athletic Union (AAU) to the outstanding amateur athlete in the United States.

seconds at the 1976 Olympics. Undefeated for the next 10 years, he won 107 consecutive hurdle finals, including the event at the 1984 Olympics. By then, the 48-second barrier had been broken 32 times, and Moses had done it 27 times. He had the 9 fastest clockings, and a world record of 47.02 seconds in August 1983. In his final race, the American won a bronze at the 1988 Olympics. Moses received the Sullivan award in 1983, and he was elected to the Hall of Fame in 1994.

PAAVO NURMI (1897–1973) won a total of 12 Olympic medals, including 9 golds and 3 silvers, from 1920 to 1928. He received 3 golds for the 10,000-meter, the individual cross-country, and the team cross-country events, and a silver in the 5,000 meters at the 1920 Olympics. In 1924, the Finnish runner won the 1,500-meter and 5,000-meter events within the space of one hour. His 5 golds that year were a record for a track-and-field athlete. At the 1928 Olympics, he won gold in the 10,000 meters and silver in the 5,000 meters and the 3,000-meter steeplechase.

AL OERTER (1936–) won gold medals for the discus throw in 4 straight Olympics, beginning in 1956. The American's most surprising Olympic victory came in 1964, when he achieved a then career-best discus throw in spite of a painful rib injury. Oerter was the first to throw the discus past 200 feet (61 meters), and he broke the world record 4 times. He made his longest throw in 1980 when he returned to competition after 8 years of retirement. He was elected to the Hall of Fame in 1974.

WILMA RUDOLPH (1940–94) overcame childhood polio to become the U.S. hero of the 1960 Olympics. At the trials, she set world records in the 200-meter event and in a preliminary 100-meter heat. At the Games, she won gold medals in both the 100-meter and 200-meter events and was also a member of the winning 4 x 100-meter relay team. During her career, she won 4 national 100-meter titles, and she won

EDWIN MOSES

PAAVO NURMI

AL OERTER

WILMA RUDOLPH

JIM RYUN

GRETE WAITZ

CORNELIUS WARMERDAM

EMIL ZATOPEK

the indoor 60-meter sprint 3 times. She received the Sullivan award in 1961 and was elected to the Hall of Fame in 1974.

JIM RYUN (1947–) was the first American to break the 4-minute mile while in high school. In 1966, he set world records in the 880-yard run, the 1,500-meter event, and the mile, and in 1967 he lowered the mile to 3 minutes 51.1 seconds, a record that stood for more than 5 years. At the 1968 Olympics he won a silver medal in the 1,500-meter event. Ryun received the Sullivan award in 1966 and was elected to the Hall of Fame in 1980.

GRETE WAITZ (1953–) won the 3,000-meter event at the 1977 World Cup. But she is most famous for setting a world record in her first attempt at the New York City Marathon, in 1978, then winning the women's division a total of 8 more times between 1979 and 1988. The Norwegian runner won the marathon at the 1983 World Cup and the silver medal in 1994 at the first Olympic marathon for women. During her career, she set 4 world marathon records as well as world records in the 3,000-meter and 5,000-meter events.

CORNELIUS WARMERDAM (1915–2001) dominated the pole vault event in the 1940's. He was the first person to clear 15 feet (4.5 meters), and he vaulted 43 times over the barrier at a time when no other athlete could clear it once. His outdoor world record of 15 feet 7.75 inches (4.77 meters) lasted for 15 years. The American pole-vaulter received the Sullivan award in 1942 and was elected to the Hall of Fame in 1974.

EMIL ZATOPEK (1922–2000) won his first Olympic gold medal in 1948 for the 10,000-meter event. At the 1952 Olympics, he won all three long-distance races—the 5,000-meter and 10,000-meter runs and the marathon. The marathon was a special achievement since he had never run that distance before. During his career, the Czech runner set a total of 18 world records.

Indoor tracks normally range in length from 150 to 200 meters, although a few are 300 meters or longer. For a running time to be considered a world record, it must occur on a track that is less than 201 meters.

Indoor tracks are frequently banked, meaning they are higher on the outside than they are on the inside. This helps runners maintain their stride and keeps them from running off the track, especially on the tight turns. The tracks are traditionally made of wood, although special coatings may also be used to improve the running surface.

As in outdoor meets, most indoor races are run in meters, again with the exception of the mile run. Because indoor tracks have limited space, some events are held that are different from those held outdoors. For example, the 60-meter dash and the 60-meter hurdles are run indoors, but they are rarely, if ever, run outdoors. And it would be unthinkable to hold the discus or javelin throws in small indoor arenas because spectators could very easily be injured.

▶ **TRACK AND FIELD FOR BOYS AND GIRLS**

Most young people who take part in track and field are members of school teams. In some communities, track clubs with volunteer coaches are also available—much like in Little League Baseball. Usually, anyone who is interested in track and field may join. Young people who are not especially fast runners are often encouraged to join, because even slow running is an excellent means of conditioning and strengthening the body. A young athlete with sufficient body weight may wish to attempt the weight throws.

Young people compete in events that are similar to those in which world-class athletes

TRACK-AND-FIELD WORLD RECORDS*

OUTDOOR

Event	Men's Record	Women's Record	Event	Men's Record	Women's Record
RUNNING			**HURDLES**		
100 meters	9.77 sec.	10.49 sec.	100 meters	–	12.21 sec.
200 meters	19.32 sec.	21.34 sec.	110 meters	12.91 sec.	–
400 meters	43.18 sec.	47.60 sec.	400 meters	46.78 sec.	52.34 sec.
800 meters	1 min. 41.11 sec.	1 min. 53.28 sec.			
1,000 meters	2 min. 11.96 sec.	2 min. 28.98 sec.	**FIELD EVENTS**		
1,500 meters	3 min. 26.00 sec.	3 min. 50.46 sec.	High Jump	8 ft ½ in (2.45 m)	6 ft 10¼ in (2.09 m)
1 mile	3 min. 43.13 sec.	4 min. 12.56 sec.	Long Jump	29 ft 4½ in (8.95 m)	24 ft 8¼ in (7.52 m)
3,000 meters	7 min. 20.67 sec.	8 min. 6.11 sec.	Triple Jump	60 ft ¼ in (18.29 m)	50 ft 10¼ in (15.50 m)
3,000-meter			Pole Vault	20 ft 1¾ in (6.14 m)	15 ft 9½ in (4.81 m)
steeplechase	7 min. 53.63 sec.	9 min. 01.59 sec.	Shot Put	75 ft 10¼ in (23.12 m)	74 ft 3 in (22.63 m)
5,000 meters	12 min. 37.55 sec.	14 min. 24.68 sec.	Discus Throw	243 ft 0 in (74.08 m)	252 ft 0 in (76.8 m)
10,000 meters	26 min. 17.53 sec.	29 min. 31.78 sec.	Hammer Throw	284 ft 7 in (86.74 m)	249 ft 7 in (76.07 m)
20,000 meters	56 min. 55.6 sec.	1 hr. 5 min. 26.6 sec.	Javelin Throw	323 ft 1 in (98.48 m)	234 ft 8⅖ in (71.54 m)
Marathon	2 hr. 4 min. 55 sec.	2 hr. 15 min. 25 sec.	Decathlon	9,026 pts.	8,358 pts.
			Heptathlon	–	7,291 pts.
RELAYS			**WALKING**		
400 meters	37.40 sec.	41.37 sec.	5,000 meters	–	20 min. 02.60 sec.
800 meters	1 min. 18.68 sec.	1 min. 27.46 sec.	10,000 meters	–	41 min. 56.23 sec.
1,600 meters	2 min. 54.20 sec.	3 min. 15.17 sec.	20,000 meters	1 hr. 17 min. 25.6 sec.	1 hr. 26 min. 52.3 sec.
3,200 meters	7 min. 3.89 sec.	7 min. 50.17 sec.	30,000 meters	2 hr. 1 min. 44.1 sec.	–
6,000 meters	14 min. 38.8 sec.	–	50,000 meters	3 hr. 40 min. 57.9 sec.	–

INDOOR

Event	Men's Record	Women's Record	Event	Men's Record	Women's Record
RUNNING			**HURDLES**		
50 meters	5.56 sec.	5.96 sec.	50 meters	6.25 sec.	6.58 sec.
60 meters	6.39 sec.	6.92 sec.	60 meters	7.30 sec.	7.69 sec.
200 meters	19.92 sec.	21.87 sec.			
400 meters	44.57 sec.	49.59 sec.	**FIELD EVENTS**		
800 meters	1 min. 42.67 sec.	1 min. 55.82 sec.	High Jump	7 ft 11½ in (2.43 m)	6 ft 9½ in (2.07 m)
1,000 meters	2 min. 14.96 sec.	2 min. 30.94 sec.	Long Jump	28 ft 10½ in (8.79 m)	24 ft 2¼ in (7.37 m)
1,500 meters	3 min. 31.18 sec.	3 min. 59.98 sec.	Triple Jump	58 ft 6 in (17.83 m)	50 ft 4⅘ in (15.36 m)
1 mile	3 min. 48.45 sec.	4 min. 17.14 sec.	Pole Vault	20 ft 2 in (6.15 m)	16 ft 1 in (4.90 m)
3,000 meters	7 min. 24.90 sec.	8 min. 29.15 sec.	Shot Put	74 ft 4¼ in (22.66 m)	73 ft 10 in (22.5 m)
5,000 meters	12 min. 49.60 sec.	14 min. 32.93 sec.	Heptathlon	6,476 pts.	–
			Pentathlon	–	4,991 pts.
RELAYS					
800 meters	1 min. 22.11 sec.	1 min. 32.41 sec.			
1,600 meters	3 min. 2.83 sec.	3 min. 23.88 sec.			
3,200 meters	7 min. 13.94 sec.	8 min. 18.71 sec.			

*Records as of 2005, recognized by the International Association of Athletics Federations (I.A.A.F.).

compete. But the events have been modified according to the age, size, and strength of these competitors. For example, high school varsity athletes compete in most of the track-and-field events except the hammer throw. The boys throw a lighter discus and shot than men do. They run a 300-meter hurdles race instead of 400 meters. And their distance runs usually do not exceed 3,200 meters.

If you wish to improve as a track-and-field athlete, it is important to have a good coach. At school, the physical education teacher who coaches the sport has probably been a track-and-field athlete. A young person who is a fast runner will find that with proper coaching, he or she will become even faster. Athletes in the field events, especially, require good coaching so that they may learn the proper techniques.

▶MODERN HISTORY OF TRACK AND FIELD

Throughout the 1900's, track and field has held a special fascination for many people because the sport is a measure of what a well-trained athlete can accomplish. In most track-and-field events, today's world records are marks that would have seemed utterly impossible to attain 50 years ago. For example, it was once believed that a human being could never run one mile in less than 4 minutes. But in a mile race in 1954, Roger Bannister of Britain set a world record of 3 minutes, 59.4 seconds, besting the old mark by 2 full seconds. The 4-minute ''barrier'' had been broken, and within a short span of years, many more runners, even some teenagers, were running a mile in less than 4 minutes. By

the early 1990's, the world record was under 3 minutes, 45 seconds, and no one seemed quite sure how fast the best milers would eventually run.

Similarly, a 7-foot-high jump was once considered a nearly impossible accomplishment for even the best male athletes. But in 1989 Javier Sotomayer of Cuba jumped 8 feet, and the women's world record has soared to nearly 7 feet. Superior training techniques, a greater knowledge of nutrition, and increased understanding of human physiology have contributed to the performance of track-and-field athletes.

Every year many important track meets take place, and over the course of a season, several new world records are usually set. A particularly significant track meet is the world championships of track and field, which takes place every two years. A gold medal—first place—in the world championships is a great prize, but the goal most desired by any track-and-field athlete is a victory in the Olympic Games, which take place in the year following the world championships.

Most of the sport's legendary heroes have been Olympic champions. Paavo Nurmi of

Track and field's legendary champions include Jesse Owens (*left*), the American sprinter and long jumper who won four gold medals in the 1936 Olympics, and Roger Bannister of Britain (*right*), who was the first runner in history to run a mile in less than 4 minutes.

Bob Mathias won four U.S. National Decathlon titles (1948–50, 1952) and was the first to capture Olympic gold in the decathlon twice in a row (1948, 1952).

Finland won nine gold medals in distance races in the 1920, 1924, and 1928 Olympic Games. In 1932, Mildred (Babe) Didrikson of the United States won the 80-meter hurdles and the javelin throw, setting world records in each. Four years later, Jesse Owens of the United States won four gold medals, a feat equaled by another American, Carl Lewis, in 1984 in the same events: the 100- and 200-meter dashes, 400-meter relay, and long jump. In 1948, Fanny Blankers-Koen of the Netherlands also won four gold medals in one Olympics: She won the 100- and 200-meter dashes and the 80-meter hurdles, and she anchored the winning 400-meter relay team. (In a relay race, the "anchor," or last runner, is usually the team's fastest athlete.) In 1948 and 1952, Bob Mathias of the United States won the decathlon. He was the first man to win the Olympic decathlon twice.

Other Olympic achievements include Czech runner Emil Zatopek's three gold medals in the 5,000 meters, 10,000 meters, and the marathon in 1952, a feat never duplicated; American Bob Beamon's 29-foot 2½-inch long jump in 1968; American Al Oerter's four consecutive gold medals in the discus throw (1956–68); the three consecutive victories of Viktor Saneyev of the former Soviet Union in the triple jump (1968–76); American Florence Griffith Joyner's three gold medals in the 100 meters, the 200 meters, and the 4 x 100-meter relay (1988); Carl Lewis' nine gold medals (1984–96), matching Paavo Nurmi's nine; and American Michael Johnson's two gold medals in the 200 meters and the 400 meters, making him the first man in Olympic history to win both events (1996).

Many outstanding performances have been set in non-Olympic meets. Eamonn Coghlan of Ireland was the first person to run under 3 minutes, 50 seconds for an indoor mile (1983). Florence Griffith Joyner was the first woman to sprint 100 meters faster than 10.70 seconds with her 10.49-second race in 1988. In 1991, Mike Powell of the United States broke Beamon's long jump mark with a leap of 29 feet 4½ inches. Yobes Ondieki of Kenya became the first to run 10,000 meters under 27 minutes with his time of 26 minutes, 58.38 seconds in 1993.

In 1993, Chinese women smashed many of the world records in distance races amid some controversy about their performances.

In 1995, Moses Kiptanui of Kenya became the first man to run the steeplechase in less than 8 minutes. Great Britain's Jonathan Edwards broke the 60-foot barrier in the triple jump at the same meet.

In the late 1990's and early 2000's, records continued to be broken as new stars emerged in the sport. Among the top athletes were Stacy Dragila (pole vault), Michael Johnson (200- and 400-meter, 4 x 400-meter relay), and Maurice Greene (50-, 60-, 100-, 200-, and 2,000-meter) of the United States; Hicham El Guerrouj (1,500- and 2,000-meter, mile) of Morocco; Cathy Freeman (100-, 200-, 400-meter) of Australia; and Gabriela Szabo (3,000-, 5,000-meter) of Romania.

JEFF HOLLOBAUGH
Editor, *Do It Sports*

TRACY, SPENCER. See WISCONSIN (Famous People).

TRADE, INTERNATIONAL. See INTERNATIONAL TRADE.

TRADE AND COMMERCE

A boy or girl offering to give a friend several small marbles in exchange for one shooter is making a bid to trade. The person making the bid is willing to give up several marbles to gain one because the shooting marble is worth more to him or her than the small marbles. The friend may have other shooters but may be running low on small marbles. If the bid is accepted, the trade is made, and both are satisfied. This is a simple form of trading called **bartering**. But it follows the pattern of all trading.

The exchange of goods and services to satisfy the needs of consumers is known as trade or commerce. "Trade" usually refers to the exchange of a particular product. For instance, people often say that a country's main trade is in coffee or tea or sugar. The word "commerce" covers all aspects of trading. In many countries there is a department of government that is responsible for seeing that trade goes smoothly.

▶ HISTORY OF TRADE AND COMMERCE

Trade began with the first exchange of goods by primitive people. At first they literally bartered grain for cloth, cloth for a knife, and so on. But bartering was not practical because traders could not always find other traders with exactly the kind of goods they wanted. People began to exchange their goods for money, which they could use, in turn to buy what they needed.

For thousands of years trading caravans or fleets of ships set out from one city and traveled to another to exchange goods. Most of the trade with other countries was in luxuries. At the height of the Roman Empire the market stalls at Rome were filled with goods from distant colonies. A wealthy Roman could buy spices, silks, and precious stones from Egypt, marble from Greece, ivory from Africa, amber from Germany, and tin from Britain. These goods commanded a high price.

With the fall of the Roman Empire, trading declined, and the people of Europe relied mainly on what they could produce at home or obtain by bartering with their neighbors. But the Crusades in the 11th, 12th, and 13th centuries introduced western Europe once again to the luxuries of the East.

The New World was discovered by European vessels looking for a sea passage to the East. Ships could sail more quickly and handle larger cargoes than the slow-moving camel caravans that followed overland trails across Asia. The discoveries of America and the sea route around Africa's Cape of Good Hope increased the possibilities of trade beyond all imagination. Different countries fought to gain control of the lands, and many people left England and Europe to set up plantations of sugar, tea, tobacco, or coffee in the New World and the Far East. But in spite of the hustle and bustle of the trading ports, vessels still carried mainly luxury goods until the end of the 18th century.

Two developments in the 19th century brought a revolution in trading systems across the world. One was the development of railroads and steamships, which could carry goods rapidly from one place to another. The second was the perfection of heavy machinery, which could produce goods cheaply and quickly. Large factories were set up. Soon it was cheaper for goods to be manufactured by one factory and shipped to different localities than for each locality to take care of all its needs itself. Different regions came to specialize in producing different kinds of goods. Our modern system of trade and commerce is based on this specialization.

▶ TRADE AND COMMERCE TODAY

Specialization is the best way of using our **productive factors:** natural resources, capital goods, and labor. Natural resources include forests, good farming land, coal, gas, or any material that is in the earth and can be turned to the use of people. Capital goods are the factories, machinery, and tools that are used to manufacture finished goods from natural resources. The term "labor" refers to the people behind the machinery. It includes the workers who invent new products and new methods of production, workers who are managers and planners, and workers who run the machines.

Not every country, nor even every region in a country, has the same kind of productive resources. Some countries have fertile, rolling farmland; others are mainly desert or mountain regions; and some may be so industrialized that little room is left for farmland.

These countries can become prosperous only by specializing and trading. People living in cities need the crops from farms. But farmers cannot harvest their crops without machinery produced by factories. And the factories cannot operate without minerals from the desert or mountain regions. By trading with one another, the different areas can use their resources to best advantage.

But people have a preference in what they buy. They buy only what they want and can pay for. This is called **consumer demand**. If all the farmers planted potatoes, the market would be flooded with potatoes, and people would not be able to find other vegetables. Therefore, farmers produce the variety of foods that consumers want. Competition for the consumer's money makes industries produce goods as cheaply and attractively as possible. The supply of goods and the demand for them change. A region may become prosperous because a new use has been discovered for a mineral deposit in the land. When the mineral is used up or is no longer needed, the region may become unproductive. This struggle to remain productive causes people to seek more efficient ways of using resources through specialization, trade, and technology. Concentrating on producing a few things means a greater output of goods. These can then be exchanged for different goods, produced in other places.

Let us take coffee, for example. The world's largest coffee producer is Brazil. How does coffee from a plantation in Brazil get to your neighborhood grocery? First, the coffee beans are picked from trees on a plantation and are sold to an exporter. An **exporter** is a person who sells a product from one country to a buyer in another country. The buyer is called an **importer**. *Portare* is the Latin word meaning "to carry." An exporter is one who carries out. An importer carries in. The importer, in turn, sells the coffee to a **wholesaler**.

The wholesaler specializes in buying coffee beans in large amounts, grinding them up, sealing certain amounts in vacuum tins, and distributing them to retailers. A retailer is a person who specializes in selling a certain type of goods to consumers. Grocery stores, drugstores, and department stores are examples of retail stores.

All these people—exporter, importer, wholesaler, and retailer—are engaged in trade and commerce.

There is a second group of persons engaged in trade and commerce. These are the people who provide such services as **transportation, insurance,** and **advertising**. A kilogram of coffee in Brazil is of no use to a buyer thousands of kilometers away. Railroads or trucks must take the coffee beans from the plantation to the exporter at a port city in Brazil. Ships then take the coffee beans to ports in other countries. Trucks carry the tins of ground coffee from the wholesaler to your local store. Machines for grinding and packaging the coffee, railroads, ships, and trucks—all are capital goods needed to carry on trade and commerce.

But it is always possible that a ship may sink or a warehouse may catch fire. To protect themselves against such a loss, shipowners, exporters, importers, and wholesalers can buy insurance from an insurance company. Finally, consumers do not know what kinds of goods are available or how much they cost unless they are told. Keeping customers informed about all the latest products is the job of advertising.

Without money, specialization would be impossible. Money acts as a common medium of exchange. All of us will accept money in return for the goods we sell and for the services we offer. We know we can always use the money to buy the things we want. This system is called a **monetary economy**. In a monetary economy there must be institutions to keep money circulating, to take care of savings, and to lend money when it is needed for new businesses.

Between the person who produces the goods and the consumer who buys the goods are a host of others—exporter, importer, wholesaler, retailer, and so on. These people must be paid for their services. When people buy coffee in a store, they are paying the grocer as well as all the other people who helped to bring the coffee from the plantation to the store. Each one plays an important part in the chain of trade and commerce.

Reviewed by GERRY OSTER
City University of New York
Bernard Baruch College

See also INTERNATIONAL TRADE.

TRADEMARKS

A trademark is a word or symbol used to identify a product or service. It may be the name of a manufacturer, such as Ford or Campbell. It may be the made-up name of a product, such as Scrabble or Twinkies. It may be a picture or symbol, such as Tony the Tiger or the NBC peacock.

If there were no trademarks, you would have trouble finding the particular brands you wanted. The "no frills" products you see in supermarkets carry no trademarks. The labels carry only **generic** names that tell what the packages contain—"dog food" or "paper towels," for example. You cannot tell who made these products. You cannot be sure they are of the same kind of quality as those you bought before. But when you buy a trademarked item that you have bought before, you know what to expect.

Generic names are ordinary words. If you look them up in the dictionary, you will find that they begin with lowercase (not capitalized) letters. Trademarks, if they appear in the dictionary at all, begin with uppercase (capital) letters.

▶TRADEMARKS ARE PROTECTED

In the United States and many other countries, laws protect trademarks. The laws prevent others from using a manufacturer's trademarked words, symbols, and slogans. They even protect the colors and package designs of trademarked products.

There are important reasons why trademarks are protected. A company may spend a great deal of money making and advertising its product. It would be unfair for another manufacturer to benefit from the advertising by using the same trademark. And other manufacturers might spoil the company's good name by putting the trademark on inferior products. The trademark is a kind of guarantee that protects the public from poor imitations.

Registration helps protect trademarks in many countries. For example, trademarks can be registered with the U.S. Patent and Trademark Office. The advantage of registration is that it provides a public record of the ownership of the trademark. It gives notice to other manufacturers. They cannot then claim that they never heard of the mark.

Registration helps the owners if they must appeal to the courts to protect their trademarks. But trademarks do not have to be registered, and thousands are not.

Courts often decide to protect a word as a trademark because it has acquired a secondary meaning. The first, or primary, meaning of a word is the meaning you find in the dictionary. But words may acquire a secondary meaning when they are closely associated with a well-known product, as the name "Jell-O" is associated with gelatin dessert.

You can tell whether a word has acquired a secondary meaning by playing a word game. When someone says a word, you answer with the first word that comes to mind. For example, if someone says "salt," you might say "pepper." If someone says "hostess," do you answer "party" or "cupcake"? What is your response to "pinto"—"horse" or "car"? When someone says "dial," do you say "telephone" or "soap"? If your answers were "cupcake," "car," and "soap," then Hostess, Pinto, and Dial have acquired secondary meanings. The courts will protect these names as trademarks whether they are registered or not.

▶CHOOSING A TRADEMARK

Any word can be used as a trademark. But if the word simply describes what the product is or what it is made of, it will not be protected. For example, one company makes crackers called Wheat Thins. But other makers of wheat crackers are free to use the word "wheat" in the names of their products.

Names like Ivory for soap and Greyhound for bus service are protected because they are not simple descriptions of products or services. The soap is not made of ivory. The buses are not pulled by greyhounds.

Names like Coppertone for suntan lotion and Dyanshine for shoe polish are riskier. The words themselves are good trademarks. Still, other manufacturers can claim that their lotions give a copper tone or that their polishes dye and shine shoes.

Manufacturers can usually use their own names as trademarks if they wish to. But this is not always so. Suppose, for example, that your name is Robert Smith. You and your brother James decide to make cough drops. May you call your product Smith Brothers

When the "Sesame Street" street sign trademark appears on a T-shirt or a toy, you know that the product is approved by the people who produce the television show. The shape and color of the McDonald's "M" is so distinctive that the trademark has its own nickname—the "golden arches." Some trademarks are just pictures. The Gerber baby and the Izod alligator symbolize their products very well with no words at all.

Cough Drops? You may not, because this has been a famous trademark for many years. If you used the same name, people could not tell which brand they were buying.

But if you and your brother made bicycles, you probably would not be stopped from calling them Smith Brothers Bicycles. Most people would not think that the cough-drop makers had suddenly begun to produce bicycles.

Would people be likely to buy a Smith Brothers Bicycle because they liked Smith Brothers Cough Drops? This is not always an easy question to answer. For example, General Motors makes a luxury car called Cadillac. It does not make dog food. But there is a dog food called Cadillac. Does the name make people think that the dog food is a luxury item?

Some companies with very well-known names have prevented others from using their names for any product. Tiffany, a New York store, has been famous for many years as a source of fine jewelry, silverware, and crystal. A film company and a restaurant were sued to prevent their use of the Tiffany name. The courts agreed that using the name in this way might hurt the store's reputation.

When a company uses a well-known name or mark, it must make sure that the public is not confused. For example, a person who saw a red cross on a package of bandages might think that the Red Cross had given its approval to the product. To make sure that this will not happen, packages of Johnson & Johnson bandages that bear a red cross also carry these words: "No connection whatever with American Red Cross."

▶HOW TRADEMARKS ARE LOST

A trademark can be lost, or become useless, when people have no other name for the type of product it identifies. This poses a problem for manufacturers of products that are the first of their kind. The product must have a name so that people will know what to ask for. But if the product goes by one name only, that name may not last as a trademark.

For example, the Bayer Company was the first to make aspirin. People who bought the product asked for "Aspirin" (the name Bayer gave its product) because there was no other name. As soon as other companies began to make and sell similar tablets, the word "aspirin" came to mean a certain type of pain reliever, not a Bayer product. Bayer might have protected its trademark if it had called the product "Aspirin Headache Tablets."

Many other words began as trademarks. For example, "mimeograph" was once a trademark. Today it refers to a way of making copies. If you wanted to make a copy of this page, would you say that you are going to "xerox" the page? The Xerox company does not want its trademark, Xerox, being used in this way. Most companies do not want their trademarks to be used as ordinary words because they may then lose the trademarks.

JESSICA DAVIDSON
Attorney

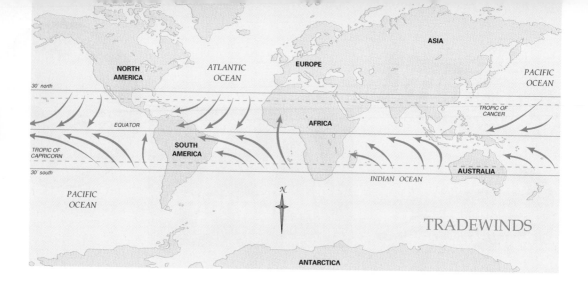

TRADEWINDS

TRADE WINDS

The trade winds are strong, steady winds that blow over the tropics and subtropics toward the equator. In the Northern Hemisphere they blow from the northeast; in the Southern Hemisphere, from the southeast. Their name came from an old nautical term, "to blow trade," which meant to blow constantly from one direction. In the days of sailing ships trade winds were important to ocean trade. That is why many people associate the name with commerce. The northeast trades aided Columbus on his voyage across the Atlantic to the West Indies. Even modern ships take advantage of these winds whenever possible.

The trade winds are the most steady of the earth's various wind systems. However, the winds do not blow in a direct, north-to-south path toward the equator. The earth's rotation causes the winds of the Northern Hemisphere to curve to their right. Thus the trades blow from the northeast rather than directly from the north. The trades of the Southern Hemisphere curve to their left and become southeast winds. This influence of the earth's rotation is known as the **Coriolis effect**. Where the trades come together near the equator, there is a belt of rising air with light winds and occasional calms. This region is called the **doldrums**.

The trade-wind belts shift slightly with the changing seasons. In summer in the Northern Hemisphere, the trade winds move slightly northward. During summer in the Southern Hemisphere, they move southward. On the average they blow from about 30 degrees north and south latitude to within a few degrees of the equator.

Effect of Trade Winds on the Environment

The trade winds typically blow over large expanses of open ocean, but when they blow over large land areas, the trade winds are quite dry. That is why the trades are sometimes called "desert makers."

When the trade winds blow long distances over the ocean, they take up a great deal of moisture. If the winds reach land on their way to the equator, they may be forced to rise over mountains, high plateaus, or other landforms. When this happens, the air cools and loses moisture, producing clouds and rain. Some of the rainiest places in the world are on the slopes of mountains in the path of the trade winds. (These slopes are called windward slopes because they are in the wind's path.) Mount Waialeale on the island of Kauai in Hawaii receives more than 450 inches (11,500 millimeters) of rainfall a year on its northeast (windward) slope.

In the Northern Hemisphere, islands in the trade-wind belt, such as the Hawaiians, have heavy rainfall on their northeastern sides. But the climate is dry on their southwestern sides. In the Southern Hemisphere the southeastern sides of islands in the trade-wind belt are rainy, and the northwestern sides are dry.

The trade winds also bring heavy rainfall to some of the mainland coasts, such as the eastern coast of Central America. Plantations of bananas and other tropical crops depend on this rain. In summer and fall, hurricanes frequently develop in the trade-wind latitudes.

HOWARD J. CRITCHFIELD
Western Washington University

See also WEATHER; WINDS.

A helicopter reporter describes traffic conditions over local radio. Such reports can alert drivers to problem areas and help them choose the best route to their destination.

TRAFFIC CONTROL

Chances are that you have been caught in a traffic jam at one time or another. You sit there in your car, crowded bumper to bumper with other cars, buses, taxis, and trucks. They all want to go in the same direction that you do, and all at the same time. But the traffic moves by inches, or does not move at all.

If you have been in a traffic jam, you understand the need for traffic control—the science of keeping traffic moving smoothly and safely. It involves making sure that there are enough roads to carry traffic and regulating the flow of traffic. The people who practice this science are called **traffic engineers**.

▶ CAUSES OF TRAFFIC PROBLEMS

Traffic problems have become worse as the number of vehicles on the roads has increased. In the United States, for example, there were more than 200 million registered cars, buses, and trucks in the late 1990's. Travel by car increased by almost 50 percent from 1970 to 1997, while truck traffic more than tripled.

Today traffic jams are a problem worldwide. The worst traffic jams often develop in and around major cities, especially during rush hours when people travel to and from work.

Traffic jams are no longer found only in cities. Many companies have moved their offices from cities to the suburbs. Often these areas do not have bus and rail lines. This means that large numbers of workers drive their own cars from suburban homes to suburban offices, using roads that were not designed or built to handle heavy traffic. Even where public transportation exists, many people prefer to drive to work, school, and shopping areas.

▶ METHODS OF TRAFFIC CONTROL

One way to lessen traffic problems is to reduce the number of vehicles on the roads. In many areas, people are encouraged to leave their cars at home and use public transportation. People can also carpool, or share rides, to work or school.

Other solutions to traffic problems include redesigning roadways to handle increased traffic, using regulations to change traffic patterns, and making better use of traffic signals and signs to control traffic movement.

Roads and Regulations. Often traffic problems can be solved by widening roads to add more traffic lanes or by building new roads. Many towns and cities have built ring roads and bypass roads for through traffic (drivers who want to pass through without stopping). This lessens the traffic on local streets and allows the through traffic to travel quickly.

Regulations also keep traffic flowing smoothly. For example, narrow city streets can be reserved for one-way traffic. Regulations may prohibit parking on busy streets during rush hours or at all times, so that the parking lane becomes an extra driving lane. And during rush hours, certain traffic lanes or entire roads can be set aside for vehicles that carry three or more people. This encourages people to carpool or take public transportation to work. Traffic regulations are enforced by the police, and violators are usually fined.

Signals and Signs. Traffic signals control the movement of pedestrians and vehicles at the intersections of busy roads. The lights of a traffic signal switch automatically from green ("go") to yellow ("caution") to red ("stop"), giving the right of way first to one road and then the other.

Traffic signals operate according to a plan selected by the traffic engineer. They may be **pretimed** or **traffic actuated.** Pretimed signals have internal clocks and are set to change at certain intervals, regardless of how much traffic is on the road. A series of pretimed signals can be set to change in sequence, so that a car can travel at a given speed without stopping.

Traffic-actuated signals change according to the amount of traffic at the intersection. Devices that detect vehicles are installed in or above the roadway. These devices tell a small computer in the signal how many vehicles are using each roadway at the intersection. The computer then adjusts the timing of the lights to suit the flow of traffic, so that more heavily traveled roads will have the right of way for longer periods of time.

Using a traffic-flow display map, a supervisor is able to unclog trouble spots on highways by adjusting the timing of certain traffic lights.

Many large cities have traffic signal systems controlled by central computers. Information from vehicle detectors is fed into the central computer, which analyzes the data and sends instructions to the traffic signals. This allows the flow of traffic to be co-ordinated over a wide area.

Traffic signs give motorists information. They warn of hazards, such as sharp turns and pedestrian crossings, and they inform drivers of regulations, such as speed limits and parking restrictions. Most countries use traffic signs with international symbols that can be understood by drivers who speak any language. The United States has its own system of shapes, colors, and symbols, many of which appear in the article DRIVER EDUCATION in Volume D.

▶HISTORY

Traffic was a problem long before the invention of the automobile. The ancient Romans built an advanced highway system throughout their empire and soon had to deal with traffic congestion. In the 1st century B.C., traffic in Rome was so heavy that the Roman leader Julius Caesar ordered the city's central areas off-limits to all vehicles except those of public officials and high-ranking citizens.

The first widely used traffic signals were **semaphores,** flaglike devices operated by hand. In 1908, Toledo, Ohio, was one of the first cities to install them. For daytime, the semaphores had movable panels with the words "stop" and "go." For night, they had red and green lenses illuminated by kerosene lamps.

The first electric traffic signal was installed in Cleveland, Ohio, in 1914. The four-way signal that we see today, with its red, yellow, and green lights, was designed about 1920. By 1931, traffic signals were in wide use.

In 1963 a computer system that controlled up to 1,000 traffic signals was installed in Toronto, Canada. Since then many cities have installed computer-controlled traffic systems to help prevent massive traffic jams in downtown areas.

KATHRYN HARRINGTON-HUGHES
Institute of Transportation Engineers

TRAINS. See RAILROADS.

TRANSCENDENTALISM. See AMERICAN LITERATURE.

TRANSFORMATION GEOMETRY. See GEOMETRY.

TRANSFORMERS

A transformer is a device that changes electrical energy. Its name comes from the word transform, which means to change.

The pressure that drives an electric current through a wire is called the voltage. A transformer changes the voltage from low to high or from high to low. At the same time it changes the current (measured in amperes) in the opposite way—from high to low or from low to high. A transformer that increases voltage is called a **step-up transformer.** One that decreases voltage is called a **step-down transformer.**

The action of transformers makes electricity available at whatever voltage is needed to do a particular job. Transformers also make it possible to transmit electricity over long distances efficiently.

▶WHERE TRANSFORMERS ARE USED

Step-up and step-down transformers are used throughout electric power systems. The largest transformers are in electric generating plants. These transformers, called generator transformers, operate with hundreds of thousands of volts of electricity. They increase voltage about 25 times before electricity is transmitted over power lines. At the same time the current is reduced to about $\frac{1}{25}$th of its value. Transformers are useful here because the lower the current, the less power loss there will be during transmission.

This very high voltage is stepped down by distribution transformers for use by city power networks and large manufacturing plants. For smaller buildings, such as homes and offices, small step-down transformers reduce the voltage still further to 115 or 230 volts. These transformers may be in the basement if the building is a large one, or on a power-line pole outside.

Inside the home, transformers raise or lower the voltage as needed. Small electric devices, such as doorbells and toy trains, use less than 25 volts. The doorbell transformer is used for safety. A visitor pressing the bell might be wet from rain or snow or might be standing in a puddle of water. If the bell or wires were broken, the visitor might get a dangerous electric shock from 115 volts of electricity. The transformer reduces the voltage to below 25 volts to prevent such accidents.

Transformers used in high-voltage systems usually are encased in tanks filled with oil. The transformer gets very hot when current flows through it, and oil insulates and cools better than air. Small transformers do not usually get so hot and can be operated in air.

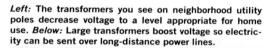

Left: The transformers you see on neighborhood utility poles decrease voltage to a level appropriate for home use. *Below:* Large transformers boost voltage so electricity can be sent over long-distance power lines.

271

►HOW A TRANSFORMER WORKS

A certain property of electricity, known as **induction,** is the basis of a transformer's operation. When a material that conducts electricity, such as copper wire, is placed near a **changing magnetic field** (a magnetic field whose lines of force are constantly changing direction), an electric current is created, or **induced,** in the material. The changing magnetic field can be produced by an **alternating electric current,** in which the flow of electrons is constantly changing direction.

A transformer is made up of two coils of wire, called the **primary winding** and the **secondary winding.** These coils are usually wound around a metal core made up of strips of steel.

When an alternating electric current enters the primary winding, it creates a changing magnetic field. That changing field induces an electric current in the secondary winding. If the secondary winding has more turns of wire than the primary winding, the voltage produced in the secondary will be higher than the voltage in the primary and the current will be lower. This is a step-up transformer. A simple step-up transformer is diagrammed below.

In a step-down transformer the primary winding has more turns of wire than the secondary winding. This causes the voltage produced in the secondary winding to be lowered and the current to be increased. The total amount of power, however, remains the same.

Volts, Amperes, and Watts

Volts, amperes, and watts are measures of electric energy. **Volts** measure the pressure that drives the electricity. **Amperes** measure the quantity of the current. **Watts** are a measure of the total amount of electrical power and are equal to volts × amps.

One hundred watts can be 1 ampere at 100 volts, 100 amperes at 1 volt, or any combination in between.

When a transformer raises the voltage, the current automatically decreases. When the transformer lowers the voltage, the current increases. But the total amount of power (watts) remains the same.

►HISTORY

The principle of induction—the basis of the transformer's operation—was discovered in 1831 by the English scientist Michael Faraday. In his experiments, Faraday proved that a moving magnet can produce an electric current. About 50 years after Faraday's discovery, transformers of the type used today were being developed.

The first successful transmission of high-voltage current by transformers took place in 1886 in Great Barrington, Massachusetts. William Stanley, an American electrical engineer, designed the system. Electric power at 500 volts was generated at a plant outside town. The voltage was then stepped up to 3,000 and sent along power lines to Great Barrington's main street. Step-down transformers then reduced the voltage, which was used for street lamps, offices, and stores.

Transformers, as well as other kinds of electrical equipment, became the focus of widespread environmental concerns in the 1970's. A group of chemicals called polychlorinated biphenyls, also known as PCB's, were used as insulators in some transformers. These chemicals were found to cause serious health problems, including cancer, when they leaked into the environment and found their way into the bodies of human beings. In 1979 the manufacture of PCB's was banned in the United States, and transformers today are no longer made with these chemicals.

HERBERT SPIES
General Electric Company

See also ELECTRICITY; MAGNETS AND MAGNETISM; WATERPOWER.

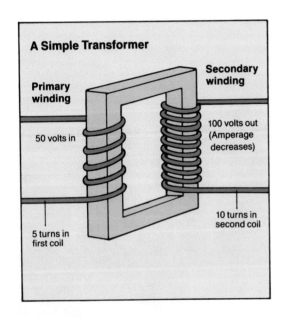

A Simple Transformer

Primary winding

Secondary winding

50 volts in

100 volts out (Amperage decreases)

5 turns in first coil

10 turns in second coil

TRANSFUSION, BLOOD

A blood transfusion is the introduction into a person's bloodstream of blood from another person. Transfusions are given mainly to replace blood that has been lost through severe bleeding. Such bleeding may occur as the result of illness, surgery, or accident.

Sometimes only a part of the blood is used for transfusions. Plasma, the liquid part of the blood, may be given alone. Transfusions of plasma are often given when people have been badly burned. In cases of severe burns, large amounts of plasma are lost from the bloodstream. The walls of the smallest blood vessels (capillaries) undergo a change that lets plasma seep out into the tissues.

Transfusions of red blood cells alone may be used to treat certain cases of anemia. Anemia is a condition in which a person has too few red blood cells or the person's red blood cells contain too little hemoglobin.

Transfusions of platelets (tiny cell-like particles that help control bleeding), of white blood cells, or of important proteins of the plasma can also be given. In some illnesses a person may lack one of these parts of the blood.

For many years doctors tried, but failed, to find a safe and successful method of giving blood transfusions. Many times transfusions caused death. In 1900 Karl Landsteiner (1868–1943), an Austrian doctor, found out why this was so. In the laboratory he mixed samples of red blood cells from one individual with serum from another. (Serum is the liquid that is left after blood has clotted.) In some cases the samples mixed without any reaction. But in other cases the red cells clumped together. In the human body this clumping causes destruction of the transfused cells, with serious consequences.

Landsteiner found that the red cells clumped because of a reaction between certain substances present in the red cells and certain substances present in the serum. He was able to classify blood into different types, or groups, depending upon the presence or absence of these substances. The groups are called A, B, AB, and O.

After the discovery of these four major blood groups, subgroups, as well as other blood groups, were found. One of the most important is the Rh group. Blood that contains a substance called the Rh factor is called Rh-positive blood, and blood without this substance is called Rh-negative blood.

Today, before people receive transfusions, their blood is tested to see if it is A, B, AB, or O and if it is Rh-negative or Rh-positive. This testing is called typing of the blood.

The blood that is to be used in a transfusion must be of the same type. For additional safety it is tested with the blood of the person who is to receive the transfusion to be sure that there is no reaction. This testing is called cross-matching of the blood.

In an emergency a person with Group O blood can give blood for transfusion to a person of any blood type. A person with Group O blood is called a universal donor. In an emergency a person with Group AB blood can receive blood of any type. A person with AB blood is called a universal recipient.

Blood can be kept refrigerated for about 3 weeks. A chemical such as sodium citrate is added to prevent clotting.

Many hospitals have blood banks, in which blood of all types is stored. When a unit of blood is needed, it is taken from the bank. Healthy people then give blood to the bank to replace the blood that is used. Most adults can give a pint of blood every 6 months.

In a transfusion a pint or more of blood is given, usually into the vein of a person's arm or leg. The blood drips through a tube leading to a needle placed in the patient's vein.

The germs that cause certain diseases, such as hepatitis (inflammation of the liver), malaria, and AIDS (acquired immune deficiency syndrome), can be passed on through transfusions. Therefore, the blood of people who have—or even once had—one of these diseases is not used for transfusion.

The germ virus that causes AIDS posed a special problem. The virus was not identified until the 1980's, and for a while there was no way to detect its presence in donated blood. Blood is now tested for AIDS antibodies, which appear in a person's blood several months after he or she was exposed to the disease. This has greatly reduced transfusion-related cases of AIDS.

Reviewed by HELEN M. ANDERSON, M.D.
St. Vincent's Hospital (New York City)

See also BLOOD; CIRCULATORY SYSTEM.

TRANSISTORS, DIODES, AND INTEGRATED CIRCUITS

The development of transistors, diodes, and integrated circuits has revolutionized electronics technology since the invention of the transistor in the 1940's. These three types of devices—known collectively as **semiconductor devices** because they are made from materials called semiconductors—exist in almost all electronic equipment. The one function all semiconductor devices have in common is their ability to control the flow of electric current. This function is the basis for the operation of computers, radio and television receivers, high-fidelity amplifiers, security networks, robot controllers, and hundreds of other electronic systems. (For an explanation of the nature of electric current, see ELECTRICITY in Volume E.)

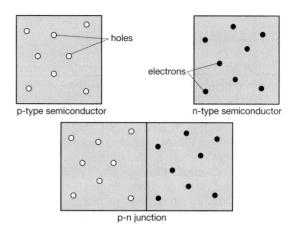

A p-type semiconductor, often made by adding a small amount of boron to a silicon base, has spaces (called holes) for extra electrons. An n-type semiconductor, often made by adding a small amount of phosphorus to a silicon base, has extra electrons. When the two types of semiconductors are put together, a p-n junction is formed.

▶ SEMICONDUCTORS

In the world of electricity and electronics, **conductors** are materials that allow current to flow easily. Copper, which is used to make electric wires, is an example of a conductor. Nonconductors, or **insulators**, are materials that do not allow current to flow very easily. Nonconducting materials are used, for example, to prevent people from getting an electric shock if they touch an electric wire.

A semiconductor is a material whose ability to conduct current can be adjusted by changing the electrical "pressure," or **voltage**, that is applied to the material by a source of electricity, such as a battery. This ability is the most important property of semiconductors. It allows them to work the way they do.

The most common semiconductor used in transistors and integrated circuits is the chemical element silicon. Silicon is one of two elements that form silicon dioxide, the main component of sand and glass. Other important semiconductors are germanium and gallium arsenide. These are somewhat less abundant in nature than silicon.

P-Type and N-Type Semiconductors

Semiconductor materials used in semiconductor devices are in the form of single crystals. This means that the position of every atom is fixed relative to every other atom in a three-dimensional pattern. This pattern is called the crystalline structure. (You can read

more about such structures in the article CRYSTALS in Volume C.)

Most solid materials are not perfect crystals. They have defects, such as misplaced atoms or impurities, that change their physical properties. For example, defects can have a great effect on the ability of a material to conduct electricity. When scientists carefully control defects, they can make materials with a wide range of useful properties.

One type of defect is especially important in silicon and other semiconductors. In a perfect crystal of silicon at room temperature, no electric current can flow. When certain impurities, called **dopants**, are carefully added to the silicon crystal, it can be made to carry electricity. However, a semiconductor, such as silicon, and a typical electrical conductor, such as copper wire, each carry electricity in a slightly different way.

In a typical conductor, every atom has one or more negatively charged electrons loosely bound to it. When a battery is hooked up to the conductor, the electrons move away from the conductor's negative end and toward its positive end. This movement of electrons creates an electric current. The electrons are called **charge carriers**, because an electric current is the flow of electric charge.

The semiconductor silicon can be made to conduct a small amount of electricity by adding a few atoms of phosphorus to the silicon crystal. Each phosphorus atom has an electron that is less tightly bound than the electrons in the silicon atoms. In the silicon crystal, these loosely bound electrons are freed from their phosphorus atoms and become charge carriers like those in a conductor. Thus an electric current can flow in the impure silicon, but not as well as in a typical conductor. This is because there are many fewer atoms with free electrons.

Adding phosphorus makes silicon an n-type semiconductor, so named because the charge carriers (electrons) are negative.

When an atom of the chemical element boron is added to a silicon crystal, the boron acts as if it has a space for an extra electron. This space will attract an electron to it, leaving a space with a positive charge at the original place of the electron.

An electron from a nearby silicon atom can fill the empty space in the boron atom. This leaves an empty space in the silicon atom. An electron from another silicon atom can fill that space, and so on. It is as if a positively charged "hole" is moving through the crystal.

The addition of boron makes the silicon a p-type semiconductor, so named because the charge carriers (holes) are positive.

▶ DIODES

If different dopants are added to neighboring sections of a silicon crystal, one section becomes a p-type material and the other an n-type. The place where the two sections meet is called a **p-n junction**, and the resulting device is called a **diode**. Diodes provide an important function used in transistors and most other semiconductor devices: Diodes conduct electricity in one direction but not in the opposite direction.

This is how a diode works. Imagine a battery hooked up to a diode. The battery's positive terminal is connected to the p-type section of the diode, and the negative terminal is connected to the n-type section. Electrons enter the n-type section from the negative terminal of the battery. Holes are created in the p-type section as electrons leave it to enter the battery's positive terminal. More electrons move from the n-type section to the p-type section, and more holes move from the p-type section to the n-type section. This movement of charge carriers (electrons and holes) creates an electric cur-

Diodes

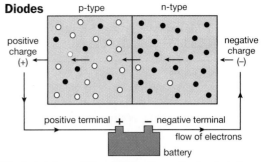

This diode is forward biased, that is, the positive terminal of a battery is connected to the diode's p-type section, and the negative terminal is connected to its n-type section. Electrons flow from the negative terminal into the n-type section. They then flow across the p-n junction and fill the holes in the p-type section. New holes are created in the p-type material as electrons are drawn toward the positive terminal. Thus, electricity can continue to flow through the junction.

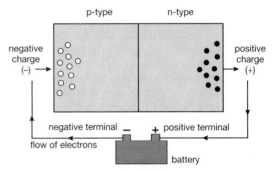

If the battery is connected in the opposite way, the diode is reverse biased. In this case, electrons leave the negative terminal of the battery and enter the p-type section of the diode, filling most of the holes. Electrons in the n-type section of the diode are drawn toward the positive terminal. This leaves very few charge carriers (electrons and holes), so little or no electricity flows across the p-n junction.

rent. As long as the battery is connected, the current flows through the p-n junction.

Now imagine that the battery is reversed. The battery's positive terminal is hooked up to the n-type section, and the negative terminal is hooked up to the p-type section. In this case, the electrons in the n-type section are drawn toward the positive end of the battery instead of the p-type section of the diode. As a result, fewer electrons move from the n-type section to the p-type section.

Likewise, electrons from the negative end of the battery flow into the p-type section of the diode and fill most of the holes. Soon there are very few charge carriers, and little or no current flows through the junction.

When an electric current is flowing through the junction, the diode is said to be forward **biased**. When no current flows, the diode is said to be **reverse biased**.

Uses for Diodes

Diodes have various uses in electronics because of their ability to pass currents in only one direction. One application of this function is **rectification**. It is used to convert alternating current (AC), which constantly switches direction, to direct current (DC), which flows in one direction. Rectifiers, which convert AC to DC, enable electronic devices that need DC to be powered from household electrical outlets, which supply AC.

As elements of transistor devices, diodes are also important in electronic communications. They are used to convert voices, images, and computer data into signals that can be transmitted via radio or cable. On the receiving end, diodes are used to convert the signals back into their original form.

A digital clock's display is make of light-emitting diodes (LED's), which glow when an electric current passes through them. Laser diodes are used to send information in the form of light pulses over long distances through glass-like optical fibers. Other diodes can detect light and convert it into electricity. Photovoltaic, or solar, cells are actually diodes with large surface areas.

▶ TRANSISTORS

Putting p-type and n-type semiconductors together in certain arrangements produces a transistor. A transistor is a semiconductor device that uses a small amount of electric power to control the flow of a larger amount of electric power. In its simpler applications, a small electric current is applied to a transistor to turn it on or off. When it is on, it acts something like a light switch—it allows the electric current to flow. When it is off, it prevents the flow of electricity.

There are two fundamental types of transistors, **bipolar transistors** and **field-effect transistors**. Both have three wires attached to them: one for the input, one for the output, and one shared by both the input and output.

Bipolar and field-effect transistors differ primarily in the way in which they achieve control of the current flowing through the semiconductor material. Both types are designed so that a small change in the electric current in one part of the transistor produces a large change in the flow of electric current in another part of the transistor. This is how tiny transistors control the flow of relatively large amounts of electric power.

Uses for Transistors

Transistors are used in a wide variety of electronic systems. They work in either of two ways: **analog mode** or **digital mode**. When transistors work in the analog mode, they amplify, or strengthen, electrical signals. In the digital mode, they function as high-speed switches.

There are two basic types of analog mode transistor amplifiers: weak-signal amplifiers and power amplifiers. Weak-signal amplifiers are used in devices such as radio receivers, television sets, and hearing aids. Power amplifiers are used in stereo sound systems and communications transmitters.

For amplifying weak signals, field-effect transistors often work better than bipolar transistors. All transistor amplifiers add some unwanted noise to signals, but field-effect transistors usually add less noise than bipolar devices. A special type of field-effect transistor, which works well when the noise must be kept to an absolute minimum, is used in receivers for space communications.

For power amplification, both bipolar and field-effect transistors are available. Bipolar devices are preferred for high-power applications. Some bipolar transistors can deliver more than 1,000 watts (1 kilowatt) of power output at audio frequencies and several dozen megahertz at radio frequencies.

Switching transistors working in digital mode are found in computers, telephone networks, and certain electrical systems. Some of these transistors, such as those in automotive electrical systems, can handle large electrical currents. Most, however, are designed to work with tiny currents.

The vast majority of switching transistors are found in computers. During the 1950's and 1960's, switching transistors replaced vacuum tubes in computer systems. The result was a tremendous improvement in efficiency and speed and a great decrease in the size of computers. In the late 1960's, technology was developed to incorporate transistors into integrated circuits. This brought about another revolution in efficiency, speed, size, and weight, making small computers that fit on desktops or in briefcases possible. Today practically all digital switching transistors in computers are microscopic regions etched into the surface of integrated circuits. In 2000, American engineer Jack Kilby was awarded the Nobel Prize in physics for his role in the invention of the integrated circuit.

▶ INTEGRATED CIRCUITS

An integrated circuit, or **IC**, is a type of semiconductor device in which many transistors are formed on one small chip of semiconducting material. The transistors are connected to each other by small metal wires on the surface of the chip. When they are arranged according to a careful plan, the interconnected transistors form useful electronic circuits.

Depending on the application of the integrated circuit, a single chip can include millions of transistors. The size of the transistors and wires on a chip can be less than a third of a micrometer. (A human hair is about 100 micrometers in diameter.)

One of the requirements for a chip's success is that all of its millions of transistors work perfectly. This is possible because of the purity and uniformity of the semiconductor material before it is doped (treated with a dopant) and also because of the processing skills for making IC's from thin semiconductor wafers, or disks. However, such a requirement limits how small IC's can be made.

Types of Integrated Circuits

Integrated circuits are classified as either **linear IC's** or **digital IC's**. These are the counterparts of the analog and digital modes of transistor operation. The term "linear" refers to a special type of analog amplification. In an amplifier, it is usually best to keep distortion to a minimum. A linear amplifier produces no distortion. Linear IC's are low-distortion amplifiers designed to work at low power levels. One common type of linear IC is the **operational amplifier**, which is used in audio devices such as tape recorders, compact disc players, and stereo tuners.

Most integrated circuits are digital IC's. These are used in computers, robot controllers, information-processing and -storage systems, communications networks, power

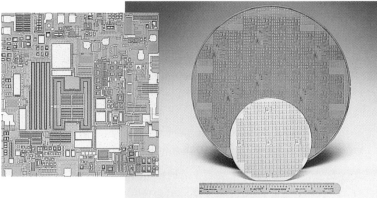

Very thin wafers (*right*) cut from cylinders of silicon are imprinted with hundreds of identical integrated circuits, or IC's. The wafers are then cut up into separate IC chips. Each chip (*left*) is then placed in a device ready to be inserted into a circuit board.

systems, and industrial processes. Two common types of digital IC's are the **microprocessor chip**, or microprocessor, and the **memory chip**.

A microprocessor contains all the circuits a computer needs to perform calculations. It is the "brain" of a personal computer. Every few years, more powerful microprocessors are developed. As IC manufacturing techniques improve, more and more switching transistors can be put onto a single chip.

A memory chip stores data as a huge array of tiny electrical charges. These charges represent sequences of a two-symbol, or binary, code. This code is based on the two bits (*bi*nary dig*its*) 0 and 1. The memory chip can easily distinguish between these two binary digits. For example, 0 might be represented by zero electrical charge, 1 by a small positive charge. Transistors in the memory chip detect the presence or absence of these charges and control the flow of current, thus determining how sequences of charges are arranged.

The capacity of memory chips keeps increasing as the manufacturing processes for IC's become more sophisticated. Some memory chips can store 1 billion bits of data (about 60,000 printed pages of text). Each year, more than 1 billion memory chips are manufactured and sold, mostly for use in computers and calculators.

▶ HOW INTEGRATED CIRCUITS ARE MADE

The manufacturing process for integrated circuits is similar in some ways to making photographs, although it is much more complex. IC's are made in batches, a large number at once. A printing process imprints the circuit patterns on the silicon wafer. This process allows IC's to be made relatively inexpensively and with a high degree of reliability. A simplified process for making an integrated circuit is described here.

Manufacture of IC's is carried out in a **clean room**. Such a room contains a thousand times less airborne dust than is found in a hospital operating room. The process begins with the growth of a silicon crystal from a hot pool of molten (melted) silicon. During growth, the crystal is doped with a precise amount of the selected impurity. Boron, for example, can be introduced to make the crystal p-type. After the crystal grows, it is sliced into wafers that may be 250 micrometers in thickness and 4 to 8 inches (10 to 20 centimeters) in diameter. The surfaces of these wafers are polished to a mirror finish.

The integrated circuits are formed on these surfaces in several similar steps. In each step a thin layer of material is added in a precise pattern by a process known as **photolithography**. First, the material to be added is put onto the entire wafer. Then the wafer is coated with a light-sensitive material known as **photoresist**. Light is projected through a precise mask, forming the desired pattern on the photoresist. The photoresist is then treated with a chemical that removes the sections that were exposed to the light. This uncovers some of the original material, which can then be removed, doped, or chemically treated. Finally, the photoresist is removed, and the process can be repeated.

After many of these photolithographic steps, the wafer has on it hundreds of identical integrated circuits. The final step is to saw the wafer into tiny chips and to place each chip into a small package with its wiring connections. In this form it is ready to be used in an electronic product.

Integrated Circuit Design

Because of the very large number of transistors and the complexity of the wiring patterns on integrated circuits, the designers of these devices have turned to a special type of computer software to assist in managing the layout complexity. The design tools are referred to as **computer-aided design**, or **CAD**, programs. Using a library of standard circuit patterns, the designers produce and test their designs in the computer before they are made into silicon chips. Before CAD programs were available, complex integrated circuits required many hours of engineering time to design. Though that time has been greatly reduced, chip design is still very expensive, which limits the variety and the complexity of the chips' functions.

▶ **THE SEMICONDUCTOR INDUSTRY**

After the transistor was invented in 1948 at Bell Telephone Laboratories in New Jersey, transistors and diodes quickly replaced many vacuum tubes in electronic equipment. IC's were invented in the late 1960's. The motivation for their development was a need to minimize the number of soldered connections in large electronic systems to improve their efficiency and operating speed.

The first practical application of IC's was in the U.S. space program. They played a vital role in the Apollo project that sent the first astronauts to the moon in 1969. The onboard computers for navigation and safety would not have been possible without IC's. Today IC's are the most important devices in the electronics industry.

Since the mid-1960's, the number of transistors in a computer chip has been doubling about every one to two years. The speed at which these chips perform calculations has been increasing at a similar rate. This trend, known as Moore's Law, may eventually decrease the sizes associated with transistors to a few hundred layers of atoms. Making reliable circuits at that scale is very difficult. However, scientists are inventing new ways of printing incredibly tiny circuits on chips using electron beams, X rays, and other methods. Computers are also being made to run much faster—for example, by cooling chips to very low temperatures. Moore's Law is expected to hold true for a number of years to come, but future advances may keep that trend going even longer.

ROBERT M. BURGER
Chief Scientist
Semiconductor Research Corporation
Reviewed by STUART K. TEWKSBURY
Chairman, Department of Electrical and Computer
Engineering, Stevens Institute of Technology

See also COMPUTERS; ELECTRONICS.

TRANSMISSIONS

Automobiles, trucks, buses, motorcycles, and other motor vehicles depend on transmissions to take power from the engine and deliver it to the wheels. In these vehicles, a gasoline or diesel engine turns a drive shaft, and the drive shaft then turns the wheels. But the engine cannot be connected directly to the drive shaft. This is because the engine must operate at certain speeds to keep from stalling, while the wheels need different amounts of speed and turning force (or torque) depending on road and driving conditions. It is the job of the transmission, which is placed between the engine and the drive shaft, to deliver the speed and torque required.

▶**WHAT A TRANSMISSION DOES**

The engine and the drive shaft rarely work at the same speed. For example, a large amount of force is needed to get an automobile moving from a standstill. The engine must operate at high speed, but the wheels must turn slowly and with great force. Less force is needed to keep the vehicle moving once it is rolling, so the engine can slow down while the wheels speed up.

The transmission uses gears to convert the power produced by the engine into the turning force and speed required by the wheels. A gear is a wheel with teeth around its rim. In a set of gears, the teeth of one wheel interlock with the teeth of the next, so that when the first gear turns, it makes the second gear turn. (You will find an article on gears in Volume G.)

The gears are able to change the strength and speed of the power produced by the engine because they are of different sizes. Suppose, for example, that the engine turns a small gear with ten teeth. That gear is connected to a large gear with twenty teeth, which powers the drive shaft. The smaller gear will turn twice as fast as the larger gear, but the large gear will have more turning force. By changing from one gear combination to another, the transmission is able to turn the drive shaft at different speeds and with different amounts of turning force.

Automobiles often have three to five gear combinations. Usually these combinations are simply referred to as ''gears'' or ''speeds.'' First or low gear combines low speed with

Location of Transmission

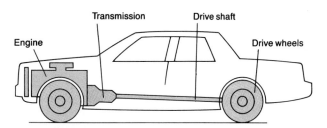

The transmission is located between the engine and the drive wheels. This car has a front engine and rear-wheel drive.

high turning power. This gear is used when a large amount of force is needed, for example, to get the automobile moving or to climb steep hills. Higher gears transmit more speed but less turning power to the drive shaft. Some transmissions have overdrive gears, in which the engine speed is actually less than the turning speed of the drive shaft. This saves fuel when the car is traveling at high speeds.

Another combination of gears reverses the turning direction of the drive shaft, allowing a vehicle to back up. And when a car stops, the gears can be disengaged, so that the engine can continue to run without moving the wheels.

▶**MANUAL AND AUTOMATIC TRANSMISSIONS**

In a vehicle with a manual transmission, the driver changes the gears. The driver first depresses a floor pedal to disengage (disconnect) the **clutch,** so that no power is sent to the transmission. The clutch is located between the engine and the transmission. Its basic parts are a **flywheel,** which is connected to the engine; a **disk;** and a **clutch plate,** which is connected to the transmission. When the clutch is engaged, strong springs hold the flywheel tight against the disk and clutch plate, so that the parts turn together. When the clutch is disengaged, the parts are pushed apart, so that the clutch plate does not turn.

Once the clutch is disengaged, the driver moves a hand-operated lever called a **gearshift.** This changes the combination of the gears in the transmission. Finally, the driver lets up the clutch pedal, so that power is restored to the transmission.

An automatic transmission shifts gears when the driver sets the gear selector on **Drive**

Manual Transmission

When the driver presses the clutch pedal, the clutch pressure plate and disk separate from the engine flywheel, disconnecting the transmission and engine. Then the driver moves the gear shift lever, which arranges the gears in the order that produces the speed and turning force required. When small gears turn large ones, the force is increased. When large gears turn small ones, the speed is increased.

Engine flywheel

Clutch disk

Springs

Gear shift

Power to drive shaft and drive wheels

Power from engine

To transmission

and presses the **accelerator** (the ''gas'' pedal). Sensors in the transmission select the correct gear according to the amount of force required to turn the wheels at the desired speed. For example, when the car first starts to move or is climbing a steep hill, the transmission shifts to low gear. At normal driving speeds on the road, the transmission is in high gear.

The driver may also set the selector on **reverse, park, neutral,** or **low.** In park, the transmission is locked, so that the wheels will not move. In neutral, the transmission is disengaged. Low prevents the transmission from shifting into higher gears. Low is used to prevent the wheels from turning at high speed on a slippery surface or when greater force is needed to move a heavily loaded vehicle.

An automatic transmission does not have a clutch. Instead, it has a type of hydraulic coupling called a **torque converter.** (To find out more about hydraulic couplings, see the article HYDRAULIC AND PNEUMATIC SYSTEMS in Volume H.) The gears are also different from those in a manual transmission. In an automatic transmission, small gears move around a central gear much as planets move around the sun. For this reason, they are called **planetary gears.** Different combinations of these complex gears deliver different speeds and amounts of turning force to the drive shaft.

ROSS OLNEY
Author, *The Shell Auto Care Guide*

Automatic Transmissions

Planet gears

Inside a ring — or internal — gear, planet gears on a carrier move around a sun gear. The speed and turning force depend on which combination of gears and carrier is moving.

Planet carrier

Ring gear

Sun gear

The engine turns the pump that moves the hydraulic fluid in the torque converter. The fluid strikes the stator and is flung out with greater force. When the force is strong enough, the fluid moves the turbine. The rotating turbine moves the planetary gears in the transmission. Automatic controls determine which units in the planetary gear sets move and which are held still. The correct turning speed and force are then passed to the drive shaft and on to the car's drive wheels.

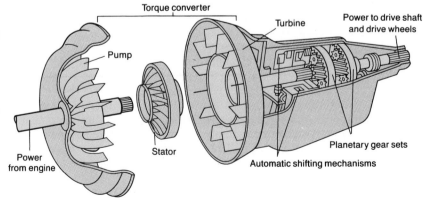

Torque converter

Pump

Power from engine

Stator

Turbine

Power to drive shaft and drive wheels

Planetary gear sets

Automatic shifting mechanisms

Fast, efficient, and reliable methods of transportation have greatly influenced the ways in which people live and are essential to economic growth in industrialized nations.

TRANSPORTATION

For thousands of years, people knew very little of the world in which they lived. Mountains, deserts, jungles, oceans, and frozen expanses of land made travel difficult. With travel slow and uncertain, different groups of people were isolated from one another.

Modern developments in transportation, however, have conquered distances and natural barriers. Today a network of transportation lines covers the earth on and under the ground, over water, and through the skies. Most of the things we eat, wear, and use each day come to us by truck, train, ship, plane, or pipeline. The people of the world are no longer isolated from one another.

▶ PRIMITIVE TRANSPORTATION

In prehistoric times, when people wanted to go from one place to another, they had to walk. When they had a heavy load to move, they carried it. Then they found it was easier to drag a load on branches or sticks that were tied together. Later they learned to build a sledge by tying beams across two runners with strips of hide. Next came the litter, which may have been the first vehicle designed to carry people. Litters were made by stretching animal skins across two poles.

Primitive people later learned how to teach animals to carry packs and pull sleds. In the Middle East the ox, donkey, and camel were trained to be beasts of burden. In the cold Arctic region, dogs and reindeer were used. In India, humped cattle and elephants were the burden bearers. The horse, which became the most common transport animal, was one of the last to be trained.

People discovered that traveling on water could be faster and easier than traveling on land. A floating log may have served as the first boat. It was later found that heavier loads could be carried on rafts made by lashing several logs together. In the Middle East, rafts were kept afloat by sheepskins and goatskins filled with air.

Wherever people could find large trees, they hollowed out logs with fire or a chisel and made long, narrow boats called dugout canoes. These boats were propelled with long poles and later with paddles and oars. An important discovery was made when it was found that the wind could be harnessed and used as power to drive boats. Different materials, such as grass mats, animal hides, or cloth, served as sails in different countries.

▶ EARLY TRAVEL AND TRADE

Some of the earliest civilizations began in Southwestern Asia and Egypt about 5,000 years ago. As people gathered together to live in cities, trade and manufacturing increased, and thus the need for transportation grew.

The Development of Land Transportation

The Sumerians, who lived in western Asia about 3000 B.C., may have been the first people to use the wheel. The earliest wheels were probably made of three wide planks held together by crosspieces, with a hole in the center for the axle. In some places, a solid disk cut from a log was used.

For many centuries the invention of the wheel had little effect on transportation, for there were few roads. Those that existed were too rutted and bumpy for long trips with a cart or wagon. Early wheeled vehicles were used as funeral wagons, military carriages, and farm carts.

Wheeled vehicles came into general use in Egypt about 1675 B.C. At that time Egypt was invaded by people from Asia called the Hyksos. The Hyksos brought with them a vehicle the Egyptians had never seen before—a spoke-wheeled chariot drawn by a horse. The Egyptians copied this design, and land travel in the Mediterranean region soon became speedier.

Most of the ancient civilizations were linked by routes in order to trade goods between them. Most of these routes were not proper roads, but merely unpaved, worn-down trails. Only cities had paved roads.

In the 1st century B.C. the Chou dynasty of China was known for its fine road systems. There were so many carriages on the roads that it became necessary to establish speed limits and other traffic regulations.

Pack animals have been used to transport people and goods for thousands of years. Today they still are used in areas that lack modern vehicles and road systems.

Of all the ancient peoples, the Romans were the finest road builders. Beginning in the 4th century B.C., the Romans built smooth, hard-surfaced roads wherever they ruled, from England to North Africa. This led to the saying "All roads lead to Rome." Many of these Roman roads were so well built that many sections of them are still in use today, particularly in England.

Progress in land transportation came to a halt after the fall of the Roman Empire in the A.D. 400's. For the next several hundred years during a period known as the Dark Ages, Europe was torn by wars, which brought an end to trade and commerce. People traveled little, and what roads there were fell into disrepair. Carriages were not used frequently, and riding on horseback became the chief means of transportation.

There were few developments in land transportation until the rigid horse collar and iron horse shoes were invented in the 900's. Before then, a horse was harnessed by straps that crossed its breast. When the horse moved forward, the straps pressed on its windpipe and choked it. Thus, the job of pulling heavy loads fell to the more solidly built oxen, which were strong but slow. With the improved horse collar, the horse could pull a heavy load without being choked. In addition, the new shoes protected the horse's hooves, enabling it to travel faster and for longer distances. These two inventions greatly speeded up transportation on land.

In Europe toward the end of the Middle Ages, trade and commerce increased, bringing about the need for better roads and improved vehicles. As a result, the coach was invented in Hungary in the 1400's. The coach, which enabled groups of people to travel together, was a closed carriage supported by leather straps between four wheels. The straps acted as springs to make the ride more comfortable. The driver sat away from the passengers in an elevated seat at the front of the coach. Stagecoach service began in Europe in the 1600's. The stagecoach traveled a regular route, stopping at set points, or stages, to change horses and allow passengers to eat and rest.

Stagecoaches came into use in the American colonies about 1756 with the setting up of a stagecoach service between Philadelphia and New York. A little more than 150 years earlier, the first settlers in the New World had found a land unmarked by roads. Wheels were unknown in America before the European settlers arrived. On farms the settlers used oxen to drag their crude two-wheeled carts. In the northern colonies, where winters were snowy, sleighs and sledges were common. Snowshoes, an Indian invention, were often used by foot travelers.

The early colonists cleared and widened trails so that goods could be transported. Slowly the settlers worked their way through forests and prairies on foot, on horseback, and in wagons. The Conestoga wagon, first built in Lancaster County, Pennsylvania, came into use about 1750. It was the most dependable freight carrier until the railroad era began. The body of the Conestoga wagon was designed with an upward slope at each end to keep the cargo from spilling out when the wagon traveled uphill or downhill. A large canvas cover over a hoop frame protected the passengers and their goods from the rain. The wagon was drawn by two to six horses or mules and could hold from 2 to 4 tons of cargo.

Roads developed slowly in the colonies because large towns were on or near seacoasts, and ships furnished the transportation between them. The roads were so bad that coaches often overturned, injuring passengers. Better methods of road construction were not introduced into the United States from England until the late 1700's.

The Development of Water Transportation

For thousands of years the roads of the sea were more easily traveled than those on land. Long before the wheel was invented or animals tamed, ships were in use on the Nile River.

The Phoenicians were the great sailors and traders of ancient times. Phoenician ships traveled from the eastern Mediterranean to the British Isles on trading voyages. Their ships, called galleys, were built of cedar wood and used square sails as well as oars. A galley could go faster and was more easily handled than a ship propelled only by a sail. Galleys were constructed with two or more banks, or rows, of oars, one above the other, extending along each side of the ship. The Phoenicians were daring seamen, and their travels to the far corners of the known world contributed a great deal to the development of trade and the spread of knowledge.

The Greeks, too, were great sea traders. Their trading vessels were known all along the Mediterranean. To protect their trading vessels against enemy attack, the Greeks learned to build large war galleys.

When the Romans set out to conquer the world, they built a powerful fleet of galleys. In great numbers the Roman ships sailed the waters along the coasts of Europe and Africa.

Sailing ships improved in the A.D. 500's with the invention of the lateen sail. The lateen sail was shaped like a triangle and ran along the length of the ship instead of across it, as the square sail did. The lateen sail could be set at various angles so that the ship could sail across or even against the wind.

With no instruments for navigation, the very early mariners sailed by landmarks and the position of the stars. Seamen tried to keep within sight of land as much as possible during their voyages. Not until the invention of navigating instruments was it possible to sail boldly out into the open ocean. The compass, first known to the Chinese, was probably used by Europeans about 1200. Besides the compass, the early mariners had some inaccurately drawn maps and charts and a few instruments for reading latitude. Crude as these aids were by today's standards, they played an important part in the explorations of Columbus, Vasco da Gama, and others. These explorations were further aided by the development of the three-masted ship, invented about 1450. Over the centuries that followed, ship design and navigation instruments were steadily improved.

In ancient times trireme galleys traveled the Mediterranean. These vessels had square sails and three rows of oars on each side and required a crew of about 200.

Exploration brought about the colonization of distant lands and peoples by the Europeans. As a result, trade flourished, increasing the need for larger and faster ships to carry raw materials and finished goods back and forth across the sea. Shipbuilders began adding more and more sails to their vessels. By the 1840's, American builders had developed a new type of sailing ship called the clipper ship. The clippers had long, slim hulls and plenty of sail area; they were the fastest ships built up to that time. But as fast as they were, clipper ships still depended on favorable winds and currents. By the end of the century, clipper ships were replaced by steel ships driven by a more dependable source of energy—steam power.

▶ **MACHINE-POWERED TRANSPORTATION**

For centuries people had only their own energy, the strength of animals, the force of the wind, and water currents to transport themselves and their supplies. When people learned to harness the power of steam, a great revolution in transportation began.

Ships

In 1787, John Fitch, an American inventor, built the first practical steamboat. Three years later he established the world's first regular steamship service between Philadelphia, Pennsylvania, and Trenton, New Jersey. The steamboat lost money on every trip. People joked about poor Johnny Fitch, who was trying to run a boat with a "teakettle." They did not understand the enormous potential of steam-powered engines. By 1838 the steamship *Sirius* had voyaged across the Atlantic, from London to New York, entirely under steam power.

In the United States, great advancements were made in sea transportation following the Civil War (1861–65). Wooden ships were gradually replaced, first by iron ships, then by steel ones (steel was lighter than iron and more durable than wood); screw propellers replaced paddle wheels; and high-speed turbines were developed. In the early 1900's, ships began operating on diesel engines.

In the 1870's the first ocean liners for passenger travel were built. Shipping lines competed to provide the fastest, most luxurious service. These luxury liners remained in service until air travel became popular.

Clipper ships, with their tall masts and enormous sails, were the fastest boats of their time. The *Flying Cloud* (*above*), built in 1851, set a record of 89 days from New York to San Francisco on its first voyage.

Ocean liners, such as the *Queen Mary* (*right*), once provided luxurious passenger service. However, in the 1960's the growing popularity of air travel forced luxury transatlantic passenger ships out of business.

In the 20th century, boats have been designed that can travel underwater and over water: Submarines, which have no practical commercial use, were first used successfully during World War I (1914–18). Today they are used primarily for military purposes and scientific research. Hydrofoils, which combine features of boats and airplanes, came into use in the 1950's. When a hydrofoil gathers speed, the hull rises above the water, supported by winglike devices. These boats can travel faster than ordinary motorboats of the same size.

Railroads

Railroad tracks were used for several hundred years before steam locomotives were invented. In the 1500's the Germans transported ore from mines in horse-drawn carts that ran on wooden rails. Similar railroad carts were used in England to haul coal from the mines to the docks.

The railroad industry began in England near the beginning of the Industrial Revolution. In 1804, Richard Trevithick built the first steam locomotive to run on tracks. It is said to have pulled 10 tons and 70 people. The first steam engines were far from perfect. They wasted fuel and frequently broke down. However, it was less expensive to repair the engines than to feed and care for horses, the most commonly used "vehicles."

The idea of railway trains soon caught on. In 1825 the first steam-powered railroad for public service, the Stockton and Darlington line, opened in England. The first railroad in the United States, the Baltimore and Ohio, opened five years later.

Within a short time after railroads were introduced, most of the coaching companies were forced out of business. The people who owned stagecoaches and hauled freight by wagons had to find new ways to make a living. As the railroads took over much of the transportation on land, and roads were used less for long-distance travel and hauling, the roads became neglected. They did not receive much public attention until the early 1900's, when the era of the automobile began.

Most American trains today are pulled by diesel or electric engines. Steam locomotives are still used in some Latin-American, Euro-

Railroad locomotives in the 1800's (*above*) burned wood for fuel, which created vast plumes of smoke. The pointed grill in front of the engine was called a "cowcatcher" because it removed obstacles from the tracks.

Modern turbo trains are called "bullet trains" because of their shape and their high speeds. Japan's *Shinkansen* system (*left*), which has been in operation since the 1960's, can travel at 160 miles (260 kilometers) an hour.

pean, and Asian countries. Trains have been developed in France, Japan, and Germany that operate on gas turbines. These turbo trains can travel at speeds exceeding 180 miles (290 kilometers) an hour.

In recent times passenger trains have had to face increasing competition from planes, automobiles, and buses. But the railroad is still the leader in freight hauling on land.

Automobiles

As early as 1769 a French artillery officer, Nicholas Cugnot, built a three-wheeled steam-powered carriage. It was so hard to steer that it ran into a wall on its trial run and was destroyed. During the 1800's a number of steam-driven carriages were produced in England and elsewhere. Steam also was the first form of power for "horseless carriages" in Amer-

ica. Electric cars briefly became popular by the early 1900's. However, they could only travel at a speed of about 12 miles (19 kilometers) an hour, and their batteries had to be recharged too frequently for practical uses.

For some years before 1890, French, English, and German inventors had been experimenting with engines that burned a variety of gases and liquid fuels. By 1885 two Germans, Gottlieb Daimler and Karl Benz, were making cars with gasoline-driven engines. Charles Duryea built the first gasoline-powered automobile in America in 1893. Soon after this car appeared, other models were introduced. Many of them were flimsy vehicles, made with a buggy body and bicycle-type wheels.

During the early 1900's, cars were owned mainly by wealthy people. Henry Ford of Detroit, Michigan, decided to make a car that most people could afford. In 1908, after some experiments, he introduced the Model T, which soon became famous.

In 1913, Ford began producing his Model T's on an assembly line, a concept that revolutionized the automobile industry. As the frame of a car passed along a conveyor belt, workers would add the individual parts to it. The efficiency of this system lowered the cost of producing the cars, which in turn made them more affordable to the average buyer. More than 15,000,000 Model T's were sold before they were discontinued in 1927.

The automobile has had a far-reaching effect on the pattern of living in the United States, Canada, and many other countries.

Henry Ford's Model T, the first mass-produced automobile, revolutionized car manufacturing. The efficiency of his assembly-line production methods made the Model T affordable to the average American.

People in the United States today depend on automobiles more than any other form of transportation. Sports cars, such as General Motors' Chevrolet Corvette (*right*), are designed to be fun as well as functional.

With cheap, easy transportation people were able to live on the outskirts of cities and drive to work. More and more suburbs have developed. Today there are many large shopping centers, motels, and drive-in restaurants, as well as theaters and banks for the convenience of motorists.

Airplanes

For hundreds of years, people tried to think of ways to fly. In 1793 the Montgolfier brothers of France built the first balloons that could carry passengers. These early balloons were made of paper and silk and were filled with heated air.

By 1900 many attempts had been made to build steam- and gasoline-powered flying machines, but none was satisfactory. Wilbur and Orville Wright of Dayton, Ohio, carefully studied the inventions and flights of others. They finally completed a gasoline-driven airplane. On December 17, 1903, on the beach of Kitty Hawk, North Carolina, the Wright brothers made the world's first successful engine-powered flight, and the airplane era had begun.

The airplane changed many of the world's habits within a relatively few years. Planes could reach the most isolated places on the globe, and at undreamed-of speed. As travel time between continents grew shorter, round-the-world travel increased. The most perishable foods could be shipped across great distances on cargo planes, and mail deliveries were speeded up.

By 1958 and 1959 a plane cruising at 300 miles (483 kilometers) an hour was no longer a wonder to marvel at, for the jet age in commercial transportation had begun. Today's jet planes cruise twice as high in the air and fly almost twice as fast as their forerunners. In addition, the newer planes are 34 to 40 percent more fuel efficient than earlier models.

Until its retirement in October 2003, the French and British Concorde was the fastest commercial jet plane. The Concorde was a supersonic transport (SST) that could reach a speed of more than 1,300 miles (2,100 kilometers) an hour, or about twice the speed of sound, and climb as high as 60,000 feet (18 kilometers).

The helicopter, another valuable vehicle in air transport, has been in use for freight, mail, industrial purposes, and passenger service since 1947. With its overhead propeller the

The Douglas DC-3 (*above*), introduced in 1936, was the first successful commercial airliner. It carried 21 passengers at 170 miles (270 kilometers) an hour and was so well built that several are still in service.

The jet airplane (*left*) is among the most influential inventions of the 20th century. Jets can carry hundreds of passengers almost anywhere in the world at an average speed of more than 550 miles (885 kilometers) an hour.

"chopper," or "whirlybird," as the helicopter is called, is able to rise straight up off the ground. It can land on a small area of land, or if equipped with pontoons, on water.

Transportation in the Cities

Both the location and the growth of cities are dependent on efficient means of transportation. Before railroads were built, most large cities were major seaports, or at least located on important navigable rivers. Railroads made it possible for cities to thrive inland.

In the 1800's, cities grew and spread out. Streets became quite crowded with horse-drawn streetcars and multi-passenger vehicles called omnibuses. It became necessary to find new methods for intercity transportation. Railroads that ran underneath or above the ground provided an answer.

The world's first subway opened in London in 1863. In spite of the soot and dirt that filled the tunnels from coal-burning steam engines, the subway was a success. In the 1870's in New York City, a steam-powered elevated railway built high above the streets began transporting passengers.

The first electrically powered railway opened in Berlin in 1881. Subways and overhead railways soon were converted to electric power, as were street vehicles. Horsecars were replaced by electric streetcars, which in turn were replaced by motor buses in the 1920's.

Highways and Traffic. To serve a constantly growing "world on wheels," many superhighways and express highways have been built. Strong bridges and tunnels that make continuous roads over or under land and water have been constructed. Roads have been built or relocated on the outskirts of larger towns and cities in order to direct the flow of traffic away from the more congested areas. Nevertheless, most of the large cities in the world have been unable to find a way to deal successfully with the steady stream of cars, buses, and trucks that clog city streets and main

In less industrialized nations, such as China (*above*), bicycles are an important form of everyday transportation. Many people there use bicycles instead of automobiles to commute to work.

Most of the world's major cities have underground railroad systems called subways (*left*). They provide rapid transit for large numbers of people and help lessen the amount of street traffic.

traffic arteries. In many of the largest cities of the world, the subway offers about the only speedy way of getting from one place to another.

Freight Transportation

Freight carriers move commercial goods from one place to another. All modes of transportation are used to transport freight. The means of transportation usually depends on the type of goods being moved and the cost and time it takes to move them.

Pipeline, an important mode of freight transportation, is rarely seen, because much of it lies 5 to 6 feet (1.5 to 1.8 meters) underground. Throughout the world, and particularly in the United States, giant pipelines carry oil, natural gas, and other products. The pipelines carry these products from the places where they are produced to industrial centers, refineries, and shipping ports. Water pipelines are also a vital part of civilization because they carry water from distant reservoirs to cities and farmlands.

A glance at a highway anywhere in the world today tells the story of the ever-increasing use of trucks for hauling goods of all kinds, from bread to heavy machinery. A method of freight hauling, called piggyback, has become important. Loaded truck trailers are placed on railroad flatcars or on ships to be transported to warehouses, factories, or distribution centers. This method makes it possible for goods not to be disturbed until they reach their final destination.

Ships are used for freight transportation whenever possible because it is the cheapest method available. Most international freight is transported by cargo ships; oil is transported by specially designed supertankers; and most bulky cargo on inland waterways is moved on flat-bottomed boats called barges. Some barges have their own engines, but most are pushed along by tugboats.

▶THE MODERN TRANSPORTATION INDUSTRY

The modern transportation industry is a very important part of the world's economy. Of the ten largest industrial corporations in the world, seven are directly related to transportation: Two of the corporations manufacture automobiles, trucks, and other vehicles; the other five refine the petroleum on which these vehicles depend.

Pipelines are a major form of transportation. They carry freight, such as oil and natural gas, from its point of origin to industrial centers, ports, and refineries.

The five largest transportation manufacturers in the United States are General Motors Corporation, Ford Motor Company, Chrysler Corporation, Boeing (Aircraft) Company, and McDonnell Douglas Corporation, a space and defense contractor. Worldwide, the five largest transportation manufacturers are General Motors; Ford; Toyota Motor Corporation of Japan; and Daimler-Benz, and Volkswagenwerk of Germany.

The transportation industry includes businesses other than vehicle manufacturing and petroleum refining. It includes retail and wholesale dealers of automobiles and automobile accessories; automobile services and garages; gasoline service stations; highway and street construction; petroleum production and shipping; and steel, glass, and tire manufacturers.

Tugboats are small, powerful vessels used to push unpowered flatbed barges carrying up to 20,000 tons of cargo. Tugboats also guide larger seagoing boats in and out of port.

The impact of the transportation industry on the economy of the United States is enormous. It accounts for almost 19 percent of the gross national product (the value of a country's goods and services). Approximately 11,139,000 people, or 9.6 percent of the country's total work force, are employed either directly in transportation or in transportation-related industries.

The Government's Role in Transportation

In the United States as well as other countries, governments play an important role in overseeing the transportation industry. For example, the United States Government issues and enforces rules concerning the safety and security of transportation systems. Among its many functions are planning, developing, and constructing transportation facilities, such as roads and bridges; certifying the fitness of pilots; regulating the transportation of hazardous chemicals and other materials; investigating public transportation accidents; issuing requirements for fuel efficiency and pollution control; and guarding against the transportation of illegal goods.

In addition, the federal government operates the nation's air traffic control system and helps state and local governments pay for the construction of highways, harbors, and mass transit systems.

The Defense Department's Corps of Engineers constructs, improves, and maintains inner harbor and port facilities. It also administers laws relating to the protection of navigable waters and wetlands. The State Department develops and approves policies and programs concerning international aviation and maritime (sea) transport. The National Transportation Safety Board conducts accident investigations and recommends improvements. The Interstate Commerce Commission regulates surface carriers engaged in interstate commerce—railroads, trucking companies, bus lines, freight forwarders, and water carriers. The National Railroad Passenger Corporation (AMTRAK) ensures a balanced national railroad system and operates approximately 240 trains a day over more than 23,000 route miles (37,000 kilometers). Agencies of the Department of Transportation include the Coast Guard, the Federal Aviation Administration, the National Highway Traffic Safety Administration, the Urban Mass Transportation Administration, and the Maritime Administration.

Dependence on Petroleum

One of the greatest problems of the transportation industry is that it depends heavily on petroleum-based products as a source of energy. The burning of such fuels causes air pollution. Of equal concern is the fact that petroleum reserves are not distributed evenly around the world.

In 1973 an energy crisis resulted when the Arab nations that supply a large part of the world's oil imposed an oil embargo (stopped shipment). This began a search for oil substitutes and more efficient vehicles. The United States imposed a 55-mile-per-hour speed limit to conserve fuel; fuel efficiency requirements for new cars were set, resulting in the development of smaller, lower-horsepower models; and to make sure vehicles were running efficiently, emissions testing and vehicle inspections began. In addition, ride-sharing and vanpool programs were set up, and more attention was paid to the development of mass transit systems. Research was done on non–oil-based fuels and oil "extenders," such as methanol and ethanol, which are made from grains and other plants.

▶ FUTURE DEVELOPMENTS

Among the primary goals of transportation technology is to develop vehicles that conserve energy and do not pollute the environment. One of the most exciting developments along these lines is the high-speed passenger train known as the maglev, or magnetic levitation vehicle, designed to travel at speeds exceeding 200 miles (322 kilometers) an hour. China unveiled the world's first commercial maglev in 2002.

Upper right: Magnetic levitation vehicles (called maglevs) are a recent development. Instead of using conventional fuels, maglevs are propelled over tracks by superconducting magnets and electrical currents.

Right: The future of air transportation may lie with the development of hypersonic Trans-Atmospheric Vehicles (TAV's), which will carry passengers the distance between New York and Tokyo in only 2 hours.

Based on the principle that like magnetic poles repel each other, maglevs travel above tracks on an electromagnetic wave, or cushion, touching down only on "takeoff" and "landing." High speed is possible because of the absence of friction. Maglevs use much less energy and produce less air pollution than the vehicles they replace.

In air transportation, dramatic changes lie ahead. A hypersonic aircraft called the Trans-Atmospheric Vehicle (TAV) could be in service in the near future. One such plane is called the Orient Express because it will be able to fly from the east coast of the United States to Japan in about 2 hours, flying at an altitude of 100,000 feet (30,480 meters) and cruising at 10,000 miles (16,100 kilometers) an hour. The Orient Express will be fueled by a mixture of hydrogen and oxygen, which emits water vapor instead of the harmful pollutants generated by other fuels. This and other new and more efficient sources of energy will eventually help us reduce our dependency on oil as well as improve the overall quality of our air in the future.

For as long as people have wanted to fly, they have wondered what it would be like to travel into outer space. In 1957 the space age began when the Soviet Union launched the first artificial satellite into orbit. Many space missions followed, but the space vehicles could only be used for one trip.

In the 1970's, however, the United States developed the space shuttle, a reusable space vehicle that can take off like a rocket and land like an airplane. The space shuttle *Columbia* was first used for commercial purposes in 1982 to launch two communications satellites. Many people continue to hope that, one day, similar vehicles will be able to carry passengers on trips into outer space.

MARY BANY
Professor of Education
California State College, Los Angeles

Updated by DOROTHY J. POEHLMAN
Chief, Information Services Branch
U.S. Department of Transportation Library

See also AIRPLANES; AUTOMOBILES; AVIATION; BICYCLING; BRIDGES; BUSES; CANALS; HELICOPTERS; HYDROFOIL BOATS; LOCOMOTIVES; MOTORCYCLES; OCEAN LINERS; RAILROADS; ROADS AND HIGHWAYS; SHIPS AND SHIPPING; SPACE EXPLORATION AND TRAVEL; SPACE SHUTTLES; SUBMARINES; TRANSPORTATION, UNITED STATES DEPARTMENT OF; TRUCKS AND TRUCKING; TUNNELS; WHEELS.

TRANSPORTATION, UNITED STATES DEPARTMENT OF

The Department of Transportation (DOT) is one of the 15 executive departments of the United States government. Its purpose is to establish policies and programs to make the nation's transportation systems safer, faster, and more efficient. These policies and programs are concerned with the planning, development, and construction of highways, mass transit systems, railroads, airports, bridges, and other transportation vehicles and facilities. In addition, the DOT sets safety standards for all types of transportation and facilities, including aircraft, automobiles, railways, ports and waterways, and oil and gas pipelines.

Organization

The DOT is managed by the secretary of transportation, who is a member of the president's cabinet. The secretary is the principal adviser to the president in all matters relating to federal transportation programs. He or she is largely focused on formulating policies, allocating resources, coordinating departmental activities, and evaluating DOT program effectiveness. The secretary, who is assisted by a deputy secretary, five assistant secretaries, a general counsel, and an inspector general, is also responsible for the overall planning and operations for each of the DOT's nine administrations, which are described below.

The **Federal Aviation Administration** (FAA) has primary responsibility for the safety of civil aviation. It develops air traffic rules and regulates the flow of air traffic. It licenses pilots and issues and enforces safety standards regarding the manufacture, operation, and maintenance of all nonmilitary aircraft and facilities.

The **Federal Highway Administration** (FHWA) provides funds for the construction and maintenance of the approximately 42,000-mile (68,500-kilometer) National System of Interstate and Defense Highways and 800,000 miles (1,290,000 kilometers) of other roadways. The FHWA also administers the Federal Highway Bridge Replacement and Rehabilitation Program.

The **Federal Motor Carrier Safety Administration** (FMCSA) develops and enforces rules and regulations aimed at reducing crashes, injuries, and fatalities involving large trucks and buses and ensures the safe and secure transportation of hazardous materials.

The **Federal Railroad Administration** (FRA) sets the safety standards for railroad operation and oversees the inspection and maintenance of railroad equipment and facilities. It also provides financial assistance to maintain passenger and freight services.

The **National Highway Traffic Safety Administration** (NHTSA) develops programs and sets safety requirements for the manufacture of motor vehicles and develops programs that are designed to reduce the number of traffic accidents and deaths and injuries on the nation's highways.

The **Federal Transit Administration** (FTA) develops programs and provides cities with funds to plan, build, and improve city mass transportation systems, such as intercity buses and subways.

The **Maritime Administration** (MARAD) develops programs to improve the efficiency and profitability of the nation's merchant marine (commercial ships). It also organizes and directs merchant ship operations in times of national emergency.

One of the duties of the Department of Transportation's Federal Highway Administration is to inspect bridges to make sure they meet safety standards.

The **Research and Special Programs Administration** (RSPA) conducts research and develops regulations to ensure pipeline safety and the safe transportation of hazardous materials. It also prepares for national transportation emergencies.

History

The Department of Transportation was created in 1966 by an Act of Congress and began operating the following year. The DOT took over many duties from the departments of Commerce, Treasury, and the Interior. The DOT's headquarters are located at 400 Seventh Street, S.W., Washington, D.C. 20590.

DOROTHY J. POEHLMAN
Chief, Information Services Branch
U.S. Department of Transportation Library

See also AVIATION (Flight Safety).

The **Saint Lawrence Seaway Development Corporation** (SLSDC) oversees the operation of the seaway within the territorial limits of the United States, between Montreal and Lake Erie.

TRAVERS, P. L. See CHILDREN'S LITERATURE (Profiles).

TREASURY, UNITED STATES DEPARTMENT OF THE

The Department of the Treasury is the principal financial institution of the United States. Its chief functions are to determine economic, financial, and tax policies; supervise national banks; mint coins and print currency; collect federal income taxes; and enforce tax laws.

The Department of the Treasury is one of the 15 executive departments of the United States government. It is headed by the secretary of the treasury, who is appointed by the president with the Senate's approval. The secretary of the treasury is the second highest ranked member of the president's cabinet (after the secretary of state).

As the government's chief financial officer, the secretary of the treasury advises the president and manages the public debt. He or she is required to make an annual report to Congress on the government's finances.

Organization

The secretary of the treasury is assisted by a deputy secretary, an undersecretary for finance, nine assistant secretaries, a general counsel (legal adviser), a treasurer, and an inspector general. These experts oversee the administration of the Treasury's ten operating bureaus, which are described below.

The **Internal Revenue Service** (IRS) is the largest of the Treasury bureaus. It evaluates and collects federal income taxes from American citizens, including employment taxes for the country's Social Security system.

The **Office of the Comptroller of the Currency** (OCC) supervises the operations of the national banks, enforces banking laws, and informs the public about banking regulations.

The **Financial Management Service** (FMS) receives and distributes all public monies, maintains financial accounts, and prepares daily and monthly reports on the government's income and expenditures.

The **Bureau of the Public Debt** manages the government's debt (money owed by the government), analyzes federal borrowing needs, and issues U.S. savings bonds.

The **Bureau of Engraving and Printing** (BEP) designs and prints all paper currency, Treasury bills, Federal Reserve notes, U.S. government bonds, and postage stamps.

The **United States Mint** produces coins and supervises the storage and distribution of the government's bullion (gold and silver).

The **Office of Thrift Supervision** (OTS) regulates the administration of savings banks and savings and loan associations.

Secretaries of the Treasury

Name	Took Office	Under President
*Alexander Hamilton	1789	Washington
Oliver Wolcott, Jr.	1795	Washington, Adams
Samuel Dexter	1801	Adams, Jefferson
Albert Gallatin	1801	Jefferson, Madison
George W. Campbell	1814	Madison
Alexander J. Dallas	1814	Madison
William H. Crawford	1816	Madison, Monroe
Richard Rush	1825	J. Q. Adams
Samuel D. Ingham	1829	Jackson
Louis McLane	1831	Jackson
William J. Duane	1833	Jackson
Roger B. Taney	1833	Jackson
Levi Woodbury	1834	Jackson, Van Buren
Thomas Ewing	1841	W. H. Harrison, Tyler
Walter Forward	1841	Tyler
John C. Spencer	1843	Tyler
George M. Bibb	1844	Tyler
Robert J. Walker	1845	Polk
William M. Meredith	1849	Taylor
Thomas Corwin	1850	Fillmore
James Guthrie	1853	Pierce
Howell Cobb	1857	Buchanan
Philip F. Thomas	1860	Buchanan
John A. Dix	1861	Buchanan
*Salmon P. Chase	1861	Lincoln
William P. Fessenden	1864	Lincoln
Hugh McCulloch	1865	Lincoln, A. Johnson
George S. Boutwell	1869	Grant
William A. Richardson	1873	Grant
Benjamin H. Bristow	1874	Grant
Lot M. Morrill	1876	Grant
John Sherman	1877	Hayes
William Windom	1881	Garfield, Arthur
Charles J. Folger	1881	Arthur
Walter Q. Gresham	1884	Arthur
Hugh McCulloch	1884	Arthur
Daniel Manning	1885	Cleveland
Charles S. Fairchild	1887	Cleveland
William Windom	1889	B. Harrison
Charles Foster	1891	B. Harrison
John G. Carlisle	1893	Cleveland
Lyman J. Gage	1897	McKinley, T. Roosevelt
Leslie M. Shaw	1902	T. Roosevelt
George B. Cortelyou	1907	T. Roosevelt
Franklin MacVeagh	1909	Taft
William G. McAdoo	1913	Wilson
Carter Glass	1918	Wilson
David F. Houston	1920	Wilson
Andrew W. Mellon	1921	Harding, Coolidge, Hoover
Ogden L. Mills	1932	Hoover
William H. Woodin	1933	F. D. Roosevelt
Henry Morgenthau, Jr.	1934	F. D. Roosevelt, Truman
Frederick M. Vinson	1945	Truman
John W. Snyder	1946	Truman
George M. Humphrey	1953	Eisenhower
Robert B. Anderson	1957	Eisenhower
Douglas Dillon	1961	Kennedy, L. B. Johnson
Henry H. Fowler	1965	L. B. Johnson
Joseph W. Barr	1968	L. B. Johnson
David M. Kennedy	1969	Nixon
John B. Connally	1971	Nixon
George P. Shultz	1972	Nixon
William E. Simon	1974	Nixon, Ford
W. Michael Blumenthal	1977	Carter
G. William Miller	1979	Carter
Donald T. Regan	1981	Reagan
James A. Baker III	1985	Reagan
Nicholas F. Brady	1988	Reagan, G. Bush
Lloyd M. Bentsen, Jr.	1993	Clinton
Robert E. Rubin	1995	Clinton
Lawrence Summers	1999	Clinton
Paul O'Neill	2001	G. W.Bush
John W. Snow	2003	G. W. Bush

*Subject of a separate article or profile. Consult the Index.

United States coins are minted in Philadelphia and Denver under the authority of the United States Mint, a bureau of the Department of the Treasury.

The **Alcohol and Tobacco Tax and Trade Bureau** (TTB) enforces laws covering the production, use, and distribution of alcohol and tobacco products. It also collects excise taxes for firearms and ammunition.

The **Community Development Financial Institution** (CDFI) helps increase the availability of credit, investment capital, and financial services available in distressed rural communities and urban areas.

The **Financial Crimes Enforcement Network** (FinCEN) supports investigations of money laundering and other domestic and international financial crimes. It also fosters cooperation between federal, state, local, and international law enforcement agencies.

History

The Department of the Treasury was established on September 2, 1789, by the First Congress. The first secretary of the treasury, Alexander Hamilton, was appointed by President George Washington. At that time, the Treasury had a staff of five people.

Headquarters for the Department of the Treasury are located at 1500 Pennsylvania Avenue, N.W., Washington, D.C. 20220.

Office of the Curator and Preservation Office
United States Department of the Treasury

See also DOLLAR; MINT.

TREATIES

A treaty is a written agreement, under international law, between two or more independent nations. Under the Constitution of the United States, this includes both a treaty ratified by the president with the advice and consent of the Senate and an executive agreement approved by the president alone. A treaty, in the broad sense, may also be a protocol, or temporary agreement, or an exchange of diplomatic notes expressing agreement on policy.

Treaties have been made since early times. About 3000 B.C. an arbitration treaty to settle a boundary dispute was concluded between the kings of two city-states of Mesopotamia. About 1280 B.C. Ramses II, Pharaoh of Egypt, and Hattushilish, King of the Hittites, made a treaty of peace, alliance, and extradition (surrender of a criminal by one state or nation to another). The Greeks and Romans developed elaborate ceremonials of treaty-making. In the Middle Ages, Emperor Charlemagne made treaties with the Muslim caliph Harun al-Rashid (764?–809).

When the European system of independent nations developed during the 15th and 16th centuries, the number of treaties grew steadily. About 10,000 treaties have been concluded since 1920, and more than that number are in force between the leading nations. Most of these are **bilateral** treaties, that is, treaties between two nations. Almost 1,000 are **multilateral** treaties, that is, treaties involving more than two nations. Some treaties, such as the United Nations Charter, join together most of the countries of the world.

Since the end of the 17th century the texts of important treaties usually have been published by the nations taking part in them. The Covenant of the League of Nations required its members to register treaties with the organization. The United Nations Charter makes the same requirement of members.

▶ CLASSES OF TREATIES

Treaties may be classified as bilateral or multilateral, according to the number of parties involved. They may also be classified according to the nature of the obligations or duties undertaken, such as lawmaking or contractual. Sometimes treaties are classified according to subject matter. For example, there are political treaties (which include territorial transfers and peace treaties), commercial treaties, and treaties for the administration of justice, the establishment of international organizations and unions, and the codification of international law.

Great peace treaties such as the Treaties of Westphalia (1648), ending the Thirty Years War, and the Treaty of Vienna (1815), ending the Napoleonic Wars, included a few articles setting up international organizations and codifying international law. But special treaties devoted to these questions were few until the second half of the 19th century. The Declaration of Paris (1856) established important rules of maritime warfare. The Geneva Convention (1864) set up the Red Cross organization to relieve the suffering caused by war. Treaties organizing the International Telegraphic Union in 1865 and the International Postal Union in 1874 (renamed the Universal Postal Union in 1878) marked the beginning of public international unions.

During the 20th century many multilateral treaties have been made. These include the Hague Conventions (1899, 1907), the League of Nations Covenant (1919), the Statute of the Permanent Court of International Justice (1920), the Kellogg-Briand Peace Pact (1928), and the United Nations Charter (1945). Many lawmaking treaties have been made under the sponsorship of the League of Nations, the United Nations, and such regional organizations as the Organization of American States (OAS), the European Communities, and the Organization of African Unity (OAU).

▶ MAKING TREATIES

Treaties may be made by an informal exchange of notes or by an agreement signed by authority of the chief executives of the nations concerned. But the most important treaties are concluded by elaborate formalities often requiring the consent of a legislative body.

Bilateral Treaties. Formalities for bilateral treaties usually include the following steps.

(1) Exchange of "full powers" of the representatives of the nations concerned, indicating the subject that they are authorized by the chief executive of their country to negotiate (work out).

(2) Negotiation, carried on in confidence.

(3) Signature (if negotiation is successful) by the negotiators of completed texts in the languages of the countries taking part. The negotiators first sign the text in their own languages.

(4) Ratification (official approval) by the respective countries, usually by the chief executives, who are often required by their nations' constitutions to obtain the consent of one or both houses of the legislature. The United States Constitution states that the president makes treaties "by and with the Advice and Consent of the Senate . . . provided two thirds of the Senators present concur." In France treaties, except for political alliances and military conventions, must be approved by a majority of both houses of the legislature. In Great Britain the Crown in Council (the reigning monarch with the Privy Council) ratifies treaties, but ordinarily the government submits them to the House of Commons for its consideration before ratification.

(5) Exchange of ratifications, the final step. In this ceremony the representatives negotiating the treaty exchange the instruments (documents) of ratification by their countries. These are carefully examined to discover whether any reservations (limitations or exceptions) have been attached. The treaty comes into force on this date, unless the text itself provides another date, past or future.

A participating country that later finds that its negotiator was the innocent victim of fraud or duress (force) at the time of ratification may declare the treaty cancelled. The use of force or pressure against a country usually is present in the case of treaties of peace ending a war. As long as war was regarded as a lawful activity, duress was not considered grounds for cancelling peace treaties. But after the Japanese seized Manchuria in 1931, United States Secretary of State Henry L. Stimson (1867–1950) declared that nations that were bound by treaty not to make war could not benefit from aggression. This meant that other countries would not recognize the results of any aggression. Stimson was referring to the Pact of Paris, or the Kellogg-Briand Pact, which was an agreement between 48 nations (including Japan) to renounce war as an instrument of national policy. He stated that treaties made as a result of aggression in defiance of the pact should not be recognized. The Stimson Doctrine was

approved by the League of Nations Assembly and has been followed ever since.

Multilateral Treaties. Multilateral treaties are concluded in much the same way as bilateral treaties. The representatives taking part meet in a conference, which may be called especially to deal with a particular subject or may be a regular meeting, such as the United Nations General Assembly. The credentials (authority to negotiate) of the representatives are accepted, and negotiations proceed by public debate, as in a legislative assembly. Usually there are some confidential discussions between the leading participants. The final text is signed by those negotiators who agree. It is then submitted to their governments for ratification. The instruments of ratification are deposited for safekeeping in a place agreed upon, such as the Secretariat of the United Nations. Often multilateral treaties may be adhered to (accepted) by representatives of countries that were not among the original signers.

▶ **ENDING TREATIES**

Treaties may be ended only by consent of the nations involved or by procedures accepted by general international law. Commercial treaties usually provide that a signer may denounce them after 1 year's notice. International organizations often provide that a member may withdraw after giving advance notice. Members of the League of Nations could withdraw on 2 years' notice. Although there is no such provision in the United Nations Charter, Indonesia withdrew in 1965, rejoining the following year.

International law recognizes that a bilateral treaty is ended if one of the signing nations ceases to exist. For example, Texas, which is today a state, was an independent republic before it joined the United States. A change in government, even by revolution, does not end a nation's existence. War between the signatory nations ends political treaties but only interrupts commercial treaties. Treaties concerning rules of war are brought into force. If one signatory power breaks the treaty, the other party may declare it no longer in force or may suspend its operation.

An important change in conditions may make a treaty out of date. This principle is known as *rebus sic stantibus*, which is Latin

SOME FAMOUS TREATIES AND ALLIANCES

Adams-Onís Treaty (Transcontinental Treaty) (1819; ratified 1821)—Between Spain and the United States. Spain ceded East Florida to the United States, and United States claims to West Florida were recognized.

Aix-la-Chapelle (1748)—Ended the War of the Austrian Succession (King George's War in America).

Alaskan Purchase Treaty (1867)—The United States purchased Alaska from Russia for $7,200,000.

Augsburg, Religious Peace of (1555)—Lutheran princes and cities in Germany were granted tolerance.

Brest-Litovsk (1918)—Ended World War I hostilities between Germany and Russia.

Bucharest (1913)—Ended second Balkan War. Bulgaria had to give up territory to Greece, Turkey, Rumania, and Serbia.

Clayton-Bulwer Treaty (1850)—Between United States and Great Britain. It provided that the two countries should have joint control over any canal built through Central America.

Concordat of Worms (1122)—The dispute over lay investiture (whether the Church or the State was to appoint bishops) was settled by the Holy Roman Emperor, Henry V, and Pope Calixtus II.

Convention of 1818—Between the United States and Great Britain. This fixed the boundary between the United States and British North America along the 49th parallel from the Great Lakes to the Rocky Mountains.

Cushing's Treaty (1844)—The first treaty between the United States and China. It opened up political relations between the two countries.

Egyptian-Israeli Treaty (1979)—Between Egypt and Israel. Formally ended state of war.

Frankfurt (1871)—Ended Franco-Prussian War. France ceded the regions of Alsace and most of Lorraine and paid a $1,000,000,000 indemnity to Germany.

Gadsden Purchase (1853)—United States bought a strip of land (today part of New Mexico and Arizona) from Mexico for $10,000,000.

Ghent (1814)—Ended the British-American War of 1812.

Guadalupe Hidalgo (1848)—Ended the Mexican War. Mexico gave up all claims to Texas and ceded New Mexico and California to the United States for the sum of $15,000,000.

Havana, Act of (1940)—An agreement among the 21 American republics that any European country that tried to transfer any of its colonies or possessions in the Western Hemisphere to another non-American power would not be permitted to do so; and if an attempt was made, an American body would take over the territory involved and administer it.

Hay–Bunau-Varilla Treaty (also called Panama Canal Treaty; 1903)—The United States leased a strip of land 16 kilometers (10 miles) wide from Panama for construction of the canal. Panama was paid $10,000,000 and given a yearly rental of $250,000.

Hay–Pauncefote Treaty (1901)—Between the United States and Britain. The United States was allowed to build the Panama Canal, thereby abolishing the Clayton-Bulwer Treaty of 1850.

Holy Alliance (1815)—Agreement first signed by Austria, Prussia, and Russia, later by all European powers except Great Britain, Turkey, and the Papal States. It was a statement of Christian brotherhood.

Jay's Treaty (1794)—Between Great Britain and the United States. It provided for British evacuation of northwestern posts.

Kellogg-Briand Pact (also called Pact of Paris; 1928)—An agreement to renounce war as an instrument of national policy and to settle disputes by peaceful means. Sixty-three countries adhered to this treaty.

Lateran (1929)—Between Italy and the Papacy. Italy recognized the independence and sovereignty of Vatican City, ending a 59-year dispute between Church and State.

Lausanne (1923)—Peace re-established between Greece and Turkey. Severe terms of Treaty of Sèvres (1920) between Allies and Turkey revised in Turkey's favor.

Lima, Declaration of (1938)—The 21 American republics asserted the solidarity of the American continent against foreign intervention or attack.

Little Entente (1920)—An alliance formed by Yugoslavia, Czechoslovakia, and Rumania.

Locarno Pacts (1925)—A series of treaties entered into by Britain, France, Germany, Italy, Belgium, Czechoslovakia, and Poland. The main treaty guaranteed the western boundaries of Germany as set by the Versailles Treaty (1919).

London Naval Agreements (1930)—The United States, Great Britain, and Japan agreed to limit naval armaments (expired 1936).

London Naval Agreements (1936)—The United States, Great Britain, and France agreed to exchange advance information on shipbuilding, and qualitative, not quantitative, limitations on naval armaments were set.

---

for "affairs remaining thus." It has been said that this principle is to be understood, if not expressed, in all treaties. Some authorities state that a signatory power may denounce a treaty when a change in conditions makes continuance of the treaty conflict with the national interest of that power. But there is another principle, known as *pacta sunt servanda,* which is Latin for "treaties must be observed." This means that even if a treaty is ended as an effective document, certain rights established by it (such as a transfer of territory or a boundary line) continue in force.

▶ **INTERPRETATION AND ENFORCEMENT**

International law provides rules for explaining the meaning of treaties. The purpose of a treaty often is expressed in the preamble, or introduction.

Language. International law provides an exact meaning for technical terms used in a treaty. Differences in language, however, often make interpretation of nontechnical terms difficult. This is true even when the texts in two languages are compared carefully before the document is signed. Before the 18th century treaties generally were in Latin. Then, up to World War I, French was the language commonly used in multilateral treaties. The League of Nations Covenant was official in both French and English. The United Nations Charter is official in French, English, Spanish, Russian, and Chinese.

Reservations. Sometimes, for various reasons, a country will ask that a certain limitation or exception be added to a treaty. This is done when the treaty is signed or ratified, and these reservations must be accepted by the

Japan attended the conference but withdrew before the final agreement was reached.

Louisiana Purchase (1803)—The United States bought the Louisiana territory from France for $15,000,000.

Neutrality Treaty (1978)—Between the United States and Panama. The Panama Canal was designated an international waterway, always to be neutral.

Nuclear Nonproliferation Treaty (1968)—Multinational agreement not to divert nuclear energy to military purposes.

Panama Canal Treaties (1978)—Between the United States and Panama. The United States gave Panama total control of the Panama Canal in 2000 and abolished the Canal Zone.

Paris (1763)—Ended the French and Indian War (the Seven Years' War in Europe). France lost most of its American possessions to Great Britain.

Paris (1783)—Ended the American Revolutionary War. The colonies won their independence from Great Britain.

Paris (1815)—Second peace ending the Napoleonic Wars between France and the Allies. It reduced France to 1789 boundaries and forced it to pay a heavy indemnity.

Paris (1856)—Ended the Crimean War between Russia and the allied powers of Turkey, France, Great Britain, and Sardinia. It halted Russian influence in southeastern Europe.

Paris (1898)—Ended Spanish-American War. Cuba was freed, and the Philippines, Guam, and Puerto Rico were ceded to the United States for $20,000,000.

Pinckney's Treaty (1795)—Between the United States and Spain. Spain recognized United States boundary claims under the Treaty of Paris of 1783. Americans were given "right of deposit" in New Orleans.

Portsmouth (1905)—Ended Russo-Japanese War. Japan's power was increased.

Pyrenees, Peace of the (1659)—Between France and Spain, which had continued fighting after the Peace of Westphalia (1648).

Rome (1957)—The founding of the European Economic Community (Common Market) by Belgium, Luxembourg, the Netherlands, France, Italy, and West Germany.

Rush-Bagot Agreement (1817)—Between Great Britain and the United States. It limited naval power on the Great Lakes and set forth a policy of peace between the United States and Canada.

Saint Germain (1919)—Between the Allies and Austria after World War I. The Austro-Hungarian monarchy was broken up, and Austria's boundaries were considerably reduced. The

independence of Yugoslavia (then known as the Kingdom of Serbs, Croats, and Slovenes), Czechoslovakia, Poland, and Hungary was recognized.

Strategic Arms Limitation Talks (SALT I) Treaty (1972)—Between the United States and the Soviet Union. The treaty set limits on their number of nuclear weapons.

Test Ban Treaty (1963)—Negotiated by Great Britain, the United States, and the Soviet Union. It was signed by 102 nations. The treaty prohibited test explosions of nuclear devices in the air, in outer space, or underwater.

Triple Alliance (1882)—Italy joined the dual alliance (formed in 1879) of Germany and Austria-Hungary.

Triple Entente (1907)—Diplomatic union of Great Britain, France, and Russia to counterbalance the Triple Alliance.

Utrecht, Union of (1579)—Union of northern Netherlands provinces that laid the foundation for what eventually became the Netherlands.

Verdun (843)—Charlemagne's empire was divided among his three grandsons. The eastern third became Germany, and the western third became France.

Versailles (1919)—Between Germany and the Allies at the end of World War I. Germany lost territory both in Europe and in the colonies and was forced to pay large reparations.

Vienna, Congress of (1815)—Division of Europe after Napoleon's overthrow. Vast territorial changes were made throughout Europe.

Washington (1871)—Between the United States and Great Britain. The *Alabama* claims and other disputes were referred to arbitration.

Washington Conference (1921–22)—Attended by Great Britain, France, Italy, the Netherlands, Portugal, Belgium, the United States, Japan, and China. Nine treaties were made. The most important of these were (1) Five-Power Naval Treaty, which set tonnage ratios in capital ships; (2) Five-Power Treaty, which concerned submarines; (3) Four-Power Treaty, by which France, Japan, Great Britain, and the United States agreed to respect one another's rights in the Pacific; and (4) Nine-Power Treaty, respecting the Open Door policy in China.

Webster-Ashburton Treaty (1842)—Between the United States and Great Britain. This treaty settled the boundary dispute between Canada and Maine.

Westphalia (1648)—Ended the Thirty Years' War. All the countries of western Europe were involved. France emerged as the dominant power.

other parties to the treaty. The usual time for this is on exchange of ratification. Difficulties arise in the case of multilateral treaties when reservations are accepted by some of the treaty signers but not by others. Often such treaties forbid reservations except to specified articles of the treaty.

Treaties are upheld mainly by the common interests and good faith of the signers. Peace treaties that were not freely accepted by the defeated party often provided for occupation of its territory by the victor over a period of years. This was done to make sure that treaty provisions were observed. Treaties often provide for arbitration of disputes, should the meaning or use of terms be questioned.

The problem of maintaining treaties in a rapidly changing world is a serious one for international law and international organizations. Treaty-making is the legislative (law-making) process of the society of nations. But the principle that an independent nation is not bound by a treaty to which it is not a party makes it very difficult to keep international law up-to-date by the treaty-making process.

Under Article 14 of its charter the United Nations General Assembly may recommend measures to meet situations, including treaty provisions, that are "likely to impair the general welfare or friendly relations among nations." However, it can only recommend measures, not enforce them.

QUINCY WRIGHT
Formerly, University of Virginia

See also EUROPEAN UNION; INTERNATIONAL LAW; INTERNATIONAL RELATIONS; LEAGUE OF NATIONS; ORGANIZATION OF AMERICAN STATES; UNITED NATIONS.

Winter | Summer

Branch

Leaves

Trunk

Roots

Trees are both beautiful and useful. Their leaves absorb carbon dioxide and release oxygen. Their roots prevent erosion by holding the soil. Food, lumber, and materials used to make paper and plastics all come from trees.

TREES

Long ago the Vikings used to tell tales of an enormous tree that supported the entire universe. The roots of this mighty tree grew down into the underworld. Its trunk held up the earth, and its evergreen boughs reached beyond the sky. Birds flew from its topmost branches, deer nibbled at its buds, and honeydew dripping from its leaves provided the gods with food.

It is not surprising that these Vikings believed in a giant tree that supported the universe, for their world really was supported by trees. Wood fires kept them warm. Blazing pine knots lit their way at night, and bark and roots gave them medicines. The log houses that sheltered them were made from trees, as were the long boats with carved dragons' heads at their prows in which the Norsemen sailed the seas.

Even in today's world of concrete and steel and atomic energy, can you imagine how life would change if trees and their products should suddenly disappear? Look out! There goes the chair you're sitting on. The pages of this book are floating away. Your pencils have vanished. Where is your baseball bat, the film for your father's camera, and your sister's plastic doll? There are no more plums and pears and cherries, no more almond cookies or apple pies.

All of these things and thousands more come from trees. But where does a tree come from?

A tree comes from a seed. Like boys and girls, elephants and daisies, a tree is alive. It is born. It breathes and grows. It drinks water and makes food. It produces seeds from which new trees grow. After a time it dies.

Trees are the largest living things and the oldest. Not even blue whales are as big as redwood or sequoia trees. Redwoods are sometimes 350 feet tall. Their relatives, the giant sequoias, have trunks so thick that 20 people with arms outstretched can barely circle them.

The scientific name of the redwood is *Sequoia sempervirens,* which means "sequoia always green." There are redwoods alive today that were tall trees when the Vikings first landed on our shores. And these are youngsters compared to the giant sequoias. Some of the sequoias now growing in northern California were saplings 3,500 years ago, at the time that Egyptian pharaohs were building temples along the Nile. Scientists now believe that some of the bristlecone pines found in California are even older. At least one gnarled bristlecone pine has been found that goes back 4,600 years!

Of course, not all trees are as ancient as the sequoias or as big. Aspens are aged at 70. Gray birches die soon after their 40th birthday. Dogwoods, whose blossoms brighten the woods in spring, may be only 20 feet tall, but they tower over the common juniper, whose topmost branches are sometimes 5 feet above the ground.

In windy places along the seashore, you may have seen dwarf forests of oak and pine and wild cherry. These Tom Thumb forests are stunted by the wind and the poor soil. If you want to smell the cherry blossoms or pick the pine cones, you have to kneel down.

White pine

Dogwood

Eastern hemlock

White
pine
leaves

Sugar
pine
leaves

Dogwood
leaf

Ginkgo
leaf

Eastern
hemlock
leaves

Utah
juniper
leaves

Sugar pine

Ginkgo

Utah juniper

Weeping willow

Bald cypress

American elm

Coconut palm

American elm leaf

Weeping willow leaf

Bald cypress leaves

Coconut palm leaves

Sequoia leaves

Spruce leaves

Cottonwood leaf

Spruce

Sequoia

Cottonwood

Sycamore

White ash

Apple

White oak

Sycamore leaf

Sugar maple leaf

White ash leaf

Apple leaf

Sassafras leaf

White oak leaf

Douglas fir leaves

Sugar maple

Sassafras

Douglas fir

Red cedar

Shagbark hickory

California laurel

Quaking aspen

Red cedar leaves

Shagbark hickory leaf

California laurel leaf

Quaking aspen leaf

American beech leaf

Joshua tree leaf

Paper birch leaf

American beech

Joshua tree

Paper birch

All trees grow from seeds. The seed puts out two shoots. One grows down into the soil to become the root. The other grows up toward the light to become the trunk and leaves. The roots absorb water and minerals, which go up the trunk to the leaves. The leaves make food, in the form of sugar, which goes down the trunk to the roots.

▶ BIRTH OF A TREE

Each kind of tree, from the giant sequoia of California to the dwarf oak on Cape Cod, starts in the same way. Have you ever found a sprouting acorn in the woods? If so, you have been present at the birth of an oak tree. The acorn is the seed of the oak. A tree in the making is packed inside its shell. After lying on the ground soaking up moisture, the shell splits and two pale shoots appear. The tree has begun to grow.

One shoot, poking through the pointed tip of the acorn, will become the roots of the tree. The other will form its trunk and leaves. The root grows down, wriggling its way into the soil. The trunk grows up, lifting its leaves toward the light. Even if you twirl the acorn around or bury it deep under the ground, the shoot that is going to be a trunk will always grow up, while the root heads down.

▶ ROOTS

Roots anchor a tree in the ground, holding it firmly in place so that it doesn't topple over when storm winds blow. The growing tip of a root is sensitive as well as strong. If it meets an obstacle, it is able to shy away and grow around the obstacle. If, however, the root has no place to turn—if it is trapped in a rock crevice—it can actually split the rock and grow through to the earth beneath.

Trees often have a long main root, or **taproot**, with hundreds of other roots and feathery rootlets branching from it. The taproot may grow a dozen feet under the ground, while its branches spread out in every direction. If you could cut away the earth, you would see more growth below the ground than above. The roots of a single sequoia can take up 3 acres, an area large enough for 16 baseball diamonds.

Some roots seem to have a life of their own. If the original tree is destroyed, they send up new trunks and leaves. These **suckers**, as they are called, grow into full-size trees. Anyone who has ever tried to get rid of an ailanthus knows that it has as many lives as a cat. If it is chopped down in the fall, half a dozen husky suckers will spring up the following year.

A few trees, particularly in the tropics, behave in just the opposite way. Instead of trunks and branches that grow up from roots, they have roots that grow down from branches. Banyan trees produce hundreds of dangling aerial roots. After a time the roots reach the earth and enter it. As they continue to grow, the aboveground part of each root becomes a trunk. The trunk develops branches—and aerial roots—of its own. In India there is a banyan tree with 3,000 trunks. A single tree has turned itself into a forest!

In a summer when there's been no rain for a long time, some people think that they can give a tree water by hosing down its leaves. Watering a tree by watering its leaves is like

Inside a tree trunk

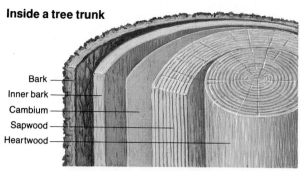

Bark
Inner bark
Cambium
Sapwood
Heartwood

The bark, a layer of dead cells, protects the tree. Each year the cambium forms two new cell layers: the inner bark, which carries food made in the leaves down to the roots, and the sapwood, which carries water and nutrients up from the roots. Heartwood is old sapwood cells that strengthen the tree.

taking a shower when you're thirsty. The shower may be pleasant, but it doesn't quench your thirst. Only water entering your mouth and trickling down your throat can do that. In the same way, a tree doesn't benefit much from a hosing until the water soaks into the earth, where the roots absorb it.

You might say that a tree drinks with its feet. Fortunately, its feet are far better equipped for the job than yours are. Its thick, strong roots and branching rootlets have millions of tiny root hairs. The **root hairs**, which are so small that you can scarcely see them without a magnifying glass, grow near the tips of the roots. They soak up water and minerals from the soil. The water then travels up into the trunk of the tree and from there to the branches and leaves.

▶TRUNKS

In its first year of life an oak tree looks like most of the other plants in a field or garden. Only when you feel its wiry stem or try to tear it do you realize that the stem is stronger than a daisy's or dandelion's. Young as it is, the stem of the oak is woody. This woody stem becomes the tree's trunk.

The outer layer of the trunk is its **bark**. The bark of young trees is always smooth. As the tree grows thicker as well as taller, its bark stretches. After a while the bark may split. Each kind of tree has its own way of stretching or splitting.

The thin, smooth bark of a beech tree can stretch without tearing. It fits around the trunk as if it were a gray kid glove. Sycamore bark, on the other hand, hardly stretches at all. Big patches of it flake off as the tree grows. The greens and whites of the inner

bark and the peeling brown outside give the tree a strange, blotchy look.

When black-locust bark splits, it forms deep ridges that run up and down the trunk. Ash bark makes a diamond-shaped pattern, while the bark of the shagbark hickory—which really is shaggy—breaks off in long strips. Almost everyone knows the chalky-white bark of the paper birch. If you peel it from a dead tree in the woods, you can write messages on it. (Taking it from a live tree may injure or kill the tree.)

Although the rough outer bark on a tree trunk is dead, it protects the living tissues inside. Just underneath the bark area is the **cambium**. This is the part of the trunk that grows. Each year the cambium builds a layer of bark on its outside and a layer of wood inside. The wood inside the cambium is called **sapwood**. Like other living things, sapwood is made up of tiny units called cells. These cells, growing one on top of another in the trunk, form pipes. The sapwood pipes are the most important part of the tree's plumbing system. They carry **sap**—which is soil water with minerals or food dissolved in it.

Sap travels between the roots, deep underground, and the topmost branches and leaves. A column of soil water with minerals in it moves up in one set of pipes. A second set of pipes brings down water with food in it. The food, which is dissolved in the water, gives every part of the tree the energy it needs to grow. Because the sap transports water and food, it is sometimes compared to the blood that circulates in our bodies.

Maple syrup comes from tree sap. Sugar maples store food during the cold months of the year, when they are not growing. Late in winter as the sap begins to thaw, farmers say, "Sap's running!" Driving hollow tubes into the sapwood pipes, they collect the sap as it drips out. The clear sap is mostly water. The farmers boil it until the water evaporates, cooking more than 30 gallons of sap to get 1 gallon of maple syrup.

Long before the time of Columbus, Indians in South. America harvested a milky juice from the sap of the Pará rubber tree. They used it to waterproof cloth and make rubber balls for games. Other trees that are tapped for their sap include the longleaf and slash pines that grow in the southern United States and the sapodilla tree of Central America. The gummy liquid that oozes from the pines is made into turpentine, while the sapodilla provides chicle for chewing gum.

The pipes in the sapwood don't last forever. Each spring the cambium builds new ones, while the old pipes slowly fill up with wastes—gums and resins, salts, and other materials. These plugged-up pipes usually become darker in color than the new wood. They form the **heartwood** of the tree.

Although the ever thickening column of heartwood is dead, it gives the tree strength. A hollow tree whose heartwood has been destroyed by fire or disease can live on. It is likely to fall in a hurricane, however.

By the time a baby oak is 4 or 5 years old, you would never mistake it for a flower. It looks like a tree. Only, what does a tree look like?

A tree usually has a single main trunk with many side branches. It grows taller from the top of its trunk. It grows wider from the tips of its branches. It doesn't send up new shoots from the ground, as lilacs or rosebushes do.

Of course, the banyan tree is an exception to these rules. So is the pussy willow, which may have several trunks, and the common juniper, which sometimes has no trunk at all but sends branches sprawling along the ground. Even botanists, the scientists who study plants, can't decide whether to call pussy willows and common junipers bushes or trees.

Although it is not hard to tell a tree from a bush or from a woody vine, not all trees are shaped alike. Each kind of tree has its own way of growing. The trunk of the apple tree often slants, making it an easy tree to climb. The trunk of the elm divides, and dozens of thin, graceful branches spray up and out like a fountain. The soldierly tulip tree grows straight, with its lowest branches sometimes 50 feet from the ground.

Even in winter many trees can be recognized by their shape. Willow branches droop, while those of the Lombardy poplar point up toward the sky. A sugar maple forms a neat oval, as if a barber had trimmed around its edges with clippers. Spruce trees are shaped like triangles. Their longest branches are at the base of the tree, their shortest at the top.

▶ LEAVES

Like all green plants, a tree makes its own food. Each leaf on a tree is a busy factory. All day long it takes in carbon dioxide from the air and water and minerals from the soil. All day long its green coloring matter, called **chlorophyll**, absorbs energy from the sun. Powered by the sunshine, the chlorophyll changes the carbon dioxide and water into sugar. The sugar made in the leaves is the tree's basic food.

This remarkable process, known as photosynthesis, is only one of a leaf's activities. Leaves also give off enormous quantities of water. Only a small fraction of the water that flows up through the sapwood pipes is used in making food. Most of the rest evaporates through millions of tiny holes on the surface of the leaves.

On a sunny summer day a middle-sized oak gives off 150 gallons of water. Although you can't see this steady spray from the leaves, you can feel the way it cools the air. In a forest where tree leaves spray thousands of gallons of water into the air, the water vapor rises and forms clouds. After a time the water that was soaked up by tree roots and evaporated from tree leaves returns in the form of rain.

In much of North America a tree's water supply is cut off in winter. After the ground freezes, trees can't release gallons of water into the air. They would need more water than they could get from the frozen ground. Like the owners of vacation cottages, who lock doors and windows and drain water pipes at the end of summer, trees must lock up, too. They do this by shedding their leaves.

If all of the leaves on a tree snapped off the way a dead twig does, there would be thousands of little wounds in the branches. Sap would ooze from the wounds, and germs might enter them. Instead, a tree gets ready for winter far ahead of time. Late in summer a double layer of cells begins to form at the base of each leaf stem. The leaves don't fall until these layers of cells are under way. It's as if the tree were bandaging its wounds before it was wounded.

At the same time, less and less sap flows into the leaves. Photosynthesis slows down, and the leaves' green coloring matter wastes away. This is when the leaves begin to wear their gaudy autumn dress.

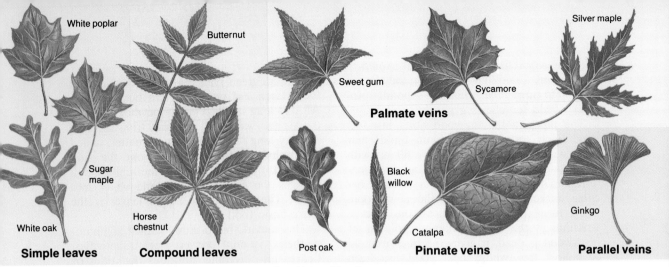

Palmate veins

White poplar

Butternut

Sweet gum

Sycamore

Silver maple

Sugar maple

White oak

Simple leaves

Horse chestnut

Compound leaves

Post oak

Black willow

Catalpa

Pinnate veins

Ginkgo

Parallel veins

Leaf Identification

Perhaps you have heard people say, "Jack Frost is painting the leaves." Jack Frost doesn't paint the leaves, nor do they "turn" orange or yellow. Small amounts of these colors were in the leaves all spring and summer, hidden from view by the bright green of the chlorophyll. The gay yellows of tulip-tree and birch leaves in the fall come from **carotene**, the same chemical that gives carrots and egg yolks their color. However, there is something new in the scarlet oak and purple ash leaves. Their reds and purples come from **anthocyanins**, coloring matter that forms in these leaves at the end of the summer.

Not all trees shed their leaves in autumn. Pines and firs and hemlocks have narrow, needlelike leaves with a thick, waxy outer covering that prevents evaporation of water. Their leaves remain on the trees for several years. When the leaves fall, new ones grow at the same time, and the branches never look bare. That's why these trees are called **evergreens**. Actually, this is a confusing name because several trees with needlelike leaves aren't evergreen at all. Bald cypresses and larch—close relatives of the pines—drop their needles in autumn, when maples and birches do.

There are also trees with broad leaves that stay green all year round. The live oak and the California laurel have leathery leaves that help the trees keep their moisture during the cold months. Palms, with their feathery or fan-shaped leaves, don't need to prepare for winter. They grow only in places where the winters are warm.

Trees have different ways of arranging their leaves. Birch and beech and elm leaves grow alternately along the branches. Maple and ash leaves always grow in pairs, directly opposite each other. You could never mistake a maple for an ash, however, because the maple leaf is all in one piece, while the ash leaf is divided into as many as 11 separate leaflets. Maple leaves—and those of poplar and oak and apple—are known as **simple leaves**. Ash trees—and hickory and horse chestnut—have **compound leaves**.

Even the veins that carry sap through the leaves grow differently. Maple and sycamore and sweet-gum leaves have what are called **palmate veins**. Their veins branch out from the leaf's stem the way fingers do from the palm of a hand. Oak and willow and catalpa leaves have a single center vein with side veins branching from it. This style of veining is called **pinnate**, after the Latin word for "feather." The ginkgo leaf is one of the few tree leaves in the world that has **parallel veins**.

There are many other ways in which tree leaves differ from one another. A willow leaf is long and pointed. A catalpa's is shaped like a heart, a sweet gum's like a star. Sycamore and apple leaves are woolly; white-oak leaves, shiny and smooth. A birch leaf has fine, sharp teeth along its edges, while beech and chestnut leaves look scalloped. Sassafras leaves have a pleasant smell, but you'll probably want to hold your nose if you crush an ailanthus leaf!

▶ BUDS

Long before the broad-leaved trees shut up shop for the winter, they get ready for the following spring. They store food in their trunks and roots, and most important, they make buds.

Many people think that buds grow in the spring, after a tree's winter rest. That's not true. The buds that open in spring start to grow almost a year earlier. At first they are no bigger than the head of a pin. Hardly anyone notices them then because they are hidden by the leaves. By the time the leaves drop, the buds are fully formed.

Buds are something like seeds. They contain leaves and stems and flowers, which are folded, pleated, and doubled over into a neat, tight package. The outside of the package is usually covered with scales. The scales keep the bud snug and dry during the winter. When spring comes and sap travels up the trunk again, the scales fall off and the bud slowly unfolds.

Usually the bud at the tip of a branch is larger than the other buds. It contains the twig-to-be, as well as a cluster of folded leaves. Most of the buds along the sides of a branch are leaf buds. Some trees wrap their leaves and flowers in the same package. Others have separate buds for flowers.

Flower buds are often shaped differently from leaf buds. Elm flowers are packed in puffy, pancake-shaped buds; elm leaves, in little cones. Dogwood buds are even more surprising. The red-brown leaf buds are thin and pointed, but the gray flower buds are round. These plump dogwood flower buds are often compared to old-fashioned shoe buttons. If you count the shoe buttons on a dogwood tree on a cold December day, you can tell the number of blossoms that will open on the tree in April or May.

Trees produce many more leaf buds than they need. A full-grown elm may have 1,000,000 buds on its branches in winter. If all of them were to open, the leaves and twigs and flowers would soon be fighting each other for light and food. Perhaps half the buds open, while the others remain on the tree. They are the tree's second team. If squirrels eat the unfolding buds or inchworms nibble on the first tender leaves, then the second team is called from the bench. If they are not needed, they fall from the branches after a year or two.

Farmers and gardeners sometimes take advantage of this overproduction of buds to

Buds form on the tips and sides of branches. Buds on the tips will produce leaves and new shoots. Buds on the sides of a branch usually produce only leaves.

change the shape of a tree. If the bud at the tip of a branch is removed, more side buds will open. The branch won't grow in length, but it will be bushier. Apple and pear trees can be trained to grow flat against a wall if side buds, which would otherwise grow outward, are pinched off. Of course, pinching off the buds can't be done only once. It has to be repeated as new buds form.

Each kind of tree makes its own kind of bud package. If you walk in the woods in winter, you will see smoky-black buds and mustard-yellow ones, and scarlet and purple and brown. The furry bud at the tip of a magnolia branch is often an inch long. The horse chestnut's end bud is almost as big. It has a sticky coating on its brown scales that bees use as a glue when they patch up their hives. Maple trees have three shiny buds at the end of each twig, a large one in the middle and a small one on either side. Beech and cottonwood buds are pointed. The tulip tree's bud is flattened at its tip. When its scales open, it looks like a duck's bill.

▶FLOWERS AND SEEDS

If pussy willow branches are put in water in a warm house, their buds begin to open late in winter and the familiar gray "pussies" appear. Soon a cluster of butter-yellow flowers pushes through the silky fur. These are the male flowers. The powdery gold dust on their tips is pollen.

Male and female pussy willow flowers grow on separate trees. When they are outdoors, the wind carries pollen to the female flower. Then a seed begins to form inside the flower. Pussy willow seeds ripen quickly. By the time the leaf buds open, little black seeds covered with fluff are ready to drift away. If they land on soft, damp earth, they grow into pussy willow trees.

The smaller trees—apple and peach and dogwood—start to bloom when they are about 5 years old. A long-lived oak, on the other hand, may not flower until it has passed its 50th birthday, while a redwood may wait 150 years and a sequoia 250 for its first seeds. So, if you know a tree that doesn't flower, just give it time—a half-century or so.

Some tree flowers are big and beautiful. The lovely magnolia flowers and the pink and white blossoms of cherry trees are called **perfect flowers**. That is, both the pollen- and seed-producing machinery grow in the same flower. The showy, sweet-smelling tree flowers are pollinated by insects. Bees hunting nectar carry pollen from the male parts of one flower to the female parts of another. When the creamy-white flowers of the linden open early in summer, so many bees buzz around them that the linden has been nicknamed Bee Tree.

The male flowers of oak and birch and hickory grow in catkins. The catkins, which are shaped like cats' tails, hang from the branches. When their pollen is ripe, it spurts out, traveling on the breeze to the smaller, upright, female flowers.

Almost all of the needle-leaved evergreens grow their seeds in cones. That is why **conifer**, which means "cone bearer," is the scientific name for this group of trees. Although pine-cones are woodier than catkins, they work in much the same way. Enormous quantities of pollen are produced by the male cones. When the pollen is ripe, the ground around the tree looks as if it had been sprinkled with yellow talcum powder.

The female cones are larger than the male. During the time that the seeds are forming, the cones remain tightly sealed. Several years may go by before the scales open and the seeds blow away. The cones of some pines stay closed even longer. Often it takes the heat of a fire to crack open jack- and lodgepole-pine cones and release the trapped seeds. After a forest fire the seeds of these pines are often the first to sprout on the burned-over land.

If the thousands of seeds that a tree pro-duces each year were to fall to the ground under the tree, few would live. The thirsty parent tree would take up the water in the soil. Its broad umbrella of leaves would shade the seedlings. In a year or two most of them would die.

Each kind of tree has its own way of spreading its seeds. The surprisingly small seeds of the sequoia sail through the air with the help of papery wings. Hemlock and spruce, ash and elm, use that same method of traveling. Maple seeds always grow in pairs. Their twin wings twirl like the blades of a helicopter as the seeds fall. Cottonwood seeds are covered with cottony down, which acts as a parachute. A stiff breeze carries them far from their parent tree.

Sweet-gum seeds grow in round, prickly balls that dangle from the branches. The ripe seeds spill out like salt from a shaker. Honey-locust seeds are packed in twisted pods that resemble pea pods. When the pods drop in winter, they skid across the icy ground.

It is hardly wise to sit under a coconut palm if its seeds are ripening. Coconuts, the largest tree seeds of all, fall with a thump. When the trees grow on sloping island beaches, the nuts often roll across the hard-packed sand to the water. As they float on the waves their hard outer covering protects them. If they are washed ashore, even after traveling hundreds of miles, they can start new coconut groves.

Apples and cherries, nuts and acorns, are too heavy to sail through the air or skid along the ground. But their seeds or seed coverings taste so good that animals help plant them. A flock of cedar waxwings gorging on cherries, a squirrel burying an acorn, a chipmunk storing hickory nuts in its burrow under the ground—they are all planting trees. So are you when you drop a peach pit outdoors or leave the core of an apple where its seeds have a chance to sprout.

▶ A LONG TIME AGO

If a botanist flying across North America in a jet plane were to bail out suddenly, he wouldn't be totally lost when he landed. He would know where he was as soon as he looked at the trees. Towering Douglas firs would tell him that he was in the West. Forests of red spruce and balsam would say

"East." If he saw longleaf pine with live oak and magnolia growing in moist places and bald cypress growing in the swamps, he would recognize the southern United States. Cottonwoods, standing tall at the edges of wheat and corn fields, would introduce the Great Plains. And one lone, scrubby Joshua tree would be enough to let him know that he was in the sandy Southwest.

Each kind of tree has its own requirements for sun and rain and soil. Douglas firs and redwoods thrive on the cool, moist air that blows in from the Pacific. They would shrivel in the dry, desert country of the Joshua tree. Bald cypresses usually grow in water. They are found in the swamps of the southeastern United States and in a few other places in the world. Longleaf pines can take poor soil, but they need warmth and sunshine. They couldn't survive the cold Maine winters that white pines like.

How did all these differences come about? Many millions of years ago the earth did not look as it does today. Continents were low, with shallow seas lapping at their shores and covering vast inland areas. There were no extremes of temperatures—and no trees.

The first real trees—the first plants to have woody trunks and seeds—appeared only after mountains began to rise and inland seas changed first into swamps and then into dry land. Some of these ancient trees were like the cycads and ginkgoes that grow today. Others developed into the needle-leaved conifers—sequoia and cypress, juniper and fir.

Sixty million years ago there were forests of sequoias in Alaska and Europe and in parts of Asia. Although these sturdy giants were able to stand the colder temperatures, their seed machinery was never very efficient. No buzzing bees gathered pollen from their woody cones, and no chattering squirrels or hungry birds scattered their seeds, for a very good reason. When sequoias first appeared, there weren't any bees or squirrels or birds.

Time passed. As new mountain ranges rose and glaciers ground them down, as it became colder in some places and hotter in others, many of the early trees vanished, as the dinosaurs did. The cycads retreated to a warmer climate. The ginkgoes survived in isolated places in the mountains of Asia. A sheet of ice thousands of feet thick destroyed the great sequoia forests. These ancient trees survived only on the western slopes of the Sierra Nevada mountains in California.

While this was happening, new kinds of trees developed that could meet the new, harsher conditions. The broad leaves of magnolias trapped the sun during short summers. Sycamores went a step further, shedding their leaves during cold winters. Poplars developed fluff-covered seeds that could travel for miles. Other trees came along—tulip, oak, and willow—each with its own way of flowering, its own way of scattering seeds.

As the earth continued to change, hundreds of different kinds of broad-leaved trees began to grow. They became more successful than the conifers. Some were able to live where it was windy or wet, others where it was cold or shady or dry. In their footsteps, smaller, flowering plants—grasses, buttercups, irises—appeared. The modern world was under way.

DOROTHY STERLING
Author, science books for children

See also FLOWERS; LEAVES; PHOTOSYNTHESIS; PLANTS.

TRENTON.   See NEW JERSEY (Cities).

TRIANGLES.   See GEOMETRY.

TRICHINOSIS.   See DISEASES (Descriptions of Some Diseases).

TRIGONOMETRY

Trigonometry is the branch of mathematics that deals with the relationships between the angles and sides of triangles. It is used to solve problems in many different fields, including physics, engineering, architecture, and surveying.

▶ **SIMILAR RIGHT TRIANGLES**

Basic to trigonometry is the relationship between similar right triangles. Similar triangles are triangles in which corresponding pairs of angles are the same size, or equal. Right triangles have one angle that measures 90°. The two triangles in Figure 1 are similar right triangles.

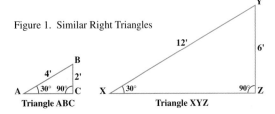

Figure 1. Similar Right Triangles

Triangle ABC   Triangle XYZ

Because triangle ABC and triangle XYZ are both right triangles, each has an angle that measures 90°. In trigonometry, an angle is commonly represented by the symbol ∠. In triangle ABC, ∠C = 90° and in triangle XYZ, ∠Z = 90°. Thus, ∠C = ∠Z. Both triangle ABC and triangle XYZ also have a 30° angle. Thus we can say ∠A = ∠X. Since triangle ABC and triangle XYZ have two pairs of equal angles, the two triangles are similar. When two triangles are similar, the lengths of their sides have the same ratio, or relationship, to one another. Look at Figure 1 again. In triangle ABC, side BC measures 2 feet and side AB measures 4 feet. The ratio between the two sides is shown as $\frac{BC}{AB}$, and $\frac{BC}{AB} = \frac{2}{4} = \frac{1}{2}$. In triangle XYZ, the ratio between the two corresponding sides will also be $\frac{1}{2}$ ($\frac{YZ}{XY} = \frac{6}{12} = \frac{1}{2}$), since the triangles are similar.

The Sine Ratio. The ratio of the side lengths that form the 30° angles in triangle ABC and triangle XYZ is called the **sine ratio**, or just the **sine**. So we can say that in triangle ABC, sine ∠A = $\frac{BC}{AB} = \frac{1}{2}$. In triangle XYZ, sine ∠X = $\frac{YZ}{XY} = \frac{1}{2}$. The sine of ∠A and the sine of ∠X are the same because the angles are both the same size. If two angles in

two right triangles are equal, then their sine ratios will be equal.

Trigonometry ratios are applied in the area called plane trigonometry.

▶ **PLANE TRIGONOMETRY**

Plane trigonometry uses the ratios between the sides of triangles to find missing angles and missing sides in a right triangle. As shown in Figure 2, the **hypotenuse** is the side of a right triangle that is opposite the 90° angle. The other two sides of a right triangle are called the **legs**.

Figure 2. Parts of a Right Triangle

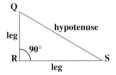

Trigonometry ratios in a right triangle are formed by comparing the lengths of any two of the three sides. The ratio is always related to an acute angle in the right triangle. An acute angle is an angle that is less than 90°. For the acute angles in any right triangle, the three most commonly used trigonometry ratios are the **sine**, **cosine**, and **tangent**. They are defined below:

$$\text{sine of } \angle S \ (\sin S) = \frac{\text{length of side opposite } \angle S}{\text{length of hypotenuse}}$$

$$\text{cosine of } \angle S \ (\cos S) = \frac{\text{length of side that is part of } \angle S}{\text{length of hypotenuse}}$$

$$\text{tangent of } \angle S \ (\tan S) = \frac{\text{length of side opposite } \angle S}{\text{length of side that is part of } \angle S}$$

There are three additional trigonometry ratios that are now rarely used: the **secant**, **cosecant**, and **cotangent**. They are defined as follows:

$$\text{secant of } \angle S \ (\sec S) = \frac{\text{length of hypotenuse}}{\text{length of side that is part of } \angle S}$$

$$\text{cosecant of } \angle S \ (\csc S) = \frac{\text{length of hypotenuse}}{\text{length of side opposite } \angle S}$$

$$\text{cotangent of } \angle S \ (\ctn S) = \frac{\text{length of side that is part of } \angle S}{\text{length of side opposite } \angle S}$$

In Figure 3 all six trigonometry ratios are shown for triangle KLM. All six ratios are based on ∠K.

The ratio between the sides of similar triangles is always equal, so the value of any trigonometry ratio is always the same for any

Figure 3. Trigonometry Ratios

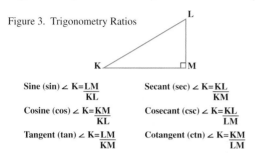

Sine (sin) ∠ K=$\frac{LM}{KL}$ Secant (sec) ∠ K=$\frac{KL}{KM}$

Cosine (cos) ∠ K=$\frac{KM}{KL}$ Cosecant (csc) ∠ K=$\frac{KL}{LM}$

Tangent (tan) ∠ K=$\frac{LM}{KM}$ Cotangent (ctn) ∠ K=$\frac{KM}{LM}$

specific angle in any right triangle. Mathematicians have calculated the values of all six trigonometry ratios, or functions, for all of the possible angles. These values can be found in mathematics textbooks and in the memory of any scientific calculator.

▶ **USING TRIGONOMETRY RATIOS TO SOLVE PROBLEMS**

In a right triangle, if you know the length of one side and the size of two of the three angles, you can use trigonometry ratios to compute the lengths of the other two sides. For example, for the right triangle in Figure 4, you can use the cosine ratio of ∠S to find the length of side RS.

Figure 4. Finding a Missing Length

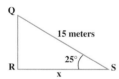

First set up the ratio:

$$\text{Cosine } \angle S = \frac{RS}{QS}$$

You know that ∠S measures 25° and side QS measures 15 meters, so:

$$\text{Cosine } 25° = \frac{X}{15}$$

The value of the cosine of 25° has been calculated to be .91, so you multiply .91 times 15 meters to get:

$$13.65 \text{ meters} = X$$

The length of side RS is 13.65 meters.

One of the applications of plane trigonometry is its use in finding the length of a distance or height that may be difficult or impossible to measure with a ruler or a measuring tape. The height of a building and the width of a river are typical examples. For instance, you can use trigonometry to find the height of the building shown in Figure 5.

Figure 5. Finding the Height of a Building

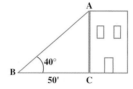

Use the same steps you followed in solving the length of side RS in Figure 4. In this case you will use the tangent of ∠B, which measures 40°. The value for the tangent of 40° has been calculated to be .84, so the height of the building will be 42 feet.

$$\text{Tangent } \angle B = \frac{AC}{BC}$$
$$\text{Tangent } 40° = \frac{X}{50} \text{ feet}$$
$$.84 = \frac{X}{50} \text{ feet}$$
$$42 = X$$

You can also use trigonometry to find the size of any angle in a right triangle by using the lengths of the sides. Problems that use other kinds of triangles are solved by using two special trigonometry formulas, the Law of Sines and the Law of Cosines, and the same six trigonometry ratios that are used with right triangles.

▶ **SPHERICAL TRIGONOMETRY**

Ancient Greek navigators used trigonometry to calculate distances on the Earth's surface. The Earth is in the shape of a sphere, and the trigonometry used to determine distances on the curved surface of the Earth is called spherical trigonometry. Spherical trigonometry continues to be used today to measure distances between cities, countries, bodies of water, and other places. Like plane trigonometry, spherical trigonometry uses the sides and angles of triangles and the same six trigonometry ratios to solve problems.

ART JOHNSON
Mathematics teacher, Nashua High School

See also GEOMETRY; MATHEMATICS; MATHEMATICS, HISTORY OF; RATIO AND PROPORTION.

TRINIDAD AND TOBAGO

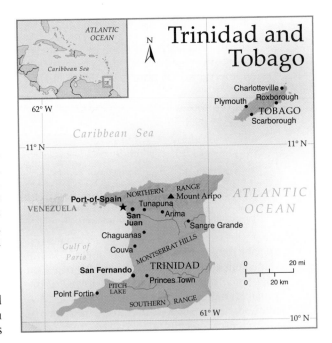

The nation of Trinidad and Tobago consists of two islands in the Caribbean Sea, situated off the northeastern coast of South America. Trinidad is much larger than Tobago and has most of the country's population. The islands were colonized at various times by Spanish, French, and British settlers and became an independent nation in 1962.

▶ **PEOPLE**

Most of the people of Trinidad and Tobago are of black African or East Indian origin. The others are mainly of European, Chinese, or mixed ancestry.

English is the country's official language. The English spoken in some parts of the islands, however, reflects the influence of Spanish, French, and African languages. Hindi, a major language of India, is spoken by some of the East Indians. French, Spanish, and Chinese are also spoken.

Most of the blacks and people of European background are Christians. The East Indians are chiefly Hindus, with smaller numbers of Muslims.

Port-of-Spain, the capital and chief seaport of Trinidad and Tobago, is one of the most modern cities in the West Indies. It is located in western Trinidad on the Gulf of Paria.

▶ **LAND**

Trinidad and Tobago are the southernmost islands of the West Indies. Trinidad, which lies closest to the South American mainland, is separated from the coast of Venezuela by the Gulf of Paria.

Trinidad makes up about 94 percent of the country's total land area. Its terrain is marked by three ranges of high hills—the Northern Range, the Montserrat Hills, and the Southern Range. The Northern Range includes the country's highest peak, Mount Aripo, which reaches a height of 3,083 feet (940 meters). Between the hills are flat or gently rolling areas of fertile land.

Tobago is a rugged, hilly island of volcanic origin. It has limited areas of level land suitable for agriculture, but draws more tourists than Trinidad. Both islands are heavily forested.

Trinidad and Tobago has a tropical climate, moderated by the trade winds. Temperatures range from 70 to 88°F (21 to 31°C). Rainfall varies from 50 to 150 inches (1,270 to 3,800 millimeters) a year, depending on location.

▶ **ECONOMY**

The country is one of the most prosperous in the Caribbean due to the production and processing of petroleum and natural gas. In addition to producing its own, Trinidad and Tobago imports petroleum for refining and export. Trinidad and Tobago also has the world's largest supply of natural asphalt (used for paving roads), at Pitch Lake on Trinidad.

Other important manufactures include chemical fertilizers, iron, steel, processed foods and beverages, cement, and textiles.

Services account for about 55 percent of the country's economy. They include personal and business services, wholesale and retail trade, finance, real estate, transportation, utilities, and communications. Businesses related to tourism, such as hotels, restaurants, and touring companies, make up a large share of the service sector.

Agriculture, once important, declined with the growth of the petroleum industry. Sugarcane is the main commercial crop. Other agricultural products include cocoa, rice, citrus fruits, coffee beans, vegetables, and poultry.

▶ **MAJOR CITIES**

Port-of-Spain, situated on Trinidad, is the nation's capital. It is the country's chief seaport and has a population of about 45,000. **San Fernando** is the largest city and a commercial center. It has a population of about 60,000. **Scarborough** is the principal town and port of Tobago.

FACTS and figures

REPUBLIC OF TRINIDAD AND TOBAGO is the official name of the country.

LOCATION: Caribbean Sea.

AREA: 1,980 sq mi (5,130 km²).

POPULATION: 1,350,000 (estimate).

CAPITAL: Port-of-Spain.

LARGEST CITY: San Fernando.

MAJOR LANGUAGE: English (official).

MAJOR RELIGIOUS GROUPS: Christian, Hindu, Muslim.

GOVERNMENT: Republic. **Head of state**—president. **Head of government**—prime minister. **Legislature**—Parliament (composed of the Senate and House of Representatives).

CHIEF PRODUCTS: Agricultural—sugarcane, cocoa, rice, citrus fruits, coffee beans, vegetables, and poultry. **Manufactured**—refined petroleum products, sugar, chemicals, steel products, fertilizer, cocoa, coffee, cotton textiles. **Mineral**—petroleum, natural gas, asphalt.

MONETARY UNIT: Trinidad and Tobago dollar (1 TT dollar = 100 cents).

▶ **HISTORY AND GOVERNMENT**

Early History. The Arawak and Carib Indians who once inhabited the islands largely disappeared after European colonization. Spain established the first settlement on Trinidad in the 1500's, after it was sighted by Christopher Columbus in 1498. Britain formally gained control of it in 1802. France acquired Tobago at the same time but ceded it to Britain in 1814. After slavery was abolished in the 1800's, laborers were brought from India, China, and Madeira to work the large sugarcane plantations, which became the mainstay of the islands' economy.

Independence. Trinidad and Tobago were politically united in 1889. The country became a self-governing member of the Federation of the West Indies in 1958. It gained complete independence in 1962.

Under a constitution adopted in 1976, Trinidad and Tobago is a republic, with a president as head of state and a prime minister as the head of government. The legislature, Parliament, has two houses: the Senate, whose members are appointed by the president, and the House of Representatives, which is elected by the people. The president is elected by members of Parliament for a 5-year term. The prime minister is usually the leader of the majority political party in the House of Representatives. Tobago has local self-government and its own legislature.

After independence, Eric Williams, founder of the People's National Movement (PNM), became the country's first prime minister. The PNM remained in power until 1986, when the multi-ethnic coalition party, the National Alliance for Reconstruction (NAR), gained control. The PNM regained control several years later, in 1991.

In 1995, Basdeo Panday, head of the United National Congress (UNC), became the first person of Indian ancestry to be appointed prime minister. In the 2001 elections, the UNC and the PNM each won the same number of seats in the House of Representatives. PNM leader Patrick Manning was appointed prime minister, but the inability to break the tie kept Parliament from meeting. Prime Minister Manning called elections in October 2002, and the PNM formed the next government after winning a majority.

Reviewed by GARTH L. GREEN
University of North Carolina, Charlotte

After years of fighting, the Greeks finally took Troy by trickery, hiding soldiers in a large wooden horse. This painting shows the capture of Troy.

TROJAN WAR

In ancient times a legendary struggle known as the Trojan War took place between the people of Greece and the people of Troy. The story of the war was told about 400 years later by the Greek poet Homer in the *Iliad.*

According to Homer, the war had its beginning when Paris, son of King Priam of Troy, stole Helen, the wife of King Menelaus of Sparta. Armies from many kingdoms of southern Greece went to war to win Helen back. Among the leaders were Menelaus' brother, Agamemnon; Achilles, who is the chief hero of Homer's story; and Odysseus. Setting out in more than 1,000 ships, the armies—perhaps 100,000 strong—sailed across the Aegean Sea. The Greeks laid siege to Troy for ten years.

Ancient Troy, or Ilium, stood on a hilltop in the western part of Asia Minor (present-day Turkey). Surrounded by walls about 16 feet (5 meters) thick, the city resisted attacks. Warriors fought for the most part as individuals rather than as armies. The outcome of a battle was often decided by a duel outside the city walls.

Troy was finally taken by trickery. The Greeks built a large, hollow wooden horse. Some of the soldiers hid inside, and the remaining Greeks sailed away. The Trojan priest Laocoön warned, "Beware the Greeks, even when they bring gifts." But the Trojans eagerly took the horse into their city. That night, when the Trojans were asleep, the Greek soldiers crept from the horse and took Troy by surprise. The rest of the Greeks returned and set fire to Troy, killing the Trojan men and taking the women captive. The Trojan hero Aeneas and a small band escaped from the burning city. Their flight was described in the *Aeneid* by the Roman poet Vergil. After ten years of wandering, described in Homer's *Odyssey*, Odysseus returned to his home. Menelaus and Helen were eventually reunited.

The Rediscovery of Troy

For many years scholars thought that there never was a city of Troy and that the Trojan War never took place. But Heinrich Schliemann, a German businessman interested in archaeology, was convinced that a mound called Hissarlik, near the Dardanelles in Turkey, was the site of ancient Troy. He began to dig at the site in 1870. Schliemann and, later, the German archaeologist Wilhelm Dörpfeld established that Hissarlik was the site of Troy and that nine settlements had stood there. Each new settlement was built directly on top of the ruins of the former one. From 1932 to 1938, a team of researchers from the University of Cincinnati excavated the site. They found that one settlement, which they called Troy VIIa, had been sacked and burned about 1250 B.C. Many scholars believe that this may have been Homer's Troy, even though 1183 B.C. is the traditional date for the end of the Trojan War.

Archaeologists dated the period of each occupation of Troy by studying the pottery and other remains. At the time of the Trojan War, the Trojans had large palaces, as well as weapons and ornaments of precious metals. Troy, a trade crossroads between the Aegean and Black seas, was a city of great importance.

Historians now believe that the Trojan War did take place, but that it did not happen exactly as the poets said it did. The real cause of the war may have been a trade dispute. In the Bronze Age, the Achaeans, a Greek people, traded in the Aegean area. They might have fought against Troy to free their trade routes from the threat of Trojan control.

Reviewed by RICHARD M. HAYWOOD
Author, *Ancient Greece and the Near East*

See also AENEID; GREEK MYTHOLOGY; HOMER; ILIAD; SCHLIEMANN, HEINRICH.

TROMBONE. See WIND INSTRUMENTS.

TROPICAL FISH. See FISH AS PETS.

TROPICAL FRUIT

Many delicious fruits grow in the tropical regions of the world. Some of the most popular are described in this article. Two others, bananas and pineapples, are the subjects of separate articles in this encyclopedia.

The **mango** is native to tropical Asia but is now grown in nearly all tropical and subtropical countries. Most mangoes are kidney-shaped, but some may be nearly round or long and thin. Mangoes also vary in size. Some are the size of a plum. Others may weigh 4½ pounds (2 kilograms) or more. At the center of the fruit is a large flat seed. Around the seed is the fleshy, fragrant, and juicy orange yellow pulp. The mango is eaten as a fresh fruit. It is also used in chutneys and preserves.

Another common tropical fruit is the **papaya**. It is native to tropical America but now grows in other tropical areas. The round or oblong fruit may be as small as a pear or as large as a watermelon. The yellow or orange flesh has a sweet, somewhat musky flavor. It has a hollow center lined with many small seeds. Papaya may be served fresh in salads, or it may be boiled and served as a vegetable. It is also used in preserves, jellies, and sherbets. The meat tenderizer called papain is an enzyme that comes from the fruit. Papaya juice is used to help relieve some digestive disorders.

The **avocado** is native to tropical America, but it now grows in many tropical and subtropical areas. Avocados may be pear-shaped or round. They range in color from green to dark purple. The greenish yellow flesh has a buttery texture and a nutty taste. The avocado is often served fresh in salads. Mashed avocados are blended with other ingredients to make guacamole, a popular Latin American dish.

The **plantain** is a type of yellowish green banana used for cooking in tropical countries. It is starchy rather than sweet and may be roasted, boiled, or baked. It is also dried and ground for use in breads, cakes, puddings, and soups.

The **breadfruit** is cooked as a vegetable. It is a sweet, starchy fruit that tastes like a sweet potato. The best types are seedless, usually round, twice the size of a grapefruit, and covered with a thick greenish rind.

The fruit of the **guava** is known especially for the delicious wine-red jelly that is made from it. The thin-skinned red or yellow fruit may be eaten by itself, sliced and served with cream, stewed, preserved, or cooked in pies.

A popular fruit of the American tropics is the **sapodilla**. It may be round, oval, or even cone-shaped. It has a thin brown skin. The flesh is yellowish brown and sweet and is eaten whole. The bark of the sapodilla tree is tapped for a milky substance that yields chicle, used in making chewing gum.

Another well-known tropical fruit of the Americas is **passion fruit**. It is an edible berry produced by a flowering vine called passionflower. The pulp of the juicy egg-shaped fruit may be eaten by itself or used to flavor frozen foods.

The **tamarind** is a tropical fruit native to Africa. The acidic brownish pulp is contained in pods. It is added to chutneys and curries and is used to pickle fish. The diluted syrup makes a beverage.

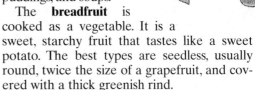

Passion Fruit

Avocado

Sapodilla

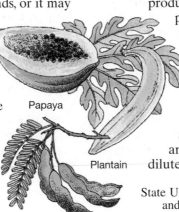

Papaya

Plantain

Tamarind

Guava

Breadfruit

Mango

Reviewed by RODNEY W. DOW
State University of New York Agricultural
and Technical College at Farmingdale

See also BANANA; FRUITGROWING; PINEAPPLE.

TROPICS. See CLIMATE; DESERTS; JUNGLES; RAIN FORESTS; ZONES.

TROTSKY, LEON. See UNION OF SOVIET SOCIALIST REPUBLICS (Profiles).

TRUCIAL STATES. See UNITED ARAB EMIRATES.

TRUCKS AND TRUCKING

Trucks are motor vehicles designed especially to transport freight. The trucking business has become an essential industry because rapid distribution of goods is important to a nation's economy. There is little that we eat, wear, or otherwise use in our daily lives that has not been carried by truck, at least part of the way, from where it grows or is made to where it is needed.

In the United States, all communities depend to some extent on truck transportation to supply their needs, and more than two thirds are served exclusively by trucks.

▶THE PARTS OF A TRUCK

Unlike automobiles, trucks are designed to haul heavy loads, frequently over great distances. In a single year, a large truck used for long-distance hauling may travel more than 100,000 miles (160,000 kilometers)—as many miles as an automobile might travel in its lifetime. This kind of truck is usually driven for about five years, and during this time it may travel more than 500,000 miles (800,000 kilometers). Trucks, therefore, are more sturdily built than automobiles and have more powerful engines. (The structure of motor vehicles is described in the article AUTOMOBILES in Volume A, and the article ENGINES in Volume E explains how engines work.)

There are two main units to the body of a truck—the driver's cab and the cargo-carrying space behind the cab.

Small, lightweight trucks usually are built so that these two units are mounted on one chassis (frame and wheels). This type of truck is called a **straight truck.** In other trucks, especially those that carry the heaviest loads, the cab, or tractor, and a cargo-carrying trailer are mounted on two separate chassis. Such trucks are called **tractor-trailers.** They are very useful, because the trailer can be hooked onto any tractor, as needed. Often the trailer has only rear wheels—the front end of the trailer rests on the tractor's chassis, over the rear wheels. This kind of trailer is called a semitrailer.

The semitrailer has a set of small retractable wheels, called dollies, at its front end. The dollies support the front end of the trailer when it is detached from a tractor. The dollies are raised off the ground when the trailer is hooked up. Some heavy long-distance trucks have a semitrailer plus a full trailer with four large wheels. These are called twin trailers. Some states also permit triple trailers.

Because truck bodies must bear heavy loads, they are supported by many wheels. The heavy truck most commonly used by the trucking industry is the ''18-wheeler,'' which has five axles—one at the front of the cab, two at the back of the cab, and two at the back of the semitrailer. Each set of two axles has two sets of double wheels on each side for extra support. Added up, they total 18.

Some trucks have all-wheel drive. This means that the engine is connected to every wheel instead of only to those at the rear or at the front, as in many automobiles. All-wheel drive is useful in mountainous areas or on soft dirt roads, where a great deal of traction is needed to move the vehicle.

A truck may have from four to 20 forward gear ratios, compared with three or four for automobiles. The lowest gear is the slowest but also the most powerful. To start off from standing position and to climb steep hills, this powerful low gear, or first gear, is used. The highest gear is the fastest gear. It is used when the truck can roll along on a level highway. On most trucks, gears must be shifted by hand, with the help of a clutch. But automatic transmissions are coming into greater use in trucks.

Lightweight trucks have hydraulic brakes like those used in automobiles. But heavy trucks have air brake systems, which use air pressure to slow down or stop a vehicle. Air brakes provide greater stopping ability.

Most heavy trucks have diesel engines. Diesel fuel has more energy per gallon than the fuels burned by gasoline engines. A truck gets a little less than six miles to a gallon of fuel (about 2.5 kilometers to a liter).

To cut down on fuel consumption, the designs of modern truck bodies are streamlined, to deflect (turn aside) the wind. This lowers wind resistance and reduces the amount of fuel needed to move the truck. One device, called an air deflector, is mounted over the cab and deflects air over the top of the trailer.

A large truck may be equipped with a ''sleeper'' built into the cab, which provides a convenient place to rest during long-distance hauls. Some custom-made sleepers even have room for a shower and kitchenette.

The dashboard of a large truck may be very simple, or it may be loaded with so many optional instruments that it resembles the cockpit of a jetliner. Trucking companies, which may own hundreds or thousands of trucks, prefer simple dashboards for the sake of economy. Owner-operators, however, may want more elaborate dashboards.

Future design advances will increase safety, comfort, and convenience for operators of trucks. Soon it will be possible to control brakes and engines by means of an on-board computer. Total operation of the vehicle will be monitored by a microprocessor. Electronic signals from a truck will be sent via satellite to company headquarters, pinpointing the truck's exact location and providing such data as speed and stops made.

▶ USES OF TRUCKS

Trucks can go anywhere there is a road, and sometimes even where there are no roads. They are fast and flexible. Unlike trains or boats, trucks are not bound to tracks or waterways. Unlike airplanes, their destinations are not limited by the need for a landing field. Trucks can pick up cargo and deliver it directly to where it is needed, when it is needed.

In agriculture, trucks are used to carry the harvest from the fields and to haul crops and livestock to market. It would be almost impossible to run a modern farm without having a truck for general hauling.

The federal government uses trucks for carrying mail and, in the armed forces, for transporting military equipment and personnel. States maintain fleets of trucks for road repairs, and local governments need trucks for fire fighting, garbage collection, and maintenance work.

In business and industry, trucks act somewhat like assembly lines, delivering raw materials to factories and distributing the finished products. They also perform the heavy work required by industries such as mining, logging, construction, and excavating.

The wide range of uses for trucks has led to the design and manufacture of many different types of trucks.

Many different kinds of trucks are manufactured to perform a wide range of activities. *Top right:* Logging trucks must be large and powerful enough to haul huge loads. *Top left:* Tow trucks are designed to pull disabled vehicles. *Above:* Pickup trucks are useful for farm work and other kinds of light hauling. *Left:* Cement trucks deliver their product to the work site, mix it, and pour it where needed. *Below:* Fire trucks are outfitted with hooks and ladders, hoses, and other equipment needed to fight fires.

▶ TYPES OF TRUCKS

Trucks are built in a variety of sizes, weights, and shapes. Some trucks—such as the pickup truck used for farm work or for small local deliveries—are not much larger than a passenger car. Other trucks are gleaming giants, 55 feet (17 meters) or more in length. They are used to haul freight long distances on the highways.

Trucks are usually classified as light, medium, or heavy. A light truck has a maximum weight of 14,000 pounds (6,300 kilograms); a medium truck weighs between 14,000 pounds and 26,000 pounds (11,700 kilograms); and a heavy truck weighs more than 26,000 pounds. These weights include both the weight of the truck itself and the weight of the load it can carry. Truck bodies are often made of lightweight materials, such as aluminum. This enables the truck to carry more freight.

Examples of lightweight trucks are pickup trucks, panel trucks, vans, and mail trucks. Among the medium-weight trucks are straight trucks used for local transportation. Fire engines and dump trucks, which are specialized trucks, may be medium or bridge the gap between medium and heavy. Some tractor-trailers may be medium weight, but most fall into the heavyweight range. The 18-wheelers and larger trucks are classified as heavy.

Much freight is carried in trucks with enclosed vans. Furniture and household goods are moved by specially designed enclosed vans. Cargo such as fresh produce and meat, which must be kept at controlled temperatures, is transported in refrigerated vans.

Tank trucks carry liquids such as gasoline, oil, chemicals, milk, and even melted chocolate. Certain types of tank trucks, called hopper trucks, carry dry bulk products such as cement powder, grain, and fertilizer.

Flatbed trucks may carry lumber, steel, or heavy machinery. Some trucks are built to transport automobiles and boats. Others are specially designed for transporting livestock.

Trucks are used extensively in road building and other construction work. Bulldozers, backhoes, and other earth-moving machinery excavate a site, and dump trucks carry away excavated dirt. Other trucks mix cement and dump it ready-made at the work area where building is going on. Another type of cement truck is the pneumatic trailer. This is a trailer with a built-in unloading device that works by air pressure. The unloader can blow about 1,500 pounds (680 kilograms) of dry cement into the mixing bins in one minute.

Besides the many kinds of trucks used for transporting goods and materials, other kinds are used for service in towns and cities. This group includes trash trucks, telephone and utility repair trucks, fire trucks, and mail vans.

Other specialized trucks include ambulances, tow trucks, bookmobiles and bloodmobiles, and vendor trucks.

▶THE TRUCKING INDUSTRY

There are two main types of truck operators: private carriers and for-hire carriers. Private carriers are businesses that own or lease trucks for hauling their own products. For example, a bakery might own one or more trucks for delivering its goods to customers.

For-hire carriers are trucking companies whose business is to transport freight belonging to others. They can operate locally, intrastate (within one state), or interstate (between states). For-hire carriers may be either common carriers or contract carriers. Common carriers offer their services to the general public. Contract carriers work for a limited number of clients under a long-term contract.

In most countries, the trucking industry is subject to government regulation. That is, the government sets standards for rates, quality of service, mergers, and other aspects of the industry. In the United States, the Interstate Commerce Commission (ICC), an agency of the Department of Transportation, regulates for-hire carriers that travel interstate. State and local governments regulate intrastate and local carriers. Certain for-hire carriers, such as those that carry farm produce or livestock, are exempt, or free, from some kinds of government regulation.

The Department of Transportation and other government agencies also set safety regulations pertaining to truck drivers, the operation of trucks, and truck equipment.

The Motor Carrier Act of 1980 partially deregulated the trucking industry. By removing many of the ICC regulations, the act made it easier for new trucking companies to enter the industry. It also removed some of the distinctions between categories of carriers.

▶HISTORY OF TRUCKING

The trucking industry began about 1900. By that time the automobile had been developed for transporting people. In time, the automobile was adapted to carry goods and freight as well. This happened wherever cars were used, but it was especially true in the United States, where goods often had to be hauled long distances to railroad lines.

At first, trucks were used in limited numbers. One reason was the lack of good roads. Trucks and automobiles raised clouds of dust on the many dirt roads. But in time, trucks as well as automobiles proved to be very practical. As the number of vehicles grew, more and better roads were built. The improved roads, in turn, made it possible to build larger trucks. The development of nationwide road systems thus was closely connected with the development of the trucking industry.

During World War I, trucks proved their usefulness for transporting supplies over long distances, and people began to realize the great potential of trucks. Until about that time, most trucks had been open-air vehicles resembling horse-drawn wagons. Tires were of solid rubber. As the use of trucks increased, roofs, doors, and windshields were added, and by 1930 most truck cabs were fully enclosed. Airfilled, or pneumatic, tires allowed trucks to travel faster and carry heavier loads.

Modern trailers appeared about 1915. These early models were all full trailers. By 1920, however, manufacturers had begun to make semitrailers. This development increased efficiency, because a semitrailer can be easily detached from a tractor, so that the tractor can be used to haul a second "semi" while the first is being unloaded.

The first trucks powered by diesel engines were built in the early 1930's. The diesel engine was a great fuel saver, but it was not widely used until after 1939 for long-haul equipment. After World War II it began to be used for smaller trucks as well.

The first workable tilt-cab, the forward tilt, was built about 1935. This type of cab is placed over the engine and can be tilted up and forward, allowing access to the engine.

During World War II, trucks again proved essential for moving troops and supplies to battlefronts. Postwar technological advances and highway improvements and the decline of railroads all contributed to the expansion of trucking. Today, trucks are firmly established as an essential mode of transportation.

JERRY BUCKMAN
Manager of Educational Services
American Trucking Association

TRUDEAU, PIERRE ELLIOTT
(1919–2000)

Pierre Elliott Trudeau became prime minister of Canada on April 20, 1968, following the retirement of Liberal Prime Minister Lester B. Pearson. Although he had relatively little political experience, Trudeau led the Liberal Party to victory in the general elections of 1968, 1972, 1974, and 1980.

Trudeau was born in Montreal, Quebec, on October 18, 1919. He received a law degree from the University of Montreal in 1943. In the 1950's he practiced law and devoted himself to liberal causes and civil rights issues.

Trudeau's rapid rise in politics began when he was elected to the House of Commons in 1965. In 1966 he became parliamentary secretary to Prime Minister Pearson, and in 1967 he was named minister of justice and attorney general. The following year he succeeded Pearson as leader of the Liberal Party.

Throughout his 15 years as prime minister, Trudeau accomplished much: He established relations with the People's Republic of China; increased trade with China and the Soviet Union; and opposed the movement to make Quebec an independent nation. In addition, he supported legislation that made French an official Canadian language, equal to English; lowered the voting age from 21 to 18; and abolished the death penalty.

The Liberals lost the 1979 election to the Progressive Conservatives but were returned

Pierre Elliott Trudeau was a popular, yet controversial, leader of Canada's Liberal Party. He was prime minister from 1968 to 1979 and again from 1980 to 1984.

to power the following year. Once again, Trudeau became prime minister. He resigned from office in 1984, having served longer than any other Canadian prime minister except William Lyon Mackenzie King. Trudeau died on September 28, 2000, in Montreal.

CHARLES BORDELEAU
Author, *Pierre Elliott Trudeau*

HARRY S. TRUMAN (1884–1972)

33rd President of the United States

FACTS ABOUT TRUMAN

Birthplace: Lamar, Missouri
Religion: Baptist
Occupation: Farmer, businessman, public official
Married: Elizabeth Virginia (Bess) Wallace
Children: Mary Margaret
Political Party: Democratic
Office Held Before Becoming President: Vice President
President Who Preceded Him: Franklin D. Roosevelt
Age on Becoming President: 60
Years in the Presidency: 1945–1953 (succeeded to the presidency on the death of Franklin D. Roosevelt, April 12, 1945)
Vice President: Alben W. Barkley (1949–1953)
President Who Succeeded Him: Dwight D. Eisenhower
Age at Death: 88
Burial Place: Independence, Missouri

DURING TRUMAN'S PRESIDENCY

Below: The surrender of Germany (1945) ended the fighting in Europe in World War II. The United Nations charter was signed in San Francisco (1945). The first atomic bomb was detonated (exploded) in a test at White Sands, near Alamogordo, New Mexico (1945). *Above:* Atomic bombs were dropped on the Japanese cities of Hiroshima and Nagasaki (1945). Japan surrendered (1945), ending hostilities in World War II. The Philippines gained complete independence from the United States (1946). The Korean War began (1950). The 22nd amendment to the U.S. Constitution was ratified (1951), limiting the president to two four-year terms of office. *Left:* Permanent headquarters of the United Nations were established in New York City (1952).

TRUMAN, HARRY S. On April 12, 1945, President Franklin D. Roosevelt died suddenly of a cerebral hemorrhage. That same day Vice President Harry S. Truman was sworn in to succeed him.

Truman became president at a particularly critical time. World War II was coming to an end, and the Cold War with the Soviet Union was in its beginning stages. The new president was immediately called on to make a number of difficult and important decisions. A man of down-to-earth directness, he learned quickly and was willing to act vigorously. As a result, he was able to establish many of the basic foreign policies adopted by the United States following World War II. These included the Truman Doctrine to restrain Communist expansion and the Marshall Plan to aid war-devastated countries. Truman also is remembered for his resistance to the Soviet blockade of West Berlin and for his action in halting Communist aggression in South Korea.

Truman's domestic policy was known as the Fair Deal program. It emphasized the need for greater employment opportunities and for increased civil rights for members of minority groups.

▶ EARLY YEARS

Harry S. Truman was born in Lamar, Missouri, on May 8, 1884. He was the eldest of three children of Martha Ellen Young and John Anderson Truman. Because his parents could not decide which of his grandfathers to name him after, they gave young Harry the letter "S" instead of a middle name.

When Harry was 6, the Trumans moved to Independence, Missouri. There he grew up, a bookish boy, so nearsighted that he had to wear thick glasses. After he finished high school, his father's financial difficulties prevented Harry from entering college. He held a number of jobs, eventually becoming a bank clerk. In 1906, at the age of 22, he went to work on the family farm, where he spent the next 11 years.

The entrance of the United States into World War I in 1917 gave Truman an opportunity to show his abilities. Soon after war was declared, he received his commission as a first lieutenant in the Missouri National Guard. In March, 1918, he left for France with the 35th Division. Truman commanded a field artillery battery in several campaigns. Throughout the fighting he managed to maintain firm discipline among his unruly men yet retain their affection. He said afterwards: "I've always been sorry I did not get a university education in the regular way. But I got it in the Army the hard way—and it stuck."

After his discharge from the Army in 1919 with the rank of captain, Truman married his childhood sweetheart, Bess Wallace. Their only child, a daughter named Mary Margaret, was born in 1924. Soon after his marriage Truman entered into a partnership with one of his army friends and opened a men's clothing store in Kansas City. But in the postwar depression of 1921 the store failed. Truman lost his life savings and owed $20,000 in debts. He refused to go into bankruptcy, however, and instead scraped for 15 years to pay off the money he owed.

▶ HE ENTERS POLITICS

Truman's friends urged him to enter politics. Like his father, he was a Democrat with strong views. In 1922, Truman won election as one of three judges of the Jackson County Court. His friends called him Judge Truman, but his duties were administrative rather than judicial. Since he felt that his new responsibilities called for a knowledge of law, he studied at night for two years at the Kansas City School of Law. In 1926 he was elected presiding judge, an office he held until 1935.

During these years Truman was allied with the notorious political machine of Kansas City boss Thomas J. Pendergast (1870–1945). In spite of this, Truman maintained his reputation as a man of strict honesty and unusual efficiency. Pendergast complained frequently that Truman was "the contrariest cuss in Missouri" but respected him as a popular vote-getter. In 1934 he backed Truman for election to the United States Senate.

During his first term in the Senate, Truman seldom spoke and was handicapped by his tie with Pendergast. With difficulty he won re-election in 1940. In his second term as a senator, however, he became famous.

Harry Truman (*right*) at the age of 4, with his younger brother, Vivian.

The Truman Committee. Truman felt that Missouri was not getting its fair share of defense contracts. He also was disturbed by reports of inefficiency and corruption in the defense program. He proposed that the Senate investigate the national defense program. A committee was formed, with Truman as chairman. It was called the Senate War Investigating Committee, but was better known as the Truman Committee. The Truman Committee became a financial watchdog for President Franklin D. Roosevelt's administration during World War II. By uncovering corruption and waste, the committee saved the government hundreds of millions of dollars—perhaps as much as $15,000,000,000. And by its efficiency it caused government officials and defense contractors to be more careful.

▶ VICE PRESIDENT AND PRESIDENT

The success of the committee and his support of Roosevelt's policies led Truman's political supporters to back him for the Democratic nomination for vice president in the election of 1944. President Roosevelt was running for a fourth term, and he and Truman were elected easily.

During his 12 weeks as vice president Truman saw little of Roosevelt. He received no

Truman with French general Charles de Gaulle in 1945.

special briefings on the major political issues, so he was not prepared for the responsibilities that fell on him when Roosevelt died on April 12, 1945. The day after Truman's inauguration he remarked to reporters: "Boys, if you ever pray, pray for me now ...."

On May 8, 1945, the unconditional surrender of the German forces ended the war in Europe. But Truman still had to win the war against Japan. In addition, the Soviets had begun taking political control of the countries of Eastern Europe. This violated the agreements reached with President Roosevelt and British prime minister Winston Churchill at the Yalta Conference.

The Atomic Bomb. In July 1945, President Truman went to Potsdam, Germany, to meet with Churchill and Soviet premier Joseph Stalin. While there, Truman received word of the first successful test of the atomic bomb. Truman made no progress with Stalin at Potsdam. However, he was able to warn Japan that unless it surrendered, it faced complete devastation. When the Japanese ignored the ultimatum, Truman ordered the atomic bomb dropped on Japan. The target, the city of Hiroshima, was struck on August 6. Despite the horrible destruction, Japan did not surrender until a second bomb was dropped on Nagasaki, on August 9.

On September 2, aboard the battleship *Missouri*, the Japanese signed the surrender documents. "Let there be no mistake about it," Truman said later. "I regarded the bomb as a military weapon and never had any doubt that it should be used." For more information, see the article WORLD WAR II in Volume WXYZ.

The United Nations. On June 26, 1945, in San Francisco, Truman had witnessed the signing of the charter establishing the United Nations. He hailed it as a "declaration of great faith by the nations of the earth—faith that war is not inevitable, faith that peace can be maintained." In this same spirit, Truman proposed international control of atomic energy to harness it for peaceful uses. But the Soviet Union refused to accept the American plan submitted to the United Nations in 1946. Instead, Soviet leaders worked at top speed to develop their own bomb.

Postwar Issues. With the long war finally over, millions of Americans were eager to return to peaceful pursuits. The armed forces were quickly demobilized (disbanded), and wartime economic controls were rapidly abandoned. In September 1945, President Truman sent Congress a message containing his recommendations for domestic legislation. Among other things, he asked for expanded social security, an increase in the minimum wage, a permanent Fair Employment Practices Act, a bill to provide full employment, and public housing and slum clearance. Additional recommendations called for federal aid to education and for health insurance, medical care, and federal control of atomic energy.

IMPORTANT DATES IN THE LIFE OF HARRY S. TRUMAN

1884	Born at Lamar, Missouri, May 8.
1890	Moved to Independence, Missouri.
1906–17	Worked on the family farm at Grandview, Missouri.
1917	Commissioned first lieutenant in Missouri National Guard.
1918	Commanded field artillery battery in France.
1919	Married Elizabeth Virginia (Bess) Wallace.
1919–21	Partner in men's clothing store in Kansas City, Missouri.
1922–24	Judge, Jackson County Court, Missouri.
1926–35	Presiding judge, Jackson County Court.
1935–45	United States senator.
1945	Inaugurated vice president January 20; became president on death of Franklin D. Roosevelt.
1949–53	Served a complete term as president.
1972	Died in Kansas City, Missouri, December 26.

Congress enacted only two of Truman's recommendations. In 1946 it passed the Atomic Energy Act, which created the Atomic Energy Commission to exercise control over the research and development of atomic energy. Congress also passed a limited version of the president's full employment program, the Maximum Employment Act, which established the Council of Economic Advisers to assist the president and issue a yearly report on economic conditions.

Meanwhile, the United States was making the difficult transition to a peacetime economy. A scarcity of goods, rising prices, and workers' strikes for higher wages led to inflation. Voters, tired of wartime and postwar shortages, gave Republicans control of both houses of Congress in 1946. And in 1947, over Truman's veto, it passed the Taft-Hartley Act, which placed certain restrictions on labor unions.

The Truman Doctrine. Gradually, Truman realized that more vigorous measures had to be taken if the spread of Communism by the Soviet Union was to be stopped. In March 1947 he became especially alarmed by Soviet pressure on Turkey and by Soviet aid to Communist guerrillas in Greece and asked Congress to provide funds for their armed forces. He also set forth the policy that came to be called the Truman Doctrine: "to support free peoples who are resisting attempted subjugation ...."

The Marshall Plan. The need to help wartorn Europe led to Truman's proposal, in July 1947, of what came to be known as the Marshall Plan, after Secretary of State George C. Marshall. Under the plan, $13 billion in aid was sent to the nations of Western Europe, which brought about their rapid economic recovery. Truman also called for aid, under his Point Four program, to developing nations of Africa and Asia. (For more information, see the biography of George C. Marshall in Volume M.)

The Election of 1948. In 1948, Truman prepared to run for election for a term as president in his own right. His Republican opponent was Governor Thomas E. Dewey of New York. In addition, the president was faced with a split in his own party.

In spite of predictions of his defeat by every poll-taker in the United States, Truman planned a vigorous campaign. He told his vice-presidential running mate, Senator Alben W. Barkley of Kentucky, "I'm going to fight hard. I'm going to give them hell." He denounced what he called the "do-nothing" Congress and appealed to voters to support welfare and civil rights legislation, aid to farmers, and repeal of the Taft-Hartley Act.

To practically everyone's surprise but his own, Truman defeated Dewey by more than 2 million popular votes and by an electoral vote of 303 to 189. (Two other parties, the Dixiecrats and the Progressives, won 39 and 0 electoral votes respectively.) The Democrats also regained control of both houses of Congress.

The Berlin Airlift, NATO, and China. In 1948, Soviet forces blockaded the western sectors of Berlin, the former capital of Germany, which had been under the control of the four main Allied powers since the end of World War II. Truman did not want to risk war by sending land convoys through the Soviet lines. Instead, he ordered that West Berlin be supplied by air, which forced the Soviets to lift the blockade in 1949. To meet any further Soviet military threats to Western Europe, Truman helped shape a new alliance called the North Atlantic Treaty Organization (NATO). For more information, see the articles BERLIN and NORTH ATLANTIC TREATY ORGANIZATION in the appropriate volumes.

Meanwhile, Truman was severely criticized for not sending massive military aid to President Chiang Kai-shek's Nationalist Chinese

Truman often relaxed by playing the piano. He is shown here playing a duet with comedian Jack Benny.

government before mainland China fell to Communist forces in 1949. The Nationalists then withdrew to Taiwan.

The Korean War. Communist North Korea invaded South Korea in 1950. Truman called for armed assistance to the South Koreans under a United Nations command headed by the United States. When Communist China came to North Korea's aid, Truman refused to allow the UN commander, U.S. General Douglas MacArthur, to bomb bases within China for fear that it might lead to all-out war. When MacArthur publicly opposed Truman's policy, the president fired him, amid great controversy.

An armistice in Korea was not achieved until July 1953, after Truman had left office. For more information, see the article KOREAN WAR in Volume JK.

Retirement. After leaving office in January 1953, Truman returned to his home in Independence, Missouri. He traveled widely, published his memoirs, and enjoyed the status of an elder statesman. He died on December 26, 1972, and was buried in Independence.

FRANK FREIDEL
Harvard University
Author, *America in the Twentieth Century*

See also KOREAN WAR; MACARTHUR, DOUGLAS; MARSHALL, GEORGE C.

TRUMBULL, JONATHAN. See CONNECTICUT (Famous People).

TRUMPET. See WIND INSTRUMENTS.

TRUTH, SOJOURNER. See ABOLITION MOVEMENT (Profiles).

TSCHAIKOVSKY, PETER ILYICH. See TCHAIKOVSKY, PETER ILYICH.

TSUNAMIS

A tsunami is a set of ocean waves caused by any large, sudden disturbance of the sea surface. ("Tsunami" is a Japanese word that means "harbor wave.") If the disturbance is near the coastline, local tsunamis can demolish coastal communities within minutes. A very large disturbance can cause destruction thousands of miles away.

Tsunamis are usually generated by large earthquakes in coastal areas. Major tsunamis are most common in the Pacific, where dense oceanic plates slide under lighter continental plates. When plates break, a quick upsurge of the ocean produces a series of waves. (To produce similar waves yourself, place your hand on the bottom of a bathtub partly filled with water. Then quickly lift your hand without breaking the water's surface.)

Tsunamis can also be caused by underwater landslides, which may accompany smaller earthquakes, and by explosive volcanoes or asteroid impacts. The 1883 eruption of Krakatau (Krakatoa) in the East Indies produced a tsunami 100 feet (30 meters) high that killed over 36,000 people. In 1997, scientists discovered evidence of a huge asteroid that landed offshore of Chile about 2 million years ago. The tsunami caused by the asteroid swept over portions of South America and Antarctica.

Since 1850 alone, tsunamis have killed over 420,000 people while causing billions of dollars of damage. Local tsunamis cause most of the devastation. They occur about once a year somewhere in the world. The December 26, 2004, tsunami killed about 130,000 people close to the earthquake and about 58,000 people on distant shores. (For more details, see the article EARTHQUAKES in Volume E.)

How Tsunamis Form. Because Earth movements and ruptures associated with large earthquakes are thousands of square miles in area, any rise of the seafloor immediately changes the sea surface. A tsunami emerges

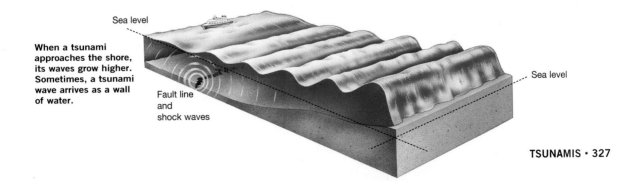

When a tsunami approaches the shore, its waves grow higher. Sometimes, a tsunami wave arrives as a wall of water.

Sea level

Sea level

Fault line and shock waves

as a set of waves whose energy is determined by the size and shape of the earthquake rupture and the nearest coastline. Because each earthquake and coastline combination is unique, every tsunami is unique.

Once formed, the tsunami travels at a speed that depends on the depth of the water below. In deep water, it travels as fast as a jet airplane. In shallow water, it slows to the speed of an automobile in the city. While the tsunami slows, its energy remains constant, so its waves grow higher. When the tsunami reaches the coastline, it unleashes its energy, causing great damage.

Warning Systems. Scientists cannot predict when and where tsunamis will start. Instead, they try to monitor tsunamis as they develop. Since 1946, the tsunami warning system in the Pacific basin has measured earthquake activity with seismographs and monitored the passage of tsunami waves with tide gauges. However, these devices do not help predict the impact of a tsunami at a particular location. Better forecasts rely on new devices: deep-ocean tsunami detectors (tsunameters). The large earthquake in 2003 near the Rat Islands, Alaska, generated a tsunami that was detected by three nearby tsunameters.

Preparedness. Understanding tsunamis can save lives. If you are at a beach and feel the shaking of an earthquake or see the ocean withdraw quickly or hear a loud roar from the ocean, immediately head inland and move to high ground. On December 26, 2004, a 10-year-old girl saved over 100 lives because she knew that a rapid withdrawal of water signaled the arrival of a tsunami. In the United States, tsunami warnings will be issued via official weather radio and local police. If you receive a tsunami warning, follow evacuation instructions.

EDDIE N. BERNARD
Director, Pacific Marine
Environmental Laboratory

TUBERCULOSIS

Tuberculosis (TB) is an infectious disease that usually affects the lungs. Common symptoms include a bloody cough and fever. Also, TB victims may appear pale and slowly waste away. In the past, these signs led people to call TB white plague or consumption, for the way TB seemed to "consume" people. Not only is TB highly lethal, it also affects a large portion of the population. About 2 billion persons have latent TB—disease that is not yet evident, even though infection is present. Each year, 8 million patients develop active disease, resulting in 2 million deaths. Regions of the world most involved include India, China, Southeast Asia, Africa, former Soviet republics, and Latin America.

TB is caused by a tiny rod-shaped bacterium that belongs to a family of soil-dwelling organisms, the mycobacteria. To survive in the soil, mycobacteria have thick, waxy cell walls that help them retain moisture and tolerate temperature changes. The walls also result in a slow flow of nutrients,

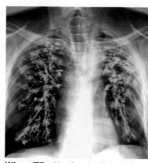

When TB attacks the lungs, it causes scarring. In this artificially colored X-ray image, the scarring is shown in green.

which leads to slow growth. These traits—protective cell walls and slow growth—shape the patterns of disease.

Progression. Mycobacteria grow slowly and produce infections that progress slowly. A long time passes between infection and the first signs of disease. In fact, many people who have latent TB will never develop active disease. Only about 10 percent will develop active TB in their lifetimes, unless the immune system is weakened.

If the immune system is weakened by the human immunodeficiency virus (HIV), latent TB is more likely to progress to active disease. Among those infected with both, 10 percent develop active TB within a year. As HIV spreads in regions where TB is common, such as Africa, more cases of latent TB progress to active disease, and death rates increase.

Transmission. Although TB can involve many organs, the disease is most common in the lungs. When patients with lung disease cough, they expel millions of bacilli into the air. Other people may inhale these bacilli and become infected.

Treatment. Drugs that cure TB have been available for 40 years, but they must be taken for at least 6 months. The drugs must be taken for a long time because antibiotics kill bacteria only when they are multiplying, so few slow-growing mycobacteria can be attacked by antibiotics at any one time.

Once drug therapy starts, the risk of transmission drops dramatically. However, if drug therapy ends too soon, the risk of spread resumes. Worse, if a patient takes just one drug, the mycobacteria may quickly develop resistance to that drug, and treatment may fail. If a series of single-drug treatments is given, resistance to one drug after another may develop. To prevent resistance, several drugs are given at the same time.

Although doctors tell patients to take their medications on a schedule, patients often make mistakes, or forget to take their drugs. If patients fall off the schedule, they may have longer illnesses. When a cure is delayed, the mycobacteria are given a chance to develop drug resistance, and there are more opportunities for disease to be passed to others.

To ensure proper drug use, directly observed therapy (DOT) is used. In DOT, a health-care worker watches the patient take every dose of medication. In extreme cases, a patient may even be quarantined (kept away from other people). Such measures are supported by public health authorities because TB is so easily transmitted through the air and may be lethal. Since 1994, DOT has been associated with a 50 percent reduction in case rates in the United States.

Prevention. The TB vaccine has been given to roughly 4 billion persons in the last 50 years. It protects infants from some life-threatening forms of TB, but it has failed to halt adult TB. The vaccine's failure is poorly understood, but this issue is being researched. Another approach used in the United States is to treat latent TB infection. If a skin test shows latent TB, the patient is encouraged to take a single drug for 4 to 9 months to prevent active disease.

MICHAEL D. ISEMAN, M.D.
Professor of Medicine
University of Colorado School of Medicine

TUBMAN, HARRIET (1821?–1913)

The American abolitionist Harriet Tubman, known as "the Moses of her people," led more than 300 fugitive slaves to freedom.

She was born Araminta Ross on a plantation in Dorchester County, Maryland, about 1821 and later took her mother's name, Harriet. From an early age she experienced the evils of slavery. Two of her sisters had been sold, and she herself had been permanently injured in a brutal attack. Tubman believed it was against God's will for people to be held in bondage. After hearing she might be sold to another slaveholder, she escaped late one night in 1849 and began the dangerous trip northward, in search of freedom. She reached Philadelphia, where she found work as a cook. Friends there told her of the Underground Railroad, a secret network of people who helped fugitive slaves reach the North.

Tubman determined that she would return to the South and rescue as many slaves as possible. In about a dozen years she made as many as 19 trips. Using the North Star (Polaris) as a guide, she led groups of refugees north along the long, dangerous road to freedom, sometimes even as far as Canada. They hid by day and traveled by night. In 1857, Tubman succeeded in liberating her aged parents and found them a home in Auburn, New York. Angry slaveholders offered rewards for Tubman's capture, but no one ever caught her.

Tubman never learned to read or write, but she became a popular speaker at antislavery meetings. During the Civil War (1861–65), she helped the Union Army as a nurse, laundress, scout, and spy. She helped gather information behind Confederate lines and encouraged slaves to join the Union forces.

In 1908 she founded a home in Auburn to help elderly and poor blacks. She continued to work to improve the lives of former slaves and also for women's rights. Harriet Tubman died on March 10, 1913. She was buried with full military honors in Auburn.

DANIEL S. DAVIS
Author, *Struggle for Freedom:
The History of Black Americans*

See also UNDERGROUND RAILROAD (Profiles).

TUCKER, RICHARD. See OPERA (Profiles).

TUCSON

Tucson is Arizona's second largest city. Surrounded by five mountain ranges, it is located a little more than 60 miles (97 kilometers) north of Mexico. The city's population is about 487,000; nearly 844,000 live in the greater metropolitan area.

The Tucson area was home to the Pima Indians long before Spanish colonists came up from Mexico in 1775 and established an army outpost there. After 1821, Tucson belonged to Mexico until the United States officially acquired the territory in 1854 after winning the Mexican War (1846–48). Tucson served as the capital of the Arizona Territory from 1867 until 1877, when the city was formally incorporated. The city began to thrive after 1910 when copper and silver deposits were discovered. In the 1950's, when air conditioning helped make the summer heat bearable, Tucson's population boomed.

Tourism is a major part of Tucson's economy. Visitors flock to its resort hotels and guest ranches to enjoy the sunshine and the warm, dry climate. The city's economy is also supported by high technology industries. Important manufactures include aerospace, optical, and electronic equipment. Copper mining

is also important. The University of Arizona is one of the city's largest employers.

Interesting places to visit include Old Tucson Studios, the Arizona–Sonora Desert Museum, Kitt Peak National Observatory, and Mission San Xavier del Bac. For visitors seeking natural beauty, the area offers Saguaro National Park, Sabino Canyon in the Coronado National Forest, and the Tucson Botanical Gardens. Cultural attractions include the Arizona Historical Society, the Tucson Symphony Orchestra, the Arizona Opera, and the Tucson Museum of Art.

TOM BEAL
Columnist, *The Arizona Daily Star*
Reviewed by CHAD KENNEDY
Tucson Metropolitan Chamber of Commerce

TULSA

Tulsa, the second largest city in Oklahoma, is located on the Arkansas River in the northeastern part of the state. The city's population is about 393,000; more than 800,000 live in the greater metropolitan area.

Tulsa was first settled in 1836 by Creek Indians, who came from Alabama. The frontier town grew rapidly as farmers, ranchers, and traders moved in from the east. The City of Tulsa was incorporated in 1898 and received

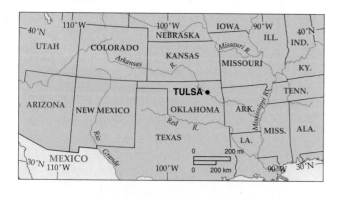

its city charter in 1908. When oil deposits were discovered in nearby Red Fork in 1901, Tulsa began to flourish; the city soon became known as the Oil Capital of the World.

Although the petroleum industry still has a strong presence in Tulsa, manufacturing and the aerospace and telecommunications industries have helped diversify the local economy. An important commercial transportation hub, Tulsa has an international airport and is a busy railroad, trucking, and interstate bus terminal. The McClellan-Kerr Arkansas River Navigation System, a 445-mile (716-kilometer) waterway, links Tulsa's inland port (in nearby Catoosa) to the Mississippi River.

The city's attractions include the Gilcrease Museum, the Philbrook Museum of Art, and the Oklahoma Jazz Hall of Fame. Educational institutions include the University of Tulsa and Oral Roberts University. Tulsa has more than 100 public parks and playgrounds.

Reviewed by Tulsa Convention and Visitors Bureau

TUNDRA

Below the north polar cap's permanent snow and ice are the Arctic's treeless plains known as the tundra. It is one of Earth's major biomes, or types of large communities of plants and animals. Tundra occurs where summers are short and cool, and winters are long and bitterly cold. Tundra is also found above the tree line in mountain alpine zones.

Tundra occupies about 3 million square miles (nearly 8 million square kilometers), or 5 percent of Earth's land surface. Large areas of Canada, Alaska, and Russia are covered by tundra.

Tundra Environment. Most Arctic tundra lies beyond the Arctic Circle, where there are long periods of continuous daylight in summer and continuous darkness in winter. In winter the temperature is often below –40°F (–40°C), and snow and ice cover the ground. Many animals hibernate or migrate, and plants are dormant (inactive). Some animals take refuge in the forest-tundra ecotone, a transition zone between the tundra and evergreen forests to the south. During the short summer, the continuous daylight melts the snow and ice, and the tundra comes alive. Even so, the average July temperature is 50°F (10°C) or lower.

Permafrost, ground that remains frozen year-round, occurs only a foot or two below the tundra surface. Because of permafrost, soils remain cold and plant roots cannot penetrate deeply. It also prevents water drainage through the soil. This means that lowland tundra areas are often wet and boggy, with many small ponds and shallow lakes.

Tundra Plants. Just beyond the tree line, tundra is dominated by shrubs of willow and dwarf birch. Farther north are mostly grasses, grasslike plants called sedges, and various herbs. In the far north is the polar desert, where mainly mosses and lichens grow.

Plant growth in the tundra is limited by the short, cool growing season and by a short supply of essential nutrients, such as nitrogen and phosphorus. Plants here take several to many years to complete their life cycles. They grow close to the ground where it is warmer and winds are less severe. To make the most of the summer, plants begin growth just as the snow is melting. The tundra buttercup even begins to flower under the snow.

Arctic tundra is covered by ice and snow most of the year. During the short, cool summer, tundra animals, such as caribou, feed on shrubs, grasses, and lichens.

Animals of the Tundra. One of the most characteristic animals of the tundra is the caribou (called reindeer in Europe and Asia). Some caribou travel hundreds of miles to spend their summers on the tundra, but they retreat south to forests during the winter.

Musk oxen are found only in the tundra. Arctic foxes, lemmings, snowy owls, and grizzly and polar bears also dwell there.

Many kinds of birds migrate to the tundra each summer to breed and also to feed on the mosquitoes and flies found there. Most of the birds leave as winter returns.

People of the Tundra. For many thousands of years, the tundra has been occupied by people who call themselves Inuit (formerly known as Eskimos). You can read more about them in the article INUIT in Volume I.

Until recently, tundra resources attracted little attention of people from the south. However, one of the biggest oil deposits in North America has been found and developed at Prudhoe Bay, Alaska, and people are searching for other Arctic oil fields. Great care must be taken to avoid damaging the tundra because it recovers from disturbance very slowly.

STEPHEN F. MACLEAN, JR.
Institute of Arctic Biology
University of Alaska

See also BIOMES.

TUNGSTEN

It is night. A sleek jet airliner climbs steeply into the dark sky as its powerful engines roar. Elsewhere in the city someone flips a switch, and light floods a room. Although these events seem unrelated, they have something in common—tungsten. This unusual metal is in the glowing filament of the electric light bulb and in the heat-resistant alloys used in jet engines.

Tungsten is a hard, brittle, whitish gray metal that has an extremely high melting point —6170°F (about 3400°C). This is the highest melting point of any metal. Tungsten is also heavy. If you filled a quart bottle (0.9 liter) with powdered tungsten, it would weigh more than 40 pounds (18 kilograms). (A quart of water weighs about 2 pounds, or 1 kilogram.) Tungsten also conducts electricity and heat fairly well.

▶**USES**

One of the most important uses of tungsten is in the making of special steels that remain strong and hard at high temperatures. An alloy steel containing 2 to 3 percent tungsten can withstand the high stresses in jet aircraft engines at 1400°F (760°C). Almost all high-speed steel cutting tools rely on tungsten to help them keep their keen edge, even under extreme friction and heat.

When tungsten unites with carbon, it forms a compound called tungsten carbide. This material is second in hardness only to diamonds. It is used in dies, machine tools, rock-crusher plates, and bucket teeth on power shovels. Tungsten carbide drill bits have enabled oilmen to drill wells 3 miles (5 kilometers) deep. In cutting tools, cobalt metal acts as a cement to hold together the hard grains of tungsten carbide. Tungsten carbide tools cut five to six times faster than the best high-speed steel tools and outlast them by as much as 10 to 1.

Although pure tungsten is very brittle, special treatment can make it ductile (able to be drawn into wire). A single pound of tungsten can be stretched into a wire 8½ miles (14 kilometers) long. The ability of this metal to be drawn so fine, coupled with its high melting point, makes it ideal for filaments in lamps and cathodes in electron tubes. Tungsten wire

FACTS ABOUT TUNGSTEN
CHEMICAL SYMBOL: W
ATOMIC WEIGHT: 183.86
SPECIFIC GRAVITY: 19.3 (about 19 times as heavy as water).
COLOR: Whitish gray.
PROPERTIES: Very hard, metallic, brittle; highest melting point of all metals.
OCCURRENCE: Never found in pure form in nature.
CHIEF ORES: Wolframite and scheelite.
CHIEF SOURCES: China, Russia, South Korea.

also is used as surgical stitching material and to make crosshairs in telescopes.

▶**HISTORY**

Although they did not know it, people were making use of tungsten as far back as the Middle Ages. Traces of tungsten in the ore made the steel of the famous Damascus swords hard enough to chop an iron spear in two and sharp enough to split a single hair. But tungsten remained unknown until the 1700's, when the Swedish chemist Karl W. Scheele (1742–86) discovered it in a mineral in 1781. It was Scheele who gave tungsten its name, which is Swedish for "heavy stone." The pure metal was isolated in 1783 by two Spanish chemists, the brothers Juan J. (1754–96) and Fausto (1755–1833) d'Elhuyar. But no way was found to extract tungsten profitably from its ore for nearly 100 years after that date.

Because tungsten cost so much to produce and was so hard to shape, there was little interest in it until the electric light bulb was invented. Then fine tungsten wire was found to be the best material for the filaments used in these lamps.

In many countries tungsten is known by the name "wolfram." This name comes from a mineral that is now one of tungsten's most important ores. Superstitious German miners of the Middle Ages believed that this mineral ate up valuable tin ore as a wolf devours sheep. Tungsten's chemical symbol, W, comes from the name "wolfram."

JOHN A. RING
Union Carbide Corporation

See also LIGHTING.

TUNISIA

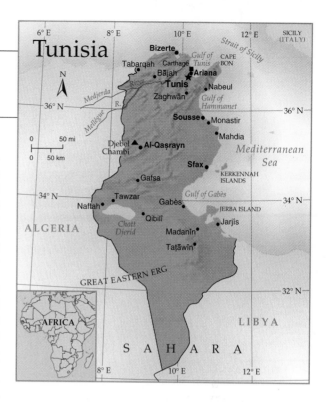

Tunisia is the smallest in area of the nations of North Africa. It is situated on the Mediterranean Sea, bordered by Algeria on the west and Libya on the southeast. Tunisia occupies the northernmost point on the African mainland, a projection of land that lies only about 86 miles (138 kilometers) across the Mediterranean Sea from the Italian island of Sicily.

Because of its location, Tunisia historically has been a crossroads between Europe and Africa and between North Africa and the Middle East. The site of the ancient city-state of Carthage, which once dominated trade in the western Mediterranean, Tunisia was later the center of the Roman Empire in Africa. The Arab conquest of North Africa in the 7th century A.D. made Tunisia a part of the Arab world. Tunisia was ruled by France from the late 19th century until 1956, when it regained its independence.

▶ **THE PEOPLE**

The Tunisians are mainly of mixed Arab and Berber descent. The Berbers inhabited the region before the arrival of the Arabs. A number of Europeans, chiefly French and Italians, also live in Tunisia.

Where the People Live. Most of the population is concentrated in the north, the country's most fertile region. More than half the people live in cities or towns; the rest live mainly in farming villages. The south, which is largely desert, has no settlements, except at occasional oases, or small fertile areas watered by natural springs. The people of this region were traditionally semi-nomadic, traveling from place to place for part of each year, seeking pasture for their sheep, goats, and camels. This way of life, however, is rapidly disappearing.

Language and Religion. Arabic is the official language of the country. French has the status of a second national language and is taught in schools and used in commerce. Islam (the religion of the Muslims) is the official state religion. The European residents are mostly Roman Catholics, and there is a small Jewish community.

A woman wearing a traditional *safsari* passes a mosque (Islamic temple) in the ancient city of Nabeul.

Fishing boats are drawn up along the shore of the harbor in Bizerte. The city is an important seaport and a popular Mediterranean tourist resort.

Many nomads have settled down in farming villages like the one in the background. Often they still use donkeys and camels to transport goods.

FACTS AND FIGURES

TUNISIA is the official name of the country.

CAPITAL: Tunis.

LOCATION: North Africa. **Latitude**—30° 13′ N to 37° 21′ N. **Longitude**—7° 32′ E to 11° 36′ E.

AREA: 163,610 km² (63,170 sq mi).

POPULATION: 6,400,000 (estimate).

LANGUAGE: Arabic (official), French, English.

GOVERNMENT: Republic. **Head of state**—president. **International co-operation**—United Nations, Arab League, Organization of African Unity (OAU).

NATIONAL ANTHEM: *Ala Khallidi* ("To Eternity").

ECONOMY: Agricultural products—wheat, olives and olive oil, barley, dates, citrus and other fruits, wine, vegetables, livestock, sugar beets, cotton. **Industries and products**—chemicals and fertilizer, food processing, building materials, tourism, steel, automobile and electrical appliance assembly, shoes, clothing, textiles, handicrafts (leather, copper, and brass objects, textiles, carpets, pottery), fishing, esparto pulp. **Chief minerals**—petroleum, phosphates, natural gas, iron, lead, zinc. **Chief exports**—crude petroleum, phosphates, clothing, textiles, olive oil, fruit. **Chief imports**—refined petroleum products, foodstuffs, machinery, iron and steel, scientific equipment, vehicles. **Monetary unit**—Tunisian dinar.

▶THE LAND

The eastern end of the Atlas Mountains divides the well-watered farmland of northern Tunisia from the dry, grassy central steppes. The south is mainly desert. Djebel Chambi, the highest point in the country, rises to 1,544 meters (5,066 feet).

The mountains and coastal plains in the north receive up to 600 millimeters (24 inches) of rain a year. Many of the forests have been cut down for firewood or to clear the land for farming. This has caused the soil to dry out or blow away in places.

In the central interior, sheep and goats graze on the sparse vegetation. Esparto grass, used in making paper and twine, grows wild in this region. Along the central coast, where there is more grass, cattle are raised. In the south, the steppes merge into the Sahara desert, where few people live.

▶THE ECONOMY

Tunisia's economy is based on a mixture of agriculture, mining, and industry. The chief crop, durum (hard) wheat, is grown in the north. Barley is grown in drier areas. The wheat is used to make *couscous*, a popular Tunisian dish. First the wheat is ground into semolina, which is like little grains of spaghetti. The semolina is then steamed, sometimes with vegetables or a little meat or fish, and served with a sauce.

Tunisia's grain crops are often affected by irregular rainfall, plagues of locusts, or the scorching sirocco wind that blows in from the Sahara. Food must often be imported. New kinds of grain that yield more food and resist weather problems are being developed.

Vineyards in the north produce grapes for eating and for making wine. Since alcoholic beverages are forbidden by the Muslim religion, most of the wine is exported. Fruits and vegetables flourish near Tunis and on the eastern coast of the Cape Bon Peninsula. Sugar beets and cotton are other northern crops.

Because the dry, sandy soil along the central coast is ideal for the cultivation of olives, olive trees have flourished in Tunisia since the time of the Romans. Tunisia is one of the world's largest producers of olive oil. Olive plantations spread like a fan around the city of Sfax. Dates, from palm trees grown on southern oases, provide the chief source of food in the desert in years of drought.

Tunisia has long been among the world's leading producers of phosphates. The making of fertilizer and chemicals from phosphates is a major industry. There are petroleum and natural gas deposits in several parts of the country and offshore, and additional large reserves were discovered early in the 1980's. Iron ore is mined in the north and west.

A pleasant climate, lovely beaches, and historic ruins have made Tunisia a popular vacation spot for Europeans. Besides tourism, the industries of Tunisia include fishing, food processing, handicrafts, and the making of building materials. To provide more jobs, the government has encouraged foreign companies to set up plants in Tunisia to manufacture goods for export. Tunisian factory workers assemble automobiles and electrical appliances and make chemicals, shoes, clothing, steel, and other goods.

▶ CITIES

Tunisia's chief cities are on the Mediterranean coast. Tunis, the largest city and the capital of the country, is a great port and center of learning. The walls of the old city have been torn down, and a new city spreads outward along wide boulevards. Along the broad,

This view of present-day Tunis shows the Place d'Afrique (Africa Plaza), with a statue of Tunisia's first president, and the broad Avenue Habib Bourguiba in the background. The building shaped like an inverted pyramid is one of the city's modern hotels.

Roman ruins can be seen in Carthage, one of the most important cities of the ancient world.

tree-lined Avenue Habib Bourguiba (named after Tunisia's first president) are banks, large hotels, cafés, and a cathedral. In the old city are the *souks,* traditional markets with little shops opening into arch-covered streets too narrow for automobiles. **Carthage**, a suburb of Tunis, has magnificent ancient ruins, including a Roman amphitheater and public baths. It is also the site of a modern presidential palace.

Sfax, the second largest city, is a busy port with many mills for processing olive oil. Other major port cities are Sousse and Bizerte. Bizerte is the northernmost city in Africa.

▶ **HISTORY AND GOVERNMENT**

Tunisia's first inhabitants were nomadic Berbers. In the 800's B.C., the Phoenicians, a people from the eastern Mediterranean, founded the city of Carthage. Carthage eventually controlled an empire that included parts of western North Africa, Spain, and Sicily, as well as Corsica and Sardinia. But a long struggle with Rome, in the Punic Wars, ended in the destruction of Carthage in 146 B.C. For more information, see the article PUNIC WARS in Volume P.

Roman rule lasted until the A.D. 400's. The Romans rebuilt Carthage, and Tunisia flourished. With the decline of the Roman Empire, waves of invaders swept over Tunisia's shores—Vandals in the 400's, Byzantines in the 500's, and Arabs in the 600's.

The first Tunisian dynasty (family of rulers) was founded in 800 by the Aghlabids. The princes of Tunisia went far afield, conquering Sicily and Egypt. But these conquests exposed Tunisia to the attacks of rival princedoms. From the 900's to the 1500's, Tunisia was ruled by a series of Muslim tribal groups—the Fatimids, the Almohades, and a Berber tribe, the Hafsids. In the 1200's and 1300's, under the Hafsids, Tunisia again flourished. Tunis gained great prosperity and importance, and its Zitouna University became a center for the teaching of Islam.

In 1574, the region became a province of the Ottoman Empire. For most of the next 300 years it had internal self-government, even though it remained part of the empire.

French Rule and Independence.   France, which already controlled neighboring Algeria, established a protectorate over Tunisia in 1883. After World War I (1914–18), the Tunisian people began to seek greater self-government, but the French rejected their demands. During World War II (1939–45), battles in Tunisia interrupted the independence movement. In the early 1950's, after negotiations failed, the Tunisians began a guerrilla war against the French. Full independence came in 1956. The Husseinite dynasty, which had ruled since 1705, ended in 1957. Tunisia then became a republic.

Tunisia Today.   The head of state and government is the president, who is elected for a 5-year term. Habib Bourguiba, the leader of the independence movement, was Tunisia's first president. The constitution was amended in 1975 to name him president for life. The president appoints a cabinet headed by a prime minister. The 189 members of the legislature, the Majlis al-Nuwaab (Chamber of Deputies), are elected to 5-year terms.

In 1987, Prime Minister Zine el-Abidine ben Ali assumed the office of president, declaring the elderly Bourguiba too ill to govern. Reforms passed in 1994 guaranteed opposition parties seats in the legislature, but Muslim fundamentalist parties were banned. Ben Ali, who ran unopposed in 1989 and 1994, won additional terms in multiparty elections in 1999 and 2004.

RUSSELL A. STONE
Coeditor, *Change in Tunisia*

The network of tunnels under a modern city carries human traffic, water, sewage, and telephone and power lines. A worker uses a laser beam to check the wall alignment during the construction of a water tunnel.

TUNNELS

Tunnels are underground passages that are used in many ways. Trains and cars travel in tunnels through mountains and under rivers and other bodies of water. City subways are a network of tunnels. Tunnels bring water to cities and carry away sewage. They also deliver the water that irrigates farms and the water that spins the turbines of electric power plants. Essential minerals are mined from tunnels dug deep in the earth.

▶ HOW A TUNNEL IS BUILT

The first step in building a tunnel is to plan its exact route. Surveyors make maps showing how deep in the earth or how far beneath a body of water the tunnel must be dug. Then geologists try to learn about the materials through which the tunnel will pass. They drill deep holes and bring up samples of what lies below the surface—hard rock, soft earth, wet earth, sand, or clay. Next the construction engineers begin work on the tunnel. Even the most skillful surveyors and geologists cannot predict every circumstance the engineers may encounter. Experienced tunnel workers know they can never be certain of what lies ahead of them beyond the **tunnel face,** the wall of rock or earth into which they are about to dig.

Building Rock Tunnels. One way to build a tunnel through rock is to blast the rock into pieces with explosives. The broken rock resulting from the explosions is removed by a process called **mucking.** Workers load the rubble into small railcars or onto trucks that haul it away, or a conveyor belt carries it off.

Another and faster way to build a tunnel through rock is to use a machine called a **mechanical mole.** On its round face, as large as the tunnel to be dug, are a number of cutting wheels with teeth made of hard steel. The face slowly revolves as jacks force it against the rock. Each cutting wheel revolves too, grinding the rock into small bits. A mechanical mole can cut through rock at the rate of several hundred feet a day.

In order to keep bits of rock from breaking off the walls, tunnels may be lined with bricks, blocks of granite, or other hard materials. A more modern method is called **shotcreting.** It uses a high-pressure air gun that sprays the rock walls with a mixture of cement and water. This mixture hardens into a lining that will keep water out of the tunnel as well.

Building Tunnels Through Soft Materials. Digging through any soft material is easier than digging through rock but presents other problems. Soft earth has a short **stand-up time,** which is the length of time a material will stand unsupported. Rock may have a stand-up time of centuries. Soft earth, clay, mud, or sand may have a stand-up time of only a few minutes—or it may have none at all. Thus tunnelers digging through such materials must take care to avoid cave-ins.

One way to tunnel through soft material is to freeze it. Pipes are driven into the soft earth, and refrigerated liquid is pumped through them until the earth freezes and becomes hard. It can then be cut out as if it were rock, and the tunnel can be lined before it has thawed out. The soft earth can also be hardened by pumping a mixture of cement and certain chemicals into it.

Another method of driving a tunnel through soft material is to use a steel **shield.** This device looks somewhat like a length of pipe a little larger in diameter than the finished tunnel will be.

The front end of the shield is pressed against the tunnel's face where the workers dig out the earth. Powerful jacks push the shield forward to keep pace with the workers' digging, so that they are always kept just inside the shield's protection.

While the workers at the front of the shield dig, other workers at the rear of the shield build a new section of tunnel lining, usually out of heavy steel arches. This lined section is left in place when the shield is jacked forward. Thus the tunnel's soft walls and ceiling are held in place at all times, first by the shield and then by the lining.

Underwater Tunneling. An underwater tunnel is built of heavy steel rings bolted together to form a huge tube. This tube must be stronger than tubes used for tunnels through soft earth because water and mud together weigh more than earth alone. The threat of collapse and leakage makes tunneling under water especially dangerous. For this reason, **sandhogs,** as underwater tunnelers are called, need the protection of a pressurized shield as they dig through the soft mud or muck below a body of water. The air pressure inside the shield is kept high enough to equal the high pressure of the water above it. This prevents water and mud from rushing into the work area.

Digging is done through doors in the shield's front wall. At the rear of the shield other workers are putting together a new section of the steel tunnel, which will be left in place when the shield is jacked forward. It can then be completed under normal pressure.

Cut-and-Cover Construction. For tunnels near the surface, such as some subway tunnels, the cut-and-cover construction method is useful. A ditch big enough to hold the tunnel is dug in the ground, and a tunnel of stone, brick, or iron is built inside it. Then the completed tunnel is covered with earth, and the surface is restored.

A similar method can be used in the bottom of a river or bay where the earth is firm enough to safely dig an underwater trench. Watertight steel tunnel sections are manufactured on shore and then floated out. They are filled with enough water to sink them into the trench. Divers bolt them together and make the joints watertight with concrete. Then the trench is filled in, the tunnel is pumped dry, and its interior is completed.

▶**TUNNEL VENTILATION**

Providing fresh air to tunnel workers has always been a problem. Once the only known method was to build air shafts up to the surface. But the development of mechanical power—steam, internal combustion, electrical—made the use of fans practical. Ventilating fans are now used on all tunnel construction jobs, to force fresh air in and draw contaminated air out.

Finished tunnels also need ventilation. Steam locomotives filled early railroad tunnels with smoke, and car windows were always shut in protection. But closed windows cannot protect car, truck, and bus riders from the deadly fumes given off by gasoline and diesel engines. In 1927, Clifford Holland, an American civil engineer, built the first underwater tunnel for motor vehicles. He designed the system now used in all such tunnels. He built two large buildings at each end of the Holland Tunnel, which runs under the Hudson River between New York and New Jersey. Eighty-four huge fans installed in those buildings can change all the air in the 1½-mile (2.4-kilometer) tunnel in 90 seconds.

▶**HISTORY**

People have used the concept of the tunnel throughout history. From ancient times to the Renaissance (about 1500), soldiers often attacked fortified cities by tunneling under their walls. Scores of prisoners have tried to tunnel their way to freedom. But such tunnels were not meant to last.

IMPORTANT TUNNELS OF THE WORLD

Name of Tunnel	Location	Approximate Length		Use
		mi	km	
Seikan	Japan	33.0	54.0	Railroad (underwater)
English Channel Tunnel	Britain-France	31.0	50.0	Railroad (partly underwater)
Laerdal	Norway	15.2	24.5	Highway
Simplon 1 and 2	Alps (Switzerland-Italy)	12.3	19.8	Railroad
St. Gotthard	Alps (Switzerland)	10.1	16.3	Highway
St. Gotthard	Alps (Switzerland)	9.3	15.0	Railroad
Rogers Pass	Canada	9.1	14.6	Railroad
Arlberg	Alps (Austria)	8.7	14.0	Highway
Frejus	Alps (France-Italy)	8.5	13.7	Railroad (first great rock tunnel)
Cascade	Washington State	7.8	12.6	Railroad
Mont Blanc	Alps (France-Italy)	7.3	11.7	Highway
Tequixquiac	Mexico	6.2	10.0	Water drainage
Shimizu	Japan	6.0	9.7	Railroad
Severn	England	4.4	7.1	Railroad (partly underwater)
San Bernardino	Switzerland	4.1	6.6	Highway

The first permanent tunnels were built about 3,000 years ago, not for the passage of people, but to carry water to towns or dry areas. Tunnels through rock were made by building a fire close to the rock face and then throwing cold water on the heated rock until it cracked and could be broken up. Another method involved driving wooden wedges into holes or cracks in the rock. The wedges were kept wet until they swelled enough to put pressure on the rock and split it into bits.

These ancient tunneling methods were still being used in the 1700's, when factories first required large-scale transportation of goods and people. From about 1760–1830 canals were built where there were no rivers to provide that transportation. Tunnels were dug to enable the canals to pass through hills.

In the 1800's railroads that replaced those canals also needed tunnels, and these were built with powerful new explosives, new equipment, and new techniques.

The First Underwater Tunnel. The first **subaqueous,** or underwater, tunnel was dug under the Thames River in London, England. It was constructed by a French-born inventor, Marc Brunel, and his son Isambard. Their Thames tunnel opened on March 25, 1843, for pedestrian use. Brunel designed the first shield and methods to line the tunnel.

The First Alpine Tunnel. The Frejus was the first tunnel dug through Europe's towering snow-peaked Alps. Engineers had always insisted that the mountains were too massive to tunnel through. But the tunneling job began in 1857 under the direction of a young Italian railroad engineer, Germaine Sommeiller. The Frejus, completed in 1871, measured 8½ miles (13.7 kilometers) from portal to portal and was the world's longest tunnel. Its tracks provided the long-desired link between Europe's northern and southern rail lines.

Japan's Seikan Tunnel. The Seikan railroad tunnel between Japan's two main islands, Honshu and Hokkaido, has a 14½-mile (23.2-kilometer) central section that has made it the world's longest transportation tunnel. The Seikan was dug 300 feet (90 meters) below the seabed of stormy Tsugaru Strait, making it the world's deepest underwater tunnel as well. It passes through nine fault zones where earthquakes often occur.

The Strait was surveyed for 25 years before plans for three separate tunnels were completed. The main one, 35 feet (10.5 meters) wide, would carry the railroad tracks. A smaller tunnel, beside the main one and connected to it at intervals, would provide ventilation, delivery of supplies, and removal of muck. Another small tunnel, called a pilot tunnel, was dug below and ahead of the others in order to discover the conditions there.

Work started from both ends of Seikan in 1971. Workers were under such high air pressure that they could work only one hour of an eight-hour shift. Accidents were frequent, and 34 lives were lost during construction.

In 1983 the two halves of the pilot tunnel met. It had been **holed through,** as tunnelers say. Two years later the main tunnel was holed through, and the first train ran through it in 1988.

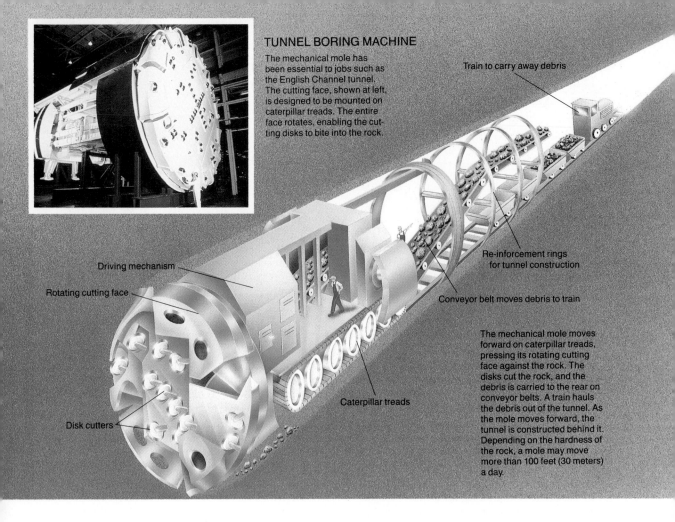

TUNNEL BORING MACHINE

The mechanical mole has been essential to jobs such as the English Channel tunnel. The cutting face, shown at left, is designed to be mounted on caterpillar treads. The entire face rotates, enabling the cutting disks to bite into the rock.

Train to carry away debris

Driving mechanism

Rotating cutting face

Disk cutters

Caterpillar treads

Re-inforcement rings for tunnel construction

Conveyor belt moves debris to train

The mechanical mole moves forward on caterpillar treads, pressing its rotating cutting face against the rock. The disks cut the rock, and the debris is carried to the rear on conveyor belts. A train hauls the debris out of the tunnel. As the mole moves forward, the tunnel is constructed behind it. Depending on the hardness of the rock, a mole may move more than 100 feet (30 meters) a day.

The English Channel Tunnel. The first tunnel under the English Channel, between England and France, was begun in 1987 and was completed in 1994, after seven years of construction and a cost of more than $13 billion. The construction of such a tunnel had been discussed for nearly two centuries, but plans had been abandoned many times. It was thought that it would cost too much, would destroy the business of cross channel ferries, or would give England's enemies too easy an invasion route. Also, tunneling was considered impossible beneath a channel 22½ miles (26 kilometers) wide at its narrowest point.

But several surveys convinced engineers that the tunnel was practical because the floor of the channel is mostly a soft limestone that would be easy to cut through. Popular demand for it grew. An association of French and English banks agreed to undertake the project, and the public was invited to buy bonds issued to help meet a cost originally estimated at $10 billion. Starting from deep shafts dug on either coast, and using newly designed cutting and drilling machines, work was finally under way on the Chunnel, as it is popularly called. When it opened to the general public in November 1994, it became, with the Seikan Tunnel of Japan, one of the two longest underwater tunnels ever built.

Engineers have experimented with new methods to tunnel through rock by using high heat to melt it, by bombarding it with water at high pressure to break it up, and by using laser beams to vaporize it. New tunnel-boring machines may someday be operated from outside the tunnel, by remote control. Thus, some future tunnels may be built without endangering the lives of those who build them.

SAM EPSTEIN
BERYL EPSTEIN
Authors, *Tunnels*

TUPPER, SIR CHARLES. See CANADA, GOVERNMENT OF (Profiles).

TURBINES

A turbine is a type of engine that is powered by water, steam, or hot gases being forced through the engine. In a turbine a series of blades are mounted at an angle on a central shaft, or pole. Liquid or gas moving over the blades causes the shaft to spin. The spinning shaft provides the power to do work. Turbines are used in hydroelectric and nuclear power plants, in rocket fuel pumps, and in the engines of large ships, military tanks, and jet airplanes.

The ancestors of the turbine are the waterwheel and the windmill. The turbine is more efficient than these ancient machines because the blades and shaft of a turbine are completely enclosed. The result is that all the liquid or gas entering the turbine has to pass through the blades. Very little of the power of the moving stream of liquid or gas is lost.

Turbines are usually classified by the substance that drives them—water, steam, or gas. They can also be described by the principle that causes the turbine wheel to turn—impulse or reaction. An **impulse turbine** is driven by the force of water, steam, or gas striking against the turbine's blades. The waterwheel is a simple impulse turbine.

A **reaction turbine** works something like a spinning lawn sprinkler. Water, gas, or steam rushing out of nozzles on the rim of a wheel provide the force to make the wheel turn.

▶ **WATER TURBINES**

The first practical turbine was a water turbine, also called a hydraulic turbine. It was invented in the 19th century by Benoît Fourneyron, a young French engineer who had entered the design in a contest for improvements in waterwheels. Fourneyron's turbine had a vertical shaft enclosed in a circular housing (outer covering). Water flowed down along the shaft and then through a set of blades located at the bottom of the shaft. As the water rushed through the blades, it turned them, which caused the shaft to rotate.

Water turbines were first used for the production of electric power in the 1870's and became important in the 1880's. Powered by water from waterfalls, rivers, or water at damsites, turbines can run electric generators cheaply and efficiently. Water turbines are now used mainly in hydroelectric power plants.

Turbines use the energy from moving water, steam, or hot gases to do useful work. This Francis turbine is used in hydroelectric power plants to produce electricity.

The most common types of hydraulic turbines in use today are the Francis turbine and the Kaplan turbine. The Francis turbine is named after James B. Francis of Massachusetts, who developed such turbines around the middle of the 19th century. In the Francis turbine the water flows inward toward the shaft through fixed (nonmoving) blades in the casing. These fixed blades guide the water toward the rotating blades on the shaft. After turning these blades, the water flows down and away.

The Kaplan turbine was invented around 1900 by Viktor Kaplan, an Austrian engineer. It looks like a big ship's propeller with four or five blades mounted lengthwise in a tunnel. The tips of the blades just clear the sides of the tunnel. The pitch, or angle, of the blades can be changed to adjust them to water currents of different speeds.

A third type of water turbine is the Pelton wheel, in which a high-speed jet of water is directed into bucket-shaped paddles on a turbine wheel. The great force of the water causes the wheel to turn.

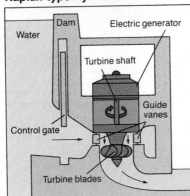

Kaplan-type Hydraulic Turbine

Dam
Water
Electric generator
Turbine shaft
Guide vanes
Control gate
Turbine blades

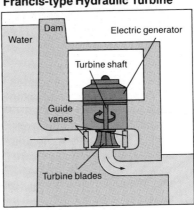

Francis-type Hydraulic Turbine

Dam
Water
Electric generator
Turbine shaft
Guide vanes
Turbine blades

Water turbines, such as the Kaplan and Francis turbines, are used mainly to produce electricity. Water flowing over the turbine blades spins a shaft in the generator, producing electricity.

▶ STEAM TURBINES

Steam turbines are powered by blasts of steam hitting the blades from a set of nozzles. In the 1600's an early example of a steam turbine was shown in a book by an Italian architect, Giovanni Branca. In Branca's drawing, a jet of steam struck paddles mounted on the rim of a wheel. The wheel turned a shaft.

During the next 250 years a number of inventors made designs of steam turbines. However, no one produced a practical steam turbine. The proper materials and tools for building steam turbines had not yet been developed.

A successful steam turbine was finally designed by the Swedish engineer Carl Gustav de Laval in the 1880's. De Laval's turbine had a circle of curved blades on a shaft. Curving the blades allowed the steam to give them a stronger push.

About the same time, another type of steam turbine was developed by an Englishman, Charles A. Parsons. Parsons used more than one circle of blades. A modern Parsons turbine may have as many as 50 rows of blades, all on the same shaft. As steam passes through a set of the moving blades, it strikes a set of fixed blades that are attached to the inside of the turbine housing. These fixed blades guide the steam so that it strikes the next set of moving blades at the best angle for the greatest possible power output.

The Parsons turbine is the most common kind of turbine for running electric generators in steam-powered electric generating plants and for propelling large ships. Nuclear power plants use steam turbines to convert the heat of the atomic reaction into electric power.

Steam Turbines and Steam Engines

Steam turbines have many advantages over conventional steam engines, which are also called reciprocating steam engines. Reciprocating steam engines have pistons and connecting rods that jerk back and forth, creating less efficient movement than the smooth spinning of the steam turbine shaft. The result is that steam turbines give more power than steam engines for the same amount of fuel. Turbines can also be built more compactly than steam engines.

Turbines do present some problems. They must be manufactured with great precision, because at the high speeds at which they turn, any vibration could shake the turbine to pieces. The water used to make the steam must be very pure, because dirt would be blasted against the turbine blades by the steam and would act as an abrasive, wearing away the blades.

A turbine cannot be run backward, as a reciprocating steam engine can. Any vehicle or ship powered by a steam turbine therefore needs some provision for backing up. There are two ways of doing this in ships' turbines. A small extra turbine can be connected to the propeller shaft and used for backing up, or the turbine can turn an electric generator, providing power for an electric motor that turns the propeller. The electric motor can be easily reversed.

Another complication is that turbines rotate many times faster than a locomotive's wheels or a ship's propellers can. Therefore, a ship or a land vehicle driven directly by a turbine must have a set of gears to slow down the motion of the propeller or the wheels.

▶ GAS TURBINES

Gas turbines belong to a group of engines called internal-combustion engines. These engines are so named because fuel is mixed with air and burned (combusted) inside the engine.

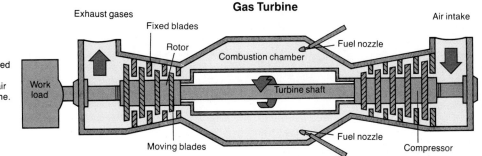

Gas Turbine

Exhaust gases · Fixed blades · Rotor · Combustion chamber · Fuel nozzle · Air intake · Work load · Turbine shaft · Moving blades · Fuel nozzle · Compressor

Gas turbines are powered by the combustion (burning) of a fuel and air mixture inside the turbine. These turbines are used to turn wheels or propellers and to run electric generators.

The expanding gases from the burning fuel act directly on the moving parts of the engine.

In contrast, steam turbines are considered external-combustion engines because fuel is burned outside the engine to boil water and produce steam, which is then piped into the engine. Water turbines involve no combustion at all—they are powered by moving water.

Turning a turbine wheel with the hot gases from internal combustion was tried as long ago as the 18th century. Not until the 20th century, however, was a successful gas turbine developed. The reason for this was that in the past no metals were known that were suitable for making the turbine blades. The intense heat of the combustion burned and pitted the blades, which either broke or bent when the turbine was running at high speeds. The problem was not solved until about the beginning of World War II, when new alloys (mixtures of two or more metals) were developed that could withstand the intense heat.

For combustion to take place, air must be forced under pressure into the gas turbine. (Air is needed for gases to burn.) A machine called a compressor does this job.

The power of a gas turbine's spinning shaft can be used for turning propellers or wheels or for running a generator. For example, turbo-prop engines in airplanes combine a turbine with a propeller. The huge engines for military ships are being changed over to gas turbines, because they are light in weight and easy to restart. Gas turbines are also being used in military tanks.

Another way to use the gas turbine is to make use of the power of the expanding gases instead of that of the rotating shaft. The turbojet airplane engine, developed in the 1930's, uses the gas turbine in this way. The thrust, or force, of the expanding gases rushing out the exhaust nozzle of the engine pushes the airplane along.

▶**OTHER TYPES OF TURBINES**

The hotter the steam or gases flowing through a turbine, the more efficient the turbine can be. A mercury-vapor turbine has been used in the search for increased efficiency by positioning it above an ordinary steam turbine. Mercury is one of the few metallic elements that is liquid at ordinary temperatures. The boiler of the turbine produces mercury vapor at 884°F (473°C). The mercury-vapor turbine has proved to be efficient, but it has drawbacks. Mercury vapor is poisonous, so that any leak in the pipes is very dangerous.

Another type of turbine is the hot-air turbine. Fuel heats air, which turns the turbine. The air is exhausted from the turbine and sent through an air compressor, which compresses the air and sends it back through the air heater again. From the heater it goes back through the turbine again. Although the hot-air turbine does not need a boiler, as does the steam turbine, its air heater is just as bulky, so that nothing is gained in compactness.

Modern windmills use the basic principle of the turbine to create electricity. Air pushes on the windmill's blades causing them to turn. The turning movement can power small electric generators, and many windmills, also called wind generators, may one day be used to provide electric power on a large scale.

L. SPRAGUE DE CAMP
Author, *Man and Power*
Reviewed by FU-KANG TSOU
Drexel University

See also ENGINES; INTERNAL-COMBUSTION ENGINES; JET PROPULSION; STEAM ENGINES.

TURING, ALAN M. See MATHEMATICS, HISTORY OF.

TURKEY

The nation of Turkey straddles two continents—Asia and Europe. Because of its location, it has played an important role in both Asian and European history. For some 600 years Turkey was the center of the great Ottoman Empire. At the height of its power, the empire stretched from east central Europe to Southwest Asia and North Africa. The modern Republic of Turkey, which was founded in 1923, retains only a part of the once vast Ottoman Empire. But it is still a country of considerable size, about as large in area as the U.S. states of Utah, Arizona, and Nevada combined.

Turkey has been an associate member of the European Union since 1963, but it was not invited to apply for full membership until 1999.

Since then, Turks and Europeans have been discussing the vital issue of Turkish national identity: Is Turkey a part of Europe, or is it part of the Middle East?

▶ **PEOPLE**

The region that is now Turkey has been inhabited by various peoples since ancient times. It was the birthplace of the Hittites, one of the earliest civilizations. Later, Greeks from Europe and Arabs and

Below: Hagia Sophia, a famous landmark in Istanbul, is one of the greatest remaining examples of Byzantine architecture. *Far right:* Turks are descended from a Central Asian people. *Right:* Kurds, a non-Turkish people, make up about 20 percent of the population.

Mount Ararat—an extinct volcano and the legendary site of Noah's Ark—is Turkey's highest peak.

other peoples from Asia settled in parts of the region. The Turks, who came from Central Asia, arrived after 1000 and eventually became the dominant people. Today Turks make up the vast majority of the population. The Kurds, a non-Turkish people, most of whom live in the southeastern part of the country, form the largest minority group, with about 20 percent of the population.

Language and Religion. Turkish, the official language of the country, is of Asian origin. At one time the Arabic alphabet was used to write Turkish, but a modified Roman alphabet is now used. Almost all the people are Muslims, and mosques (Muslim houses of worship) are found throughout the country.

Education. Primary, secondary, and college education are free. Primary education is compulsory for children age 6 to 14. There are high schools in all the larger towns and cities. Technical schools, teacher-training schools, and colleges provide further education. Turkey has a number of universities. The largest is the University of Istanbul. Several new universities were founded in the 1990's.

Way of Life. The Turkish way of life combines both European and Asian traditions. In appearance and dress most Turks resemble Europeans, while Turkish food, arts and crafts, and folktales are more likely to reflect Asian influence.

A favorite dish is *shish kebab*—small pieces of meat (lamb or beef) and onions roasted on a spit over charcoal pits. The Turks first learned to make coffee in Yemen during the 1500's, after they conquered the Arabian Peninsula. They took coffee back to Turkey and later introduced it to Europe.

▶ **LAND**

Asian Turkey and European Turkey are separated by the strait of Bosporus, the Sea of Marmara, and the strait of the Darda-

nelles. These narrow strips of water form one of the world's most strategic waterways.

Land Regions. Asian Turkey, called Anatolia (Anadolu in Turkish), is often referred to as Asia Minor. Two major mountain ranges cross it in an east-west direction. In the north the Northern Anatolian Mountains (the Pontic mountain system) follow the Black Sea coast. In the south the Taurus Mountains follow the coast of the Mediterranean Sea. These two mountain ranges meet in the eastern Anatolian highland. Mount Ararat, an extinct volcano that is the country's highest peak, is located there, near the border with Iran and Armenia. According to legend, it was the location of Noah's Ark. South of the eastern highland, low hills and plains join the plains of Syria and Iraq.

The Anatolian plateau lies between the Northern Anatolian Mountains and the Taurus Mountains. In the west it gives way to a low fertile plain, one of the best agricultural areas in the country.

European Turkey, or Thrace, is all that remains of what was once a vast Turkish empire in Europe. Thrace, an area of low plains and hills, has a rugged coastline. Low mountains extend from the Bulgarian border along the Black Sea coast.

Rivers and Lakes. The Kizil Irmak and the Sakarya rivers flow through Asian Turkey into the Black Sea. A shorter, curving river, flowing into the Aegean Sea, is called Menderes, from the ancient Greek word meaning "to meander." The Seyhan, Ceyhan, and Orontes rivers in the south are used for

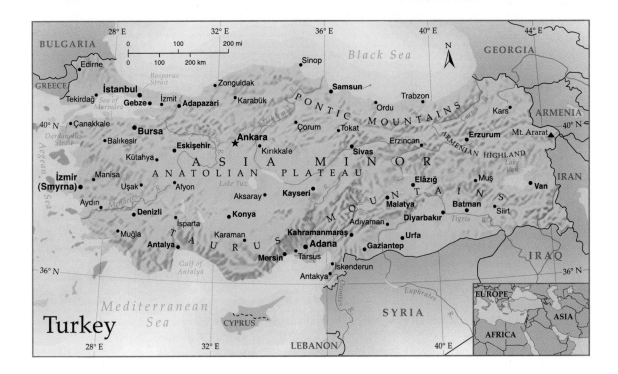

Turkey

irrigation. Lake Van and Lake Tuz, both salt lakes, are Turkey's largest lakes.

Climate. The climate of European Turkey and coastal Asian Turkey is mild, with cool, rainy winters and warm, dry summers. Winter temperatures seldom fall below freezing, and frost and snow are rare. Summer temperatures average 75°F (24°C). The western coast gets about 25 inches (650 millimeters) of rain annually. In the east, rainfall is much greater.

The Anatolian plateau has cold winters, with more than 100 days of frost every year. Summer days are hot, but the nights are cool. Annual rainfall is between 10 and 17 inches (250 and 430 millimeters). April and May are usually the wettest months in this area.

The eastern part of Asian Turkey has one of the most extreme climates in the world. Winter temperatures of –40°F (–40°C) have been recorded. Snowfall is very heavy. Summers are hot, with daytime temperatures rising to over 100°F (38°C).

Natural Resources. Coal, copper, and iron ore have been mined in Turkey since ancient times. Chromium, boron, and some petroleum are also produced. Turkey's petroleum deposits supply only a fraction of its needs; the rest must be imported.

▶ **ECONOMY**

Turkey's economy, the largest in the Middle East, ranks among the world's top twenty.

Services. The service sector employs 38 percent of the total workforce. Among these workers are bankers, real estate brokers, salespeople, teachers, and government personnel. Tourism is a very important part of the economy. Tourist-related services employ about 3 million people.

FACTS and figures

REPUBLIC OF TURKEY (Türkiye Cumhuriyeti) is the official name of the country.

LOCATION: Southeastern Europe and southwestern Asia.

AREA: 301,382 sq mi (780,580 km²).

POPULATION: 67,300,000 (estimate).

CAPITAL: Ankara.

LARGEST CITY: Istanbul.

MAJOR LANGUAGE: Turkish.

MAJOR RELIGIOUS GROUP: Sunni Muslim.

GOVERNMENT: Republic. **Head of state**—president. **Head of government**—prime minister. **Legislature**—Grand National Assembly.

CHIEF PRODUCTS: Agricultural—tobacco, cotton, grain (wheat, corn, barley, rice), olives, sugar beets, legumes, citrus fruits, livestock (chiefly sheep and goats). **Manufactured**—textiles and clothing, processed foods, automobiles, steel, lumber, paper. **Mineral**—coal, chromium, copper, boron, petroleum.

MONETARY UNIT: Turkish lira (1 lira = 100 kurus).

Manufacturing. Encouraged by government investment, Turkish industry has grown rapidly in recent years, and exports of industrial goods now exceed agricultural exports in value. Industry employs about 14 percent of the workforce. Textiles and clothing are the most important manufactured products, followed by processed foods, automobiles, steel, lumber, and paper.

Agriculture. About 40 percent of the workforce is engaged in agriculture. Wheat, grown mainly on the Anatolian plateau, is the major crop. Other important cereals are corn, barley, and rice. The chief export crops are cotton, grown on the Mediterranean coast, and tobacco, grown on the coasts of the Aegean and Black seas. Other commercial crops include tomatoes, figs, raisins, olives, hazelnuts, pistachio nuts, and citrus fruits.

Large parts of the country, especially in the Anatolian plateau, are used only as grazing land. The raising of sheep and goats is an important part of the economy. Sheep are a major source of meat in Turkey. Goat's milk is used to make cheese. Sheep wool is used in the textile industry, and goat hair is made into mohair.

Transportation. More than 5,000 miles (8,000 kilometers) of railways connect Turkey with all parts of Europe and the Middle East. All of the country's important cities are linked by rail. There are still twice as many unpaved roads as paved ones, but many all-weather roads have been built in recent years. Because of Turkey's long coastline, travel along the coast by steamship is also very popular. Istanbul and Izmir are the two chief port cities. Air transportation is growing in importance. International flights stop at Istanbul, Ankara, and Adana.

Communication. Less than one-third of the population owns a television or radio. But telecommunications systems, cellular telephones, and Internet service are on the rise. The two most important newspapers are *Cumhuriyet* (the Republic) and *Hürriyet* (Freedom).

▶ MAJOR CITIES

Istanbul is situated on both sides of the Bosporus, in Europe and in Asia. It is the largest city in Turkey. For about 470 years Istanbul was the capital of Turkey. Although no longer the capital, it has remained the country's major port and most important commercial center. For more information, see the article ISTANBUL in Volume I.

Ankara is the capital of Turkey and the nation's second largest city. Once known as Angora, the city is situated in the central part of the Anatolian plateau. The older part of the town was an ancient trading center. The newer town was built by Kemal Atatürk (1881–1938), the Turkish republic's first president. Outside the new town is a magnificent monument marking Atatürk's burial place.

Izmir (Smyrna) is located on the Aegean Sea. It is the second most important port in Turkey, exporting mainly agricultural products, such as tobacco and cotton.

▶ CULTURAL HERITAGE

For more than one thousand years, Constantinople (present-day Istanbul) was the center of culture for the Eastern Roman Empire. After the Turks captured the city in 1453,

Below: Traditional hats, slippers, and wooden boxes are displayed at a market stall. *Right:* Women harvest cotton on the Anatolian plateau. Cotton is one of Turkey's chief export crops.

the area that is now Turkey fell under the influence of the Ottoman Turks. For information on the art from the Byzantine period, see the articles BYZANTINE ART AND ARCHITECTURE; ISLAMIC ART AND ARCHITECTURE; and OTTOMAN EMPIRE in the appropriate volumes.

▶ GOVERNMENT

Turkey is a republic, governed under a constitution approved in 1982. It provides for a parliamentary form of government, consisting of a president, a prime minister, and a legislature, the Grand National Assembly. Legislators are elected by the people to 5-year terms.

The president, who is elected by the Grand National Assembly for seven years, is head of state and commander in chief of the armed forces and has wide executive powers. The president appoints the prime minister from among the members of the National Assembly. The prime minister leads the Council of Ministers, or cabinet, and heads the day-to-day activities of the government.

The Sultan Ahmed Mosque, built in the 1600's during the time of the Ottoman Empire, is nicknamed the Blue Mosque for the blue tiles that decorate its interior.

Turkey is divided into 81 provinces. Each has a governor appointed by the president and an elected council.

▶ HISTORY

Some 3,000 years ago the country now known as Turkey was divided into several kingdoms, including that of the Hittites. About 1200 B.C. many Greeks began to migrate to Turkey. Later, both Asian and European Turkey were conquered by the Persians, who in turn were driven out by the Macedonian Alexander the Great in 333 B.C. After the death of Alexander several small kingdoms rose and fell in Turkey. They all were conquered eventually by the Romans, who divided Turkey into several provinces and built many cities.

The Byzantine Empire. In A.D. 330 the Roman emperor Constantine chose Byzantium as his eastern capital. Byzantium, renamed Constantinople, became the most important city in the Byzantine, or Eastern Roman, Empire. The Christian religion and much of the ancient Greek civilization survived here and were passed on to other parts of Europe and Asia.

During the 1000's, the first Turkish tribes, called Seljuks, came from Central Asia and settled in what is now central and eastern Turkey. The Seljuks were followers of the Islamic religion. They attacked the Byzantine Empire and set up a Muslim state in Asian Turkey.

The Ottoman Empire. The Ottomans, another group of Turkish tribes from Central Asia, arrived in the 1200's and conquered what remained of the Seljuk states. By 1360 they had conquered much of what is now European Turkey. Constantinople held out until 1453, when it, too, fell to the Ottoman Turks. The Ottoman Empire reached its height during the 1500's. Slowly, however, the empire began to decline. By the late 1800's and early 1900's, it had lost most of its territories. The final breakup of the empire came after World War I (1914–18). As one of the defeated powers, the empire was forced to give up its remaining non-Turkish lands. The chief victorious powers, France and Britain, occupied Istanbul for a time, and in 1919, Greek troops invaded Turkey's Aegean coast.

Republic of Turkey. With the Ottoman government helpless, a Turkish general, Mustafa

Kemal, organized a temporary government whose forces expelled the Greeks in 1922. The last sultan, Mehmed VI, was deposed, and in 1923, Kemal established a Turkish republic, with its capital in Ankara. Kemal became its first president. Adopting the surname Atatürk ("Father of the Turks"), he helped transform Turkey into a modern nation.

After Atatürk's death in 1938, his Republican People's Party was led by Ismet Inönü, who served as president until 1950. From 1950 to 1960, Turkey was governed by the Democratic Party, with Celal Bayar as president and Adnan Menderes as prime minister. In 1960 the government was overthrown by the military under General Cemal Gürsel. A civilian government was restored in 1961, with Gürsel as president and Inönü as prime minister.

In 1965, Süleyman Demirel, head of the Justice Party, became prime minister. He governed until 1971, when he was forced to resign by the military. Bülent Ecevit, leader of the Republican People's Party, became prime minister in 1974.

In 1980, after a series of weak governments proved unable to cope with the nation's problems, General Kenan Evren took over the government. He became president under a new constitution in 1982, serving until 1989, when Turgut Ozal was elected president. Ozal was succeeded after his death in 1993 by Süleyman Demirel. Tansu Çiller became Turkey's first woman prime minister in 1993.

The Cyprus Situation. In 1960, the island of Cyprus became an independent country, with Turkey, Greece, and Great Britain guaranteeing its independence and unity. However, some Greek Cypriots wanted to unite all of Cyprus (including its Turkish population) with Greece. In 1974, to stop the proposed union with Greece, Turkish prime minister Ecevit ordered the occupation of northern Cyprus, home to most of the Turkish Cypriots. Turkish troops have remained in Cyprus ever since 1974, and relations between Turkey and Greece have long been strained as a result.

In 1923, Mustafa Kemal established the Turkish republic and adopted the surname Atatürk ("Father of the Turks").

Recent Events. In 1995 Necmettin Erbakan, leader of the Welfare Party, became Turkey's first Islamic fundamentalist prime minister since independence. But tensions mounted with members of the military, who objected to Erbakan's pro-Muslim policies. Erbakan was forced to resign in 1997, and the Welfare Party was later banned. In 1999, a new coalition government, headed by former prime minister Bülent Ecevit, took power. Other major events of 1999 included the capture of Kurdish leader Abdullah Ocalan, who had led violent rebellions against the Turkish army since 1984.

In May 2000 Ahmet Necdet Sezer succeeded Demirel as president. He backed democratic reforms that would help Turkey's chances of gaining entry into the European Union (EU). In 2002, parliament passed one such reform by abolishing the death penalty (in peacetime) and by eliminating restrictions on freedom of speech, press, religion, and assembly. That year, the Justice and Development Party (AKP) won an impressive majority of seats in parliament. But their leader, Recep Tayyip Erdogan, was barred from becoming prime minister because he had once been convicted of stirring up religious hatreds. His deputy, Abdullah Gul, was named prime minister in his place. In 2003, President Sezer approved certain constitutional changes that allowed Erdogan to assume the role of prime minister.

In early 2003, as the United States planned to invade Iraq to search for forbidden weapons of mass destruction, Turkey agreed to open its airspace to U.S. air forces. It declined, however, to let the United States use Turkey as a launching site for ground troops. That April, a devastating earthquake in southern Turkey claimed the lives of dozens of schoolchildren.

ALEXANDER MELAMID
Author, *Turkey*
Reviewed by WILLIAM OCHSENWALD
Virginia Polytechnic Institute and State University

See also BYZANTINE EMPIRE; CYPRUS; HITTITES; ISTANBUL; OTTOMAN EMPIRE.

TURKEYS

Turkeys are large birds of the Phasianidae family, which also includes pheasants, grouse, peafowl, and partridges. Native to North America, turkeys live in forests, swamps, and grasslands from the Canadian border to Mexico and from the east coast to the Midwest. Isolated populations are found from the Midwest to the west coast. A separate species, the smaller and more colorful ocellated turkey, is found in Central America. This article discusses only the North American species.

Characteristics of Turkeys. Turkeys have long, robust bodies with long necks and small, mostly bare heads. Their feathers are primarily black and brown; wing feathers have light and dark bands, and body feathers are iridescent. Turkeys are fast runners, but they will also fly to evade predators or reach a roost up in a tree.

The adult male turkey, called a **gobbler** or a **tom**, weighs about 18 pounds (8 kilograms) and is about 4 feet (1.2 meters) long from head to tail. A "beard" of long, thin feathers hangs from its breast, and its featherless head is colored in shades of white, blue, and red.

The female turkey, or **hen**, weighs about half as much as the tom. Its head has a few small feathers, and it may have a short beard.

The Life of Turkeys. Wild turkeys eat insects, grass seeds, green leaves, and many kinds of fruit and seeds from shrubs and trees. They will scratch in the leaves on the ground during fall and winter to find food.

In the spring, the gobbler fans out his tail, struts back and forth, and gobbles—a warbling call—to attract hens. After mating, the hen lays about twelve brown-spotted eggs in a well-hidden nest on the ground. The gobbler does not take part in nesting or caring for the young.

After four weeks of incubation, the young turkeys, called **poults**, hatch. Poults are able to fly when they are only 8 days old. They also are able to find their own food. Although poults remain under the hen's care for their first summer, more than half are caught by predators. Wild turkeys fortunate enough to avoid predators may live to be 2 or 3 years old. Human hunters also kill turkeys but not in great numbers.

Conservation. The wild turkey was widely hunted for food by early settlers in the

The male wild turkey is distinguished by his colorful head. He struts and gobbles to attract the attention of the less colorful and smaller female.

United States. In later years turkeys were hunted to be sold in markets. Commercial hunting ended in the late 1800's, but by then the wild turkey had already disappeared from most of America's woodlands.

One of the first wildlife conservation programs, begun in the 1930's, was to capture wild turkeys where they were still plentiful and release small flocks where they no longer existed. The restocked turkeys flourished. Wild turkeys now live in every U.S. state except Alaska (where winters are too cold for turkeys to survive). There are now more than 5 million wild turkeys in the United States and Mexico. Small populations are found in southern Canada and in Germany.

The Domestic Turkey. The domestic turkey is the only important domestic animal that originated in the New World. Native people tamed wild turkeys in Mexico about 2,000 years ago, and a few were carried to Europe by Spanish explorers in the early 1500's. Since then the domestic turkey has been raised in captivity worldwide, particularly on poultry farms for commercial use. For more information on turkey farming, see POULTRY in Volume P.

Domestic turkeys come in a variety of colors, including white, black, and reddish brown. They are typically larger and heavier than wild turkeys, and they are unable to run quickly or fly.

LOVETT E. WILLIAMS, JR.
Author, *The Book of the Wild Turkey*

TURKMENISTAN

Turkmenistan is one of the five countries—along with Kazakhstan, Kyrgyzstan, Tajikistan, and Uzbekistan—that formerly made up the region known as Soviet Central Asia. It declared its independence from the Soviet Union, which has since ceased to exist, in 1991. Historically, Turkmenistan was the home of independent nomadic peoples, who until recent times had no government structure of their own beyond tribal federations.

The People. The Turkmen (or Turkmens, Turkomans, or Turkmenians, as the people have variously been called) make up some 77 percent of the population. Uzbeks and Russians are the largest minorities. Uzbeks make up about 9 percent of the population and Russians make up about 7 percent. In religion, the Turkmen and Uzbeks are Muslims, the Russians Eastern Orthodox Christians. The Turkmen language is closely related to Turkish. A rich Turkmen oral literary tradition also exists, based on epic songs and poetry.

In their way of life, the Turkmen are more of a confederation of tribes than a modern nation. The largest and most powerful of the tribes is the Tekke, followed by the Ersary and the Yomuk. The tribes are divided into subtribal groups, which are divided into clans. The old class divisions of nobles, members of the middle class, and former slaves still sur-

vive. The Turkmen see themselves as warlike and aristocratic in comparison to their settled neighbors, who in turn think of Turkmen as uneducated and primitive.

The Land and Economy. Turkmenistan is bordered by Afghanistan on the south, by Iran and the Caspian Sea on the west, and by Ka-

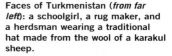

Faces of Turkmenistan (*from far left*): a schoolgirl, a rug maker, and a herdsman wearing a traditional hat made from the wool of a karakul sheep.

Most of Turkmenistan consists of the forbidding desert of the Kara Kum. The country's only fertile region lies along its border with Iran in the southwest. Because of the dry climate, livestock raising was long the mainstay of the economy, although cotton is grown in irrigated areas. Beneath the barren surface of the land, however, are valuable deposits of oil and natural gas.

zakhstan and Uzbekistan on the north and east. Most of Turkmenistan consists of the great desert of the Kara Kum. A narrow strip of fertile land lying along the Kopet-Dag range, on the Iranian border, is the most densely populated region. Ashkhabad (Ashgabat), the capital and largest city, with a population of about 400,000, is situated in the foothills of the Kopet-Dag.

Turkmenistan has a dry, continental climate, with extremely hot summers and cool to cold winters. Rainfall is sparse.

Economically, the people traditionally relied on livestock raising, including cattle and karakul sheep, from which the valuable Persian lamb is obtained. Rug making was a traditional Turkmen handicraft. Under the Soviets, cotton growing was introduced in irrigated areas and the region's large deposits of oil and natural gas were developed. Industry is based on mining and the manufacture of building materials, chemicals, and textiles.

FACTS and figures

TURKMENISTAN is the official name of the country.

LOCATION: Central Asia.

AREA: 188,455 sq mi (488,100 km²).

POPULATION: 3,600,000 (estimate).

CAPITAL AND LARGEST CITY: Ashkhabad. (Ashgabat).

MAJOR LANGUAGES: Turkmen, Russian.

MAJOR RELIGIOUS GROUP: Muslim.

GOVERNMENT: Republic, with a president and parliament.

CHIEF PRODUCTS: Cotton, livestock (cattle and karakul sheep), oil, natural gas, building materials, chemicals, textiles.

Early History. Like other parts of Central Asia, the early history of what is now Turkmenistan was marked by successive invasions of Turkic tribes; Arabs, who converted the people to the Muslim religion; and Mongols. The region fell to the empire of Tamerlane in the 1300's, then to Uzbek and Persian dynasties, and finally came under the rule of the states of Khiva and Bukhara, where the Turkmen served as mercenary troops and were influential in court politics.

Russian and Soviet Rule: Independence. The Russians conquered the region between 1875 and 1885, but not before the Turkmen stubbornly defended their freedom. Following the decisive battle of Geok-Tepe (1879), however, the Tekke tribe was subdued, and the others soon followed.

After the Soviets came to power following revolutions in 1917, they erased the old administrative units in Central Asia and established republics based on ethnic division. Local resistance was only slowly put down, and the Turkmen Soviet Socialist Republic came into being in 1924. Under Soviet Communist rule, Turkmenistan, like other parts of the Soviet Union, was subjected to forced collectivization of agriculture, religious discrimination, and political purges. Soviet political reforms in the late 1980's led to demands for greater self-rule and then to full independence, which was proclaimed in late 1991, as the Soviet Union was breaking apart.

MICHAEL RYWKIN
City University of New York, City College
Author, *Moscow's Muslim Challenge: Soviet Central Asia*

See also articles on the other Central Asian republics.

TURKS AND CAICOS ISLANDS

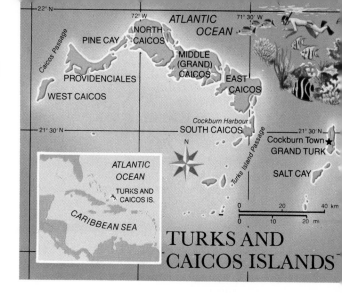

The Turks Islands and the Caicos Islands are two neighboring groups of low-lying coral islands in the Atlantic Ocean—about halfway between Miami, Florida, and Puerto Rico. They have often been called the "forgotten islands." But their pleasant climate, beautiful coral reefs, and uncrowded white sandy beaches now attract growing numbers of tourists. Over 30 islands, many very small in size, make up the territory, which has been a British dependency for about 300 years.

▶ PEOPLE

Only eight of the islands are inhabited—Grand Turk, Salt Cay, South Caicos, North Caicos, East Caicos, Middle (Grand) Caicos, Providenciales, and West Caicos. The people are mostly of black African descent. English is the official language. Education is free and compulsory for children between the ages of 7 and 14.

▶ LAND AND ECONOMY

Geographically, the two groups of islands are a continuation of the Bahamas chain. They are separated from the Bahamas by the Caicos Passage and from each other by the Turks Island Passage. There are eight larger islands and many cays (small low islands). Because all the islands are small, there are few roads or automobiles. People travel between islands by boat or small plane. The capital is Grand Turk.

There is little agriculture on the islands. The soil is not very fertile, and the rainfall is irregular. The reefs abound with fish. Lobster, dried conch meat, and conch shells are the leading exports. Tourism provides a growing number of jobs, but many people leave the islands in search of work.

▶ HISTORY AND GOVERNMENT

The islands were sighted by the Spanish explorer Juan Ponce de León about 1512. They were uninhabited when salt traders from Bermuda claimed them for Britain in the late 1600's. The islands were attacked by Spain and France in the 1700's, but Britain kept control. Loyalist planters fleeing the rebellious American colonies went to the islands in 1776. They later abandoned their plantations, but their former slaves remained. At various times during their history, the islands were ruled from other British colonies in the area: Bermuda, the Bahamas, and Jamaica. Today the islands have their own governor, who represents the British monarch and is responsible for foreign affairs, defense, and internal security. Local affairs are handled by the governor, the Executive Council, and the Legislative Council.

THOMAS G. MATHEWS
Association of Caribbean Universities
and Research Institutes

TURNER, FREDERICK JACKSON. See WISCONSIN (Famous People).

FACTS and figures

TURKS AND CAICOS ISLANDS is the official name of the dependency.

LOCATION: Atlantic Ocean, southeast of the Bahamas.

AREA: 166 sq mi (430 km²).

POPULATION: 16,000 (estimate).

CAPITAL AND LARGEST TOWN: Grand Turk (also called Cockburn Town).

MAJOR LANGUAGE: English.

MAJOR RELIGIOUS GROUP: Protestant.

GOVERNMENT: British dependency. **Head of state**—British monarch, represented by governor. **Head of government**—chief minister. **Legislature**—Legislative Council.

CHIEF PRODUCTS: Corn, beans, cassava, citrus fruits, fish. **Monetary unit**—U.S. dollar (1 dollar = 100 cents).

TURNER, JOHN NAPIER (1929–   )

On June 30, 1984, John Napier Turner was sworn in as the 17th prime minister of Canada. He had been elected by the Liberal Party to succeed Pierre Elliott Trudeau, who was stepping down after more than 15 years as party leader and head of government. But Turner held office for only a short time. In the September 1984 elections, the Liberals were overwhelmingly defeated by the Progressive Conservatives, led by Brian Mulroney.

John Turner was born on June 7, 1929, in Richmond, Surrey, England. His father, a journalist, died when John was 2. His mother, a Canadian, moved the family to Ottawa, where she became a government economic adviser during World War II.

Turner was graduated from the University of British Columbia, where he was the Canadian champion in the 100-yard dash. From 1949 to 1951 he studied law at Oxford University, in England, on a Rhodes Scholarship.

After another year of study at the Sorbonne in Paris, he joined a Montreal law firm in 1954.

The ambitious young lawyer joined the Liberal Party in 1960 and was elected to Parliament in 1962. He represented the Montreal riding (district) of St. Lawrence–St. George until 1968, followed by the Ottawa-Carlton district. Turner ran for the Liberal Party leadership in 1968 but finished a distant third to Trudeau, who became prime minister. In the Trudeau government, Turner held several important cabinet positions—solicitor general, justice minister, and finance minister.

In 1975, Turner returned to private law practice but kept his following in the Liberal Party. When Trudeau resigned as prime minister in 1984, Turner was elected party leader, which automatically made him prime minister.

In 1988 elections, Turner again lost to Mulroney and the Conservatives. He announced his resignation as party leader the next year.

Reviewed by DESMOND MORTON
University of Toronto

TURNER, JOSEPH MALLORD WILLIAM (1775–1851)

Joseph Mallord William Turner was one of England's greatest landscape painters. He was born in London on April 23, 1775, the son of a barber. He began to draw at an early age. By the time he was 14, he was accepted into the painting school of the Royal Academy.

Turner's interest in light, atmosphere, and water can be seen in *Peace: Burial at Sea* (1842).

Turner liked to be alone, and he loved nature. He would sit by the water or in the woods for hours, staring and memorizing. He painted what he remembered—not exact details but impressions. By the age of 24, he was a successful artist.

Turner traveled throughout Britain, painting picturesque scenes, but the countryside was not varied enough for him. He wanted to paint nature at its boldest and most dramatic. So he traveled abroad. He loved the sea and the colors of the sea. Once, during a storm, he was strapped to the mast of a ship so that he could study the angry waves.

After a trip to Italy in 1819, Turner changed his style of painting. He could now afford to paint only for himself and to experiment. He paid little attention to objects and began trying to depict atmosphere and light. He painted sky and water bathed in light or blown by wind. His paintings suggest the work of the later French impressionists. Turner died in London on December 19, 1851.

HERBERT B. GRIMSDITCH
Fleetway Publications (London)

TURNER, NAT.   See SLAVERY (Profiles).

TURTLES

A turtle is an animal in armor. Much of its body lies within a protective shell, which has openings for the turtle's four chunky legs, short tail, and head. When danger threatens, many turtles pull legs, tail, and head into the shell. But unlike some animals that live in shells, such as hermit crabs and snails, a turtle cannot crawl out of its shell. The shell is part of the turtle's body.

All turtles belong to the class of backboned animals known as reptiles. This class also includes snakes, lizards, and crocodiles. Turtles are the oldest group. The first turtles crawled about on earth more than 250,000,000 years ago. Turtles have changed very little since that time.

Turtles are found in almost all temperate and tropical regions of the world. Many turtles spend all or most of their lives in fresh water. They may live in swamps, ponds, running streams, or even roadside ditches. They come up on dry land to sun themselves or to lay eggs. Other turtles live completely on land. Still others live in warm seas, sometimes following warm currents far northward.

The name "turtle" is often used to identify those animals that live in water. The name "tortoise" frequently refers to a turtle that lives on land. The American Indian name "terrapin" usually refers to small freshwater turtles, especially those used for food. But these groupings are not strictly scientific. In this article, all of these animals will be referred to generally as turtles, though the proper name for a specific animal, such as Galápagos tortoise, will be used.

There are some 250 kinds of turtles. They range in size from tiny bog turtles about 3 inches (7 centimeters) long to leatherbacks almost 9 feet (2.5 meters) long that weigh 1,500 pounds (680 kilograms).

▶A TURTLE'S SHELL

A turtle's shell is made of two parts that are joined at the sides by bony bridges. The upper part of the shell is called the **carapace,** from a Spanish word for "shield." The lower part is called the **plastron,** from an Italian word for "breastplate."

The carapace and the plastron are made up of many small, flat, bony shields, or plates. These plates are fused with (joined to) the tur-

The Eastern box turtle (*top*) is typical of most land turtles. It has short, stumpy legs and a hard shell made up of small, bony plates. Some aquatic turtles, such as the Florida soft-shelled turtle (*middle*), lack bony plates and have smooth, leather-like shells. The hawksbill turtle (*bottom*) has limbs designed for swimming in the open sea. This turtle was once widely hunted for the beautiful outer covering on its shell, known as tortoiseshell.

tle's backbone and ribs and parts of its shoulders and hips. The bony plates are covered with broad, thin scales called **laminae.** The laminae are made of material something like your fingernails. (The hawksbill sea turtle was once hunted and killed for this material, which was called tortoiseshell. Before plastics were developed, tortoiseshell was widely used for combs, the frames of eyeglasses, and other objects.) The laminae give a turtle its color. Depending on the kind of turtle, this color may be brown, black, or olive green. (The plastron is usually lighter than the carapace.) These dull colors blend perfectly with a turtle's usual surroundings.

Some turtles, however, have brightly colored markings. Spotted turtles are covered with polka dots. More spots develop as the turtles get older. Painted turtles have bright red, yellow, or orange borders on their smooth olive or dark-brown shells. The colors are so bright that they look as though they were painted on. The bright colors may help turtles find one another. Scientists have discovered that turtles see colors and are especially sensitive to red.

Turtle Defenses

As a rule, turtles that spend all or part of their time on land rely on their hard shell to protect them from the teeth and claws of hungry animals. Otters, raccoons, crocodiles, snakes, bears, and large birds are some of the animals that prey on turtles. A typical land turtle draws its head, tail, and legs into its shell for protection. The stout, scaly legs form a sort of armored door. Other turtles, such as the freshwater box and mud turtles, can shut up their shell completely. The plastron of these turtles is hinged and, when closed, fits firmly against the carapace.

Mud and musk turtles defend themselves by hissing and withdrawing into their shells. They have a further means of defense. They can give off a bad-smelling yellow fluid called musk. Some scientists think this odor may also serve to attract a mate. Other turtles squirt out water or body wastes when bothered.

A few turtles drive off their enemies by biting and clawing. The snapping turtles, for example, are quick to attack with a vicious bite. A snapper has a small plastron. Its legs, tail, and neck do not fit into the shell. However, the snapper has other defenses. Its tail is armed with a ridge of spines, and its snapping jaws take care of the front end. The soft-shelled turtles also rely on their sharp claws and crushing jaws for defense.

How Turtles Breathe

The turtle's rigid shell prevents the animal from breathing in the usual way, that is, moving the ribs to fill the lungs with air. The turtle's ribs are firmly fixed to the inside of its shell, so in order to breathe the turtle uses two special sets of muscles. One set pulls the other body organs away from the lungs, filling the lungs with air. Then a second set of muscles pulls the organs against the lungs, forcing the air out.

One deep breath may last a turtle several hours. Some freshwater turtles can remain underwater for several days (except during hibernation, when they can remain underwater for several months). They do this by lying still on the bottom, thereby using up very little oxygen. Some kinds can even take a little oxygen from the water, as a fish does, by using specialized body tissues.

In climates where the ground and water freeze in winter, turtles survive the cold by hibernating. They may burrow in the muddy bottoms of ponds or streams or crawl under decaying vegetation. When a turtle hibernates, it uses up very little oxygen. Even if it spends months underwater, a hibernating turtle does not have to come up for air. Its body does not have the same oxygen needs that it has when the turtle is active during the warmer months.

▶ HOW TURTLES MOVE

Turtles are famous for the slowness of their movements. And most turtles do move slowly on land, their legs sprawled awkwardly out to the sides. A box turtle, for example, heaves

The Galápagos tortoise is one of the world's largest land turtles. Because Galápagos can survive for long periods without any food or water, sailors used to take them on voyages as a fresh food source before the days of refrigeration.

its body along, clawing at the ground, with its toes spread wide apart. If it falls on its back, it has a hard time righting itself.

The turtles that live entirely on land are the slowest and most awkward of all turtles. They have high, domed shells and stumpy legs that end in small feet. Most of these turtles walk on the tips of their toes. This is true of the largest land turtles as well as the smallest. A giant tortoise of the Galápagos Islands in the Pacific may have a weight of 500 pounds (227 kilograms) or more to move.

In water, however, turtles move more easily. Most freshwater turtles are good swimmers. They have webbed feet and smooth, arched shells. Strangely enough, freshwater turtles can move more quickly on land than most land turtles can. The members of one family can even run. These are the soft-shelled turtles, which have a soft, leathery skin (instead of horny scales) covering the bony plates.

Ocean turtles move awkwardly on land. But in water they swim steadily along with strong, winglike strokes of their huge flippers. A sea turtle, such as a hawksbill, a loggerhead, or especially the green turtle, is somewhat streamlined. Its body is heart-shaped, tapering toward the tail. Its front flippers are longer and stronger than the hind ones.

▶DIET

Most turtles will eat anything they can catch. This may be earthworms, snails, slugs, insects, mussels, shrimps, fish, frogs, or even small birds and mice. The ocean-dwelling green turtle feeds mainly on seaweeds. Land turtles, too, often eat plants. Map turtles, mud and musk turtles, snapping turtles, and most other water-dwelling turtles eat dead animals from time to time.

A turtle has no teeth. However, its beak has sharp edges and its jaws are strong. A turtle seizes its prey and holds the wriggling creature in its beak. If the prey is too large to be swallowed whole, the turtle uses its claws to tear off pieces until the food is small enough.

Land turtles feed as they go, shearing off bits of leaves, flowers, or fruits when they feel hungry. The green sea turtle grazes on underwater plants. Other sea turtles actively swim after jellyfish, crabs, and other slow-moving creatures. Freshwater turtles for the most part hunt in a different way. They lie on the bottom

of a pond or river and wait for something to come along. This is what the snapping turtles do, for example. Because they are poor swimmers, these animals hide in the mud. But when a snapper sees something moving in the water, such as a fish or the legs of a bird, its long neck darts out and its sharp beak grabs the prey.

▶REPRODUCTION AND LIFE CYCLE

Turtles may mate on land or in the water, depending on the species. After a single mating, female turtles may store sperm in their bodies and lay fertilized eggs for several years.

All turtles lay eggs on land. They lay their eggs in warm, sunny places, usually not far from water. The eggs of most turtles are oval, but some are round. Some eggs have soft, rubbery shells; others have hard, brittle shells. They may be as large as tennis balls or as small as kidney beans. The eggs are usually white.

All turtles lay their eggs on land. Biologists study nesting sites to help determine if there is a decline in the population of certain threatened species.

Instincts guide sea turtle hatchlings directly into the sea. Scientists are unable to explain fully these instincts, which also guide sea turtles on long migrations to nesting sites.

When a female turtle finds a good spot to lay her eggs, she starts digging, first using one hind leg and then the other. When the hole is as deep as her legs can reach, she starts laying her eggs. Most turtles lay from two to 25 eggs at a time. Sea turtles may lay 150 or more.

When all the eggs are laid, the female turtle fills in the nest with sand or dirt. Once she has completed her task of concealing the nest, the female turtle goes back into the water or moves away through the underbrush. She has no further interest in her eggs.

The beginning of a turtle's life is a very dangerous time. Bears, skunks, raccoons, and other animals may dig up and eat the eggs. And even if the eggs hatch, birds, lizards, and other hungry animals may gobble up the tiny young turtles. People also use turtles for food. Many kinds of turtles and turtle eggs are eaten throughout the world.

If the young turtles survive until adulthood, they may live a long time. Turtles live longer than any other animal except people. Some turtles are known to have lived more than 100 years. But a very large turtle is not necessarily an old one. Turtles reach their full size in less than ten years. After that, turtles continue to grow, but very slowly.

▶ INSTINCTS AND MIGRATION

All turtles have good eyesight and hearing. They also have a good sense of smell and touch. In addition, some—and perhaps all—turtles have a sense that seems unrelated to the usual senses. This sense is more like an instinct. It is responsible for controlling turtle behavior during various stages of the animals' lives. For example, when water turtles of any kind hatch, the hatchlings promptly make their way to water. They do this even when they cannot see the water. Scientists think that a turtle can somehow distinguish the difference between light over water and light over land.

Some green turtles seem to have a "compass sense." They may cross more than 1,000 miles (1,600 kilometers) of water to their nesting grounds on Ascension Island, an island halfway between Africa and South America. The turtles arrive at Ascension in December. They remain there until June, laying eggs every twelve days. Scientists tagged some females during one nesting season. Later a few of the tagged turtles were found feeding on seaweeds off the coast of Brazil. Three years later some of the females returned to the island beach where they were tagged. They laid their eggs in the same stretch of beach.

Such long-distance migrations still puzzle scientists. They know that strong ocean currents carry the young turtles to the coastal waters of Brazil. But why do the turtles return to Ascension Island? And how do they find their way there—against the current—during the thousand-mile journey? Perhaps some day we will better understand the behavior of these fascinating reptiles.

Reviewed by ARCHIE CARR
University of Florida
Author, *Handbook of Turtles*

See also HIBERNATION; HOMING AND MIGRATION.

TUVALU

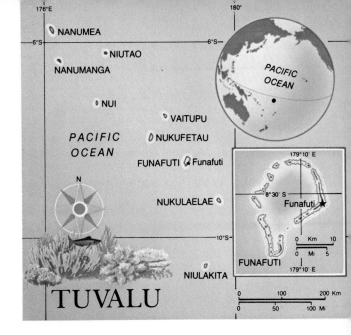

TUVALU

Tuvalu is one of the world's smallest nations. It consists of nine small islands, eight of which are permanently inhabited, situated in the southwestern Pacific Ocean. Formerly governed by Britain as the Ellice Islands, Tuvalu gained its independence in 1978.

People. The Tuvaluans are Polynesians, related to the people of the Pacific islands of Samoa and Tonga. Their language is Tuvaluan, but English is also widely used. The islanders are Christians, belonging mostly to Protestant denominations.

Land and Climate. Some of the islands of Tuvalu are low-lying atolls—ring-shaped islands of coral enclosing a lagoon. The others are reefs, or ridges of rock, coral, and sand. The most heavily populated island is Funafuti, site of the capital, also called Funafuti. The other islands, in order of population, are Vaitupu, Niutao, Nanumea, Nukufetau, Nanumanga, Nui, and Nukulaelae. Niulakita has no permanent inhabitants.

The climate is warm and humid, with an average high temperature of 86°F (30°C). Rainfall is heavy but varies with the seasons.

FACTS and figures

TUVALU is the official name of the country.

LOCATION: Southwestern Pacific Ocean.

AREA: 10 sq mi (26 km²).

POPULATION: 9,000 (estimate).

CAPITAL: Funafuti.

MAJOR LANGUAGES: Tuvaluan, English.

MAJOR RELIGIOUS GROUP: Christian (mostly Protestant).

GOVERNMENT: Constitutional monarchy. **Head of state**—British monarch, represented by a governor-general. **Head of government**—prime minister. **Legislature**—Parliament.

CHIEF PRODUCTS: Copra (dried coconut meat), taro, bananas, breadfruit, fish.

MONETARY UNIT: Tuvaluan and Australian dollars are both used (1 T or A dollar = 100 cents).

Economy. Farming and fishing are the islands' main economic activities. Coconuts are the chief crop. They provide both food and the country's major export, copra (dried coconut meat). Taro (a starchy root), bananas, and breadfruit are staple food crops. Money sent home by Tuvaluans working abroad is an additional and important source of income.

History and Government. Spanish navigators first sighted the islands in the 1500's, but there was little contact with Europeans until the 1800's. The islands became a British protectorate in 1892, and part of the British Gilbert and Ellice Islands Colony in 1915.

The Ellice Islands were politically separated from the Gilbert Islands in 1975 and gained independence as the nation of Tuvalu in 1978. (The Gilbert Islands won independence as the Republic of Kiribati in 1979.)

Tuvalu's head of state is the British monarch, represented in the islands by a governor-general, who must be a native Tuvaluan. The legislative body is the Parliament, which is composed of twelve members elected for 4-year terms. The head of government is the prime minister, who is elected from among the members of the Parliament. In 2000, the United Nations approved Tuvalu's application for membership.

HAROLD M. ROSS
St. Norbert College (Wisconsin)
MICHAEL R. GOLDSMITH
University of Waikato (New Zealand)

See also KIRIBATI.

TWAIN, MARK (1835–1910)

The author, humorist, and lecturer Mark Twain is regarded as one of America's greatest writers. His insight into human nature, his humor, and his use of everyday American language have made his novels and stories among the best loved in American literature.

Mark Twain was born Samuel Langhorne Clemens on November 30, 1835, in the village of Florida, Missouri. When Sam was 4, his parents moved the family to nearby Hannibal, on the banks of the Mississippi River. Growing up in Hannibal, Sam became enchanted with the life and lore of the great river. The Mississippi was a lifelong fascination, and it provided the material for many of his greatest books. Sam later took the name Mark Twain as a reminder of life on the Mississippi—when riverboat crews charted the depth of the river, they would cry "mark twain!" to indicate a measure of 2, or twain, fathoms (12 feet).

Young Sam left school at the age of 11 to become a printer's apprentice. He worked in Hannibal for a newspaper published by his brother, Orion, and then found jobs in St. Louis, New York, and Philadelphia. After a year in Iowa, again working for Orion, Sam was drawn back to the Mississippi. In 1857, traveling down the river, he persuaded the steamboat captain to teach him how to pilot. After earning his license, he served as a river pilot until the Civil War, when the Mississippi was closed to commercial traffic.

After serving with the Confederate Army for two weeks, Clemens quit and set out for the western frontier in 1861. For the next several years, he lived with Orion in the Nevada Territory, trying his hand at gold mining, the lumber business, and other unsuccessful ventures. On the strength of humorous sketches he had been writing about his adventures in the West, Sam landed a job with a newspaper in Virginia City, Nevada. He began signing his articles "Mark Twain."

Twain moved on to San Francisco in 1864, joining the staff of *The Morning Call* and writing for two local magazines. In 1865 a New York magazine published his short story about a California frog-jumping contest, called "The Celebrated Jumping Frog of Calaveras County." The story made him famous overnight. During the next several years,

Mark Twain created two memorable characters in American literature: Tom Sawyer and Huckleberry Finn.

Twain began lecturing and continued his writing as a travel correspondent for several publications. In 1867 he sailed on the *Quaker City* to Europe and the Middle East, sending back comic but insightful letters about his experiences. The letters were later made into a book, *The Innocents Abroad* (1869), which won him worldwide attention and financial freedom.

In 1870, Twain married Olivia Langdon, the sister of a fellow traveler on the *Quaker City*. In 1871 the couple moved to Hartford, Connecticut. The house they built there was a Victorian-style mansion, with an ornate design that suggested a Mississippi River steamboat. It was their home for twenty years.

The Hartford years were the most creative in Twain's writing career. There and in Elmira, New York, where the family spent summers, he produced many of his most important works. *The Adventures of Tom Sawyer* (1876), *Life on the Mississippi* (1883), *The Adventures of Huckleberry Finn* (1884), *A Connecticut Yankee in King Arthur's Court* (1889), and other books made him one of the best-known and most prosperous authors of his time. Twain also went on long lecture tours, packing auditoriums across the United States and Europe. And when he was not working, he enjoyed spending time with his three daughters—Susy, Clara, and Jean. As young girls, Twain's daughters loved to act out his stories, especially *The Prince and the Pauper* (1882).

Despite his great success, Mark Twain suffered deep disappointments during his later years. He lost his entire fortune in two unsuccessful business investments—a publishing firm and a new kind of typesetting machine. That forced him to move his family to Europe, where they could live more cheaply. Then, while he was away lecturing, his daughter Susy died of meningitis. Twain's outlook darkened, and his writing became gloomy and pessimistic. His wife's health also began to fail, and she died in 1904. Jean, his youngest daughter, died five years later.

In the last months of his life, Mark Twain recalled that he had been born when Halley's comet was shooting across the night sky. "It will be the greatest disappointment of my life if I don't go out with Halley's comet," he said. The day after he saw Halley's return, on April 21, 1910, Twain died at his home in Redding, Connecticut.

JEFFREY H. HACKER
Author, *Carl Sandburg*

Excerpts from two of Twain's best-loved works follow.

▶ **THE ADVENTURES OF TOM SAWYER**

When Tom reached the little isolated frame schoolhouse, he strode in briskly, with the manner of one who had come with all honest speed. He hung his hat on a peg and flung himself into his seat with businesslike alacrity. The master, throned on high in his great splint-bottom armchair, was dozing, lulled by the drowsy hum of study. The interruption roused him.

"Thomas Sawyer!"

Tom knew that when his name was pronounced in full, it meant trouble.

"Sir!"

"Come up here. Now, sir, why are you late again, as usual?"

Tom was about to take refuge in a lie, when he saw two long tails of yellow hair hanging down a back that he recognized by the electric sympathy of love; and by that form was *the only vacant place* on the girls' side of the schoolhouse. He instantly said:

"I stopped to talk with HUCKLEBERRY FINN!" The master's pulse stood still, and he stared helplessly. The buzz of study ceased. The pupils wondered if this foolhardy boy had lost his mind. The master said:

"You—you did what?"

"Stopped to talk with Huckleberry Finn."

There was no mistaking his words.

"Thomas Sawyer, this is the most astounding confession I have ever listened to. No mere ferule will answer for this offense. Take off your jacket."

The master's arm performed until it was tired and the stock of switches notably diminished. Then the order followed:

"Now, sir, go and sit with the *girls!* And let this be a warning to you."

The titter that rippled around the room appeared to abash the boy, but in reality that result was caused rather more by his worshipful awe of his unknown idol and the dread pleasure that lay in his high good fortune. He sat down upon the end of the pine bench and the girl hitched herself away from him with a toss of her head. Nudges and winks and whispers traversed the room, but Tom sat still, with his arms upon the long, low desk before him, and seemed to study his book.

By and by attention ceased from him, and the accustomed school murmur rose upon the dull air once more. Presently the boy began to steal furtive glances at the girl. She observed it, "made a mouth" at him and gave him the back of her head for the space of a minute. When she cautiously faced around again, a peach lay before her. She thrust it away. Tom gently put it back. She thrust it away again, but with less animosity. Tom patiently returned it to its place. Then she let it remain. Tom scrawled on his slate, "Please take it—I got more." The girl glanced at the words but made no sign. Now the boy began to draw something on the slate, hiding his work with his left hand. For a time the girl refused to notice; but her human curiosity began to manifest itself by hardly perceptible signs. The boy worked on, apparently unconscious. The girl made a sort of non-committal attempt to see it, but the boy did not betray that he was aware of it. At last she gave in and hesitatingly whispered:

"Let me see it."

Tom partly uncovered a dismal caricature of a house with two gable ends to it and a corkscrew of smoke issuing from the chimney. Then the girl's interest began to fasten itself upon the work and she forgot everything else. When it was finished, she gazed a moment, then whispered:

"It's nice—make a man."

The artist erected a man in the front yard, that resembled a derrick. He could have stepped over the house; but the girl was not hypercritical; she was satisfied with the monster, and whispered:

"It's a beautiful man—now make me coming along."

Tom drew an hour-glass with a full moon and straw limbs to it and armed the spreading fingers with a portentous fan. The girl said:

"It's ever so nice—I wish I could draw."

"It's easy," whispered Tom, "I'll learn you."

"Oh, will you? When?"

"At noon. Do you go home to dinner?"

The Adventures of Tom Sawyer tells of the escapades of an imaginative and mischievous boy growing up in a small town on the Mississippi River. This illustration is from the first edition, published in 1876.

"I'll stay if you will."

"Good—that's a whack. What's your name?"

"Becky Thatcher. What's yours? Oh, I know. It's Thomas Sawyer."

"That's the name they lick me by. I'm Tom when I'm good. You call me Tom, will you?"

"Yes."

Now Tom began to scrawl something on the slate, hiding the words from the girl. But she was not backward this time. She begged to see. Tom said:

"Oh, it ain't anything."

"Yes it is."

"No it ain't. You don't want to see."

"Yes I do, indeed I do. Please let me."

"You'll tell."

"No I won't—deed and deed and double deed I won't."

"You won't tell anybody at all? Ever, as long as you live?"

"No, I won't ever tell *any*body. Now let me."

"Oh, *you* don't want to see!"

"Now that you treat me so, I *will* see." And she put her small hand upon his and a little scuffle ensued, Tom pretending to resist in earnest but letting his hand slip by degrees till these words were revealed: *"I love you."*

"Oh, you bad thing!" And she hit his hand a smart rap, but reddened and looked pleased, nevertheless.

Just at this juncture the boy felt a slow, fateful grip closing on his ear, and a steady lifting impulse. In that vise he was borne across the house and deposited in his own seat, under a peppering fire of giggles from the whole school. Then the master stood over him during a few awful moments, and finally moved away to his throne without saying a word. But although Tom's ear tingled, his heart was jubilant.

▶THE CELEBRATED JUMPING FROG OF CALAVERAS COUNTY

"Well, there was a feller here once by the name of Jim Smiley, in the winter of '49—or maybe it was the spring of '50—I don't recollect exactly . . . but anyway, he was the curiousest man about always betting on anything that turned up you ever see, if he could get anybody to bet on the other side, and if he couldn't he'd change sides. Any way that suited the other man would suit *him*—any way just so's he got a bet, *he* was satisfied. But still he was lucky, uncommon lucky; he most always come out winner. He was always ready and laying for a chance; there couldn't be no solit'ry thing mentioned but that feller'd offer to bet on it and take ary side you please, as I was just telling you. If there was a horse-race, you'd find him flush or you'd find him busted at the end of it; if there was a dog-fight, he'd bet on it; if there was a cat-fight, he'd bet on it; if there was a chicken-fight, he'd bet on it; why, if there was two birds setting on a fence, he would bet you which one would fly first; or if there was a camp-meeting, he would be there reg'lar to bet on Parson Walker, which he judged to be the best exhorter about here, and so he was too, and a good man. If he even see a straddle-bug start to go anywheres, he would bet you how long it would take him to get to—to wherever he was going to, and if you took him up, he would foller that straddle-bug to Mexico but what he would find out where he was bound for and how long he was on the road. . . . He ketched a frog one day and took him home, and said he cal'lated to educate him; and so he never done nothing for three months but set in his back yard and learn that frog to jump. And you bet you he *did* learn him, too. He'd give him a little punch behind, and the next minute you'd see that frog whirling in the air like a doughnut—see him turn one summerset, or maybe a couple if he got a good start, and come down flat-footed and all right, like a cat. He got him up so in the matter of ketching flies, and kep' him in practice so constant, that he'd nail a fly every time as fur as he could see him. Smiley said all a frog wanted was education and he could do 'most anything—and I believe him. Why, I've seen him set Dan'l Webster down here on this floor—Dan'l Webster was the name of the frog—and sing out, 'Flies, Dan'l, flies!' and quicker'n you could wink he'd spring straight up and snake a fly off'n the counter there, and flop down on the floor ag'in as solid as a gob of mud, and fall to scratching the side of his head with his hind foot as indifferent as if he hadn't no idea he'd been doin' any more'n any frog might do. You never see a frog so modest and straightfor'ard as he was, for all he was so gifted."

Twins may be identical, with exactly the same physical traits, or fraternal, with no more in common (except age) than ordinary sisters and brothers. Most of the twins in this photograph are identical. Two fraternal pairs in the two back rows are easy to spot.

TWINS

Twins are two individuals who were born to the same mother at about the same time. Multiple births—the birth of more than one offspring at a time—are rare among humans. Twins occur only once in about 90 births.

Most twins are either identical or fraternal. Each type is the result of a different occurrence during the reproductive process. (For more information on how humans reproduce, see the article REPRODUCTION (Human Reproduction) in this encyclopedia.)

All human beings develop inside the mother's body from an egg that has been fertilized by the father's sperm. **Identical** twins occur when a fertilized egg splits in two. Each half develops into a fetus with identical sets of genes—the chemical molecules that determine what traits a person will inherit. Because they have the same genetic makeup, identical twins have the same physical characteristics, such as sex, color of hair, skin, and eyes, body weight, and height. They may also possess similar personalities, ambitions, and tastes.

No one knows what makes an egg split to produce identical twins. They seem to occur randomly, at a rate of about four sets for every 1,000 births. About one third of all twins are identicals.

Fraternal twins develop from two separate eggs that were fertilized at about the same time by separate sperm. (Normally a woman's body releases only one egg at a time for fertilization.) Fraternal twins are no more alike than non-twin brothers and sisters. They may be the same sex or opposite sexes. They may be very similar in looks and personality or quite different.

Fraternal twins occur more often than identical twins, and the tendency to have them seems to run in families. Other factors increase a woman's chances of having identical twins—for example, if she is between the ages of 34 and 40 or has had other children. The frequency of fraternal twins varies with the race of the mother. Asians produce about one set of twins for every 155 births, while Caucasians produce one set for every 90 births. Among blacks and American Indians the rate is one set for every 78 births. One of the highest rates for fraternal twins occurs among the Yoruba tribe of Nigeria, who produce about one set for every 22 births.

There are other types of twins besides identical and fraternal, but they are extremely rare. Also rare are conjoined twins, the so-called "Siamese" twins, who are always identical. Another unusual type of identical twins are "mirror-image" twins. They have exactly the same features but in reverse—one twin may be left-handed and the other right-handed, for example. Mirror-image twins came very close to being conjoined, because the egg splitting occurred very late in the twinning process.

▶ OTHER MULTIPLE BIRTHS

Three infants born to the same mother at the same time are called triplets. Four are called quadruplets, and five are quintuplets. Triplets occur only once in 7,500 births, quadruplets once in 650,000 births, and quintuplets once in 57,000,000 births. Within a set of multiples, any two individuals may be identical twins. Or, all the members of a set of triplets, quadruplets, or quintuplets may be identical, meaning that one egg has divided into three, four, or five identical parts.

In recent years, the frequency of twins and other multiple births has increased due to the use of fertility drugs by women who have been unable to become pregnant. These drugs sometimes cause a woman's body to release more than one egg at a time, increasing the chance of multiple birth. Any multiples that result are always fraternal, because they have developed from separate eggs.

▶ RESEARCH WITH TWINS

The close similarity of identical twins makes them very interesting to researchers. For years, scientists have tried to determine the influences of heredity and environment on human behavior. Do people think and act in certain ways because they were born with fixed personality traits, inherited from their parents? Or are their personalities shaped by their surroundings and way of life—their families, friends, schools, levels of income, and so forth? To find out, researchers at the University of Minnesota brought together pairs of identical twins who had been raised apart since infancy. Because the twins had been born with the same genetic makeup, any differences would have to be due to the different environments in which they were raised.

The study compared the twins' behavior, intelligence, personalities, interests, values, and even their physical characteristics. Some surprising similarities were discovered, leading many scientists to conclude that heredity has a greater influence on behavior than had previously been supposed.

One of the first pairs of identical twins to be investigated were so strikingly alike that they amazed the scientists. Jim Springer and Jim Lewis came to be known as the Jim twins. They had never met until researchers brought them together when they were 39 years old. But, they discovered, both had the same kind of job, interests, and hobbies. Both had been married twice, first to women named Linda and then to women named Betty. One Jim had named his son James Allan; the other had a son named James Alan. Both had owned dogs named Toy. The two Jims had even spent vacations at the same 300-yard stretch of beach in Florida. They also had identical pulse rates, blood pressure, and sleep patterns. The researchers found remarkable similarities between many other pairs of re-united twins.

▶ BEING A TWIN

Most twins like growing up with a partner. Identical twins often enjoy confusing family and friends, who find it difficult to tell them apart. Frequently, twins have a special bond that makes them closer than ordinary brothers and sisters. Many twosomes say that at times they even know each other's thoughts and feelings.

But being a twin can also present problems. The special closeness that twins share may interfere with the development of other relationships. And twins do not always enjoy being treated exactly alike. Parents of twins should take care to treat each child as an individual, and twins themselves must work to develop separate interests. However, because twins always have a best friend, most of them say that being a twin is terrific.

KAY CASSILL
President, The Twins Foundation
Author, *Twins: Nature's Amazing Mystery*

See also GENETICS; REPRODUCTION (Human Reproduction).

JOHN TYLER (1790–1862)

10th President of the United States

FACTS ABOUT TYLER

Birthplace: Charles City County, Virginia
Religion: Episcopalian
College Attended: College of William and Mary, Williamsburg, Virginia
Occupation: Lawyer
Married: Letitia Christian (died 1842); Julia Gardiner
Children: Tyler had 8 children by Letitia Tyler and 7 by Julia Tyler
Political Party: Whig (originally Democratic)
Office Held Before Becoming President: Vice President
President Who Preceded Him: William Henry Harrison
Age on Becoming President: 51
Years in the Presidency: 1841–1845 (succeeded William Henry Harrison, April 6, 1841, after Harrison's death in office)
Vice President: None
President Who Succeeded Him: James K. Polk
Age at Death: 71
Burial Place: Richmond, Virginia

John Tyler

DURING TYLER'S PRESIDENCY

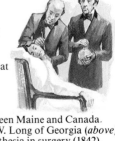

The Webster-Ashburton Treaty with Great Britain was signed (1842), settling the disputed boundary between Maine and Canada. Dr. Crawford W. Long of Georgia (*above*) used ether anesthesia in surgery (1842), but the results of his discovery were not reported until 1852. The first message by telegraph (*below*) was sent (1844) by Samuel F. B. Morse in Washington, D.C., to Alfred Vail in Baltimore, Maryland. The message was "What hath God wrought!" Congress approved the annexation of Texas (1845). Florida joined the Union as the 27th state (1845).

TYLER, JOHN. When President William Henry Harrison died in office on April 4, 1841, John Tyler became the first vice president in American history to be elevated to the presidency. He came to power at a time when the new Whig Party was badly divided. The Northern Whigs, led by Senator Henry Clay of Kentucky, favored government aid to industry, a national bank, and government funds to build roads and canals. The Southern Whigs, headed by John Tyler, believed that government was best when it governed least. Many of them, like Tyler himself, were ex-Southern Democrats who had joined the Whigs in the 1830's because of their dislike of Democratic President Andrew Jackson. The Southern Whigs favored states' rights. They had more in common with the Southern Democrats, led by South Carolina Senator John C. Calhoun, than with the Northern Whigs.

No sooner had Tyler taken office than he became involved in a personal and political feud with Senator Henry Clay. This dispute split the Whigs further and made Tyler's years in the White House bitter and difficult ones. Indeed, he spent much of his time vetoing, or disapproving, bills that the Clay Whigs had pushed through Congress. As a result, Tyler was expelled from the Whig Party. He was the only U.S. president to have been ousted by the party that had nominated and elected him.

After that, Tyler worked more closely with the Southern Democrats. With their aid, he was able to accomplish much in the field of foreign policy. In 1842 he and Secretary of State Daniel Webster negotiated the Webster-Ashburton Treaty with Britain, which settled the boundary between Maine and Canada. More important, in 1845, Tyler brought about the annexation of Texas to the United States. He considered this his most important contribution. It made up for all the defeats and disappointments he suffered in the presidency.

▶ EARLY YEARS

John Tyler was born at Greenway plantation in Charles City County, Virginia, on March 29, 1790. Tyler's mother died when he was 7,

Letitia Christian Tyler (*above*), John Tyler's first wife, died in the White House in 1842. In 1844, Tyler married the 24-year-old Julia Gardiner (*right*), becoming the first president to marry while in office.

and the boy was raised by his father, Judge John Tyler, who later served as governor of Virginia. As a youth, Tyler was frail and never in very good health. He was, however, an excellent student. He graduated from the College of William and Mary in nearby Williamsburg in 1807. He then studied law and in 1811 began to practice in Richmond. That same year, at the age of 21, he was elected to the Virginia state legislature.

Letitia Christian Tyler. In 1813, Tyler married Letitia Christian, the daughter of a Virginia planter. They had eight children. She was an invalid when Tyler became president and made only one public appearance, at her daughter Elizabeth's marriage in 1842.

▶HIS POLITICAL CAREER

Except for the years 1834 to 1844, when he called himself a Whig, John Tyler was a lifelong Democrat. He was elected to almost every office open to a professional politician. From 1811 to 1816 and again from 1823 to 1825 he sat in the Virginia House of Delegates. From 1816 to 1821 he served in the United States House of Representatives. He was elected governor of Virginia in 1825, but he resigned in 1827 to enter the United States Senate. There he remained until 1836. In that year he resigned his Senate seat and left the Democratic Party rather than support policies of President Andrew Jackson that he believed unconstitutional. In 1836 he ran for vice president. Defeated, he returned to the Virginia

House of Delegates in 1838. He was serving as Speaker of that body when the Whigs nominated him to run as vice president with William Henry Harrison of Ohio in the exciting "Tippecanoe and Tyler too" campaign of 1840. "Tippecanoe" was a nickname for Harrison, who had won the Battle of Tippecanoe against the Shawnee Indians in 1811.

Tyler's nomination was designed to balance the ticket. The Whigs thought it a shrewd idea to put a man who was a former Southern Democrat on their ballot to draw votes in the South. They did this knowing that Tyler's political principles were not supported by Harrison, Clay, or the Northern Whigs. Thus, when Harrison suddenly died in office, the surprised Whigs were faced with a man in the White House who opposed much of their program. Clay quickly set out to drive Tyler from the party and from the presidency. He wanted the presidency for himself in 1844.

▶TYLER'S POLITICAL PRINCIPLES

Throughout his long political career John Tyler held rigidly to certain beliefs. He could be a very stubborn man when he believed he was right. He thought that only educated men who owned property should have the vote. He was very upset when General Andrew Jackson appeared on the political scene in the years between 1824 and 1828 as the popular leader of the common people. Tyler never trusted Jackson. He worried that a military man in the White House might bypass the Constitution and establish a military dictatorship.

Tyler felt that each state should run its own affairs and that the federal government should stay within the powers assigned to it in the Constitution. Like most Southern politicians of that day, he also believed in low tariffs, or taxes on imports.

Regarding slavery, John Tyler accepted the institution as he found it. He did not think that slavery was good; he simply felt that to abolish it overnight would create more problems for the Southern whites than it would solve for the Negro slaves. He favored gradual abolition of slavery.

He strongly opposed the powerful Bank of the United States. This national bank was a partnership between private business and the federal government. Tyler argued that it was an unequal partnership. He also felt that the very existence of the bank was unconstitutional. He pointed out that while the government deposited its money in this bank, it was actually run by the small group of wealthy businessmen who controlled most of the stock. Tyler charged that these men ran the bank more in their own selfish interest than in the public interest. He demanded that the government withdraw its money from the Bank of the United States and put it in various state banks. This would (and eventually did) ruin the Bank of the United States. He was happy, therefore, to see President Jackson remove the government's funds in 1833, although he did not like the way Jackson went about it.

▶ **HIS ADMINISTRATION**

Tyler had scarcely settled into the White House when Henry Clay decided to drive him out of it. The Kentucky senator produced two bills to re-establish the Bank of the United States. He knew Tyler would veto these bills, and he was right. During the political warfare that followed the bank bill vetoes, Clay persuaded all of Tyler's Cabinet, except Webster, to resign in a body. He hoped this would cause the President to quit his office in panic and disgust. But Tyler calmly appointed a new Cabinet and stood firm. Then Clay had Tyler thrown out of the Whig Party. By October, 1841, the Tyler administration was a shambles.

Annexation of Texas

Tyler wanted Americans to remember him for some great accomplishment. Because of his break with Clay, he knew that the divided Whig Party could get little done in domestic matters. For this reason he turned to the annexation of Texas, which was then an independent republic and previously had been part of Mexico. Many Southern Whigs and Democrats around the President wanted annexation because it would bring another slave state into the Union. Tyler did not want it for this reason. Instead, he saw annexation as an opportunity to expand American trade into the Southwest and as a chance to bring most of the world's cotton production under the American flag. But above all he wanted the annexation of Texas to rescue the historical prestige of his sagging administration.

Between 1843 and 1844 Tyler and his new secretary of state, Abel P. Upshur (1791–1844), secretly worked out an annexation treaty with the Republic of Texas. Unfortunately Upshur was killed in an accident in February, 1844. John C. Calhoun then be-

---

IMPORTANT DATES IN THE LIFE OF JOHN TYLER

1790 Born at Greenway plantation, Charles City County, Virginia, March 29.

1807 Graduated from the College of William and Mary.

1811– Served in the Virginia House of Delegates.
1816

1813 Married Letitia Christian.

1816– Served in the United States House of
1821 Representatives.

1823– Served in the Virginia House of Delegates.
1825

1825– Governor of Virginia.
1827

1827– United States Senator
1836

1838– Speaker of the Virginia House of Delegates.
1839

1841 Inaugurated as vice-president of the United States, March 4.

1841 Took office as 10th president, April 6, after death of President William Henry Harrison on April 4.

1844 Married Julia Gardiner.

1845 Retired from the presidency, March 3.

1861 Served as president of Peace Conference; delegate to the emergency Virginia State Convention.

1861– Served in House of Representatives of the
1862 Provisional Congress of the Confederate States of America.

1862 Died in Richmond, Virginia, January 18.

came secretary of state. Calhoun unwisely linked Texas annexation to the expansion of slavery. This was a political blunder in an election year. The treaty quickly became involved in sectional politics, and the Senate turned it down. Many senators wanted to wait and see how the people felt on the annexation issue in the coming elections of 1844.

Meanwhile, Tyler had formed a small third party with the slogan "Tyler and Texas." He knew he himself had no chance of re-election in 1844. He created his party only to force the wavering Democrats to support annexation. He agreed to withdraw from the race if James K. Polk and the Democrats would pledge annexation in their platform and stick to their promise. When Polk agreed to this bargain, Tyler quit the campaign. He threw his support to Polk, who defeated Clay by a narrow margin. The President-elect then urged the Democrats in Congress to support Tyler's Texas treaty. Congress finally approved the treaty in February, 1845, and an overjoyed Tyler signed it just before he left office. Throughout the whole annexation debate Tyler showed great political skill and patience.

Julia Gardiner Tyler

Letitia Christian Tyler, the President's first wife, died in the White House in September, 1842. A few months later, Tyler began courting 23-year-old Julia Gardiner, a beautiful and wealthy New Yorker. When they were married in New York City on June 26, 1844, Tyler became the first president to be wed while in office. He was 30 years older than his bride. As First Lady, the new Mrs. Tyler captivated Washington with the size and brilliance of her White House receptions.

▶YEARS OF RETIREMENT

From 1845 to 1861, Tyler and his second wife spent peaceful years at Sherwood Forest, his plantation on the James River below Richmond, Virginia. Seven children were born to them there. Lively dinners and dances and fox hunts were held. About 70 slaves worked the corn and wheat fields of the sprawling estate. Tyler was an excellent farmer. He experimented with new fertilizers, and the harvests were good. But Julia always managed to spend more money then the plantation brought

in. The Tylers were in constant financial trouble as a result of large expenditures for entertainment, clothes, and travel.

Sherwood Forest seemed a model Southern plantation. No whips or lashes were ever used on the slaves there. The slaves appeared happy and contented, and there were no runaways. But all this was deceiving. When the Union Army overran the proud estate in 1864, the slaves quickly and gladly departed. Before they left, they sacked and plundered the main house.

▶SECESSION AND CIVIL WAR

As the Civil War approached, John Tyler was on the side of moderation. He thought that the problems of slavery and the expansion of slavery into the territories could be solved by compromise rather than by a bloody civil war. When South Carolina seceded in December, 1860, and the Confederate States of America was formed on February 8, 1861, Tyler was saddened.

Although he was now 70, tired, and sick, he agreed to leave retirement to serve as president of the Peace Conference, which met in Washington, D.C., on February 4, 1861. He soon saw, however, that this last attempt to preserve the Union was doomed to failure. At this point he returned to Richmond and became an outspoken secessionist. His vain hope was that if Virginia joined the Confederacy, the border states would follow its lead. This would make the enlarged Confederacy so strong that the federal government would not dare risk a war. Thus peace would be preserved, and Virginia would not become a battleground. Tyler wanted Virginia's secession to preserve the peace; not peace to preserve the Confederacy. He was willing to sacrifice the Union to prevent bloodshed.

Following Virginia's secession on April 17, 1861, Tyler was elected to the House of Representatives of the Confederate Provisional Congress. This was the last of his many political offices. He was serving in this post when he suffered a stroke and died in a Richmond hotel on January 18, 1862. He was 71. He died in debt and in doubt, branded a traitor by the very government he had once headed.

ROBERT SEAGER II
Author, *And Tyler Too: A Biography of John and Julia Gardiner Tyler.*

TYPE

Type is the name given to all printed characters. Every letter, number, punctuation mark, or other character you read in books, magazines, newspapers, and the like is printed from type. This page you are now reading includes 2,751 type characters.

It is difficult to think of a world without type. Before the 1400's, all reading materials were written out by hand. Johann Gutenberg's invention of movable type and the printing press in the 1440's is considered one of the greatest developments in history because it put information in the hands of many people instead of just a few.

▶TYPEFACES

There are thousands of typeface designs. They may be plain or fancy, **dark** and **heavy** (called boldface), or light and slender, *formal* or informal, expanded or condensed. Some are easier to read than others. Most textbooks and scholarly works are printed in a plain typeface that will not distract the reader. *Formal announcements, such as wedding invitations, may be set in more ornamental typestyles.*

A typeface is a style of type with unique design features. A complete set of type in a particular typeface is called a **font.** A font contains all the letters of the alphabet (upper and lower case), numerals, punctuation marks, and other characters that might be used in one size of a certain typeface.

There are four basic categories of typefaces: roman, sans serif, italic, and script.

Roman. Roman typefaces were first designed to imitate the handwritings of ancient Roman scribes. Nicolas Jenson, a French printer, developed the first roman typeface in 1470. Today there are hundreds of roman styles to choose from, but they all have certain characteristics in common: They are perpendicular (they do not slant); they are generally easy to read; and they have serifs (short strokes that finish off the ends of each of the characters).

Some of today's most popular roman typefaces were designed centuries ago by old masters: Jenson's typefaces are still used; Garamond, a typeface designed by a French printer, Claude Garamond, in 1530 is still quite popular today; and in the 1700's, En-

---

ROMAN

We the people of the United States,
Baskerville

We the people of the United States,
Caslon Old Face No. 2

We the people of the United States,
Garamond

SANS SERIF

We the people of the United States,
Futura Book

We the people of the United States,
Helvetica

We the people of the United States,
Univers 55

ITALIC

We the people of the United States,
Baskerville Italic

We the people of the United States,
Caslon Old Face No. 2 Italic

We the people of the United States,
Helvetica Italic

SCRIPT

We the people of the United States,
Brush Script

We the people of the United States,
Kaufmann Script

We the people of the United States,
Linoscript

---

glish typefounders William Caslon and John Baskerville each designed typefaces that are still outstanding examples of style and readability.

Sans Serif. The Bauhaus school of design in the 1920's believed that true beauty meant less ornamentation. Thus type designers of that period, such as Paul Renner, created typefaces without the short end strokes, or serifs (*sans* means "without" in French). Sans serif typefaces are popularly used to call attention to type in newspaper headlines and advertisements. Among the most popular styles in

Japanette
20-point Japanette

MOORE COMPUTER
16-point Moore Computer

Abbott Old Style
16-point Abbott Old Style

BUFFALO BILL
20-point Buffalo Bill

Delphin
18-point Delphin

Claudius
24-point Claudius

BROADWAY
18-point Broadway

Moore Swash
24-point Moore Swash

STENCIL
18-point Stencil

use today are Futura (designed by Renner), Helvetica, and Univers.

Italics. In 1490, Aldus Manutius, a Venetian printer, designed italics, a tightly set style of type that slants to the right. It was specially designed to fit a lot of information in small, compact books. Today most typefaces, such as Baskerville and Garamond, have an italic version, which is used mostly for emphasis and to indicate foreign words.

Script. In 1643 a Parisian printer named Pierre Moreau designed a typeface that imitated handwriting. This typeface, called script, had connecting lines that joined the letters together. Today script typefaces, such as Bank Script, are used for special emphasis and formal announcements.

▶ **TYPE SIZES**

Type measurements are based on the American point system. A **point** is about ¹⁄₇₂ inch, or .013837 inch (.351459 millimeter) wide or high; a **pica** contains 12 points; and there are approximately 6 picas to the inch (25.4 millimeters).

The spacing between words may be adjusted to make lines of equal length. This is called **justifying** the lines. The spacing between lines of type also may vary. Adjusting line spacing is called **leading.** The text on this page is set in 10-point Times Roman typeface with 1 point of leading between the lines.

▶ **TYPESETTING**

Typesetting is the process of setting type in the proper order to make up a printing surface. All type is classified as either **hot** or **cold.** Hot type is the traditional kind of metal type that was used by printers for centuries. Hot type is made (cast) by pouring molten (melted) metals into type molds. Examples of cold type include wood blocks; rubdown type (hardened ink on wax paper); strike-on composition (typewriting); and photographic type.

Before typesetting machines were invented, all type was set by hand, even for newspapers and magazines. In hand typesetting, a person called a **compositor** would arrange pieces of type into words, lines, paragraphs, and pages for printing. In front of the compositor were shallow wooden trays divided into small, open boxes. Each box held the type for one letter or character. Letters that were used most often were kept closest to the compositor. Setting type by hand was slow work. As the demand for printing increased, people tried to invent machines that would set the type faster. Between 1820 and 1883, about 200 kinds of typesetting machines were built, mostly in the United States.

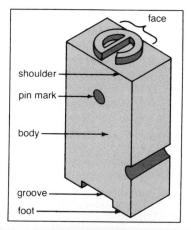

Traditional metal type (*right*) is called "hot type" because it is made from molten (melted) metals. It has been replaced in popularity by photographic type, a form of "cold type." Photographic type is produced by shining a light beam through master images of type characters contained on rotating drums or disks (*below*). The light exposes the type characters onto film.

face
shoulder
pin mark
body
groove
foot

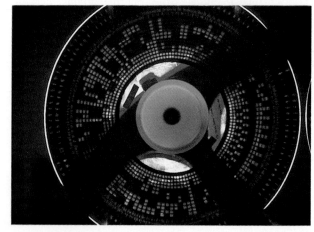

Today some small print shops still set type by hand, but most commercial typesetting is done by high-speed, computer-driven photo-typesetting machines. **Phototypesetting** is a method of setting type using the photographic process. Text is not set into metal type; it is recorded onto film instead. The process involves shining a light through a master type image onto photographic paper or film.

Type characters can be keyboarded into the computer or "read" by Optical Character Recognition (OCR) scanners that translate type characters into digital information and record it on magnetic tape or disks. (For more information on how type is printed, see the article PRINTING in Volume P.)

▶HISTORY

As early as A.D. 868 the Chinese printed a book called the *Diamond Sutra* by pressing inked, individually carved wooden blocks against mulberry-bark paper. Movable pieces of type made from hardened clay were in use in China and Korea as early as the 11th century, but they were too fragile to be practical. By the 13th century, bronze type had emerged in China, Korea, and Japan. There is no known connection, however, between these inventions and the development of movable type in Germany in the 1440's.

In the late 1800's, Ottmar Mergenthaler, an American inventor, developed the first successful automated typesetting machine. It was called the Linotype because it could produce an entire "line of type" in one solid piece of metal, called a slug. Three years later, another American, Tolbert Lanston, invented the Monotype machine, which cast type characters individually.

In the 1920's the Teletypesetter was invented. This automated machine used paper tape that had holes punched out in coded patterns. These patterns "told" the machine to drop certain type character molds into place. It remained the fastest typesetting method until phototypesetting was developed in the 1950's.

Phototypesetting has revolutionized the typesetting industry by making it faster and more economical than ever before. Advancements in computer technology continue to improve typesetting methods for the future.

JOHN LUKE
President, Type Directors Club

See also BOOKS (Book Design).

TYPEWRITERS

Typewriters are writing machines that imprint letters, numbers, and other symbols on paper. Using a typewriter is faster and less tiring than writing with a pen or pencil. In addition, the results are clearer and easier to read than most handwriting. Because of these advantages, typewriters are used daily in many areas of life.

The typewriter is an essential business tool. In most companies all letters, bills, orders, reports, and lists of merchandise must be typed. Even the smallest company owns at least one typewriter, and larger firms often have hundreds. Computers and word processors, which have keyboards much like those of typewriters, are also used in business.

Newspaper reporters use typewriters or word processors to write and edit their stories. Doctors' and dentists' offices have typewriters for filling out patient records and preparing bills and orders for medical supplies. Most school offices are equipped with typewriters

Typewriters are valuable tools for both home and office use. This portable model is equipped with an electronic memory that allows easy correction of typing errors.

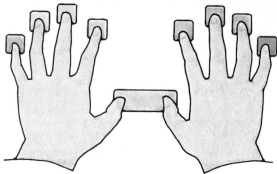

The touch system of keyboarding is the most effective way to operate a typewriter or computer keyboard. The keyboard is memorized, and the fingers are placed in a certain position on the keys. In the correct starting position, the fingers of the left hand rest lightly on the A, S, D, and F keys. Those of the right hand rest on the J, K, L, and ; keys. From these "home" keys, each finger reaches to press other keys. The color coding in this diagram shows which fingers are used to press which keys. Either thumb can press the space bar.

or computers. Typewriters are also found in many homes, where they are used by students as well as by other family members.

High schools have long offered typing courses. The growing importance of computers has made keyboarding (the technique of using a typewriter or computer keyboard) a valuable skill for younger students. Today, keyboarding may be taught in junior high schools and even in the early elementary grades.

▶ HOW TYPEWRITERS WORK

A typewriter has a keyboard, a set of type bars or a typing element containing the type for each letter and other writing symbol, an inked or carbon-film ribbon to imprint the letter on the paper, and a carriage, on which the paper is rolled and held in place.

The typewriter keyboard is made up of keys labeled with the letters of the alphabet, punctuation marks, numbers from 0 to 9, and symbols such as the dollar sign ($) and the percent sign (%). The typist presses the key labeled with the letter (or other symbol) he or she wishes to reproduce. This activates the corresponding letter on the type bar or typing element inside the machine, which then strikes

the typewriter ribbon, leaving an imprint of the letter on the paper. Pressing a letter key will result in a small (lowercase) letter unless the shift key is also pressed. To type a capital (uppercase) G, for example, the typist holds down the shift key while pressing the G key. To type in all capitals, the shift key can be locked in position.

When the end of a line is reached, the typist returns the carriage by means of a handle or return key. This also moves the paper up to start the next line. A space bar moves the carriage forward one space at a time and is used to make spaces between words. A typewriter usually has a tabulator, a key or button that can be set to move the carriage forward a certain number of spaces. A backspacer moves the carriage backward one space at a time.

Most typists learn the touch system of keyboarding, which involves memorizing the keyboard and placing the fingers in a certain position on the keys. All the fingers of both hands are used, and either thumb can be used to press the space bar. The touch typist does not have to look at the keyboard and can type very quickly and accurately. With practice, some touch typists can type more than 100 words a minute.

KINDS OF TYPEWRITERS

A **manual** typewriter is one that is not powered by electricity. All the power required to make the type strike the ribbon (and paper) is supplied by the typist's hands. (The word "manual" means "by hand.") On a manual, the type is contained on type bars, which rise up and strike the ribbon, one at a time, when the typist presses each key. Today most typewriters are powered by electricity, and manual typewriters are used less and less. But manuals have certain advantages over electric typewriters. They are less expensive and easier to repair and can be used anywhere, even where no electricity is available.

On an **electric** typewriter, the work of moving the type to the ribbon is done by an electric motor, so the typist need only touch the keys very lightly. For this reason electric typewriters are speedier and less tiring to use than manuals. They also have many automatic features, including a return key that can be used without removing the hand from the keyboard. Certain keys, such as those for spacing and underlining, repeat automatically when held down. Many electric typewriters have automatic correction keys that use specially treated ribbons to remove mistakes. Some electric typewriters have type bars, but most print with a ball- or wheel-shaped typing element. With a typing element, the carriage does not move back and forth. It stands still, and the typing element moves across the paper. Typewriters with this feature take up less space and vibrate less than those with traditional carriage returns. The typing element can easily be removed and replaced with one that prints a different style of type, such as italics or script.

Many electric typewriters are equipped with electronic memory, like that of a computer. These **electronic** models range from typewriters with a two-line memory to automatic typewriters that can type programmed material at rates of 200 words a minute or more. Many automatic typewriters have erase mechanisms that remove typing errors from the memory and from the typewritten page at the same time. Some electronic typewriters have dictionary programs that provide correct spelling. Word processors, the most advanced of these machines, combine a typewriter keyboard, a screen, and a small computer. More information on word processors can be found in the article COMPUTERS in Volume C.

Manual typewriters use type bars to imprint letters on paper (*top*). Most electric models use typing elements, either ball-shaped (*middle*) or wheel-shaped (*bottom*).

Portable typewriters are useful for students and travelers. They are smaller and lighter than standard typewriters and are easy to carry. Portable typewriters may be either manual or electric.

Typewriters are available in nearly every language, including Arabic and Hebrew, which are written from right to left, and Chinese. Models are available that type special characters, such as musical notes, foreign language accents, mathematical notations, and pharmaceutical symbols.

Typewriters can help people with disabilities. Several kinds of typewriters are made for the blind. One has a standard keyboard, but the letters are raised so that they can be felt by the typist. Another kind writes in braille, the special language of the blind. The teletypewriter, or TTY, helps deaf people make and receive telephone calls. The machine is connected to the telephone. The sender dials the person he or she wishes to contact and types the message on the teletypewriter. The message is sent through the telephone wires and is typed out automatically on the receiver's teletypewriter.

▶HISTORY

The growth of business and industry in the 19th century led to a need for a machine that could write letters and other paperwork quickly and efficiently. Early inventors produced some odd "writing machines." One device used a piano keyboard, and in another the type was mounted on the teeth of a comb.

The first practical typewriter was produced in 1873 in Milwaukee, Wisconsin, by Christopher Latham Sholes, with the help of fellow inventors Samuel Soule and Carlos Glidden. This early typewriter, called the Sholes and Glidden, printed only capital letters, and the typist could not see the letters as they were being typed. The carriage was returned by means of a foot treadle. The keyboard arrangement, however, was almost identical to that used today. The Remington Company, a maker of sewing machines and guns, manufactured 1,000 of these machines, and the typewriter industry had begun. One of the first Sholes and Glidden machines was sold to the American author Samuel Clemens, better known as Mark Twain. His *Life on the Mississippi* is believed to be the first typed manuscript to be given to a publisher.

As time went on, Remington produced more and more typewriters, and improvements were made. Remington's second model, produced in 1878, introduced lowercase letters. Later, the shift key was added, and the foot treadle was replaced by a hand-operated carriage return. In 1893, Franz Wagner designed a typewriter, later produced by the Underwood Company, that permitted the typist to see what was being written as it was typed. Other manufacturers also added to the development of better typewriters in those early years.

Early typewriters were large and boxy, and a typist was not able to view the work as it was being typed. A foot treadle was used to return the carriage.

The typewriter revolutionized business procedures. It also was a major factor in bringing women into the business work force, which until then had consisted only of men. Remington began training women to operate and demonstrate their machines. When a company bought a typewriter, it also hired one of these skilled operators. The women were known by the same name as the machine they used. Soon, business schools all over the United States were training women "type-writers."

In 1902 the Blickensderfer Company introduced the first electric typewriter, and others were produced in the 1920's and 1930's. These early electrics had many flaws, and it was not until after World War II that electric typewriters became popular. In 1961, International Business Machines Corporation (IBM) introduced the "Selectric," which was the first typewriter to use a typing element instead of type bars. Since then, typewriters have become more automatic. Designers are now experimenting with an automated typewriter that can type a message as it is being spoken.

CAROL H. BEHRMAN
Author, *The Remarkable Writing Machine*

TYPHOID FEVER. See DISEASES (Descriptions of Some Diseases).

TYPHUS. See DISEASES (Descriptions of Some Diseases).

Index

HOW TO USE THE DICTIONARY INDEX

See the beginning of the blue pages in Volume 1.

Taj Mahal (tomb in Agra, India) I:139; T:12
  Asian architecture A:367
  Islamic architecture I:356–57
  picture(s) A:438e; I:116; K:293; T:12
    marble pillar I:138
Tajumulco (volcano, Guatemala) G:396
Takakkaw Falls (British Columbia) B:406b; W:59
Take-apart puzzles P:553
Take-out service (in restaurants) R:187
Tala (meter of Indian music) I:143
Talas, Battle of (751) B:103f
Talbot, William Henry Fox (English inventor) P:211
Talc (mineral) C:560; M:315, 317
Tale of Genji, The (by Lady Murasaki) J:41, 52–53
Tale of the Heike, The (Japanese literary work) J:53
Tale of Two Cities, A (novel by Dickens) D:152
Tales of Hoffmann, The (operetta by Jacques Offenbach) O:54,
    163–64
Taliban (former ruling force in Afghanistan) A:42, 43, 44, 45
  Qaeda, Al Q:2
  terrorism, war on T:116–17; U:205
Taliesin East (Wisconsin home of Frank Lloyd Wright) W:200
Taliesin West (Arizona home of Frank Lloyd Wright)
  picture(s) W:326
Talismans (jewelry believed to hold magical powers) G:72;
    J:98
Talking books (recorded books for the blind) B:258
Talking drums (musical instruments) A:77, 78
Talking Heads (American rock group) R:264
Talk shows (television programs) T:70
Tallahassee (capital of Florida) F:260, 263, 264, 269, 274
  picture(s) F:271
Tallapoosa River (Alabama) A:132, 133
Tallchief, Maria and Marjorie (American ballerinas) O:95
  profile
Talleyrand-Perigord, Charles Maurice de (French statesman)
    A:13
Tallgrass Prairie Preserve (Oklahoma) O:90
Tallies (for counting) N:397, 403
Tallinn (capital of Estonia) E:324
  picture(s) E:325
Tallis, Thomas (English composer) C:283
Tallit (prayer shawl) J:147
Tallmadge, James (American statesman) M:381
Tallow (fat from cattle and sheep) O:79, 80
  candles made of C:96
  lighting, history of L:232
  soapmaking D:140
Tall ships (sailing ships) S:153
Talmud (body of literature that records Jewish laws and
    traditions) J:104, 144, 148; R:147; T:13
  attacks against in the Middle Ages J:105
  dietary laws J:146b
Talons (claws of birds of prey) A:276
Tamanduas (mammals) A:296
Tamaraus (hoofed mammals) B:430
Tamarind (tropical fruit) T:317
  picture(s) F:285; T:317
Tamarins (monkeys) M:68, 420, 421, 422
  picture(s) P:457
Tambora (drum) D:340
  picture(s) D:339
Tambourine (drum) D:339; M:551; P:149
Tambura (musical instrument) I:143
Tamburlaine the Great (play by Marlowe) M:104
Tamerlane (Timur; Timur-Lenk) (Mongol conqueror)
  India, history of I:131
  Islamic painting I:357
  tomb in Samarkand I:356
  Uzbekistan U:257
  picture(s) W:263
Tamil (language) I:140, 141
Tamil Nadu (formerly Madras state) (India) I:125; M:14
  picture(s)
    temple I:118

Tamils (a people of Sri Lanka and Madras) M:14; S:413,
    416
Taming of the Shrew, The (play by Shakespeare) S:139
Tammany Hall (Democratic Party organization)
  Nast's cartoons about C:127; N:17
Tampa (Florida) F:268, 269, 270
Tampere (Finland) F:137
Tam'si, Tchicaya U (Congolese poet) A:76d
Tana, Lake (Ethiopia) E:331; L:33; N:260
Tanana (Indians of North America) I:188
Tananarive (Madagascar) *see* Antananarivo
Tanana Valley (Alaska) A:147, 151
Tandem bicycles B:175–76
Tandem harrow (farm machine) F:54
Tandja Mamadou (president of Niger) N:252
Taney, Roger Brooke (American jurist) C:335; D:323
Tanga (Tanzania) T:19
Tanganyika (former republic, now part of Tanzania) T:16, 19
Tanganyika, Lake (east central Africa) B:457, 458; L:26,
    33
Tang dynasty (ancient China) A:242; C:269
  China, art of C:274, 277
  pottery P:410
  picture(s)
    ceramic vase C:266
Tangelo (citrus fruit) O:189
  picture(s) O:186
Tangent (ratio in trigonometry) T:312, 313
Tangerine (citrus fruit) O:189
  picture(s) O:186
Tangier (Morocco) M:460
Tanglewood (near Lenox, Massachusetts) *see* Berkshire Music
    Festival
Tango (Latin-American dance) L:72
  picture(s) L:47
Tangram (puzzle) P:553, 554
Tangshan (China)
  earthquake E:41
  picture(s)
    earthquake E:38
Tanguy, Yves (French artist) M:395
  picture(s)
    Mama, Papa Is Wounded! (painting) S:518
Tani Buncho (Japanese artist)
  picture(s)
    Hibiscus (painting) W:55
Tanka (Japanese verse form) J:52
Tank cars (of railroads) R:84
  picture(s) R:83
Tankers (airplanes) U:110
Tankers (ships) S:155, 159
  liquefied natural gas (LNG) tankers N:60
  oil spills P:175–76; W:65–66
  picture(s) F:486; L:317; P:175
Tanks (armored combat vehicles) T:14–15
  battles B:103f
  United States Army U:105
  World War I W:287
  diagram(s) T:15
Tank trucks T:320
Tank vessels (ships) *see* Supertankers
Tannenberg, Battle of (1914) W:283
Tannhäuser (opera by Richard Wagner) O:164
Tannin (Tannic acid) (vegetable compound) A:386; D:375;
    L:110, 111; T:34
Tanning (of leather) L:110
Tanoan Pueblos (Indians of North America) I:183
Tantalum (element) E:177
Tantalus (in Greek mythology) G:367
Tantrayana Buddhism *see* Vajrayana Buddhism
Tanui, Moses (Kenyan runner)
  picture(s) T:254
Tanumafili II, Malietoa (head of state of Samoa) W:125

fog and smog due to inversion of   F:291
gases, properties of   G:56, 58–59
How hot is the sun?   H:87
how ocean temperature is measured   O:31
infrared radiation   L:221
injury caused by extremes of heat and cold   F:162
inversion in air pollution   A:123; E:303–4; F:291
Jupiter   P:279
liquid gases   L:253
liquids, properties of   L:254
Mars   P:279
matter, changes in volume of   M:172
measurements   W:116
Mercury   M:230; P:276
moon   M:454
Neptune   P:282
ocean temperature and coral reefs   C:556
ocean temperature measurement   O:38
ocean water becomes colder as depth increases   U:21
Pluto   P:282
record highest and lowest in world   W:95
record highs and lows in Asia   A:443
record highs in Africa   A:49
record lows in Siberia   S:170
Saturn   P:280; S:55
seed germination affected by cold   E:397
shells show temperatures in the past   I:15
in space   S:356
stars   S:428, 429–30, 431
sun   S:490, 491, 492, 495
temperature range in which life exists   A:263; L:201
thermometers   T:163–64
thermometers as weather instruments   W:87–88
Uranus   P:281; U:232
Venus   P:276; V:303a
volume affected by change in temperature   M:174
water temperature limits where fish live   F:182
winds caused by temperature   W:186, 187, 188
world's highest recorded in Sahara   S:7
world's lowest recorded in Antarctica   A:292
Temperature, body see Body temperature
Temperature inversion   A:123; E:303–4; F:291
   diagram(s)   A:123
Tempering (of metals)   M:236; W:191
Tempest, The (painting by Giorgione)   G:210
   picture(s)   G:210; I:399
Tempest, The (play by Shakespeare)   S:139
Tempietto, The (in the courtyard of San Pietro in Montorio, Rome)
   picture(s)   I:397
Templates (used in mechanical drawing)   M:200
Temple, Shirley (American actress and public official)   M:492
   profile
   picture(s)   C:33
      Shirley Temple doll   D:270
Temple Mount (Jerusalem)   J:82
   picture(s)   J:82
Temples (buildings used for religious services) see also
      Mosques; Pagodas
   ancient civilizations   A:230
   Buddhist sculpture   C:277
   Chavín (Andean temple center)   I:168
   Diana of Ephesus   W:218
   Egypt, ancient   A:365–66; E:107, 108, 111–12, 117
   Greek temples   A:367–68; G:346, 348
   Hinduism   A:367; H:140–41, 142
   India, art and architecture of   A:366; I:139
   Judaism   J:145
   Khmer civilization   A:243
   Kyoto (Japan)   K:312
   Temple of Fortune (Praeneste, Italy)   R:318
   Temple of Heaven (Beijing, China)   B:127c
   Temple of Jerusalem   J:84, 103, 148
   Temple of the Emerald Buddha (Bangkok)   B:47
   ziggurats   A:230, 365

   picture(s)
      Beijing (China)   A:366
      Buddhist temples   B:426; I:138
      Greek temples   G:349
      Hindu temples   H:141; I:118, 138
      Maya temple   G:397
      Mormon Temple (Salt Lake City)   M:457
      Roman temple (Baalbek, Lebanon)   L:119
      Temple of Apollo (Corinth, Greece)   G:340
Temple Square (Salt Lake City, Utah)   U:250
   picture(s)   U:250
Tempo (musical term)   M:537, 539
   orchestra conducting   O:198, 199
Temporal lobes (of the brain)   B:365
Temptation of Saint Anthony (painting by Hieronymus Bosch)
   picture(s)   D:363
Temptations (American musical group)   R:262c
Tempura (Japanese dish)   J:29
Tenant farmers see also Sharecroppers
   English migration to America   T:167
Tenants (living in rental housing)   H:190; R:112d
Ten Commandments (Decalogue)   T:72–73
   Hebraic faith, foundation of   J:102
   Judaism, beliefs of   J:144
   Moses   M:469; R:147
Tenders (of locomotives)   L:285
Tendons (cords joining muscles to bones)   B:279, 280;
      F:160; M:518
Tendrils (of plants)   L:117; P:305
Tenebrism (style in art)   B:64, 66; S:384
Tenement houses   H:194
Tenerife (island, Spain)   S:373
Teng Hsiao-ping (Chinese political leader) see Deng Xiaoping
Tennessee   T:74–87
   Civil War   C:338, 340, 342
   Knoxville International Energy Exposition   F:17
   Memphis   M:217
   Nashville   N:16
   Scopes trial   S:84
   westward movement   W:142
   map(s)   T:85
   picture(s)
      country music   T:75, 80
      farm   T:76
      Great Smoky Mountains   T:75, 77
      Great Smoky Mountains National Park   T:82
      Lookout Mountain   T:82
      Memphis   M:217; T:75, 78, 82
      Nashville   N:16; T:83
      Shiloh National Military Park   T:82
      TVA dam   T:78
Tennessee, University of   T:79
   picture(s)
      women's basketball   T:79
Tennessee River (United States)   T:74, 76, 81
   Alabama   A:132, 133
   Kentucky   K:214, 221
   Mississippi   M:352
   TVA dam system   D:21
Tennessee-Tombigbee (Tenn-Tom) Waterway project   A:132,
      136; M:352, 357; T:81
Tennessee Valley Authority (TVA)   N:138h; T:76, 79, 83, 87
   Kentucky   K:226
   Roosevelt, Franklin D.   R:323
   system of dams   D:21
   picture(s)
      dam   T:78
Tenniel, Sir John (English cartoonist and illustrator)   C:119,
      232, 233; I:80
Tennis   T:88–99
   Evert, Chris   F:274
   Gibson, Althea   G:205
   Hispanic Americans   H:147
   Jacobs, Helen Hull   A:404–5

Tennis (cont.)
  London   **L:**296
  Olympic sport   **O:**108
  paddle tennis   **P:**11
  platform tennis   **R:**37
  table tennis   **T:**2
  picture(s)
    Hall of Fame   **R:**220
Tennis ball sponge
  picture(s)   **S:**411
Tennis Court Oath (in French Revolution)   **F:**468
Tennyson, Alfred, Lord (English poet)   **T:**100–101
  "Crossing the Bar"   **T:**100
  English literature of the Victorian period   **E:**284
  figures of speech   **F:**122
  "Lady of Shalott," excerpt from   **T:**101
  lullabies   **L:**337
  odes   **O:**52
Tenochtitlán (now **Mexico City**) (capital of the Aztec empire)
    A:575, 578; **I:**172–73; **M:**248, 253
  Cortés, Hernando   **C:**559
  famous ancient cities   **C:**317
  Montezuma II   **M:**443
Tenoners (machine tools)   **F:**515
Tenor (male voice)   **C:**282; **V:**377
Tenor drum   **D:**338
Tenpins (bowling game)   **B:**348–50
Tense (of verbs)   **P:**93
Tension (in physics)   **B:**432
Tenskwatawa (Shawnee Indian prophet)   **H:**42; **I:**177, 204
Tentacles
  coelenterates   **J:**72, 73, 75
  coral polyps   **C:**555
  jellyfish   **A:**280
Tent caterpillars
  picture(s)   **B:**483; **I:**247
Tenth Amendment (to the United States Constitution)   **B:**182,
    183; **S:**436
Ten Thousand Leaves (Japanese poetry collection) *see*
    Man'yoshu
Tenth planet (belief of some experts)   **S:**340d
Tents
  backpacking   **H:**135
  camping   **C:**44
  circus tents   **C:**307
  houses that move   **H:**189
  Inuit   **I:**275
Tent stitches (in needlepoint)   **N:**100
Tenure of Office Act (United States, 1867)   **J:**118
Tenzing Norgay (Sherpa guide and mountain climber)   **E:**371;
    H:136, 138; **M:**499
Tenzin Gyatso (14th Dalai Lama) *see* Dalai Lama
Teosinte (wild grass that was developed into maize)   **B:**213;
    P:442
Teotihuacán (Mexico)   **A:**244; **I:**167, 169; **M:**253; **P:**558
  picture(s)   **A:**244
Tepees *see* Tipis
Tepehuan (Indians of North America)   **I:**183
Tequendama Falls (Colombia)   **W:**59
Tequestas (Indians native to Florida)   **F:**271
Tequila (alcoholic drink)   **M:**241
Terabytes (of computer-stored information)   **C:**481
Terai (southern part of Nepal)   **N:**108
Terbium (element)   **E:**177
Terborch (Ter Borch; Terburg), Gerard (Dutch painter)   **D:**365
Terbrugghen, Hendrick (Dutch artist)   **D:**365
  picture(s)
    Saint Sebastian (painting)   **D:**367
Teredo worms *see* Shipworms
Terence (Roman playwright)   **D:**299; **L:**75
Tereno (Indians of South America)   **I:**197
Teresa, Mother (Roman Catholic nun)   **C:**9, 324
Teresa, Saint (of Ávila) (Spanish nun and writer)   **S:**18d
  profile, 388

Tereshkova, Valentina Vladimirovna (Soviet cosmonaut)
    A:467; **S:**346 *profile*
  picture(s)   **S:**346
Terman, Lewis (American psychologist)   **I:**253
Terminals (connecting posts of batteries)   **B:**103b
Terminals (of airports)   **A:**126–28
Terminal velocity (maximum speed of a falling body)   **F:**34;
    G:323
Termites (insects)   **H:**262; **I:**234, 237; **P:**497
  picture(s)   **I:**246
Terms (of arguments in logic)   **L:**290
Terms (of fractions)   **F:**397
Ternary form (design for writing music)   **M:**533
Terns (birds)   **A:**284; **B:**240 *see also* Arctic terns
Ter-Petrosyan, Levon (Armenian president)   **A:**422
Terracing (in agriculture)   **E:**319; **G:**100
  Bhutan   **B:**155a
  picture(s)   **E:**299
    China   **C:**261
    Indonesia   **A:**92–93; **G:**281
    Japan   **J:**35
    Nepal   **N:**107
    Pakistan   **P:**38
    Philippines   **N:**62
    Yemen   **Y:**359
Terra-cotta (fired, usually unglazed clay)   **P:**408
  Chinese tomb figures   **A:**356; **C:**259; **P:**410
  early African sculpture   **A:**70–71; **P:**411
  Renaissance sculpture   **S:**100
  picture(s)
    African sculpture   **A:**72, 75; **P:**411
    Chinese tomb figures   **A:**242, 356; **P:**409
    toy horse from ancient Cyprus   **T:**251
Terrapins (turtles)   **T:**355
Terrariums (gardens under glass)   **H:**269; **T:**102
Terrazzo (decorative flooring)   **C:**166
Terrell, Mary Church (American reformer)   **W:**215 *profile*
  picture(s)   **W:**215
Terrestrial Planet Finder   **P:**282
Terrestrial telescopes   **O:**181
Terriers (dogs)   **D:**242, 248
  picture(s)   **D:**244
Territorial Courts   **U:**170–71
Territorial expansion of the United States   **T:**103–13;
    U:180–81, 183–84; **W:**270
  Alaska purchase   **A:**157
  Arizona   **A:**402
  Florida becomes a state   **F:**272, 274
  Hawaii   **H:**62
  Louisiana Purchase   **L:**329–30
  Manifest Destiny concept   **M:**239a–239b
  Mexican War   **M:**239a–239b
  Northwest Ordinance (1787)   **W:**140–41
  outlying areas of the United States   **U:**84–85
  overland trails   **O:**268–82
  Panama Canal   **P:**48
  public lands   **P:**516–17
  Puerto Rico   **P:**531–32
  Spanish-American War   **S:**392c–392d
  Texas, annexation of   **P:**375; **T:**367–68
  westward movement   **W:**140–44
Territoriality (of animals)
  birds   **B:**227
  iguanas   **I:**60
Territorial rights (in publishing)   **B:**324
Territorial waters (directly off a nation's shores)
  Arctic region   **A:**381
  fishing industry   **F:**221–22
Territories (in the Commonwealth of Nations)   **C:**461
Territory (of the United States)   **I:**256; **U:**88
Terrorism   **C:**585; **T:**114–16 *see also* Bombings; Terrorism,
    war on; Terrorist attacks on the United States
  Chechen terrorist acts   **R:**373
  food safety   **F:**335

Thirteen American colonies (cont.)
 municipal government **M:**514–15
 Oglethorpe founded Georgia **O:**61
 Penn, William **P:**125
 Pitt, William, Earl of Chatham **P:**265
 Plymouth Colony **P:**344–47
 prisons, history of **P:**481
 Raleigh established Roanoke Island **R:**101
 Revolutionary War, events leading to **R:**194–98
 slavery, development of **S:**194
 Smith, John, and the Jamestown colony **S:**205
 taxation **T:**25
 territorial expansion **T:**103, 106
 textiles, history of **T:**145
 westward movement **W:**140–42
 Zenger, John Peter, wins fight for free press **Z:**380
Thirteen Classics (ancient Chinese texts) **C:**278
Thirteen-lined ground squirrels (rodents) **R:**275
Thirteenth Amendment (to the United States Constitution)
 U:157
 abolition movement **A:**6, 6b
 Anthony, Susan B. **A:**299
 civil rights **C:**326, 328
 Civil War **C:**347
 Emancipation Proclamation led to **E:**201
 ratified after Lincoln's death **L:**246
 slavery abolished in the United States **A:**79b, 79g, 79h
Thirty-five millimeter cameras **P:**202, 206, 214
Thirty-Six Views of Mt. Fuji (series of prints by Hokusai)
 H:159d
Thirty-Three Immortals (Uruguayan patriots) **U:**241
Thirty Tyrants (of ancient Greece) **A:**221
Thirty Years' War (1618–1648) **C:**293; **G:**160; **N:**121;
 R:231; **T:**179
Thjórsá (river in Iceland) **I:**35
Thomas, Clarence (American jurist) **S:**508 *profile*
 picture(s) **U:**171
Thomas, Dylan (Welsh poet) **E:**288; **P:**349; **T:**180
Thomas, George Henry (U.S. army general) **C:**342, 343
Thomas, Helen (American wire service reporter) **J:**139 *profile*
Thomas, Isaiah (American publisher) **N:**415
Thomas, Jesse Burgess (American statesman) **M:**381
Thomas, Petria (Australian swimmer) **O:**119
Thomas, Piri (Puerto Rican writer) **H:**147
Thomas, Saint (one of the 12 Apostles) **A:**328, 329; **M:**14
Thomas, William I. (American sociologist) **S:**231
Thomas à Becket *see* Becket, Saint Thomas à
Thomas à Kempis *see* Kempis, Thomas à
Thomas Aquinas, Saint *see* Aquinas, Saint Thomas
Thomism (system of thought created by Saint Thomas Aquinas)
 R:289
Thompson (Manitoba) **M:**82, 85
Thompson, Benjamin (American-born British scientist)
 H:88–89; **P:**234; **T:**180
 picture(s)
 Thompson's cannon **H:**88
Thompson, David (Canadian explorer) **B:**407; **C:**82; **F:**522
 profile; **I:**56
Thompson, Era Bell (American journalist) **N:**335 *profile*
Thompson, Francis Joseph (English poet) **E:**285
Thompson, Jenny (American swimmer) **O:**107 *profile,* 119
Thompson, Sir John Sparrow David (Canadian prime
 minister) **C:**76 *profile*
Thompson, John T. (American inventor) **G:**423
Thompson, Stith (American folklorist) **F:**312
Thompson, Tommy G. (American political figure) **W:**207
 profile
Thompson seedless grapes **G:**297
Thompson's gazelles **A:**282
Thompson submachine guns *see* Tommy guns
Thoms, William John (English folklorist) **F:**312
Thomsen, Christian Jürgensen (Danish museum curator)
 A:359
Thomson, Bobby (American baseball player) **B:**93

Thomson, Charles (American Revolutionary War patriot)
 G:329
Thomson, James (English poet) **E:**278
Thomson, Sir Joseph John (English physicist) **P:**236, 238
 profile
 atoms **A:**486
 picture(s) **P:**238
Thomson, Robert William (British inventor) **T:**210
Thomson, Tom (Canadian painter) **C:**73; **O:**137
 picture(s)
 The Jack Pine (painting) **N:**40
Thomson, Virgil (American composer and music critic)
 O:149; **U:**209
Thomson, William *see* Kelvin, Lord
Thor (Norse god) **N:**279
 picture(s) **M:**569
Thoracic duct (of the lymphatic system) **L:**349
Thoracic vertebrae (of the spine) **S:**183
Thorax (chest cavity of animals)
 ants **A:**319
 bees **B:**116
 beetles **B:**124
 insects **I:**230, 231
 shrimps **S:**167
Thoreau, Henry David (American writer) **A:**209–10; **T:**181–83
 nature, study of **N:**70
 Transcendentalism **A:**210
 Walden, excerpt from **T:**182–83
 picture(s) **A:**210
Thorium (element) **E:**167, 177; **R:**65, 74
Thorndike, Edward Lee (American psychologist) **D:**157; **P:**507
Thorns (on plants) **P:**305, 316; **W:**104
Thornton, William (American architect) **C:**104
Thorny oysters (mollusks)
 picture(s) **S:**150
Thorny whelks (mollusks)
 picture(s) **S:**149
Thoroughbred horses **H:**233, 236, 239; **I:**318
 picture(s) **H:**241
Thoroughbred racing *see* Horse racing
Thorpe, Ian (Australian swimmer) **O:**119
Thorpe, Jim (James Francis Thorpe) (American athlete) **O:**114;
 T:183
 picture(s) **O:**114
Thor's Hammer (rock formation in Bryce Canyon National Park)
 picture(s) **U:**243
Thorvaldsen (Thorwaldsen), Bertel (Danish sculptor) **C:**552
Thorvaldsson, Eric *see* Eric the Red
Thoth (Egyptian god of writing and knowledge) **E:**108
Thought *see* Thinking
Thousand and One Nights *see* Arabian Nights
Thousand Islands (in Saint Lawrence River, Canada–United
 States) **C:**55; **N:**213; **O:**124
 picture(s) **O:**132
Thrace (region of Greece and European Turkey) **G:**333, 338;
 T:345
Thrasher (songbird)
 picture(s) **G:**133
Thrasybulus (ancient Greek leader) **A:**221
Thread (for sewing) **N:**97; **S:**129
Threatened species (of plants and animals) **E:**208
Three Age System (of organizing archaeological artifacts)
 A:359
Three Baskets (Buddhist writings) *see* Tripitaka
Three Children, Story of the (apocryphal book of the Bible)
 B:164
"Three Crows, The" (folk song) **F:**322, 323
Three-cushion billiards **B:**180
3-D archery (sport) **A:**362
Three-dimensional animation **A:**289
Three-dimensional design **D:**137
Three-dimensional geometry *see* Solid geometry
Three-dimensional laser images **P:**272
Three-dimensional motion pictures **M:**494
Three-dimensional photographs **C:**466–67; **P:**208

Tides T:193–97
  biological clock **B:**193
  Canada's Bay of Fundy **C:**57; **N:**138, 350
  Earth's oceans **E:**18–19
  earth tides **T:**197
  hurricanes cause higher than usual tides **H:**305
  moon's gravitational pull **M:**450
  ocean water, movement of **O:**19
  tidal power plants **E:**222
  water is a source of power **W:**53
  picture(s)
      gravity **G:**325
Tidewater (coastal region of United States) **N:**308; **V:**346
Tidewater glaciers **G:**222
Tied notes (in musical notation) **M:**535
Tie-dyeing (technique for dyeing cloth) **D:**377; **T:**143
  picture(s) **T:**142
Tiempo, El (Colombian newspaper) **C:**406
Tien Shan (mountain range, Asia) **K:**313–14
Tientsin (Tianjin) (China) **C:**265; **T:**197
Tie plates (of railroad tracks) **R:**78
Tiepolo, Giovanni Battista (Italian painter) **I:**402; **P:**24
  picture(s)
      ceiling of Episcopal Palace (Würzburg, Germany)
      I:402
Tierra del Fuego (South America)
  Argentina **A:**382, 386, 386b
  climate **S:**282
  Indians, American **I:**199
  "Land of Fire," why so named **C:**252
Tie-stalls (type of barn housing for cattle) **D:**6
Tiffany, Louis (American artist and glassmaker) **A:**316; **S:**418
Tiffany glass
  picture(s) **A:**316; **G:**235; **S:**418
Tiflis (capital of Republic of Georgia) *see* Tbilisi
Tiger, The (nickname for Georges Clemenceau) **C:**355
"Tiger, The" (poem by William Blake)
  picture(s) **E:**278
Tiger beetle
  picture(s) **B:**126; **I:**230
Tiger Cubs (Boy Scout program) **B:**356
Tigers **T:**198
  cats, wild **C:**144, 145, 146, 147, 150
  circus acts **C:**307
  reproduction **M:**68
  Siberian tigers **R:**363
  picture(s) **A:**283, 438d; **C:**141, 150; **T:**198
      circus act **C:**309
      fur **C:**149
"Tigers" (countries with rapidly developing economies)
  S:332
Tiger salamanders (animals)
  picture(s) **L:**201
Tiger's eye (gemstone) **G:**74
Tiger sharks **S:**144
Tiglath-Pileser I (king of Assyria) **A:**462
Tigranes I (Armenian king) **A:**422
Tigreans (a people of Ethiopia) **E:**316, 330
  picture(s) **E:**316
Tigre People's Liberation Front **E:**333, 334
Tigrinya (language) **E:**316
Tigris-Euphrates valley (southwest Asia) **A:**230, 231–33,
  453
  Babylonia **B:**5
  Iraq **I:**312, 315–16
  Mesopotamia **M:**231–32
  Sumer **S:**487
  picture(s)
      farmer plowing **A:**346
Tigris River (Asia) **B:**15; **I:**312; **M:**300; **R:**246
Tihama (region, Saudi Arabia) **S:**58c
Tijuana (Mexico) **M:**247
Tikal (Guatemala) **A:**229, 243; **M:**184
  picture(s) **G:**397

Tikrit (Iraq)
  picture(s) **I:**316a
Tilden, Bill (American tennis player) **T:**97 *profile*
  picture(s) **T:**97
Tilden, Samuel Jones (American politician) **E:**132; **H:**68, 70
Tile games **G:**15–16
Tiles *see* Ceramics
Tiling (design of interlocking shapes) *see* Tessellation
Till (soil deposited by glaciers) *see* Glacial till
Till Eulenspiegel (German folk hero) *see* Eulenspiegel, Till
Tilley, Sir Samuel L. (Canadian statesman) **N:**138g
Tilling (of the soil) **F:**48–49, 53–55, 56; **V:**287
Tillotson, John (English archbishop) **O:**191
Till Plains (Illinois) **I:**64, 146
Till Plains (Ohio) **O:**64
Tilsit, Treaties of (1807) **N:**12
Tilt-cabs (of trucks) **T:**322
  picture(s) **T:**318
Tilting (contest of knights)
  picture(s) **K:**274
Timbales (drums) **D:**340
  picture(s) **D:**339
Timber *see* Forests and forestry; Lumber and lumbering; Trees;
  Wood
Timber-framed houses **H:**192
Timberline (Tree line) (altitude above which trees cannot grow)
  A:378
Timber wolves *see* Gray (timber) wolves
Timbre (in music) **B:**71; **M:**533, 537
Timbuktu (Mali) *see* Tombouctou
Time **T:**199–204
  animals' sense of **H:**202
  base-60 system used in measurement **M:**162; **N:**406;
  S:487
  calendar **C:**13–17
  changes with speeds near speed of light **R:**142
  clocks **C:**369–72
  fossil story of past time **F:**383–88
  Greenwich standard time **G:**374b
  international date line **I:**266
  measurement **W:**115–16, 117
  relativity **P:**231
  time management **T:**205–6
  using maps to find time **M:**96
  watches **W:**45–46
  table(s)
      geological time scale **E:**25
Time (magazine) **J:**140; **M:**20
  Einstein, Albert, named person of the 20th century by
  E:120
Time deposits (banking) **B:**56
Time fuses (of explosive shells) **G:**425
Time locks **L:**283–84
Time Machine, The (novel by H. G. Wells) **S:**80
Time management **T:**205–6
Time of Troubles (in Russian history) **R:**369
Timepieces *see* Clocks; Watches
Time reversal (theory) **T:**204
Times Beach (Missouri) **H:**72; **W:**65
Time shifting (recording television programs for later viewing)
  V:332d, 332i
Time signature (in musical notation) **M:**535, 537
Times-Mirror Company **L:**308
Times Square (New York City)
  picture(s) **H:**160; **N:**231
"Times that try men's souls" (from the words of Thomas Paine in
  The Crisis) **P:**13; **R:**202
Time travel (theory) **T:**204
Time zones (geographical areas within which the same standard
  time is used) **I:**266; **R:**89; **T:**202–3
Timing (bowling) **B:**349
Timing devices (to operate machinery) **C:**369
Timmins (Ontario) **O:**133
Timon of Athens (play by Shakespeare) **S:**139
Timor (province, Indonesia) **I:**209, 212

Timor, East (Timor-Leste)   **A:**457; **I:**209, 212; **T:**207–8
  map(s)   **T:**207
  picture(s)   **T:**207
    flag   **F:**240
    independence celebration   **T:**208
Timothy I and II (books of the New Testament)   **B:**166, 167
Timpani (kettledrums)   **D:**339–40; **O:**194
  orchestra seating plan   **O:**196
  percussion instruments   **M:**551; **P:**148
  picture(s)   **M:**551; **O:**195
Timpanogos Cave National Monument (Utah)   **U:**250
Timucuans (Indians native to Florida)   **F:**271; **J:**10
Timur the Lame (Mongol conqueror) *see* Tamerlane
Tin (metal)   **E:**178; **T:**209
  alloys   **A:**192
  antiques   **A:**316b
  bronze   **B:**409–10
  coated steel   **I:**337
  Malaysia is world's leading producer   **A:**442; **M:**57
  soldering   **W:**118
  picture(s)
    Bolivian tin mine   **B:**309
    japanned tin coffee pot   **A:**316a
    lantern   **F:**296
  table(s)   **M:**235
Tinamou (bird)
  picture(s)   **B:**234
Tin cans (containers)   **T:**209
Tinchebray, Battle of (1106)   **H:**107
Tinctoris, Johannes (Flemish musician and musical theorist)
      D:372
Tinder (for fires)   **F:**142
Tin Drum, The (novel by Günter Grass)   **G:**182
Tinea *see* Ringworm
Tingi Hills (Sierra Leone)   **S:**172
Tin-glazed pottery   **P:**411, 412
Tinian (island, Pacific Ocean)   **W:**313, 317
Tin Lizzie (automobile) *see* Model T
Tinoco Granados, Federico (Costa Rican political leader)
      C:567
Tin Pan Alley (nickname for the center of American popular
      music)   **U:**208–9
Tinplate (steel sheeting with a thin coating of pure tin)   **I:**337;
      T:209
Tintoretto (Venetian painter)   **P:**23; **T:210**
  picture(s)
    Christ in the House of Martha and Mary (painting)
        T:210
Tints (of colors)   **C:**426
Tionontati (Indians of North America)   **I:**175
Tip-dyeing (of furs)   **F:**503
Tipis (tent dwellings of North American Indians)   **H:**189;
      I:180
Tippecanoe, Battle of (1811)   **H:**42; **I:**157, 204
  picture(s)   **H:**43
"Tippecanoe and Tyler, too" (campaign slogan for Harrison)
      H:43
Tipping, origin of the word   **R:**186
Tippit, J. D. (American police officer)   **O:**246
Tipplers (pigeons)   **P:**178
Tiptoe (manner of walking)   **F:**81
Tiranë (Tirana) (capital of Albania)   **A:**159, 161
Tires   **T:**210–12
  automobiles, technical advances in   **A:**544
  rubber   **R:**344, 346
  truck tires, improvements in   **T:**322
Tiridates III (Armenian king)   **A:**422
Tiros (Television Infrared Observation Satellite) (weather
      satellite)   **W:**91
Tirpitz, Alfred von (German admiral)   **W:**284 *profile*
Tirso de Molina (Spanish dramatist)   **S:**388
Tirthas (Hindu places of pilgrimage)   **H:**141
Tiso, Jozef (Slovak political leader)   **S:**202

Tissue (in living things)   **L:**200
  animal kingdom   **K:**254
  grafting   **I:**97
  human body   **B:**275
  plants   **K:**256
  proteins important for growth and repair   **N:**423
  picture(s)   **B:**199
Tissue cultures (used in the study of viruses)   **V:**368
Tissue paper   **C:**402; **P:**57
Tissue-plasminogen activator   **G:**84–85
Tissue typing (for organ transplants)   **O:**226
Tisza River (eastern Europe)   **H:**296
Titan (moon of Saturn)   **H:**310; **P:**280, 281; **S:**52, 58, 360
  picture(s)   **S:**58
Titania (moon of Uranus)   **P:**281; **U:**233
Titania (queen of the fairies, in *A Midsummer Night's Dream* by
      Shakespeare)   **S:**138
Titania's Palace (dollhouse)   **D:**263–64
Titanic (British steamship)
  Astor, John Jacob IV, died in sinking   **A:**464
  iceberg accidents to ocean liners   **I:**18
  radio's role in saving lives   **I:**284
  submersible investigated wreckage   **E:**416
  underwater archaeology   **U:**20
  What caused the *Titanic* tragedy?   **O:**33
  picture(s)   **O:**33
Titanic (motion picture, 1997)   **O:**33
Titanium (element)   **E:**178
  supersonic planes have skins of   **S:**502
  table(s)   **M:**235
Titano, Mount (San Marino)   **S:**35
Titans (in mythology)   **G:**201, 361, 362; **M:**571
Tithe (tax)   **M:**457
Tithonus (in Greek mythology)   **A:**87
Titian (Venetian painter)   **I:**398; **R:**169; **T:212–13**
  Giorgione, assistant of   **G:**210
  Madonna with Saints and Members of the Pesaro Family
      (painting)   **P:**23
  master of oil technique   **P:**23
  picture(s)
    Madonna with a Rabbit (painting), detail from   **T:**213
    *Madonna with Saints and Members of the Pesaro
        Family* (painting)   **P:**22
Titicaca, Lake (Peru–Bolivia)   **B:**307; **L:**33–34; **P:**161, 162;
      S:281
  ancient civilization developed at the lake   **A:**244; **B:**306
  Andes have highest large lake in the world   **A:**250
  picture(s)   **B:**306; **L:**33; **S:**280
Titles (forms of address)   **A:**21–22
Titles (in publishing)   **P:**525
Title search (of land ownership)   **R:**113
Tito, Dennis (American businessman and space tourist)
      S:356
Tito, Marshal (Josip Broz) (Yugoslav political leader)   **T:213;**
      Y:364, 365, 368, 369
  Croatia   **C:**589
  Serbia and Montenegro   **S:**126
  picture(s)   **Y:**364
Titograd (Serbia and Montenegro) *see* Podgorica
Titus (book of the New Testament)   **B:**166, 167
Titus Andronicus (play by Shakespeare)   **S:**139
Titus Flavius Sabinus Vespasianus (Roman emperor)   **R:**316,
      317
Titusville (Florida)   **S:**340
Tiv (people of Nigeria)   **F:**300, 302
TiVo (video recording service)   **V:**332i
Tivoli Gardens (amusement park, Copenhagen, Denmark)
      C:551; **P:**78
Tiwa (Native American language group)   **I:**183
Tiwanaku (early Indians of Bolivia)   **I:**170
TKO (technical knockout, in boxing)   **B:**350b
Tlacopán (city in Aztec empire)   **A:**578
Tlatelolco (city in Aztec empire)   **A:**575

Tlingit (Tlinkit) (Indians of North America)   A:150, 156; I:188
  picture(s)
    carving on house   I:188
T lymphocytes *see* T cells
TNT (Trinitrotoluene) (explosive)   E:422; N:375
Toad of Toad Hall (play by A. A. Milne)   M:311
Toads   A:222–24; F:476–78; H:128; W:145
  picture(s)   A:222; G:91
Toadstools (mushrooms)   M:529
  picture(s)
    bioluminescence   B:205
Toamasina (Madagascar)   M:9
"Toaster, The" (poem by William Jay Smith)   F:123
To a T (saying)   T:1
Toba (Indians of South America)   I:198
Tobacco   T:214–15
  Alcohol and Tobacco Tax and Trade Bureau   T:294–95
  American colonies   C:414; T:177
  avoiding health hazards   H:75
  cancer   C:93, 95
  drug abuse among young people   D:330
  Jamestown crop   J:23; V:358
  Kentucky   K:222
  "money crop" for Virginia colony   T:170
  related to some vegetables   V:290
  seeds   P:313
  smoking   S:207
  picture(s)   A:91; K:219
    Missouri farm   M:368
    South Carolina farm   S:303
    virus infection   V:367
Tobacco mosaic virus   V:362, 363
  picture(s)   V:361, 362, 367
Tobago *see* Trinidad and Tobago
Tobey, Mark (American painter)   W:57
Tobit (apocryphal book of the Bible)   B:163
Toboggans (sleds)   B:270
  picture(s)   U:76
Toccata (musical form)   M:540
Toddy cats (animals) *see* Palm civets
Toes (parts of the feet)   F:79, 81–82, 84
  hoofed mammals   H:216
  primates, characteristics of   P:455
Toffee (candy)
  picture(s)   C:97
Tofutti (frozen dessert)   I:22
Toga (Roman dress)   C:375; R:312
Toggles (fasteners)   N:3
Toggling (method of drying leather)
  picture(s)   L:111
Togo   T:216–17
  map(s)   T:216
  picture(s)
    flag   F:241
    woman spreading corn to dry   T:216
Togo Mountains (Togo)   T:216
Toilets (Water closets)   H:194
  campsite latrines   C:47
  water conservation   W:74
Toilet water (perfumed liquid)   P:150
Toiyabe Range (mountains, Nevada)   N:124
Tojo, Hideki (Japanese prime minister)   W:294, 303 *profile*, 317
  picture(s)   W:303
Tokaimura (Japan)   N:372
Tokamak (machine used to produce a nuclear reaction)   N:368
Tokelau (Pacific island group)   P:10
Tokens (small objects)   N:397
To Kill a Mockingbird (book by Harper Lee)   A:143
Toklas, Alice B. (American literary figure)   S:446
Tokugawa Ieyasu (Japanese statesman and shogun) *see* Ieyasu
Tokugawa period (in Japanese history)   J:43–45, 52, 53

Tokyo (capital of Japan)   T:218–20
  earthquake (1923)   E:40
  Japan's major city   J:43, 45
  World War II   W:300, 317
  picture(s)   A:438d; C:311; J:36
    convenience store   T:219
    Ginza   J:26; T:218
Tokyo Stock Exchange   S:456
Tokyo Tower (Tokyo, Japan)   T:219, 220
Tolbert, William R., Jr. (president of Liberia)   L:168
Toledo (Ohio)   O:72, 75
Toledo (Spain)   S:376
Toledo, Alejandro (president of Peru)   P:165
Toledo, Montes de (Spain)   S:372
Toledo swords   I:337
Toledo War (between Ohio and Michigan territory)   O:75
Tolerance (for drugs)   D:331, 332; N:15
Tolerance, Edict of (1781, granted religious freedom to Austria)   A:524
Toleration Act (Maryland, 1649)   M:133; T:177
Toleware (painted tin objects)   A:316b
Tolkien, J. R. R. (English author)   T:220–22
  fairies   F:12
  The Hobbit, excerpt from   T:221–22
Tollbooths, automated   A:532
Toller, Ernst (German playwright)   D:304
Toll roads *see* Turnpikes
Tolowa (Indians of North America)   I:187
Tolstoi, Leo (Russian novelist, philosopher, and social reformer)   F:115; N:360; R:114, 382; T:222
Toltecs (Indians of North America)   A:244, 578; I:172
Tom (male turkey)   T:350
Tomahawk cruise missile   U:114
  picture(s)   E:162
Tomatoes   T:223; V:289, 290, 291
  genetic engineering   G:85; V:370a
  most popular vegetable   A:91
  picture(s)   T:223
    genetic engineering   B:213
Tomba, Alberto (Italian skier)
  picture(s)   S:184e
Tombaugh, Clyde W. (American astronomer)   A:471; P:341
Tombigbee River (Alabama–Mississippi)   A:132; M:352
Tomb of the Unknown Soldier *see* Unknown Soldier
Tombolos (sandbars that tie islands to the mainland)   M:138
Tombouctou (Timbuktu) (Mali)   A:66; M:61, 62
  picture(s)   A:79d; W:265
Tombs *see also* Catacombs; Cemeteries
  African guardian figures   A:72
  Celtic graves   C:164
  China, ancient   A:242
  Chinese tomb figures   A:356; C:277; P:409–10
  Egyptian art and architecture   A:365; D:70; E:108, 110–17
  funeral customs   F:493
  Italian sculpture   I:392
  Japanese tomb figures   P:410
  Korean murals   K:297
  Mausoleum at Halicarnassus   W:218–19
  pyramids   P:556–58
  Taj Mahal   T:12
  tomb-mosque of Sultan Hasan   I:356
  Unknown Soldier   U:227
  picture(s)
    Celtic crosses in Ireland   I:322
    Chinese tomb figures   A:356; C:277; P:409
    Egyptian tomb painting   E:103
    Neanderthal grave   P:440
    tomb of Emperor Humayun   D:103
Tombstone (Arizona)   A:400
Tombstones (source for genealogical research)
  picture(s)   U:127
Tomislav (Croatian king)   C:589
Tom Jones (novel by Fielding)   E:279–80
Tommy (rock opera by the Who)   R:263

Torsion bars (of suspension systems)   A:551
Torsion waves (of earthquakes) see S-waves
Torso look (in fashion design)   F:65
Tortillas (Mexican food)   B:385; C:558; F:333; M:241
   Guatemala   G:395
   picture(s)
      with grasshoppers   F:332
Tortoise beetle   B:125
Tortoises see Turtles
Tortoiseshell   T:355
Torts (wrongful acts that are not crimes)   L:87
Tortuga (Caribbean island)   C:114
Tortugas see Dry Tortugas
Torture (of people)   R:290
Torvill, Jayne (British ice dancer)   O:107 *profile*
   picture(s)   O:107
Tosas (dogs)   D:250
Tosca (opera by Giacomo Puccini)   O:164
Toscanini, Arturo (Italian conductor)   T:245
Tosks (a people of Albania)   A:159
Tossa del Mar (the Costa Brava, Spain)
   picture(s)   S:372
Tostig (Saxon ruler)   V:343
Totable Tornado Observatory
   picture(s)   W:90
Total impulse (of a rocket)   R:259
Total internal reflection (in optics)   F:106
Totalitarianism (government control by directed election of a
      small group)   G:274
   Fascism   F:63–64
   Nazism   N:78–81
Totality (of an eclipse)   E:51, 52; M:448
Totem poles   I:189; O:127
   British Columbia   B:406b
   Canada's Northwest Coast Indians   C:71
   Totem Bight State Historical Park (Alaska)   A:148
   picture(s)   A:148; C:68; W:19, 228
Totems (emblems)
   Australian Aborigines   A:7
   prehistoric religions   R:147
Toubkal, Jebel (highest peak in Morocco)   M:460
Touch, sense of   B:290
   dogs   D:243
   dolphins   D:276
   fish   F:194
   insects   I:235
   nervous system   N:118
   sharks   S:143
   spiders   S:402
   used by the blind   B:257
Touchback (in football)   F:354, 355
Touchdown (in football)   F:357
Touché (French word for "hit," scoring point in fencing)   F:87
Touch football   F:361
Touch holes (of muzzle-loading weapons)   G:416
"Touching by the king" (medieval remedy for tuberculosis)
      M:206
Touch-me-not (plant)   W:106
   picture(s)   W:105
Touch system (of keyboarding)   T:372
Toughness (of gems)   G:70
Toulon (France)   N:10
Toulouse (France)   F:410
Toulouse-Lautrec, Henri de (French artist)   I:80; T:245–46
   Divan Japonais (lithograph)   G:306
   graphic arts: color lithography   G:308
   posters   P:402
   postimpressionism in France   F:431
   picture(s)
      Jane Avril (poster)   T:245
Toungoo dynasty (of Burma)   M:561
Touraco (bird) see Turaco
Tour de France (bicycle road race)   B:177; P:72
   picture(s)   E:341; F:411
Touré, Ahmed Sékou (Guinean political leader)   G:406b

Touré, Amadou Toumani (president of Mali)   M:62
Touring kayaks (boats)   K:199
Tourism see also Hostels and hosteling; individual city,
      province, state, and country articles
   buses   B:461
   hotels and motels   H:256–59
   Italy's most important industry   I:384
   Los Angeles   L:306
   national parks   N:56–57
   Nevada   N:122, 130, 136
   Niagara Falls   N:242, 243
   ocean liners   O:30–33
   railroads   R:81, 82
   space tourism   S:356
   whale watching   W:153
   picture(s)
      railroads   R:81
Tourist industry see Tourism
Tourmalines (gems)   G:70, 71, 75
   picture(s)   G:70
Tournaments (Tourneys) (medieval mock battles)   K:274
   duels of the Middle Ages   D:349
Tour of the Waterfalls of the Various Provinces (series of prints
   by Hokusai)   H:159d
Touro Synagogue (Newport, Rhode Island)   R:220
   picture(s)   J:145; R:220
Tours, Battle of (732)   B:103f; F:412; R:288; S:375 see also
   Charles Martel
   picture(s)   S:376
Toussaint, Pierre (American slave)
   picture(s)   I:92
Toussaint L'Ouverture (liberator of Haiti)   H:11; T:246
   slavery   S:196 *profile*
   picture(s)   H:11
Tow (monofilament fibers)   F:112
Towa (Native American language group)   I:183
Tower, John (United States senator)   I:310
Tower Bridge (London)
   picture(s)   L:291
Tower Falls (Wyoming)   W:59
Tower of Babel see Babel, Tower of
Tower of London see London, Tower of
Towers (in architecture)
   bell towers (campaniles)   I:393
   Eiffel Tower (Paris)   P:72
   Tower of London   L:292
   picture(s)
      Eiffel Tower (Paris)   P:69
Town crier (town officer who makes proclamations)
   picture(s)   V:307
Townes, Charles (American inventor)   I:283 *profile*
   picture(s)   I:283
Town gas (fuel)   C:390
Town houses   H:193, 195
Town meeting (assembly of town inhabitants to transact public
   business)   C:417; M:515; N:139; T:173; V:316
Towns (units of municipal government)   M:515–16
   Lost Springs (Wyoming) is smallest incorporated town in
      United States   W:334
   New England states' political units   C:518
   Puritan legacies   P:551
Townshend, Pete (English rock musician)   R:263
Townshend Acts (Britain, 1767)   R:196
Township (territorial unit)   M:515
Towton, Battle of (1461)   H:110
Tow trucks
   picture(s)   T:320
Toxicology   F:372–73; P:515
Toxic substances see Poisons
Toxic Substances and Disease Registry, Agency for (United
   States)   H:79; P:514
Toxoid (substance that opposes toxin)   D:203, 211; V:260
Toy dogs   D:246, 260
Toynbee, Arnold (English historian)   E:288
Toynbee Hall (English settlement house)   A:21

Toyota Corona (automobile)
picture(s) A:545
Toyotomi Hideyoshi (Japanese warrior and statesman) see
Hideyoshi
Toys T:247–51
automobile models A:534–35
dollhouses D:260–65
dolls D:266–72
folk art F:295
gyroscope G:436
kaleidoscope K:172
kites K:266b–270
tops T:240
picture(s)
Rhode Island industry R:218
trade show F:15
Toy Story (motion picture, 1995) A:291
picture(s) A:288
Trace elements (required by living organisms in tiny amounts)
F:96; N:425; O:17; V:371
Trace fossils (evidence of ancient animals' activities) F:382
Tracers (radioactive elements) G:61
Tracery (ornamental pattern work) D:75; F:509; G:267–69
picture(s) G:268
Trachea (in respiratory system) see Windpipe
Track and field (sports) T:252–63 see also the names of
athletes
Griffith Joyner, Florence L:308
jogging and running J:111
Lewis, Carl O:106
Olympic Games (2004) O:120
Owens, Jesse O:284
Thorpe, Jim T:183
world records T:261
Tracking (of rockets) R:260
Tracking dogs D:256
Tracking network, Apollo S:340k
Tracking stations (to follow path of a space vehicle) S:340d
Tracks (for athletic events) T:253, 261
Tracks (for railroads) R:77–80, 86–87; T:285
diagram(s) R:78
Tracks (in sound recording) S:266–67
Tracks (of armored tanks) T:14
Tractarians see Oxford Movement
Traction elevators E:185
Tractor (of a truck) see Cab
Tractors (farm machines) F:53–54, 60
earth-moving machinery E:30, 32
tractor pulls F:14
picture(s)
tractor pull F:14
Tractor-trailers T:318
Tracy, Spencer (American actor) W:207 profile
Trade and commerce T:264–65 see also Communication;
Harbors and ports; International trade; Tariff; Trade
routes; the industries and products section of country
articles
agriculture, advances in F:337
ancient civilizations A:228, 230, 236, 237, 240
Britain's lifeblood U:54, 57
China, ancient A:242
cities, growth of C:316–17
colonial America C:419, 420, 421
distribution of natural resources stimulates trade
N:65–66
East India Company E:47
European Union E:368–69
fairs and expositions, importance of F:13–18
fur trade in North America F:519–24
guilds G:403–5
Indian Ocean I:161
Indians, American I:166, 167, 169, 170, 171, 175,
178, 188, 190
international trade I:270–71

ivory trade I:416
Maya A:243–44
Middle Ages M:292–93
money and monetary systems M:412–15
Open-Door Policy M:193–94
prehistoric people P:442
river commerce and trade R:239
seventeenth century W:266
silk trade S:174
spice trade H:120–21
stocks and bonds S:454–59
textile trade, development of T:143–46
transportation, influence on T:281–82, 284
triangular trade (New England–West Indies–Africa)
S:194
Trojan War, cause of T:316
Trade books (publishing term) B:323; C:228; P:523–24
Trade cults see Cargo cults
Trade Expansion Act (United States, 1962) K:209
Trade fairs see Trade shows
Trademarks C:457; D:333; T:266–67
Trade names (of synthetic fibers) N:437, 440
Trade routes T:264, 282
Gama, Vasco da, and a sea route to India E:405–6
Great Lakes and Saint Lawrence Seaway G:326–28;
S:14–15
Panama Canal P:49–51
silk trade S:174
spice trade H:120
Traders Descending the Missouri (painting by Bingham)
picture(s) O:268
Trade shows (of products) F:15–16
development of S:455
fashion modeling M:385
Frankfurt Book Fair P:525
Trades Union Congress (TUC) L:12, 18
Trade Union Act (United States, 1868) L:12
Trade unions see Labor unions
Trade winds T:268
belt in North America N:291
earth's prevailing wind systems W:188–89
El Niño W:83
map(s) T:268
Trading posts F:379; O:276
Tradition see also Folklore; Legends; Superstition
fundamentalist beliefs and practices F:492
Traditional economics E:58
Traditionalist Judaism see Orthodox (Traditionalist) Judaism
Traditional practitioners (of medicine) D:238–39
Traditional religions (of Africa) A:57
Trafalgar, Battle of (1805) E:249; N:11, 104
Trafalgar Square (London) L:294
picture(s) L:293
Traffic control T:269–70
automated traffic lights A:532
bicycles and bicycling B:178
city problems C:319; T:288–89
computerized cars of the future A:556
National Highway Traffic Safety Administration T:293
police P:364
preventive measures for accidents S:3
railroads R:86
Trafficking (of a manuscript) B:326
Tragacanth gum R:185
Tragedy (form of drama) D:297
Greek D:299; G:356
Shakespeare's tragedies S:134
Tragical History of the Life and Death of Dr. Faustus (play by
Christopher Marlowe) M:104
Tragicomedy (form of drama) D:297
Trail drives see Cattle drives
Trail End State Historic Site (Sheridan, Wyoming) W:342
Trailers (for trucks) R:83, 90; T:318–19, 322
Trailers (movable homes) C:44

Trailing arbutus (Mayflower)
   picture(s) **M:**137; **N:**351
Trail of Tears (forced migration of Cherokee Indians) **G:**145;
   I:179; **O:**90, 94; **S:**122
   Alabama **A:**140
   North Carolina **N:**319
   picture(s) **U:**182
Trails, hiking **H:**136
   national scenic trails **N:**55
   picture(s)
      Appalachian National Scenic Trail **N:**49
Trails, overland (in American history) *see* Overland trails
Trained fruit trees **F:**483–84
Trained nurses *see* Registered nurses
Training (of dogs) **D:**259, 260
Training schools (for youthful offenders) **P:**482
Trains (series of gears in timepieces) **C:**369–70; **W:**45
Trains, railroad *see* Railroads
Traitors (spies) **S:**407
Traits (inherited features) **G:**77, 80
Trajan (Roman emperor) **R:**316
Trajectory (of artillery) **G:**425
Trajectory (of spacecraft) **S:**340L
Trajkovski, Boris (president of Macedonia) **M:**4
Tramp clown *see* Character clown
Tranquilizers (drugs) **D:**331
Transactinide elements **E:**170
Trans-Alaska Pipeline (from Prudhoe Bay to Valdez) **A:**152,
   158; **P:**172
   picture(s) **A:**152; **E:**219
Trans-America Building (San Francisco, California)
   picture(s) **S:**31
Transantarctic Mountains (Antarctica) **A:**292
Trans-Atmospheric Vehicles (hypersonic aircraft) **T:**292
   picture(s) **T:**291
Trans-Canada Highway **B:**405; **C:**66; **N:**138c, 143; **O:**130;
   P:462
Transcaucasia **A:**440
   Azerbaijan **A:**573–74
   Georgia, Republic of **G:**147–48
Transcendentalism (philosophy) **A:**210; **R:**304; **T:**181
Transcontinental railroad (United States) **R:**89; **U:**255
   Chinese immigration to the United States **A:**459; **O:**228
   Golden Spike National Historic Site (Utah) **U:**250
   picture(s) **R:**89; **U:**187, 255; **W:**144
Transcontinental Treaty (Adams-Onís Treaty) (1819) **A:**17;
   M:426; **T:**107–8
Transcription (process by which messenger RNA is made)
   B:299
   diagram(s) **B:**299
Transduction (of viruses) **V:**366
Transepts (parts of churches) **A:**369; **C:**134
Trans-fatty acids **O:**80
Transfer printing **D:**378
Transfiguration (of Jesus Christ) **J:**87
Transfiguration, Church of the (Kizhi, Russia)
   picture(s) **R:**375
Transformation geometry **G:**125–26; **M:**169
   picture(s) **G:**126
Transform boundaries (in geology) **E:**12
Transformers (of electric currents) **E:**145; **T:**271–72
Transfusion, blood **T:**273
   ancient Incas **B:**262
   blood types **B:**261
   Drew, Charles R. **D:**325
   how AIDS spreads **A:**100b
Transgenic animals and plants **G:**83, 91
   cotton **C:**569
   mice **G:**82, 85
Transhumance (grazing practice) **H:**138
Transistor radio batteries *see* Nine-volt batteries
Transistors (electronic devices) **T:**276–77, 278
   computer circuits **C:**491, 492
   impurities in crystals **M:**153

   inventions **I:**277, 285
   New Jersey research **N:**179
   properties of crystals **S:**250
   radio **R:**60
   science, milestones in **S:**74
   telecommunications **T:**49
   thermometers **T:**164
   picture(s) **E:**158
Transit (in astronomy)
   Mercury **M:**230
   picture(s)
      Mercury **M:**230
Transit advertising **A:**32
Transitional forms (in evolution) **E:**373–74
Transitional Tool Period (stage in tool use) **T:**234–35
   picture(s) **T:**235
Transition zones (between two types of climate) **C:**364
Transitive verbs **G:**289; **P:**93
Transit malls (city areas which ban automobiles) **B:**460
Transits (instruments that measure angles) **O:**182–83; **S:**520
   picture(s) **S:**519
Transjordan (former name of Jordan) **J:**132; **P:**41
Translation (motion in transformation geometry) *see* Slide
Translation (process by which cells assemble amino acids)
   B:299
   diagram(s) **B:**299
Translational joints (of robot arms) **R:**253
Translational slides (landslides) **A:**558
Translations (of speech or writing from one language to another)
   B:157–58
Transmarine Council (Portuguese colonial rule of Latin America)
   L:58
Transmigration of the soul *see* Reincarnation
Transmission (of Biblical materials) **B:**156–57
Transmission electron microscopes **E:**163–64; **M:**155, 285
   picture(s) **M:**285
Transmissions (in motor vehicles) **A:**540, 548–49; **G:**66;
   T:279–80, 319
Transmitters (in electronics)
   radar systems **R:**38, 73
   radio **R:**53
   telephones **T:**53, 55
   television **T:**61, 62
   diagram(s)
      telephones **T:**53
Transmutation (change of one element to another through
   radioactive decay) **R:**64
Transonic flight (approaching the speed of sound) **S:**499
Transparent materials **L:**141–51, 213; **P:**322
Transpiration (in plants) **L:**117
Transplanting (in gardening) **G:**40
Transplants, hair **H:**6
Transplants of body organs and tissues *See* Organ transplants
Transponder (radar device) **A:**569; **R:**105; **T:**66
Transportation **T:**281–92 *see also* Bridges; Canals;
   Communication; Harbors and ports; Navigation; Roads
   and highways; Subways; Trade routes; Tunnels; the
   transportation section of country, province, and state
   articles
   affects the food supply **F:**351
   Africa **A:**64
   African Americans' civil rights **A:**79L, 79m, 79n
   airplanes **A:**108–21
   airports **A:**126–29
   automobiles **A:**539–56
   aviation **A:**559–72
   bicycling **B:**175–78
   buses **B:**460–61
   canals **C:**88–90
   cities and suburbs, traffic problems of **C:**319, 320
   elevators and escalators **E:**185–88
   environment, effect on **E:**304
   fruit, shipping of **F:**485
   fuel, methods of transporting **F:**490

helicopters, uses of **H:**105
Industrial Revolution in America **I:**224
inventions in **I:**280, 281, 284
kinds of industry **I:**225
lumber and lumbering **L:**339–40
mass marketing **M:**88
methods for conserving energy **E:**223
Mississippi River **M:**357
motorcycles **M:**498–99
New York City **N:**232–33
North America **N:**303–4
ocean liners **O:**30–33
petroleum products, transportation for **P:**172
pioneer life **P:**259–60
pneumatic systems **H:**314
Pony Express **P:**383–84
postal service **P:**396–402
railroads **R:**77–90
refrigeration **R:**135
river commerce and trade **R:**239
Saint Lawrence Seaway **S:**15
ships and shipping **S:**153–59
trade and commerce **T:**264, 265
traffic control **T:**269–70
Transportation, United States Department of **T:**293–94
trucks and trucking **T:**318–22
vector-borne diseases and **V:**285
vegetable shipping **V:**290, 292
water transportation **W:**57
wheels **W:**159–60
Transportation, United States Department of **J:**122; **P:**447;
T:293–94
Transportation Corps (of the United States Army) **U:**102
Transport planes **U:**109
Transposition (in music) **M:**537
Transposition ciphers (in secret writing) **C:**393
Trans-Siberian Railroad **A:**452; **R:**364; **S:**170
picture(s) **R:**365
Transuranium elements **E:**170
Transvaal (historical province of South Africa) **B:**302; **S:**272
Transverse Ranges (California) *see* Los Angeles Ranges
Transylvania (Romania) **R:**297, 299, 300
Transylvania Land Company (in Kentucky) **K:**225
Transylvanian Alps (southeastern Europe) **R:**297
Transylvania University (Lexington, Kentucky) **K:**217
Traoré, Moussa (president of Mali) **M:**62
Trapassi, Pietro (Italian poet) *see* Metastasio, Pietro
Trap-door spiders **S:**404, 405
Trapeze artists (in a circus) **C:**310
picture(s) **C:**309
Trapezoids (geometric forms) **G:**122
Trappers (fur traders) **F:**519–24
Trapping (for furs) **F:**501, 502 *see also* Hunting
Traprock (Trap) (igneous rock) **N:**171
Traps (bends in pipes) **P:**340
Traps (in fishing industry) **F:**220
Traps (rock formations that hold petroleum) **P:**168
diagram(s) **P:**168
Trauma center (hospital equipped to treat people with
life-threatening injuries) **H:**248
Travel *see also* Tourism; the places of interest section of
country, province, state, and city articles
bicycling **B:**175
camping **C:**44–49
hiking and backpacking **H:**134–36
hostels and hosteling **H:**254–55
hotels and motels **H:**256–59
ocean liners **O:**30–33
passports and visas **P:**96
Polo, Marco **P:**380
Public Health Service, inspection by **P:**514–15
vaccination **V:**261
Travel and Tourism Industries, Office of (United States) **C:**455
Traveling cranes (machines) **H:**159c
Travers, Morris William (British chemist) **N:**106

Travers, P. L. (British author and actress) **C:**235 *profile*
picture(s) **C:**234
Traviata, La (opera by Verdi) **O:**164–65
Travis, William B. (American hero of the Alamo) **T:**139
Travois (Native American vehicle) **I:**180
Trawls (fishing nets) **F:**218; **S:**168
picture(s) **F:**219
Tread (of tires) **T:**211
Treading water **S:**532
Treason (act of betraying one's country)
Arnold, Benedict **A:**426
Burr's arrest for treason **B:**456
Treasure Island (book by Stevenson) **M:**563
Treasure State (nickname for Montana) **M:**428, 429, 432
Treasure trove *see* Buried treasure
Treasury, United States Department of the **M:**340; **P:**447;
T:294–95
Treaties (agreements between nations) **T:296–99** *see also* the
names of treaties, as Paris, Treaty of, 1783
disarmament **D:**182
foreign service **F:**371
Geneva Conventions **G:**93
genocide, United Nations definition of **G:**96
inter-American treaties based on Monroe Doctrine **M:**427
international law **I:**267
Paris, many treaties have been signed in **P:**68–69
president of the United States, treaty-making powers of
P:452
Senate's responsibility for ratification **U:**142
Treatises (long written articles) **E:**321
Treble clef (G clef) (in musical notation) **M:**534
Tree ferns **F:**94
Tree frogs
picture(s) **A:**266; **F:**476, 477
Tree Grows in Naples, A (painting by de Kooning)
picture(s) **M:**396
Tree kangaroos **M:**115
picture(s) **M:**114
Tree line *see* Timberline
Tree pythons
picture(s) **A:**266
Tree-ring dating *see* Dendrochronology
Trees **T:300–311** *see also* Forests and forestry; Lumber and
lumbering; the names of trees
acid rain's effects **A:**9
Christmas trees **C:**297–98
cork bark **C:**557
drought worsened by cutting trees **D:**329
felled by beavers **B:**110–11
forests and forestry **F:**374–77
fruitgrowing **F:**481–85
holidays to plant trees **H:**161, 162
leaves **L:**112–18
marked trees for the British Navy **L:**338
nut trees **N:**431–36
papermaking **P:**53, 58
rain forests **R:**99–100
ring counting method of dating **A:**357
rings can provide clues about past climate **C:**363
state **U:**80 *see also* individual state articles for pictures
swamps **W:**146
Why is a tree or an American flag sometimes placed on the
highest part of a building under construction? **B:**436
wood **W:**222–27
picture(s)
lightning strikes **T:**186
natural world of a tree **N:**69
ring counting method of dating **P:**312
Trefoil (three-leafed clover, emblem of Girl Guides and Girl
Scouts) **G:**215
Tremblay, Michel (Canadian writer) **C:**87
Tremolite (mineral) **A:**438c
Tremolo (in music) **M:**537
Trenches (field fortifications) **F:**378, 379; **W:**282
picture(s) **W:**276

Trenches (in the ocean floor)   E:12, 18; O:21
Trenching machines   E:31–32
Trent, Council of (1545–1563)   C:293; G:377; R:132, 291
Trentino (Italy)   I:390
Trenton (capital of New Jersey)   N:174; R:202
  picture(s)   N:175
Trenton, Battle of (1776)   W:40
Trepanation (Trephining) (surgical procedure)   M:206; S:512
Trésaguet, Pierre-Marie (French road builder)   R:248
Très riches heures (prayer book illustrated by the Limbourg
    brothers)   F:423
Trevi Fountain (Rome, Italy)   F:394; R:306
  picture(s)   R:306
Trevino, Lee (American golfer)   G:259 profile
  picture(s)   G:259
Trevithick, Richard (English inventor)   A:539; L:287; R:87;
    S:445; T:285
Trezzini, Domenico (Italian architect)   R:376
Triacetate fibers   F:110
Triad (musical chord)   M:533, 537
Trial, The (novel by Kafka)   G:182
Trial balance (in bookkeeping)   B:312
Trial by jury (in the Sixth Amendment to the United States
    Constitution)   B:182; L:90
Trial by Jury (operetta by Gilbert and Sullivan)   G:208
Trial (Petit) jury   J:163
Trials (in law)   C:575–76
  journalism, issues in   J:137
  jury   J:163–64
  juvenile crimes   J:170
  law enforcement   L:90
  Magna Carta guaranteed jury trials   M:26
  picture(s)
    court officer swearing in a witness   L:88
Triangle (in geometry)   G:121; T:312–13
  diagram(s)   G:121
Triangle (musical instrument)   M:551; P:149
  picture(s)   M:551
Triangle (used in mechanical drawing)   M:200
Triangle Shirtwaist Company fire (New York City, 1911)   F:146
Triangular numbers   N:382, 387–88
Triangular trade (New England–West Indies–Africa)   S:194
Triangulation (in surveying)   O:182; S:520
Trianon, Treaty of (1920)   H:299; W:291
Triassic period (in geology)   E:25, 28
  dinosaurs   D:166, 170–71, 172, 174
  mass extinction   E:425, 426
  plants   F:387
  picture(s)
    dinosaurs   D:166
    drifting continents   G:113
  table(s)   F:384
Triatomine bugs   V:284
Tribal homelands (Bantustans) (South Africa)   S:269, 270
Tribes and tribal life
  Africa   A:60–61
  Arabs   A:344
  clothing, development of   C:372
  dance celebrations   D:22
  economics   E:58–59
  Germanic or Teutonic   M:289
  Gypsies   G:434–35
  Indians, American   I:162–201
  jungle life   J:158
  Kyrgyzstan   K:313
  Turkmenistan   T:351
Tribhuwan (king of Nepal)   N:110
Triborough Bridge (New York City)   N:233
Tribunals (military courts)   T:117
Tribunes (Roman officials)   R:311, 313
Tributaries (of rivers)   R:235
Tribute (payment)
  ancient civilizations, characteristics of   A:228
  Andorra's payment to France and Spain   A:252–53

Aztec society   A:244, 576
  Hittites   H:155
  pirates   P:263
Tribute Money, The (fresco by Masaccio)
  picture(s)   P:20
Tricarboxylic acid cycle (TCA cycle) (in metabolism)   B:186
Triceps muscles   M:518
  picture(s)   M:519
Triceratops (dinosaur)   D:176
Trichinosis (muscle infection)   D:207
Trickle method (of irrigation)   I:341
Trick Mules Puzzle   P:553
Trick or treat (Halloween custom)   H:13
Tricks
  magic   M:22–25
  number tricks   N:392
Trickster tales
  African stories   A:76b
  coyote in Native American folktales   F:316
  Hermes in Greek mythology   G:362
  Loki in Norse mythology   N:278
  Native American folktales and mythology   F:307;
    M:571–72
Triclinic crystal system (in chemistry)   C:604
  picture(s)   C:603
Triconodon (prehistoric mammal)
  picture(s)   P:434
Tricornes (hats)   C:377
Trictrac (game) see Backgammon
Tricuspid valve (of the heart)   H:80
Tricycle gear (airplane landing gear)   A:114
Trident (missile)   U:114
Trieste (bathyscaphe)   U:27
Trieste (Italy)   I:385, 390
Triggerfish   F:188, 199, 200–201
Triglav, Mount (Slovenia)   S:203
Triglycerides (fats and oils)   B:296; O:79–80
  diagram(s)   B:297
Trigonometry (branch of mathematics)   M:157; T:312–13
  mathematics, history of   M:163, 164
Triiodothyronine (hormone)   H:227
Trill (in music)   M:537
Trillium (Wake-robin; Birthroot) (plant)
  picture(s)   O:125
Trilobites (extinct sea-dwelling creatures)   E:27; F:385, 387
  picture(s)   E:26, 425; F:382
Trim (page size)   B:325
Trimarans (three-hulled boats)   S:8
Trimmers (tools)   L:342
Trimming the sails (on a sailboat)   S:11
Trim tabs (control surfaces of an airplane)   A:114
Trinidad (Bolivia)   B:308
Trinidad and Tobago   T:314–15
  Caribbean Sea and islands   C:113, 114, 115
  Latin America   L:49, 50, 51
  map(s)   T:314
  picture(s)
    flag   F:241
    Port-of-Spain   T:314
Trinitrotoluene see TNT
Trinity (Christian doctrine)   C:287; P:490; R:148, 283
Trinity College (Hartford, Connecticut)   C:513
Trinity River (Texas)   T:127
Trinity Site (New Mexico)   N:188
Triodes (three-part vacuum tubes)   R:58
Tripe (variety meat)   M:196
Tripitaka (Three Baskets) (sacred Buddhist writings)   B:424,
  425
Triple Alliance (Germany, Austria-Hungary, Italy)   W:277
Triple Alliance, War of the (1864–1870)   P:65; S:295
Triple Crown (in horse racing)   H:234
Triple crown (in horse racing)   K:227
Triple Dip (screen print by Ben Shahn)   G:306
Triple Entente (France, England, and Russia, 1907)   W:278

Triple jump (track event)   T:257
    world record   T:261
Triplets (multiple birth)   B:3; T:364
Tripods (in photography)   P:202
Tripoli (capital of Libya)   L:188, 189
    picture(s)   L:189
Tripoli (Lebanon)   L:121
Tripoli, County of (Crusader state)   C:600
Tripolitania (region of Libya)   L:188
Trip to the Moon, A (motion picture, 1902)   M:487; S:83
Trireme galleys (ships)
    picture(s)   T:283
Trisomy 21 *see* Down syndrome
Tristan da Cunha Islands (in South Atlantic)   I:368
Tristan und Isolde (opera by Richard Wagner)   O:165
    romance by Gottfried von Strassburg   G:176
Tristram (knight of King Arthur's court)   A:438; F:436
Tristram Shandy (novel by Laurence Sterne)   E:280
Tritemnodon (prehistoric mammal)
    picture(s)   P:434
Triticale (grain)   G:286
Tritium (form of hydrogen)   A:486; H:316; N:367, 375
Triton (moon of Neptune)   N:113; P:282; S:52; V:386
    picture(s)   N:113
Triton shell
    picture(s)   S:149
Triumph (ceremonial entrance of a victorious general into a
    city)   P:61
Triumph of Divine Providence, The (fresco by Cortona)
    B:64–65
    picture(s)   B:63
Triumvirate (Roman government)   A:317; R:315–16
Trivial Pursuit (game)   G:17, 21
Trobriand Islands (in the South Pacific Ocean)   A:304
Trochees (metrical feet in poetry)   P:351
Trogon (bird)
    picture(s)   B:235
Troilus and Cressida (play by Shakespeare)   S:139
Troilus and Criseyde (poem by Chaucer)   C:191
Trois Frères, Les (cave, France)   P:437
Trojan asteroids   C:450
Trojan horse (in Greek mythology)   G:369; T:316
    picture(s)   G:368
Trojan War   G:340, 368–69; T:316
    Homer's poems   G:354–55; H:184
    Iliad   I:61
    picture(s)
        painting of capture of Troy   T:316
Trolley cars *see* Streetcars and trolleycars
Trolling (in fishing)   B:268; F:219
Trollope, Anthony (English novelist)   E:286
Trombone (musical instrument)   M:550; O:194, 196; W:185
    picture(s)   M:550; W:185
Tromsø (Norway)   N:348
Trona (mineral)   W:338, 340
Trøndelag (region of Norway)   N:345, 346
Troodos Mountains (Cyprus)   C:616
Trooper of the Plains (sculpture by Remington)
    picture(s)   U:130
Trooping the Colour (British military spectacle)   H:165; U:50
Troops (social groups of monkeys)   M:422
Troop units (United States Army)   U:103, 104
Tropical depressions (cyclones)   H:302
Tropical fish (as pets)   F:204
Tropical fruit   T:317
    fruitgrowing   F:481
    pineapple   P:249
Tropical Prediction Center (Miami, Florida)   W:93
Tropical public health   P:515
Tropical rain forests *see* Rain forests
Tropical storms   H:302, 304
Tropical year   T:202
Tropics (torrid zone)
    agriculture   A:91, 92

    climates   C:362
    dams and global warming   D:20
    jungles   J:157
    ocean life   O:23, 26
    plant varieties   P:293
    rain forests   R:99–100
    picture(s)
        birds   B:245
Tropinin, Vasili (Russian painter)   R:377
Tropisms (movements of plants in response to stimuli)   E:395;
    K:256; L:197
    picture(s)   P:314
Tropopause (atmospheric boundary)   A:481–82
Troposphere (bottom layer of Earth's atmosphere)   A:481–82;
    E:21; J:93; W:79
Trot (gait of a horse)   H:234–35
    picture(s)   H:232
Trotsky, Leon (Russian revolutionist)   U:37 *profile*, 41, 42
    picture(s)   U:37
Trotting races *see* Harness racing
Troubadours and trouvères (French poet musicians)   F:436,
    444; M:297
Trough collector systems (solar energy)   S:240
Trout (fish)   F:213; I:53; N:183; R:177
    picture(s)   F:211, 213
    table(s)
        United States aquaculture production   F:208
Trouvères *see* Troubadours and trouvères
Trovatore, Il (opera by Verdi)   O:165
Trovoada, Miguel (president of São Tomé and Príncipe)   S:41
Troy (ancient city of Asia Minor)   A:441; G:368–69; I:61;
    S:59; T:316
Troyes, Chrétien de (French poet) *see* Chrétien de Troyes
Troyes, Treaty of (1420)   E:241; H:109, 293
Troy pound (measure of weight)   F:18; W:115
Truce, flag of   F:247
Truce of God   F:103
Trucial States *see* United Arab Emirates
Truck cranes (machines)   H:159c
Truckee (Paiute Indian chief)   O:280
Truckee River (California–Nevada)   N:124, 125; O:280
Trucks (frames holding a locomotive's small wheels)   L:286
Trucks and trucking   T:318–22
    dump trucks   E:32
    Federal Motor Carrier Safety Administration   T:293
    forklift trucks   H:159c
    freight carriers   T:289
    ore trucks   M:323
    railroad "piggyback" service   R:83, 84, 85, 90
    refrigeration systems   R:135
    right-side steering wheels for mail carriers   P:398
Trudeau, Pierre Elliott (prime minister of Canada)   C:85; T:322
    picture(s)   C:74; T:322
Trudgen (swimming stroke)   S:536
Trudgen, John (English athlete)   S:536
True Cross (symbol of the Crusades)   C:598
True Story of Ah Q, The (book by Lu Xun)   C:279
Truffaut, François (French film director)   M:494
Trujillo (Peru)   P:163, 164
Trujillo Molina, Rafael Leonidas (Dominican political leader)
    D:283
Truk (Pacific island) *see* Chuuk
Truman, Bess Wallace (wife of Harry S. Truman)   F:178
    picture(s)   F:178
Truman, Harry S. (33rd president of the United States)
    T:323–27; U:196–97
    atomic attack on Japan   J:47; W:317, 318
    Harry S. Truman Home   M:366
    Harry S. Truman Library-Museum   M:370
    vice presidency   V:330 *profile*
    White House   W:166
    picture(s)   M:378; P:452; T:323
        with Benny, Jack   T:326
        childhood   T:324

Truman, Harry S.
   picture(s) (cont.)
      with de Gaulle, Charles **T:**325
      "Dewey Defeats Truman" headline **U:**196
      Harry S. Truman Home **M:**370
      with Stalin at Potsdam Conference **S:**419
Truman Doctrine (foreign policy) **C:**400; **M:**110; **T:**326; **U:**197
Trumbo, Dalton (American film writer) **U:**13
Trumbull, John (American painter) **C:**521 *profile;* **U:**128
Trumbull, Jonathan (American political leader and Revolutionary War patriot) **C:**521 *profile*
Trumka, Richard (American labor leader)
   picture(s) **L:**3
Trümmelbach Falls (Switzerland) **W:**59
Trumpet (musical instrument) **M:**550; **O:**194, 196
   picture(s) **M:**550; **W:**185
Trumpeter swans (birds) **D:**348
   picture(s) **B:**231, 236
Trumpet shell
   picture(s) **S:**149
Trunk (of the elephant) **E:**180
Trunks (of trees) **T:**306–7
Trunnions (gun barrel supports) **G:**425
Truss (in architecture) **B:**439
Truss bridges **B:**396
   table(s)
      notable bridges of the world **B:**400
Truss type (of airplane fuselage) **A:**110
Trust (in people) **L:**194
Trust departments (at banks) **B:**57–58
Trusteeship Council, United Nations **U:**66
Trusts and monopolies *see* Monopolies and trusts
Trust territories
   United Nations **U:**66
   United States **T:**113; **U:**85
Trust Territory of the Pacific Islands **P:**7; **T:**113; **U:**85
   Caroline Islands **P:**87
   Marshall Islands were part of **M:**113
   Micronesia, Federated States of **M:**280
   Palau was the last territory **P:**40b
Truth (philosophical principle and value) **L:**194
   Is the news truth? **N:**198
   myth and truth **M:**575–76
Truth, Sojourner (American antislavery speaker) **A:**6a *profile*
   grave in Battle Creek (Michigan) **M:**262
Truth quark (subatomic particle) *see* Top quark
Trypsin (digestive enzyme) **D:**164
Tryptophan (amino acid) **V:**370c
Tsar (title of Russian rulers) *see* Czar
Tsarskoye Selo (Russia) *see* Pushkin (Russia)
Tsavo Park (Kenya) **A:**53
Tschaikovsky, Peter Ilyich (Russian composer) *see* Tchaikovsky, Peter Ilyich
Tsetse flies **T:**17; **V:**284
   picture(s) **V:**285
Tshombe, Moïse Kapenda (African political leader) **C:**503
Tsientang Kiang (tidal bore, China) **T:**197
Tsimshian (Indians of North America) **A:**150, 156; **I:**188
Tsiolkovsky, Konstantin Eduardovich (Russian scientist) **R:**257
Tsiranana, Philibert (Malagasy president) **M:**9
T-square (used in mechanical drawing) **M:**200
Tsugaru Strait (Japan) **T:**339
Tsunameters **T:**328
Tsunamis (sometimes called **Tidal waves**) **E:**41; **H:**53; **O:**19; **T:**327–28
   South Asia (2004) **A:**457; **B:**465; **I:**134, 212; **T:**152, 327
Tsushima Strait, Battle of (1905)
   picture(s) **J:**45
Tswana (a people of Botswana) **B:**344
TTY's *see* Teletypewriters
Tuamotu Islands (Pacific Ocean) **P:**10
Tuareg (a people of Africa) **B:**453; **M:**61, 62; **N:**251, 252; **S:**7

Tuataras (reptiles) **N:**238–39; **R:**180
   picture(s) **E:**211; **R:**180
Tuatha de Danann (fairies) **F:**11
Tub, The (drawing by Degas)
   picture(s) **I:**105
Tuba (musical instrument) **M:**550–51; **O:**194, 196
   picture(s) **M:**550; **W:**185
Tubac (Arizona) **A:**402
Tubal ligation (surgical sterilization of a woman) **B:**250b
Tubb, Ernest (American singer) **C:**571
Tube anemones (coelenterates) **J:**77
Tube feet (of starfishes) **S:**426–27
   picture(s) **S:**426
Tuberculosis (disease) **D:**188; **L:**345; **M:**206; **T:328–29**
   Bissell, Emily Perkins, fought against **D:**100
   cows are inspected for **D:**212
   Koch finds a way to test for **K:**291
   medieval remedy for **M:**206
   picture(s)
      bacterium **M:**206
      X-ray of infected lungs **D:**204; **T:**328
Tuberous roots **G:**41
Tubers (underground stems) **G:**41; **P:**304, 305
   garden selection **G:**29
   potatoes **F:**329; **P:**403–4
Tubes, steel **I:**337
Tubing (water sport)
   picture(s) **N:**211
Tubman, Harriet (abolitionist leader) **T:329;** **U:**16 *profile,* 17
   African American history **A:**79f
   picture(s) **U:**16
Tubman, William Vacanarat Shadrach (president of Liberia) **L:**168
Tu B'Shevat (Jewish holiday) *see* New Year of the Trees
Tubules (in the kidneys) **K:**243, 244
Tubulidentata (order of mammals)
   picture(s)
      aardvark as example **M:**72
Tuck (diving position) **D:**225
   picture(s) **D:**224
Tucker, Richard (American opera singer) **O:**141 *profile*
Tucker, Tanya (American singer) **C:**573
Tucker, William (first African American born in what is now the United States) **A:**79c
Tuck Everlasting (book by Natalie Babbitt) **C:**239
Tucson (Arizona) **A:**396, 397, 399, 401, 402; **T:**330
   picture(s) **W:**79
Tucumán (Argentina) **A:**386b
Tudjman, Franjo (Croatian president) **C:**589
Tudor, Antony (English choreographer) **B:**31, 33
Tudor, House of (English royal family) **E:**242–44; **H:**114
Tudor style (in English architecture) **E:**258
   picture(s) **E:**258
Tuesday (day of the week) **D:**46
   Mardi Gras (fat Tuesday) **C:**116; **R:**154
Tuff (a rock) **R:**267; **V:**383
Tufting (carpet weaving process) **R:**355
Tugboats **S:**155
   picture(s) **R:**239; **T:**290
Tugela Falls (South Africa) **W:**58, 59
Tug of war (game)
   picture(s) **O:**114
Tuileries, Jardin des (Paris) **P:**70
Tuition (paid to universities and colleges) **U:**224
Tukano (Native American language) **I:**197
Tuktut Nogait National Park (Northwest Territories, Canada) **N:**343
Tukulor (a people of Africa) **M:**179; **S:**117
Tukulti-Ninurta I (king of Assyria) **A:**462
Tula (Toltec city, Mexico) **A:**244, 578
Tularemia (disease) **T:**192; **V:**284
Tulips (flowers) **G:**42; **M:**262; **P:**305
   picture(s) **E:**350; **G:**36, 43; **N:**119; **P:**304
      Oregon crop **O:**209

Turkey
> picture(s) (cont.)
>> people **T:**344
>> pottery **P:**410
>> shepherd women **M:**298

Turkeys (birds) **P:**417; **T:350**
> picture(s) **B:**218; **P:**416; **T:**350

Turkey vultures **V:**394

Turkish crescent (percussion instrument) **P:**149
> picture(s) **P:**149

Turkish language **M:**299; **T:**345

Turkish Ottoman Empire see Ottoman Empire

Turkmen (Turkomans) (a people of Asia) **A:**43; **T:**351

Turkmenistan **T:351–52; U:**34
> map(s) **T:**351
> picture(s)
>> flag **F:**241
>> people **T:**351

Turkmen language **T:**351

Turkomans (a people of Asia) see Turkmen

Turks (a people of Asia) **A:**444; **T:**345
> Azerbaijan **A:**573, 574
> battles **B:**103d
> Byzantine Empire conquered by **B:**494, 496
> Crusades against **C:**598–600
> Union of Soviet Socialist Republics **U:**34, 35, 36
> Uzbekistan **U:**257–58
> picture(s) **T:**344

Turks and Caicos Islands (Caribbean Sea) **T:353**

Turku (Åbo) (Finland) **F:**137, 138, 139

Turmeric (spice product) **R:**184

Turn (motion in transformation geometry) **G:**126

Turn-and-bank indicator (in airplanes) **A:**118

Turner, Benjamin (American politician)
> picture(s) **U:**143

Turner, Frederick Jackson (American historian) **W:**207 profile

Turner, John Napier (Canadian prime minister) **C:**85; **T:354**

Turner, Joseph Mallord William (English painter) **T:354**
> English landscape painting **E:**262; **P:**27
> impressionism, influence on **I:**105
> modern art **M:**387
> watercolor painting **W:**56
> picture(s)
>> "Fighting Temeraire" Tugged To Her Last Berth (painting) **E:**262
>> Peace: Burial at Sea (painting) **T:**354
>> The Snow Storm (painting) **P:**26
>> View of Lucerne (painting) **W:**56

Turner, Nat (American preacher and leader of a slave revolt) **A:**79f; **S:**197 profile; **V:**360

Turnips **A:**98; **V:**287, 290

Turn of the Screw, The (book by Henry James) **J:**20

Turnpikes (toll roads) **R:**249

Turnstones (birds)
> picture(s) **B:**235

Turpentine **D:**341; **R:**184

Turquino, Pico (highest peak in Cuba) **C:**607

Turquoises (gems) **G:**69, 74, 75
> picture(s) **E:**409; **G:**74; **N:**127

Turret (machine gun mounting) **T:**14

Tursiops see Bottlenose dolphins

Turtle (early American submarine) **C:**514; **S:**473
> picture(s) **S:**474

Turtle Mountains (North Dakota–Manitoba) **N:**324

Turtles **T:355–58**
> Galápagos Islands (Ecuador) **E:**67
> hero in African trickster tales **A:**76b
> life spans **A:**83
> pets **P:**179
> reptiles **R:**180
> sea turtles **H:**199, 202; **O:**25
> picture(s)
>> biologist studying nesting site **T:**357
>> Eastern box turtle **T:**355
>> Florida soft-shelled turtle **T:**355
>> Galápagos Islands (Ecuador) **E:**66; **T:**356
>> giant tortoise **R:**180
>> hawksbill turtle **T:**355
>> migration route **H:**201
>> sea turtles **P:**9; **T:**357
>> snapping turtle **W:**145

Tuscan Sea see Tyrrhenian Sea

Tusitala ("teller of tales") (nickname for Robert Louis Stevenson) **S:**449

Tuskalusa (Native American chieftain) **A:**139

Tuskegee Airmen (African American pilots in World War II)
> picture(s) **W:**292

Tuskegee Institute (Alabama) **A:**79h, 138; **C:**130; **W:**28

Tuskegee University (Alabama) **A:**135

Tusks (of animals)
> elephants **E:**181
> hoofed mammals **H:**216, 218, 220
> ivory **I:**415–16
> narwhals **W:**151
> walruses **W:**6

Tusk shells (mollusks) **M:**407; **S:**151
> picture(s) **S:**151

Tutankhamen (Egyptian king) **A:**352; **E:**109
> picture(s)
>> tomb **A:**352
>> treasures from his tomb **A:**115; **D:**70; **E:**99

Tutsi (a people of Africa)
> Burundi **B:**458, 459
> genocide of **G:**96; **U:**71
> Rwanda **R:**388, 389

Tutti (musical term) **M:**537

Tuttle Creek Lake (Kansas) **K:**179

Tutwiler, Julia Strudwick (American educator and social reformer) **A:**143 profile

Tuvalu (Pacific island group) **T:359**
> picture(s)
>> flag **F:**241

Tuyeres (in a Bessemer process furnace) **I:**333

Tuz, Lake (Turkey) **T:**346

TVA see Tennessee Valley Authority

Tvardovsky, Alexander (Russian poet) **R:**384

TV Guide (magazine) **M:**20

TV Ontario (television network) **O:**130

Twa (a people of Rwanda and Burundi) **B:**458, 459; **R:**388

Twain, Mark (Samuel Langhorne Clemens) (American writer) **A:**212; **T:360–62**
> "The Celebrated Jumping Frog of Calaveras County," excerpt from **T:**362
> children's literature **C:**236
> circus **C:**310
> description of the Mississippi River **M:**364
> home (Hannibal, Missouri) **M:**366
> humorous observations quoted **H:**292
> Mark Twain House (Hartford, Connecticut) **C:**514
> novels **F:**115; **N:**360
> quoted **Q:**22
> quoted on dogs **D:**250
> Tom Sawyer, The Adventures of, excerpt from **T:**361–62
> typewriters, history of **T:**374
> picture(s) **M:**378
>> The Adventures of Huckleberry Finn **N:**361
>> house (Hartford, Connecticut) **C:**514

Tweed, William Marcy (American political boss) **C:**127; **N:**17, 233 profile

Tweed carpets **R:**355

Tweed River (England–Scotland) **E:**233; **U:**52

Tweeters (of loudspeakers) **H:**133; **S:**267b

Twelfth Amendment (to the United States Constitution) **E:**132; **U:**156–57; **V:**326–27

Twelfth Night see Epiphany

Twelfth Night, or What You Will (play by Shakespeare) **S:**139

Twelve Apostles see Apostles, The

Twelve labors of Heracles (in Greek mythology) **G:**365–67

Twelve Million Black Voices (book by Wright) **W:**327

PHOTO CREDITS

The following list credits the sources of photos used in THE NEW BOOK OF KNOWLEDGE. Credits are listed, by page, photo by photo—left to right, top to bottom. Wherever appropriate, the name of the photographer has been listed with the source, the two being separated by a dash. When two or more photos by different photographers appear on one page, their credits are separated by semicolons.

T

Cover © Barbara Penoyar—Photodisc Green/Getty Images
3 The White House Collection, © copyright White House Historical Association; This painting by Ken Marschall has been taken from *The Discovery of the Titanic* by Dr. Robert Ballard, published by Warner—Madison Press Books and is protected by copyright as provided.
4 The White House Collection, © copyright White House Historical Association
5 The Granger Collection
6 The Granger Collection
7 © David R. Frazier
8 © SuperStock
9 © Chris Stowers—Panos Pictures
10 © Egert—Bavaria Bildagentur
11 © Naomi Duguid—Asia Access
12 © Steve Vidler—Leo de Wys
13 © Israel Talby—Woodfin Camp & Associates
16 © age fotostock/SuperStock; © Thomas Schmitt—The Image Bank/Getty Images; © Albert Normandin—Masterfile.
17 Digital Vision Ltd./SuperStock
18 © David Else—Lonely Planet Images
19 © Alison Wright—Corbis
21 Victoria and Albert Museum—Art Reference Bureau; Courtesy of The Metropolitan Museum of Art, Cloister Collection, Gift of John D. Rockefeller, 1937; Paris Museum, Versailles—Art Reference Bureau.
22 Courtesy of Museum of Contemporary Crafts of American Craftsmen's Council
23 UPI/Corbis-Bettmann
24 The Alan Mason Chesney Medical Archives of The Johns Hopkins Medical Institutions
26 © Danielle Pellegrini—Photo Researchers
27 © E. R. Degginger—Animals Animals; © Biophoto Associates/Science Source/Photo Researchers; © Rod Planck—Photo Researchers; © Michael Ederegger—DRK Photo; © Phil Degginger—Animals Animals.
30 The White House Collection, © copyright White House Historical Association

32 The White House Collection, © copyright White House Historical Association; The Granger Collection.
34 © Luis Villota—The Stock Market
35 © Topham—The Image Works
36 The Bettmann Archive
37 © Ken Sherman—Bruce Coleman Inc.
39 © Barry Gay—The Image Bank
45 © Bill Foley—Bruce Coleman Inc.
47 Bettmann—Gendreau/Corbis
48 © Jon Feingersh—The Stock Market
49 © Donna Cox/Bob Patterson—NCSA, University of Illinois at Champaign
50 © Intel Corporation
51 Brown Brothers
54 Archive Photos
55 © Gary A. Conner—PhotoEdit; © Myrleen Ferguson—PhotoEdit; © Bruce Laurance—Liaison Agency.
56 Loral Space & Communications Ltd.; © Dan Bosler—Stone.
57 Ryan Steinberg & Family, Adam Block, NOAO, AURA, NSF; © Tony Freeman—PhotoEdit; © Tony Freeman—PhotoEdit.
59 University of California & W. M. Keck Observatory
60 © Gianni Tortoli—Photo Researchers
61 © SONY; Ted Horowitz—The Stock Market; © Jose L. Pelaez—The Stock Market.
63 © Eric Berndt—Midwestock
65 © Everett Collection
66 © Courtesy, Philips Electronics
67 © Shahn Kermani—Liaison Agency; © Michael Newman—PhotoEdit.
68 © Mark Richards—PhotoEdit
70 © CBS Photo Archive; © Archive Photos; © Archive Photos.
71 © Richard Termine—Children's Television Workshop; © Fotos International/Archive Photos; © Everett Collection; © Warner Bros./Archive Photos.
72 SuperStock
75 © Werner Bertsch—Bruce Coleman Inc.; © Jim Amos—Photo Researchers; © Frank Siteman—New England Stock Photo.
76 © John Elk III—Stock, Boston
77 © Bruce Roberts—Photo Researchers
78 © William Johnson—Stock, Boston; Memphis Convention & Visitors Bureau.
79 © Jonathan Daniel—Allsport
80 © Chad Ehlers—Photo Network; © Jeff Greenberg—Photo Researchers.
81 © William Strode—Woodfin Camp & Associates; © Karen Kasmauski—Woodfin Camp & Associates.
82 © Jim Schwabel—New England Stock Photo; © Phyllis Picardi—Photo Network; © Dennis MacDonald—Photo Network; © Nancy Hoyt Belcher—Photo Network.
83 © Andre Jenny—New England Stock Photo
86 Brown Brothers; UPI/Corbis-Bettmann.
87 Brown Brothers
88 © Mark Thompson—Allsport; © Clive Brunskill—Allsport.
89 © Art Seitz—Liaison Agency
90 © Trevor Jones—Allsport
91 © Focus on Sports
92 © Bob Martin—Allsport
93 © Focus on Sports
95 © Focus on Sports; © De Waele/Photo News—Liaison Agency; © Focus on Sports.
96 © AP/Wide World Photos; © Steve Powell—Allsport; UPI/Corbis-Bettmann; © Caryn Levy—Allsport; © Tony Duffy—Allsport; © Clive Burnskill—Allsport; © Focus on Sports; © Chuck Solomon—Focus on Sports.
97 AP/Wide World Photos; © Hulton Deutsch—Allsport; © Focus on Sports; © Steve Powell—Allsport; UPI/Corbis-Bettmann; © Bob Martin—Allsport; © Focus on Sports; UPI/Corbis-Bettmann.
98 © Rick Stevens—AP/Wide World Photos
99 © Focus on Sports
100 The National Gallery, London
101 The Granger Collection
102 © George H. Harrison—Grant Heilman Photography
103 The Butler Institute of American Art
105 From the collection of the Louisiana State Museum Collection
108 The Anne S. K. Brown Military Collection, Brown University Library
111 Library of Congress
116 © al-Jazeera—AP/Wide World Photos
117 © Sergei Grits—AP/Wide World Photos
118 © Jim Cronk
125 © Chad Ehlers—Photo Network; © SuperStock; © Lindsay Hebberd—Woodfin Camp & Associates.
126 © Robert E. Pelham—Bruce Coleman Inc.; © Lindsay Hebberd—Woodfin Camp & Associates; © Michael Shedlock—New England Stock Photo.
128 © Alan Blank—Bruce Coleman Inc.
129 © SuperStock; © Michael Shedlock—New England Stock Photo.
130 © Carolyn Brown—Photo Researchers
131 Texas Medical Center; © Jan Halaska—Photo Researchers; © Charles Thatcher—Stone.
132 © Robert E. Daemmrich—Stone; © John Elk III—Bruce Coleman Inc.; © Michael J. Howell—New England Stock Photo.
133 © Lindsay Hebberd—Woodfin Camp & Associates
134 © SuperStock
137 © Jean Higgins—New England Stock Photo
138 UPI/Corbis-Bettmann; The Granger Collection.
139 UPI/Corbis-Bettmann; The Granger Collection.
140 Brown Brothers
141 The Textile Museum, Washington, D.C., 91.729; Trans. No 2314 (5). Courtesy Department Library Services, American Museum of Natural History; Neg. No. 103814. Courtesy Department Library Services, American Museum of Natural History.
142 The Textile Museum, Washington, D.C., (1995.5.4), The Ruth Lincoln Fisher Memorial Fund.
143 © Erich Lessing—Art Resource; © Reno Gazette-Journal, Lisa J. Tolda—AP/Wide World Photos.
144 © UCLA Fowler Museum of Cultural History. Photo by Denis J. Nervig; The Textile Museum, Washington, D.C. 1977.18.
145 Arizona State Museum, University of Arizona. L. F. H. Lowe, photographer; Old Economy Village, Ambridge, PA; Philadelphia Museum of Art: Given by Joseph B. Hodgson, Jr.
147 The Bettmann Archive
148 © Buddy Mays—Travel Stock; Travel Pix/Taxi/Getty Images; © K. Hanel—The Zefa Collection/Masterfile.
150 © Steve Vidler—SuperStock; © Bruno Barbey—Magnum Photos.
151 © Steve Vidler—SuperStock
152 © Hulton/Archive by Getty Images
153 Courtesy of Pilgrim Society
154 Courtesy of the Norman Rockwell Museum, Permission of Norman Rockwell Estate
156 © Frank Jensen—The Stock Solution; © Arena Stage, Washington, D.C.; © David M. Thum—Playhouse Square Foundation.
157 © Fabian—Corbis-Sygma; © Mary Kate Denny—PhotoEdit.
158 © M. Franck—Magnum Photos; © Anna E. Zuckerman—PhotoEdit.
160 UPI/Corbis-Bettmann; © Peter C. Jones/Alex Gotfryd—Corbis-Bettmann.
161 Corbis-Bettmann; Hulton Deutsch Collection Limited—Woodfin Camp & Associates.
163 © Roy Vazquez
166 The Granger Collection
167 The Granger Collection
168 The Granger Collection
171 The Granger Collection
172 The Granger Collection
174– The Granger Collection
175
177 The Granger Collection
179 The Granger Collection
181 The Granger Collection
182 The Bettmann Archive
184 © Thomas Ives
186 © Richard E. Orville—State University of New York at Albany; © Adrian Davies—Bruce Coleman Inc.
188 Copyright 1932, 1960, James Thurber, from The Seal in the Bedroom, published by Harper and Row.
189 © Li Wei—Imaginechina; © Keren Su—Danita Delimont, Agent; Keren Su—Danita Delimont, Agent.
190 © Keren Su—Danita Delimont, Agent
191 © SuperStock
192 © Runk/Schoenberger—Grant Heilman Photography
193 © George Whitely—Photo Researchers; George Whitely—Photo Researchers.
196 Nova Scotia Power Corporation
198 © Erwin & Peggy Bauer—Bruce Coleman Inc.
199 © H. Armstrong Roberts
200 © Photo Researchers
207 © John Banagan—Lonely Planet Images
208 © Dita Alangkara—AP/Wide World Photos
209 © Carl Frank—Photo Researchers
210 Alte Pinakothek, Munich—Artothek
211 Goodyear Tire and Rubber Company
213 The Louvre, Paris—Art Resource
214 © William Kerr Collins
216 © Betty Press—Woodfin Camp & Associates
217 Grolier International, Inc.
218 © SuperStock
219 © Katsumi Kasahara—AP/Wide World Photos
221 Illustrated by Lidia Postma from A. Tolkien Bestiary—Mitchell Beazley Publishers
223 © Jarrold Norwich
227 © Mitch Mandel—Rodale Stock Images; © Eduardo Fuss.
228 © Tom Pantages (all photos on page).
229 © Eduardo Fuss (all photos on page).
230 © Tom Pantages (all photos on page).
231 Makita U.S.A., Inc. (all photos on page).
240 Toy Collection: Museum of the City of NY; John Kane—Silver Sun Studio.
241 © Tim Marshall—Time magazine
243 © Vic Bider—Photo Network
244 © Jim Russell—First Light
245 The Museum of Modern Art, New York, Gift of Mrs. John D. Rockefeller, Jr., 1946
247 © Joachim Messerschmidt—Leo de Wys
248 Courtesy, Fisher-Price; Courtesy, Lego Systems, Inc.; The Little Tykes Company.
249 © Richard Hutchings—Photo Researchers
250 Lionel Trains, Inc.; © James Wilson—Woodfin Camp & Associates.
251 The Bettmann Archive; The Metropolitan Museum of Art, The Cesnola Collection: purchased by subscription, 1874-1876.
252 © Iundt-Ruszniewski—Sportschrome, Inc.; © Paul J. Sutton—Duomo; © Michel Gouverner—Liaison Agency; © Aray Mortimorf—Allsport.
253 © Mike Powell—Allsport
254 © Paul J. Sutton—Duomo
255 © Steven E. Sutton—Duomo
256 © Victor Sailer—Sailer Ltd.
257 © Focus on Sports
258 © Victor Sailer—Sailer Ltd.; © Steven E. Sutton—Duomo.
259 © Tony Duffy—Allsport; © Tony Duffy—Allsport; © Dave Cannon—Allsport; © Mike Powell—Allsport; © Tony Duffy—Allsport; © Lynne Sladky—AP/Wide World; © Michel Spingler—AP/Wide World.
260 UPI/Corbis-Bettmann; Allsport; Hulton Deutsch/Allsport; Allsport; UPI/Corbis-Bettmann; Allsport; AP/Wide World; Hulton Deutsch/Allsport.
262 Historical Pictures Service; UPI/Bettmann Newsphotos; AP/Wide World Photos.
263 UPI/Bettmann
267 Children's Television Workshop; Gerber Products Company; Izod Ltd.; McDonald's.
269 © Peter Poulides
270 Mark Richards—© Time magazine
271 © Ed Rosenberger—The Stock Solution; © Mark E. Gibson.
277 © Reprinted with the permission of Analog Devices, Inc. (all photos on page).
281 © Cameramann International Ltd.
282 © Alan Oddie—PhotoEdit
283 The Bettmann Archive
284 The Mariners' Museum, Newport News, Virginia; © John Elk III—Bruce Coleman Inc.
285 The Bettmann Archive; © Comstock—Miller Services Ltd.
286 © Henry Austin Clark, Jr.; General Motors Corporation—Chevrolet Division.
287 The Bettmann Archive; © Randa Bishop.
288 © Michael K. Nichols—Magnum Photos; © David M. Doody—The Stock Solution.
289 © Steve McCutcheon
290 © Doug Wilson—The Stock Solution
291 © Kaku Kurita—Liaison Agency; NASA.
293 Robert C. Moore—State of Connecticut
295 © Cameramann International Ltd.
301 © Arthur W. Ambler—National Audubon Society; © John H. Gerard; © John H. Gerard; © John H. Gerard; © V. R. Johnston—Photo Researchers; © Russ Kinne—Photo Researchers; © Paul W. Nesbit—National Audubon Society.
302 © Stephen Collins—Photo Researchers; © FPG International; Franklin R. Schmidt—Courtesy of A. Polonsky Estate; © David Muench; © McIntyre—Annan; © Josef Muench; © Josef Muench.
303 © Irvin L. Oakes—Photo Researchers; © Stephen Collins—Photo Researchers; © Chuck Abbott—Rapho Guillumette; © John H. Gerard; © A. C. Shelton—A. Devaney, Inc.; ©